THE PDMA HANDBOOK OF NEW PRODUCT DEVELOPMENT

THE PDMA HANDBOOK OF NEW PRODUCT DEVELOPMENT

SECOND EDITION

Edited by
Kenneth B. Kahn

ASSOCIATE EDITORS
George Castellion
Abbie Griffin

WILEY

JOHN WILEY & SONS, INC.

For general information on our other products and services or for technical support, please contact our Customer Care Department within the United States at (800) 762-2974, outside the United States at (317) 572-3993 or fax (317) 572-4002.

Wiley also publishes its books in a variety of electronic formats. Some content that appears in print may not be available in electronic books. For more information about Wiley products, visit our web site at www.wiley.com.

Library of Congress Cataloging-in-Publication Data:

The PDMA handbook of new product development/edited by Kenneth B. Kahn.— 2nd ed.
   p. cm.
   Includes bibliographical references.
   ISBN 0-471-48524-1 (cloth : alk. paper)
   1. New products—United States—Management—Handbooks, manuals, etc. 2. Product management—United States—Handbooks, manuals, etc. I. Title: Handbook of new product development. II. Kahn, Kenneth B. III. Product Development & Management Association.
   HF5415.153.P35 2005
   658.5'75—dc22

                                                                                2004002261

Printed in the United States of America

10 9 8 7 6 5 4 3

CONTENTS

INTRODUCTION

Kenneth B. Kahn

The editors' goal was to put together a guidebook to help practitioners make improved decisions when traveling through the difficult landscape typical of new product development. Modeled after the first edition published in 1996, the second edition of *The PDMA Handbook of New Product Development* updates core chapters with current knowledge and adds new chapters to cover the many changes in the new product development (NPD) landscape over the last eight years. While the term "product" is used, material in this handbook is intended for practitioners in product and/or service development situations.

Who This Book Is For

The following extract from a reader's review of the first edition on Amazon.com provides insight into who will benefit from this book:

> To whom can I recommend this book? To anyone who wants to increase his or her own scope of knowledge in this field and is able to compare his or her own experience to this book.

This handbook is written for people involved in the development of new products and services who have a keen interest in increasing their knowledge of the topic.

How to Use This Book

No NPD guidebook can anticipate the uncharted terrain into which a new product's developers may occasionally stumble. While this handbook offers concise, map-like detail about individual topics, it is also similar to a compass. As a compass, it will enable you to find your bearings no matter where in the topography you unexpectedly find yourself.

Of course, each reader of this handbook will have different interests. We recommend that first-time readers skim the table of contents and the introductions for each of the seven sections. Once oriented, explore the topics that are of interest to you or in which guidance is necessary.

Here's the Book's Structure

The first five sections follow the general flow of product development in most firms. In practice, this flow is not compartmentalized and the tasks associated with one section may overlap with the tasks of other sections. The sixth section provides a view into two areas where the PDMA is creating new knowledge to close the gap between NPD theory and practice. An appendix and a glossary are offered as well. The appendix provides a description of and contact information for the PDMA. The glossary contains terms commonly used in NPD, but that are seldom gathered in one book.

Part I Before You Get Started (1)

Part II Organizing the Development (108)

Part III Getting Started (188)

Part IV Doing the Development (335)

Part V Finishing the Job (443)

Part VI PDMA Research on NPD (525)

Appendix About the Product Development & Management Association (PDMA) (567)

The PDMA Glossary for New Product Development (572)

ACKNOWLEDGMENTS

Writing and editing this handbook has been, in common with other PDMA projects, an all-volunteer activity. All the authors and editors volunteered their time and talent, taking time from already full professional calendars. One or more experts in the subject reviewed each chapter anonymously. Responsibility for a chapter's content lies with each author, but the editors thank our expert reviewers for their on-target comments and suggestions:

Ned Anscheutz

Dave Bacehowski

Robert Brentin

Warren Butler

Charles Chase

Richard Clark

Mark Deck

C. Anthony di Benedetto

Scott Edgett

Kim Elliott

Edon Fisher

Dan Flint

Frank Franzak

Jerry Groen

Nancy Hahn

Tom Hardy

Mary Jane Hellyar

Kathy Hofius

Beth Hunt

Judy Hunt

Gerald Katz

George Kingston

Stefan Kohn

Peter Lawrence

Stephen Markham

Marsha McArthur

Lee Meadows

Mark Meyer

James Miller	Preston Smith
Gregory Moores	Stephen Somermeyer
Robert Morais	Frederick Squires
Jeffrey Morrison	Chris Storey
Beebe Nelson	Edward Takacs
Richard Notargiacomo	Stefan Thomke
Paul O'Connor	Hamsa Thota
Jeff Pinegars	Melissa VanRyzin
Mary Pochobradsky	Thomas Verhulp
Wayne Pollack	Francis Via
Alan Rae	Jeffrey Willis
Anne St. Clair	Janet Zuffa

We also appreciate the support the Board of directors of the Product Development & Management Association gave to the editors throughout the production of this book. Among the PDMA's other products are its Web site (www.pdma.org), the award-winning *Journal of Product Innovation Management,* the award-winning *Visions* magazine, the *PDMA ToolBooks* (published by John Wiley & Sons, Inc.), its New Product Development Professional Certification program, and conferences and workshops. In addition, the PDMA Foundation creates and delivers actionable knowledge, such as the Comparative Performance Assessment Study (see Chapter 36), for better decisions in new products management. Additional information on the PDMA is in the appendix.

Finally, we appreciate the support that our publisher, John Wiley & Sons, Inc., has provided. Robert J. Argentieri gave timely counsel, and his assistants, Shannon Effinger and Naomi Rothwell, ably shepherded this multiauthored manuscript through the editorial process.

Editor: *Associate Editors:*
Kenneth B. Kahn   George Castellion
University of Tennessee   SSC Associates

                                                      Abbie Griffin
                                                      University of Illinois, Urbana-Champaign

Kenneth B. Kahn, Ph.D. is Associate Professor of Marketing in the Department of Marketing and Logistics at the University of Tennessee, Knoxville, and is a cofounding director of UT's Sales Forecasting Management Forum, which emphasizes education and research in the areas of sales forecasting and market analysis. His teaching and research interests concern product development, product management, sales forecasting, and interdepartmental integration. Dr. Kahn has published in a variety of journals, including the *Journal of Product Innovation Management*, and is author of the book *Product Planning Essentials*. His industrial experience includes serving as an industrial engineer and project engineer for the Weyerhaeuser Company, and as a manufacturing engineer for Respironics, Inc.

George Castellion, SSC Associates, provides custom marketing research to a wide range of clients in business-to-business product management. He specializes in working with clients in the early stages of product development to quickly find reliable answers to questions about potential customers, competitors, and the new product's marketplace.

Dr. Castellion founded his marketing research practice, SSCA, in 1985 after a business career in the chemicals industry. As a practitioner, he was first an inventor and manager of technology groups. Then, he moved into marketing, where he held senior positions with profit responsibility for both established and new products.

Besides his business experience, George Castellion is a past president of the PDMA. He currently serves on the editorial board of the *Journal of Product Innovation Management* and is VP, Development, of the PDMA Foundation's *Comparative Performance Assessment Study* of product development practices.

Abbie Griffin is a professor of Business Administration at the University of Illinois, Urbana-Champaign. Dr. Griffin's research focuses on measuring and improving the process of new product development, including the marketing techniques associated with developing new products. She is the former editor of the *Journal of Product Innovation Management*, and sits on the board of directors of Navistar. Prior to becoming an academic, she worked in product development at Corning Glass Works, was a consultant with Booz, Allen and Hamilton, and started her career as an engineer at Polaroid Corporation. She is an avid quilter and hiker.

PART ONE

BEFORE YOU GET STARTED

If you don't know where you are going, any road will take you there.

CHARLES DODGSON, ENGLISH MATHEMATICIAN, 1865

Quantitative studies of successful products versus unsuccessful ones since the early 1970s enable researchers to pinpoint the critical reasons for success. Chapter 1 summarizes these studies and discusses the circumstances, facts, and influences that separate winning products from losers.

A skillfully assembled strategy chooses where a product will compete and why it can win. Chapter 2 addresses the new product strategy set of choices developers make when building a plan of action for converting a new product concept into a product.

Increased growth in both revenue and profit from new products occurs for firms employing portfolio planning and management. Chapter 3 gives a program for leading, carrying out, tracking, and managing a new product portfolio.

Knowing how to design the set of processes making up new product development (NPD) is only of partial value. Chapter 4 addresses the challenges that arise in implementating the NPD processes set, which is not a trivial problem.

One of these process implementation challenges is identifying just who owns a process. Is it the process champion, the process sponsor, the process manager, or is ownership a dual role? In the viewpoint of Chapter 5's author, an enduring NPD process is "owned" by its practitioners.

The fuzzy front end of NPD begins when a customer need is known and a technology exists to fill that need. A review is provided in Chapter 6 of three different approaches to the fuzzy front end, depending on whether the product is incremental, platform, or breakthrough.

The PDMA viewpoint is that products can be either tangible goods or intangible services, and are often a combination of the two. The authors of Chapter 7, while not disagreeing with this view, believe that understanding what distinguishes services and makes them unique is the first step in strengthening new service development.

CHAPTER ONE

NEW PRODUCTS—WHAT SEPARATES THE WINNERS FROM THE LOSERS AND WHAT DRIVES SUCCESS

Robert G. Cooper

1.1 Introduction

Product innovation—the development of new and improved products—is crucial to the survival and prosperity of the modern corporation. According to a recent American Productivity and Quality Control (APQC) benchmarking study, new products launched in the last three years currently account for 27.5 percent of company sales, on average (American Productivity & Quality Center, 2003; Cooper, 2003). And product life cycles are getting shorter: a 400 percent reduction over the last 50 years, the result of an accelerating pace of product innovation (Von Braun, 1997). But many products do not succeed: the same APQC study reports that just over half (56 percent) of businesses' new product development (NPD) projects achieve their financial goals, and only 51 percent are launched on time.

The central role of NPD in business strategy coupled with the poor NPD performance results in many firms has led to a quest for the factors that drive performance and product innovation success (see box). Understanding why new products succeed and why some businesses are so much better at NPD is central to effective new product management: it provides insights for managing new product projects (for example, are certain practices strongly linked to success?), and clues to new product selection (what are the telltale signs of a winner?). This chapter reports the findings from a myriad of studies

---

The Quest for the Critical Success Factors

The keys to new product success outlined in this chapter are based on numerous research studies into why new products succeed, studies of why they fail, comparisons of winners and losers, and benchmarking studies of best performing businesses. Many of these investigations have been reported over the years in the PDMA journal, the Journal of Product Innovation Management. *Some of the most revealing of these studies have been the large sample, quantitative studies of successful versus unsuccessful new products (for an excellent review, see Cooper, 2001, and Montoya-Weiss and Calantone, 1991). They began with Project SAPPHO in the early 1970s, followed by the NewProd series of studies, the Stanford Innovation Project, and more recently studies in countries outside of North America and Europe. Many are referenced. More recently, several large benchmarking studies of best practices have provided yet other insights into how to succeed at NPD (American Productivity & Quality Center, 2003; Cooper, 2003; Griffin, 1997). This long tradition of research has enabled us to pinpoint the critical success factors—those factors which separate winners from losers, which are outlined in this chapter.*

---

into what makes new products winners and what makes some businesses more successful at NPD.

1.2 Critical Success Factors at the Project Level

1.2.1 Striving for Unique Superior Products

Superior and differentiated products—ones that deliver unique benefits and superior value to the customer—is the number one driver of success and new product profitability. Their success rates are reported to be three to five times higher than for "me-too," copycat, reactive, and ho-hum products with few differentiated characteristics. (Note that the "customer" buys the product; the "user" uses the product; the two are not necessarily the same, although often the terms are used interchangeably).

That differentiated, superior products are key to success should come as no surprise to product innovators. Apparently it isn't obvious to everyone: study after study shows that "reactive products" and "me-too" offerings are the rule rather than the exception in many businesses' new product efforts, and the majority fail to produce large profits!

> *Superior and differentiated products—ones that deliver unique benefits and superior value to the customer—are the number one driver of success and new product profitability.*

What do these superior products with unique customer or user benefits have in common? These winning products:

√ Feature good value for money for the customer, reduce the customer's total costs (high value-in-use), and boast excellent price/performance characteristics
√ Provide excellent product quality, relative to competitors' products, and in terms of how the user measures quality
√ Are superior to competing products in terms of meeting users' needs, offer unique features not available on competitive products, or solve a problem that the customer has with a competitive product
√ Offer product benefits or attributes easily perceived as useful by the customer, and benefits that are highly visible

Best-performing businesses emphasize these factors in their NPD efforts. The APQC benchmarking study cited above shows that the Best Performers are much stronger in terms of offering important benefits, a superior value proposition, and better value for the customer in their new products (see Figure 1.1). (APQC, 2003; Cooper and Kleinschmidt, 2003) (Here "Best Performers" are businesses whose NPD efforts were superior on a number of performance metrics: profitability; meeting sales and profit objectives, time efficiency, and the ability to open up new windows of opportunity–see APQC, 2003; Cooper and Kleinschmidt, 2003).

A point of distinction: *benefits* are what customers or users value and pay money for; by contrast, *attributes* are product features, functionality, and performance—the things that engineers and designers build into products. Often benefits and attributes are connected, but sometimes the designers get it wrong, so that added product features and performance do not yield additional benefits for customers/users.

The management implications are clear:

• First, these ingredients of a superior product (see Figure 1.1) provide a useful checklist of items to assess the odds of success of a proposed new product

Critical Success Factors at the Project Level
1. *Striving for Unique Superior Products*
2. *A Strong Market Orientation—Market Driven, Customer Focused*
3. *Predevelopment Work—the Homework*
4. *Sharp, Early, and Stable Project and Product Definition*
5. *Planning and Resourcing the Launch*
6. *Quality of Execution of Key Tasks from Idea to Launch*
7. *Speed—But Not at the Expense of Quality of Execution*

Critical Success Factors—People and Environment
1. *The Way Project Teams Are Organized*
2. *The Right Environment—Climate and Culture*
3. *Top Management Support*

Strategic Critical Success Factors
1. *A Product Innovation and Technology Strategy for the Business*
2. *Leveraging Core Competencies—Synergy and Familiarity*
3. *Targeting Attractive Markets*
4. *Focus and Sharp Project Selection Decisions—Portfolio Management*
5. *The Necessary Resources*

A Multistage, Disciplined New Product Idea-to-Launch Process

project: they logically become top priority issues in a project screening checklist or scorecard.

- Second, these ingredients become challenges to the project team to build into their new product design. Note that the definition of "what is unique and superior" must be based on an in-depth understanding of customer or user needs, wants, problems, likes, and dislikes. This leads to success factor #2 below.

What about competitive advantages gained via elements other than product advantage? These include brand-name or company reputation, superior marketing communications (advertising and promotion), a superb sales force or distribution channel, superior technical support and tech service, or simply product availability. The limited evidence available suggests that the impact of

FIGURE 1.1 PRODUCT ADVANTAGE—IMPACT ON PERFORMANCE.

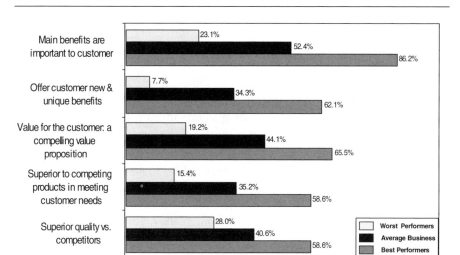

Percent of Businesses Whose New Products Have Product
Advantage vs. Competitive Products

nonproduct advantage pales in comparison to the impact of product advantage—it has less than half the effect. The message is evident: by all means, strive for advantage via nonproduct elements—every advantage helps! But don't pin your hopes on these elements alone: whenever you hear yourself saying "Our company's reputation, brand name, or sales force will make this product a winner," be on guard.

1.2.2 A Strong Market Orientation—Market Driven, Customer Focused

A thorough understanding of customers' needs and wants, the competitive situation, and the nature of the market is an essential component of new product success. This tenet is supported by virtually every study of product success factors. Conversely, a failure to adopt a strong market orientation in product innovation, an unwillingness to undertake the needed market assessments, and leaving the customer out of product development, spells disaster; these are the culprits found in almost every study of why new products fail!

A provocative finding of a number of studies is that, not only does a strong customer focus improve success rates and profitability, but it also leads to reduced time-to-market (Cooper, 2001). Contrary to myth, taking a little extra time to execute the market analysis and market research in a high-quality fashion does not add extra time; rather it pays off, not only with higher success rates, but also in terms of staying on schedule and achieving better time efficiency.

Sadly, a strong market orientation is missing in the majority of firms' new product projects. Detailed market studies are frequently omitted (in more than 75 percent of projects, according to one investigation). Further, marketing activities are the weakest-rated activities of the entire new product process, rated much lower than corresponding technological actions. Moreover, relatively few resources and little money are spent on the marketing actions (except for the launch), accounting for less than 20 percent of the total project.

A market orientation must prevail throughout the entire new product project (Griffin and Hauser, 1996; Olson, Walker, Ruekert, and Bonner, 2001):

√ *Idea generation:* Devote more resources to market-oriented idea generation activities, such as focus groups and voice-of-the-customer (VoC) research with customers to determine customers' generic needs and/or their problems. Use the sales force to actively solicit ideas from customers and develop relationships with innovative or lead users.

√ *The design of the product:* Often, market research, when done at all, is done too late—after the product design has already been decided and simply as an after-the-fact check. Note that market research must be used as an input to the design decisions and serve as a guide to the project team before they charge into the design of the new product. Determine customer/user needs at the outset, starting with a user needs-and-wants study: this usually means VoC research—listening to the customer or user to understand his/her problems and to determine his/her unarticulated needs, wants, and desires. And in tandem, conduct a competitive product analysis (competitive benchmarking) to determine competitive product strengths and weaknesses, and to identify competitive strategies (e.g., pricing, distribution). For more information on VoC and on market research, see Chapters 14 and 18.

√ *Throughout the entire project:* Customer inputs shouldn't cease at the completion of the predevelopment market studies. Seeking customer inputs and testing concepts or designs with the user is very much an iterative process—"spiral development." Keep bringing the customer into the process to view facets of the product via a series of concept tests, rapid-prototype-and-tests, customer trials, and test marketing, verifying all assumptions about the winning design. Leave nothing to chance. For more information on interacting with customers, see Chapter 16.

Even in the case of technology-driven new products (where the idea comes from a technical or laboratory source), the likelihood of success is greatly enhanced if customer and marketplace inputs are built into the project soon after its inception.

1.2.3 Predevelopment Work—the Homework

Homework is critical to winning. Countless studies reveal that the steps that precede the actual design and development of the product make the difference between winning and losing. Successful firms spend about twice as much time and money on these vital up-front activities:

√ Initial screening—the first decision to get into the project (the idea screen).
√ Preliminary market assessment—the first, quick market study.
√ Preliminary technical assessment—the first and quick technical appraisal of the project.
√ The detailed market study, market research, and VoC research (described earlier).
√ The business and financial analysis just before the decision to "go to development" (building the business case).

Another issue is the *balance* within the homework phase. Best Performers strike an appropriate balance between market/business-oriented tasks and technical tasks, while poor performers tend to push ahead on the technical side, and pay lip service to marketing and business issues in the early phases of the project (APQC, 2003; Cooper, 2003). Figure 1.2 shows how much better Best Performers execute the homework activities, especially the early-stage marketing/business tasks. Surprisingly, most firms confess to serious weaknesses in the "up-front" or predevelopment steps of their new product process. Pitifully small amounts of time and money are devoted to these critical steps: only about 7 percent of the dollars and 16 percent of the effort.

"More homework means longer development times" is a frequently voiced complaint. This is a valid concern, but experience has shown that homework pays for itself in reduced development times as well as improved success rates:

√ First, all the evidence points to a much higher likelihood of product failure if the homework is omitted. So, the choice is between a slightly longer project or greatly increased odds of failure.
√ Second, better project definition, the result of sound homework, actually speeds up the development process. One of the major causes of time

FIGURE 1.2 QUALITY OF EXECUTION OF KEY EARLY-STAGE ACTIVITIES.

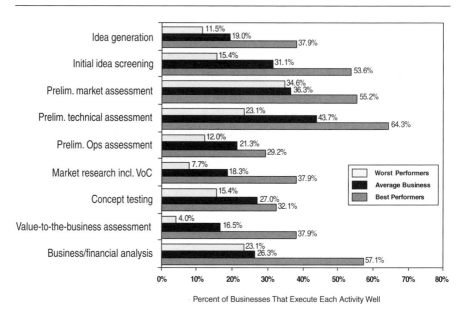

Percent of Businesses That Execute Each Activity Well

slippages is projects that are poorly defined as they enter the development stage: vague targets and moving goalposts.

√ Third, given the inevitable product design evolution that occurs during the life of a project, the time to make the majority of these design improvements or changes is not as the product is moving out of development and into production. More homework up front anticipates these changes and encourages them to occur earlier in the process rather than later, when they are more costly.

The message is evident. Don't skimp on the homework! If you find yourself making the case that "we don't have time for the homework," you're wrong on two counts: first, cutting out the homework drives your success rate way down, and second, cutting out homework to save time today will cost you in wasted time tomorrow. It's a "penny wise, pound foolish" way to save time. Make it a rule: no significant project should move into the development stage without the actions described above completed and done in a high-quality way. Figure 1.2 provides a useful checklist of early-stage activities that should be built into your new product project or NPD process.

1.2.4 Sharp, Early, and Stable Project and Product Definition

Two of the worst time-wasters in a NPD project are "project scope creep" and "unstable specs." Scope creep means that the definition of the project constantly changes: it might begin as a single customer project, then be targeted at multiple users, and finally end up being a platform for a new family of projects. Similarly, unstable specs means that the product definition—product requirements and specifications—keeps changing throughout the development stage; thus, the technical people chase elusive development targets—moving goalposts—and take forever to get to the goal.

Securing a sharp, early, stable, and fact-based product definition during the homework phase is a solution. How well the project and product are defined prior to entering the development stage is a major success factor, having a positive impact on both profitability and reduced time-to-market. Some companies undertake excellent product and project definition before the door is opened to a full development program. This definition includes:

√ Definition of the project's scope (e.g., domestic versus international; new product item versus platform development, etc.)
√ Specification of the target market: exactly who the intended users are
√ Description of the product concept and the benefits to be delivered to the user (including the value proposition)
√ Delineation of the positioning strategy, including target price
√ A list of the product's features, attributes, requirements, and specifications (prioritized: "must have" and "would like to have")

Unless these five items are clearly defined, written down, and agreed to by all parties prior to entering the development stage, then your project faces tough times downstream: your odds of failure have just skyrocketed by a factor of three! Here's why:

• Building in a definition step forces more attention on the up-front or pre-development activities, a key success factor (described previously).
• The definition serves as a communication tool and guide. All parties' agreement or "buy in" means that each functional area involved in the project

> *Securing sharp, early, stable, and fact-based product definition during the homework phase is one of the strongest drivers of cycle time reduction and new product success.*

has a clear and consistent definition of what the product and project are and are committed to it.

- This definition also provides a clear set of objectives for the development stage of the project and the development team members: the goalposts are defined and clearly visible.

1.2.5 Planning and Resourcing the Launch

Emerson once said, "build a better mousetrap and the world will beat a path to your door"; the problem is that Emerson was a poet, not a businessman. Not only must the product be a superior one, but it must also be launched, marketed, and supported in a proficient manner. A high-quality launch is strongly linked to new product profitability, and effective after-sales service is central to the successful launch of the new product (Di Benedetto, 1999; Mishra, Kim, and Lee, 1996; Song, and Parry, 1996).

The message is this: don't assume that good products sell themselves, and don't treat the launch as an afterthought. Just because the launch is the last step in the process, never underestimate its importance. A well-integrated and properly targeted launch does not occur by accident, however; it is the result of a *fine-tuned marketing plan*, properly backed and resourced, and proficiently executed. There are five requirements for an effective market launch plan:

1. The development of the market launch plan is an *integral part of the new product process:* it is as central to the new product process as is the development of the physical product.
2. The development of the market launch plan *must begin early* in the new product project. It should not be left as an afterthought to be undertaken as the product nears commercialization.
3. A market launch plan is only as good as the *market intelligence* on which it is based. Market studies designed to yield information crucial to marketing planning must be built into the new product project.
4. The launch must be properly resourced—with both people and dollars. Too often, an otherwise great new product fails to achieve it sales goals simply because of an underresourced launch.
5. Those who will execute the launch—the sales force, technical support people, other front-line personnel—must be engaged in the development of the market launch plan and should therefore be members of the project team.

This ensures valuable input and insight into the design of the launch effort, availability of resources when needed, and buy-in by those who must execute to the product and its launch—elements so critical to a successful launch. Hultink and Atuahene-Gima, 2000) For more information on launch, see Chapter 30.

1.2.6 Quality of Execution of Key Tasks from Idea to Launch

More emphasis is needed on completeness, consistency, and quality of execution in the new product process. Certain key activities—how well they are executed and whether they are done at all—are strongly tied to profitability and reduction in time-to-market. Particularly pivotal activities include: the vital homework actions outlined earlier (factor #3) and market-related activities (factor #2). But proficiency in most activities in the new product process has an impact on outcomes, with successful project teams consistently doing a better-quality job across many tasks (Mishra, Kim, and Lee,1996; Song and Parry, 1996; Song and Montoya-Weiss, M. M., 1998).

There is a *quality crisis*, however, in product innovation. Investigations reveal that the typical new product project is characterized by serious errors of omission and commission:

- Pivotal activities, often cited as central to success, are omitted altogether. For example, more than half of all projects typically leave out detailed market studies and a test market (trial sell).
- The quality of execution ratings of important activities are also typically low. In postmortems on projects, teams typically rate themselves as "mediocre" in terms of how good a job they did on these vital activities. Witness the high proportion of businesses that confess to poor quality of execution in Figure 1.2—for example, only 18 percent of businesses do a good job on market research for NPD, only 26 percent handle the business analysis well, idea screening is proficient in only 31 percent of businesses, and so on.

The best way to double the success rate of new products and, at the same time, reduce development time is to strive for significant improvements in the way that the innovation process unfolds. The solution that some firms have adopted

---

There is a quality crisis in NPD: key tasks are skipped over and too many tasks are done in haste and/or poorly executed. Often, this quality issue stems from underresourced projects—doing too many projects for the limited resources available.

is to treat product innovation as a process: they use a formal *idea-to-launch product delivery process*. And they build into this process quality assurance approaches: for example, they introduce checkpoints and metrics into the process that focus on quality of execution, ensuring that every action is executed in a high-quality fashion, they carefully define requirements and expectations for the project team in the form of stage activities and gate deliverables, and they make certain best-practice actions mandatory—such as VoC research, stable product definition, and solid up-front homework—actions that are often omitted, yet are central to success.

1.2.7 Speed—But Not at the Expense of Quality of Execution

Speed is a competitive weapon. Speed yields competitive advantage—being the first on the market means that there is less likelihood that the market or competitive situation has changed, and it results in a quicker realization of profits. So, the goal of reducing the development cycle time is admirable. A word of caution here, however: speed is only an interim objective; the ultimate goal is profitability. While studies reveal that speed and profitability are connected, the relationship is anything but one to one! Further, there is a dark side to speed: often the methods used to reduce development time yield precisely the opposite effect, and in many cases are very costly: they are at odds with sound management practices (Crawford, 1992). The objective remains successful products, not a series of fast failures! Additionally, an overemphasis on speed has led to trivialization of product development in some firms, too many product modifications and line extensions, and not enough real new products. For more information on speed, see Chapter 12.

Some of the principles that project teams embrace in order to reduce time-to-market include:

- Do the up-front homework and get an early and stable product and project definition, based on facts rather than hearsay and speculation. This saves time downstream.
- Build in quality of execution at every stage of the project. The best way to save time is by avoiding having to cycle back and do it a second time.
- Effective cross-functional teams are essential for timely development. "Rip apart a badly developed project and you will unfailingly find 75 percent of slippage attributable to: 'siloing,' or sending memos up and down vertical organizational 'silos' or "stovepipes" for decisions; and sequential problem solving" (Peters, 1998).
- Use *parallel processing*: the relay race, sequential, or series approach to product development is antiquated and inappropriate for today's fast-paced projects.

- In combination with parallel processing, use *spiral development*: that is, a series of build-and-test spirals, constantly checking the product with the customer or user. These iterations begin with the concept test in Stage 2 (see Figure 1.6) and end with the full field trials (beta tests) in Stage 4.
- Prioritize and focus—do fewer projects, but higher value ones. By concentrating resources on the truly deserving projects, not only will the work be done better, but it will also be done faster.

1.3 Critical Success Factors—People and Environment

1.3.1 The Way Project Teams Are Organized

Product innovation is very much a team effort! Do a postmortem on any bungled new product project and invariably you'll find each functional area doing its own piece of the project, with very little communication between players and functions—a fiefdom mentality, and no real commitment of players to the project. Many studies concur that how the project team is organized and functions strongly influences project outcomes (Cooper, 2001). The APQC study finds that Best Performers organize their NPD project teams with the following elements (see Figure 1.3) (American Productivity & Quality Center, 2003; Cooper, 2003):

1. *A clearly assigned team of players for each significant NPD project—people who are part of the project and do work for it:* What is surprising is that this practice is not evident in almost all businesses today. But this is true: only 61.5 percent of businesses have clearly assigned teams for NPD, with Best Performing businesses outdoing the worst by two to one.
2. *Cross-functional project teams, with team members from Technical, Sales, Marketing, Operations, and so on:* This is a practice now embraced by the great majority of businesses. Here, team members are not just representatives of their function, but rather *true members of the project team*, shedding their functional loyalties and working together in an integrated fashion to common goal.
3. *Cross-functional cooperation within the team (e.g., not too much time and effort wasted on politics, conflicts, inter-departmental prejudices, etc.):* Surprisingly this is a moderately weak part of most businesses' new product efforts, with only 43.7 percent of businesses reporting good cross-functional cooperation within NPD project teams.
4. *The project team remaining on the project from beginning to end—not just on the project for a short-while or a single phase:* Almost half of businesses practice this team

FIGURE 1.3 THE WAY NPD PROJECT TEAMS ARE ORGANIZED.

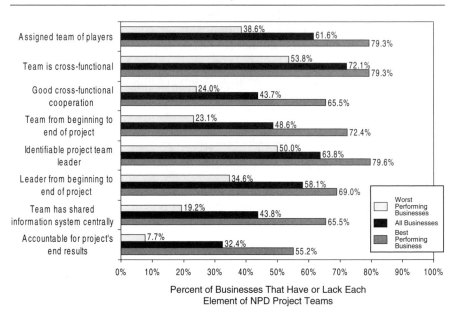

approach, and it is particularly evident among Best Performers. This practice also enhances project team accountability.

5. *A clearly identified team leader:* A person who is in charge and responsible for driving the project.

6. *A project leader responsible for the project from idea through to launch:* This person carries the project right through the process and not just for one or a few stages; poor performers are weak here.

7. *A central shared-information system for project team members:* This practice entails a centralized communication system that permits the sharing of project information and allows several team members to work concurrently on the same document, even across functions, locations, and countries. This is a particularly strong facet of Best Performers, with almost two-thirds having such a system.

8. *Project teams accountable for their project's end result:* For example, they are responsible for ensuring that projects meet profit/revenue targets and time targets. Team accountability is a pivotal best practice and, indeed, strongly separates Best from Worst Performers by a factor of eight to one!

Product development must be run as a multidisciplinary, cross-functional effort. While the ingredients of good organizational design should be familiar ones, surprisingly many businesses have yet to get the message. For more information on teams, see Chapter 9.

1.3.2 The Right Environment—Climate and Culture

A second organizational success ingredient is a positive climate for innovation. Such a climate has many facets and includes an environment where . . .

√ Intrapreneurs and risk taking behavior are supported and encouraged
√ Senior management is not afraid to invest in the occasional risky project
√ New product successes are rewarded and recognized (and failures are not punished)
√ Team efforts are recognized, rather than individuals
√ Senior managers refrain from "micromanaging" projects and second-guessing the project team members
√ Project review meetings are open (the entire project team participates)

The APQC study finds that most businesses are quite weak on almost all of the above elements of a positive climate, with typically less than one-third of businesses employing these practices (but Best Performers do!) (American Productivity & Quality Center, 2003; Cooper, 2003). Some other practices that also drive performance, but are rarely seen, include making resources and time available for creative people to work on their own projects (e.g., via free "scouting time" or bootstrapping funds), allowing the occasional "unofficial project," permitting "skunk works" projects outside the official bureaucracy, and having an idea submission scheme in place (here, employees are encouraged to submit new product ideas and are rewarded or recognized for good new product ideas).

1.3.3 Top Management Support

Top management support is a necessary ingredient for successful product innovation. Top management's main role is to *set the stage* for product innovation,

> *A positive climate and culture that supports product innovation is one of the strongest discriminators between Best and Worst Performers.*

to be more of a "behind-the-scenes" facilitator, and much less of an actor, front and center.

Senior management must make the long-term commitment to product development as a source of growth; it must develop a vision, objectives, and strategy for product innovation. It must make the necessary resources available to product development and ensure that they aren't diverted to more immediate needs in times of shortage. And management must commit to a disciplined process to drive products to market.

Most importantly, senior management must be engaged in the new product process, reviewing projects, making timely and firm go/kill decisions, and if a go decision is made, making resource commitments to project teams. Management also must empower project teams and support committed champions by acting as mentors, facilitators, "godfathers," or sponsors of project leaders and teams.

1.4 Strategic Critical Success Factors

1.4.1 A Product Innovation and Technology Strategy for the Business

We live in turbulent times. Technology advances at an ever-increasing pace, customer and market needs are constantly changing, competition moves at lightening speed, and globalization brings new players and opportunities into the game. More than ever, businesses need a product innovation and technology strategy to help chart the way (Cooper, 2000).

Having a new product strategy for the business is clearly linked to positive performance (APQC, 2003; Cooper, 2003). The ingredients of such a strategy with the strongest impact on performance include:

1. *The role of NPD in achieving the overall businesses goals:* Strategists recommend that one should link the NPD goals of the business to the overall business goals, so that the role of NPD in achieving business goals is clearly articulated.
2. *Clearly defined NPD goals:* Best practice suggests that a business should clearly define its longer-term goals for new products—for example, what percentage of the business's sales or profits or growth will come from new products over the next three or five years.
3. *Definition of strategic arenas—areas of strategic focus on which to concentrate NPD efforts:* Focus is the key to an effective NPD strategy! Here, businesses typically do a solid job, with the majority designating strategic arenas—markets, product areas, industry sectors, or technologies—in order to help focus their NPD efforts.

4. *Strategic buckets:* Studies of portfolio management point to earmarking buckets of resources—funds or person-days—targeted at different project types or different strategic arenas to ensure strategic alignment of NPD with business goals (Cooper, Edgett, and Kleinschmidt, 2002). Best Performers fare much better here: 41.4 percent of Best Performers (and only 15.4 percent of Worst) employ the strategic buckets approach.

5. *Product roadmap in place:* A product roadmap is an effective way to map out a series of initiatives in an attack plan. A roadmap is simply a management group's view of how to get where they want to go or to achieve their desired objective (Albright and Kappel, 2003; McMillan, 2003). The roadmap is a useful tool that helps management make sure that the capabilities to achieve their objective are in place when needed.

6. *Long-term commitment:* Does the business have a long-term view of its NPD efforts? Or is product development largely a short-term effort, with an absence of longer-time-horizon projects? Many businesses have deficiencies here, with only 38.1 percent of businesses having a longer-term new product strategy. But the majority of Best Performers do so.

7. *More innovative projects:* Best-performing businesses undertake a higher proportion of more innovative NPD projects, while the Worst Performers have a very timid NPD project portfolio. The breakdown is shown in Figure 1.4.

1.4.2 Leveraging Core Competencies—Synergy and Familiarity

"Attack from a position of strength" may be an old adage, but it certainly applies to the launch of new products. Where new product synergy with the base business is lacking, new products fare poorly on average.

Synergy, or *leverage,* is a familiar term, but exactly what does it translate into in the context of new products? Synergy means having a strong fit between the needs of the new product project and the resources, competencies, and experience of the firm in terms of . . .

√ R&D resources (for example, ideally the new product should leverage the business's existing technical competencies)
√ Marketing, selling (sales force) and distribution (channel) resources
√ Manufacturing or operations capabilities and resources
√ Technical support and customer service resources
√ Market research and market intelligence resources
√ Management capabilities

These six synergy ingredients become obvious checklist items in a scoring model used to prioritize new product projects. If the synergy score is low, then there

FIGURE 1.4 BREAKDOWN OF PROJECTS BY PROJECT TYPE— BEST VS. WORST.

	Best Performers	Worst Performers	Average Business
Promotional developments & package changes	5.89%	12.31%	9.45%
Incremental product improvements & changes	28.21%	40.42%	32.74%
Major product revisions	25.00%	19.15%	21.97%
New to the business products	24.11%	20.00%	24.16%
New to the world products	15.89%	7.42%	10.23%

Note: Does not add quite to 100% down a column due to a small percentage of "other" projects.

must be other compelling reasons to proceed with the project. Synergy is not essential, but it certainly improves the odds of winning.

Familiarity is a parallel concept to synergy. Some new product projects take the company into unfamiliar territory: a product category new to the firm; new customers and unfamiliar needs to be served; unfamiliar technology; a new sales force, channels, and servicing requirements; or an unfamiliar manufacturing process. Sadly, the business often pays the price: step-out projects tend to fail, so beware the unknown!

The encouraging news is that the negative impact here is not as strong as for most factors. New and unfamiliar territory certainly results in lower success rates and profitability, on average, but the rates are not dramatically lower.

The message is this: Sometimes it is necessary to venture into new and unfamiliar markets, technologies, or manufacturing processes. Do so with cau-

The ability to leverage core competencies along with the familiarity of the project to the company are important project-screening criteria.

tion, and be aware that success rates will suffer, but note that the odds of disaster are not so high to deter making the move altogether.

1.4.3 Target Attractive Markets

Market attractiveness is an important strategic variable and plays a role in notable strategy models, such as Porter's "five forces" model and the two-dimensional GE-McKinsey map or business portfolio grid. In the case of new products, market attractiveness is also important: products targeted at more attractive markets are more successful (Cooper, 2001; Mishra, Kim, and Lee, 1996, Song and Parry, 1996).

There are two dimensions of market attractiveness:

1. *Market potential:* Positive market environments, namely large and growing markets—markets where a strong customer need exists for such products and where the purchase is an important one for the customer
2. *Competitive situation:* Negative markets characterized by intense competition, on the basis of price, high quality, and strong competitive products; and competitors whose sales force, channel system, and support service are strongly rated

The message is this: Both elements of market attractiveness—market potential and competitive situation—have an impact on the new product's fortunes, and both should be considered as criteria in any scoring scheme for project selection and prioritization. For more information on market analysis and segmentation, see Chapter 13.

1.4.4 Focus and Sharp Project Selection Decisions—Portfolio Management

Most companies suffer from too many projects, often the wrong projects, and not enough resources to mount an effective or timely effort on each (Cooper and Edgett, 2002). This stems from a lack of adequate project evaluation and prioritization, with negative results:

1. First, scarce and valuable resources are wasted on poor projects.
2. Second, the truly meritorious projects don't receive the resources they should. The result is that the good projects are starved for resources, and move at a crawl.

The desire to weed out bad projects coupled with the need to focus limited resources on the best projects means that tough go or kill and prioritization decisions must be made. This results in a sharper focus, higher success rates, and shorter times-to-market. Project evaluations, however, are consistently cited as weakly handled or nonexistent: decisions involve the wrong people from the wrong functions (no functional alignment), no consistent criteria are used to screen or rank projects, or there is simply no will to kill projects at all—projects are allowed to take on a life of their own.

What some companies have done is to redesign their new product processes: they have created a funneling process, which successively weeds out the poor projects, and they have built in decision points in the form of tough "gates." At gate reviews, senior management rigorously scrutinizes projects, and makes go or kill and prioritization decisions. The use of visible go/kill criteria at gates improves decision-making effectiveness; fortunately, certain project characteristics have been identified that consistently separate winners from losers, which should be used as criteria in scorecard format for project selection and prioritization. A typical list of criteria includes some of the important success factors cited above:

1. *Strategic:* How well the project aligns with the business's strategy and how strategically important it is
2. *Competitive and product advantage:* Whether the product is differentiated, offers unique benefits, and represents a compelling value proposition
3. *Market attractiveness:* How large and growing the market is and whether the competitive situation is positive (not intense, few and weak competitors)
4. *Leverage:* Whether the project leverages the business's core competencies, such as marketing, technology and manufacturing
5. *Technical feasibility:* The likelihood of being able to develop and manufacture the product. Is this new science and a technical complex project? Or a technology repackage?
6. *Risk and return:* The financial prospects for the project (e.g., net present value (NPV), internal rate of return (IRR), time-to-profit) versus the risk.

Project selection and picking winning new product initiatives is only part of the task, however. Another goal is selecting the right *mix and balance* of projects in your NPD portfolio, seeking strategic alignment in the portfolio, and ensuring that the business's spending on NPD mirrors its strategic priorities. Many businesses have moved to more formal *portfolio management systems* to help effectively allocate resources and prioritize new product projects (Cooper, Edgett, and Kleinschmidt, 2000; Cooper, Edgett, and Kleinschmidt, 2002). For more information on a new product's strategy, see Chapter 2.

1.4.5 The Necessary Resources

Too many projects simply suffer from a lack of time and monetary commitment. The results are predictable: much higher failure rates. Some facts:

- A strong market orientation is missing in the typical new product project, and much of this deficiency is directly linked to a lack of marketing resources available for the project.
- Another serious pitfall is that the homework doesn't get done. Again, much of this deficiency can be directly attributed to a lack of resources: simply not enough money, people, and time to do the work.

The reason: As the competitive situation has become tougher, companies have responded with restructuring and doing more with less; so, resources are limited or cut back (Cooper and Edgett, 2003). This short-term focus takes its toll. Certain vital activities, such as market-oriented actions and predevelopment homework are highly underresourced, particularly in the case of product failures.

Best-practice companies commit the necessary resources to new products much more so than do most firms. Figure 1.5 reveals that while NPD resources are in short supply across the board—with less than 30 percent of businesses indicating "sufficient resources" from four key functional areas—Best Performers appear to be much better resourced. Equally important, these resources are focused and dedicated, with project team members not working on too many projects or doing other tasks. Indeed, about half the Best Performers have a *ring-fenced product innovation group* that does nothing but work on new products (this is a *dedicated* cross-functional group—technical, marketing, even sales and operations—whose full-time job is to work on new product projects and that typically reports to a senior executive). Finally, resources must be available early in the project in order to undertake the essential up-front homework and early-stage market research outlined in Section 1.2.

1.4.6 A Multistage, Disciplined New Product Idea-to-Launch Framework

A systematic new product framework—such as a Stage-Gate® process[1]—is the solution that many companies have turned to in order to overcome the

[1] Stage-Gate® is a registered trademark of Product Development Institute Inc. in the U.S.A.; see: www.prod-dev.com.

FIGURE 1.5 PROJECT TEAM FOCUS AND DEDICATED RESOURCES.

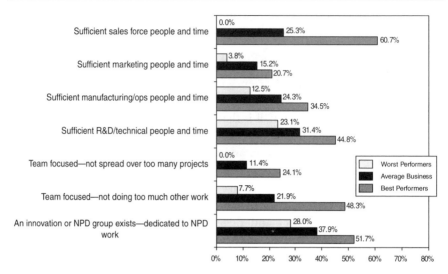

Percentage of Businesses That Have Sufficient
Resources Allocated to NPD Projects

deficiencies that plague their new product programs (Cooper, 2001; Griffin, 1997; Lynn, Skov, and Abel, 1999; Menke, 1997). Stage-Gate® frameworks are simply roadmaps or "play books" for driving new products from idea to launch, successfully and efficiently. About 68 percent of U.S. product developers have adopted Stage-Gate® frameworks, according to the 1997 PDMA best-practices study (Griffin, 1997). The 2003 APQC benchmarking study reveals that 73 percent of businesses employ such a framework and identified a stage-and-gate process as the strongest best practice, employed by almost every Best Performing business (APQC, 2003; Cooper, 2003). And the payoffs of such frameworks have been frequently reported: improved teamwork, less recycling and rework, improved success rates, earlier detection of failures, a better launch, and even shorter cycle times (by about 30 percent).

Leading companies have adopted a Stage-Gate® framework, a method developed by the author, to accelerate new product projects from idea to launch.

The goal of a robust NPD process is to build the best practices outlined previously into a single process or model, so that these factors or practices happen by design, not by accident. A typical NPD process is shown in Figure 1.6, which breaks the innovation process into stages (Cooper, 2001). Each stage consists of a set of concurrent, cross-functional and prescribed activities, undertaken by the cross-functional team. Best practices, such as up-front homework and VoC research are built into the various stages. A set of deliverables is the result of each stage.

Stage 1. Scoping: A quick investigation and sculpting of the project. This first and inexpensive homework stage has the objective of determining the project's technical and marketplace merits. Stage 1 involves desk research or detective work—little or no primary research is done here. Prescribed activities include preliminary market, technical assessment, and business assessment (see Figure 1.2).

Stage 2. Build the Business case: The detailed homework and up-front investigation work. This second homework stage includes actions such as a detailed market analysis, user needs and wants studies to build

FIGURE 1.6 AN OVERVIEW OF A TYPICAL STAGE-GATE® PROCESS.

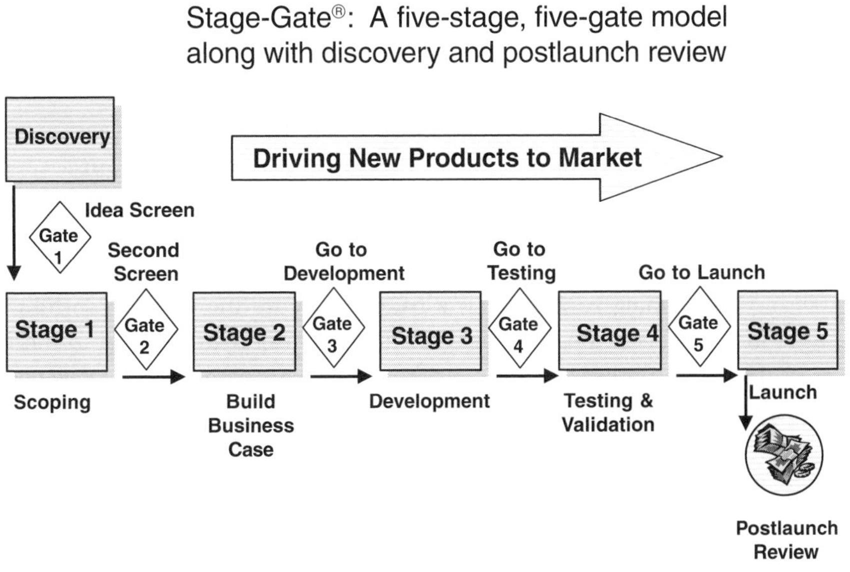

Stage-Gate®: A five-stage, five-gate model along with discovery and postlaunch review

in VoC, competitive benchmarking, concept testing, detailed technical assessment, source of supply assessment, and a detailed financial and business analysis. The result is a *business case*—a defined product, a business
justification, and a detailed plan of action for the next stages

Stage 3. Development: The actual design and development of the
new product. Stage 3 witnesses the implementation of the development
plan and the physical development of the product. Lab tests, in-house
tests, or alpha tests ensure that the product meets requirements under
controlled conditions. The "deliverable" at the end of Stage 3 is a prototype product that has been lab tested and partially tested with the customer.

Stage 4. Testing & validation: The verification and validation of the
proposed new product, its marketing and production. This stage tests and
validates the entire viability of the project: the product itself via customer
tests, beta tests, or field trials; the production process via trial or limited
production runs; customer acceptance by way of a test market or a trial
sell. Also, the financial justification required prior to full launch is obtained.

Stage 5. Launch: Full commercialization of the product—the beginning of full production and commercial launch and selling. The postlaunch plan—monitoring and fixing—is implemented, along with early
elements of the life-cycle plan (new variants and releases; continuous improvements).

Some 12–18 months after launch, the Post Launch review occurs: the performance of the project versus expectations is assessed (team accountability is
a key review issue), along with reasons why events occurred and what lessons
were learned; the team is disbanded and recognized; and the project is terminated.

Preceding each stage is a gate. These are the quality control checkpoints
in the process, opening the door for the project to proceed to the next stage.
Here, the project team meets with senior management, the gatekeepers, seeking
approval and resources for their project. Each go/kill gate in Figure 1.6 specifies
deliverables (what the project team must deliver for that gate review), criteria
for a go decision (for example, a scorecard as outlined above, upon which the
go/kill and prioritization decisions are based), and outputs (an action plan for
the next stage, and resources approved).

1.5 Summary

Generating a continuous stream of new product successes is an elusive goal. But the quest goes on, because the goal is so important to business success. This chapter has provided an overview of some of the key drivers of new product performance, and hence insights into how to win at new products.

References

Albright, R. E. and Kappel, T. A., "Roadmapping in the Corporation," *Research-Technology Management* 46(2): 31–40 (March–April, 2003).

American Productivity & Quality Center. *Improving New Product Development Performance and Practices*. Houston, TX.: APQC 2003 (www.apqc.org/pubs/NPD2003).

Cooper, R. G. *Winning at New Products: Accelerating the Process from Idea to Launch*, 2nd edition. Reading, MA.: Perseus Books, 2001.

Cooper, R. G., "Product Innovation and Technology Strategy" in the "Succeeding in Technological Innovation" series, *Research-Technology Management* 43(1): 28–44 (January–February 2000).

Cooper, R. G. and Edgett, S. J., "The dark side of time and time metrics in product innovation," PDMA's *Visions* XXVI (22): 14–16 (April–May 2002).

Cooper R. G. and Edgett, S. J. "Overcoming the crunch in resources for new product development," *Research-Technology Management* 46(3): 48–58 (May–June 2003).

Cooper, R. G., Edgett, S. J., and Kleinschmidt, E. J., *Best Practices in Product Development: What Distinguishes Top Performers*. Ancaster, ON, Canada: Product Development Institute Inc., 2003 (www.prod-dev.com).

Cooper, R. G., Edgett, S. J., and Kleinschmidt, E. J., "Portfolio Management: Fundamental to New Product Success," in The *PDMA Toolbox for New Product development*, edited by P. Beliveau, A. Griffin and S. Somermeyer. New York: John Wiley & Sons, Inc., 2002, pp. 331–364.

Cooper, R. G., Edgett, S. J., and Kleinschmidt, E. J., *Portfolio Management for New Products*, 2nd edition. Reading, Mass: Perseus Book, 2002.

Crawford, C. M., "The hidden costs of accelerated product development," *Journal of Product Innovation Management* 9(3): 188–199 (September 1992).

Di Benedetto, C. A., "Identifying the key success factors in new product launch," *J. Product Innovation Management* 16(6): 530–544 (November 1999).

Griffin, A., *Drivers of NPD Success: The 1997 PDMA Report*. Chicago, IL.: Product Development & Management Association, 1997.

Griffin, A. and Hauser, J., "Integrating R&D, and Marketing: a review and analysis of the literature," *Journal of Product Innovation Management*, 13: 191–215 (1996).

Hultink, E. J. and Atuahene-Gima K., "The effect of sales force adoption on new product selling performance," *J. Product Innovation Management* 17(6): 435–450 (November 2000).

Lynn G. S., Skov, R. B., and Abel, K. D., "Practices that support team learning and their impact on speed to market and new product success," *J. Product Innovation Management* 16(5): 439–454 (September 1999).

McMillan, A., "Roadmapping—Agent of Change," *Research-Technology Management*, 46(2): 40–47 (March–April 2003).

Menke, M. M., "Essentials of R&D strategic excellence," *Research-Technology Management*, 40(5): 42–47 (September–October 1997).

Mishra S., Kim, D., and Lee, D. H., "Factors affecting new product success: cross country comparisons," *J. Product Innovation Management* 13(6): 530–550 (November 1996).

Montoya-Weiss, M. M. and Calantone, R., "Determinants of new product performance: a review and meta-analysis," *Journal of Product Innovation Management* 11(5): 397–417 (November 1994).

Olson, E., Walker, O., Ruekert, R., and Bonner, J., "Patterns of cooperation during new product development among marketing, operations and R&D: implications for project performance," *Journal of Product Innovation Management* 18(4): 258–271 (2001).

Peters, T. J. *Thriving on Chaos*. New York: Harper & Row, 1988.

Song, X. M. and Parry, M. E., "What separates Japanese new product winners from losers" *J. Product Innovation Management* 13(5): 422–439 (September 1996).

Song, X. M. and Montoya-Weiss, M. M., "Critical development activities for really new versus incremental products," *J. Product Innovation Management* 15(2), 124–135 (March 1998).

Von Braun, C. F. *The Innovation War*. Upper Saddle River, NJ: Prentice Hall, 1997.

Dr. Robert G. Cooper is president of the Product Development Institute Inc., Professor of Marketing at the School of Business, McMaster University in Hamilton, Ontario Canada, and also ISBM Distinguished Research Fellow at Penn State University's Smeal College of Business Administration.

Dr Cooper is a world expert in the field of new product management and the father and developer of the *Stage-Gate®process*, now widely used by leading firms around the world to drive new products to market. Bob is a thought-leader in the field of product innovation management: he has published more than 95 articles in leading journals on new product management, with many award winners, and he has also written six books on new product management, including the popular *Winning at New Products: Accelerating the Process from Idea to Launch.*

CHAPTER TWO

A NEW PRODUCT'S DEVELOPMENT STRATEGY: FORMULATION AND IMPLEMENTATION

George Castellion

2.1 Introduction

New product strategy, discussed in this chapter, addresses the set of choices that developers make when building a plan of action for converting a new product concept into a product. The plan addresses issues that, when resolved, can create value for desirable customers and can capture value for the developers' business unit (BU). A skillfully assembled development strategy can play a major role in developing a new product concept. It includes choosing where the product will compete and explaining why it can win. It helps set direction and focuses the development work.

In 1997, the PDMA reported on the role of strategy in a comparative performance analysis of new product development (NPD) at 383 firms. Analysis showed the "Best" firms are more likely to start each NPD project with strategy-building than are the "Rest" of the firms. Best firms also needed only 3.5 ideas for success, compared with the 8.4 ideas needed by the Rest (Griffin, 1997:5).

A good strategy is a path of action that, when a company is developing a new product concept, answers the following question: "Are we doing the right things, when developing this idea, to create value for desirable customers and to capture value for our BU?" Designing and carrying out an effective strategy for developing a product concept isn't easy. It involves homework, common sense, and unbiased choices of the major benefits of the new product and understanding why potential customers value these benefits.

There are five guidelines (see Section 2.2.3) for developers to use when making a new product's development strategy:

1. Devise a strategy for each development project.
2. Make sure that the strategy is aligned with the BU's product development strategy.
3. Orient the strategy toward creating unique benefits and superior value to the customers.
4. Balance this orientation against maximizing the long-term value captured by the BU.
5. Express the sense of the strategy in a product protocol or a value proposition.

This chapter contains an introduction, two main sections, and a summary. The material included in this chapter assumes that your firm has made and has committed to strategic choices as to the businesses the firm should be in. It also assumes that your BU has made and has committed to strategic choices on how it will compete. Recognizing the central role that strategy plays in the successful development of a product concept, other chapters in this handbook include more insights on development strategy.

> *"Strategy has to do with the selection of specific positions. An effective strategist can sometimes find a place to stand in a deep lake; alternatively, ineffective ones sometimes drown in lakes that are on average shallow."* *(Mintzberg, Ahlstrand, and Lampel, 1998:297)*

The first main section discusses *strategy formulation*. It begins by relating this topic directly to something increasingly familiar and important to practitioners: value-based management and sustainable growth. Underpinning strategy formulation is the close connection between a new product's development strategy and its long-term ability to capture value for the BU. Improving or adding attributes to a product concept may persuade potential customers to put a significantly higher benefits score on the product compared with competitive offerings. However, long-term the BU must capture, in one form or another, enough of the value created for customers to justify investment in the concept's development.

Next, this section uses "the blind men and the elephant" description of strategy formation proposed by Mintzberg, Ahlstrand, and Lampel (1998) to classify ten separate ways that strategy formation can be approached. Mintzberg and his colleagues (1998:3) begin their book with the following statement. "We are the blind people and strategy formation is our elephant. Since no one has had the vision to see the entire beast, everyone has grabbed hold of some part or other and 'railed on in utter ignorance' about the rest. . . . Yet to comprehend the whole we also need to understand the parts."

At the end of this section is a discussion of the five guidelines for development groups to use when putting together a strategy for developing a product concept into a new product. These guidelines review some familiar terms in the new product lexicon: the unique superior product, the product protocol, and the value proposition.

Successfully working out a good strategy for developing a new product concept does not guarantee successful implementation. The second main section outlines three categories of implementation issues: people, processes, and politics.

2.2 Strategy Formulation

New product strategy formulation answers the following questions for a product idea's developers:

- Who are the target customers for the new product?
- Which three or four critical benefits of the product create enough value for the target customers to choose to buy the new product rather than competitive offerings?
- How can we produce these benefits cost-effectively and correctly price the product?

A product development group makes day-to-day strategy decisions in two arenas:

1. Choices that create value for the product's customers.
2. Choices that capture for the BU an acceptable share of the value created.

The competitive advantage of the BU may rest on a foundation of tangible and intangible assets such as patents, proprietary technology, brand equity, skills, and a product development process that's right for the unit. The development group needs to employ these assets to create superior value for target customers and to capture enough of this value over the long term to produce a superior economic profit.

2.2.1 Value-Based Management (VBM) and Sustainable Long-Term Profitable Growth

The VBM view of new products melds management accounting and marketing management. During the past 20 years, firms across the world have increasingly adopted VBM practices.[1] In this economist-centered view, the new product captures economic profit when the return on capital employed by the BU over the life cycle of the product exceeds the cost of capital.[2] To create the largest long-term economic profit, the three or four critical benefits of the new product must be produced cost-effectively and priced correctly.

Figure 2.1 shows one way of viewing a product concept's potential to manage pricing and costs. *Relative Price*, on the y-axis, measures the differences in value drivers that customers notice and will pay for when comparing the new product to competitive products' value drivers. It is also a measure of the attractiveness of the target customers' market. *Relative Economic Cost*, on the x-axis, measures the economic cost (operating costs plus the cost of capital) to the BU to produce the new product compared to competitors' economic costs.

The new product concept represented by A in the upper-right quadrant has exceptional advantages in both price and cost to produce. New product

> *"Economic rent (economic profit) is what firms earn over and above the cost of the capital employed in their business. The terminology is unfortunate . . . but it doesn't matter. The concept does. The objective of a company is to increase its economic rent, rather than its profit as such"* (Kay, 1999:3)

[1] See, for example: McTaggart, Kontes, and Mankins, 1994; Drucker 1995; Kay, 1999; Doyle, 2000; Haspeslagh, Noda, and Boulos, 2000; Roslender and Hart, 2000:15; Pitman, 2003:41–46. Haspeslagh et al. (2000) surveyed managers at 106 of firms who have adopted VBM. The firms were in North America, Europe, Japan, and South Korea. The managers reported the impact of VBM on the following new product decision issues. Increasing penetration of existing markets for the firm's products: Impact = 5.9. Moving into new product areas in existing markets: Impact = 4.9. Entering new markets: Impact = 4.8. Diversifying into unrelated products and markets: Impact = 4.3.

Impact was measured on a seven-point scale. Managers who considered VBM's impact as very negative = 1. Managers who considered VBM's impact as very positive = 7.

[2] Cost of capital is calculated using a risk multiplier that includes both the business risk and the financial risk. It is estimated using the Capital Asset Pricing Model in which the cost of capital is the weighted average of the after tax cost of debt and the BU's cost of equity. (McTaggert, Kontes, and Mankins, 1994:310–312)

FIGURE 2.1 A NEW PRODUCT'S POTENTIAL TO CREATE AND CAPTURE ECONOMIC PROFIT.

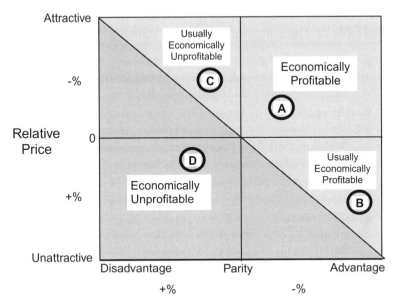

Circles A, B, C, D represent positioning of new product concepts at the end of predevelopment homework (Section 2.2.3.1). *Relative price,* expressed as % of the average price. It is measured by subtracting the average price of competing products from the price target customers are forecasted to pay for the new product. The difference is divided by the average price and multiplied by 100. *Relative economic cost,* expressed as % of the average cost. It is measured by subtracting the average economic cost (operating costs plus the cost of capital) to supply competitive products from the economic cost to supply the new product to the target customers. The difference is divided by the average economic cost and multiplied by 100.

concept B is within an area usually economically profitable and could represent a winning new product with outstanding benefits competing in a mature market. Product concept C, in the right side of the upper-left quadrant, is in an unsustainable profitable position. It could represent a new product competing in an emerging market. For later platform extensions the BU needs to move the product to an advantaged relative cost position. New product concept D, in the lower-right quadrant, could be a new product designed to put a technical stake in the ground or for image-building purposes by the BU. Long-term, product D needs to move an advantaged relative cost position and, if possible, at the same time improve the value created as judged by the BU's target customers.

2.2.2 Schools of Thought on Devising a Strategy

The field of strategic management first came to practitioners' notice in the 1960s. The field continues to evolve through creative tension between prescriptive and descriptive schools of thought. Prescriptive schools give definite, precise directions on what makes up ideal behavior in forming strategies. Descriptive schools are concerned with seeing how, in practice, strategies are formed.

Seasoned NPD practitioners are aware of the need to balance prescription and practice when forming a strategy for developing a product concept into a product. They do not expect to create a path of action by identifying, planning, and influencing all the key variables in advance. However, they can produce a path that encompasses a process of learning and discovery, a path challenging the developers to achieve desired results in a timely fashion.

Such practitioners avoid "satisficing." (Satisficing refers to making a decision without making a believable effort to search for alternatives. [Simon, 1997: 118]) The unfortunate result of satisficing is adopting a development strategy

TABLE 2.1 THREE GROUPS OF SCHOOLS OF THOUGHT ON STRATEGIC FORMATION (MINTZBERG, AHLSTAND, AND LAMPEL, 1998:CHAPTER 1).

Three Groups of Schools of Thought on Strategy Formation	
Group I—Contains only one school—integrates the nine other schools	
Configuration School	Describes the development group's stable state and its surrounding context as *configurations* prescribes *transformation* when warranted
Group II—Three schools that pr*escribe* how strategies should be formed	
Design School	Prescribes a process of *conception*
Planning School	Prescribes a *formal* process
Positioning School	Prescribes an *analytical* process
Group III—Six schools that *describe* how strategies are, in fact, made	
Entrepreneurial School	Describes a *visionary* process
Cognitive School	Describes a *mental* process
Learning School	Describes an *emergent* process
Power School	Describes a process of *negotiation*
Cultural School	Describes a *collective* process
Environmental School	Describes a *reactive* process

for a new product by default, rather than constructing one that will maximize a new product's potential for producing superior, long-term, economic profit.

A recent field review of more than 2000 papers on strategy-making found three groups of schools of thought on devising a strategy (Mintzberg et al., 1998). These authors give this advice on which school of thought to choose when working out a strategy: "There are categories out there, but they should be used as building blocks, or, better still, as ingredients of a stew." When creating a path of action for developing a new product concept, the *Configuration School* can serve as the container in which some of the schools act as main ingredients and others act as seasonings. Stirring the stew is the value-based management spoon.

2.2.2.1 The Configuration School as a Container for Other Schools of Thought.

The Configuration School describes strategy-making as thoughtful consideration of each of the schools of thought at its own time, in its own place. It integrates the messages of the other nine schools and recognizes when it is fitting to make the transformation from one way of thinking about strategy-making to another.

Most of the time, developers use the Configuration School perspective to sustain stability of the configuration that provides a successful path of action for developing a new product concept. However, for each concept, developers must remain alert and recognize when transformation to another path of action would be helpful. Seasoned practitioners not only recognize when transformation is proper but also are skilled at setting it up within the BU without destroying productive features and assets of the earlier way of making strategy.

Product developers are familiar with Miles and Snow's classification of an organization's behaviors into four configurations: *defenders, prospectors, analyzers,* and *reactors* (Miles and Snow, 1994). Each of these configurations has a characteristic strategy for establishing a connection to its chosen market.

A *defender* BU seeks stability. They chose a path of action aimed at sealing off a portion of the market to create a stable state. Product development concentrates on a limited set of products to serve a narrow piece of the addressable market.

A *prospector* BU seeks out innovative new product and market opportunities. Product development is constantly looking for new opportunities and ways of responding to emerging marketing needs.

An *analyzer* BU follows a plan of action balanced between the imperatives of the defenders and the prospectors. An analyzer's strategy for developing a new product concept seeks to minimize risk while maximizing the opportunity for profit.

FIGURE 2.2 CREATING A NEW PRODUCT'S DEVELOPMENT STRATEGY.

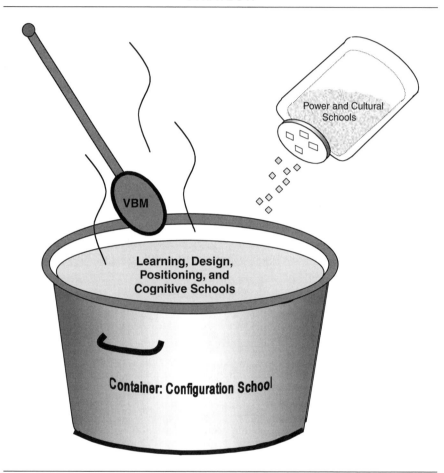

Power and Cultural Schools

VBM

Learning, Design, Positioning, and Cognitive Schools

Container: Configuration School

Strategy-making stew in the Configuration School container. Key ingredients are insights from the Learning, Design, Positioning, and Cognitive schools of thought on strategic-making and seasoned insights from the Power and Cultural schools.

A *reactor* BU responds with new products only when it is forced to do so by competition in the marketplace. As a result, the long-term economic profit created by reactors' NPD efforts suffers compared to that of the other three configurations.

Developers' Alert: Configurations are useful because they are relatively easy to understand and teach. However, reality is always more complex than the view of any one school. Make sure that, within the Configuration School container, contributions from all relevant schools of thought are brought in as main ingredients or seasonings.

2.2.2.2 Main Ingredients in the New Product's Development-Strategy Stew.

- *The Learning School:* In this school, strategies emerge as people, sometimes acting individually but more often collectively, come to learn about the external environment as well as their BU's abilities for dealing with it. Cooper's observations on the strong correlation of predevelopment homework with new product success (see Chapter 1) follow the teachings of the Learning School. Core competencies and venturing are terms used in this school. *Developers' Alert:* the challenge for developers employing this school, as a main ingredient, is to recognize when enough is known to commit to exploiting what has been learned so far.
- *The Design School:* This school seeks to reach a fit between internal abilities and the environment. This is an influential school in NPD, with emphasis on simple and informal strategy-making. Terms used in this school are SWOT (*Strengths* and *Weaknesses* of the BU and the *Opportunities* and *Threats* in the BU's external environment), distinctive competence, and competitive advantage. *Developers' Alert:* This school views strategy-making as mainly a process of conception rather than a process of learning. Developers need to ask the question: "How can my BU be so sure of its strengths and weaknesses in product development without learning how potential customers and competitors view the BU's strengths and weaknesses?
- *The Positioning School:* This school argues that only a few positions in an industry's marketplace are desirable. This is an influential field in NPD, drawing on both military strategy and the field of economics. "Competitive analysis," "portfolio," "five forces," "star," "cash cow," and "dog" are key phrases in this school. *Developers' Alert:* This school overplays the influence of external conditions and downplays internal skills. Positioning should support the strategy-making process, not be the process. What looks like a star may be a black hole and often a dog can be a BU's best friend.
- *The Cognitive School:* This school focuses on subconscious biases in the complex and creative decision-making acts that result in strategies. Individuals often display judgmental biases, such as "anchoring" or "overconfidence," when processing information gathered for strategy making (Russo and Schoemaker, 2002). Some firms use the Myers-Briggs instrument to help staff product development teams with individuals having different cognitive styles (Stevens et al., 1999). *Developers' Alert:* this school is coming along fast as a key ingredient when creating a new product's development strategy, but is

currently characterized more by its potential than its contribution to NPD strategy-making.

2.2.2.3 Schools for Seasoning the New Product's Development-Strategy Stew.

- *Power School:* This is an unconcealed emphasis on power and politics for negotiating strategies favorable to particular interests. Power and politics pervade new product development. Holahan and Markham (see Chapter 10) discuss the benefits of incorporating insights from the Power School. *Developers' Alert:* power can have a positive role in strategy formulation, but it can also be a source of much waste and distortion.
- *Cultural School:* This school concerns itself mainly with the influence of culture on preserving strategic stability, or sometimes, in actively resisting strategic change. It sees a BU as a collection of assets and skills. The success of new products developed by these BUs is based on a BU's distinctive assets and skills. *Developers' Alert:* this school equates strategic advantage with organizational uniqueness and can lead to arrogance and a new product's development strategy that is blind to moves by competitors and customers.

2.2.2.4 Schools Where Caution Is Recommended When Adding to the Development-Strategy Stew.

- *Environmental School:* This school sees the environment as a set of abstract forces to which the organization must react or perish. *Developers' Alert:* this school has a restrictive view of strategic choice, since its dimensions of the environment are often vague and abstract.
- *Planning School:* This school is rooted in the Design School but is more formal and linear. *Developers' Alert:* the world has to hold still while planning unfolds.
- *Entrepreneurial School:* This school focuses on the leader of the development group, the firm, or the BU and stresses vision based on intuition, judgment, wisdom, experience, and insight. *Developers' Alert:* when a strategy runs into difficulty, this school's cure is to get a new leader.

2.2.3 Five Guidelines for Development Groups Creating a New Product's Development Strategy

1. *Devise a strategy for each new product development project:*
   Why? In comparative performance studies of new product success, the Best firms set strategy for each NPD project (Griffin, 1997:5). Not all NPD

projects run with good strategies produce successful new products. However, devising a strategy before beginning development increases the likelihood of success.

How? Skilled builders of a product concept's development strategy draw on all ten schools of thought on strategic management. Insight from the Configuration School should be the major container for the strategy stew for developing a product concept into a new product. Major ingredients of the stew are insights from the Learning, Design, Positioning, and Cognitive Schools. Seasoning the new product's development strategy are insights from the Power School and the Cultural School.

Working out strategy is a crucial skill in product development. It calls for performing high-quality homework before formulation and looking for insight on benefits and pricing without being numbed by data overload. Successful developers at best-performing firms spend twice as much time and money on predevelopment work than do developers at the worst-performing firms (see Chapter 1). In *value-to-the-business assessment*, a key homework task for strategy-making, 38 percent of best performers performed this task well. However, only 4 percent of the worst performers did a high-quality, value-to-the-business assessment. (see Chapter 1, Figure 1.2)

Strategy-making homework consists of a conscientious completion of six tasks before starting development work. The first task is conducting a screening of product concepts for exploiting a new product opportunity. The second is completion of a preliminary study of the marketplace for the product concept if it is developed into a product. The third is a quick technical appraisal of possible development work. Next is an introductory marketing research study describing potential customers' wants, needs, and willingness to buy a product developed from the concept (see Chapters 13 and 14). Then, possible competitive products are identified. Finally, a preliminary business and financial analysis of the new product is prepared based on what is known at this point.

2. *Make sure that the strategy is aligned with the firm's and the BU's product development strategies.*

Why? Many firms have mission statements to guide the whole firm in creating and capturing value. In addition, the firm may assign platform strategies to a BU. Platforms evolve where several new product development projects are close together and share some strategic needs. Platforms may share a common technology or a category, either product type or customer, or they may share a brand. Within the BU there may also be product line strategies and expansion strategies (Crawford and Di Benedetto, 2003; McGrath, 2000).

How? Two chapters in this Handbook deal with how developers can create support for the new product's development strategy within the firm and the BU. (see Chapters 4 and 10) Ensuring that this strategy is integrated with the firm's mission statement and the BU's platform strategies makes the creation of support easier.

Integrated strategies take care to define the following matters: (1) structure, what goes where, (2) responsibilities, who is responsible for which essentials of development, and (3) timing, which essentials precede others and how often each essential is performed (McGrath, 2000).

Crawford and Di Benedetto (2003) warn that developers framing a new product's development strategy "had better take into consideration all the baggage that comes from corporate and platform strategies." Section 2.3.3 of this chapter has more to say about dealing with this "baggage."

3. *Orient the strategy toward creating unique benefits and superior value to the customers.*

Why? Developing a product delivering unique benefits and superior value to potential customers is the number one reason for a new product's success. (see Chapter 1) Growth of a BU through the introduction of new products depends on convincing desirable customers that these products offer superior value when compared to competitive products.

How? Desirable customers for a new product may include existing customers in the market for improved products, new customers in the market, or potential customers in markets new to the BU. Completing the six homework tasks outlined in the first guideline helps the company discover the value of the unique benefits of a product concept for the customer. The objective is to gain up-to-date knowledge on where value lives in the chain from the new product to the customers' end users.

4. *Balance this orientation against maximizing the long-term value captured by the BU.*

Why? The economic profit captured by the BU over the life cycle of the new product must exceed the cost of capital employed to develop and launch it. If it doesn't, then the new product strategy is unacceptable in the VBM view.

How? As with the second guideline, the goal is to gain up-to-date knowledge on financial issues where it is essential to resolve some of the confusion before starting development. Techniques suitable for forecasting sales are covered in Chapter 23. Financial analysis tools for estimating value created and economic profit are described in Higgins (2001:231–317), Doyle (2000:32–68), and McTaggart et al. (1994:313–329).

5. *Express the sense of the strategy in a product protocol or a value proposition.*

Why? These written statements serve as guides for trade-off decisions as knowledge gained during development influences the new product's potential for value creation and economic profit. Such a statement is needed whether development advances by a relay from one department to another or concurrently by a multifunctional team.

A *product protocol,* described by Crawford and Di Benedetto (2003), is a document prepared after completing financial analysis in the strategy-making homework. It states what major benefits the product will deliver to the customer and how the BU will capture exemplary economic profit through that delivery. The protocol documents trade-off decisions made in producing the protocol. It states how developers arrived at the choices they made when setting the specifications of the protocol and what prompted those decisions. The protocol also spells out the target market for the product and positioning of the product in that market compared with competitive products.

A product's *value proposition,* described by Reinertsen (1997:174), is a brief—25 words or less—statement clearly explaining the mission of the group developing a product concept. As a distillation of the strategy-making stew, a compelling value proposition provides clear decision-making answers to the now familiar two questions: Why should customers buy this product rather than its competitors? How will we produce and deliver this unique and superior value in a way that produces economic profit for the BU?

For the development group, the value proposition focuses on the three or four unique benefits—the value drivers—desirable customers in attractive markets consider when making their buying decision. It also focuses on the one or two ways of superior value creation by which the BU will capture economic profit.

A compelling value proposition uses another principle from economics, Pareto's Rule. In this application of the rule to a new product, the development group has clear guidance for focusing on the 80 percent of the value of the product that comes from 20 percent of the benefits. It keeps the group from having to hew their way through a laundry list of do's and don'ts on the product's attributes. The briefness of the proposition also makes it easier to

> *"Devise and maintain a clearly stated, focused strategy. . . . It begins with a simple, focused value proposition that is rooted in deep, certain knowledge about your company's target customers and a realistic appraisal of your own capabilities"* (Nohria et al., 2003:45)

keep in mind when making many small trade-off decisions as development work advances.

2.3 Strategy Implementation

Implementation issues fall into three categories: people, processes, and politics. Successful implementation of a new product strategy can often be more difficult than putting together the strategy.

2.3.1 People

A proverb states, "Show me and I will forget. Teach me and I will remember. Include me and I will understand." The people charged with doing the development work should be included in the work of building a product protocol or a value proposition. Doing so means more effective trade-off decisions during development.

Individuals have work habits and judgmental biases formed by their formal training or learned in past development projects. Each new product strategy means a change in work habits. Understanding the strategy behind a new product's development can produce productive change in ingrained work habits.

Beyond work habits, personality differences and diverse backgrounds in people can either strengthen or impede implementation of a strategy. Through training, teams composed of people of different personality types and mixed experiences can form development teams that are more cohesive and effective than homogeneous teams. (See Chapter 9.)

Another people problem is assigning individuals to development groups without considering the time or motivation they have to focus on implementation.

> The middle managers studied here typically complained that a new implementation effort required additional demands on their time, with no relief from normal job responsibilities and no monetary incentives for the effort itself, leaving them to be evaluated primarily on the basis of their traditional tasks (Noble, 1999:27).

2.3.2 Processes

Implementing a product development framework warrants a separate chapter in this handbook (see Chapter 4). In addition, Chapter 6 discusses the differences in processes used to develop incremental, platform, and radical products. When a development group is transforming from an ineffective process to a more effective process, make sure to include enough time, training, and motivation for the switch or else only the surface appearance of the process will change.

2.3.3 Politics

"Things in The Company aren't always what they seem, and often they work better that way"

(RITTI AND LEVY, 2003:30)

In every BU there are disputes between groups during strategy implementation about such issues as who "owns" the communication channel with potential customers, and why wasn't the most "capable person" put in charge of the development project. Insight from Chapter 10 helps in understanding the conditions within BUs that result in political behavior. Chapter 10 also suggests ways of using politics to carry out a new product strategy.

Ritti and Levy (2003) in *The Ropes to Skip and the Ropes to Know* devote a book to the dangers of ignoring politics and to the leverage in making politics work for you within an organization. There are no short or simple explanations for the behaviors described. However, the descriptions, and the prescriptions for making political leverage work positively, ring true for people familiar with the cultural characteristics of North American development groups involved in new product strategy implementation.

2.4 Summary

Building a clear and realistic path of action for transforming a product concept into a successful new product calls for making clear choices about where the product will compete and why it will win. It needs unambiguous explanations why this strategy will create superior value for the customer and capture sustainable value for the BU.

Product developers must work out a strategy for each NPD project before beginning development. Doing this helps the developers match or exceed the performance of the Best firms in translating ideas into successful products. This strategy needs to be aligned with the BU's new product strategy. It must create value for customers and capture enough of that value to produce an economic profit for the BU as the strategy plays out through the product's life cycle.

The Configuration School of thought on strategy-making integrates the teachings of the other nine schools of thought. The Configuration School prizes strategies that preserve a configuration. However, it also recognizes the need for managed transformation to another configuration when that is the best long-term course.

Five guidelines for building a new product's development strategy are recommended for development groups. Devise a strategy for each new product development project. Make sure that the strategy is aligned with the BU's product development strategy. Orient the strategy to create unique benefits and superior value to the target customers. Balance this orientation against maximizing the economic profit captured by the BU. Express the sense of the strategy in a product protocol or value proposition.

Successful implementation of a new product strategy can often be more difficult than putting together the strategy. Implementation issues fall into three categories: people, processes, and politics. The people doing the development need to be involved with strategy-making. When moving from an ineffective to a more effective development process make sure that enough time, training, and motivation are included when making the switch or else only the surface appearance will change. Finally, ignoring politics and the "baggage" that comes from a firm's mission statement and a BU's platform strategies can be dangerous.

References

Crawford, C. Merle and Di Benedetto, C. Anthony, *New Products Management* 7th Edition. New York, NY McGraw-Hill, 2003.

Doyle, Peter, *Value-Based Marketing: Marketing Strategies for Corporate Growth and Shareholder Value.* Chichester, England, John Wiley & Sons, 2000.

Drucker, Peter F., "The Information Executives Truly Need," *Harvard Business Review* 73(1): 54–62 (1995).

Griffin, Abbie, *Drivers of NPD Success The 1997 PDMA Report.* Chicago, IL, 1997.

Haspeslagh, P., Noda, T., and Boulos, F., "Are You Really Managing for Value?" INSEAD Working Paper (http://ged.insead.edu/fichiersti/inseadwp2000/2000-67.pdf), 2000.

Higgins, Robert C., "Part IV. Evaluating Investment Opportunities," *Analysis for Financial Management* 6th Edition, New York, NY: McGraw-Hill, 2001.

Kay, John, "Mastering Strategy," *Financial Times (London)* 9/27/99 (http://www.johnkay.com/strategy/135), 1999.

McGrath, Michael E., *Product Strategy for High-Technology Companies* 2nd Edition, New York, NY: McGraw-Hill, 2000.

McTaggart, James, Kontes, Peter, and Mankns, Michael, *The Value Imperative: Managing for Superior Shareholder Returns,* New York, NY: The Free Press, 1994.

Miles, Raymond E. and Snow, Charles C., *Fit, Failure, and the Hall of Fame.* New York, NY: The Free Press, 1994.

Mintzberg, Henry, Ahlstrand, Bruce, and Lampel, Joseph; *Strategy Safari: A Guided Tour Through The Wilds of Strategic Management.* New York, NY: The Free Press, 1998.

Noble, C. H., "Building the Strategy Implementation Network," *Business Horizons* (November-December 23–28, 1999).

Nohria, Nitin, Joyce, William, and Roberson, Bruce, "What Really Works," *Harvard Business Review* 81(7) (2003).

Pitman, Brian, "Leading for Value," *Harvard Business Review* 81(4) 41–46 (2003).

Reinertsen, Donald G., *Managing the Design Factory: A Product Developer's Toolkit*. New York, NY: The Free Press, 1997.

Ritti, R. Richard and Levy, Steve, *The Ropes to Skip and the Ropes to Know: Studies in Organizational Behavior* 6th Edition. New York, NY: John Wiley & Sons. 2003.

Roslender, Robin and Hart, Susan J., "Integrating Management Accounting and Marketing in the Pursuit of Competitive Advantage," presented at the Proceedings of the Sixth Interdisciplinary Perspectives on Accounting Conference, Manchester, England (http://les.man.ac.uk/IPA/papers/117.pdf), 2000.

Russo, J. Edward and Schoemaker, Paul J. H., *Winning Decisions*. New York, NY: Random House, 2002.

Simon, Herbert A., *Administrative Behavior: A Study of Decision-Making Processes In Administrative Organizations* Fourth Edition. New York, NY: The Free Press, 1997.

Stevens, Greg, Burley, James, and Divine, Richard, *Journal of Product Innovation Management* 16:455–468 (1999).

George Castellion, SSC Associates, provides custom marketing research to a wide range of clients in business-to-business product management. He specializes in working with clients in the early stages of product development to quickly find reliable answers to questions about potential customers, competitors, and the new product's marketplace.

Dr. Castellion founded his marketing research practice, SSCA, in 1985 after a business career in the chemicals industry. As a practitioner, he was first an inventor and manager of technology groups. Then, he moved into marketing, where he held senior positions with profit responsibility for both established and new products.

Besides his business experience, George Castellion is a past president of the PDMA. He currently serves on the editorial board of the *Journal of Product Innovation Management* and is VP, Development, of the PDMA Foundation's *Comparative Performance Assessment Study* of product development practices.

CHAPTER THREE

NEW PRODUCT PORTFOLIO PLANNING AND MANAGEMENT

Marvin L. Patterson

3.1 Introduction

Business leaders have two overarching objectives for their new product programs. First, they expect their investments in new products to create growth for the enterprise. Increases in revenue and profits created by a steady stream of new products are needed to fund growth of the business. Second, business leaders expect their new product efforts to increase the competitive strength of the firm, both now and in the future.

An effective new product program is, however, the result of many factors. New technology and R&D inventiveness are important, but these alone cannot ensure business success. Effective portfolio-planning and management activities are also needed to: (1) aim the new product program at a profitable and suitable future, and (2) ensure the continuing effectiveness of current projects.

New product expenses are often the largest investments that a business enterprise makes and, as with any investment, they should be managed carefully—with due diligence. Yet, in many firms, new product activities get too little mind share from business leaders. The discussion that follows will outline key activities related to the effective tracking and management of these investments, which the business leadership team must own and carry out effectively.

3.2 Portfolio Planning and Management— A Useful Framework

An effective new product program is essentially a system for rapidly gathering and assimilating information and then systemically adding value to it until it describes how to sell, make, use, and support an exciting new product or service (Patterson, 1999). From another perspective: "The ability to learn faster than your competitors may be the only sustainable competitive advantage" (De Geus, 1988).

The portfolio planning and management framework depicted in Figure 3.1 is one of the key learning systems in the business enterprise. Business leaders need to lead, carry out, track, and manage this essential system.

This framework includes new product portfolio activities, shown inside of the dashed boundary, as well as other support functions and related efforts

FIGURE 3.1 PORTFOLIO PLANNING & MANAGEMENT WITH RELATED ACTIVITIES.

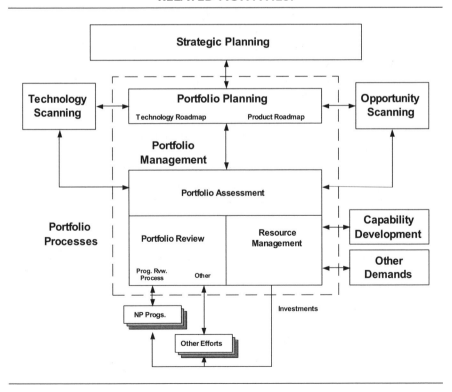

shown outside this boundary as context. The portfolio work that concerns the business leadership team includes a strategic process, labeled "portfolio planning," and several tactical tasks under the heading of portfolio management. Tactical tasks include portfolio assessment, resource management, and portfolio review.

The overarching objective of this system is to transform the business strategy of a company into effective and specific new product investments. To be effective, these investments must be directed at profitable and suitable business opportunities, and they must involve competitive, perhaps newly emerging, technologies and practices. When added together, the portfolio of investments the firm makes in new products and services should move the enterprise from its present state into a strategically desirable future. Each of these investments must result in a well-planned and managed project activity that first defines the most competitive response to an opportunity and then quickly and effectively transforms this definition into a deliverable product or service.

A second overall objective of this system is to provide strategic guidance to the firm's various capability development activities. These activities might include: (1) hiring new employees, (2) training and development for the existing workforce, (3) gaining new tools, (4) developing new business processes, (5) adding new manufacturing abilities, or (6) developing new strategic partnerships. Achieving this second objective will ensure that the firm's capacity to compete improves steadily over time.

The sections that follow describe each of the portfolio activities. A couple of definitions will be useful in this discussion.

- *Portfolio:* The set of R&D projects, technology, and new product efforts currently funded and underway.
- *Roadmap:* A "moving belt" representation of future products or technologies versus time, starting now and extending into the future. Included in a roadmap are projects in the current portfolio, as well as unfunded efforts envisioned for the future.

In *portfolio planning,* members of the business leadership team in a company or business unit should own creation and execution of a portfolio planning process. The objective of this process is to create a strategic plan for new products and technologies that is responsive to the firm's overall business strategy. This plan sets the desired direction for future product and technology investments (Cooper, 1998). The financial future of the enterprise is, to a large degree, fixed by this process. Key outputs from this activity include: (1) a roadmap of future products and services, (2) a roadmap for future technology efforts, and

(3) high-quality decisions on whether or not to add candidate new product or technology efforts to the current portfolio (Wilyard, 1987). Other useful results might include business insights such as market segmentation models and market-related business cycle understanding.

Each company needs to design its own portfolio planning process to fit the nature of its business and to compliment the relationships the firm typically preserves with its customers, key vendors and strategic partners. In general terms, however, each portfolio planning process needs to gather and analyze internal and external information related to markets and technologies of interest to the firm. Information of interest will include: (1) conditions and trends in current markets, (2) factors related to emerging markets, (3) the state and actions of competing firms, (4) local, national, and global business conditions and trends, (5) trends and other factors related to technologies of current interest, and (6) emerging technologies and technical trends that might be of interest in the future. Ideally, all members of the firm's business leadership team, from the CEO or business unit general manager on down to first line managers, will take part in gathering and processing this information. Members of the team at each level will see issues from different and valuable perspectives. Effective integration of these multiple perspectives leads to stronger product and technology strategies.

Another important element of most portfolio planning processes is the integration of market and technology perspectives. Primary responsibility for the product roadmap will belong to the marketing function, whereas technology roadmap planning will belong to the R&D function. At various points in the process, these two functions should come together to share and integrate what they have learned. The resulting product roadmap will thus be responsive to R&D's understanding of technology developments, and technology strategies will reflect the firm's knowledge of current and future market factors.

A third common attribute of portfolio planning is a periodic review and approval of the resulting product and technology roadmaps by top management. Depending on circumstances this might be done as often as once a quarter, or only once a fiscal year.

Portfolio management is a set of activities that includes portfolio assessment, resource management, and portfolio review.

The primary objective of the portfolio assessment activity is to ensure that the current set of new product and technology investments: (1) is likely to provide anticipated returns, (2) moves the firm along desired strategic directions, and (3) continues to reflect the best possible use of available resources in view of changing conditions. A second objective of this activity is to evaluate the learning rate of the enterprise for relevant market and technology issues.

Depending on the results of this evaluation, business leaders may decide to focus a small fraction of available resources on specific investigation activities to ensure that the enterprise is learning faster than its competitors in key areas. These decisions would trigger projects in either the Opportunity Scanning or Technology Scanning functions outside the dashed boundary in Figure 3.1.

A subset of the business leadership team does the portfolio assessment. Working together as a portfolio management team, this group should periodically meet, perhaps once a month, to perform this evaluation. In this meeting they should share, integrate, and bring to bear what they have individually learned about external and internal circumstances relevant to the current portfolio. They should consider each project in the portfolio and compare its current state: (1) to what was promised during its first proposal, and (2) to alternative investments that might use the same resources. The portfolio management team might take the following actions: (1) continue to invest in the current portfolio without change, (2) provide guidance or redirection to individual projects in the portfolio, or (3) cancel current investments whose performance has fallen too far below expectations or that are no longer likely to create needed returns.

The responsibility for resource management efforts is distributed among managers in the various new-product-related functions—for example, R&D, marketing, manufacturing, quality, and finance—with oversight by the portfolio management team. The overall objective for these activities is to ensure that available resources, both internal and external, are effectively applied to achieve new product portfolio goals. Achieving this objective requires: (1) a good understanding of the workload implied by the current portfolio and by proposed additions, and (2) clear understanding of the inherent capacity of each department and vendor to perform new-product-related assignments.

Portfolio review accomplishes the following objectives: (1) ensures that each new product investment remains on track relative to expectations, (2) enforces a sense of urgency and accountability among project personnel, (3) provides opportunities for midcourse correction of project direction or performance, and (4) discovers excellent performance and provides proper and timely recognition. Periodic project reviews vary in frequency from once a month to once a quarter. Project phase-gate reviews are driven by project progress and provide portfolio managers with an opportunity to judge a project's accomplishments compared with published expectations. All members of the business leadership team should also look for less formal opportunities, such as hallway conversations or management by wandering around, to stay abreast of issues and developments related to new product activity.

3.3 New Product Portfolio Roles and Responsibilities

Setting up clear ownership of essential roles and responsibilities is crucial to effective portfolio planning and management. This section outlines important roles and suggests where ownership might best be placed.

Process ownership: Company executives should define a portfolio management team responsible for the overall process of portfolio planning and management. The team should delegate the tasks of developing and carrying out the various parts of portfolio planning and management. However, they must assume overall responsibility for the effectiveness of the integrated process and for the results that it produces. If any part of the process performs short of expectations, this group should detect the problem and take corrective action.

Portfolio ownership: The portfolio management team also should own the efficacy of the current portfolio of new-product-related investments. All parts of the portfolio are their responsibility. This includes: (1) the expected financial impact, (2) the implied strategic direction, (3) the overall balance, and (4) the expected competitive impact. Portfolio balance (Item 3) is an important part of the portfolio that will be specific to each business (Cooper, 1998). The balance may reflect how investments are spread between market segments addressed by the firm. Alternatively, it might reflect how investment is spread between high-risk, breakthrough projects and incremental product development projects. If the current portfolio falls short in any of these areas, the portfolio management team should assume responsibility for detecting and correcting the situation. The gateway between product and technology roadmaps and the portfolio is the decision process used to evaluate candidate projects. The portfolio management team should own and carry out this process as well and use it to keep control over the contents of the portfolio.

Setting strategic directions: The responsibility for setting up an effective strategic direction for new product efforts is distributed throughout the business leadership team. The R&D function has primary responsibility for creating the technology roadmap, whereas marketing should assume ownership of the product roadmap. Each of these efforts should, however, strive to integrate the best strategic insights from members of the business leadership team at all levels. The portfolio management team should act as overseer, reviewing and approving the product and technology roadmaps.

Once strategic product and technology directions have been established, the portfolio management team should address the question, "What capabilities do we need to support this future?" The answers might imply adding new capabilities, closing down some that currently exist, or perhaps setting up new relationships with vendors or strategic partners. In the 1990s, for instance, the Hewlett-Packard Company found that the shift to microprocessor control of instruments left it with too many electrical engineers (EEs) and not enough software engineers. An internal educational curriculum was developed to "retread" EE's, and turn them into effective software engineers. Over several years, hundreds of EE's volunteered for the program, which ran until the imbalance in the workforce was corrected. New product and technology roadmaps should provide long-term guidance for capability development efforts. The portfolio management team needs to make sure that this information is communicated to others in the enterprise and applied as appropriate.

Resource management: The manager of each functional department involved in new-product-related activity should be able to estimate the resource impact of a proposed new project and decide whether it can be supported. In some departments, this can be as simple as deciding if the right person can be made available. In other functions, such as R&D, this may need a sophisticated estimation tool that embodies models of typical project resource profiles versus time. In either case, accurate feedback to the portfolio management team concerning resource availability is crucial. New projects should be added to the portfolio only when the needed resources are available.

Knowing who is working on what is a second and important responsibility in resource management. In many firms, new projects often begin by "spontaneous combustion." Perhaps an interesting idea in the engineering ranks leads to experimentation, which leads to a working prototype. Higher-level managers are sometimes unaware of this activity until they are presented with an accomplished fact—a working system that has perhaps cost hundreds of hours of engineering effort. A certain freedom for experimentation is desirable and can lead to important learning, even breakthroughs. This activity should be a conscious part of the R&D investment portfolio, though, not clandestine behavior. A key part of the portfolio management responsibility is ensuring that the R&D investment is being spent as intended.

3.4 Assessment of Portfolio Planning & Management Capability

Previous sections have outlined key elements of the portfolio planning and management process and described roles and responsibilities that must be implemented. This section addresses the critical success factors for performance related to this important business process. The intent is to provide business leaders with information and insights useful in evaluating the performance of their own firm.

A comprehensive evaluation of portfolio planning and management capability requires measuring levels of achievement in four critical performance areas: (1) strategic direction, (2) portfolio level of merit, (3) project execution, and (4) new-product-related resources. A sparse set of quantitative tools are available for appraising performance in these areas but, in general, they do not offer enough breadth and depth to achieve the comprehensive assessment wanted here (Cooper, 1998; Patterson, 1999). Instead, a largely subjective approach is suggested—that of comparing a firm's performance to the earmarks of ideal performance, as described below. The following paragraphs outline key symptoms of success in each of these four performance areas.

Strategic direction: Regular, well-planned and -executed strategic discussions occur that involve key members of the business leadership team. A process is in place that creates product and technology roadmaps and periodically updates them (Wilyard, 1987). These roadmaps exist and are current. Each roadmap is supported by a coherent, insightful, well-explained rationale. The new product and technology strategies provide bold objectives for the firm, are exciting, and extend well beyond the reach of current markets and currently applied technologies. The near-term strategies are stable and produce competitive, exciting, and fruitful candidates for addition to the R&D portfolio. The current new product and technology strategies reflect integrated and broadly held perspectives on relevant market and technological factors. New product efforts commonly achieve high revenue gain and profitability that meets or exceeds targets. The strategies provide clear, consistent direction for capability development efforts. The portfolio management team has determined the three most important new-product-related performance issues that keep the firm from being more competitive, has initiated corrective actions, and is measuring progress on these efforts.

Portfolio level of merit: Targets and forecasts exist for the business return expected from each project in the portfolio. A roll-up of this data, such as the new product vintage chart depicted in Figure 3.2, shows that the current portfolio will support the firm's targets for financial growth (Patterson, 1998). Guidelines for portfolio balance exist and are evident in the nature of the current portfolio (Cooper, 1998). The value propositions for the projects in the portfolio, as an integrated set, promise excellent progress in chosen strategic directions. There are clear signs that the enterprise is learning faster than its competitors in key areas and that the current portfolio of projects will be effective in growing competitive capability. Each new product effort in the portfolio has clear targets for performance factors such as: (1) revenue gain, (2) project cost, (3) unit manufacturing cost, (4) reliability, and (5) serviceability. Project schedules and budgets are best estimates of expected performance, not constraints imposed politically from the top down.

FIGURE 3.2 VINTAGE CHART REPRESENTATION SHOWING PORTFOLIO IMPACT.

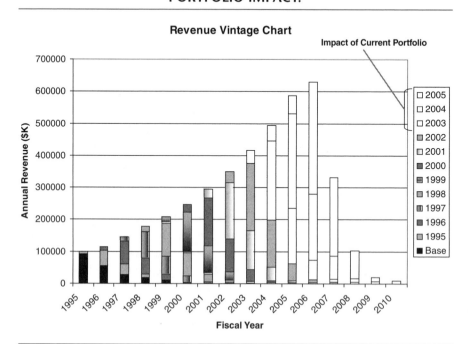

Project execution: Published plans exist for each product and technology project, and they are current and realistic. Means for tracking estimates of schedule and budget over time have been implemented, and the data show that these estimates are stable for most projects (Patterson, 1999). The few projects that display unstable estimates get close management scrutiny. Projects are managed through an institutionalized phase-gate process that aligns well with the firm's new product business model. The quality of project deliverables for each development phase is routinely assessed relative to published norms and is found acceptable. The requirements and performance levels for each new product are stable and well managed. The value proposition of each project in the portfolio—to the firm's customers, and to the firm itself—is well documented and tracked with other project attributes.

Project teams include strong representation from the R&D, marketing, manufacturing, and quality functional departments. These teams are led well, effectively integrated, highly motivated, and largely in agreement about project issues. Each individual has enough time to do good work. Project managers vigorously discourage "shortcuts," such as skipping design reviews or subsystem tests. Major performance shortfalls, compared with project targets, are rarely discovered in final project phases.

New-product-related resources: The firm is viewed as a preferred employer by new product professionals throughout the industry. Attrition is low, especially among top performers, and this is a source of pride throughout the enterprise. The working environment is free from fear so everyone, including each individual contributor, feels comfortable speaking out and raising issues. The performance of individuals on each project often yields "nice surprises"; "nasty surprises" are rare. All individuals in the new-product-related workforce invest a substantial part of their time—on the order of 40 hours or more per year—in professional development activity, gaining important new job-related skills.

Project teams move quickly enough to create a reasonable level of scrap as they go, but costly, stress-induced errors are rare. Each new product team works hard, but keeps the resilience needed to work harder in a crisis. The firm is skilled in setting up and managing strategic partnerships that compliment its core competencies. These alliances are fruitful and substantially strengthen competitive capability. Root causes for chronic new product program bottlenecks are understood, corrective steps are underway, and progress is being measured and tracked.

Assessment technique: Evaluation of a firm's portfolio planning and management capability involves comparing its performance with the idealized attributes described in each of the four sections above. This comparison includes two important elements: (1) evaluating how close or far a firm is from ideal performance levels, and (2) identifying the most important gaps between actual and ideal performance.

A simple 1 to 5 scale can be used to evaluate performance relative to each attribute described above:

1 = Our performance threatens the firm's long-term existence.

2 = Our performance causes us to lose ground to competitors.

3 = Our performance is enough to stay abreast of competitors.

4 = Our performance is a competitive advantage.

5 = Our performance is world class, a key differentiator for our firm

Each member of a firm's business leadership team should first perform this evaluation separately, then the group should meet to discuss and integrate the results. During this discussion all individuals should summarize their perspectives on the key areas of strength and performance shortfall as they see them and offer a rationale for their scoring. Next, the group should discuss collectively each of the noteworthy performance areas. The goal is to achieve a shared perspective on the firm's strengths and weaknesses and to understand the diversity in views among members of the business leadership team.

The most critical performance gaps should be used to establish the strategic direction for performance improvement efforts. The group should prioritize the shortfalls in their portfolio planning and management capability and pick only the three most important issues as a focus for attention. An owner should be designated for each issue to initiate the generation and execution of action plans. As progress is made in these performance improvement efforts, additional issues can be pulled from the list to be addressed by follow-on efforts. This process needs to continue, with occasional reassessment of current performance, until an effective portfolio planning and management capability has finally been established.

3.5 Summary

A system view of portfolio planning and management has been presented that embodies four key components:

- Portfolio planning
- Portfolio assessment
- Resource management
- Portfolio review

The business objectives for each of these components were presented, and the roles of business leaders in carrying out these activities were described. The suggested owner of this system—the group eventually responsible for its effective design, implementation, and operation—has been identified as the portfolio management team, a designated subset of the firm's business leadership team. The critical success factors for effective portfolio planning and management were discussed, and a technique for assessing the performance of this crucial business process was outlined. Finally, a model for setting up effective performance improvement initiatives was suggested that provides needed strategic direction, focus, and ownership.

Every firm that develops new products and services has each element in the portfolio planning and management process already in place, either purposefully or unconsciously. New product investments are selected, either deliberately and insightfully or otherwise. An investment portfolio exists that will create a return, either substantial or disappointing. Project teams create results, either efficiently or haphazardly. New product releases carry the firm to its future, either along a well-chosen path or one that more resembles a random walk. The difference in business performance between one firm and the next is often determined by the degree of planning and effort invested in making these existing process elements effective.

Business leaders can achieve significant gains in the long-term financial and competitive strength of their firm by improving portfolio planning and management performance. These improvements will provide substantial gains in business performance, including faster growth in revenue and profit and in the firm's ability to learn faster than its competitors. Overhauling this business process, though, requires knowledge, persistence, and hard work. The ideas presented here can provide an effective framework for this worthwhile effort.

References

Cooper, Robert G., Edgett, Scott J., and Kleinschmidt, Elko J., *Portfolio Management for New Products*. Reading, MA: Addison-Wesley, 1998.

De Geus, Arie P., "Planning as Learning," *Harvard Business Review* 70–74 (March/April 1988).

Patterson, Marvin L., "From Experience: Linking Product Innovation to Business Growth," *Journal of Product Innovation Management (JPIM)*, 15(5): 390–402 (September 1998).

Patterson, Marvin L., *Leading Product Innovation: Accelerating Growth in a Product-based Business.* New York NY: John Wiley & Sons, 1999.

Wilyard, Charles II and McClees, Cheryl W., "Motorola Technology Roadmap Process," *Research-Technology Management* 13–19 (September–October 1987).

Marvin L. Patterson is founder and president of Innovation Resultants International (IRI), a firm dedicated to helping client companies achieve greater business success through more competitive new product innovation. Prior to establishing IRI, Marv enjoyed a 20-year career at the Hewlett-Packard Company (HP). When he left HP he was director of Corporate Engineering, an internal consulting group focused on improving the competitiveness of HP's own worldwide new product development efforts.

Marv has written two books on managing new product development: *Leading Product Innovation: Accelerating Growth in a Product-based Business* (John Wiley & Sons, 1999), and *Accelerating Innovation: Improving the Process of Product Development* (John Wiley & Sons, 1997). He has served on the board of trustees for the National Technological University and on the board of directors of the American National Standards Institute (ANSI). Marv received his B.S.E.E. and M.S.E.E. degrees from the University of Washington, and is a graduate of the University of Michigan Executive Program.

CHAPTER FOUR

IMPLEMENTING PRODUCT DEVELOPMENT

Paul O'Connor

4.1 Introduction

As other chapters point out, a set of processes make up an overall framework for NPD. It includes product line planning (Miller, 2000; O'Connor, 2003; Meyer and Lehnerd, 1997), new concept generation (see Chapter 17 and Koen et. al., 2000), phase-gate development (see Chapter 1 and O'Connor, 1994), product life-cycle management (see Chapter 33), and portfolio and pipeline management (see Chapter 3 and O'Connor, 2003). Knowing the details of the framework, however, is only of partial value. The main challenge is in realizing consistent use. As trivial as it sounds, organizations must first use the framework consistently before they realize the desired benefits.

Some organizations focus improvement efforts only on their phase-gate (development) processes, seeking mainly to drive speed-to-market. Yet, a phase-gate process drives single projects from concept to launch. There are two fundamental problems with this. First, few organizations develop only one NPD project at a time, and second, the very nature and quality of concepts delivered into development has enormous influence on project execution and resulting strategic impact. Clearly, phase-gate processes need to be supplemented with portfolio and pipeline management, as well as with front-end and back-end subprocesses.

Carrying out an effective NPD framework does not happen effortlessly. Consider, for example, that during the 1970s Toyota reported taking almost

> *Gaining rapid acceptance and consistent use of the NPD framework across the organization is the main challenge of implementation.*

seven years to put a simple development process in place (O'Connor, 1994). Such implementations are unacceptable in today's environment. How well organizations implement is as important as what they implement.

4.2 A Closer View of Implementation Issues

Organizations are unique in culture, strategy, skills, competition, technologies, and structure. Therefore, the details of a full framework will differ from organization to organization. It is from these details that unique challenges arise. A look at some of the nuances of an NPD framework, shown in Figure 4.1, helps clarify some of the many issues.

FIGURE 4.1 FULL NPD FRAMEWORK.

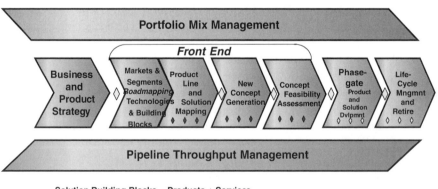

Front to Back NPD Framework

Portfolio Mix Management

Front End

| Business and Product Strategy | Markets & Segments Roadmapping Technologies & Building Blocks | Product Line and Solution Mapping | New Concept Generation | Concept Feasibility Assessment | Phase-gate Product and Solution Dvlpmnt | Life-Cycle Mngmnt and Retire |

Pipeline Throughput Management

Solution Building Blocks = Products + Services

◊ = Top Management Portfolio Decisions

♦ = Project Team Decision (and Judgment) Flow

Throughout the framework, managers must judge and choose. Based on this judging and choosing, concepts will be terminated, recycled, or advanced. Many of the decisions will be influenced by each concept's fit with business and product strategy. Note the implication: *managers need a common understanding of product strategies.* Top management, therefore, must commit to and clearly explain the strategies. Poor articulation of strategy can be harmful to gaining consistent use of the framework. A director of technology at a multinational chemical company described the effects of poor articulation of product strategy. He shared that in his business unit "as soon as a big customer says that they want us to do a new product for them, all resources get shifted to that project." Unless the objective is to satisfy that customer at all costs, both strategy and process are being sidestepped. Adherence to strategy enables a good decision flow on which NPD workflows can align.

In front-end subprocesses, certain concepts needing technology research may need to advance to a technology development process (Ajamian and Koen, 2000), rather than through the NPD framework. Similarly, line extensions and incremental improvements may avoid the concept generation subprocess and go to full development. Good routing of projects becomes critical to organizational use. A blanket decree that all projects must follow the same path is a surefire way to inhibit process use. Clearly, more flexibility is needed. For example, Harley Davidson routes its NPD projects into six different "bins" according to complexity and risk. Such implementations fix boundaries or guidelines defining pathways for different project types.

When settling pathways, some issues will likely surface: What makes a line extension different from a new product? What makes up platform developments and how should they be handled? How should complexity and risk be measured? How will resource conflicts be addressed? Resolving these issues makes each framework unique.

Projects entering development often need greater resources than those in the Front-end. Often, the challenge is that the development pipeline is full. For the new entry to advance, some project will have to share resources. Figuring out which resources to share requires knowledge of who is to be working on which project during future time periods. To do all this requires seasoned project management skill. Once again, those performing implementations must confront issues: How do you set up resource management capabilities? What software systems might help? When should an enterprise system be implemented? How should project priorities be established? How should resources and leaders be assigned to teams?

These issues merely skim the surface and serve to underscore the challenges of customizing the framework to an organization. More important, the scope

> *The best time to resolve implementation issues is during design, not during use.*

and number of issues suggest the need to resolve them during design. Waiting to face issues during use might seem the quickest path to setting up a new approach. Doing so, however, creates the slowest path to gaining consistent use of the framework.

4.3 What Is Implemented

There are three basic components to any NPD framework: the decision flow, the workflow, and supporting systems and practices. It is necessary to understand these components to carry out processes effectively.

4.3.1 The Decision-Making Process

A key benefit of the framework is that it enables organizations to manage risk: the risk of individual projects and the total risk of the portfolio of projects. It does this by requiring decisions at certain milestones. Investment of resources should be in-

> *Top management participation throughout the decision flow is critical to an effective NPD framework.*

creased for good projects and be decreased or stopped for poor projects at each milestone. To justify investments and disinvestments, they must align with strategy. Good implementations, therefore, require setting up decision flows that (1) use specific criteria, (2) align with the product strategy, (3) evaluate the risk of a project by itself and within the full NPD portfolio, and (4) enable management to reallocate resources quickly. This approach is not just applicable to the development subprocess. Decision flows must cross the full framework.

4.3.2 Cross-Functional Workflow

The workflow across functions is another part of an NPD framework. Just as the decision-making should align with the strategy, the project activities should align with the decision flow. Two central questions for designing and performing workflow are:

- What information or insight is needed to overcome the criteria hurdles at each decision point?
- What are the fastest, most efficient methods or activities for assembling this knowledge?

Work activities will differ from one sub-process to another. Also, the best activities within a subprocess will differ from project to project. A well-designed workflow provides guidelines for teams and project con-

> *Workflows should facilitate the work of teams, not bog them down with unnecessary tasks.*

tributors, not commands to conduct specific tasks. For example, the process for a consumer packaged goods company may show a concept test in the first stage of activity. Yet, the method used for creating the concept may have avoided the risk that the concept test was intended to mitigate. In such cases, skipping the activity is sensible. The team's goal is to pass decision criteria, not to conduct predetermined tasks.

4.3.3 Organizational Systems and Practices

Often, organizations have embedded systems or practices that hinder NPD. Pitney Bowes confronted this issue as they transitioned from electromechanical to digital systems. They needed significantly improved product development practices to make the transition. Yet, as they set up new processes, cost accounting methods hindered their efforts. Full cost accounting needed overhead to be shared equally across products and development projects. But the new digital products did not need the overhead required for electromechanical systems. Financial evaluations of new digital projects were unfairly burdened with overhead they did not create, thus decreasing their attractiveness.

Financial practices are not the only practices that hinder implementation. Figure 4.2 lists some organizational systems and practices that can influence an organization's ability to use a framework consistently.

Organizations can speed up NPD process implementation and benefit accrual by following a simple rule: *reduce hindering systems and practices before establishing new driving forces.* Consider the consequences of doing the opposite. Suppose that you set up a million dollar bonus (driving force) for a team should it launch

> *Focus on changing systems and practices that slow NPD before setting up new systems and practices aimed at speeding NPD.*

FIGURE 4.2 SELECTION OF ORGANIZATIONAL SYSTEMS AND PRACTICES.

- Compensation Practices
- Enterprise Information Systems
- Planning Cycles and Budgeting
- TQM; ISO and Regulatory Processes
- Sales incentives and compensation
- Performance Metrics
- Pilot Manufacturing

a product on time. But the organization may also have in place a time-consuming quality management practice (hindering force). Driven by the reward, the team will likely do everything it can to get around the practice. But at what risk? Will there be negative fallout on other NPD projects? A better approach is to streamline the rigid practice (the hindering force) during process design, before setting up the bonus (the driving force.)

4.4 Process Is Business Entity Specific

Typically, business units within corporations implement their own NPD framework. Alignment with a common strategy is difficult at a corporate level. Here, often the only resource shared is money. Each business unit has its own mission and resources, and needs its own decision flow, workflow, and support systems. More important, each business unit must accept and use its NPD process for itself.

Corporate staffs, however, can help NPD implementations and improvements. For example, General Electric, DuPont, and Procter & Gamble each have or have had central groups that provide support to the business units. These groups provide

Customize the NPD framework for each business unit. One process does not fit all.

internal consulting, facilitation, and secondary information to the business units. NPD processes in these organizations may have a common look, but the details are business unit specific.

4.5 Acceptance Precedes Process Use

The speed of implementation and benefit accrual is dependent on many factors. The most critical is the commitment and involvement of the business unit's top management. An organization's willingness to change comes from this commitment. Involvement by senior management results in a dialogue that helps form the needed political alliance among the business unit's top functional leaders toward all decision criteria. Consider the "hands-off" approach by the president of a major electronics components manufacturer. After considerable strategic planning, the president stated to key managers that because of significant devaluation of their products, R&D and Marketing needed to improve NPD outputs. In the end, though, the president did not participate in the new framework assessment or design. The result was the postponement of NPD improvement. The president's lack of involvement decreased the odds that his direct reports would support NPD improvement.

4.6 Potential Impediments to Full Implementation

Some managers will perceive the framework as time-consuming and rigid (Cooper, 2001). These perceptions can slow an organization's acceptance of the framework. Flexibility, speed, and potency must be central themes. The workflow should facilitate concurrent and streamlined activities. Paths should be built where teams can skip activities. The decision flow should be fluid, changing in response to opportunities and possible shifts in strategy.

Because perceptions are important, many companies give their NPD framework, subprocesses, and specific practices with names that avoid rigid connotations. Consider, for example:

- FIRST (Fast Innovation Requires Strategy and Teamwork) at Reynolds Consumer Products, a business unit of Alcoa
- PROPEL (Phase Review of Products for Excellence and Leadership) at Eaton Engine Components
- ATOM (Accelerate To Market) at SC Johnson and Sons
- SixDays™ (model used in project definitions) at Dow Chemical's Polyolefin Business Unit product specification™
- FAST (Front end concept generation process) at Appleton Papers

> *Position the process as fast, flexible, and potent. The design must match the promise.*

The purpose of these names is to position the NPD approach as fast, flexible, and powerful. This accelerates acceptance and use of the framework.

4.7 Change: From Current to Desired NPD Process

The toughest issues in implementation are people-oriented ones. Implementations challenge the interests of some managers by requiring them to conduct work or make decisions differently. While many contributors may embrace change, they may not embrace the specifics of all of the desired changes.

Implementations require that organizations move from a current state of NPD to a desired state. To do so, individuals need motivation to make the transition. They must believe that the desired change is worth the effort. The change equation in Figure 4.3 (Beckhard and Harris, 1987) illustrates this.

Movement toward a fast and flexible framework happens when the organization perceives the equation as true. Organizations whose managers believe that they are successful often have challenging implementations. Why should their organizations change if, for example, earnings are at an all-time high? The pain is not

> *Work the change equation to start and to sustain implementations.*

FIGURE 4.3 ORGANIZATIONAL CHANGE EQUATION.

Change will occur when:

$$P_{cn} + G_{desired} > COC_{econ, psy}$$

Where:

P_{cn}	= perceived pain of current NPD practices
$G_{desired}$	= perceived gain of new NPD Framework
$COC_{econ, psy}$	= perceived cost of change, both economic and psychological

apparent. In such cases, the answer lies in getting top leadership to embrace and articulate the future consequences of the current state. Jack Welch at GE was a master at this (Slater, 1998) He would induce the perception of pain and gain through improvement. measures and performance reviews, even though the business had stellar performance.

4.8 Beginnings: Analyze the Old and Envision the New

Implementation advocates need to make sure that the pain plus the gain continually remains greater than the perceived cost of change. This requires gathering, analyzing, and disseminating information related to each of the three contributing factors in the change equation.

To begin implementations, organizations should assess their current state (and pain) of NPD. One approach is to review a set of NPD projects. For each project, managers should map the flows for work, decisions, and communications. Analysis can reveal insights about delays, decision-making, the interface with (or lack thereof) customers, and success rates. The purpose is to identify the root cause of the pain. Some areas often influencing benefit accrual from NPD are shared in Figure 4.4.

Understanding best practices is also important. Start by conducting literature research. The chapters in this handbook, especially Chapter 36 describing first results of the PDMA Foundation' Comparative Performance Assessment Study (CPAS), are helpful guides (see also Belliveau et al., 2002). Benchmarking can complement the literature review. Such external comparisons should focus on the how's, why's, and consequences of the decision flow, workflow, and

FIGURE 4.4 SOME KEY AREAS INFLUENCING BENEFIT ACCRUAL.

- Creativity and Innovation
- People behavior
- Predicting and Forecasting
- Prioritization methods and practices
- Project definitions and judgments
- Project leadership
- Project management capability
- Specification development
- Voice of the Customer

subsystems. Benchmarking a single company, however, may be problematic, because some companies may execute one subprocess better than other subprocesses.

Outside experts and consultants can contribute positively to the understanding of each of the change equation variables. With insights about NPD influences and experience in doing assessments, independent experts can facilitate identifying the pain, articulating the gain, and delineating a path forward. An outsider's independence from the organization can also facilitate implementation activities and dialogue with senior managers that may be politically awkward for internal managers. Strong facilitation will speed design and deployment, enabling organizations to realize benefits sooner.

4.9 Participative Design Leads to Acceptance and Usage

Separating the jobs of process design from those of deployment is a common mistake in implementations. It is better to think of design and deployment as one. Handing an already designed process to an organization and telling everyone to use it is a surefire means of creating strong resistance to the implementation. Intel experienced this when they set up a software support system to support NPD. The system dictated the process, which was not the way that managers wanted to do work or make decisions. Declaring that the system needed too many "clicks" to carry out the needed work, the organization removed the system within 18 months of deployment.

Involve those who will be using a component in the design of that component. This does not mean that they should be left on their own. Facilitation, guidance, coordination, and starting templates are necessary to good implementation. Nonetheless, contributors on NPD teams should be involved in the design of the workflow. The controllers of the systems (usually direct reports to top management) should be participants in the design or redesign of support systems. Similarly, the business unit's top management should be involved in creating decision criteria and designing the decision flow. Management's involvement, not just their blessing, speeds benefit accrual.

A good example of setting up implementation was seen at Appleton, a billion dollar paper producer. To carry out design and deployment, a set of teams, overlapping in membership, was established. The goal was simple: involve the key people in each element of implementation and make sure all that teams were aware of each other's progress and issues. The business unit leader and an outside consultant coordinated team activities.

Implementations can have many work groups contributing to design and deployment. Table 4.1 shows contributors and their responsibilities. All participants need to meet periodically to integrate the work of all teams. An imple-

TABLE 4.1 IMPLEMENTATION CONTRIBUTORS AND RESPONSIBILITIES.

Contributor	Who	Responsibility
Portfolio Management Team (PMT)	Business leader; top functional managers	Create, use portfolio and gate criteria Work as gatekeepers and portfolio managers
Workflow Design Teams (WFDT)	NPD project contributors representing all functions	Design workflow aligning with decision criteria
Systems and Practices Team (SPT)	Direct reports to top functional managers, overseers of systems and practices	Identify, mitigate hindering systems and practices Process improvement
Process Implementation Manager	Key manager, NPD adept, good influence/ communication skills	Coordination of implementation activities
Outside Expert and Facilitator	One or more experienced consultants	Provide guidance, knowledge, independence, methods, and templates

mentation manager and outside expert should work to coordinate and facilitate the work groups.

Tackling all subprocesses concurrently at the start of implementation is a mistake. Organizations typically already have in place some elements of each subprocess. To chart the fastest path, managers must recognize current capability maturity and practices within and across subprocesses. An implementation plan should start with current capabilities and build progressively on each. For example, certain portfolio and pipeline management activities may need other front-end practices to already be in place first. Because one component may be dependent upon another component, the order of implementation is important. Executing a coordinated implementation plan speeds up benefit gains by enabling more consistent use of components when the components are ready to be used.

Motorola battled the tendency to "install a full system that does it all." Key resource managers reported that some executives wished to "blast through" the issues of improving NPD by simply installing a system that the vendor declared would support and drive all aspects of NPD. It sounded simple. Unfortunately, the approach would have left too many aspects of NPD unaddressed. The managers then had to convince top management that the organization was not yet prepared to deploy it. This took much work. They had to gather information and show how certain components were needed before others and that deploying an enterprise system would worsen the need for all components.

Top management involvement is key to participative design. Implementation managers need to build consensus among top management on the specific criteria that comprise the decision flow. A strong start is to conduct a workout session with top management on strategy, constraints, and new product objectives. The output of the session is a set of criteria for evaluating projects across subprocesses. After the session, management should amend and alter the criteria as needed. The goal is to align the workflow, to create a means of managing the risk of the portfolio of projects, and to decide how to assign resources across projects.

Participative design ensures that the framework matches the culture. The result is that the change will be closer to the norms of the organization, helping to speed consistent use. This is not to imply that culture should not change. Rather, the change should be orchestrated to avoid negative behaviors.

> *Those who will be using a component of the framework should be involved with the design of that component.*

4.10 Designing Improvement Into the Process

The resulting framework should also provide a means for improvement and increased proficiency. Several mechanisms help. Tracking work and decisions throughout the framework provides valuable insights and rich data. Analysis of the documents and data may reveal reoccurring challenges. Metrics on projects and the process provide another source of valuable data. Table 4.2 lists some potential metrics that the organization may wish to track.

4.11 Process Ownership

Ownership of the framework is an important for continuous improvement. Without ownership, improvements will wane, and process use will become inconsistent. Often, an individual manager, assigned as the process manager or coordinator, assumes full responsibility. Yet making an

> *Build continuing improvement into the NPD framework to ensure continuous benefit gains.*

TABLE 4.2 POTENTIAL METRICS FOR NPD FRAMEWORK IMPROVEMENT.

• Time to react (to knowledge of opportunity or threat)	• Project duration as a function of project complexity.
• Time to breakeven	• $ Investment per subprocess
• Slippage from schedule	• Number of programs stopped
• Number of programs completing process (to launch)	• Core team turnover
• Capacity (resource use)	• Risk
• Financial returns on programs	• Participation in each subprocess (person-yrs per function)

individual solely responsible for improvements can be self-defeating. It allows key functional leaders to get "off the hook." A better approach is to share ownership and responsibility across functions. One way to do this is to assign improvement responsibility to the systems and practices team (see Table 4.1) along with the process manager. The team would report regularly to top management on process metrics, hindrances, and improvement activities. These responsibilities should also be anchored with individual performance evaluation measures.

4.12 Summary

Gaining consistent use of a full NPD development framework is challenging. It requires aligning processes with strategy, involving contributors from across the organization, and positioning the process correctly. Once implemented, though, the framework will have a significant impact on launching more, successful products to the marketplace—simpler, better, faster.

References

Ajamian, G. and Koen, P. "Technology Stage Gate: A Structured Process for Managing High-Risk New Technology Projects" in P. Belliveau, A. Griffin, S. Somermeyer, eds. *The PDMA Toolbook of New Product Development.* New York: John Wiley & Sons, 2000.

Beckhard, R. and Harris, R. *Organizational Transistions: Managing Complex Change,* Reading, MA: Addison Wesley Publishing, 1987.

Belliveau, P. Griffin, A., and Somermeyer, S. eds. *The PDMA Toolbook of New Product Development.* New York: John Wiley & Sons, 2002.

Cooper, R., Edgett, S., and Kleinschmidt, E. *Portfolio Management for New Products* 2nd Ed., Reading, MA: Perseus, 2001.

Cooper, R. G., *Winning at New Products: Accelerating the Process from Idea to Launch* 3rd Ed. Reading, MA: Addison-Wesley, 2001.

Eureka, W. E. *Introduction to QFD: Collection of Presentations and Case Studies* Detroit, MI: American Supplier Institute, 1987.

Gorchels, L. *The Product Manager's Handbook: The Complete Product Management Resource* Lincolnwood, Illinois: NTC Business Books, 1998.

Griffin, A. "PDMA Research on Product Development Practices: Updating Trends and Benchmarking Best Practices." *The Journal of Product Innovation Management* 14(6): 429–458 (1997).

Koen, P., Ajamian, G., Boyce, S., Clamen, A., Fisher, E., Fountoulakis, S., Johnson, A., Puri, P., and Seibert, R. "Fuzzy Front End: Effective Methods, Tools, and Techniques" in P. Belliveau, A. Griffin, S Somermeyer, eds. *The PDMA Toolbook of New Product Development*. New York: John Wiley & Sons, 2000.

Meyer, M. and Lehnerd, A. *The Power of Product Platforms: Building Value and Cost Leadership* New York: The Free Press, 1997.

Miller, C., (2000) "Hunting for Hunting Grounds: Forecasting the Fuzzy Front End" in P. Belliveau, A. Griffin, S Somermeyer, eds. *The PDMA Toolbook of New Product Development*. New York: John Wiley & Sons, 2002.

O'Connor, P. "Spiral-Up Implementation of NPD Portfolio and Pipeline Management" in P. Belliveau, A. Griffin, S Somermeyer, eds. *The PDMA Toolbook of New Product Development*. New York: John Wiley & Sons, 2004.

O'Connor, P. "Product Line Planning" Adept Group Limited Newsletter Ponte Vedra Beach, Florida (Spring 2003).

O'Connor, P. "Implementing a Stage-gate Process: A Multi-Company Perspective," *Journal of Product Innovation Management* 11: 183–200 (1994).

Repenning, N., Goncalves, P., and Black. L "Past the Tipping Point: The Persistence of Firefighting in Product Development," *California Management Review*, 43(4): 44-63 (2001).

Slater, M. *Jack Welch & The G.E. Way: Management Insights and Leadership Secrets of the Legendary CEO.* New York: McGraw-Hill, 1998.

The pictorial model is a modification of full Front-to-Back Architecture of NPD developed by Paul O'Connor, The Adept Group; Beebe Nelson, Working Forums; and Robert Gill, InterMatrixPDP.

Paul O'Connor is an expert in product development productivity. He has conducted assignments, implementation initiatives, and benchmarking activities with numerous firms around the world. Mr. O'Connor is managing director of The Adept Group, a firm he founded in 1984. Paul is also a past president of the Product Development and Management Association and teaches portfolio and pipeline management for various organizations.

CHAPTER FIVE

PROCESS OWNERSHIP

Dr. W. M. Watson

5.1 Introduction

The enduring new product development (NPD) process must be "owned" by all of its practitioners, otherwise the process will fail. Establishing NPD process ownership, though, is often a difficult and confusing phenomenon. Regardless of the type of organization, whether a strictly hierarchical model or a matrix structure, demarcation of who owns what within the NPD process is essential.

In most companies, existing leaders assume new process owner roles. These leaders may have both old and new roles—and frequently more than one new role. Confusion over which "hat" that leader is wearing at any given time can derail implementation of the new process. Clear definition of roles and a visible practice of the process help avoid this confusion (see also Chapters 4 and 10).

Three central ownership roles need especially to be identified. These may be called the process champion, the process sponsor, and the process manager. The purpose of this chapter is to define what each of these essential roles represent and their importance to creating, implementing, and sustaining a successful NPD process. Other emergent roles that depend on the particular NPD model are also considered.

5.2 The Process Champion

Change seldom happens without a champion. Because new product development may represent elements of change for any organization, a visible process champion is needed to initiate such change.

The successful process champion is someone not only universally known but also widely admired by company personnel. A senior manager frequently serves this role, but anyone who has visibility and company trust can be a process champion. Because visibility and trust are key factors, not all senior managers may be able to effectively serve as process champions. The effective process champion is one who relies on perseverance and persuasion more than political power: the champion wins trust that the NPD process is superior to other alternatives (see Chapter 10).

The finest process champions know when to be in front of the audience and when to be a part of the audience. The successful process champion also is an expert promoter and natural leader. The promoter needs to push the NPD process as the vehicle for product innovation. The natural leader knows when to stop promoting the process and to start encouraging the practitioners.

Organizations are frequently not well organized to deliberately choose process champions. Rather, process champions emerge. Senior management needs to ensure that the right champion is enabled to work in the right change effort.

> *The process champion owns the initiation of the NPD process.*

5.3 The Process Sponsor

Implementation requires resources, and it is the process sponsor who is ready to back the NPD process with the resources that it needs to thrive. The effective process sponsor delivers the appropriate people and physical resources to the NPD process and its individual projects when and where the next steps call for them.

The likely candidate for process sponsor is either someone who controls these resources directly or has considerable influence with those who do. Primary candidates are traditional managers of the design or development functions. As the NPD process is institutionalized, the process sponsor's span of control over resources is likely to grow. Management, therefore, needs to take this into ac-

> *The process sponsor owns the smooth operation the NPD process.*

count when identifying a candidate for process sponsor. The immediate position may remain somewhere in the current management hierarchy, but this leader will likely play a larger role in future process-oriented initiatives.

5.4 The Process Manager

The process manager is the "keeper" of the NPD process. In this role, the process keeper must be process expert, unabashed promoter, and tireless improver. The process manager becomes the recognized expert at all aspects of the NPD process. He or she must understand the NPD process, company capabilities, portfolio, pipeline, and projects. Process managers may be considered the "conscious of the process."

The emphasis on "process" suggests recruiting someone with a background in engineering, science, or the total quality management movement (TQM). Strong process managers are often those who have experience in developing company products, and therefore, know the pitfalls and can envision best practices.

Because the position of process manager is a new one in most organizations, the temptation exists to simply add this role to an existing position. This is almost always a deadly mistake. Someone should be appointed process manager as his or her primary responsibility. Except in very small NPD organizations, this should be a full-time responsibility during the implementation of a new NPD process. Secondarily, special projects can be added after the new process is substantially underway.

The process manager frequently serves as "defender of the NPD process." Because of process erosion, which is a serious threat to efficient product innovation, the process manager is often in the difficult position of defending the process

> *The project manager owns the implementation and improvement of the NPD process.*

while developing improvements to that process. Issues related to timelines stretching, budgets ballooning, and pressures to slide past the requirements must be addressed immediately, if not resisted.

5.5 Roles Specific to the Process Model

Additional roles that share ownership of the NPD process are specific to the process model that the organization is using. Prevalent examples include project leaders, portfolio managers, resource (or pipeline) managers, gatekeepers, and the process analyst.

5.6 Project Leaders

The NPD process in most companies is based on multifunctional project teams. Working together for at least the development of a single new product, these teams need robust leadership to proceed efficiently from the beginning of new product development in the Fuzzy Front End through Commercialization stages. Project leaders typically replace one or more levels of management in the conventional R&D organization, although project leaders do not all come from that background. Good leadership skills in organizing the work of project teams can be found everywhere in business organizations. And many projects need special functional knowledge from unique corners of that organization. Frequently, project leaders are tasked with building team loyalty without full control over every team member's time and attention.

The jury is still out on keeping the same project leader throughout the project. Changing the team leader is always a disruption, and some organizations put special effort into maintaining leadership continuity throughout the life cycle of NPD projects. Other organizations deliberately migrate team leadership as the focus of the project begs different skills.

> *The project leaders own the effective operation of their project teams.*

5.7 Portfolio Managers

The NPD process models identify the need to manage the portfolio of all development projects underway at any given time. Best practice suggests that this task be undertaken by a multifunctional set of portfolio managers. Collectively, portfolio managers own the control of the size and shape of the entire NPD project portfolio. Portfolio managers typically serve in other roles within the business organization so that the NPD portfolio can be well matched to the overall business strategy.

The Project Review model, as described by Crawford (1984), emphasizes the importance of an explicit "contract" between an NPD project and the managers of the overall portfolio. The portfolio manager therefore works closely with the process champion and process sponsor to confirm "contractual" de-

> *The portfolio managers own the robustness of the portfolio of active development projects.*

tails. The viability of this contract is owned by the portfolio managers, but if the project no longer fits in the portfolio of next products, then the contract will be abrogated and the project killed.

5.8 Resource Managers

NPD process models identify the need to manage the NPD resources, which include skilled people, physical equipment, market analysis capabilities, field-testing opportunities, first customer contacts, and so forth. Best practice suggests that the sum of these resources be viewed as a pipeline, and the shape of this pipeline be characterized by the resources presently available to the NPD effort. The flow in the pipeline is the portfolio of the development projects currently underway. A resource manager is therefore tasked with pushing as many projects through the available pipe as quickly as possible. This task is often called "pipeline management."

Resource managers work as a team. Their leader is the process sponsor, and they hold frequent meetings and maintain specific lines of communications to keep them in constant touch with the pipeline. This team is an active owner of the project

> *The resource managers own the effective deployment of people and physical resources.*

assignments. Resource managers also are typically project leaders or gatekeepers because all three roles need to be in touch with the realities of available resources.

5.9 Gatekeepers

Gatekeepers are usually drawn from the ranks of functional managers and have strong knowledge of the various complexities involved in getting new products into the marketplace. They serve as referees of deliverables from project teams, and often make critical gate decisions.

> *The gatekeepers own key decisions at project gates.*

When the gatekeepers approve moving a project on to the next development stage, the process sponsor and resource managers respond by finding and assigning the needed people and physical resources. These leaders co-own the often vexing problem of making the project's needs fit in the current pipeline.

Gatekeepers are also commonly expected to act as coaches to project teams.

5.10 Process Analyst

A specialized role appears when the NPD process emphasizes the importance of quantitative information. Process models based on total quality management

> *The process analyst owns the scorekeeping.*

(TQM), cycle time management (CTM), and portfolio management devour large amounts of in-process and output data. A process analyst is needed to generate the necessary process metrics and guide the flow of process information.

5.11 Wearing Two Hats

NPD organizations are often never able to assign just one role to most personnel. The great value of a more formal NPD process lies in addressing the confusion that naturally surrounds the multiple roles that many personnel are expected to play. Roles can be played tacitly or explicitly. "I wear two hats" is the common explanation of many operational controversies; if the hats have names, the heated discussion can turn to dialogue between process roles and co-owners, and the process moves forward.

Some best practices suggest that where roles are not clear, the process is not clear. And where the process is not clear, organizations have been unable to take full advantage of other best practices. Developing better new products, faster, and with fewer resources comes only to those who are willing to invest up front in a clearer NPD process.

Some dual roles include the following: the process sponsor can be the process champion. In the flatter management hierarchies of smaller organizations, this is a natural way to initiate the change to process-centered new product development. On the other hand, combining the roles of process manager and process sponsor has typically delayed—sometimes thwarted—the implementation of a new NPD process. Thus, there is an apparent need to see the give and take between the two leaders of the changes in new product development to gain confidence in those changes.

The process manager also frequently serves as the process analyst. This is especially appropriate during implementation of the process.

Many leaders serve as gatekeepers and as portfolio managers, but this may promote confusion because a portfolio manager's criticism of a project would be made in a gatekeeping setting, and such criticism would not be about the gate deliverables, but rather, the shape of the portfolio. Project leaders and gatekeepers also are frequently resource or pipeline managers, led by the process sponsor and process manager.

5.12 NPD Process as Part of the Culture

The NPD process, over time, becomes an expected part of the organizational culture. Naturally, the process is looked to for aid in solving new problems with portfolios and individual projects. However, roles in the process evolve too.

For instance, the role of the process champion becomes increasingly invisible as the culture itself champions the NPD process. In a learning organization, the NPD process champion would transition to new corporate change initiatives.

Another evolution would be the role of the process manager. This role would become less taxing and less time-consuming because personnel would understand what responsibilities they individually and collectively own. Accordingly, the process manager would concentrate on metrics and improvements. One process manager may be able to serve that role for several related business units or for several related business processes. Full implementation of an NPD process should provide impetus for rethinking new technology development, new business development, technical service, sales development, and other business activities as key business processes; the experience of the process manager would be useful in addressing these issues.

The role of the process analyst could also be broadened. The data for analyzing pipelines and portfolios would become more readily available and more credible. As a consequence of more and better data, gatekeepers, portfolio managers, and resource managers would be more willing to make careful data-based decisions. While gatekeepers and resource managers may find their roles easier, their roles may become more time-consuming. This is so because the organization would expect the individuals in these roles to take strong ownership of their decision-making responsibilities as a result of greater confidence in achieving value from the product innovation process.

5.13 Summary

The successful NPD process is "owned" by all who participate in it. Three central leadership roles must be clearly identified: The process champion owns the initiation of the new process; the process sponsor lines up the necessary resources and owns the smooth operation of the process; and the process manager owns the implementation and improvement of the process. Other roles emerge, depending on the NPD process model adopted. Inevitably, many participants have more than one role in the process. They must be clear about which "hat" they are wearing at any particular time.

To conclude, the overarching mantra for process ownership can be simply stated: the NPD process owned by its practitioners endures.

References

Cooper, R. G., "Third-Generation New Product Processes," *J Prod Innov Manag* 11: 3–14 (1994).

Crawford, C. M., "Protocol: new tool for product innovation," *J Prod Innov Manag*, 1: 85 (1984).

Griffin, A., "PDMA Research on New Product Development Practices: Updating Trends and Benchmarking Best Practices," *J Prod Innov Manag*, 14: 429–458 (1997).

Dr. W. M. Watson is a principal of Inngenuity LLC, builders of custom tools for successfully implementing the best practices of product innovation. Until recently, Dr. Watson was New Opportunities Process Manager in the Coatings business of the Rohm and Haas Company. There, he had developed products for the Graphic Arts industry, championed the Total Quality movement, and pioneered the Stage-Gate model of NPD. He was educated as a physical chemist at Georgia Tech, the ETH-Zurich, and the University of Illinois.

Dr. Watson believes that successful change is 1 part theory, 10 parts detail, and 100 parts implementation.

CHAPTER SIX

THE FUZZY FRONT END FOR INCREMENTAL, PLATFORM, AND BREAKTHROUGH PRODUCTS

Peter A. Koen

6.1 Introduction

The innovation process may be divided into three areas: the Fuzzy Front End (FFE), the New Product Development Portion (NPD), and commercialization as indicated in Figure 6.1. Most projects, once the concept is defined in the FFE, are managed in the NPD portion using the traditional "Stage-Gate®" (see Chapter 1) process.[1] However, three separate strategies and processes are typically involved in the FFE for incremental, platform, and radical projects. The objective of this chapter is to provide the reader with an overview of each of these strategies and processes.

6.2 What Is the Front End?

The FFE is defined by those activities that come before the more formal and well-structured NPD process (Koen et. al., 2002). Even though there is a continuum between the FFE and the new product development, the activities in the FFE are often chaotic, unpredictable, and unstructured. In comparison, the

[1] Stage-Gate® is a registered trademark of the Product Development Institute, Inc.

FIGURE 6.1 THE INNOVATION PROCESS MAY BE BROKEN INTO THREE PARTS: THE FUZZY FRONT END (FFE), NEW PRODUCT DEVELOPMENT (NPD), AND COMMERCIALIZATION.

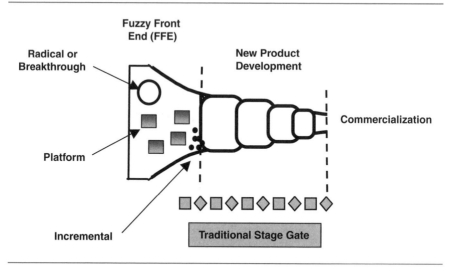

new product development process is typically structured, which assumes formalism with a prescribed set of activities and questions to be answered.

Most companies utilize either a formal "Stage-Gate®" (see Chapter 1) or "PACE® approach" (McGrath and Akiyama, 1996) for managing product development. A schematic of the "typical" five-stage five gate model is shown in Figure 6.2. Many companies consider the FFE to include the first two stages and be completed at Gate 3 with a business plan, which includes the product specifications as well as business and financial analysis and detailed project management plans. However, the traditional Stage-Gate® process was designed for incremental product development and ". . .may be inappropriate. . ." (Cooper, 2001:151) when applied to platform or breakthrough projects.

6.3 What are Incremental, Platform, and Breakthrough Products?

The Wheelwright and Clark (1992) typology shown in Figure 6.3 may be used to characterize incremental, platform, and breakthrough products. It characterizes products based on the extent of product and process change. Break-

FIGURE 6.2 TYPICAL FIVE-STAGE, FIVE-GATE MODEL OF STAGE-GATE®.

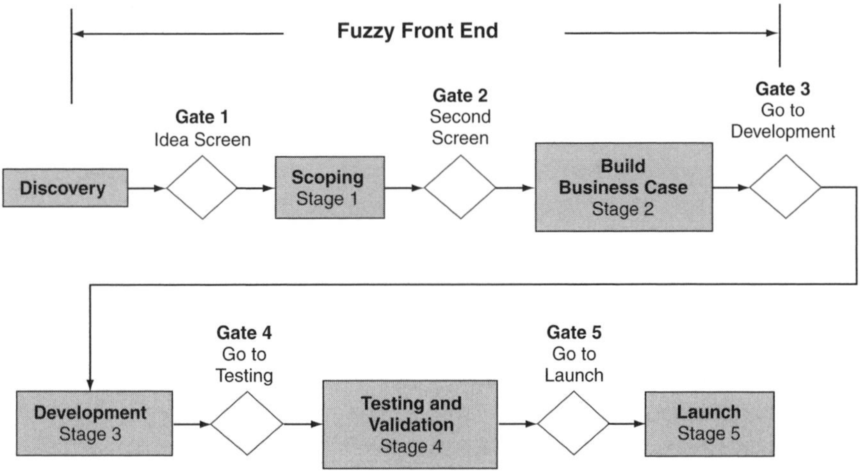

From *Winning at New Products* by Robert G. Cooper, copyright 1993 by Perseus Books, L.L.C. Reprinted with permission of Perseus Books P, a member of Perseus Books, L.L.C.

throughs involve substantive product and process change. Incremental products require little product or process change. Between these two extremes are platform products. Incremental products are generally considered to be cost reductions, improvements to existing product lines, additions to existing platforms, and repositioning of existing products introduced in markets well known to the company, with well-identified customer needs using technology in which the company already has expertise. Platform products (Meyer and Lehnerd, 1997) establish a basic architecture for a next generation product or process and are substantially larger in scope and resources than incremental projects. An example of a platform product would be Kodak's disposable single-use 35 mm camera (called the Fun-saver). An incremental extension would include a stretch version of the camera (i.e., panoramic) and a waterproof version. Breakthrough products (i.e., those new to the company or the world) typically offer a 5–10 times or greater improvement in performance combined with a 30–50 percent or greater reduction in costs (Leifer et. al., 2000). Breakthrough products typically involve high risk technologies (i.e., inventions yet to occur), while platform products involve less risky technologies. Polaroid's development of an instant film camera would be considered to be a breakthrough product, involving the

FIGURE 6.3 TYPOLOGY OF NEW PRODUCTS (WHEELWRIGHT AND CLARK, 1992), INDICATING THE DIFFERENCES BETWEEN INCREMENTAL, PLATFORM AND BREAKTHROUGH PRODUCTS.

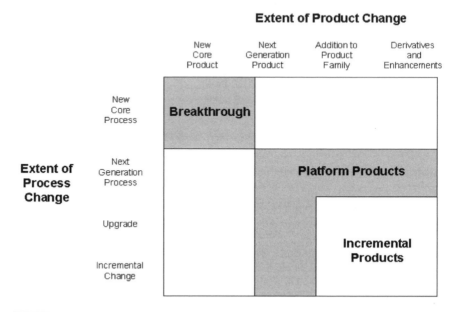

development of special chemicals that would allow the film to develop within a short period of time.

The FFE strategies and processes for each of these product categories are discussed in the next three sections.

6.4 Fuzzy Front End for Incremental Products

New product ideas for incremental products are usually determined from the overall strategic planning process or as part of an idea suggestion program. Once identified, they go through Stage 1 (see Figure 6.2)—which is a "gentle" screen that evaluates the strategic fit, market attractiveness, technical feasibility and the identification of any killer variables. The gatekeepers are often not senior management, but technical and marketing people. Resources, people, and monies are assigned to the project to perform both an initial market and technical assessment. The purpose of this stage is to determine if the idea still looks feasible to pass through Gate 2—which is a more rigorous screen. If the project passes through Gate 2, a detailed business case is developed, which includes market definition and segmentation, product positioning, a product win statement, product specifications, market entry strategy, technology and operational strategy, and a financial analysis. In-depth market investigations are done in this stage to understand both segmentation and customer needs. Competitive assessments, along with intellectual property evaluations, which determine both freedom to operate and ability to gain a competitive advantage, are also analyzed. The developed business case is then evaluated in Gate 3, typically by a senior management team, and allowed to continue into product development if the project, relative to other projects, is expected to have the appropriate level of impact on the company's project portfolio. Most often, the decisions on incremental projects are based on the financial attractiveness of the project. The gate committee will then empower a multifunctional team to begin product development based on the specifications detailed in the Stage 2 business case. An example of an incremental product might be the addition of a color screen to an existing PDA line, which in the past, only included black and white screens, though the assumption is that the new screen will fit into the existing architecture (i.e., size, power characteristics, and functionality) such that the new product can use essentially the same manufacturing line, parts, and molds as the black/white PDA. This process flows nicely for incremental products, which are already part of the overall strategic planning process. Incremental and unplanned ideas, which are out of the strategic planning cycle, often need to fight for resources to get through Gate 1. Some companies have "seed-stage" funds available to Gate 1 decision makers so that some resources may be applied to these early-stage ideas. Without some resources, it is often difficult for those investigating the new product idea to gain the market, customer, and competitive knowledge so that it can survive a Gate 2 review.

Many companies maintain a Web-enabled idea generation process on their intranet so that any individual may submit ideas. This process works effectively if these ideas are reviewed periodically with frequent feedback being given, ideally within two weeks, to the submitter. Though many companies have become disenchanted with the process as it becomes overwhelmed with ideas and feedback time lengthens to months or ceases to exist. Recently, several companies have been successful at using Web-enabled idea generation with targeted "idea events." For example a company might be interested in hearing specifically about ideas for achieving a 10–15 percent cost reduction in a major product line. The "event" would be open to anyone in the company and would occur over a specific time period–say two months. Monetary incentives (e.g., a percentage of the cost savings) typically result in a large number of submissions—though this can often distract key people from working on their own projects, which may have an even larger payback for the company.

6.5 Fuzzy Front End for Platform Products

The traditional Stage-Gate® processes, discussed previously, was designed for a single product—not the development of a platform product possibly requiring a multimarket, multiproduct plan, which will share common architecture and have common systems and interfaces.

A classic example of a platform product was Black and Decker's development of a new common universal motor with a fixed width and variable length that could be used in all of the their products (i.e., drills, sanders, circular saws, hedge trimmers, etc.) instead of hundreds of different motors manufactured on different production lines. The result of this change in product architecture was Black and Decker being able to market a lighter and more profitable drill at half the price! As a result, Black and Decker gained dominant market share and drove many competitors out of business (Meyer and Zack, 1996). McGrath (2001:54) indicates that ". . .failures in high tech companies frequently can be traced to an incomplete platform strategy. . ."

The FFE for developing a new platform starts out with a strategic vision of what the company wants to develop. This vision can come from the need to develop a new generation product to make a current one obsolete. For example, Xerox realized that digital technology was a major threat to their lens-based copier line and needed to develop a new generation of copiers and printers based on digital technology. Black and Decker (Meyer and Lehnerd, 1997), in the example indicated earlier, felt that they needed to dramatically revitalize their product line as a result of less-expensive offshore manufacturers making inroads into their market, the rising cost of labor and materials, which were decreasing their margins, and higher standards of safety that required major redesigns of their products. Black and Decker's strategic vision was to redesign all of the power tools at the same time, redesign manufacturing to achieve a substantial cost advantage, and meet the new regulatory requirements at no increase in price to the consumer. Alternatively, the vision can come from the need to develop a new product platform so that the company may expand into a new market. An example would be Honda's strategic vision to use its competences in automobile engines to develop lawn mowers and motorcycles.

Product strategies to meet the strategic vision in this later example are often supplemented with acquisition strategies when new market channels are needed.

The vision needs to be aligned with the business, though, the strategic vision may be a catalysis for changing the business charter. For example, a product vision indicating the desire to develop motorcycles would require the business charter to change. Lynn and Akgun (2001) indicate that an effective vision should have three components: (1) clarity (refers to having a well-articulated and easy-to-understand target), (2) support (implies commitment from people throughout the organization to support the vision), and (3) stability (refers to having the vision remain stable over time).

Developing a platform and accompanying product strategy based on the strategic vision typically is done in the following four chronological steps. Though this effort should *not* be undertaken until there is consensus between the team and senior management on the strategic vision.

1. *Segmenting and understanding the market:* Before specific concepts can be developed, the platform team needs to clearly understand how the market is segmented, the unmet customer needs, and strength of the competitors within each segment.
2. *Developing initial product concepts:* Product concepts that satisfy the customers' needs and build on the core competencies, capabilities, or channels of the company. A concept (Koen et. al. 2002) is not a product, but a well-defined form, including both a written and visual description, which includes its primary features and customer benefits combined with an understanding of the technology needed. A product concept for the Black and Decker example could consist of rough sketches of a common motor and how it could integrate and be part of drills, sanders, and circular saws. Ultimately, the product concept needs to build on the unique skills of the company so that competitive advantage and favorable margins may be achieved. Multiple product concepts are developed then reevaluated to assess their attractiveness to the market and the company.
3. *Developing the product family:* Once the initial concepts are determined a product family with its accompanying product roadmap (Wheelwright and Sasser, 1989) is developed. For example Hewlett-Packard's Product roadmap of its inkjet printers consisted of its Deskjet (i.e., the initial offering) followed by the Deskjet Plus, the Deskjet writer for Macintosh, and then the Deskjet 500, and so on.
4. *Determining the economic case:* Ultimately, a business case needs to be developed for the product platform and needs senior management approval. Although the first product released from the product platform may have a negative

return on investment, since it may have to absorb considerable R&D and operational expenses, which are part of the overall platform plan. Traditional "hurdle rate" calculations need to be done on the entire product family with its stream of products based on a common architecture rather than on the initial offering.

Typically, the platform plan, with its first product is evaluated at Gate 3, with subsequent incremental extensions following the traditional Stage-Gate® process. The overall process, typically, is an intensive effort that involves 3–5 people for often as much as six months, though the project can often be shortened to 2–3 months if many of the members of the team are committed on a full-time basis. The reader is referred to a couple of classic books (Meyer and Lehnerd, 1997; McGrath, 2001) and several articles on platform development (Meyer and Mugge, 2001; Meyer and DeTore, 1999; Meyer and Seliger, 1998).

6.6 Fuzzy Front End for Breakthrough Products

Breakthrough products (i.e., those new-to-the-company or new-to-the-world) typically either begin with a strategic vision or are identified and promoted by an individual/product champion (Markham, 2002).

Examples of breakthrough products that have occurred as a result of a strategic vision are SmithKline & French's Tagamet® and Corning's catalytic converter. Tagamet® (Nayak and Ketteringham, 1986), the first billion dollar drug in the pharmaceutical industry, began with a vision of developing a new class of drug, called H_2 antagonists, for healing ulcers more quickly and painlessly than previous drugs. SmithKline & French agreed to support this vision. The project began in 1964 with a budget of $2.5 million. The product was not released until 1976, 12 years after the initial effort. This project succeeded as a result of the brilliance and tenacity of the research team combined with a senior management vision that was clear, stable, and supported. Corning achieved a huge success in developing the successful ceramic substrate for catalytic converters. Corning senior management set forth a compelling vision to develop the next generation of catalytic converters when they realized the huge potential that resulted from the reduced emission requirement of the Clean Air Act. These factors were so compelling that Corning, in 1970, directed hundreds of scientists and engineers to focus on this single challenge. The resulting product has been used on more than three hundred million automobiles. Technology development in these high-risk projects are often managed by a Technology ·

Stage-Gate (Eldred and Shapiro, 1996; Eldred and McGrath, 1997; Ajamian and Koen, 2002) process, which involves many of the characteristics of the traditional Stage-Gate® process, but encompass methodologies to mange the risk and uncertainty of dealing with discoveries that have not yet occurred. Standard financial methods for analyzing these types of projects do not work well. A summary of risk methodologies and other techniques are discussed by Koen et. al. (2002).

Many discoveries are accidental and often establish entirely new markets. Perhaps the classic example was the development of the Post-it® Note (Nayak and Ketteringham, 1986), a journey that began when Spence Silver recognized that he had invented, in 1968, an unusual glue that was more tacky than adhesive. Despite visiting almost every division in 3M, he could not find any use for it. In fact he had to wage a battle even to get the invention patented— which 3M reluctantly did—but only in the United States. It was not developed further until 1974, when Art Fry, a colleague of Silver's, dropped his hymn book and the slips of paper that he had used to mark places in the hymn book fluttered to the floor. Art Fry had his "eureka!" moment and envisioned the concept that is now a huge business for 3M.

While accidental discoveries are a common occurrence in most companies, it is critical that the culture of a company allow individuals freedom to try their ideas without sacrificing their career. While 3M did not financially support Silver's quest when he first discovered this unique adhesive—they did not prevent him from trying to find an opportunity to use it—provided that he still met his expected duties. Perhaps this is best described as a "caring" organization (von Krough, Icihjo, K., and Nonaka, I., 2000). "Care" may be thought of as the way that parents nurture their children. In another words, the culture needs to value the individual and provide a degree of trust that he or she will do the right thing. Care could be considered the soil in which accidental discoveries need to germinate. Without it, they will quickly die. And even with it only a few seeds will germinate into truly breakthrough products. Zein and Buckler (1997), in their study of 13 innovative companies, found that these companies valued the individual and had an environment that was conducive to high personal motivation. Similarly, Prather (2000), based on his work at DuPont, found that trust and openness that allows people to speak their minds and offer contrasting opinions was important for maintaining an environment conducive to innovation. In summary, having an organization that values and trusts the individual is a necessary condition for allowing individual discoveries that may lead to a breakthrough, which may or may not be aligned with the strategy of the corporation, to germinate.

6.7 Summary

The overall objective of this chapter was to provide the reader with a more holistic view of the FFE and an understanding that it includes not only incremental idea generation, but also platform and breakthrough development. The Stage-Gate® process is an effective tool for accelerating incremental product development. However, it cannot be directly used for the FFE of platform or breakthrough products. Platform products need to begin with a strategic vision, which will lead to a family of products based on an in-depth understanding of the market and how the companies core competencies and capabilities can be used to build competitive advantage. A robust method for developing new and sustaining existing platforms is typically associated with the most innovative companies. Breakthroughs start out with a similar strategic vision, but are usually associated with technologies that require new discoveries. These projects may be managed during the discovery efforts by the Technology Stage Gate Process. Many breakthrough discoveries occur by accident. However, these innovations can only succeed in a caring organization.

References

Ajamian, G. and Koen, P. A., "Technology Stage-Gate: A Structured Process for Managing High Risk, New Technology Projects," In P. Belliveau, A Griffen and S. Sorermeyer, eds. *PDMA Toolbook for New Product Development*. New York: John Wiley & Sons, 267–295, 2002.

Booz, Allen and Hamilton, Inc. *New Product Management for the 1980's*. New York: Booz Allen and Hamilton, Inc., 1982.

Cooper, R. G. *Winning at New Products*, 3rd ed., Perseus Publishing, Cambridge, MA, 2001.

Eldred, E. W. and M. E. McGrath. "Commercializing new technology—I." *Research—Technology Management:* 41–47 (January–February 1997).

Eldred, E. W. and A. R. Shapiro. "Technology Management," In M. E. McGrath, ed. *Setting the PACE in Product Development*. Boston: Butterworth and Heinemann, 1996.

Koen, P. A. Ajamian, G., Boyce, S., Clamen, A., Fisher, E., Fountoulakis, S., Johnson A., Puri. P., Seibert, R., "Fuzzy-Front End: Effective Methods, Tools and Techniques," in P. Belliveau, A Griffen and S. Sorermeyer, eds. *PDMA Toolbook for New Product Development*. New York: John Wiley & Sons, 2–35, 2002.

Leifer, R., McDermott, C. M., O'Connor, G. C., Peters, L. S., Rice, M., and R. W. Veryzer. *Radical Innovation*. Massachusetts: Harvard Business Press, 2000.

Lynn, G. S. and Akgun, A. E., "Project visioning: Its components and impact on new product success." *Journal of Product Innovation Management*, 18: 374–387 (2001).

Markham, S. K., "Product Champions: Crossing the Valley of Death," in P. Belliveau, A Griffen and S. Sorermeyer, eds. *PDMA Toolbook for New Product Development*. New York: John Wiley & Sons, 119–140, 2002.

McGrath, M. E., *Product Strategy for High-Technology Companies*," 2nd ed. New York: McGraw-Hill, 2001.

McGrath, M. E. and C. L. Akiyama "PACE: An Integrated Process for Product and Cycle Time Excellence," in M.E. McGrath, eds. *Setting the PACE in Product Development*, Butterworth Heinemann, Boston, 1996.

Meyer, M. H. and DeTore, A., "Product development for services," *Academy of Management Executive*, 13(3): 64–76 (1999).

Meyer, M. H. and Lehnerd, L., *The Power of Product Platforms*, New York: The Free Press, 1997

Meyer, M. H., and Mugge, P. C., "Make Platform Innovation Drive Enterprise Growth," *Research Technology Management*, 44(1): 25–39 (2001).

Meyer, M. H. and Seliger, R., "Product Platforms in Software Development," *Sloan Management Review*, 40(1): 61–63, 1998.

Meyer, M. H., and Zack, M. H., "The Architecture of Information Products," *Sloan Management Review*, 37(3): 43–59 (1996).

Nayak, P. R. and Ketteringham, J. M., *Breakthroughs*. San Diego, CA: Pfeiffer and Co., 1994.

von Krogh, G., "Care in Knowledge Creation," *California Management Review*, 40(3): 133–153, (1998).

Prather, C. W. "Keeping Innovation Alive After the Consultants Leave," *Research Technology Management* 43(5): 17–22 (September–October 2000).

Wheelwright, S. C. and Clark, K. B., *Revolutionizing Product Development*. New York: Free Press, 1992.

Wheelwright, S. C. and Sasser, W. E. "The new product development map," *Harvard Business Review*, 112–125 (May–June 1989).

von Krough, G., Icihjo, K., and Nonaka, I. *Enabling Knowledge Creation*. Oxford: Oxford University Press, 2000.

Zien, K. A. and Buckler, S. A. From experience dreams to market: crafting a culture of innovation. *Journal of Product Innovation Management*, 14:274–287 (1997).

Peter Koen is currently employed as a full-time associate professor in the Wesley J. Howe School of Technology Management at Stevens Institute of Technology in Hoboken, New Jersey. He is currently director of the Consortium for Corporate Entrepreneurship (CCE) at Stevens, whose mission is to stimulate highly profitable activities at the "Fuzzy Front End" of the innovation process (www.frontendinnovation.com). Peter is actively engaged in research directed at Best Practices in Front End, determining how companies organize around breakthroughs in large corporations and knowledge creation flow. He has 19 years of industrial experience, including new product development responsibility at both large and small companies. His academic background includes a BS and MS in mechanical engineering from New York University in 1965 and 1967, respectively. In addition, he holds a Ph.D. in biomedical engineering from Drexel obtained in 1975 and a professional engineering license.

CHAPTER SEVEN

SERVICE DEVELOPMENT

Thomas D. Kuczmarski and Zachary T. Johnston

7.1 Introduction

Services are fundamentally different from products and need unique considerations in their creation and development. The best approach for developing innovative new services, however, remains a systematic and iterative process that is intimately based upon solving customers' problems and meeting their needs. This disciplined approach ensures higher customer satisfaction, reduced development costs, and eventually more impact in the marketplace.

Service development has its own set of distinct characteristics, challenges, and processes that need to be distinguished from traditional product development. For example, the "manufacturing" process of service development is the service operations support or "delivery" process that creates the customer's experience. Customers play a direct role in the service delivery process, making their involvement in development that much more essential. In addition, because the success of service delivery is highly influenced by the person or technology that interfaces with the customer, minimizing variation in delivery quality and consistency is critical for success.

As our society continues to change and evolve at an accelerated pace, customer expectations change with the times as well as the capabilities of service providers. Because total customer experience is the defining success criteria for services, rapidly changing needs and higher expectations add a level of complexity to service development in the twenty-first century. This chapter will outline the unique aspects and emerging trends of service development and a customer-driven service development process.

7.2 How Service Development Is Different

Despite its pervasive use in today's business lexicon, the word "service" is widely misunderstood. What exactly constitutes a service? What is unique about a service compared to a product? What is the relationship between services and products?

The lack of understanding surrounding the word "services" leads to misfocused and inefficient new service efforts.

Since the answers to these questions remain unclear to much of the business world, the majority of service development efforts are misfocused and inefficient. Understanding what differentiates services and makes them unique is the first step in enhancing new service development.

The four unique-to-service qualities that help to define the word "service" are summed up in the four "I's": Individualized, Intangible, Instantaneous, and Inseparable.

1. Services are individualized to a given customer.
2. Services are intangible.
3. Customer reaction and evaluation is instantaneous.
4. Services can only be thought of as a holistic sum of their parts—they are inseparable.

Founded in 2000 on the premise of offering a superior customer experience, JetBlue Airways has quickly established itself as the premier airline service provider in the nation. They are a case study example of a service company that intimately understands the four "I's" of service development, and they have reaped the rewards. JetBlue was named the best domestic airline and best value-for-cost airline by Conde Nast Traveler in 2002 along with countless other accolades. As each of the four "I's" is discussed below, it is easy to see how JetBlue has consciously addressed these unique aspects of service development.

7.2.1 Individualized

The most glaring difference between services and products is that one particular customer consumes any given service differently than the next. Because service delivery is inevitably subject to variation, and consumers all have different behavioral idiosyncrasies, the exact delivery/consumption interplay will rarely ever replicate itself the same way twice. By definition, services mean doing something for someone else, not producing a product for mass consumption. This becomes one of the most critical elements to any successful service: the extent to which the provider can deliver a unique, "customized" experience to each customer rather then apply a generic, one-size-fits-all solution. In 2002, a Kuczmarski and Associates survey of Fortune 500 managers and directors found that, although they were hesitant to admit it, the number one corporate innovation strategy during the past three years had been cost cutting. Cost cutting to innovate? This telling finding underscores the Wall Street pressures on companies to meet their numbers and poses a potential barrier to successfully implementing this individualized approach to services.

Despite strong economic pressures in the airline industry, JetBlue has been able to overcome this trap while its competitors have blindly fallen into it. Instead of resorting to cost-cutting initiatives, JetBlue enhanced services and amenities such as free real-time television, more comfortable seats, friendlier and more accommodating ticket agents and flight crews, and a more personalized Web site. These services allow customers to have individualized flying experiences, making them feel better about the service they are provided rather than simply being one of the herd. In fact, at its inception, CEO David Neeleman proclaimed that his plan was to bring "humanity back to air travel." In other words, he wants to make his customers feel valued as individuals.

7.2.2 Intangible

While it may seem elementary, it is important to underscore that services are not products, but rather intangible interactions or experiences. Take, for example, a trip to the doctor's office, a quote for car insurance, or an afternoon spent at the ballpark watching a baseball game. While all of these services leave the customer with something of value, there is certainly nothing concrete for them to pull out of their pockets and show to their friends.

This unique aspect of service swings open the doors for both opportunities and challenges in development. Because there is nothing tangible for consumers to evaluate beyond memories or receipts, the experience itself is what is evaluated and reevaluated down the line. The key point—the experience—is the essence of successful new service development. For this reason, services need to leave a lasting positive impression, satisfy customers' expectations, and be responsive to customer feedback in order to ensure continued success. Developing services, therefore, requires a different approach from that used for new products.

Take JetBlue's continued development of industry-leading safety measures. While customers will only occasionally utilize these services, safety in the air is highly valued. For this reason, JetBlue was the first airline to introduce "paperless cockpit" flight technology, the first to install bullet-proof doors in the cockpit, and the first and only airline to install cameras in the passenger cabin. These services are not only intangible, they are also largely unrecognized by customers during their actual flight. It is the mere knowledge of these precautions that enhances customers' overall flight experience. The company's quick response to 9/11 and the changing expectations and desires of their customers clearly demonstrates their understanding of the need to be flexible and adaptable in delivering an effective service.

7.2.3 Instantaneous

Another significant defining feature of services is the instantaneous and ongoing nature of their evaluation. At every point of contact with a customer, new opinions and expectations are formed. Service providers have the advantage of being able to assess these evaluations and make actionable decisions based on this feedback much more quickly than product developers. It is imperative to capture these feelings and opinions as they happen to most effectively tailor services and make revisions accordingly.

Again, JetBlue understands the importance of services responding instantaneously. The company provides numerous contact points for feedback and solicits opinions, good or bad, at every point in their service chain. Whether it is on their Web site, at a ticket counter or even in-flight, they constantly try to get real-time evaluations in hopes of better meeting the changing needs and wants of their customers.

7.2.4 Inseparable (Yet Individual)

"Inseparable" underscores the fact that services are a collective sum of their individual parts, spanning every point of contact with the customer. When a service is performed, the event is evaluated holistically rather than at each separate stage in the service chain. For example, the overall experience when flying on JetBlue encompasses the ticket purchase online or over the phone, the check-in process, the flight itself, and luggage retrieval. If there is a disconnect in service quality at one of the contact points, the whole service experience is negatively affected. Service development, therefore, needs to address the holistic aspect of services and the interplay between their numerous customer contact segments.

While, overall, services are an indivisible part of their whole, it is important to keep in mind the individual nature of any given service in the development process. For example, as an overall company approach, JetBlue tries to uphold the same quality standards throughout their service. However, each service segment is addressed separately to figure out how to best tailor it to adhere to the overall corporate service theme.

The individualized aspect of services is evident in services that accompany a product. In fact, over the last few years many companies that have traditionally been fueled by the high quality of their products have been emphasizing ancillary services to competitively differentiate their products. Over the last few years, Lexus has shifted its business model to emphasize the service aspect of their dealerships. While the Lexus brand still stands for luxury, the company has successfully expanded it to include high quality, reliable service as well. Now, the brand "Lexus" stands for a luxurious experience, not just a luxury car. Recently, BMW has followed suit and has started offering free lifetime maintenance for all of its 5-series vehicles. Again, the service is offered as a complement to the product to help bolster the overall company message and experience realized.

7.3 The Service Development Process

Perhaps the single most important aspect of service development, one that is absolutely imperative for success, is a staged development process that hinges on the involvement of and input from customers and employees. A staged development process (see Figure 7.1) is one that manages new services as they move through various phases of development, from problems and ideas to concepts and launch. While the overall strategy for new service development should closely mirror that used for developing new products, service development requires a unique, hands-on approach due to the complex, variant nature of service delivery. After a foundation is set that links the overall corporate strategy to the creation of new services, the development process differentiates itself from that used in new product development in both subtle and extreme ways.

7.3.1 A Corporate Innovation Strategy

While many executives would view creating a new services strategy a "no brainer," it is surprising how many fail to execute this step properly. Just as the foundation of a structure lays the base upon which to

> *A new services strategy lays the strategic platform upon which to create new services.*

FIGURE 7.1 ESSENTIAL STEPS FOR A SUCCESSFUL NEW SERVICES DEVELOPMENT PROCESS.

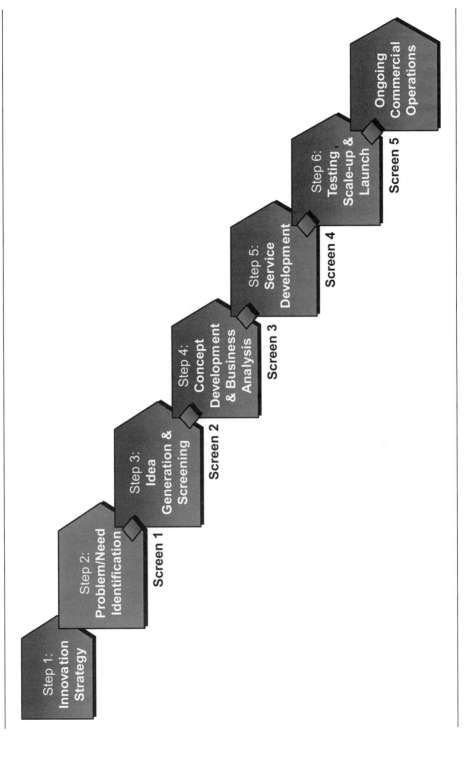

build, a new services strategy lays the platform upon which to create new services. If you don't know what strategic roles you want new services to play within your organization, this will lead to haphazard and disjointed service creation, and it will be difficult to evaluate their success.

An effective new services strategy should have four main elements:

1. A resource strategy, which outlines the financial and human resource requirements for successful new service creation
2. The financial growth gap that new services are expected to fill over the next five years
3. The new service vision and the strategic roles that new services must satisfy
4. Screening criteria to be used for moving ideas and concepts though the development process

Without a well-articulated strategy, companies will often fall into the trap of supporting too many or too few projects. This results in under- or overutilized innovation resources, leading to reduced morale among service providers and thus reduced service quality. It cannot be stressed enough how important employee morale and motivation are in the creation of new services. Without the enthusiastic support of employees, often the very people who deliver the service to customers, new services are doomed to failure.

The financial growth gap helps determine the magnitude of the new service efforts that a company will attempt to fulfill. For example, refer to the financial growth gap illustrated in Figure 7.2. A large gap usually dictates breakthrough new services both inside and outside the company's current market or category. This point of reference prepares companies for the degree of risk they will be undertaking.

Similarly, the new service vision and strategic roles provide qualitative benchmarks to help guide problem exploration and development. They provide specificity to the growth gap by defining "what's in" and "what's out" from a new service development perspective.

And finally, the screening criteria help separate the winners from the losers, prioritize concepts, and ensure continued overall alignment with the strategy and roles. The criteria provide metrics across a variety of categories to help companies understand the relative attractiveness of various initiatives.

7.3.2 Service Development and Shaping: The Voice of the Customer

Once the foundation is in place, actual service development can begin. The first stage is problem identification and exploration. It is here that acutely felt

FIGURE 7.2 FINANCIAL GROWTH GAP.

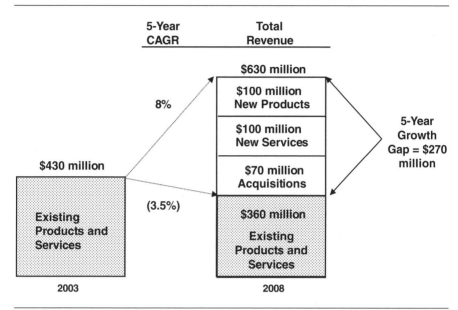

problems, frustrations, and issues of customers and noncustomers are uncovered. By utilizing a range of qualitative research techniques, you can help better zero in on and identify customers' biggest problems and frustrations, which often serve as the foundation against which new solutions can be generated. This "needs and wants" focus can be broad (e.g., category service usage processes or routines) or narrow (e.g., service feature, benefit, or dissatisfactions). The problem identification stage is arguably the most important stage of service development because it establishes the foundation for the development of breakthrough new services by identifying creative, customer-based problems and opportunities.

The second stage of service development is targeted new service ideation and conceptualization. The first objective is to generate dozens of new solution ideas that address those needs, wants, problems, and frustrations uncovered in

---

Identifying customers' biggest problems and frustrations up front is arguably the most important stage of new service development.

problem identification. Participants in ideation should include customers and noncustomers as well as a cross-functional mix of employees. After ideas have been condensed and shaped, the screening criteria is used to determine what ideas should move on to conceptualization. Once this screening has taken place, the highest potential concepts are then turned into concept statements, shaped and tested with customers, and evaluated financially though rigorous business analyses.

In the mid-1990s, just as our society was teetering on the edge of the Internet explosion, Cincinnati Bell Telephone found itself in the dark about many of its customers rapidly emerging needs. In a process very similar to the one described earlier, the company went out to the market to learn more about their customers' needs, problems, and frustrations in this brave new Internet age. What they discovered was that the communication power of the Internet was allowing more people to work from their homes than in the past. However, when a customer would call his/her business line, that customer would get a busy signal when the computer was in use. The company's concern was missed new business, frustrated customers, and the appearance of being a one-person shop. The most compelling solution that surfaced in postresearch ideation sessions was a service that provided call waiting while customers were online, eventually called CallManager. This allowed customers to remain uninterrupted and still get important calls. Cincinnati Bell was the first to offer this revolutionary service, which gained them high customer satisfaction and helped to establish them as a pioneer in the competitive telecommunications industry.

7.3.3 Employee Involvement and Service Blueprinting

Because so much of a service's success or failure will hinge on it's successful delivery, it is absolutely essential to involve delivery staff in the early problem identification and ideation sessions. These staff members have been "in the trenches," dealing with

> *Staff members have one of the best frames of reference for identifying unmet customer needs and frustrations.*

customer feedback and complaints, giving them one of the best frames of reference for unmet needs and frustrations. Additionally, these are the people who will ultimately transform an illusive service concept into a tangible customer-valued "product," and involving them from the beginning will improve their morale and motivation, thereby improving delivery.

In addition to having these staff directly involved throughout the process, another effective way of engaging them is by having them create service blueprints that map interactions, contact points, and routs of delivery for service ideas. For all services that have moved through to conceptualization, a service processes map, a graphical representation of the delivery process, including all possible contact points, should be created. It should map out the sequential flow of activities and interactions, both those that are visible and those that are not visible to the customer. The first, initial draft should map out different possibilities for points of contact and service delivery. These different alternatives can then be tested once a prototype is ready. In addition, this will allow staff to better visualize their role in the overall service delivery process, making them feel like a valued, essential part of a larger team.

Let's look at the touch points involved in a newspaper experience for a customer. The billing process, ease of holding delivery during vacation, quality of the editorials, delivery of the newspaper to the doorstep, appeal of separate sections of the newspaper, and the like represent pieces of the total experience pie. While the black-and-white product is the core offering, all of the services that surround it are indeed inseparable and help to shape the collective experience. A service blueprint will help the newspaper company both identify all these different touch points and map out possible modes and styles of interactions for every key customer involvement situation. This map will help show the linkages among the different service and product attributes and help give employees a sense of their purpose in the overall value proposition that the company is offering.

Figure 7.3 illustrates a blueprint for a newspaper home delivery service. As shown, this delivery service has many "one-time" interactions. That is, after the initial contact and agreement on services to be rendered, the subsequent interactions are essentially delivery, billing, and maintenance. Therefore, after a customer has made a decision to purchase the service, it is imperative for the company to keep the customer satisfied at every future touch point. A breakdown at merely one of the many points of interaction will subject the whole newspaper home delivery service to cancelation. In short, the New Service Blueprint allows one to determine all the customer points of contact and related company actions to ensure that none are overlooked.

7.3.4 Prototype and Beyond: Differentiation through Delivery

The next major stage is prototype development and launch. In this stage, concepts that pass through screens are then turned into full-scale prototypes and detailed market test and launch plans and service delivery plans are developed. The highest potential service concepts are then brought to life and refined and tested with customers. After being tested, tweaked, and validated by customers,

FIGURE 7.3 NEW SERVICE BLUEPRINT: NEWSPAPER HOME DELIVERY.

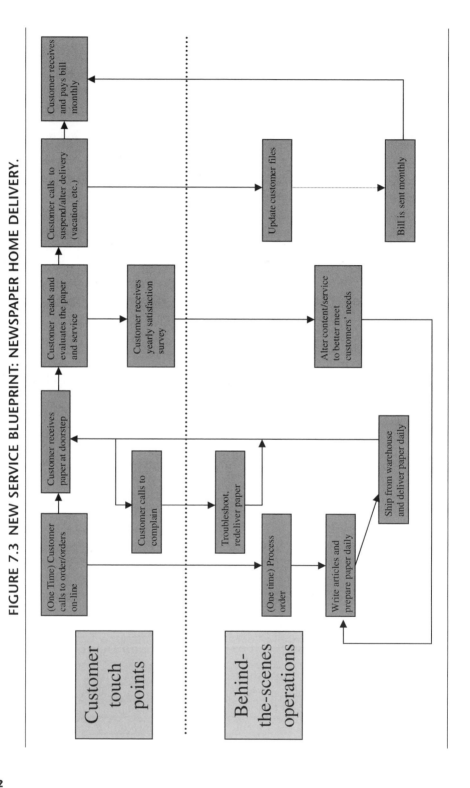

The launch of a new service is essentially never-ending.

the services are ready for launch in accordance with a specified roll-out plan. This plan must take into account a number of factors, including screening criteria, the new services strategy, and prototype testing results.

Prototype testing is one of the most essential elements of new service development. Unfortunately, many service companies will omit the prototype testing and jump directly from concept to launch. This could not be more deleterious to successful service creation. Because services are largely unpatentable, are extremely susceptible to replication, and require few barriers to entry, it is imperative to garner customer feedback on a new service in order to improve and tweak it before undertaking a full-scale public launch. Failure to do so can result in unsatisfied customers and leave an organization vulnerable to competition. This is devastating, not only because of the financial ramifications of lost investment, but also because it is damaging to the creative mindset and chance of future risk taking and success.

The launch is another unique aspect to service creation because it is essentially never-ending. When a product is launched, a company's hard work is essentially over; it is exactly the opposite with services. A service needs constant monitoring and assessment to make sure that it is still addressing relevant consumer needs in the most efficient and effective way possible. There is always room for improvement with services, so constant customer feedback is essential.

In addition, while it is easy to predict the reception that a new product will receive after launch (through qualitative and quantitative research with a representative sample of customers and possible customers), with services it is much more difficult. Although it is possible to test a service much like a product, often the service's value proposition is highly influenced by network externalities; that is, often the value of a service is directly related to the number of people who use it. For example, email services become increasingly valuable as more people use email as a primary mode of communication. While some network effects may be unforeseeable prior to launch, it is possible to mitigate this lack of information by testing plausible market occurrences related to service usage in prototype testing—that is, there is the need to test the variability in usage with customers prior to launch (in a "for instance" manner) in order to determine its effect on the service's overall value. The possible presence of network externalities, either positive or negative, also calls for constant customer feedback and monitoring after launch—only with a continuous understanding of the changing value propositions of the services provided can a company effectively reevaluate the service offered.

In 2002, Volunteer Hospitals of America (VHA), a nationwide, member-driven health-care consulting company, launched a new service called, "Transforming the ICU," a service aimed at helping its members better equip and more effectively use their Intensive Care Units. Conducting both on- and off-site research with its members to better understand what makes an ICU as effective and efficient as possible, VHA leveraged what they learned to help bridge the gap between its best- and worst-performing hospitals. After the launch, however, VHA's work did not cease. A dedicated team continued to conduct research on best-in-class ICUs and continuously updated the service's specifications and procedures to make sure it was in line with cutting-edge research. Because the world of medicine has such a swiftly moving frontier, it was essential for VHA to keep as current as possible. This constant monitoring of "Transforming the ICU" leveraged their main point of difference, their large member and knowledge base, and helped to further differentiate them from their competitors.

7.3.5 Training as Part of the New Service Development Process

Services, unlike products, are ultimately delivered either by people or with the assistance of people. Because all people are unique and respond differently in given situations, certain measures must be taken to ensure that employees have the resources and knowledge to act in the best interest of the company. Training of employees should revolve around three main areas:

1. The company's corporate strategy and the service's strategic role
2. Crisis management and troubleshooting
3. The actual delivery of the service

First, only with an ingrained knowledge of the strategic role or objective of the service under the larger umbrella of corporate strategy can employees make decisions that will tie into the overall company objectives. Training them to see the larger picture will help ensure that they have the company's goals in mind in every decision made. Second, employees need to be trained in extensive crisis management and troubleshooting situations. Only when they are well versed in the plausible mishaps will they be able to respond in a consistent and appropriate manner. It is imperative to invest in extensive training for the basic delivery of the service. Learning by doing is not an acceptable approach in service development because this will lead to alienated customers and lost business.

7.4 Emerging Trends in Service Development

Another characteristic unique to services is the alacrity with which they move and adjust to societal trends. While certain products continue to demonstrate their value decade after decade, few services stand this test of time because people's expectations and needs are in constant flux. There are two notable trends that have acutely affected service development over the last decade: the development and utilization of technology and the blurring of the lines between products and services.

7.4.1 Technology

Increasing technology has had an impact on service development at its core by elevating both service development capabilities and customers' expectations. These two forces work both for and against each other in the service development equation: as technology increases, providers are able

> *Increased competition due to technological advances calls for greater differentiation through unique, personalized service delivery.*

to better meet the demands of their customers, who, in turn, continue to increase their expectations of minimum standards. The ultimate consequence of this technology/expectations cycle is that service providers cannot ever be content with their technology advances or rest on their innovation laurels, because companies are now constantly susceptible to competitive offerings and unsatisfied customers.

The increasing capabilities of service providers are best exemplified by the rise in use of the Internet as a means of interfacing with customers. The Internet has provided both businesses and customers with unprecedented reach at an extremely low cost. While this allows customers much more information in an easy-to-use format, the main impact is on the ease of feedback collection for the service provider. They now have a captive audience from whom they can solicit feedback and suggestions, helping them provide better, more-responsive service to their customers. Other technologies have had similar effects, such as cell phones, email, personal digital assistants (PDAs), the global positioning system (GPS), and powerful software applications.

While these new technologies have certainly helped innovative companies expand their boundaries and improve their services, they have also made it much simpler and cheaper for others to replicate competitors' actions. The fast follower is now able to play "catch up" at a price and time frame significantly less than those of the pioneer. Due to this phenomenon, it is imperative that companies test and shape new services prior to launch to ensure that they meet and exceed customers' expectations and requirements. If appropriate, they should also consider filing for a service mark as another source of competitive insulation. Failure to act prudently allows competitors the opportunity to capitalize on months or years of hard work and innovation without the time or financial investment. Companies first to market with a properly tested and shaped new technology stand to gain market share and block competitors, while companies who hastily rush to market with an imperfect technology will at first succeed, but ultimately fail as competitors flood the market. This increased competition also calls for a greater attention to personalized, unique service delivery as a means to further differentiate yourself.

An example demonstrating the dangers of technology and new service development is the story of Webvan, an online grocery shopping and delivery service. Webvan took a great idea, allowing customers to order and receive groceries and other goods without leaving the comfort of their home, but did not exercise patience when developing, testing, and perfecting their service delivery. Thus, their service ultimately failed as other providers were able to come in and offer higher-quality services at a much lower cost.

7.4.2 The Blurring of Products and Services

Another major trend in service development that continues to grow is the blending of products and services into a "full experience," rather than standing as individual entities. This emerging viewpoint is similar to services being "Inseparable" from their congruous parts but is much more literal. For example, when you buy a cell phone, are you buying a product or a service? Well, the phone itself is certainly a product, but it is only useful with the accompanying service.

This line has continued to blur as people have become more time crunched and concerned with convenience and simplicity. For instance, when you order pizza, are you paying for the actual pizza or more for the convenience of the delivery? When you order a newspaper from the *Chicago Sun-Times*, are you paying more for the paper itself or the convenience of the delivery and online bill pay? People now place more value on these interconnected and interrelated services that accompany many products.

This thinking has distinct ramifications for service development. Service providers should never underestimate the importance of the service they provide merely because it is ancillary to the product. America's reliance on convenience has shifted this paradigm to the point where a once supplemental service can now be the defining benefit of a product/service combination. Extensive customer research is needed to determine the changing role of a specific service in the overall value proposition of the product/service package.

7.5 Summary

This chapter has looked at the defining features of service development and outlined an effective process for the creation of breakthrough new services. While service development shares many common threads with product development, there are stark differences that call for a unique approach. In addition to the need for a staged process and continuous customer involvement, extensive testing and feedback during the prototype and launch stage and the need for comprehensive employee training are the hallmarks of a successful new services process.

Thomas D. Kuczmarski is the president of Kuczmarski & Associates, a Chicago-based consultancy specializing in new product and service innovation. He is the cofounder of the Chicago Innovation Awards, an annual event that recognizes the ten most innovative new products and services developed in the Chicago area. Mr. Kuczmarski also teaches Managing New Product Development at Northwestern University's Kellogg Graduate School of Management and is the author of numerous books, including *Innovation* and *Managing New Products (3rd edition)*.

Zachary T. Johnston is a consultant at Kuczmarski & Associates. He specializes in assisting clients in strategic new product and service development and designing customer-centric branding strategies. He has extensive experience in service industries and with business-to-business companies. Mr. Johnston has been published in journals such as *Marketing Management* on the topics of corporate innovation strategies and how to create an innovation mindset.

PART TWO

ORGANIZING
THE DEVELOPMENT

A bad beginning makes a bad ending.

EURIPIDES, GREEK PLAYWRIGHT, 438 BC

Companies develop innovative new products in three broad categories: incremental, platform, and breakthrough. New arrangements, described in Chapter 8, separate mainstream incremental development from the other two. However, this separation is not so distant that what emerges from platform and breakthrough development becomes irrelevant to the mainstream.

Teamwork is not a new idea but now, more than ever before, product development practitioners must pay attention to effective teamwork. The skills outlined in Chapter 9 move beyond threshold competencies to skills for building fast and flexible teams. Such teams can work dynamically and creatively toward objectives in a changing environment.

Getting approval for product development actions is not just a rational exercise of telling others that a project is important. Rather, it is a means of creating support. Chapter 10 helps practitioners cope with political behavior at the company and department levels by focusing on their interaction with other practitioners, with the departments with whom they must work, and with management.

Given a clean sheet of paper, how would you design a new product development process that brings to together the following qualities? The process brings to bear the best talent you need for success. It has costs that are competitive globally. And, finally, it offers enough edge to change the game on the competition. Distributed development, the topic of Chapter 11, describes what many firms are employing to respond to this question.

Many practitioners approach rapid product development with unrealistic, distorted, or unclear objectives, so they are disappointed with the results they achieve. Chapter 12 clarifies the objectives of such a process, frames the talents and skills needed, and discusses pitfalls that have misled many other practitioners in their search for development speed.

CHAPTER EIGHT

INNOVATION IN LARGE COMPANIES: APPROACHES AND ORGANIZATIONAL ARCHITECTURE

Peter A. Koen

8.1 Introduction

This chapter provides an overview of the overall approaches and organizational architecture for innovation in large corporations. An overall typology for how companies approach innovation is indicated in Figure 8.1. On the ordinate is the focus of the innovation effort—which may be internal or external. Internal innovation effort refers to the development of products or services that grow the current businesses. External innovation is used to imply innovation efforts that are occurring in other companies that, because of their synergy, become prime candidates for acquisitions, mergers, alliances, and co-development. The term "external innovation" is also used in the context of a product or service innovation developed for a new business external to the corporation. An example of this would be the development of a "spin-off" company, such as Face2Face, which has unique applications in facial analysis and animation built on technologies developed by Lucent—but which does not fit with any of Lucent's current businesses. On the abscissa is the funding— whether it is from a strategic business unit (SBU) or from the corporation. Organizational structures for new product development will be explored in three of the areas. Mergers and acquisitions, joint alliances, and codevelopment activities (top-left box) are not discussed in this chapter.

FIGURE 8.1 OVERALL TYPOLOGY OF CORPORATE ORGANIZATIONAL STRUCTURES WHERE INNOVATION MAY OCCUR.

Focus of Innovation		
External	Mergers and Acquisitions, Joint Alliances and Codevelopment Ex: Division acquires or purchases an equity position	Corporate Venturing Ex: Corporate Venture Fund for external ventures in specific technology or industry sectors
Internal	SBU Business Development Ex: Projects are developed within the SBU	Central Research Laboratory Ex: Research Center funded by corporation to work on high risk technologies Corporate Business Development Ex: Venture Fund for funding internal projects
	SBU	Corporate

Funding

8.2 Product Development Within a Strategic Business Unit

The majority of product development within most corporations occurs within a SBU—which is responsible for its profit and loss, is aligned with industries, and has a well-defined value chain and customer distribution channel. Figure 8.2 illustrates an overall architecture for managing innovation. This section begins with a discussion of different parts of the architecture and ends by indicating the constituencies needed to manage the overall process.

8.2.1 Innovation Vision

The process begins with an innovation vision, which is consistent with the SBU strategy. A good example is the innovation vision that led to the development of the Hewlett-Packard (HP) inkjet printer. In the mid-1980s the market for HP's dot-matrix printer was being eroded by two market forces. Laser printers emerged, which were more expensive, but offered higher-quality printing, and began taking market share at the high end. Less-expensive dot-matrix printers were also emerging, which were reducing market share and margins in the low

FIGURE 8.2 OVERALL PRODUCT DEVELOPMENT ARCHITECTURE THAT EXISTS WITHIN A STRATEGIC BUSINESS UNIT.

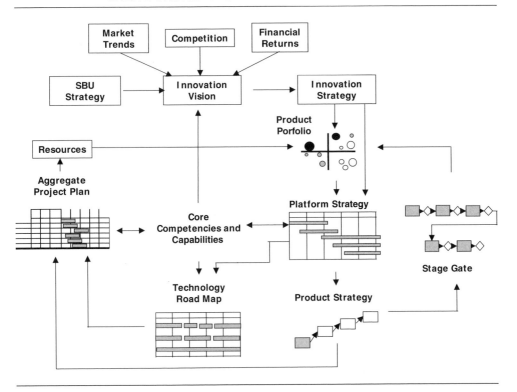

end. As a result HP, in September 1985, developed an innovation vision for the printing SBU to develop products with print quality closer to that of laser printers, but at a price that would compete directly with the lower-priced dot-matrix printers. Another example is how Sony created the first "Walkman®" by setting a seemingly impossible vision in 1952 of a "pocketable radio"—at a time when transistors were only being used in military applications. Still another example is the innovation vision developed by Kodak, which was to expand their product line to include a one-time-use disposable camera, where the film would be packaged in an inexpensive plastic case that the consumer would return directly to the photofinisher. This innovation vision ultimately resulted in the development of Kodak's very successful FunSaver camera. The innovation vision will need to capture not only the new platforms—as discussed above—but also innovations needed to sustain the current business as well as visions for radical or breakthrough projects.

The overall innovation vision is bounded by five forces, as illustrated in Figure 8.2:

- *Overall SBU strategy:* The overall strategy defines the mission, value chain, and market channels of the SBU. The innovation vision needs to be consistent with the SBU strategy, although in some cases the SBU strategy may need to change because of the vision. For example, envisioning a new market channel for an existing product is likely to cause strategy modification.

- *Core competencies and capabilities:* Competitive advantage is achieved when a company has unique core competencies (Prahalad and Hamel, 1990) and capabilities (Stalk et al., 1992) that are valuable, rare, immutable, and non-substitutable. Competencies are a unique set of skills which provide significant competitive advantage to the corporation. For example, Honda's expertise in engines is a core competence (Prahalad and Hamel, 1990). In contrast, capabilities are a bundle of skills embodied throughout the corporation that allow it to achieve competitive advantage—where no single skill represents a competence. An example is "cross-docking" (Stalk et al., 1992), which is a capability that Wal-Mart possesses that allows them to continuously deliver full truck loads of goods to central warehouses where they are repacked and dispatched to stores without ever sitting in inventory. This sophisticated inventory system is supported by a private satellite communication system that sends daily point-of-sale reports to its 4000 vendors and a transportation system that includes 19 distribution centers supported by 2000 Wal-Mart-owned company trucks. In this way Wal-Mart is simultaneously able to minimize overall inventory and product cost, while maximizing inventory turns at their stores.

- *Market trends:* The innovation vision needs to be consistent with the current and future market trends and unmet customer needs.

- *Competitive forces:* Understanding of the competitive landscape is also critical because many competitors are vying for the same or similar product landscape. Intellectual property developed by competitors may block the company's ability to develop products built on an already patented technology.

- *Financial or economic goals:* One of the goals of the innovation vision is to achieve the revenue growth and profitability within the investment parameters of the SBU. Many companies fail to test whether their innovation vision will achieve their financial objectives.

Product development needs to begin with a well-defined innovation vision, which leads to an innovation strategy, which in turn, defines the product and platform strategy.

8.2.2 Innovation Strategy and Portfolio

Next, an innovation strategy is developed based on the innovation vision. The innovation strategy expresses the products and services that are needed to meet the innovation vision. This strategy is "operationalized" into a product portfolio. Ultimately, it is a senior management responsibility to determine project selection and resource allocation. Cooper et al.'s (2001) classic book on portfolios and Chapter 3 are suggested for readers who are not knowledgeable on the subject. The overall purpose of a portfolio is to:

- *Maximize value:* What projects will maximize the overall return based on the business objective of short- or long-term profitability, return on investment, economic value, or strategic objective?
- *Achieve project balance:* Effective portfolio management will achieve a balance between long-term and short-term projects, high vs. low risk projects, and various project types (i.e., maintenance and fixes, cost improvements, incremental, platform, and radical products.)
- *Ensure strategic alignment:* The main goal of the portfolio is to achieve strategic alignment with the innovation strategy so that all projects are "on strategy."
- *Choose the right projects:* Ultimately, most companies have too many projects. The overriding goal of effective portfolio management is to balance projects and resources.

8.2.3 Platform and Product Strategy

The innovation strategy determines both a platform and product strategy. Platform products (Meyer and Lehnerd, 1997) establish a basic architecture for a next generation product or process and are substantially larger in scope and demand for resources than incremental projects. An example of a platform product would be HP's Deskjet® printer. The first Deskjet® printer established overall technology and manufacturing architecture. Incremental extensions include the Deskjet ®Plus, which offered cost and quality improvement followed by the Deskjet® 500C which enabled color printing. Dual cartridges, one for black and one for color, were added to the Deskjet® 550C. Portable printing was part of the Deskjet® 300 version. The 600 platform was an entirely new design built around a new core patented ink technology, which could produce deeper blacks and more vivid colors. The new ink affected the entire platform architecture, including the mechanical subsystems and required a complete rework of the electronics. The product generation map for the inkjet printers is illustrated in Figure 8.3.

FIGURE 8.3 PRODUCT GENERATION MAP FOR THE ORIGINAL DESKJET PLATFORM.

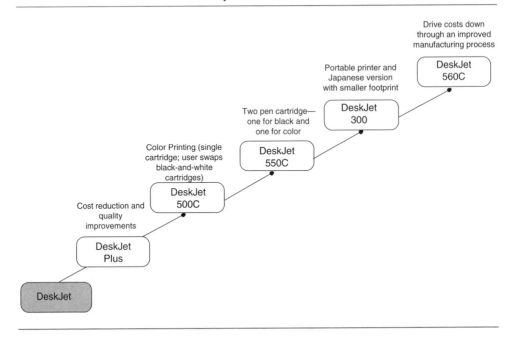

The platform strategy leverages the core competencies and capabilities of the company and defines the overall aggregate project plan and resources needed. This information is then evaluated against the innovation strategy, since adequate resources typically are not available to staff all of the projects. The innovation strategy is then modified and continuously refined so that resources match the portfolio, platform, and product strategies (see Figure 8.2).

> *Companies that develop platforms built on the core competencies and capabilities of the firm typically achieve a greater return from their investment than those that primarily focus on incremental products built on continuing extensions of their existing products.*

8.2.4 Stage-Gate® and Technology Roadmapping

Another part of the innovation architecture is the management of individual projects. These are typically managed by a "Stage-Gate®"[1] (See Chapter 1) process. A schematic of the "typical" five-stage five-gate model is shown in Figure 8.2. Each project is assessed at each gate with the results compared with other projects during a project portfolio assessment.

The technology roadmap is also considered to be a critical element of the product development architecture since it provides a roadmap into the future. Technology is not only related to time, but also linked directly to the product strategy. An example of a technology roadmap for the Motorola cell phone is shown in Figure 8.4. An excellent series of articles on technology roadmapping is contained in a recent issue of *Research-Technology Management* (Albright et al., 2003).

8.2.5 Constituencies for Managing the Process

The overall product development process as outlined in Figure 8.2 is managed by five different constituencies:

- *Senior management:* Senior management (i.e., SBU president, vice presidents of R&D, Marketing, Finance, and Operations) is responsible for determining the innovation vision and platform and product strategy and utilizes the portfolio to determine if their strategy is on plan. They often serve as gate-keepers in the Stage-Gate® process from the Business Case Gate—typically Gate 3—until commercialization. In this role, the gatekeepers have the responsibility to approve and allocate resources to projects in development. In some cases, Gate 1, the idea screen, and Gate 2, the scoping screen, are the responsibility of an R&D/marketing planning team. The senior management role as a gatekeeper has wide diversity in companies, though it is generally accepted that they need to be part of the decision-making process for large platform and breakthrough projects.
- *R&D management:* R&D Management in both the SBU and the corporate research laboratory are responsible for the technology roadmap, developing, licensing, or acquiring the technologies contained in the roadmap.
- *Process owner:* A process owner is critical for managing the overall product development process. He or she facilitates and acts as a coach/mentor to

---

[1] Stage-Gate® is a registered trademark of the Product Development Institute, Inc.

FIGURE 8.4 TECHNOLOGY ROADMAP FOR THE CELLULAR PHONE INDICATING CUSTOMER AND TECHNOLOGY REQUIREMENTS ON THE ORDINATE AND CURRENT TECHNOLOGIES THAT ARE ENVISIONED FOR NOW AND IN THE FUTURE ON THE ABSCISSA.

Core Technology Area	Last Year	Now	+ 1 year	+ 2 year	+ 3 year	Vision
Weight/Size						
Interface ASIC	5735 Chip		ACA	Integ call signal proc	Single Bread-board Chip	Soft Radio
DSP	1832					
Audio codec	CMOS					
Audio Front End	Bipolar discrete					
Microcontroller	8 bit CISC	16 bit CISC	microcontroller			
Housing	1.7mm thick		1.4mm		1.2mm	
'PWB	6 layer 1.5mm		6 layer 1mm		4 layer 0.8mm Flex	Molded in
Ease of Use						
Display	2 Line LCD	4 Line LCD		VGA	Touch Sensitive	Voice Interface
User Interface	Navigation Keys					
Software	Menu Driven		Configurable		Customer adaptive	
Talk Time						
Battery	NiCd – 4.6V			NiMH – 3.,6V		Alter Tech
Power Supply	Linear (50% eff)		Switching (80% eff)			99% eff
RF Power Amp	Module		MMIC-3V			
RF Radio	Triple Conversion		Double Conversion		Homodyne	Tunable Homodyne
Antenna	Dual Band, High Gain		Diversity			
Audio Quality						
Voice Coders	V celp		ITU, Qcelp13			
DSP noise algorithms	Expander		IS-99 Data BER Improvement/echo cancel			
Microphone	First Order Gradient (FOG)				Steering Array	
Receivers	Piezoelectric	Noise Canceling earpiece, miniaturized				

Reprinted by permission of the Industrial Research Institute, Inc.

teams and assures that the overall process is running efficiently. Having a full-time process owner is critical in most companies. Cooper (2001:348) indicates that ". . .there has never been a successful installation of a Stage-Gate® process without a process manager. . ."

- *Portfolio manager:* A number of companies have a portfolio manager who helps evaluate the project portfolio and keeps information current and accurate on the multiple projects being worked on by the company. In some companies, the process owner also plays the role of the portfolio manager.
- *Product line planning team:* Meyer and Mugge (2001) indicate that IBM has staffed a specialized team to plan and determine the future platforms. Col-

> *The overall product development process in an SBU needs to be lead by five constituencies: (1) senior management, (2) R&D management, (3) process owner, (4) portfolio manger, and (5) product line planning team.*

lectively, they evaluate the company's competencies, capabilities, common architectures, and customer needs and trends in order to identify the next platform. This team typically reports to senior management.

8.3 Corporate Venturing

Corporate venturing organizations are organizations that fund and establish businesses based on technology advances having broad applications outside the market strengths of the parent company. This is an organizational structure that goes through hot and cold phases almost on a ten-year cycle. The reader is encouraged to review articles by Chesbrough (2000) and Miles and Coven (2002) for a more extensive discussion.

The standard for external corporate venturing is embodied in Lucent's new ventures group (Chesbrough, 2001). The unit created a portfolio of 26 companies valued in excess of $200 million with an impressive internal rate of return of 70 percent (Chesbrough, 2001). Despite their success, the unit was sold when Lucent became strapped for cash. Overall, despite the financial success, the lack of a direct link between the ventures and shareholder value represents the Achilles heel of this approach. Creating new businesses outside the value chain of the parent company does not seem to be sustainable—even when a workable process and organizational structure, like that developed at Lucent, has been developed.

> *Corporate Venturing is moving from the creation of new businesses in new markets based on financial return to more strategic investments. For example, Intel Capital supports start-ups that make products that need even more powerful processors.*

Perhaps the value of external corporate venturing lies in making more strategic investments. Chesbrough (2002) provides several examples from Intel, Mircosoft, and Merck—who make investments to support the strategy of the parent company rather than to create financial returns in new businesses in new markets. Intel Capital, the investment arm of Intel, invests in start-ups making products that require ever more powerful microprocessors—thereby stimulating sales of the newest chips. Microsoft has set aside $1 billion to invest in companies that help advance its .Net architecture. Merck's investments are in start-ups that develop technologies that reduce the time it takes to bring a new drug to market.

8.4 Corporate Research Laboratory and Corporate Business Development Group

Both the corporate research laboratory (CRL) and business development group fall into this area. The CRL's traditional mission has been to develop and prove the feasibility of high-risk exploratory research that would have significant benefit to the corporation. Traditionally, these units were relatively independent of the SBUs—being funded through a corporate tax and free to pursue high-risk technologies. However, considerable reorganization in most CRL's occurred during the latter part of the 1990s, when firms placed more emphasis on them to produce bottom line results. Most companies increased the SBU ". . .focused level of funding from between 30–50 percent to up to 70–80 percent. . ." (Glass et al., 2003:25). This has resulted in a much stronger alignment of the CRL with the SBU.

Several organizational structures designed to achieve better SBU alignment are being utilized. The relationship manager and individual initiative model are discussed in a recent article by Glass et al. (2003). The relationship manager reports directly to the head of the CRL. This person's responsibility is to focus on the relationship between the CRL and SBU and ensure that the goals of the SBU are met so that the SBU obtains value and maintains its funding commitment to the CRL. In the more effective examples, the rela-

> *Corporate research laboratories (CRL) typically have projects that are jointly funded by both the corporation and the strategic business unit (SBU). To achieve success a relationship manager, reporting directly to the head of the CRL, is often utilized to foster effective collaboration between the CRL and SBU.*

tionship manager reports directly to the head of the CRL, but does not have a line responsibility so that his or her focus is mainly on the CRL-SBU relationship. Typically, the best relationship managers were long-term researchers who were well respected by both the CRL and the SBU. In the individual initiative model, individual networking between the CRL and SBU is strongly encouraged. It is the researchers' responsibility to work with the SBU. In addition, the performance review system combined with the financial reward system needs to reinforce these individual interactions. This method only works effectively when there already exists a strong culture of CRL-SBU interaction.

The second structure is the business development group, whose mission is to develop new businesses that are built on the core competencies and capabilities of the organization, but are corporately funded. The overall goals of these units are to create "greenfield units," which are kept somewhat distant from operating SBUs. Bower and Christensen (1995), in their classic *Harvard Business Review* article on disruptive technologies, advocate establishing an independent organization for managing and creating new businesses. A well-documented example is Procter and Gamble's corporate business development group (Whitney and Amiable, 1997), which put aside $250 million of seed money to develop at least one major business per year. While they have handed off five projects to the business sectors, they have yet to develop a profitable business because the SBUs have had difficulty allocating people to the new project. This transition from the internal corporate venture group to the existing businesses is a classic problem of having separated business development units that are funded by the corporation. The Achilles heel of these autonomous organizations will probably continue to impede their transitioning to the mainstream business.

What organizational architecture is needed in order to deliver on breakthrough projects if the one discussed previously doesn't work? A number of companies have begun to adopt a new model for achieving breakthroughs that are jointly conceived and funded by the SBU and the corporation. In this way, the SBU does not feel that it is sacrificing its current business to pursue this large but potentially risky project. The value of this approach is that it allows the SBU to share its core competences and capabilities and business acumen with the new project. Early results from several companies indicate that this approach appears to be very successful and avoids the transition problem experienced by the internal venture group. Four characteristics for success have emerged:

- *Senior management commitment:* Senior management commitment to dedicate the resources and provide a culture to sustain projects that are high risk and may displace the current business is a necessary condition.
- *The use of full-time heavyweight project teams (Clark and Wheelwright, 1992)*: The "emergencies" of today will quickly prevent the team from doing the heavy lifting without full-time commitment. In addition, the team needs to be populated with participants who have credibility and political savvy in the

organization so that the new high-risk concept can survive the expected corporate immune response.

- *Future opportunities which are based on market and technology trends:* In other words, looking for where the "puck" is going as opposed to where it has been. Perhaps Seagate's leadership in the disk drive market (Bower and Christensen, 1995) would not have evaporated had they been watching the market trend to smaller drives.

- *Building on the core competencies and capabilities of the company:* Ultimately, the breakthrough needs to be sustainable and provide value to the company. Leveraging the core competencies and capabilities of the company allows this to happen.

Two additional models, separate from the CRL and the traditional business development group, have been emerging. The first is a separate autonomous organization for creating and managing disruptive businesses. This approach is advocated by Bower and Christensen (1995), in their classic Harvard Business Review article and in their new book (Christensen and Raynor, 2003) on disruptive technologies. Two models for disruptive business are presented. The first is a low-end-margin business, which eventually disrupts the high-end business through up-market migration. An example is steel minimills that make steel in electric arc furnaces. Because of the uncertainty of the process and the varying chemistry, the quality of the steel initially produced in 1975 was low. The only market the minimills could enter was the low-end low-quality rebar market. Integrated steel mills gladly gave up this market because of the low margins. Over time (from 1975 to 1995), minimills improved their steel-making capability and moved up-market to the extent that they have forced most integrated steel mill industry into bankruptcy. Existing SBUs will consistently reject low-end-margin business in its initial stages because of its low profitability.

The second disruptive business model is when the initial customer is a nonconsumer. An example of this is the angioplasty business. (Angioplasty is a method for expanding the coronary arteries via a balloon catheter that is

---

Business development groups, jointly conceived by both the SBU and the corporation, are emerging in order to avoid the transitioning problems of totally separated groups. Characteristics for success of these new groups include: SBU senior management commitment, heavyweight project teams, opportunity analysis based on market and technology trends, and leveraging the company's core competencies and capabilities.

> *The SBU product development structure supports ongoing businesses, and while efficient, has difficulty creating entirely new businesses with high returns. Corporate venture groups and business development groups are needed to support the development of "breakthrough" projects.*

threaded into the heart through a leg artery.) In 1985, angioplasty was a new procedure being performed by cardiologists to repair low-complexity single-vessel coronary blockages. Open-heart surgery, performed by cardiac surgeons, was required for more complex multivessel coronary blockages. The cardiologist would be considered a nonconsumer. This was a new procedure that provided cardiologists with a new source of revenue, and cardiac surgeons did not see this as a threat, since cardiologists were able to correct only very minor coronary blockages. Over time (between 1985 and 2000), angioplasty has become more sophisticated, can handle complex multivessel disease, and has now decreased the number of open-heart surgeries being performed. Once again, sustaining SBUs would reject this nonconsumer business model because the niche is initially too small and does not support mainstream SBU customers. Based on these findings, Christensen and Raynor (2003) posit that both low end-margin and nonconsumer businesses be separated from existing SBUs, since their initial strategies and values will always lead to rejection by the mainstream SBU.

The second emerging business model is referred to as "open innovation" (Chesbrough, 2003), where the company more actively looks for ideas and new products, which provide a fit with the company's value chain, with a much larger focus on external innovation. Procter and Gamble has created a new position called "Director of External Innovation" whose goal is to increase innovation acquired from external sources by 50 percent in the next five years from their current estimated 10 percent in 2002 (Chesbrough, 2003). Companies such as CISCO and Nokia have a long tradition of actively looking for and acquiring already proven technologies rather then investing in internal development. Perhaps the Director of External Innovation needs to be another SBU management constituency added to the list indicated in Section 8.2.5.

8.5 Summary

Three separate structures for developing new products are discussed. Unfortunately none appears to be a panacea. The SBU product development

> *Christensen and Raynor (2003) advocate that a separate and autonomous business development group is required for the low-end-margin and nonconsumer disruptive businesses, since they will be consistently rejected by the SBU as either not providing enough profit or serving the wrong customer. Over time, these disruptive businesses have the potential for replacing the SBU business.*

structure (bottom-left box in Figure 8.1) supports ongoing businesses, and while efficient, has difficulty creating entirely new businesses with high returns. In addition, the relentless quest to support ongoing customer requests for incremental extensions often drowns the effort needed to focus on new platform and breakthrough projects. Bower and Christensen (1995:53) indicate that mainstream business ". . .fail—not because they make the wrong decisions, but because they make the right decisions. . ." and relentlessly focus on today's customer needs rather than tomorrow's market trends.

The external venture group (top-right box in Figure 8.1) was posited as a method to create new businesses for the corporation based on new technologies created by the firm—but which did not easily fit into existing SBUs. Unfortunately, this concept does not appear to be sustainable in public companies, since the stock market does not to reward companies for building entirely new businesses outside their value chain—despite the good financial returns that these units have demonstrated. Perhaps the sustaining role for these external venture groups will be more strategic than financial as indicated by the Intel, Merck, and Microsoft venture examples.

The "optimum" overall organizational structure of the internal ventures group (bottom-right box in Figure 8.1) has yet to emerge. One approach being adopted by a number of companies is projects jointly conceived of by the SBU and the corporation, but in which the team members are isolated from their "day-to-day" activities. They are allowed to work on the project, almost exclusively, but within their existing SBUs. The people in this latter organizational structure are isolated from the emergencies of the day, but not the competencies, capabilities, and personal networks that are often needed to create the breakthroughs for the future. This model fits with projects that aligned with the strategy of the SBU. The second approach, being advocated by Christensen and Raynor (2003) is for disruptive businesses. These do need to be separated from existing SBUs, since the SBU will consistently reject them.

The corporate research laboratory (bottom-right box in Figure 8.1) is going through a similar transition from an independent and separated research organization to one that is better aligned and jointly supported by the SBU. This new model should decrease the classic transition problem discussed previously in this chapter.

Getting to new platform and breakthrough projects will continue to be a struggle for companies. However, new structures, discussed in this chapter, are beginning to emerge that simultaneously allow separation from mainstream incremental product development and are yet not so distant that their results become irrelevant to the mainstream businesses.

References

Albright, R., Farrukh, C., Kappel, T., McCarthy, R., McMillan, A., Mitchell, R., Phall, R., Probert, D., and Radnor, M., "Technology Roadmapping," *Research Technology Management*, 46(2): 26–59 (2003).

Bower, J. L. and C. Christensen, "Disruptive Technologies: Catching the Wave," *Harvard Business Review*, 43–53, (January–February 1995).

Chesbrough, H. "Lucent Technologies: The Future of the New Ventures Group," *Harvard Business Review*, Case N9-601-102 (2001).

Chesbrough, H., "Designing Corporate Ventures in the Shadow of Private Venture Capital," *California Management Review*, 42(3); 31–49, (Spring 2000).

Chesbrough, H., "Making Sense of Corporate Venture Capital," *Harvard Business Review*, 4–11, (March 2002).

Chesbrough, H., "The Era of Open Innovation," *MIT Sloan Management Review*, 35–41, Spring (2003).

Christensen, C. M., *The Innovator's Dilemma: When New Technologies Cause Great Firms to Fail*, Harvard Business School Press, Boston, (1997).

Christensen, C. M. and Raynor, M. E., *The Innovator's Solution: Creating and Sustaining Successful Growth*, Harvard Business School Press, Boston, (2003).

Clark, K. B. and Wheelwright, S. C., "Organizing and Leading Heavyweight Development Teams," *California Management Review*, 34, 9–28, Spring (1992).

Cooper, R. G. *Winning at New Products*, 3rd ed., Cambridge, MA: Perseus Publishing, 2001.

Cooper, R. G., Edgett, S. J. and Kleinschmidt, E. J., *Portfolio Management for New Products*, 2nd ed., Reading, MA: Perseus Books, 2001.

Glass, J. T., Ensing, I. M. and DeSanctis, G., "Managing the Ties Between Central R&D and the Business Units," *Research Technology Management*, 46(1), 24–31 (2003).

Meyer, M. H. and Lehnerd, L., *The Power of Product Platforms*, New York: The Free Press, 1997

Meyer, M. H., and Mugge, P. C., Make Platform Innovation Drive Enterprise Growth," *Research Technology Management*, 44(1): 25–39 (2001).

Miles and Covin, "Exploring the Practice of Corporate Venturing: Some Common Forms and Their Organizational Implications," *Entrepreneurship: Theory and Practice*, Spring 2002

Prahalad, C. K. and Hamel, G., "The Core Competence of the Corporation," *Harvard Business Review*, 79–90, (May–June 1990).

Stalk, G., Evans, P. and Shulman, L. E., "Competing on Capabilities: The New Rules of Corporate Strategy," *Harvard Business Review*, 57–68, March–April (1992).

Whitney and Amiable, "Corporate New Ventures at Proctor and Gamble," *Harvard Business Review*, Case 9-897-088 (June 1997).

Peter Koen is currently employed as a full-time associate professor in the Wesley J. Howe School of Technology Management at Stevens Institute of Technology in Hoboken, New Jersey. He is currently director of the Consortium for Corporate Entrepreneurship (CCE) at Stevens, whose mission is to stimulate highly profitable activities at the "Fuzzy Front End" of the innovation process (www.frontendinnovation.com). Peter is actively engaged in research directed at Best Practices in Front End, determining how companies organize around breakthroughs in large corporations and knowledge creation flow. He has 19 years of industrial experience, including new product development responsibility at both large and small companies. His academic background includes a BS and MS in mechanical engineering from New York University in 1965 and 1967, respectively. In addition, he holds a Ph.D. in biomedical engineering from Drexel obtained in 1975 and a professional engineering license.

CHAPTER NINE

MANAGING PRODUCT DEVELOPMENT PROJECT TEAMS

Hans J. Thamhain

9.1 Introduction

Teamwork is not a new idea. However, the process of team-building has become more complex. It requires more specialized management skills as bureaucratic hierarchies decline and horizontally oriented teams and work units change. More than at any other time in history, product development managers must pay attention to effective teamwork.

This has strong implications for organizational process and leadership. Not too long ago, product management was widely considered a "management science." Most managers ensured successful integration of their product development projects by focusing on properly defining the work, timing, and resources, and by following fixed procedures for project tracking and control.

Today, these skills are still necessary. However, they have become threshold competencies and are not sufficient to guarantee product success. Today's business world needs *project teams* who are fast, are flexible, and can work dynamically and creatively toward objectives in a changing environment (Bhatnager, 1999; Jasswalla and Sashittal, 1999; Thamhain, 2001).

To work this way requires effective networking and cooperation among people from different organizations, support groups, subcontractors, vendors, government agencies, and customer communities. It also needs the skill to deal with risks caused by technological, economic, political, social, and regulatory changes.

Often the project manager becomes a social architect who understands how organizational and behavioral traits interact and uses this understanding to move the work forward. This manager provides overall project leadership for developing multidisciplinary task groups into unified teams, and fostering a climate conducive to involvement, commitment, and conflict resolution. Table 9.1 summarizes typical managerial responsibilities and challenges of today's project team leaders. (Project managers can use Table 9.1 as a tool for self-assessment, including setting-up performance measures, training, and organizational development needs.)

9.2 What We Know About Project-Oriented Teamwork

Vitually all product managers recognize the critical importance of effective teamwork to project performance. In fact, the basic concepts of organizing and managing teams go back to biblical times. However, it was not before the discovery of important social phenomena in the classic Hawthorne studies in 1939 that a theoretical framework of the work group emerged.

9.2.1 Redefining the Process

In today's complex multinational and technologically sophisticated environment, the self-directed team has become the *project team* (Fisher, 1993; Nurick, 1993; Thamhain and Wilemon, 1999; Kruglianskas and Thamhain 2000).

Team-building takes a collection of individuals with different needs, backgrounds, and expertise and transforms them into an integrated, effective work unit. In this transformation process, the goals and energies of individual contributors merge and focus on specific objectives. When describing an effective project team, managers stress that high performance depends on the reasons graphically summarized in Figure 9.1. Team-building is a constant process that requires leadership skills and an understanding of the organization, its boundaries, authority, power, and motivation.

9.2.2 Team Life Cycle

The life cycle of a project team spans across the complete product development project, not just a particular phase. For example, the team responsible for creating a new search engine for Yahoo!, integrates activities ranging from assess-

TABLE 9.1 RESPONSIBILITIES AND CHALLENGES OF PROJECT TEAM LEADERS.

- Bringing together the right mix of competent people which will develop into a team
- Building lines of communication among task teams, support organizations, upper management, and customer communities
- Building the specific skills and organizational support systems needed for the project team
- Coordinating and integrating multifunctional work teams and their activities into a complete system
- Coping with changing technologies, requirements, and priorities while maintaining project focus and team unity
- Dealing with anxieties, power struggle and conflict
- Dealing with support departments; negotiating, coordinating, integrating
- Dealing with technical complexities
- Defining and negotiating the appropriate human resources for the project team
- Encouraging innovative risk-taking without jeopardizing fundamental project goals
- Facilitating team decision-making
- Fostering a professionally stimulating work environment where people are motivated to work effectively toward established project objectives
- Integrating individuals with diverse skills and attitudes into a unified workgroup with unified focus
- Keeping upper management involved, interested, and supportive
- Leading multifunctional task groups toward integrated results in spite of often intricate organizational structures and control systems
- Maintaining project direction and control without stifling innovation and creativity.
- Providing an organizational framework for unifying the team
- Providing or influencing equitable and fair rewards to individual team members
- Sustaining high individual efforts and commitment to established objectives

ing the business opportunity to product research, feasibility analysis, development, technology transfer, product rollout, marketing, and support services. The work also involves market surveys, licensing, subcontracting, acquisitions, and offshore developments. The need for close integration of activities across the entire project life cycle needs the team to stay together for most of the product's life cycle, rather than just for a particular phase of the development.

The primary mission of this Yahoo! product development team may focus on the system design and software development phase. However, the team also supports activities, ranging from exploring and analyzing the new product idea, to licensing, subcontracting, technology transfers, and field services. This creates

FIGURE 9.1 CHARACTERISTICS OF A HIGH-PERFORMING PROJECT TEAM IN ITS ORGANIZATIONAL ENVIRONMENT.

managerial challenges in dealing effectively with resource leveling, priority conflicts, and long-range multifunctional commitment.

9.2.3 Toward Self-Direction and Virtual Teams

As present-day organizations evolve, traditional bureaucratic hierarchies decline and horizontally-oriented teams and work units become increasingly important to effective project and product management. At the same time, the team leader's role as supervisor dwindles in favor of more *empowerment* and *self-direction* of the team, as defined in Table 9.2.

Advances in information technology make it feasible and effective to link team members "electronically" creating a *virtual team* environment, as described in Table 9.3. *Virtual product teams* and *virtual project organizations* are powerful managerial tools in today's work environment; they are especially useful for efforts which are associated with risk, uncertainty, creativity, and team diversity. These were also the work environments that first moved from traditional hi-

TABLE 9.2 SELF-DIRECTED TEAMS.

Definition: A group of people chartered with specific responsibilities for managing themselves and their work, with minimal reliance on group-external supervision, bureaucracy, and control. Team structure, task responsibilities, work plans, and team leadership often evolve based on needs and situational dynamics.

Benefits: Ability to handle complex assignments, requiring evolving and innovative solutions that cannot be easily directed via top-down supervision. Widely shared goals, values, information and risks. Flexibility toward needed changes. Capacity for conflict resolution, team-building, and self-development. Effective cross-functional communications and work integration. High degree of self-control, accountability, ownership, and commitment toward established objectives.

Challenges: A unified, mature team does not just happen, but must be carefully organized and developed by management. A high degree of self-motivation and sufficient job, administrative and people skills must exist among the team members. Empowerment and self-control might lead to unintended results and consequences. *Self-directed* teams are *not* necessarily *self-managed*, they often require *more* sophisticated external guidance and leadership than conventionally structured teams.

erarchical team structures and tried more self-directed and network-based virtual ideas (Fisher, 1993).

9.3 Measuring Project Team Performance

"A castle is only as strong as the people who defend it." This Chinese proverb also applies to the business enterprise. Organizations are only as effective as their unified team efforts. However, team performance is difficult to measure.

9.3.1 Project Performance Measures

Despite cultural and philosophical differences among organizations, managers surveyed (Thamhain and Wilemon, 1997) agreed on measures of overall project performance that are driven by specific project team characteristics conducive to project performance. In this survey, about 1000 product managers and project leaders were asked to list and rank-order factors that are critical to the success of their new product developments. On average, each respondent listed five measures. The first number shows the percentile of managers or team leaders that ranked the measure among the top four factors on their list of critical factors. The second number points to the percentile of respondents that included the measure on their list:

TABLE 9.3 VIRTUAL TEAMS.

Definition: A group of project team members, linked via the Internet or media channels to each other and various project partners, such as contractors, customers, and regulators. Although physically separated, technology links these individuals so they can share information and operate as a unified project team. The number of elements in a virtual team and their permanency can vary, depending on need and feasibility. An example of a virtual team is a project review conducted among the team members, contractors, and a customer, over an Internet Web site.

Benefits: Ability to share information and communicate among team members and organizational entities of geographically dispersed projects. Ability to share and communicate information in a synchronous and asynchronous mode (application: communication across time zones, holidays, and shared work spaces). Creating unified visibility of project status and performance. Virtual teams, to some degree, bridge and neutralize the culture and value differences that exist among different task teams of a project organizations.

Challenges: The effectiveness of the virtual team depends on the team members' ability to work with the given technology. Information flow and access are not necessarily equal for all team members. Information may not be processed uniformly throughout the team. The virtual team concept does not fit the culture and value system of all members and organizations. Project tracking, performance assessment, and managerial control of project activities are often very difficult. Risks, contingencies and problems are difficult to detect and assess. Virtual organizations often do not provide effective methods for dealing with conflict, power, candor, feedback, and resource issues. Because of the many limitations, more traditional team processes and communications are often needed to augment virtual teams.

1. Delivering agreed-on results	90%	100%
2. Time-to-market	74%	96%
3. On-budget performance and resource utilization	68%	94%
4. Overall quality and customer/sponsor satisfaction	67%	91%
5. Responsiveness and flexibility to requirements/changes	42%	60%
6. Innovative product implementation, differentiation	37%	58%
7. Dealing effectively with risk and uncertainty	28%	37%
8. Positioning the organization for future business	11%	23%
9. Stretching beyond planned goals	5%	11%
10. Organizational learning and benefits to future projects	3%	6%
11. Other critical success factors	0%	5%

These measures can be used to fine-tune performance targets for a specific project and set up the basis for a *team performance contract*. This is an important precondition for unifying project teams to obtain needed results.

9.3.2 Team Effectiveness Measures

Team characteristics drive project performance. However, this relationship is not "linear." Project performance is influenced by many "external" factors, such as technology, socioeconomic factors, and market behavior, as shown in Figure 9.1, making it difficult to see the intricate cause-and-effect relationships. Yet, project performance is not random. Field research (Thamhain and Wilemon, 1997) suggests specific characteristics of a high-performing team, such as those shown in Table 9.2, correlate favorably with project performance.

For the benefit of convenient benchmarking, Table 9.4 breaks the characteristics of a high-performing team into four categories: (1) work and team structure, (2) communications and control, (3) team leadership, and (4) attitude and values. Teams that score high on these measures are also seen by upper management as most effective in dealing with cost, quality, creativity, schedules, and customer satisfaction. They also receive favorable ratings on other, more subtle measures of team performance, such as speed, flexibility, change orientation, innovative performance, high morale, and team spirit.

Understanding the association between team characteristics and project performance is significant in several areas. First, it offers insight about what an effective team environment looks like. Second, it provides a starting point and framework for identifying and removing performance barriers, an important building block for further organizational development.

9.4 Breaking Down Barriers to High Team Performance

Four sets of interrelated variables influence project teams' performance. All four sets can be stacked into each other, as shown in Figure 9.2. This simple model breaks down the complexity of teambuilding and its managerial process into smaller parts.

1. *Drivers and barriers:* These are key reasons for success, which directly influence team performance. The degree of project success is primarily determined by the strength of specific driving forces and barriers related to *leadership,*

TABLE 9.4 BENCHMARKING YOUR TEAM PERFORMANCE.

Work and Team Structure
- Team participates in project definition, work plans evolve dynamically
- Team structure and responsibilities evolve and change as needed
- Broad information-sharing
- Team leadership evolves based on expertise, trust, respect
- Minimal dependence on bureaucracy, procedures, politics

Communication and Control
- Effective cross-functional channels, linkages
- Ability to seek out and process information
- Effective group decision-making and consensus
- Clear sense of purpose and direction
- Self-control, accountability, and ownership
- Control is stimulated by visibility, recognition, accomplishments, autonomy

Team Leadership
- Minimal hierarchy in member status and position
- Internal team leadership based on situational expertise, trust, and need
- Clear management goals, direction, and support
- Inspires and encourages

Attitudes and Values
- Members are committed to established objectives and plans
- Shared goals, values, and project ownership
- High involvement, energy, work interest, need for achievement, pride, self-motivated
- Capacity for conflict resolution and resource-sharing
- Team-building and self-development
- Risk-sharing, mutual trust, and support
- Innovative behavior
- Flexibility and willingness to change
- High morale and team spirit
- High commitment to established project goals
- Continuous improvement of work process, efficiency, quality
- Ability to stretch beyond agreed-on objectives

---

job content, personal needs, and the general work environment, as shown in Table 9.5. Collectively, the items in Table 9.5 explain over 85 percent of the variance in project team performance.

2. *Managerial leadership:* These influences are derived from managerial actions and the image of sound leadership. Ingredients include authority, motivation, autonomy, trust, respect, credibility, and friendship. They influence both the drivers and barriers, and team behavior.

3. *Team environment:* The strongest single driver of team performance and project success is a *professionally stimulating team environment,* characterized by interesting and challenging work, visibility, and recognition of achievements, growth potential, and good project leadership.

FIGURE 9.2 MODEL OF INFLUENCES ON TEAM PERFORMANCE.

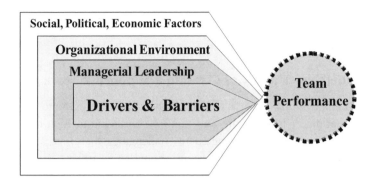

TABLE 9.5 STRONGEST DRIVERS AND BARRIERS TO PROJECT TEAM PERFORMANCE.

Drivers	Barriers
1. Professionally interesting and stimulating work	1. Communication problems
2. Recognition and sense of accomplishment	2. Lack of team definition, role conflict and confusion
3. Team spirit, mutual trust, and respect	3. Poor qualification of team/project leader
4. Team agreement on clear project plan/objectives	4. Unclear team leadership, power struggle
5. Low conflict and prompt problem resolution	5. Lack of team member commitment
6. Qualified, competent team personnel	6. Conflict among team members or with support organizations
7. Good project direction and team leadership	7. Different values and objectives perceived by team members
8. Good interpersonal relations and shared values	8. Poor trust of, respect for, and credibility of team leader
9. Effective cross-functional cooperation and support	9. Inability to deal with project risks and contingencies
10. Professional growth potential	10. Insufficient resources
11. Management involvement and support	11. Insufficient rewards
12. Work-life harmony	12. Lack of professional challenge and interest
13. Effective project support system	13. Lack of senior management interest, involvement, and support
14. Project visibility and priority	14. Shifting goals and priorities
15. Stable organizational goals, business plans, and job security	15. Unstable project environment, anxieties, poor job security

4. *External business environment:* The *social, political, and economic factors* of the firm's external environment affect all other influences derived from the team environment, managerial leadership, and immediate drivers/barriers to team performance.

9.4.1 Leadership: The Art of Creating a Supportive Work Environment

Managers must foster a work environment encouraging to their team members. Creating such a climate and culture conducive to high-quality teamwork involves multifaceted management challenges, which increase with the complexities of the project and its organizational environment.

No longer is technical expertise or good leadership alone enough. To manage product teams effectively, managers need skills across a broad range of skills and sophisticated organizational support. It is important for project leaders to understand, identify, and minimize the various barriers to team development.

What does all this mean to managers in today's competitive product development environment with high demands for efficiency, speed, and quality? Given the realities of technical complexities, cross-functional dependencies, and the need for innovative performance, more and more project leaders have to rely on information from and judgments by their team members for developing solutions to complex problems. Especially with decision processes spread throughout the team and solutions often evolving incrementally and iteratively, power and responsibility is shifting from managers to the project team members, who take higher levels of responsibility and authority for and control over project results.

These teams become *self-directed*, gradually replacing the traditional, hierarchically structured project team. As a result, product development processes rely strongly on group interaction, resource- and power-sharing, group decision-making, self direction, accountability, and control. Self-directed teams can rarely be led "top-down." Leading them successfully requires interactive team management skills and senior management support. Tools such as the Project Maturity Model and the Six Sigma Project Management Process can serve as framework for analyzing and fine-tuning the team development and management process.

9.4.2 Managing Team Formation and Development

No work group comes fully integrated and unified in their values and skill sets. These skill sets need nurturing and development. Managers must realize that the organizational dynamics involved during the various phases of the team development process. They must understand the professional interests, anxieties, communication needs, and challenges of their team members and anticipate them as the team goes through the various stages of its development.

Team leaders must adapt their managerial style to the context of each product development project and each phase of the project's life cycle. Many of the problems that occur during the formation of the new project team or during its life cycle are normal and often predictable. However, they present barriers to effective team performance. The problems must be quickly identified and dealt with. Team leaders must recognize what works best at each stage, and what is most conducive to the team development process. Tools such as the four-stage Situational Leadership Model® of team development, originally developed by Hersey and Blanchard, can help in identifying the leadership style and organizational support needed in creating effective and expedient team developments.

>   ***Team formation and start-up:*** Early project stages, such as *team formation* and *start-up*, are especially turbulent and prone to anxieties, confusion, and conflict. Often, a directive leadership style is most effective. To help the team pass quickly through the first two stages of their development, two actions are important. First, provide clear guidelines on the project's mission, its objectives, and its requirements. Second, create the necessary back-office support for the project team.

>   ***Team development toward full integration:*** Once the people of the work group have settled into their roles, settled on communications networks, and begun to work as a self-directed, unified team, a *participative leadership* will produce most favorable results. Once fully integrated among all stakeholders, the team has little need for external managerial intervention and can work effectively with a minimum degree of supervision and administrative support. However, keeping such a delicate team equilibrium, focus, and commitment requires a sophisticated leadership style and continuous attention to the human side of the product development process.

The effective team leader is a social architect who understands how organizational and behavioral variables interact. The leader can foster a climate of active participation and minimal conflict. This requires carefully developed skills in leadership, administration, organization, and technical expertise. It further requires the project leader's ability to involve top management, to ensure organizational visibility, resource availability, and overall support for the new project throughout its life cycle.

9.5 Recommendations for Effective Team Management

Managing product development teams is not for the weak and faint of heart. A few specific recommendations may help managers in setting up working conditions conducive to multidisciplinary task integration and to building high-performing project teams.

- *Early project life cycle team involvement:* Team involvement, early in the project's life cycle, will have a favorable impact on the team environment, building enthusiasm toward the assignment and team morale, and will eventually improve team effectiveness. Because project leaders have to integrate various tasks across many functional lines, proper planning requires all stakeholders' participation. These stakeholders include support departments, subcontractors, and management. Modern project management techniques provide the framework and tools for effective cross-functional planning and for organizing the work for effective execution. Such techniques include phased project planning and Stage-Gate® concepts.

- *Define work process and team structure:* Successful project team management requires an infrastructure conducive to cross-functional teamwork and technology transfer. This includes properly defined links, task responsibilities, reporting relations, communication channels, and work transfer protocols. The tools for systematically describing the work process and team structure come from the conventional project management system. Here are some of these tools: (1) *a project charter* defining the mission and overall responsibilities of the project organization, including performance measures and key links; (2) *a project organization chart* defining the major reporting and authority relationships; (3) *a responsibility matrix* or *task roster;* (4) *a project interface chart,* such as the N-squared chart (cf. Buede, 1999); (5) *job descriptions.*

- *Develop organizational interfaces:* Overall success of a project team depends on effective cross-functional integration. Each task team should clearly understand its task inputs and outputs, interface personnel, and work transfer mechanism. Team-based reward systems can help to simplify cooperation with cross-functional partners. Team members should be encouraged to check out early feasibility and system integration. Quality function deployment (QFD), N-squared charting, and well-defined phase-gate criteria can be useful tools for developing cross-functional linkages and promoting inter-disciplinary cooperation and alliances. It is critical to include in these links all the support organizations, such as purchasing, product assurance, and legal services, as well as outside contractors and suppliers.

- *Staff and organize the project team:* Project staffing is a major activity, usually conducted during the project formation phase. Because of time pressures, staffing is often done hastily and before defining the basic work to be performed. The result is team personnel that is suboptimally matched to the job needs, resulting in conflict, low morale, suboptimum decision-making, and eventually poor project performance. While this lack will cause problems for any project organization, it is especially unfavorable in a product development environment that relies on strong cross-functional teamwork and shared decision-making, built on mutual trust, respect, and credibility. Team personnel with skill sets poorly matched to job needs are seen as inept. This affects the trust, respect, and credibility among team members, and eventually team performance. For best results, project leaders should *negotiate the work assignment* with their team members one-to-one, at the start of the project. These negotiations should include the overall task, its scope, objectives, and performance measures. A thorough understanding of the task needs develops often as the result of personal involvement in the front-end activities, such as needs analysis, bid proposals, project planning, link definition, or overall product planning. This early involvement also has positive effects on the buy-in toward project objectives, plan acceptance, and unifying the task team.

- *Communicate organizational goals and objectives:* Management must communicate and update the organizational goals and project objectives. The relationship and contribution of individual work to the overall product development, the business plans, and the importance to the organizational mission must be clear to all team personnel. Senior management can help in unifying the team behind the project objectives by developing a "priority image," through their personal involvement, visible support, and emphasis on project goals and mission objectives.

- *Build a high-performance image:* Building a favorable image for a project, with high priority, interesting work, importance to the organization, high visibility, and potential for professional rewards is important for attracting and holding high-quality people. Senior management can help develop a "priority image" and communicate the key features and management guidelines for specific projects. Besides, fixing and communicating clear and stable top-down objectives helps in building an image of high visibility, importance, priority, and interesting work. Such a pervasive process fosters a climate of active participation at all levels, helps attract and hold quality people, unifies the team, and minimizes conflict.

- *Build enthusiasm and excitement:* Whenever possible, managers should try to adjust to the professional interests and wishes of their personnel. Interesting and challenging work is a view that can be enhanced by the visibility of the work, management attention and support, priority image, and the overlap of personnel values and perceived benefits with organizational objectives. Making work more interesting leads to increased involvement, better communication, lower conflict, higher commitment, stronger work effort, and higher levels of creativity.

- *Define effective communication channels.* Poor communication is a major barrier to teamwork and effective project performance, especially in concurrent engineering environments, which depend widely on information-sharing for their concurrent execution and decision-making. Management can make the free flow of information easy, both horizontally and vertically, by workspace design, regular meetings, reviews, and information sessions. In addition, modern technology, such as voice mail, email, electronic bulletin boards, and teleconferencing, can improve communication, especially in complex organizational settings.

- *Create proper reward systems:* Personnel evaluation and reward systems should be designed to reflect the needed power equilibrium and the authority and responsibility sharing needed for the concurrent engineering organization to work effectively. Creating a system and its metrics for reliably assessing performance in a product development environment is a great challenge. However, several models, such as the Integrated Performance Index (Pillai, Joshi, and Rao, 2002), have been proposed and provide a potential starting point for customization. A QFD-philosophy, whereby everyone recognizes the immediate "customer" for whom a task is performed, helps to focus efforts toward desired results and customer satisfaction. This customer-orientation should exist, both downstream and upstream, for both company-internal and -external customers. These "customers" should score how the deliverables they received perform and, thus, have a major influence on the individual and team rewards.

- *Ensure senior management support:* It is important that senior management provides the proper environment for a project team to work effectively (Prasad, 1998, 2002). At the onset of a new project, the responsible manager needs to negotiate the needed resources with the sponsor organization, and gain commitment from management that these resources will be available. An effective working relationship among resource managers, project leaders, and senior management critically affects the credibility, visibility, and priority of the engineering team and their work.

- *Build commitment:* Managers should ensure team members' commitment to their project plans, specific objectives, and results. If such commitments appear weak, managers should discover the reason for such lack of commitment of a team member and try to change possible negative views. Apprehensions and fear of the unknown are often a major reason for low commitment (Stum, 2001). Managers should look into the potential for insecurities, find out the cause, and then work with the team members to reduce these negative views. Conflict with other team members and lack of interest in the project may be other reasons for such lack of commitment.

- *Manage conflict and problems:* Product development activities are disruptive to any organization. Conflict is unavoidable. Project managers should focus their efforts on problem avoidance. That is, managers and team leaders, through experience, should recognize potential problems and conflicts at their onset, and deal with them before they become big and their resolutions consume much time and effort (Haque, 2003).

- *Conduct team-building sessions:* A mixture of *focus-team* sessions, *brainstorming, experience exchanges*, and *social gatherings* can be powerful tools for developing the work group into an effective, fully integrated and unified project team. (Thamhain and Wilemon, 1999) Such organized team-building efforts should be conducted throughout the project's life cycle. Intensive team-building efforts may be especially needed during the formation stage of a new project team. Although formally organized, these team-building sessions are often conducted in an informal and relaxed atmosphere to discuss critical questions such as (1) how are we working as a team? (2) what is our strength? (3) how can we improve? (4) what support do you need? (5) what challenges and problems are we likely to face? (6) what actions should we take?, and (7) what process or procedural changes would be worthwhile?

- *Provide proper direction and leadership:* Project managers and team leaders can influence the attitude and commitment of their people toward the project objectives by their own actions. Concern for the project team members and enthusiasm for the project, can foster a climate of high motivation, involvement with the project and its management, open communications, and willingness to cooperate with the new requirements and to use them effectively.

- *Foster a culture of continuous support and improvement:* Successful project management focuses on people behavior and their roles within the project itself. Companies that effectively manage product development have cultures and support systems that demand broad participation in their organizational developments. Encouraging management throughout the enterprise to be proactive and aggressive toward change is not an easy task. It is important to set up support systems—such as discussion groups, action teams, and suggestion systems—to capture and leverage the lessons learned, and to identify problems as part of a continuous improvement process. Tools such as the Project Maturity Model and the Six Sigma Project Management Process can provide the framework and toolset for analyzing and fine-tuning the team development and its management process.

9.6 Summary

Succeeding in today's ultracompetitive world of business is not an easy feat. No single set of broad guidelines exists that guarantees success. However, the success of team-based product development is not random! A better understanding of the criteria and organizational dynamics that drive project team performance can assist managers in developing a better insight into the organizational process and critical success factors that drive product team performance.

One of the most striking findings is that many of the factors that drive project team performance are derived from the human side. The strongest testimonies of new product success come from organizations that satisfy personal and professional needs—that is, the most significant influences to creativity and overall team performance come from the work itself. People who find their assignments professionally challenging, leading to accomplishments, recognition, and professional growth, also work more effectively in a product development team setting. A professionally stimulating environment also lowers communication barriers and conflict and strengthens the wish to succeed.

Other influences to project team performance come from organizational processes that have their locus outside the project organization. In fact, many of these influences are controlled by senior management. Organizational stability, availability of resources, management involvement and support, personal rewards, and stability of organizational goals, objectives, and priorities, are all derived from organizational systems that are controlled by general management. Project team leaders must work with senior management to ensure an organizational ambience conducive to effective teamwork. Leaders of successful product teams create a sense of community across the whole enterprise; that is, they understand the factors that drive team performance and create a work environment conducive to such a behavior. Effective project leaders can inspire their people and make everyone feel proud of being part of the product team and the company as a whole. Both clarity of purpose and alignment of personal and organizational goals are necessary for a unified team culture to emerge. Encouragement, personal recognition, and visibility of the contributions to customer and company values help to sustain the team focus and commitment to the project objectives as an integrated part of the total enterprise.

References

Bhatnager, A., "Great teams," *Academy of Management Executive*, 13(3): 50–63 (August 1999).

Buede, D. M., *The Engineering Design of Systems: Models and Methods*, New York: John Wiley and Sons, Inc., 1999.

Fisher, K., *Leading Self-Directed Work Teams*, New York: McGraw-Hill, 1993.

Haque, B., Pawar, K., and Barson, R., "The application of business process modeling to organizational analysis of concurrent engineering environments," *Technovation*, 23(2): 147–162 (February 2003).

Jassawalla, A. and Sashittal, H., "Building collaborate cross-functional new product teams," *The Academy of Management Executive*, 13(3): 50–63 (August 1999).

Kruglianskas, I. and Thamhain, H., "Managing technology-based projects in multinational environments," *IEEE Transactions on Engineering Management*, 47(1): 55–64 (2000).

Nurick A. and Thamhain, H., "Project team development in multinational environments," in *Global Project Management Handbook* in D. Cleland, ed., New York: McGraw-Hill, 1993.

Pillai A, Joshi A., and Raoi, K., "Performance measurement of R&D projects in a multi-project, concurrent engineering environment," *International Journal of Project Management*, 20(2): 165–172 (February 2002).

Prasad, B., "Toward life-cycle measures and metrics for concurrent product development," *International Journal of Computer Applications in Technology*, 15(1/3): 1–8 (2002).

Prasad, B., "Decentralized cooperation: a distributed approach to team design in a concurrent engineering organization," *Team Performance Management*, 4(4): 138–146 (1998).

Stum, D., "Maslow revisited: building the employee commitment pyramid," Strategy and Leadership, 29:(4): 4–9 (July/August 2001).

Thamhain, H., "Team management," Chapter 19 in *Project Management Handbook*, edited by J. Knutson, New York: John Wiley & Sons, 2001.

Thamhain, H. and Wilemon, D. "Building effective teams for complex project environments," *Technology Management*, 5(2): 203–212, 1999.

Thamhain, H. and Wilemon, D., "Building high performing engineering project teams," *The Human Side of Managing Technological Innovation* edited by R. Katz. New York: Oxford University Press, 1997.

Hans J. Thamhain is Professor of Management at Bentley College in Waltham, Massachusetts. He has held engineering and project management positions with Verizon/GTE, General Electric, Westinghouse, and ITT. Dr. Thamhain is well known for his research and writings in project management. He has written over 70 research papers and five professional reference books in project management. Dr. Thamhain is certified as Project Management Professional, PMP, and New Product Development Professional, NPDP, and is the recipient of the IEEE Engineering Manager of the Year 2000 Award.

CHAPTER TEN

INFLUENCE AND POLITICS IN PRODUCT DEVELOPMENT

Stephen K. Markham and Patricia J. Holahan

10.1 Introduction

Getting approval for product development activities is not just a rational exercise of telling others that a project is important; rather, it is a process of creating support. Product development professionals not only have to be skillful in specific disciplines, (e.g., engineering, marketing, project management, and team building), but they must also be adept at political maneuvers. Moving across the "Valley of Death" between technical development and commercialization is a difficult endeavor requiring both processes and political astuteness (Markham, 2002: Markham et al., in press).

This chapter will help product development professionals cope with political activity at the company and departmental levels by focusing on the relationships among product development professionals, the departments with whom they are interdependent, and management. Product development activity within an organization may comprise an entire department, formal multifunctional teams, ad-hoc teams, or just a person with an idea. Regardless of how product development is composed, the need for political activity is similar. One must always convince others of the value that a specific product development effort has for the firm, so that the necessary resources and backing are obtained.

In this chapter, we discuss political behavior and the product development process. Then, we introduce a model that explains why product development may be viewed as political activity and how political strength can be developed. Finally, we suggest several means by which product development teams and professionals can exert influence within the context of the product development process.

10.2 Political Behavior in Product Development

The terms *power, influence,* and *political activity* often conjure up negative images of force and manipulation, and in their worst expression these views are correct. Many product development professionals have seen cases in which superior projects are terminated due more to "political" rather than rational reasons. Contrary to the idea that political behavior is always a mechanism for unfair and unjust allocations of resources, politics may serve a useful role within the organization. Product development personnel in many firms make liberal use of political activity and influence tactics to the benefit of their firms. Below we describe how product development teams and professionals exert influence in the product development process.

The champion, (Markham, 2000) the product development team, and the use of product development processes such as Stage-Gate® processes[1] can all be viewed as mechanisms for exerting influence. Champions influence management and others by convincing them that their project has an attractive payoff for the organization. For example, champions may promote their projects as critical to the organization across several dimensions, such as filling a neglected market niche, leading the competition in time-to-market or product specifications. Champions may argue that devoting resources to their project provides strategic advantage such as reducing the uncertainty of future technological or product advances. Research has found champions protect projects from ending, gain added resources for their project, and help project performance (Markham, Green, and Basu, 1991; Markham, 1998). Clearly, champions are immersed in political activities.

Champions, however, do no work alone (Markham, 2000). Often champions are supported by multifunctional teams (see Chapter 9), which perform the tasks involved in developing new products. Team members support, protect, and promote the project and exercise influence through political activity. Dedicated team members are often able to secure needed information and resources, and gain acceptance and support for their project. Team members

---

[1] Stage-Gate® is a registered trademark of the Product Development Institute, Inc.

exert influence by engaging in boundary-spanning activities, which include seeking support and acceptance and bargaining with other units, selling the project to others, protecting the project from criticism, and so on (Ancona and Caldwell, 1990).

Political activity surrounds product development decisions because they involve the allocation of resources and control, and issues of strategic direction. As a decision-making tool, the product development process is a focal point of political activity. Shepherding a project from one stage to the next involves a high degree of political activity by the champion (Markham and Aiman-Smith, 2001), the sponsor, and the team. The team must convince management that the project has met the gate's requirements. This often has to be done in the presence of those who would like to see the project ended. Getting approval for the next gate is not just a matter of presenting information but often also includes generating support from various people in the organization.

10.2.1 Product Development Processes Are Powerful Political Tools

Not only is the product development process an arena for political behavior, it is also a political tool. Controlling the product development process is a form of political behavior. Product development shares control of the process with management. Although management decides, product development personnel provide the information and help set the boundaries. In approving and supporting a stage-gate process, management effectively transfers some control (power) of product decisions to an agreed set of boundaries devised by people involved in product development. Not only is this a major focus of political activity, but it is also a significant transfer of power to product development.

Product development also devises other programs to commit management to a course of action defined by predetermined sets of boundaries. These kinds of programs include: developmental shoot-outs, skunkworks, critical factors selection, and so on. It is asking a lot for management to commit to a course of action not yet specified. One must have great power to hold management to this arrangement. Many product developers become frustrated because management does not live up to its commitment. Management often makes autocratic decisions contrary to the agreed-on boundaries. This is so because management does not feel that product development has delivered worthwhile projects to decide about.

Therefore, product developers must take care to understand, manage, and deliver on management expectations. Too often, product developers see the product development process as just a functional process. A logical means to develop products. In reality, it is a power-laden activity that attracts the interest of the whole organization. Future production strategies and costs as well as future sales and marketing programs must follow product development. The process binds management to make choices about resources that affect the whole company. Thus, the whole company may feel it has a stake in the process. If developers don't understand the political nature of the development process, they are blind to much what is going on the company and in product development.

The question must be asked why the company would invest so much power in product development. Having power allows product development to react early to the business environment in ways that other parts of the organization may not see. Having power also allows product development to help set the agenda and keep new revenue streams before the organization. Product development is in a strong position if they recognize the impact they have on the rest of the organization. When developers do not recognize the wide range of issues they affect and respond properly, they will be relieved of their political power. Developers, relegated to a lesser role, are constantly frustrated that other people are making the real decisions in the company. The Strategic Contingencies Model of Political Behavior will identify how to recognize political behavior and how to cultivate political power.

10.3 Strategic Contingencies Model of Political Behavior

The strategic contingencies model of power and influence identifies issues, activities, and resources that are critical for organizations to achieve their goals (Salancik and Pfeffer, 1977). The model has two parts. The first part explains why some activities in organizations are political in nature; the second part explains how and why a specific subunit, such as product development, accrues political power in the organization.

10.3.1 Level of Political Activity

According to the strategic contingencies model, several conditions result in political behavior in organizations (see Figure 10.1) (Pfeiffer, 1981). Each of these conditions is discussed below. From this discussion it will become clear that several of these conditions are characteristic of the product development process.

1. *Goal differences:* Functional areas such as marketing and production may not share the same goals and objectives as product development. Differences in

FIGURE 10.1 PREDICTORS OF POLITICAL BEHAVIOR.

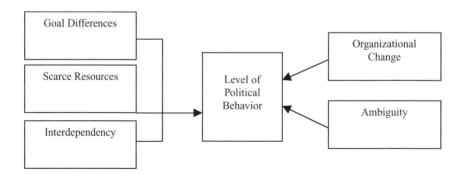

goals, metrics, and priorities between departments are common. These differences may result in conflicts as each group competes to achieve its respective goals.

2. *Scarce resources:* All organizations are constrained by a finite set of resources such as money, technology, expertise, and so on. Product development activities will of necessity compete with each other and with the functional areas for resources.

3. *Interdependency:* When two or more departments are interdependent, they depend on each other for some needed resource (e.g., material, expertise, or informational resource). This interdependency can create conflict as each group tries to develop dominance over the others. When many departments depend on a single department for a needed resource, the power of that department is enhanced.

4. *Ambiguity:* Product development is risky. Outcomes are never certain. Projected market share, revenues, performance, and profits often are merely a best guess. In ambiguous circumstances, defining the problem becomes a contest of opinions. Without objective information, each group will try to define the problem in a way that is rewarding to its own department. Front-end innovation, for example, represents a highly ambiguous situation.

5. *Organizational change:* Changes in the firm's competitive strategy, downsizing, reengineering, turnarounds, mergers, takeovers, transfers, and automation all threaten settled power structures. Change realigns the organization with the environment, creating new areas of importance and erasing settled areas. Power shifts as departments and projects gain and lose strategic importance.

Each of these conditions results in political activity.[2] Therefore, the more prevalent these conditions the greater the political activity. For example, if product development's goals and functional goals conflict, political activity will increase as each competes to achieve their goals. Similarly, the more departments have to compete for scarce resources, the more political activity one can expect. In addition, ambiguous or changing conditions give rise to political activity as each department attempts to secure resources for itself. There is little doubt that the product development setting in many organizations is ripe for political behavior.

10.3.2 Level of Product Development Power

Understanding the causes political activity is essential in assessing the political reality of product development. Nevertheless, the reasons that political activity arises cannot tell us how much political power product development has or how to create more. The second part of the strategic contingencies model explains how product development can accrue political power in the organization (Pfeiffer, 1981; Salancik and Pfeiffer, 1977).

The strategic contingencies model states that power accrues to departments that address strategic issues or critical problems for the firm. Therefore, a department will accrue power when it (1) helps the firm cope with uncertainty, (2) gains scarce resources for the firm, (3) is depended on by other departments or is central (i.e., perceived as strategically important) to the firm, and (4) is nonsubstitutable. (see Figure 8.2). For example, in fast-paced high-technology industries, time-to-market is likely to be a strategic contingency for the firm that helps provide scarce resources (revenue). Departments that help deliver products to market fast will accrue power.

Below are some observations about each of these strategic contingencies and recommendations for how product development may increase its power vis-à-vis these contingencies. Note that these observations may not hold true for your company. Analysis and recommendations are company specific. There are no "silver bullets" here, only approaches.

1. *Cope with uncertainty:* When product development is perceived as enabling the firm to better cope with uncertainties, it will accrue power. Major

---

[2] Political activity involves activities to acquire, develop, and use power and other resources to obtain the preferred outcome when there is uncertainty or disagreement about choices (Markham and Kingon, in press).

FIGURE 10.2 STRATEGIC CONTINGENCIES THAT DETERMINE SUBUNIT POWER.

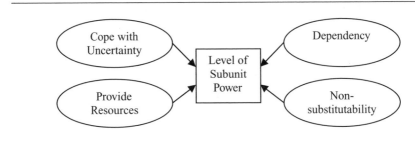

sources of uncertainty in organizations today include technological advances, competitors' actions, and shifting customer demand. In many firms, product development plays a major role in dealing with these uncertainties.

a. In the short run, product development may be viewed as a cause of uncertainty, since it usually has several projects, any one of which may fail. Remind management that new products will account for greater revenues in the future (Markham, 2002) and that product development programs rather than individual projects must be funded.

b. New products also have strategic implications for market positioning and competition. Short-term perspectives often focus inward, which increases uncertainty because of neglecting competitive market information. Supply others with market intelligence about rapid changes and developments in the market. Offer recommendations about how product development faces market challenges rather than how a new technology can be researched.

2. *Provide scarce resources:* When product development provides scarce resources to the firm, it will accrue power. Although others may argue that product development uses resources, successful new products account for an ever-larger portion of revenues. It should be argued that product development is a source of resources (revenues in this case) not just an expense.

a. As well as producing revenue-generating products, product development should be efficient and cost-effective. Also, accounting practices should reflect the cost and revenues associated with each project so the financial contribution of product development is not lost. Product development needs to portray itself as a profit center rather than a cost center. This might be done by keeping track of the overall figure for gross profit from new products minus the cost of product development.

3. *Dependency:* Product development will accrue power to the extent the firm or other departments within the firm depend on product innovations. There are many reasons that a department may depend on product development, such as bringing new products to market quickly, or supplying inputs for other departments, such as new products for marketing to sell or for operations to produce. To understand how other departments depend on product development, one must recognize critical issues facing the organization and how product development addresses those issues. For example, national and international competition has increased the rate of product introductions. Competitive threats are based both on new technologies that provide for new product platforms having price and performance advantages and on market research that provides increasing customization for different market segments. As product development becomes recognized as the resource to cope with these issues, the firm becomes dependent on product development.

4. *Nonsubstitutability:* To the extent that product innovation is important and cannot be undertaken in other departments, power will accrue to product development. The capacity to work multifunctionally helps product development preserve its unique position.

    a. Providing information about competitors' product offerings is a way that product development builds credibility. Explain that shortened product life cycles mean shorter revenue streams. In financial terms, explain how future revenue streams will depend more and more on new products. Explain, in market and strategic terms, the need to be first to the customer. Explain the advantage of keeping or gaining a competitive position for add-on sales and services. Raising these issues helps others to recognize the critical need for a proper level of product development.

The environment often settles what is critical for a given company. These critical contingencies take many forms: high-quality products, timely delivery, low costs, supplier retention, efficient distribution, good industrial relations, regulatory issues, and availability of capital, to name a few. Any one of these issues may be critical for your company. Since product development is only one of many "voices" in an organization, it must convince management and other departments that it deals with uncertainty, delivers scarce resources, and solves critical problems. The strategic importance (i.e., perceived criticality of new products to the firm's viability) varies across different companies. This is why product development wields varying degrees of power across different companies. Nonetheless, understanding the strategic contingencies model has significant implications for assessing the power that product development has as well as how to generate more influence.

In summary, product development must determine what is important for the firm and what it can do to aid the firm. The observant reader will probably respond, "but that is what I am already doing." The point here is not to change any intents but rather to be sensitive about how things get done in the organization by understanding what is important to decision makers. Engaging in political behavior does not necessarily mean that one is engaging in any form of dishonest or manipulative behavior. Quite the opposite. The more open and honest one is at framing issues about critical problems, the more effective one will be in influencing others.

10.4 Influencing Others

People in product development often lament and even react bitterly to how political their companies are, yet take little action to be successful political operators. Projects receive attention and resources based on their proponents political abilities. Learning to influence others is a critical product development skill if you want your project to receive fair treatment.

Before trying to gain influence, however, one must assess of the sources of political activity as well as have an accurate understanding of one's own sources of political activity. The section on "Level of Political Activity" (see Figure 10.1) provides guidance for assessing the source of political behavior and how pervasive it will likely be. The content of your influence attempt must be properly directed. For example, there can be a big difference between having different goals and being interdependent. Both conditions give rise to political behavior that may be indistinguishable. Nevertheless, the solution for agreeing on what course to take (goal) and who is going to do what part (interdependence) are different. Not having a clear understanding of the source of the problem is a common reason for increasing conflict.

Knowing the source and degree of political activity is only part of the equation. One must also understand how much political power one has and how to get more (Salancik and Pfeiffer, 1977) Finding agreement on goal differences could lead to different approaches, depending on how much power one has. An assessment of the source of your power is a mustIt might come from being able to cope with risk, providing resources to others, others dependence on you, and being the only one who can provide an answer (see Figure 10.2). If you can't explain your source of power other people probably can't see it or will choose to ignore it. Your political power is in the minds of your targets—not just your own. Knowing how others perceive you is critical. You must assess where your power base is and then explain it to others so that they can see it and so they know that you know it too. Presentations showing criticality on one or more dimensions of power is a necessary first step. When you are first preparing such a presentation, the chance of delusional thinking is high. Make the presentation to several friendly people before exposing to outside people.

10.4.1 Teams and Political Influence

In this section, we examine how product development teams cope with political activity by dividing political tasks between members. Although we often see champions as driving a project, in fact champions and teams work together (see Chapter 9). In the next section, we examine how individuals use relationships and tactics to garner project support.

When we think about influence techniques, we usually focus on personal influence tactics, which we discuss in the following section. In product development, however, we must also think of the influence techniques as team activities. Ancona and Caldwell empirically traced a list of external team activities and found they fell into four categories, each of which represents a team member role (Ancona and Caldwell, 1990). As a list of team activities, this conceptualization of roles and responsibilities is especially relevant to discussing political activity in product development. Table 10.1 details these roles and responsibilities. Although it was not originally meant to be a political guide, most of the activities are political in nature. Each team must have someone accepting these informal role responsibilities or the project is disadvantaged. Table 10.1 should be used as a checklist of political activities for team leaders to ensure that the team will be able to cope with its political environment. If a project team is considering how to organize its political efforts, this list is a good place to start. This list is for external roles and not a guide for team roles and responsibilities for getting the internal work done.

10.4.2 Individual Influence Tactics

Not only must we prepare teams for political activity, but we must also help individuals develop skills to influence others. How one actually influences others remains a persistent and difficult question. There are two streams of thought about how people influence others to support product development projects.

TABLE 10.1 BOUNDARY-SPANNING ROLES AND RESPONSIBILITIES IN PRODUCT DEVELOPMENT.

Ambassador: Protect and persuade
- Absorb outside pressure for the team
- Protect the team from extra work and requests
- Persuade others of team importance
- "Talk up" the team
- Acquire resources
- Assess support and opposition to the project
- Gather information about company strategy useful to the team

Task Coordinator: Coordinate and negotiate with outsiders
- Resolve design problems
- Coordinate tasks with outside groups
- Negotiate with others on delivery dates
- Review product design with outsiders

Scout: Scan competitor, market, and technology developments
- Scan inside and outside company for marketing ideas
- Collect technical information from outside the firm
- Find out what competing firms are doing with similar projects

Guard: Avoid releasing information
- Keep news about team secret until appropriate
- Avoid releasing information to protect team's image or project
- Control the release of information to present the profile wanted

First is that influence is contained within the relationship between the influencer and their target. The second stream of thought is that successful influence depends upon choosing the correct method of influence or influence tactics.

Direct tests of relationship and tactics conclusively reveal that the relationship between people is more important than tactic choice. In fact, when influence tactics are used, the less compliant targets became over time (Markham, 1998). Since the quality of relations is the strongest predictor of compliance with a request for support rather than the merits of the projects, the old adage of "it's not what you know but who you know" takes on literal meaning. Influence, then, becomes a social activity. Not all product development professionals are adept at social interactions. Similarly, they may not have extensive enough networks to provide sufficient resources for their projects. Therefore, product development management should provide training and practice for their subordinates in developing and sustaining relationships and networks. Similarly, by knowing that some product developers may lack sufficient networks, managers may take action to include people in networks both internally and externally and to make their own networks available.

Although the level of compliance with a request resides in the relationship and not the choice of tactic, this does not mean that tactic choice is not important. Picking the wrong tactic can destroy relationships. For example, just because one has established a relationship with someone does not mean that being coercive is a good idea. Picking the appropriate tactic given the nature of the relationship is important to maintaining that relationship.

Although there are many anecdotal methods offered as influence techniques, David Kipnis and his colleagues (Kipnis and Schmidt, 1982) developed an empirically derived list of influence tactics. In addition, Kipnis determined which tactics work best in attempting to influence superiors and subordinates. Table 10.2 summarizes his findings.

The most often used tactic is reasoning; it is also the most successful. This suggests that a straightforward, open approach should be the foundation of all attempts at influence. Coalition building relies on the influence of other people to bring pressure on the target. Although generally successful, this may cause resentment if someone feels that he or she is being forced to comply. Ingratiating must be used cautiously; pandering or patronizing people could result in resistance rather than assistance. On the other hand, developing good will can be a sincere and mutually beneficial situation. Like reasoning, bargaining is straightforward, yet the person complies because of the benefits of the exchange not because he or she believes that the request is the best action to take. Assertiveness may be used with subordinates, but it is a dangerous tactic with superiors. Using higher-ups in the organization brings direct pressure from the target's superior to comply with a request. Such tactics are seldom appreciated and may result in active resistance in other areas. Like the use of higher authority and assertion, the use of sanctions has a negative connotation and may be counterproductive in the long run. Gaining support for product development

TABLE 10.2 INFLUENCE TACTICS AND THEIR APPLICATIONS.

Tactics	Behavior	Application
Reason	Use fact to develop a logical argument	Sup & Sub
Coalition	Mobilize other people in organization	Sup & Sub
Ingratiation	Impression management and good will	Sup & Sub
Bargaining	Negotiate to exchange benefits and favors	Sup
Assertiveness	Take a direct and forceful approach	Sub
Higher Authority	Gain support from higher levels	Neither
Sanctions	Use rewards and punishments	Neither

Sup = Superior, Sub = Subordinate

activities is a long-term prospect, and forcing someone to do something may not be in the best interests of the product development organization in the long run.

10.5 Summary

Since product development decisions usually represent change for an organization, political activity almost always will surround product decisions. Product development personnel, therefore, engage in much political behavior, such as championing, Stage-Gate® processes, and using teams. By helping the organization cope with critical strategic contingencies, product development can make a strong contribution to the organization. To do this, however, product development professionals must learn to help the organization cope with uncertainty, gather scarce resources, and solve critical problems. In this way, product development helps define the agenda and influence the organizational mission and objectives.

Departments persuasive at convincing top management that they are important in dealing with critical problems are the most likely to get needed resources. If the most persuasive subunits are indeed dealing with critical issues, political activity is positive. Unfortunately, the political process that helps a firm align itself with the environment is the same political process that can misdirect resources. Helping the product development function to exercise influence to enable the firm achieve its goals is what this chapter is all about.

References

Ancona, D. G., and Caldwell, D., "Beyond Boundary Spanning: Managing External Dependence in Product Development Teams," *Journal of High Technology Management Research*, 1(2): 116–135 (1990).

Kipnis, D., and Schmidt, S., *Profile of Organizational Influence Strategies*. San Diego: University of Associates, 1982.

Markham, S. K., "A Longitudinal Examination of How Champions Influence Others to Support Their Projects," *Journal of Product Innovation Management*, 15(6): (1998).

Markham, S. K., "Championing and Antagonism as Forms of Political Behavior," *Organization Science*, 11(4): 429–447 (2000).

Markham, S. K., "Moving Technology From Lab to Market," *Research Technology Management*, 45(6): 31–42 (November–December 2002).

Markham, S. K. and Aiman-Smith, L. A., "Product Champions: Truths, Myths and Management," *Research Technology Management*, 44(3): 44–45 (May–June 2001).

Markham, S. K., Green, S. G., and Basu, R., "Champions and antagonists: relationships with R&D project characteristics and management." *Journal of Engineering and Technology Management* 8: (1991).

Markham, S. K. and Griffin, A., "The breakfast of champions: Associations between champions and product development environments, practices, and performance." *Journal of Product Innovation Management*, 15(5): (1998).

Markham, S. K. and Kingon, A. I., "Turning Technical Advantage into Product Advantage," in *PDMA New Product Development Toolbook II* edited by Paul Belliveau, Abbie Griffin, and Stephen Somermeyer. New York: John Wiley & Sons, in press.

Page, A. L., Assessing new product development practices and performance: establishing crucial norms. *Journal of Product Innovation Management* 10(4): 273–290 (1993).

Pfeffer, J., *Power* in *Organizations*. Boston: Pitman, 1981.

Salancik, G. R. and Pfeffer, J., "Who gets power-and how they hold on to it: A strategic-contingency model of power." *Organizational Dynamics* (Winter 1977).

Stephen K. Markham, North Carolina State University, holds a Ph.D. in organizational behavior from Purdue University and an MBA from the University California, Irvine. Presently, he is an associate professor of Management at North Carolina State University (NCSU), where he teaches courses in technology management. Dr. Markham's research focuses on commercializing technology and the roles people take in product/process development teams. Dr. Markham is director of the Center for Innovation Management Studies (CIMS) and also codirector of the Technology, Education and Commercialization (TEC) program at NCSU. The TEC program seeks to commercialize technology through the cooperative efforts of university, private, and government agencies.

Patricia J. Holahan, Stevens Institute of Technology, holds a Ph.D. in organizational behavior from Purdue University. Presently, she is an associate professor of Management at Stevens Institute of Technology, where she teaches graduate courses in the management of technology, and organizational design and theory. Dr. Holahan also holds an appointment as a senior research associate with the Stevens Alliance for Technology Management, where she conducts research on the management of multifunctional product development teams and advises corporate sponsors on issues related to the transfer of management technologies. Dr. Holahan also works as a consultant to several major corporations, advising them on issues related to team-based work designs and team reward and recognition systems.

CHAPTER ELEVEN

DISTRIBUTED NEW PRODUCT DEVELOPMENT (DNPD)

Stefan Heck and T. J. Grewal

11.1 Introduction

Put aside for a moment thoughts of your current product development process, organization, and capabilities and think of how you would answer the following:

> Given a clean sheet of paper, how would you design a new product development process that brings to bear the best talent you need for success, has costs that are competitive globally, and offers sufficient competitive edge to change the game on the competition?

Individual answers to this question will be unique, but across the group of responses we suspect that many of the answers will share some common traits. For instance, it will involve the use of both in-house and third-party specialists who are further down the experience curve or simply cheaper. Development will be multiregional drawing on the expertise of different centers of excellence. The process will involve teams with different capabilities to collaborate on product development. What this "answer" defines is distributed new product development (DNPD):

> **DNPD Definition:** The separation and optimization of activities performed during a single product development process (i.e., product ide-

ation, development, launch), across multiple geographic locations. These locations may either be within a single corporate entity, be within subsidiaries, or involve the use of third parties.

Today, the use of DNPD varies across industries. Industries such as the aerospace and automotive industries have seen a dramatic shift in the last decade as product development has become quite distributed across design, engineering, and prototype manufacturing both in-house and with suppliers. Other industries (e.g., software, pharmaceuticals, consumer products) are increasingly heading down the path of greater distributed development.

The benefits of distributed development vary by product and industry, but can be very significant. For example, a semiconductor company has saved nearly 60 percent of design costs by putting designers and layout engineers in India. An automotive company can save millions by leveraging R&D investments made by parts suppliers. New technology entrants in China are rapidly closing product capability gaps with global market share leaders by leveraging ODMs and design talent in Taiwan. Each of these companies has gained a strategic edge over its competitors and cemented its leadership position by designing a DNPD process optimized to what matters economically for its industry.

If you are a product development manager, it is becoming increasingly important for you to develop your own DNPD strategy, both for current operations and as part of a longer-term roadmap that you can work toward. This chapter is focused on helping you understand the benefits, common challenges, and best practices to incorporate into your own program. Other chapters identify these new practices (see Chapter 1) and point out internal political pitfalls to avoid (see Chapter 10).

11.2 Basic Beliefs

Our work across industries has led us to three basic beliefs about distributed product development:

The use and importance of DNPD is increasing: This is driven by the economic advantages of specialization (see our five advantages below) and new enablers (IT systems, tools). The other driver is globalization: Demand is becoming more homogenous across regions.
Time-to-market, economic cost, and pricing pressures are becoming more acute.

DNPD is a challenging effort to master and success requires a clearly formulated approach: Even those who have well-entrenched DNPD experience continue to face challenges and must proactively manage risks. To earn the rewards of DNPD, you must invest to manage the process proactively rather than simply let it grow through acquisition or incremental decisions. This begins with a comprehensive review of your strategic goals, development needs, and internal capabilities, and an assessment of external assets (current and emerging).

DNPD is not a panacea for fundamental product development skill gaps nor is it for every company: The basic factors of new product development success remain unchanged (e.g., opportunity identification, innovation, process excellence, and discipline). While DNPD can be applied to strengthen specific areas of weakness, it is not a replacement for a weak process overall. Also, the applicability of DNPD is conditional on the characteristics of your product, the capabilities of your organization, and the characteristics of your industry.

One clarification: Though it may involve third parties, DNPD is not simply "outsourcing." Outsourcing is tasking a third party to perform a very specific function wholesale with limited collaboration if any. On the other hand, DNPD is a collaborative effort around a project with comparatively loose boundary conditions that may or may not change during the effort.

11.3 The Benefits of DNPD

Based on our analysis and discussions with practitioners using distributed processes, DNPD can offer up to five distinct benefits to a company: lower development costs, access to greater capabilities and specialized skills, shorter development times, better risk management, and improved product targeting (see Figure 11.1). Obviously, the nature and magnitude of each benefit will vary according to your company and industry situation (more on that in Section 11.4). As you try to determine the applicability of DNPD for your projects, it is important to review the types of benefits you might achieve.

11.3.1 Lower Development Costs

There are three levers for lower development costs: labor costs, productivity gains, and focused R&D investments leveraging existing products/services:

FIGURE 11.1 DNPD LEVERS.

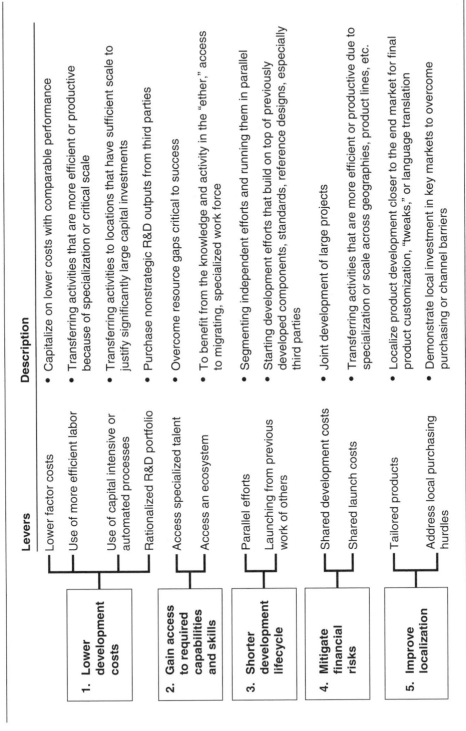

Levers		Description
1. Lower development costs	Lower factor costs	• Capitalize on lower costs with comparable performance
	Use of more efficient labor	• Transferring activities that are more efficient or productive because of specialization or critical scale
	Use of capital intensive or automated processes	• Transferring activities to locations that have sufficient scale to justify significantly large capital investments
	Rationalized R&D portfolio	• Purchase nonstrategic R&D outputs from third parties
2. Gain access to required capabilities and skills	Access specialized talent	• Overcome resource gaps critical to success
	Access an ecosystem	• To benefit from the knowledge and activity in the "ether," access to migrating, specialized work force
3. Shorter development lifecycle	Parallel efforts	• Segmenting independent efforts and running them in parallel
	Launching from previous work of others	• Starting development efforts that build on top of previously developed components, standards, reference designs, especially third parties
4. Mitigate financial risks	Shared development costs	• Joint development of large projects
	Shared launch costs	• Transferring activities that are more efficient or productive due to specialization or scale across geographies, product lines, etc.
5. Improve localization	Tailored products	• Localize product development closer to the end market for final product customization, "tweaks," or language translation
	Address local purchasing hurdles	• Demonstrate local investment in key markets to overcome purchasing or channel barriers

- Labor factor costs, taking advantage of lower paid, often equally skilled individuals is a common occurrence and a very attractive option in labor-intensive industries. For example, in software development, coding developer resources can be $\frac{1}{3}$ to $\frac{1}{4}$ the expense per FTE in India or Eastern Europe when compared to North America.
- Improved productivity through the use of focused design or development centers that specialize in a specific capability or development step. Note that the capability may not be particularly sophisticated (e.g., plastic mold making) but simply benefit from increased productivity due to scale. Higher utilization from concentration of projects and accumulation of experience both favor dedicated centers.
- Use of design centers that have made substantial capital investments that would be cost-prohibitive for companies to make on their own and support a private development process (e.g., automated drug testing equipment, pilot fabrication lines for semiconductor design)
- Rationalizing your internal R&D portfolio, choosing to "buy" or license the outputs of R&D investments made by others instead of making the R&D investment in house. This is especially relevant for components that you may consider nonstrategic or where you do not have or need a distinctive advantage.

11.3.2 Gain Access to Distinctive Capabilities and Skills

Success of product development efforts are ultimately driven by the skills and capabilities of your development teams. Yet even for the most successful organizations, attracting, retaining, and motivating best-in-class talent is very difficult, especially across the board. DNPD offers two types of solutions to these challenges:

- Access to specific skills by remote hiring or through contractual arrangements with third parties or the people themselves. Usually the conditions creating this need are: the skills are too difficult to attract in-house (personal preferences or geography), are only needed occasionally and do not justify the required investment, or are so specialized that resources are scarce.
- Access to a broader ecosystem, joining a community that is a recognized center of excellence and on its own attracts the best talent and innovation (e.g., Silicon Valley for high-tech management, Boston for pharmaceutical research, Southern California for automotive design). Presence in this location allows a company to be "in the flow" of the critical resource/skill in question. Evaluation of which ecosystems are a priority is advised, especially

for situations where there are competing locations (e.g., where your competitor has a presence, historical versus emerging centers of excellence).

11.3.3 Shorter Development Life Cycle

A DNPD program provides an opportunity to parallelize or pipeline development steps to levels that are usually beyond what the organization could do internally. One can also use previously developed technologies as a launch pad to save overall development time serve. The advantages of this time saving vary according to the situation, but there are well-documented cases of:

- First-to-market advantages to secure market share through innovation (for example, Palm versus Microsoft in PDAs).
- First-to-market pricing advantages (the microprocessor example of 95 percent price decline over 12 months, 75 percent of value in first three months).

11.3.4 Mitigate Risks of Significantly Sized Development Programs

Within certain industries, the financial risks of new development programs have become so large that it becomes challenging for the company to afford multiple efforts. As a result, the number of projects declines while the risk of each remaining project increases. Sharing risks across partners during the development cycle offers a way to resolve both issues. For example, in commercial OTC pharmaceutical products, the average cost of successful drug development (research thru phase III) is increasing and can be up as high as $800 million. The same drug could then cost an additional $800 million for the first two years of market launch.

By sharing activities among multiple parties, DNPD offers a risk management strategy at different phases of the development process.

- At innovation/ideation, companies can access fostered innovation via investments or other contractual mechanisms (e.g., pharmaceutical companies funding external research teams).
- During product refinement stages, outsourcing to third parties can often mean the more efficient use of funding dollars (e.g., pharmaceutical companies using clinical research organizations to design, deploy, and monitor drug trials).
- At market launch, seeking partners that share risks and rewards and bring unique assets to bear to help in the success of the product. For example, comarketing agreements between pharmaceutical companies that share risks,

while leveraging assets of each company (e.g., different channels, different geographies).

11.3.5 Improve Product Targeting for Success in Local Markets

There are two types of end-market influencers that DNPD can address for greater success: the first is driven by the needs of the consumer, the second a more political circumstance prevalent in certain industries.

- Products, and especially product platforms, like the Audi A4 platform used in Audi and Volkswagen cars all over the world, have greater global reach today than ever before. However, most require tweaks to address end-market nuances. Distributing this component of end-market expertise to local players allows a better understanding of the end-market, and from a central point of view across many geographies, allows the development of a more robust platform.
- For industries that involve a significant scale of operations, involvement of local companies in the development process often demonstrates commitment to the local market, reducing possible objections at the time of purchasing (e.g., in military procurement, regulated industries, and protectionist countries).

In summary, there is a broad spectrum of advantages offered by DNPD, the value of which is dependent on your specific goals and situation. Consider each of these potential benefits as you think through product development in your industry and for your specific product types in the next section.

11.4 Suitability of DNPD to Your Development Projects

Despite the spectrum of benefits that DNPD offers, they will only be achieved if the intrinsic of the product or your goals are suited for DNPD. What works for one company may not necessarily work for others. So instead of following the behaviors of other companies, as a rule, each company should evaluate the applicability of DNPD against the three dimensions of product, company, and industry attributes (see Figure 11.2).

11.4.1 Product Attributes

Does the product, and the development steps needed, lend themselves to being distributed? More specifically:

FIGURE 11.2 EVALUATING USE OF DNPD.

DNPD should be considered if . . .

Product attributes	
• **Product modularity**	• Product is very modular • Each component can be discretely defined • Component development can be parallelized
• **Advance specification**	• Technical requirements and component interfaces can be defined a priori, are not evolutionary in design
• **Sequence of development**	• Sequence of product development does not need to be linear
• **Labor intensity**	• Labor is a high component of overall R&D effort • Assets/tools people need to perform functions are small/easily movable
• **End product usage**	• End product is a component used by the customer in their products • End product is fungible, manipulated by customers for their own use
Company attributes	
• **Skills and capabilities**	• Resource gap in capability areas vital to success • Finding the talent is not possible within required timelines • Talent is accessible at third parties or specific regions where there are no company operations today
• **Culture**	• Cross-staffed teams are frequently assembled, operating, and then disbanded • Strong push for best-in-class solutions, whether in-house or external
• **Systems and infrastructure**	• Systems to share, collaborate, and manage development process are in place, widely used
Industry attributes	
• **Innovation pool**	• There is a vibrant community of innovation and associated capital support • Significant product developments have emerged from this pool in the past • The pool is an enticing option for employment for the most skilled individuals
• **Centers of excellence**	• There are established centers of excellence in which the company has no presence • There are emerging centers of excellence that the company has an opportunity to influence
• **Innovation as primary value driver**	• Innovation is valued more than efficient integration or economic efficiency
• **Relative spend on R&D**	• R&D is number 1 or 2 in expense category • A marginal improvement in R&D spend has disproportionate improvement in net income, creates comparative advantages against competitors

Product modularity: Is the project modular? Are there discrete components that come together to form the final product?

- The more different and separable the components are, the more applicable DNPD becomes.

Advance specification: Can the technical requirements and the interfaces or connection points for each of the components be defined a priori, or do they evolve during the development process?

- Well-defined components are most naturally suited to distributed development, though this does not remove the importance of closely monitoring change control procedures.
- Products that are more evolutionary in design process can still be distributed, but require substantial investment in time and support to maintain the levels of interaction needed between teams.

Sequence of development: Is it feasible to make parallel the development of individual components? How much time could be saved and what financial impact would a shorter development cycle provide?

- Parallel efforts are well suited for DNPD programs, particularly if they lead to more focus for individual team members. This focus often leads to improved performance or more efficient development.

Labor intensity: Is the development process labor intensive? Are the tools used by R&D individuals mobile, easy to transfer between locations?

- Labor-intensive projects are often good candidates for DNPD where centers of excellence and specialization can be built (in-house) or leveraged (third party).

End product usage: Is the end product stand-alone in its usage, or is it a component of a larger offering developed by your customer?

- Component products could be part of a larger overall DNPD effort to be leveraged with your customers, providing access to new innovations or better economics if developed in conjunction with your customer.

11.4.2 Company Attributes

Does the company lend itself to the nature of distributed development? DNPD is a particularly viable alternative when there is both a compelling need to seek out talent not available in-house or at current sites, and a supporting culture and infrastructure to make DNPD collaboration work. The evaluative questions you need to ask of yourself for each of these factors are:

Skills and capabilities: Are the in-house skills and capabilities sufficient to address needs and are they best-in-class for areas that are truly strategic?

- If leading talent is naturally attracted to an environment different from the one your company can offer (e.g., small or independent businesses) or offers today (e.g., U.S.-focused company trying to enter a new market), use DNPD as a mechanism to access this talent pool and forge relationships.
- If needed talent is very specialized, and required only on occasion, use DNPD as a way of "renting" the talent before you "buy" (if "buy" is an option at all).

Culture: Does the company have the necessary culture to accept and adopt distributed development? For DNPD success, an organization typically:

- Has a strong bias toward working on teams that form and disband frequently
- Has a "best-in-class" mentality and a willingness to accept something that is "not invented here"
- Rewards collaboration and joint goals rather than individual performance evaluation or "genius inventors"

Systems and infrastructure: Are the people and information processes able to handle the complexities of distributed development? For DNPD efficiency, an organization needs to be able to:

- Share information among development teams in a timely manner
- Have visibility to complications, and have processes in place to understand the ripple effects of any complications on other components of the development project

11.4.3 Industry Attributes

Does the nature of the industry lend itself well to support DNPD, and given the size of your company, can you use of DNPD to create strategic advantages (e.g., reduced cost of development, reduced time, increased product innovation)? Industries where DNPD is a natural fit have the following characteristics:

Innovation pool: Is there a vibrant community of innovation that is sufficiently funded with associated capital support to act as a pool of innovation for the industry (e.g., start-ups, small to medium-sized businesses)? Have significant product innovations emerged from this pool in the past? Is the pool an enticing employment option for your most skilled individuals?

- Companies may find that they need to proactively access these innovation pools to remain competitive using a distributed approach to feed and develop project efforts (e.g., research funding, education sponsoring).

Centers of excellence: Have a diverse collection of centers of excellence emerged across the globe for specific components of the product development process (e.g., location of design of each subcomponent)?

- DNPD efforts are ways to both access and extend the influence centers of excellence can provide.

Innovation as primary value driver: Is value is driven by innovation or aggressive cost reduction not by superior integration?

- For companies where innovation is the primary driver, a DNPD model can allow more leveraged access to innovation that occurs elsewhere, coupled with processes that then feed innovations into a development process owned and managed by you.

Relative spend on R&D: Is R&D a significant component of spend in your industry segment? Would a sustained comparative advantage in R&D productivity create substantial competitive advantages overall (e.g., net income, rate of product introductions)?

- DNPD can be one method to increase overall R&D productivity, leading to either more output per dollar spent, or less overall spending, which in many industries represents a significant portion of net income returns.

11.5 Common Risks and How to Recognize the Danger Signs

Based on review and the assessment of companies with DNPD programs across several industries and with varying levels of DNPD experience, a common set of risks became apparent. The three most often recited risks were longer than expected development times; projects that were "off spec," missing market needs or needing rework; and jeopardizing the long-term ability of the company to remain competitive.

1. *Longer than expected development times* or greater than expected costs because of the inefficiency of DNPD processes, primarily driven by the lack of visibility between process checkpoints. In contrast to a nondistributed environment,

the frequency and richness of interactions is often diluted in a DNPD environment. Ad-hoc interactions, common in nondistributed environments are either gone or very infrequent, with greater importance being placed on structured interactions to review progress. This is often a hard skill to learn for companies not accustomed to DNPD efforts because it requires changes in behaviors. Common warning signs that suggest you should pay close attention to this risk include:

- Many teams in multiple geographic locations, perhaps in time zones that make communication more challenging
- Abnormally long periods of time between formal interactions, especially between development teams working on integral components
- Absence of informal communication "chatter" between development groups or even emergence of an "us" vs. "them" view of other groups
- Surprise discoveries (good or bad) during formal checkpoints

2. *Variation from original specifications* because of development difficulties when the elements supporting the specification are distributed among different teams. For instance, the fuel consumption of a car is a function of the engine design, overall weight of the car, and drivetrain design. Challenges such as this require collaborative problem-solving and a mechanism for making trade-offs systematically (e.g., design review board). Often compromises must be made, but they should not be determined in absence of a broader discussion that assesses the impact of each alternative. Common warning signs that suggest you pay close attention to this risk include:

- Very small development teams working independently, but being collectively responsible for a key product attribute, although neither team owns the specifications outright
- Lack of investigation and rigor when a product specification is changed or inability to fully specify requirements up-front in a way that all parts of the team can understand
- Discovery of specification changes too late in the process to reverse course

3. *Jeopardizing future capabilities of the organization* by making short-term decisions of what development process are distributed to third parties without first assessing the long-term implications. DNPD decisions made in haste can leave an organization open to the risk of losing key design skills required to remain competitive, the loss of IP rights that form the basis of competitive positioning, and weakened negotiating power with customers/suppliers as the source of development value shifts to third parties. Common warnings signs include:

- Absence of a systematic review of capabilities and make/license/partner/ buy decisions

- Teams that are fragmented to the point where there is no critical mass of expertise in any one location
- Absence of guidelines and monitoring of development managers contracting with third parties for components of the development process
- Failure to assess external partners for their own policies for IP protection, confidentiality for the company as a whole and for individual employees

11.6 Ten Keys to Implementing DNPD Successfully

From our experience and from the experience of the practitioners we have spoken with, a set of ten key success factors become evident, grouped loosely into three categories: identifying the opportunity, determining the required team organization, and driving execution. Together, these help you avoid the risk of delayed or failed projects and the temptation to overdistribute your core capabilities.

Identify opportunities:

1. Apply DNPD only to projects that are well suited to distributed design
   - Assess the situation against the three dimensions of product, company, and industry characteristics (see Section 3).
   - Be clear on what benefit you are trying to capture and set explicit targets (see Section 2).
2. Identify locations and resources best suited for specific components/activities
   - Proactively scan the market for available talent and centers of excellence.
   - Focus both on the skills needed today and the skills you will need tomorrow to remain competitive.
   - Contrast available resources against those of your competitors. Is there an opportunity to make greater than step-change advances?
3. Retain strategically important aspects of R&D in-house:
   - Categorize components of your process as:
     - Strategic: source of value creation, protect at all costs
     - Important: temporary source of value but distinctiveness expected to erode slowly
     - Nondistinctive: capabilities are widely available, not the source of value creation
   - Evaluate your skills capabilities against each category discussed and align them appropriately. For "strategic" issues, ensure that you have sufficient

skills and capabilities to execute the project, or at minimum a plan to resolve any gaps.

Team organization:

4. Always establish a "prime" group in the design effort and avoid distributing authority in equal amounts:
   - Design authority into your DNPD organization; ensure that the necessary sponsors have committed to your authority model.
   - Design a systematic process for resolving issues prior to the project's start—do not make things up as you go along.
   - Avoid authority models that can lead to deadlock situations when a decision is needed. Odd numbers of decision-makers, or a single decision-maker typically work best.
5. Design into the process sufficient number of interface points:
   - Plan in advance formal reviews of progress. Predefine the nature of each discussion and the expectations for each participant.
   - In addition to formal checkpoints of progress, initially overinvest in less-formal, one-on-one reviews with individual teams that take place more frequently.
6. Overinvest in up-front design specification where possible:
   - Avoid any vague specifications to be defined during the process, particularly for components that are distributed to a third party.
   - Measure and track performance against initial specifications. Make or accept changes only after evaluating the implications and alternatives.

Execution:

7. Use standardized collaborative design tools across your development teams
   - Normalize on a standard set of tools prior to project start. Include the training of individuals prior to project start.
   - Drive the acceptance of tools with third parties, and discourage "special circumstances" where noncompliance is accepted.
8. Apply rigorous stage and gating methodology:
   - Predefine the stages and conditions of moving through each gate.
   - Design stages at both the overall project and the subcomponent level.
9. Deploy strong controls to ensure on-time completion:
   - Design mechanisms to provide you leverage over individual development teams.

- Use contractual penalties and incentives to motivate the behaviors of third parties (e.g., bonuses for early completion, fines per day for late completion).

10. Ensure visibility between organizations to track linkages:
    - Identify and monitor closely all interdependent efforts.
    - Focus as much on the information flows between groups as you do on the product flow or progression.

11.7 Summary

If you are in a global or globalizing industry, you will inevitably have competitors who find ways to take advantage of lower-cost locations, specialized expertise, or other leading-edge components. You will have to do the same to compete, but only *after* you have ensured that your organization is good at innovation and good at executing process.

Stefan Heck is a principal in the Silicon Valley office of McKinsey & Company and a leader of McKinsey's semiconductor and product development practices. He has led over two dozen engagements in the United States, Europe, and China on product development for clients throughout the high-tech value chain, including development tool providers, component vendors, OEMs, and software companies, as well as medical devices, consumer products, and aerospace companies. Stefan holds a Ph.D. in philosophy and cognitive science from the University of California, San Diego, and a B.S. in symbolic systems from Stanford University.

T. J. Grewal is an engagement manager in the San Francisco office of McKinsey & Company and a member of the McKinsey's high-tech and product development practices. T. J. holds an M.B.A. from McMaster University and a B.A. from York University.

CHAPTER TWELVE

ACCELERATED PRODUCT DEVELOPMENT: TECHNIQUES AND TRAPS

Preston G. Smith

12.1 Introduction

Many managers approach rapid product development with unrealistic, distorted, or unclear objectives, so they are disappointed with the results they achieve. This chapter clarifies objectives, frames the capabilities and skills needed, and discusses pitfalls that have misled many managers in their search for development speed.

Time-to-market is such an alluring goal that providers of various techniques often list faster development as one of their technique's benefits. They are partially correct, but their technique may not speed up the aspect of development that you need. Also, many of the other chapters in this book provide the basic ingredients of rapid development, but they must be adapted in certain ways to provide significant improvements in speed. The goal of this chapter is to enable you to become a "smart shopper" for accelerated development techniques and to read the rest of this book with greater sensitivity to the time-saving potential of the tools it provides.

12.2 Time-To-Market Is Not Free

The first trap that awaits you is to assume that faster development is always desirable. Speed has its price, which might be paid by higher product cost, greater development expense, a reduced product feature set, higher risk, organizational changes and training, or staff burnout. Perhaps the easiest way to see this is to ask why you aren't moving faster now. If there were no impediment, you would already be taking advantage of speed techniques. You and your colleagues are smart, and most of the techniques are well known. Whether or not you have vocalized it, you know there is a price to be paid somewhere. Sometimes, the price is not worth benefit to be gained. Even if it is, if you continue to accelerate long enough, you will eventually reach this barrier.

The classic trade-offs of cycle time are against the first three items listed: higher product cost, greater development expense, and reduced product performance or feature set. These are illustrated in Figure 12.1. The six trade-offs pointed out here by the arrows can be calculated for each of your projects, as described in Chapter 2 of Smith and Reinertsen (1998). For instance, the most common trade-off is between cycle time and development expense, a value known as the cost of delay. The cost of delay may be less than $1000 per day, but for major projects in large companies, it can exceed $1 million per day in pretax profit. Using this value, you can wisely trade off time against money by hiring contractors, using airfreight liberally, and buying test equipment generously to cover peak loads. Likewise, using your project's trade-off value for time against the product feature set, your team can—on a cross-functional basis— prudently balance the features provided against the time available.

These classic trade-offs need not always be traded off against each other. For instance, you can gain on speed and development expense simultaneously, as shown in Figures 1-7 and 1-8 of Smith and Reinertsen (1998). However, in this case, you will pay in some other way, such as through process or organizational changes or in training. Also, beware of the "faster is cheaper" trap discussed at the end of the chapter.

Although you should be cautious about applying development speed where it isn't warranted, it is a valuable capability to possess. It is a potent arrow in your quiver for the projects that demand it. Besides, it is perhaps the best overall measure of the health of your product development capability. Think about sporting events: most of them are conducted as races against time, and for good reason. Anybody can walk, swim, or bicycle a kilometer, given enough time, but only the best can do it faster than anybody else. To win a race, everything must be in the best of condition: your skills, your weight, your mental attitude, your equipment, and the logistics supporting you—whether you are competing in sports or in the marketplace. If you can develop a product quickly, you probably can develop it to be superior in any other way you wish as well.

FIGURE 12.1 NEW DEVELOPMENT PROJECT TRADE-OFFS. EVERY DEVELOPMENT PROJECT REQUIRES TRADE-OFFS AMONG THESE FOUR ATTRIBUTES, AND YOU CAN CALCULATE THEM, EFFECTIVELY PUTTING CONVERSION VALUES ON EACH OF THE SIX ARROWS TO HELP YOU MAKE BETTER TRADE-OFF DECISIONS.

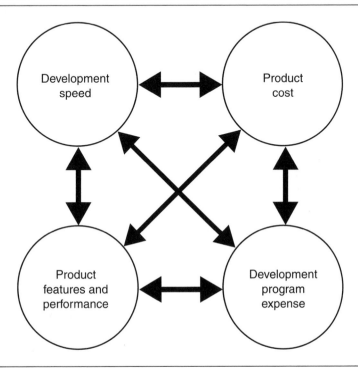

Source: Developing Products in Half the Time; Preston G. Smith and Donald G. Reinertsen; copyright © 1998 Preston G. Smith and Donald G. Reinertsen; this material is used by permission of John Wiley & Sons, Inc.

12.3 Types of Time-To-Market

Much of our confusion about improving cycle time stems from differing notions about how cycle time is measured. When does your cycle begin and when does it end? For example, one company did a wonderful job at cutting their cycle time in half, from the time they approved the project until the product was available for sale. However, they did this by bolstering front-end activities to reduce uncertainty later. When we added the extra front-end time back in, there was no net improvement. So, they decided that they needed to start measuring time earlier, when the product opportunity arose, and this changed their whole approach to shortening cycle time.

In addition, when organizations launch a cycle time initiative, they are seldom specific about the aspect of cycle time they wish to improve. To focus attention on suitable tools, the organization needs a clear business objective for speeding up development. Here is a sampling of the possibilities:

- *All-out speed:* This can be important in certain high-tech markets where products become outmoded quickly.
- *Minimizing schedule variation:* Many products depend on hitting a certain launch window, such as those that are seasonal or holiday related and those launched through an annual trade show. Predictability is more important than raw speed here.
- *Improving agility:* Many acceleration techniques also allow you to make changes, such as product features changes, more easily and later without disrupting the launch date. This is a potent weapon in a chaotic world.
- *Avoiding mistakes and rework:* Some delays stem from mistakes, so some managers concentrate on the mistakes to save not only time but also other wasted resources as well.
- *Improving productivity:* Although this is not actually a time-to-market objective, it is often the unspoken objective of managers who turn to accelerated development in order to obtain more new products from their resources or to cut expenses.
- *Overcoming sagging revenues or market share:* The thinking here is short-term and sales driven: if we could just get some new products out quickly now, we could overcome weak financial results. There is little long-term interest in improving business processes.
- *Sticking to schedule:* Many organizations exhibit poor schedule discipline, which means that development projects, meetings, and everything else simply happen whenever they happen. Basic schedule discipline will help them greatly.

None of these seven reasons is likely to fit your situation exactly. Please use them as a starting point to develop your objective in speeding up your development. Once you have created your rationale, share it with everyone in your organization. This will align everyone on techniques and approaches that will head your organization in this direction. Perhaps more importantly, it will diffuse potential rumors that can undercut your efforts, such as, "This is just a ploy to squeeze more work out of us" or, "Quality doesn't matter anymore.

Let's skip non-value-adding steps such as voice-of-the-customer research or product reliability testing." (Such misinterpretations are covered later.)

12.4 Time-To-Market Tools and Techniques

This section is a survey of the tools, techniques, and approaches for shortening development cycle time. Many of these are covered in greater detail in other chapters, and the references at the end of this chapter provide added detail. The other chapters and references are often aimed at objectives other than cycle time, however, so please adjust the tools to gain significant cycle time benefit. For example, the first group below, Process Control Approaches, is often focused on ensuring that all steps of the process are completed with the objective of maximizing the product's marketability. This is a laudable goal, but you may find there are certain steps that contribute more to cycle time than to product marketability, so your objective may suggest cutting out or adjusting these steps. However, you do so in concert with other parts of the organization, realizing the costs and benefits of these steps. Furthermore, you may decide not to cut out these steps from your next project, because the costs and benefits associated with them differ for the next project.

An important and popular technique is redesigning your development process, mainly by overlapping activities; see Smith and Reinertsen (1998, Chapter 9) for details. In contrast, the other techniques listed below are often not so obvious.

12.4.1 Process Control Approaches

Most organizations that regularly develop products now have some sort of a phased development process, such as Stage-Gate®, Product Life Cycle, or Customer-to-Customer (C2C). These processes often claim to accelerate development, but their real emphasis is on consistency rather than speed. For example the primary reference on Stage-Gate® is Cooper (2001), whose subtitle is "Accelerating the Process from Idea to Launch." However, the objective of Cooper's book is primarily on creating a product that "wins" in the marketplace and secondly on aiming development resources at the organization's biggest opportunities. Speed plays a minor role.

Phased development processes divide development into sequential phases that allow management to check certain deliverables at the end of a phase and decide whether the project should be admitted to the next phase. This renders it easy for management to track progress, but speed suffers:

- The process is necessarily sequential.
- It is difficult or impossible to overlap activities between phases.
- Time is inevitably lost in completing reviews at gates (see Figure 12.2).
- The team is in limbo about the next phase until the last one has been approved.

The team being in limbo is an important point, because it sends the team mixed messages. Management has probably told the team that this project is urgent and that everything should be done to complete it quickly, yet management holds up the project until they decide whether the business wishes to continue with it. It is difficult to keep team momentum in high gear under such circumstances. The term *tollgate*, used by many firms for phased development systems,

FIGURE 12.2 EACH SUBSYSTEM HAS DIFFERENT TIMING NEEDS. WHEN PHASE GATES ARE USED, THE ORGANIZATION MUST WAIT FOR THE SLOWEST SUBSYSTEM AT EACH GATE. THERE ARE OTHER MORE SIGNIFICANT BUT LESS OBVIOUS DELAYS CONNECTED WITH PHASE GATES.

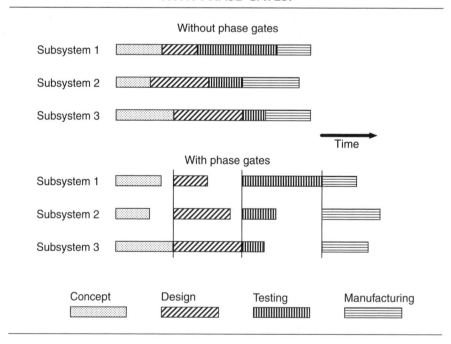

is apropos: stop and pay your toll before we will admit you to the next section of the turnpike.

There are ways of reducing these impediments to speed. Cooper (2001) proposes fuzzy gates. Note that fuzzy gates undermine the character of phased systems in that each phase is intended to be an escalating step of project investment, so management should independently decide at each gate whether they wish to continue the project investment. However, reality sides with fuzzy gates, because it is not practical to stop a project at a gate while awaiting a review. Will you lay off the team at the gate and hire a new one if you decide to fund the next phase? Momentum continues, but the team is hobbled—not a fast way to run a project.

An alternative is to announce that the project will continue at full speed presuming gate approval. But this is no different from having no gates, because management always has the choice to kill the project at any time. Also, you can minimize the impact of gate delays by having fewer gates. The project history of most organizations shows that, usually, projects are actually killed at only a couple of gates that involve particularly large resource commitments. Conclusion: consider these gate issues and design your process carefully to reflect what you wish to actually happen at your gates.

There are two ways of avoiding phased development processes. One is to shift the burden of controlling progress to the team. Phased processes are attempts to build judgment into the process rather than letting it stay with the team. A team that makes most of its own decisions can move much faster— and it usually makes much better decisions, because it has more accurate, fresher information from which to operate. One way of accomplishing this is by using development agreements between the team and management. As explained in Chapter 14 of Smith and Reinertsen (1998), these are essentially contracts between the team and management that specify the team's and management's authority and obligations. A similar and more recent approach is the bounding box, essentially a management by exceptions technique in which certain critical parameters of the project, such as profit margin, project budget, product performance level, and launch date, are negotiated as the bounding box. The team is free to move ahead unimpeded by phase boundaries as long as it stays within the box. Management regularly checks that the team remains within the box, and it is also the team's responsibility to notify management quickly if it finds that it is leaving the box. For more on bounding box, see Smith (2004).

Another way of avoiding phased development is to fundamentally change its sequential basis. Software development has done this by moving from its former waterfall (sequential) process to an inherently iterative one, as described by Kruchten (2000). Koen et al. (2002) found that a sequential model was inappropriate for front-end activities in product development, so they created a relationship model for these initial product development activities that clearly avoids sequential implications.

Eppinger (2001) has taken this one step further to show that product design is an inherently iterative process for all but the simplest products; that is, product design, by nature, is not sequential but instead depends on going back and revisiting earlier assumptions and adjusting them until the whole design is in balance. This occurs because there are points in the process where the designer does not have enough information to proceed and so must make some assumptions that are most likely partially wrong. This is no reflection on the designer but rather a characteristic inherent to innovation.

For more on product development processes, see Chapters 1, 4, 6, and 8.

12.4.2 Project Management Tools

Increasingly, product development is being viewed as a project to be managed. Project management has been reinforced in some companies by moving to program management, which brings more of a business perspective to the project. Other firms are formalizing project management through a project office structure, as covered by Englund, Graham, and Dinsmore (2003).

The basic project management skills of planning, scheduling, budgeting, and creating work breakdown structures are valuable for effective, fast product development. Certainly, the concept of critical path is essential to managing a fast-moving project, and Leach (2000) has extended critical path to the concept of critical chain.

As you apply project management to speed up product development, however, keep four things in mind:

- The project manager must have authority to take action. In some companies, the project manager is more of a clerk who knows exactly which activities are on the critical path but has no power to move them along. This is frustrating for the project manager and provides the organization with little time-to-market benefit. Managing an accelerated project is about people skills and empowerment as much as it is about the tools of scheduling, work breakdown structure, and the like.
- Project management provides effective tools for estimating and planning project schedules, but some marketing-driven organizations ignore these and dictate unrealistic schedules based on market pressures. This leads to disbelief, chaos, and weakened morale at the working level; in general, it back-

fires. In order for project management to be useful, you must believe in its tools.

- Employ project management software, but don't become subservient to it. Do not plan too far into the future, subdivide activities too finely, or spend time on the computer updating the project model when working directly with project staff would move the project ahead faster.
- Establish a baseline schedule and do not alter it. The temptation is great to update the baseline when the project is replanned, but then the project tends to keep slipping as the past is forgotten.

Related material appears in Chapter 10.

12.4.3 Team Techniques

A high-performance team is perhaps your most potent tool for accelerating a project, but high-performance teams are rare and demanding. Virtually all organizations developing products today would claim to employ a development team. However, most of these "teams" are what Katzenbach and Smith (2001) would call an effective group. An effective group has the basic skills to conduct effective meetings and respect members' contributions. But they are not knit together to achieve performance. There are two ways to achieve greater performance. One is called a single-leader discipline by Katzenbach and Smith (notice that they are quite restrictive about applying the term *team*, and would not apply it here). In this structure, the leader basically makes the decisions—normally after consulting with members—and remains accountable for them. In the team discipline, the team *jointly* makes decisions and produces work products. In the team discipline, a team member cannot fail; only the team can fail, since members are locked together by joint goals and work products. The team discipline takes more work to set up, and it can be an uncomfortable environment, since a member is accountable for others' shortcomings. See Figure 12.3 for elaboration of these three options.

Katzenbach and Smith suggest explicitly choosing the structure independently for each project, based on its requirements. The team discipline can greatly accelerate projects that can employ its strengths, but it has a higher setup investment. In general, product development projects gain from moving beyond the effective group, because they can benefit from joint work products.

However, recognize that product development projects, even within an organization, vary greatly in their need for team performance. Highly innovative breakthrough products and new platforms would benefit from investing in the team discipline, but an effective group could probably handle a repack-

FIGURE 12.3 THREE TEAM OPTIONS. FOR EACH PROJECT, EXPLICITLY CHOOSE THE ONE THAT PROVIDES THE BEST BLEND OF PERFORMANCE (SPEED) VERSUS SETUP EFFORT.

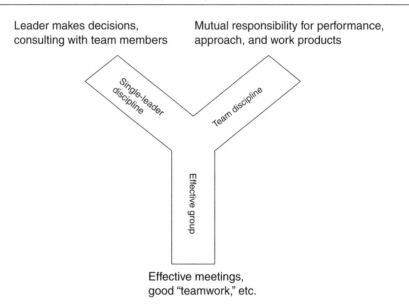

Leader makes decisions, consulting with team members

Mutual responsibility for performance, approach, and work products

Single-leader discipline

Team discipline

Effective group

Effective meetings, good "teamwork," etc.

Adapted from *The Discipline of Teams* by Jon R. Katzenbach and Douglas K. Smith; copyright © 2001 by Jon R. Katzenbach and Douglas K. Smith. Used with permission of Jon R. Katzenbach, Senior Partner of Katzenbach Partners LLC.

aging effort more efficiently. See Smith and Reinertsen (1998, pages 141–148) for more on tailoring your team structure to the project at hand.

Another major factor in the team's ability to move quickly is co-location. In the twentieth century, this meant having all critical members (engineering, marketing, manufacturing, and perhaps finance, procurement, regulatory, and others) physically close enough together to overhear each other's conversations. In the twenty-first century, with global organizations, global markets, development outsourcing and alliances, and new communication tools, many teams try to co-locate "virtually," with mixed results. Smith and Blanck (2002) discuss the pitfalls of dispersed teams and suggest means of improving their effectiveness. These include:

• Using as much partial co-location as possible, for example, by gathering at the start of the project, gathering all team members at each site close together, and identifying the heavy communication partners and co-locating them

- Deciding, as a team, on protocols to overcome the major delays involved in communicating at a distance, such as by specifying that an email will receive a reply within four hours, even if the answer must be incomplete
- Not depending on technology to overcome distance but only to be an enabler of enhanced people skills.

For more on teams, see Chapter 9.

12.4.4 Product-Related Tools

There is more to rapid development than process, organization, and project management. Many opportunities exist in the product itself. Developing a deep understanding of the customer and how the product is likely to be used is critical. This allows you to make quick but wise decisions in balancing the benefit offered by a feature against the time required to develop it. To do this, you must also know your project's economic trade-off rules, as shown in Figure 12.1. Moreover, a team that understands its customers will be able to reach such conclusions on the fly, rather than by consulting with the marketing department and conducting a new round of market research. In many cases, the project will be accelerated as a result, because you will conclude that a certain feature is no longer worth developing—at least not in this version of the product. In other words, rather than the common scope creep, you will enjoy wise scope shrinkage. For details, see Chapter 5 of Smith and Reinertsen (1998).

Another opportunity overlooked by many developers is the structure, or architecture, of the product and related opportunities to roll out feature sets incrementally rather than as a do-everything megaproject. Chapters 4 and 6 of Smith and Reinertsen (1998) describe the details.

Note that these tools are related: in order to effectively shrink the product scope on the fly and roll out incremental feature packages wisely, you will need a full-time marketing member co-located with your high-performance team, as suggested in the previous section.

12.4.5 Staffing Techniques

Too many projects proceed at half pace simply because they are half-staffed or staffing ramps up slowly, and often the worst bottlenecks are not in R&D. This is probably the most prevalent opportunity for improving cycle-time performance dramatically. Many firms are working on twice as many development projects as they could staff fully, which generally means that each project proceeds at half of the pace than it could if fully staffed. Often, management has a poor conception of its development capacity or the extent to which it is overloading the system. The medicine is simple but bitter: eliminate half of the projects for now, staff the remainder fully and finish them. Then—and only then—start some more. For a fuller explanation and for an illustration of what happens when you split people between projects, see Chapter 11 of Smith and Reinertsen (1998).

For more, see Chapters 1 and 9.

12.5 Time-To-Market Traps

As you proceed to accelerate your product development, you should be aware of some traps that await you so that you can respond to them wisely. Here are the main ones.

12.5.1 Scaring or Rewarding People

This area is a minefield. Many managers try to motivate the team with an aggressive time-to-market mandate. Although Swink (2002) shows that an explicit project objective is a critical success factor—and many teams have no project objective—to be effective, the objective must be ambitious while also being seen as achievable and compelling *by the team*. *Compelling* means that it is an outside milestone that everyone appreciates as being critical to the business.

Rewards for the team or for individuals can be effective, but just as often they backfire. See Smith and Reinertsen (1998:135–138) for details. Perhaps surprisingly, Swink's research (2003) shows that rewards for speed generally *slow down* development projects.

12.5.2 Skipping Steps

Many of us were well trained as children that "haste makes waste." From this, we jump to the conclusion that rapid development can be accomplished only by skipping its time-consuming steps, as Crawford (1992) discusses. An effective development process is scalable, so that it can be adjusted to the needs of each project by deleting steps if their total cost outweighs their benefit. But skipping steps arbitrarily without considering their total cost is not the route to effective development, and it will not save time in the end.

12.5.3 Process Eliminates Mistakes

Some organizations try to build a watertight development process that will eliminate mistakes, and they thereby hamstring their development teams, preventing the obvious mistakes but also most opportunities to move quickly—and even to innovate outside of narrow boundaries. You will be much faster, while catching a more robust variety of mistakes, by empowering the team to run its project, as discussed earlier under "Process Control Approaches."

12.5.4 Product Development Is Engineering

Because the majority of the labor that goes into product development is normally technical, there is a great tendency to relegate product development to engineering. However, most of the opportunities to cut cycle time are cross-functional in nature, for example, scope creep problems. If you really want to accelerate development, look at the interdepartmental interfaces first.

12.5.5 Faster Is Cheaper

The beginning of this chapter emphasizes that rapid development is not free—you will pay for it in one way or another. Many managers blissfully assume that if they can develop a product in half the time, their labor expense will diminish commensurately. They do not comprehend that one of the most powerful tools in rapid development is fully staffing the team with full-time participants, which will roughly double their labor burn rate, although it will prevail for only half as long. In addition, a co-located team and a team following the team discipline will generally incur extra start-up costs and require higher-quality (more expensive) staff and more training.

Furthermore, even if these premiums did not exist, it is dangerous to assume that faster means cheaper. Under this assumption, management will starve the team for the resources needed to move to faster modes, and they will never see the acceleration they desire. It is much better to be relatively lavish in the beginning and then cut back after you have demonstrated success.

12.5.6 Outcome Outweighs Approach

Some hard-pressed managers turn to rapid development as a panacea to bring one badly needed new product to market sooner. They succeed at this, but because they have concentrated on the destination, they haven't noticed the route they have taken, and they cannot repeat it. If you want to build a repeatable rapid development capability, your first product through this approach must be subservient to developing the approach.

A large part of rapid development is in developing certain skills by team members and management as they proceed. These skills are a valuable, scarce asset. If you do not focus on developing skills, you will have nothing at the end besides your new product.

12.5.7 Technology Accelerates Development

Speeding up development is hard work. Some purveyors of technologies suggest that their technologies will reduce your development time. Technologies, such as computer networking, videoconferencing, product data management software, and computer-aided design (CAD), can support an improvement, but the core of the change must be in management styles, team makeup and behavior, and similar items that cannot be purchased and installed so easily. Start shopping for technology *after* you have chosen the management tools you plan how to implement projects. Also, allow extra time in your first couple of projects that use the new technology to learn it and work the kinks out of it.

12.6 Conclusion

Although you have many large opportunities to accelerate development, achieving results will require persistent hard work. Many different tools are available to you, and few of these are esoteric or obscure. The tools generally reinforce each other, so plan to combine them. Freely adapt them to your objectives, strengths, weaknesses, resources, and markets. Finally, recognize and celebrate the value of the asset you are creating, because this will fuel further progress.

References

Cooper, Robert G., *Winning at New Products*. Cambridge, MA: Perseus Publishing, 2001.

Crawford, Merle C., "The Hidden Costs of Accelerated Product Development," *Journal of Product Innovation Management*, 9(3):188–199 (September 1992).

Englund, Randall L., Graham, Robert J., and Dinsmore, Paul C. *Creating the Project Management Office*. San Francisco: Jossey-Bass, 2003.

Eppinger Steven D., "Innovation at the Speed of Information," *Harvard Business Review* 79(1): 149–158 (January, 2001).

Katzenbach, Jon R. and Smith, Douglas K., *The Discipline of Teams*. New York: John Wiley & Sons, Inc., 2001.

Koen, P., et al., "Fuzzy Front End: Effective Methods, Tools, and Techniques," in P. Belliveau, A. Griffin, and S. Somermeyer, eds. *The PDMA Toolbook for New Product Development*. New York: John Wiley & Sons, Inc., 2002.

Kruchten, Philippe. *The Rational Unified Process*, 2nd Ed. Reading MA: Addison-Wesley, 2002.

Leach, Lawrence P., *Critical Chain Project Management*. Norwood, MA: Artech House, 2000.

Smith, Preston G., "Concurrent Product Development Teams" in D. I. Cleland, ed. *Field Guide to Project Management*, 2nd Edition. New York: John Wiley & Sons, Inc., 2004.

Smith, Preston G. and Blanck, Emily L., "From Experience: Leading Dispersed Teams," *Journal of Product Innovation Management*, 19(4): 294–304 (July 2004).

Smith, Preston G. and Reinertsen, Donald G. *Developing Products in Half the Time*. New York: John Wiley & Sons, Inc., 1998.

Swink, Morgan. "Product Development—Faster, On-time," *Research-Technology Management*, 45(4): 50–58 (July–August 2002)

Swink, Morgan. "Completing Projects On-Time: How Project Acceleration Affects New Product Development," *Journal of Engineering and Technology Management*, 20(4): 319–344 (December 2003).

Preston G. Smith, as a principal with the consultancy New Product Dynamics, has specialized in accelerated product development for 20 years, and he has helped dozens of companies in 23 countries to adopt the techniques covered in this chapter. His book, *Developing Products in Half the Time*, and his article, "Reaping Benefit from Speed to Market," have been instrumental in helping many firms to bring their new products to market faster and more effectively. Preston has also served 20 years as an engineer and manager in both small and large companies. He holds an engineering Ph.D. from Stanford University and is a Certified Management Consultant.

PART THREE

GETTING STARTED

Know your enemy, know yourself, and your victory will not be threatened. Know the terrain, know the weather, and your victory will be complete.

SUN TZU, CHINESE GENERAL, 510 BC

Understanding customers, markets, and their needs and requirements is a critical first step when developing a new product. Chapter 13 introduces qualitative and quantitative techniques for analyzing and segmenting relevant markets. High-performing firms use these tools to assure they target the most valuable opportunities for product development.

Firms that ignore customers, or only talk to them in general terms, risk wasting money and time. The risk lies in developing solutions to problems that do not exist, as far as desirable customers are concerned. Chapter 14 shows how to talk with prospective customers and elicit unique information from them to be used to distinguish your product from those of your competitors.

Contextual research is a new, but proven, way of creating information about what people actually do, instead of what they say they might do. The use of the contextual tools and techniques described in Chapter 15 results in development of innovative products that resonate with the needs of prospective customers.

Many practitioners herald customer interaction as essential for successful innovation. Others lambaste it as a useless exercise because information from customers is often unreliable, misleading, fuzzy, and imprecise. Chapter 16 outlines methods for helping firms align themselves with the axiom "To be successful, firms should know their customers better than their customers know themselves."

Effective new product ideation is more structured, more aggressive, and more intellectually demanding than most ideation procedures. Approaching ideation and concept generation with an attitude of "rigorous openness," as sketched out in Chapter 17, provides a focus interconnected with creativity and screening.

The quantitative market research tools discussed in Chapter 18 are variations of the traditional survey, in which customers give numerical responses to objective questions. The strengths and weaknesses of some methods of data collection, including the newest, Internet-based market research, are set forth with recommendations on how to match the right tool to the information needed.

Chapter 19 delineates the "getting to the best first" method of understanding the value of a firm's patent portfolio. This screening process provides an organized database that makes it easier to identify a firm's intellectual property for NPD.

The eventual goal of technology management is to place in order and focus research and development efforts on technology opportunities today that will positively influence corporate revenue in the future. Chapter 20 highlights the advantages of a defined technology management process.

CHAPTER THIRTEEN

MARKET ANALYSIS AND SEGMENTATION FOR NEW PRODUCTS

Douglas G. Boike, Ben Bonifant, and Tony Siesfeld

13.1 Introduction

This chapter will summarize the key techniques associated with analyzing the relevant markets for a new product development effort and introduce the concept of market segmentation as a means to find out a coherent set of requirements. The need to understand the target markets for new product development efforts has long been recognized as critical to success. "Putting" customer needs and requirements into the design and development of new products and services increases the chances of success for new product introductions. Customer insight improves innovation. There are qualitative and quantitative techniques available for use today to develop the fact base—the data—necessary to find this insight. Armed with sound data, many means exist to drive the segmentation of your market. Finally, a logical series of steps exist to guide such a market analysis effort as a critical input to a new product development effort.

13.2 Need for Market Analysis and Segmentation

Understanding customers and markets and their needs and requirements has long been recognized as critical to the success of a new product development effort. In Chapter 1 of this book, Cooper summarizes the results of his research, which clearly points out a strong correlation between sound market understanding and new product development effort success. He states, "A thorough understanding of customers' needs and wants, the competitive situation, and the nature of the market is an essential component of new product success. This finding is supported in virtually every study of new product success factors."

Mercer Management Consulting, in a study performed with *R&D Magazine* (Deck, 1994), examined the differences between high- and low-performing product development organizations. Across a range of measures, the research revealed that high-performing companies differentiated themselves through their collection and use of customer understanding information. Figure 13.1 summarizes the practices that have been shown to be statistically significant in explaining what makes a company become a high performer.

In summary, the linkage between sound market analysis and understanding and new product success is well demonstrated. Successful companies have rec-

FIGURE 13.1 SUMMARY OF KEY MARKET ANALYSIS PRACTICES DIFFERENTIATING LOW-PERFORMING COMPANIES FROM HIGH-PERFORMING COMPANIES.

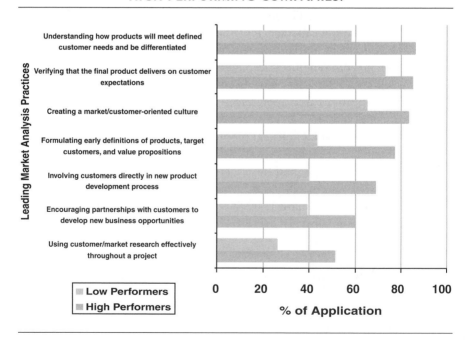

ognized this and have added steps such as "Strategy Development" and "Concept Screening" to their product development processes (Griffin, 1997).

More companies are making "Customer Focus" a higher priority in their product development processes. These companies display this philosophy through differentiated attention to customer priorities throughout product development:

- Continually refining insights into the customer needs, behaviors, preferences, expectations, and economics
- Focusing value propositions on meeting those needs and achieving a comprehensively superior customer experience
- Effectively capturing, analyzing, and spreading knowledge to embed customer understanding throughout the organization
- Dynamically focusing resources on, and aligning measurement and reward systems with activities that maximize long-term customer value

13.3 Setting Up the Foundation: Who Are Your Customers? What Is Your Product?

It is hard to argue against the point that customer information is a critical input to a successful product development system. However, there must be some boundaries that limit which customers and products are considered. To increase the odds of new product success, the company typically must either have some existing relationship with a given set of customers or some expertise within a selected product area. Thinking broadly about current customers and products can provide useful boundaries for targeting market understanding.

13.3.1 Who Are Your Customers?

It seems simple enough to identify the customer. For many markets, the definition of a customer is the traditional "consumer" or "household" view, which characterizes an "end user" of a product or service. However, few situations are that simple, as Figure 13.2 shows. Consumer products are not usually sold directly by the manufacturer to the end users. Instead, channel partners such as retailers or distributors consolidate products and create a purchase environment. Manufacturers often struggle with designing value propositions that meet channel partner requirements, while concurrently focusing on meeting needs of the end users. For some, the retailer is the most important customer because consumers are loyal to the channel and will buy whichever brands they carry.

FIGURE 13.2 RANGE OF POTENTIAL CUSTOMER TYPES.

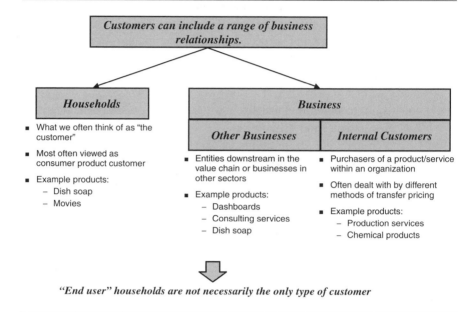

"End user" households are not necessarily the only type of customer

For others, the retailer is simply a vehicle. The consumer's willingness to search for the product (across channels) means that the important customer relationship is with the end user.

Some environments are even more complex. For example, in the pharmaceutical industry, the patient is the last consumer of the product, but the doctor has a dominant role in product selection. Meanwhile, insurance companies strive to put in place controls that highlight a cost/benefit balance that may differ from that of the patient or doctor. Manufacturers in this environment must understand the influence of each group and address the priorities of the primary decision makers.

A different set of challenges exists when the customer is not an individual consumer at all, cases where businesses sell to other businesses (B2B). When selling to businesses, there are typically fewer customers, but each individual transaction involves participation from a much larger number of decision-makers. Besides, each of these decision-makers is likely to have a focused area of expertise and unique set of priorities. For example, a producer of aircraft engine parts likely has a much smaller customer base to understand than a producer of laundry soap. For each sale, the customer requirements likely involve complex technical capabilities and specific cost targets. Engineers and pilots may be involved in evaluating technical performance, and regulatory compliance. Individuals from purchasing will be interested in pricing and the arrangements of terms. Finally, logistics experts from the supply chain group are likely to be called in to evaluate whether the supplier's service commitments will be satisfactory. Selling into this environment involves evaluating the priorities of each of these decision-makers, judging how these factors will be balanced, and communicating trade-offs across the customer's organization.

Finally, an existing customer may not be the proper or target customer for the new product choices under consideration. A financial services company designing an advisory and money management offering to attract high net worth people is actively seeking to attract those not currently customers to become ones. Likewise, a freight forwarding company that wants to protect existing ground delivery might develop a tracking and logistics service to appeal to the COO, someone not typically seen as the customer for the shipping services otherwise provided.

In all of these examples, the critical step is to identify the decision-makers and address value propositions to their needs. Sometimes, the first step in market understanding is building knowledge about who makes product choices and how others act as influencers.

13.3.3 What Is Your Product?

The traditional view of a product has changed. It has moved from the tangible manufactured good or contracted service to a consideration of the total utility (e.g., total experience) created through the customer's experience of interacting with a company and its offerings. The product development organization must, then, decide how broad a definition of product will be applied to new concept development. For many, this means stepping away from a product-centered view and beginning with an unconstrained consideration of customer needs. For example, computer hardware providers are discovering that uninterrupted service (uptime), service guarantees, and easy integration of new devices into the existing network are often far more important than the technical aspects of new features or functions. Once these needs are understood, the team can begin to identify value propositions that could satisfy those needs and priorities. To define a suitable scope for the product concept, the team should begin with a series of questions similar to the following (see Chapters 14–16):

- Broadly speaking, why does the customer use our products?
- What are the customers' needs and priorities during the entire process of introduction to, acquisition, use, and disposal of products to satisfy their need for my product?

- Where are there opportunities to better satisfy those needs and priorities?
- What capabilities does our organization have (or could be acquired by our organization) that could be applied to provide these value propositions?

The product development team must discover how broad a set of customer needs will be considered. For most organizations an increasingly holistic view of the customer experience must be considered. This opens up new opportunities to satisfy unmet needs and allows companies to defend against market encroachment from suppliers in neighboring sectors.

13.4 Basic Approaches to Market Analysis for New Product Development

Many techniques exist for analyzing market characteristics and customer requirements. They fall into two broad classes: qualitative methods and quantitative methods. The qualitative techniques typically draw insights from an in-depth understanding of a small set of customers (see Chapters 14 and 15). Here, the goal is to identify customer priorities in an open environment. The researcher uses qualitative techniques to build new hypotheses and gain understanding in new areas. Quantitative methods are more often used to test hypotheses and forecast the "size" of the demand for different products under different conditions (see Chapters 18 and 23). Here, a more generalized level of customer understanding is gained by posing a structured set of questions to a larger number of respondents. Insights on particular value propositions can be drawn, and differences among segments of customers can be identified.

13.4.1 Qualitative Techniques (see Chapters 14 and 15)

Often, the starting point is a qualitative analysis of the market dynamics. These approaches are applied when the goal is to gain an understanding of the basic market and customer needs, leading trends and issues, and the emerging priorities that might be addressed by an innovative value proposition. The range of qualitative techniques can be clustered into three research categories. These span a spectrum of market focus, analytical rigor, and investment level:

- *Industry analogies:* In many market environments, a good starting point for understanding needs and concepts is to study a representative industry analogy. The thesis here is that emerging market needs in the industry being studied might already have been faced in an analogous industry and that effective solutions might already have been developed. For example, the growth of "frequent buyer" clubs in many consumer sectors closely resembles the original "frequent flyer" concept developed in the early 1980s by the airlines. The need in all cases has been to strengthen customer loyalty and buying behavior. The solution in nearly all cases has been to put in place tracking and reward programs aimed at reinforcing the buying behavior wanted by the product- and service-providing companies. The qualitative analysis techniques involved here include mapping common characteristics to the industry analogues and research into the successful solutions developed in those industries.

- *Focus groups:* Focus groups are one of the most common techniques used to develop a sound understanding of market needs and requirements and begin the development of useful product/service concepts. In nearly all cases, focus groups involve a facilitated group discussion of prospective users and/or buyers in a target market. An agenda of topics and issues is used to lead the discussion. However, the facilitator takes care to allow free and open discussion of needs and ideas. The group discussions are generally recorded or carefully monitored to ensure that all the learning is captured. Focus groups are often used as the first step technique in a systematic exploration of market needs and characteristics. For most consumer products, focus groups are relatively easy to set up and inexpensive, while producing valuable and insightful results. In B2B settings or when the targeted decision-maker is often hard to gain access to (for example, doctors or government purchasing representatives). Here, focus groups may represent a large research investment and warrant even greater levels of planning and oversight.

- *Ethnography:* Ethnographic research is often the next step in a systematic market needs study. This form of research involves careful monitoring and observations of actual product/service users in live-use settings. The goal of such careful research is to explore the behavior of users with current products and services and note the difficulties that they meet and how they most often compensate for the difficulties. A classic example of such research is provided by Bell Labs research in the late 1970s diagnosing the need for cordless phones. In this research, the behavior of phone users clearly showed the need for a "cordless" phone as people sought to move about and complete tasks while still tethered by a phone cord. To conduct such research, a carefully structured environment and monitoring system is required. Videotaping or other recording techniques are often employed. A careful and insightful analysis of the observations is then required to "see needs" that may not be obvious on first glance.

In summary, qualitative research often forms the foundation for a sound but basic understanding of a market and its dynamics. Qualitative research is often followed by more detailed quantitative analysis aimed at confirming hypotheses and testing specific product concepts.

13.4.2 Quantitative Techniques (see Chapter 18)

There are three basic approaches for conducting more analytic market research:

- *Preference surveys:* Preference surveys are fairly straightforward in design, querying for measures of satisfaction and/or need using simple statements and/or tables. Preference surveys are designed to gather insights on the factors that underlie customer decision-making. By using questions that have the respondent express preferences, rank alternatives, or grant points to different options, these types of surveys yield quantifiable information on what drives customer decision-making. This approach provides an efficient assessment of a broad set of customer needs, preferences and requirements and yields critical insight into the elements of a new product or service that matter most to customers. One limitation of this technique is that people often do not know what is important to them; their stated preferences can be misleading.
- *Attribute experiments:* An effective approach to overcoming the weakness of a preference survey is to design a survey-based experiment, forcing customers to chose between potential products or services. Such surveys can be designed to draw out statistically significant insights about how individual product features or differences in the attributes of a value proposition influence customer choices. Figure 13.3 shows the range of techniques available for use in attribute experiments. The simplest technique involves direct questioning about individual features and attributes—often called self-explicated sampling. More sophisticated approaches such as conjoint analysis are designed to measure the value of specific attributes. With even more up-front design, choice analysis can be employed where specific attribute combinations can be tested and assessments can be made concerning the trade-offs that customer's make. In practice, all these techniques can be very powerful, extracting statistically significant relationships that can help analyze a very complex set of market needs or attributes of a product design. The key is to understand what techniques are most appropriate to the task. One limitation is that these experiments provide customers with "perfect information" about a product. In the real world, there are some who are not aware of a new product or, being aware, cannot obtain them. Real-world limits to awareness and access means that these experiments tend to overstate likely demand for a new product.

FIGURE 13.3 RANGE OF TECHNIQUES FOR AN EXPERIMENTALLY DESIGNED SURVEY.

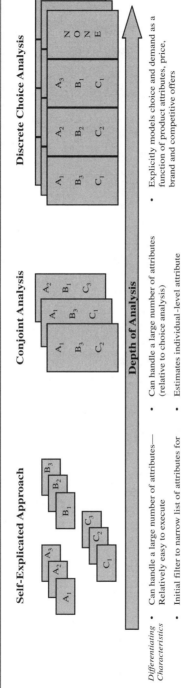

Self-Explicated Approach

Conjoint Analysis

Discrete Choice Analysis

Differentiating Characteristics

Self-Explicated Approach:
- Can handle a large number of attributes— Relatively easy to execute
- Initial filter to narrow list of attributes for subsequent conjoint or choice analysis
- Best used to obtain reactions to a particular offering in a noncompetitive context, for example, an improved service level at a particular hotel, situations where there are numerous attributes to be measured (i.e., early stages of product development)

Conjoint Analysis:
- Can handle a large number of attributes (relative to choice analysis)
- Estimates individual-level attribute utilities (can be used as a basis for segmentation)
- Requires small sample size (relative to choice analysis)
- Best suited to markets with features more likely to be non-numerical.

Discrete Choice Analysis:
- Explicitly models choice and demand as a function of product attributes, price, brand and competitive offers
- Provides a more realistic choice task for survey respondent
- Well suited to markets where competitive differences play a significant role (e.g., branding or pricing studies) and the competitive set is well defined . . . as well as situations where decisions are made on the basis of relatively few attributes that are well known

Depth of Analysis

- *In-market-based research:* Of course, the best information is gained by putting the value proposition in front of customers in the environment where real customer choices will be made. In-market-based research is focused on actual user and/or market response to a new value proposition. Again, the design of the test depends on whether the goal is to test a particular offering or if there is a need to evaluate the influence of including individual features. The goal of in-market research may be simply to validate a relatively mature new product concept prior to introduction. On the other end of the spectrum, sampling can also be used to test various combinations of features and pricing in an effort to uncover the statistically significant relationships driving customer need and behavior. Credit card companies often employ in-market testing to understand how consumers will respond to variations in offers (fee levels, introductory interest rates, late payment penalties) and the design of the marketing device (envelope graphics, salutation, marketing partner). Using insights from the in-market experiments, the provider company is able to complete the design of the feature package (or packages), pricing, promotion, and method of communicating with the customer. Critical components of successful in-market experiments include an accurate data collection methodology and an approach for interpreting the results of the test. In-market tests should almost always include a control cell. The control cell provides a means of interpreting the test results by offering a comparison to a market that is similar in all aspects except those being tested. Sometimes experiments are expensive—because the cost of a prototype is high or the risk of losing a customer too great to bear. This limitation makes in-market experiments most suitable for fairly high transaction, mass market situations.

In summary, the application of quantitative research techniques can yield very valuable insights and analytical data to support a coherent understanding of market needs. The results of these models are often the inputs to financial models that are used to evaluate whether to continue investment in a new product or service.

13.5 Choosing the Right Technique

Armed with this range of techniques, a new product development team should select the most suitable research tools for their situation. The tools selected should reflect the level of understanding of the market the team currently has and the stage of development for the value proposition. Figure 13.4 depicts the best application of these tools based on the current market understanding.

FIGURE 13.4 BEST PRACTICE APPLICATIONS OF MARKET RESEARCH TOOLS.

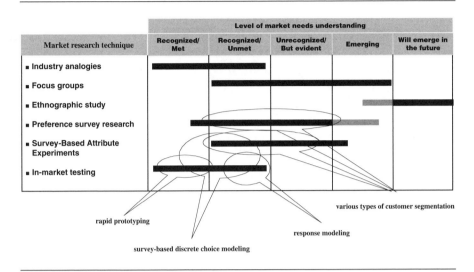

Figure 13.5 shows a typical application sequence of these market research tools. At the onset of a development effort, a team might choose to conduct an early broad survey as a means to first characterize the market and its needs. For some of the emerging areas, this might be coupled with an ethnographic study to better understand user behavior and unmet needs. Following this early exploration, a series of focus groups might be arranged to seek input on specific issue areas uncovered in the first round of research. The team then uses this information to form a series of new product concepts. The concepts then need to be tested using varying levels of survey research, potentially extending into a designed survey instrument that can be analyzed statistically. Finally, with a sound product concept in hand, the team will often choose to conduct in-market research with the nearly mature product or service.

13.6 Segmenting Your Market

Armed with a sound understanding of the market as a whole, segmentation is often an important next step. For most companies, the days are gone when they could view their customers as a homogeneous group that could be attracted, served, and retained in the same way. In most markets, customers are

FIGURE 13.5 EXAMPLE OF APPLICATION SEQUENCE FOR MARKET RESEARCH TOOLS.

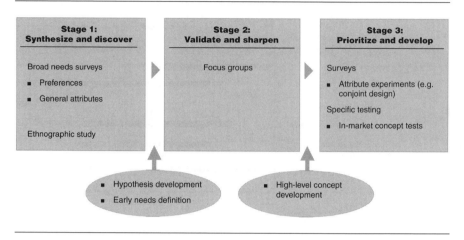

not all the same. They respond to different offers, require different service levels, and return different profits. All customers are not created equal in needs, behaviors, and profitability. Improving a company's focus on the most profitable customers can provide enormous returns. Segmentation analysis takes market and customer analysis to the next level by differentiating between customer groups and understanding the drivers of customer behavior on a segment by segment basis. Because product concepts are designed to meet underserved customer priorities, segmentation often precedes the identification of innovative value propositions. A customer-focused company manages its customer portfolio as closely as any other asset.

13.6.1 Criteria for Segmentation

Segmentation is fundamentally about de-averaging the customer base. It is the process of dividing a market into distinct groups of buyers that are similar in the way that they perceive, value, use, and/or buy the product or service being developed. Similarities within the segment are contrasted with differences across segments. The best segmentation schemes use several types of inputs in order to be both actionable and meaningful. Figure 13.6 summarizes a range of typical segmentation criteria. As the figure illustrates, the various types of criteria provide different utility. For example, understanding behavioral segments is useful for building knowledge about today's customers, but may not reveal

FIGURE 13.6 SAMPLING OF POTENTIAL CUSTOMER SEGMENTATION CRITERIA.

Criteria Type	Behavioral	Demographic	Psychographic	Preferences
Sample Data	• Type of product/service purchased • Number of products/services purchased • Features purchased • Frequency of purchase • Where/how purchased • Price Paid	• Age • Gender • Ethnicity • Family status • Education • Geography • Work status	• Personality traits • Values • Lifestyle • Attitudes	• Motivations to purchase • Perceptions of product/service and purchase experience • Requirements • Ideals • Barriers
Pros	• Easy to identify customers based on observable characteristics	• Actionable due to easily identifiable prospects • Data is easy to collect	• Provides great understanding of "need" addressed by product/service • Allows for more effective marketing positioning • Possible to predict behavior	• Allows for tailoring of value proposition
Cons	• Difficulty in identifying new prospects	• No insight into "needs'" • Hard to predict future behavior	• Not easily observable • Hard to identify new prospects • Hard to gather information	• Hard to identify new prospects • Hard to gather information

203

opportunities to meet the needs of new segments. Demographic segments are easy to target but offer less insight on making tailored value propositions. Psychographic segmentation provides a good understanding of how the product satisfies customer needs but these segments may be more difficult to target.

A sound segmentation analysis should provide meaningful differentiation in customer characteristics and provide a tool for acting on those insights. Product development groups should pay particular attention to segments of customers who are early adopters of innovations. These customers often have unusual sets of needs that make them pilots for the entire market. Recognizing the needs of this group and designing products and services that satisfy those needs can keep the company ahead of competitors.

13.6.2 Example of a Segmentation Model

Figure 13.7 presents a good example of a potential segmentation analysis result. This example is taken from a retail banking situation and shows the detail and insight that is possible from a careful analysis of several types of segmentation criteria. As can be seen, four segments are identified and distinguished based on needs/preferences, psychographics, behaviors and demographics. Figure 13.8 then shows how each segment can then be targeted with tailored product and service offerings. Finally, Figure 13.9 provides a framework to analyze which segments to focus on in planning a business strategy and new product development effort. Clearly, a company is best advantaged when it builds capabilities that match those in demand by valuable customer segments.

In summary, segmentation analysis is a tool used to understand the differences between groups of customers. It reveals clusters of customers who perceive, value, use, and/or buy products and services in ways that allow design of differentiated value propositions. The most valuable segmentations are based on multiple inputs and result in meaningful and targetable customer segments. It is important, however, to recognize that analytically based segmentation may often conflict with traditional market views—and, therefore, care must be taken to ensure organizational buy-in before continuing too far into implementation. Ultimately, the goal is to drive business strategy and new product development efforts.

13.7 Getting Started

Many customer-focused organizations strive to make the processes described above an ongoing part of how business is conducted. These organizations are

FIGURE 13.7 ILLUSTRATIVE CUSTOMER SEGMENTATION MODEL.

Target Segments	Bank Junkies	Personal Touch	Automated Bankers	Credit Card Users
Needs/Preferences	• Believe the branch is necessary for some transactions • Highly value convenience – 24 x7 service, ATMs, home banking • Like dealing with only one bank	• Believe branch is necessary for most transactions • Value convenience • Like personal touch • Concerned about the safety of their money	• Do not believe branch is necessary • Highly value convenience • Low value placed on personal touch • Prefer to use PC for all transactions	• Believe branch is necessary • Like personal touch • Value convenience • Do not want to consolidate all business in one bank
Psychographics	• Overcommitted • Like to try new technologies • Worried about money • Willing to take more time to save money	• Consider themselves "people" persons • Prefer to stick with tried and true technologies	• Not "people" persons • Overcommitted • Like to try new technologies • Unwilling to spend time or money for quality or convenience	• Consider themselves "people" persons • Not overcommitted • Satisfied with economic situation
Behaviors	• Few deposits and investment products owned • Above average loan products owned • Very frequent transactors	• Above average deposit products owned • Below average loan and investment products • Most transactions in branch	• Above average ownership of deposit, loan, and investment products • Use ATMs and touch -tone phone services frequently	• High number of bank products owned, including mutual funds and stocks • Most bank transactions are credit card transactions
Demographics	• Average income and debt • More single, younger • Work full-time • College-educated	• Low income and debt • High assets • Female • Retired, married, or widowed	• High income and debt • Married with young children • Male • Highly educated	• Average income and high debt • Homeowners • Highly educated • Married with older children
The Target Customer				

FIGURE 13.8 ILLUSTRATIVE CUSTOMER SEGMENTATION STRATEGY.

Banking Payment Preferences Example

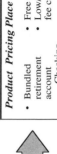

"Retired Segment" Information

- *Prefer to use checks whenever possible*
  - *Low tech*
  - *Not interested in electronic payment*
- *Credit cards also acceptable*
  - *Have resources to pay off bill*
- *Used to having free retirement checking*
- *Believe in convenience of bank and want one-stop shopping*
- *Need investment management services*
- *Go to bank frequently*
  - *Friendliness key factor in customer satisfaction*

Acquisition

Product	Pricing	Place	Promotion

• Bundled retirement account
  –Checking
  –Credit card
		• Free checking
		• Low/no annual fee credit cards
			• AARP-type lists
			• Advertise in retired journals
				• Position as brand for retired people

Development

Product	Pricing	Place	Promotion

• Offer no fee credit card for those who do not have
• New services for retired
  –Legal advice
  –Trusts
  –Etc.
		• Bundled pricing structure	• Retail primary channel	• Retail promotions/ teller introductions

Retention

Product	Pricing	Place	Promotion
• Assign personal advisor		• Competitive pricing–checking and credit card • Higher pricing for more value added	• Retail primary channel	• Offer periodic rewards for spending and multiple accounts

FIGURE 13.9 SEGMENTATION IMPACT ON NEW PRODUCT STRATEGY.

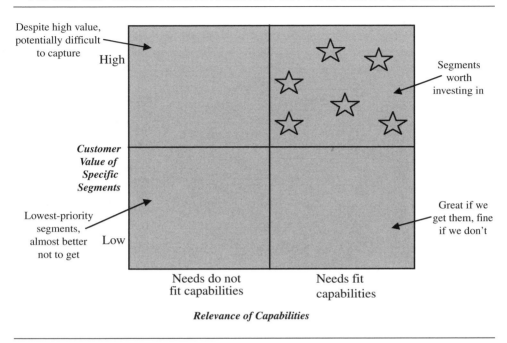

always learning from meetings with customers. New concepts are continually being tested and refined. Eventually, these organizations develop almost a reflex for translating customer priorities to new product concepts. When this occurs, the organization builds a growing advantage over those competitors who have a less-effective link between customer understanding and new product development.

To become a successful customer-focused company, a strong "test and learn" capability must be established (see Figure 13.10). Figure 13.11 shows a typical application sequence of these market research tools. At the onset of a development effort, a team might choose to conduct an initial broad survey as a means to first characterize the market and its needs. For some of the emerging areas, this might be coupled with an ethnographic study to better understand user behavior and unmet needs. Following this initial exploration, a series of focus groups might be arranged to solicit input on specific issue areas uncovered in the first round of research. The team then uses this information to form a series of new product concepts. The concepts then need to be tested using varying levels of survey research, potentially extending into a designed survey

FIGURE 13.10 ESTABLISHING A "TEST AND LEARN" CAPABILITY.

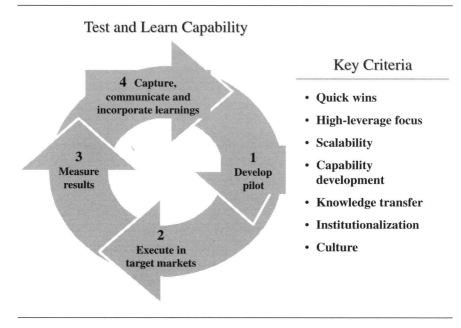

FIGURE 13.11 THE ROLE OF MARKET RESEARCH AND ANALYSIS IN A NEW PRODUCT DEVELOPMENT PROCESS.

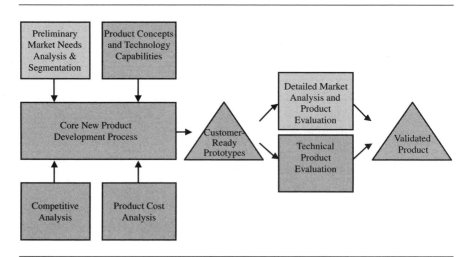

instrument that can be analyzed statistically. Finally, with a sound product concept in hand, the team will often choose to conduct in-market testing with the nearly mature product concept.

Best practice research reveals the importance of continually going out to the market for understanding and testing new product/service concepts. This iterative "test and learn" process leads an organization to an always current understanding of its markets and customers. It also provides insight on which competitor actions are having a meaningful impact on the market. Further, it allows the company to discontinue products no longer valued by customers, freeing up resources to support better-performing products and the development of new products.

Market research and analysis needs to play a role throughout the product development process. It is perhaps more important, however, to ensure that market needs analysis and segmentation inform the early stages. This early understanding is crucial to ensure the correct set of requirements is placed in front of the development team and that investment is focused on the highest-return opportunities.

Once a working set of product and/or service prototypes is in hand, a focused market validation and product testing step must also be completed to ensure that the product delivers on its original commitments to satisfy customer needs. This in-market testing of new product prototypes needs to be an ongoing component of organizational learning. It should be applied to product after product, concept after concept.

13.8 Summary

This chapter has summarized the key techniques associated with analyzing the relevant markets for a new product development effort and has introduced the concept of market segmentation as a means to establish a coherent set of requirements. As we have reviewed, high-performing new product organizations are using these tools to ensure that they are targeting the most valuable areas of opportunity and that their efforts have the highest possible probability of commercial success. As customers expect value propositions that increasingly match their priorities and as competitors battle to be the first to meet those demands, effective customer focus will continue to grow in strategic importance. The qualitative and quantitative techniques summarized in this article represent the initial tool kit for building these capabilities.

References

Cooper, R. G., *Winning at New Products: Accelerating the Process from Idea to Launch*, 3rd Edition. New York: Perseus Publishing, 2001.

Deck, M., "Why the best companies keep winning the new products race." *R&D*, 4LS–5LS (1994).

Griffin, A., *Drivers of New NPD Success: The 1997 PDMA Report*. Chicago: Product Development & Management Association, 1997.

Douglas G. Boike is president of Triad Consulting, Inc., a management consulting firm focused on process improvement in manufacturing and new product development. He formerly was a director with Mercer Management Consulting, responsible for its new product development and manufacturing practice. He has also held operations and technology management positions with Xerox Corporation and B/E Aerospace. Dr. Boike has held a number of positions within the PDMA, most recently serving as secretary/treasurer of the PDMA Foundation. Dr. Boike earned a Ph.D. in Engineering Science from Dartmouth College, a M.Eng. in engineering management from Rochester Institute of Technology, and a B.A. in physics from Kalamazoo College.

Ben Bonifant is a practice director with Campbell Alliance in Raleigh, NC. He has been a consultant to leaders of global pharmaceutical and biotechnology organizations, as well as decision makers of large private equity funds. He has extensive experience in determining the implications of external market changes to the design and priorities of sales organizations. A major focus of Mr. Bonifant's work has been developing programs that enable organizations to close the gaps between existing capabilities and processes and the capabilities and processes required to achieve success. Mr. Bonifant earned an M.B.A. from the Stanford Graduate School of Business and a B.S. in mechanical engineering from Duke University.

Tony Siesfeld is a director with Mercer Management Consulting's Strategy Group and heads its Customer Science Unit. He is a trustee of the Marketing Science Institute, an academic and business consortium. His responsibilities range from the design and execution of primary customer research for clients considering new product or service introduction to better understanding the dynamics of customer buying decisions. He earned his Ph.D. in psychology and M.S. in statistics from Stanford University.

CHAPTER FOURTEEN

OBTAINING CUSTOMER[1] NEEDS FOR PRODUCT DEVELOPMENT

Abbie Griffin

14.1 Introduction

Products and services that don't solve peoples' problems, or don't solve them at a competitive cost, fail. Motorola discovered this with Iridium. Iridium's general purpose was to "enable wireless communication worldwide." However, in developing a solution to this general problem, potential customers were not asked about the details of or the specifics of what that means. Thus, the technology solution chosen—satellite delivery to a bulky phone requiring a large antenna for in-car use that was very expensive to buy or use—did not meet the physical functionality customers wanted simultaneously with the

> *The most successful new products match a set of fully understood consumer problems with a cost competitive solution to those problems.*

---

[1] "Customer" in this chapter refers to current customers, competitor's customers, potential customers, and all others who have unsolved problems and unmet needs. Customers can be individuals interested in meeting their own needs, or people in firms trying to solve business needs. They can be seeking either product or service solutions to their problems.

communications functionality. The result was predictable: the demise of Iridium, with an $8 billion development write-off.

The most successful product development efforts match a set of fully understood customer problems to a cost-competitive solution to those problems. "The devil is in the details," as they say. Palm's first Palm Pilot® was successful because the development team interacted extensively with potential users to understand the details of both form and function. Functionally, they identified that people were using a combination of computer- and paper-based organizing and memory tools, and the mix changed depending upon whether they were at or near their computer or away from it. The solution to these problems was to create an organizing "system" with both computer-based and remote capabilities rather than just a stand-alone product. They determined the frequency of use of each of the organizing capabilities, and designed the product so that those most frequently used were the easiest to get to. Finally, they thought about how people might want to carry the remote device around. Because men frequently carry date books and other notes in their pockets, especially shirt pockets, they designed the Palm to fit in the smallest shirt pocket made, which happens to be on Brooks Brothers shirts. The result of their development efforts was a wildly successful product that changed the way people organized their lives.

New product success can be obtained by following one of two paths. On one path, the firm first acquires a complete understanding of the complex set of needs surrounding a problem for which a set of customers would like a better solution. They then develop a product or service that solves the set of problems. This is the path that the Palm team took. Alternatively, firms can develop products that do new things, are based on new technology, or have new features, and then see if they solve enough problems to make people want to buy the product at the price the firm can afford to charge. Motorola developed Iridium using the second path. Although teams can be successful this way, it is a riskier path to success.

On the one hand, firms that ignore customers, or only talk to them in general terms, risk wasting money developing solutions to problems that do not exist or for which potential customers already have an adequate solution. On the other hand, interacting with and talking to customers truly can be misleading if one asks them for information that they inherently are not able to provide. The key is to talk to customers using appropriate methods and asking questions that customers can answer and that can provide information useful for developing new products. This chapter presents information and qualitative market research methods to help product development teams understand customer needs (see also Chapter 15).

14.1.1 Information Customers Cannot Provide

Customers cannot tell firms exactly what products to develop. They cannot provide the details of exactly what the future blockbuster product for your firm should look like, the features it should have, or the technologies it should contain. If you find someone who can—hire that person! He/she is doing the job your development team should be doing. That is, that person understands his/her problems fully and has the technical capability to translate those needs into yet-to-be-developed technologies and forecast the features that will advantageously deliver those needs in the future.

Customers also cannot provide reliable information about anything they have not experienced, or with which they are not personally familiar. By definition, customers are not familiar with technologies that have not been commercialized. They cannot be familiar with a new product the firm may be thinking of developing and thus generally cannot provide reliable information when asked to react to a concept or prototype. This is especially true for radial or new to the world products. They will, of course, provide answers to questions (most people want very much to be helpful). In reacting to product concepts without experiencing them, some customers may try to imagine how they think they really will feel. Others will just tell you what they think you want to hear. Information derived from unknowledgeable customers is at best inaccurate and at worst is an irrelevant fantasy. To act upon it is extremely risky.

14.1.2 Information Customers Can Provide

Customers can provide reliable information about the things with which they are familiar and knowledgeable or that they directly have experienced. A customer can provide the subset of the needs information that is relevant to them in an overall category of customer problems. They can articulate the problems and needs they have. They can indicate the products and features they currently use to meet their needs, where these products fall short of solving their problems, and where they excel. The only way that a full set of customer needs for a product area can be obtained is by coming to understand the detailed needs of a number of customers, each of whom contributes a piece of the needs information.

14.2 Basic Principles for Obtaining Customer Needs

The objective of this chapter is to define and present techniques for obtaining the qualitative customer needs necessary to start product development. These

> *Current customers and potential users can provide reliable information about the*
> *problems and needs they experience, those that are relevant to them. For each person,*
> *this is a subset of the full set of information needed for effective product development.*

needs can be used for quantitative market research later in the project (see Chapter 18). More important, this information provides the detailed understanding of the functional nuances to the development team that will dictate the engineering trade-offs they make during product development. The techniques presented focus on producing rich, detailed, context-specific information and ensuring that this information is transferred completely to those who need it, the development team.

14.2.1 Defining Customer Needs

Customer needs are the problems that a product or service solves and the functions it performs. They describe what products let you do, not how they let you do it. For example, many businesspeople have a need to "be able to do any work I want, wherever I am." General needs and problems are fairly stable, they change only slowly, if at all, over time.

Features deliver the solutions to peoples' problems. Features are the ways in which products function—a portable PC delivers a partial solution to being able to work wherever I want. So does taking a secretary and all one's paper files on a trip, but although this was a preferred solution for some in past millennia, this is not a particularly feasible solution today. As this example demonstrates, features change more rapidly than general needs.

Customers have general problems for which they need a solution and that relate to the overall product function. For example, a portable PC must "let me connect to the Internet." The dominant feature that delivers the solution to this need is the laptop's modem, although both high-speed local area networks (LANs) and "wi-fi"® (wireless fidelity) solutions now are becoming available.

Customers also have very specific needs or aspects of the overall function that a successful product must also meet. These more detailed needs, which may be related to a particular feature or technical solution, often are specific to the particular contexts in which the product is used (see Chapter 15). For instance, portable PCs are used in many different venues. Some of the detailed needs include "let me connect to the Internet. . ." ". . .from my office," ". . .from a hotel room," ". . .when I am overseas," and my personal favorite ". . .while sitting next to the hotel pool."

Customer problems generally are very complex, and frequently different needs conflict. At the same time I want to be able to connect to the Internet in all those different venues, I also want to be able to shove the laptop into my briefcase and know that I have everything I need with me wherever I go. Therefore, needing several different cables and peripheral connection devices is not a useful solution for me. I will never end up with everything I need on my business trip. The development team thus needs to have a good understanding of the relative importance of all the contexts and ways in which the product will be used, misused, and abused to select the most appropriate feature set for their product. It is first uncovering and understanding and then delivering against these detailed needs that differentiates between product successes and failures.

No product is perfect. Each product is a compromise, delivering only partially against a complex set of customer needs for any function. Products consist of sets of features that deliver extremely well against some needs, adequately against others, and not at all against others. For example, the modem on my laptop does not allow me to connect to the Internet when I'm sitting by the pool, although it works just fine for the other contexts. While the modem's connection speed (slowness) is adequate for me for my Internet usage, it is not for others. Those who need higher Internet speed are likely to already have adopted high-speed direct connections in their laptops. As different firms develop new technologies and features, product compromises shift across the set of customer needs. Because of both technology and competitor evolution, features tend to change over time. However, customer needs tend to be far more stable than features. Providing product development teams a rich understanding of the complex and detailed customer needs and problems prepares them to select the best technology and feature set compromises in the future to continue delivering successful products for the firm.

The four C's of good statements of customer needs and problems:

- *Customer language:* They are not the words of the team and do not contain company-specific or technical jargon.
- *Clear:* They are easily understandable by all, over time. Some teams even create dictionaries with detailed definitions of terms and phrases.
- *Concise:* They are not too wordy. They contain only the words necessary to describe the need.

> *Understanding features leads to today's dominant products; understanding needs leads to tomorrow's dominant products*

- *Contextually specific:* They include all contextual references and provide situational details. For example, "The PC lets me see what I'm working on when I'm flying at night."

14.2.2 From Whom to Obtain Needs

Only the people involved with the details of how a problem affects the day-to-day way they perform their job or live their lives can provide you with their needs. And only the people who interact with, use, or are affected by the operation of a particular product can provide you with the details of how that product excels at or fails to solve their problems. A purchasing agent cannot identify the logistical and physical problems that a grocery clerk has operating a point-of-sale scanner system. Nor can they help you understand the difficulty of the procedure the general manager of the grocery store must go through to produce a daily income statement or rectify the store's inventory position at the end of the month using the software associated with the scanner system. In the same vein, a mother cannot provide adequate information about the athletic protector her son needs for playing baseball, nor can she even provide concrete details about the feminine hygiene needs of her newly adolescent daughter. The details of customer needs and problems must be gathered directly from the people who have them.

14.2.2.1 Special Considerations in Business-to-Business Markets. Gathering detailed information generally is more difficult in business-to-business markets because most products affect multiple groups of people. Because no one can provide accurate information about something they don't actually experience, several different groups must be investigated to obtain complete information about the detailed issues surrounding a function (McQuarrie, 1998). Grocery store general managers only partially understand the ergonomic and other customer needs of their check-out clerks. They have general information, but not the details that will help firms differentiate between acceptable and superior products. Having to investigate multiple groups' needs increases the cost and effort associated with obtaining good, complete product development market research for business-to-business markets.

14.3 Techniques for Deeply Understanding Customer Needs

Firms can obtain detailed understanding of customer needs through at least three market research techniques:

- Be an involved customer who has those needs and problems.
- Critically observe and live with customers who have those needs.
- Talk to customers with those needs.

Table 1 summarizes the main aspects of these techniques. Additional techniques that provide alternative methods for understanding needs can be found in Chapters 15, 16, and 17.

14.3.1 Be a User: Be an Involved Customer of Your Own and Competitor's Goods and Services

Being a user is the simplest technique for uncovering needs.

14.3.1.1 What to Do and Keys to Success. An enormous amount of customer needs knowledge and understanding can be gained by putting every development team member in situations where he/she is actively involved customers with the problems your firm is trying to solve. Also, when your firm already has a product commercialized in a particular functional area, encourage team members to use your products and all competitive products routinely in "everyday" as well as "extraordinary" situations.

At one company, both men and women work on the product development team for a feminine hygiene pad product. Teams at this company are known for the lengths to which they go to try to fully understand and identify with customer problems. The entire team personally tests their own and competitors' current and new products. Male team members have worn pads underneath armpits and in shoes to test chafing and odor-elimination characteristics. They also have worn these pads in the anatomically appropriate area, with and

---

Different techniques for understanding needs produce different kinds of information. No one technique is sufficient to produce a full understanding of customer and potential user needs.

TABLE 14.1 SUMMARY OF TECHNIQUES FOR OBTAINING NEEDS.

Needs Uncovering Techniques	Information Obtained	Major Benefits	Major Drawbacks
Be a User	• Tacit knowledge • Feature trade-off impacts on product functionality	• Knowledge depth • Generates irrefutable belief in identified needs	• Hard to transfer knowledge to others • Time and expense
Critically Observe Users	• Process Knowledge • Tacit knowledge	• Learn customers' language • Find unarticulated needs	• Time and expense • Must translate observations into words
Interview Users for Needs	• Large volumes of details • Context-specific needs	• Speed of information collection • Breadth of information	• Ability to elicit reliable tacit and process needs • Viewed as "Marketing's job"

without having doused the pads with liquid to simulate various normal-use conditions.

Team members at another firm in the point-of-sale scanner system market work full shifts as check-out clerks several days a year in different kinds of stores. Stores readily agree to assign the development people shifts because they do not have to compensate them and because they hope to get improved products. By working full shifts, development personnel learn about shift start-up and close-out, the effects of different payment modes, breakage, and fatigue, and are exposed to a random day's worth of the strange things that can happen in a check-out line that can affect the operator and the system. Operating a system in a laboratory setting just does not provide the same breadth of interaction experience.

Routine continual personal gathering of customer information is not feasible for all product areas. It is highly unlikely that many or even any, individuals on those teams developing, for example, stents that open plaque-clogged arteries, will be qualified to perform heart catheterizations. However, with a little imagination it is possible to do far more than many firms encourage development teams to do.

14.3.1.2 What Kind of Information Is Obtained. Having employees become actively involved customers is the best way, sometimes the only way, to transfer "tacit" information into the product development team. Tacit information is knowledge someone has but cannot or does not articulate. It is the intuitive aspect of the knowledge a person has about their needs. Becoming a routine customer for all the various products in the category also may be the most efficient way to drive home to development teams the trade-offs firms have made in their products and the effects that trade-off decisions have had on product function.

GM misses out on opportunities to inexpensively imbue employees with a great deal of competitive and daily ownership information by some of its policies. GM requires that any employee traveling on business for the firm and renting a car rent a GM car. Development team members miss out on great opportunities to inexpensively see how other firms' design differences affect performance. In addition, GM provides managers with new cars and then assumes responsibility for maintaining those cars. Because of this policy, senior people at GM lose an appreciation for how recalls and having to maintain a car over time causes problems for customers—especially for dual-income families who are short on time.

14.3.1.3 Codicils. Although this is a good technique to bring rich data into the product development team, it is only one of several techniques that should be used, because of several inherent problems:

> *By actively using products, developers are exposed to needs that are "tacit" and difficult to extract verbally from customers.*

- The firm must learn how to transfer one person's experience and knowledge to others. A means of codifying experiences must be found.
- If experiences are not well documented, retaining personal knowledge becomes a critical problem if in your organization team members frequently shift product areas or end markets or leave the firm.
- Project management must take steps to ensure that individuals do not think that their own needs are representative of the market. They will differ from the "average" customer in unexpected ways.
- Encouraging team members to be customers takes time, money, and personal effort. Obtaining cooperation from team members requires management support and example.

14.3.2 Critically Observe and Live with Customers

Critically observing customers demonstrates how your true customers' needs differ from your perception of their needs.

14.3.2.1 What to Do. Product developers who cannot become customers may be able to live with customers, observing and questioning them as they solve a set of problems (see Chapter 15). Developers of new medical devices for doctors usually cannot act as doctors and personally test devices in patients. However, they can observe operations, even videotape them, and then debrief doctors about what happened and why they took particular actions later, with or without viewing the videotape simultaneously.

Sometimes observing customers in their natural settings leads directly to new products or features (Lilien et al. 2002). Development team members at Chrysler observed that many pickup truck owners had built holders for 32-ounce drinks into their cabs, so the 1995 Ram truck comes with cupholders appropriate for 32-ounce drinks. In other instances, observation only points out the problem, and the team must still determine whether the problem is specific to that person or applies across the a large part of the target market, and if so, develop an appropriate solution. Another Chrysler engineer had watched the difficulty his petite wife had wrestling children's car seats around the family minivan. It took him several years to convince the firm that his leap to a solution—integrating children's car seats into the cars' seating system—would solve a major problem for a large number of customers. It did.

14.3.2.2 Keys to Success.
Critical observation, rather than just casual viewing, is the key to obtaining information by watching customers. Critical observation involves questioning why someone is performing each action rather than just accepting what they are doing.

The best results are achieved when team members spend significant time with enough different customers to be exposed to the full breadth of problems that people encounter. They must spend enough time observing customers to uncover both "normal" and "abnormal" operating conditions. In addition, using team members from different functions is important because people with different training and expertise "see" and pay attention to different things.

14.3.2.3 What Kind of Information Is Obtained.
Living with customers is an effective way to identify tacit information and learn customers' language. It is also the most effective means for gathering work-flow or process-related information. These customer needs are particularly important for firms marketing products to other firms. The products and services they develop must fit into the work flows of those firms, which means that the work flows must be understood fully. Even when questioned in detail, people frequently forget steps in a process or skip over them. Although forgotten by or unimportant to the customer, these steps may be crucial to product design trade-offs.

14.3.2.4 Codicils.
Observing and living with customers is not especially efficient. It's inherent problems include:

- Gathering information broadly requires significant team time and expense. Actions unfold slowly in real time.
- Observation or even unobtrusive videotaping may change people's behavior: "natural" actions may not be captured.
- The team again has to turn actions and behaviors into words, reliably capturing customer needs verbally.

When new products must fit into work flows or customer processses, critically observing customers is crucial to effective development.

14.3.3 Talk to Customers to Get Needs Information: Capturing the Voice of the Customer

By talking to customers, development teams can gather customer needs faster and more efficiently than by emulating or observing customers.

14.3.3.1 What to Do. A structured, in-depth probing, one-on-one, situational interview technique called voice-of-the-customer (VOC) research can uncover both general and very detailed needs of customers (Griffin and Hauser, 1993; Zaltman and Coulter, 1996). The way questions are asked in this method differs significantly from standard qualitative techniques such as focus groups in four ways. VOC:

- Is grounded in reality. Customers only talk about situations and experiences they actually have had. This keeps customers from fantasizing inaccurately about things they know nothing about.
- Uses indirect questioning, rather than direct questions. Thus, rather than asking customers "What do you want" directly (as frequently happens in focus groups), VOC indirectly discovers wants and needs by walking customers through the ways they currently obtain or acquire and use products and services to fulfill particular needs.
- Asks questions from a functional orientation, not a product or feature orientation. For example, one study asked customers about the various ways that they transported food they had prepared at home to another place and stored it for some period of time before later consuming it. This is the general function that picnic baskets, coolers, and ice chests fulfill. Asking about the function rather than a product yields information about many different and unexpected products that customers use to perform this function, including knapsacks and grocery store bags. Detailed probing draws out the specific functions, needs, drawbacks, and benefits of each product. Most important is delving into *why* various features of the products are good and bad. What problem does each of these features solve, and at the same time, does a particular feature cause any other problems? Probing the why uncovers the needs.
- Inquires about multiple situations or contexts in which the customer faced a particular problem, because the information desired is the breadth and depth of needs details.

One advantage of interviewing is that many different use situations can be investigated in a short period of time, including a range of both "normal" and "abnormal" situations. Each different use situation provides information about additional dimensions of functional performance that a customer expects. A good way to get started is to ask each customer to tell about the last time he/she used a product that fulfilled the function. The food transporter study began: "Please tell me about the most recent time you prepared food in your home, to be shared by you and others, then took the food outside your home and ate it somewhere else later." By asking customers to relate what they did, why they did it, what worked well, and what did not work well about what they did, both detailed and general customer needs are obtained indirectly.

After a customer relates his/her most recent experience, the person is asked about how he/she fulfilled the function in a series of other potential use situations. These use situations are constructed by the team to attempt to cover all the performance dimensions within which customers will expect the product to function. For example, customers were asked about the last time they took food with them:

- On a car trip
- To the beach
- To a football or baseball game
- On a romantic picnic

- On a bike trip
- Hiking or backpacking
- Canoeing or fishing

They also were asked to relate the most disastrous and marvelous (best) times they ever took food with them. Although no customer had experienced all of these situations, the food transporting and storing needs resulting from each situation were fully uncovered by the time 20 people had been interviewed (Griffin and Hauser, 1993).

14.3.3.2 Keys to Success. Although VOC is not difficult, it approaches the task of gathering needs differently than traditional focus group or other qualitative market research techniques. It results in a much larger list of far more detailed and context or situation-specific needs, because the objective is to obtain a level of detail that enables teams to make engineering trade-offs during product development. There are several keys to being successful in obtaining the voice of the customer.

Buried in the stories that consumers relate about specific use in stances are the nuggets of detailed needs which a superior product must deliver.

It is critical to ask customers about functions (what they want to do), not features (how it is done), because only by understanding functional needs can teams make the appropriate trade-offs in technologies and features as they become feasible in the future. It is continual probing as to "why" something is wanted or works well that gets at the underlying needs.

A second key is that the VOC only covers reality. If someone has never been on a romantic picnic, that person cannot be asked about what they would like in this situation because they do not know. What they would relate would be fantasy.

The final key to success is to ask detailed questions about specific instances of use. General questions produce general needs. General needs are not as useful in designing products as are the details of problems. Customers are very capable of providing an excruciating level of detail when they are asked to relate the story of specific situations that have occurred in the last year.

14.3.3.3 What Kind of Information Is Obtained. Both the details of customer problems as well as the more general functional needs are obtained with VOC. Through indirect questioning, customer needs that relate to technical design aspects can be obtained, even from nontechnical customers. For example, by relating how their car behaves in various driving situations (flooring the accelerator at a stop sign, traveling at city speeds around 35 mph, and traveling at interstate highway speeds), even senior citizens can provide information that determines the gear ratios governing the speeds at which an automatic transmission shifts gears, even though they may have no idea how their transmission works.

14.3.3.4 Codicils. As with all customer needs gathering methods, VOC has weaknesses.

- The development team obtains a better understanding of a full set of detailed needs if the team interviews customers rather than outsourcing it to a market research group.
- Some customers are completely inarticulate. Getting conversation out of them is like pulling teeth. It always seems that one of the first two customers the team interviews will be inarticulate.
- Extreme care must be taken to maintain the words of the customer and not immediately translate one particular problem into a solution before understanding the full set of needs.
- Tacit and process-related needs may not be complete.

14.4 Practical Aspects of Gathering Customer Needs

Regardless of which technique is used to gather customer needs, the development team will be interacting with customers, which always involves some risk (see Chapter 16). By structuring and planning the interactions carefully, firms can increase the probability that both the team and the customer will benefit. This will increase the likelihood that a particular customer will agree to work with the firm in the future.

14.4.1 How Best to Work with Customers

The most basic principle behind working with customers is that they should be involved so that the firm can learn from them. If product features already are defined, and customer needs are gathered after that, to "prove" they have specified the "right" product, they likely are wasting money. Gathering customer needs makes sense only if the task is completed before the product is specified.

Customers will be most willing to interact with the development team if they see how they can benefit. For most household markets, that generally means that customers receive money for interviews or observation periods. Development teams investigating business-to-business markets may find that they can provide benefit to customers by helping them gain an understanding of their own end customers.

Most firms have a portfolio of products that they have already commercialized. If the product development team collects customer needs themselves rather than contracting with a market research firm to gather the data anonymously, most or all of the customers interviewed will be familiar with at least some of their current product line. Some customers, especially in business-to-business markets, may spend the first 10 to 15 minutes of an interview venting their anger and frustration at current products. The team needs to be careful not to get defensive during this tirade but to listen to what the customers say and try to find out why these items bother them. Once customers understand that the team is talking to them in order to serve them better in the future by developing better products, and once they have vented their immediate anger, they generally calm down and gladly answer questions.

14.4.2 Pitfalls to Avoid When Interacting with Customers

There are several pitfalls to avoid when gathering information from customers. The first is that the team is not there to sell, even if a salesperson is on the interview team. They are strictly on a fact-finding mission. Selling will both use up the limited time you can schedule with each customer and erode their willingness to interact.

The second pitfall to avoid is not talking to enough customers to obtain a complete set of needs. Only observing one firm's business processes or only talking to your firm's people as surrogates for actual customers is almost more dangerous than not interacting with customers at all. No one customer provides a full set of customer needs for any product area. Interaction with about 20 customers is required to obtain about 90 percent of customer needs (Griffin and Hauser, 1993).

Finally, several steps must be taken to ensure that the results the team has obtained are used. Gathering information that does not affect the product development effort wastes the time and energy of the team as well as the firm's money. Results are more likely to be used when the users of the information are involved in the data gathering. Both technical specialists and managers find the data more believable if they assist in collecting the information. Data that are in a usable form are also more likely to be used in the development. Data that are buried in a report are less likely to be used than those that are pasted all over the walls of the development area. Reminders of what was learned can never hurt.

14.5 Summary

No one technique provides all the customer needs that product development seeks. Tacit needs are best conveyed by being a customer. Process-related needs are best identified by critical observation of customers. In-depth interviewing is the most efficient means to obtain masses of detailed needs, but may not provide the tacit and process-related information. Unfortunately, few projects can afford the time and expense of fully implementing all these processes. When personnel are fairly stable, management may be able to implement an ongoing customer-need-generating process, which works to provide product developers continuously with customer interactions. Otherwise, it is best for development teams to use the most appropriate customer-need-generating technique(s), given the informational requirements, budget, and time frame for their project.

References

"Griffin, Abbie and Hauser, John R., "The voice of the customer." *Marketing Science* 12(1): 1–27 (1993).

Lilien, Gary L., Morrison, Pamela D., Searls, Kathleen, Sonnack, Mary, and von Hippel, Eric. "Performance Assessment of the Lead User Idea-Generation Process for New Product Development." *Management Science* 48(8): 1042–1059 (2002).

McQuarrie, Edward F., *Customer Visits: Building a Better Market Focus*, 2nd Ed. Thousand Oaks, CA: Sage Publications, 1998.

Zaltman, Gerald and Hige Coulter, Robin. "Seeing the voice of the customer: Metaphor-based Advertising Research." *Journal of Advertising Research.* 35(4): 35–24 (1996).

Abbie Griffin is a professor of Business Administration at the University of Illinois, Urbana-Champaign. Dr. Griffin's research focuses on measuring and improving the process of new product development, including the marketing techniques associated with developing new products. She is the former editor of the *Journal of Product Innovation Management*, and sits on the board of directors of Navistar. Prior to becoming an academic, she worked in product development at Corning Glass Works, was a consultant with Booz, Allen and Hamilton, and started her career as an engineer at Polaroid Corporation. She is an avid quilter and hiker.

CHAPTER FIFTEEN

CONTEXTUAL RESEARCH FOR NEW PRODUCT DEVELOPMENT

Chris V. Conley

15.1 Introduction

Exercisers throw a towel over the treadmill console. Office workers paste FedEx label holders on the front of a filing box. DayTimer® users clip printouts to the cover of their binders. Dry-erase calendar users keep a second calendar and wait until the last day of the month to erase the previous weeks' outdated information. Identifying and understanding everyday customer behaviors like these are the foundation of contextual research, a relatively new research technique introduced in this chapter. Contextual research uses information about what people do, rather than what they think, to drive new product development that is innovative and naturally resonates with other people in the same situation.

In what ways does your company come to understand customers' needs? Or do you already have a good handle on them? Surprisingly, even with the spectacular growth of market research over the past two decades, many companies resist conducting research on and with their customers. It is understandable why this is so. For one, it is hard to accept that "the market" may somehow hold more information than the company who owns a significant share of it. For another, through its normal operational activities such as sales and technical support, companies feel they are "hearing" the customer's voice. The challenge doesn't seem to be knowing more about the market, but keeping up with requests from customers. Finally, to many professionals, marketing research seems just to confirm what managers think they know already. The growth of "validation studies," in which a company tries to confirm that a product very far along in development will succeed in the market, is evidence of this trend.

While understandable, these beliefs and the resulting behavior are surprising given that so many new products fail or never provide an adequate financial return. It would seem that companies would begin to realize that they do lack some insight about the market and that the yearly addition of new features, the lowering of cost, or the introduction of a derivative model is not an adequate development engine that leads to significant business growth.

Innovative products drive business growth. Innovative products, by definition, are ones that provide new value and are readily adopted by the market. They are elusive because what clearly provides new value may be too complex and costly for customers to understand and adopt. What customers will easily adopt is often an in-

> *The context is simply the everyday situation of use and includes the environment, the people, their goals and processes, and other products.*

cremental improvement or a reduction in cost. Developing new products that provide new value and are easy to adopt requires deeper insight.

This chapter introduces contextual research as one key research method that gives the type of information companies can use to develop innovative product ideas that provide new value and resonate with customers to foster adoption. Contextual research is a market research method that has developed out of ethnography, the social science method used to understand cultures other than one's own. This chapter uses the term "contextual research" as opposed to "ethnographic research" to distinguish between the aims and techniques of market research and those of social science.

Quite simply, contextual research gathers information about everyday situations, or contexts. Most often, these contexts are the places where your products and services exist or would like to exist. They involve the people, the places, and the activities in which your product exists. Most often, the context is the context of use by the ultimate end user(s), but in fact, can be anywhere along the supply and distribution chain. Although many companies know what contexts their products and services go into, few spend time experiencing or studying them. It is a lost opportunity, because the context can provide tremendous insight and lead directly to innovative ideas.

15.2 The Shift from Product to Context

At the core of this method is a shift of focus away from the product itself to the product's context of use. Focusing on the product leads to incremental improvements such as adding a feature, changing the color, or reducing the cost. The product itself doesn't provide the information to inform the question of innovation. While there may be value in these improvements, none of them leads to significantly new product lines and new market growth. Unfortunately, most new product development focuses on exactly these kinds of improvements, and this is one reason so many companies falter over time.

A contextual viewpoint broadens what the company looks at in relation to its products or services. The context includes the people involved, activities and processes surrounding the product, inputs and outputs of those activities, other products used in conjunction or simply that are present, and environmental conditions. Figure 15.1 illustrates this difference between product and context-centric viewpoints.

> *Contextual research broadens a company's view while maintaining a connection to what matters to its customers.*

With a focus on the context, the *role* of the product gets more attention than its function and features. A useful analogy is a stage set. There are actors, a story, the set, props, and interactions. The props, likened to products, are there to serve a purpose, to support the story. A theater audience is more apt to tolerate makeshift props than customers are willing to accept products that are poorly suited to their context. Developing this metaphor a bit further, we can liken a service-oriented business to the scene of the play. Everything in the

FIGURE 15.1 DIFFERENCES IN SCOPE BETWEEN PRODUCT-CENTRIC AND CONTEXT-CENTRIC VIEWPOINTS.

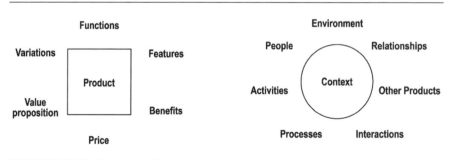

context helps determine the successful communication and delivery of the experience, just as in the service business.

In contextual research, the company foregoes a limiting focus on its products and services to better understand the context in which they play a role. This new focus reveals opportunities for improvement and growth.

15.3 Where Contextual Research Comes From

Contextual research is based on the ethnographic methods of anthropology. Ethnography is the scientific description of human culture. The results of ethnographic research in the social sciences contribute to social theory and may influence government policy.

In the late 1980s, Lucy Suchman, an anthropologist at the Xerox Palo Alto Research Center (PARC), did doctoral research on the use of a newly developed copying machine. Xerox claimed the machine was easy to use, despite its considerable complexity—a Xerox commercial implied that the only thing one needed to learn was how to push the Start button.

In her study, Suchman gave the participants (technology PhD's and Nobel Laureates) the task of making fifteen double-sided copies of an article from a bound book. Most participants could not complete the task, and those who did spent the better part of an hour figuring it out. It became clear from the research footage that the machine was extremely hard to understand. In her dissertation, Suchman highlights the need for the developers of technical systems to consider issues that affect the design of the system outside of the system itself. In this case, looking at the people and their tasks helped reveal significant problems with the performance of the product, the feedback from machine, and the structure of the instructions that were meant to be helpful.

After Suchman's work, researchers from Xerox PARC became more involved in corporate sponsored ethnographic research. One of these projects involved understanding air traffic control rooms for Steelcase, the largest manufacturer of contract furniture in the U.S. The research showed how the air traffic controllers interacted with equipment and with each other, what was of importance to them, and how they communicated. Steelcase has continued to use and develop ethnographic methods to understand the workplaces for which they build products and services.

15.4 A Few Critical Principles of Contextual Research

Obviously, developers of new products and services aren't interested in constructing social theories, so the ethnographic method isn't applied in exactly the same way. Contextual research can be thought of as the commercially-oriented outgrowth of ethnography.

Contextual research differs from ethnography primarily in the time taken to conduct a study, the rigor of data analysis, and the intended use of its outputs. However, several key principles of the ethnographic method apply to contextual research:

- Empathy for your subjects is necessary in order to understand their experience.
- Rapport with your subjects is necessary in order to see true behavior and values, not just stereotypes.
- The subjects and their context lead the exploration and the identification of what is important.
- Focus on what the subjects actually do as opposed to their opinions.
- General patterns and insightful criteria for innovation result from small sample sizes and rich, qualitative data.

While these principles sound simple, they are surprisingly different, if not in direct conflict, with the principles used in common market research techniques.

15.4.1 Empathy

Empathy is defined as identification with and understanding of another's situation. As simple as it sounds, our natural behavior is different from this. Imagine the last time you and your colleagues saw someone using your product or service in a way that

> *"Improper" and modified uses of a company's products should be seen as latent innovations calling attention to themselves.*

was not intended. A common response is laughter and/or irritation, and an immediate reaction to characterize the user in negative terms: ill-informed, ignorant, or not a real customer for example. We criticize or correct customers when we see them using our products improperly and not doing the right thing.

In contrast, an empathetic viewpoint requires a question rather than a label. Why are they using the product in that way? What goal do they have? What is their mental model of the product's use? What is it about the situation that leads to this behavior? The goal is to identify with the situation, to see beyond the user doing things "incorrectly" and to gain insight about the conditions. The insight gained through an empathetic viewpoint opens to new ideas for supporting and changing the situation rather than the user.

15.4.2 Rapport with People

Rapport is a relationship, especially one of mutual trust or emotional affinity. Developing rapport with people in their context of use is required to get high-quality information that is deeper and more meaningful than information that typically results from formal customer interviews, questionnaires, and surveys.

Developing rapport is difficult because of how we view ourselves as professionals and how we view customers. Our professional selves are different from our personal selves. Just think of the differences in behaviors and perceptions of each other during the normal work day and on a weekend company picnic. Colleagues who remain in work mode are thought to not be able to relax or let their guard down. In contextual research, one must be very personable, not represent one's company or professional role, in order to build trust and connection with people in a very short time frame.

We normally view customers with the same level of formality that we view our professional selves. Even more abstractly, customers are seen as market segments (see Chapter 13). This strongly conditions our interactions with customers and how we interpret their comments and suggestions. It keeps us from seeing them as everyday people in their day-to-day activities, goals, and troubles as concretely as customers experience them. It keeps us from entering into conversations that accept the fact that our product works particularly well *for the customer.* With rapport, a research participant willingly tells you what's really going on, what they really think, and how they really feel about things. The ability to develop rapport must be done regardless of the research participant's role, background, socioeconomic class, or any other aspect of their situation.

15.4.3 Customers Lead the Discussion

Normal research preparation involves significant design of questionnaires (see Chapter 18). In an effort to standardize answers and provide a robust data set, questions and answers are predetermined. The flow of the questions is also considered when structuring the overall interaction. In contextual research, the questions

> *People don't necessarily know what they do on a day-to-day basis nor can they describe it in any significant level of detail— seeing what people actually do is the only way to know.*

and answers are not designed. Rather, the researcher designs how she will get the participants to show, demonstrate, or simply do their everyday activities. Fieldwork in contextual research varies by the degree to which one observes behavior and interacts with the participants. In pure observation, participants simply go about their daily activity—there are no questions or guidance from the researcher. It is most practical, however, to have interaction between the researcher and participant. A document called the field protocol, rather than a questionnaire, guides the interaction between researcher and participant.

15.4.4 A Focus on Activity and Behavior

"Can you show me how you do that?" This should be the most common probing statement in contextual research. Behavior rather than opinions or specific answers to questions is the focus of developing data.

A company making baby strollers held focus groups in which mothers articulated what they liked and didn't like about their strollers. "I love mine, it's a Peg Perego." The result of the work was a collection of potential improvements, all incremental, but no significant new ideas about strollers. Subsequently, the company had the mothers bring their babies and strollers to the research facility so they could actually use and demonstrate them. As soon as the first "exercise" was given, problems with the strollers became painfully apparent. A mother holding her child couldn't fold the stroller to put it in the trunk of a car. With a bag of groceries and the child seated in the stroller, steering with one hand was difficult and ergonomically harmful. The results of this activity-based research was a series of innovations, including one-handed steering that received a utility patent.

15.4.5 Results from Small Samples and Rich, Qualitative Data

One of the most methodologically challenging principles of contextual research is that it deals with qualitative data and the number of participants are few, perhaps one or two dozen. The data are normally video recordings, a set of notes, pictures, and physical samples of things from the environment. Qualitative data are normally used just to "get a sense" of what people in a market think. But in contextual research, qualitative data provide the specific means for new innovations.

Unfortunately, marketing managers frequently are loath to base big ideas on small sample sizes. The normal tendency is to increase the number of interviews to get more data. Rather than making the data more reliable, this often just increases the time and resources necessary to conduct, collate, and deliver the research results. This tendency also works against developing rapport with participants because as the sample size goes up, the ability to engage equally from the first through to the last participant goes down.

Contextual research delivers valuable results with relatively small samples sizes.

It is surprising, however, that intriguing patterns develop in as few as 5 to 7 interviews. While difficult to explain, especially to professionals used to large samples sizes, there has been research to demonstrate small sample size effectiveness. It has been shown that 90 percent of the full set of customer needs was developed with 20 qualitative interviews of a heterogeneous set of customers (Griffin and Hauser, 1993). Indeed, after more than 100 studies over the past decade, it is clear that the fundamental insights about the context and innovative ideas that result can be developed with small samples. Of course, quantitative surveys to validate the ideas that go into development should be a normal part of the process.

These five principles of contextual research are key to developing data and insights from the data that lead to innovative products. The customer's context must be approached with an intentional naiveté, which is certainly not a typical behavior for successful professionals. To make the most of contextual research, one must transform the ordinary into the exotic, constantly asking, "what is the customer doing here?" and "why is this seemingly everyday activity interesting?" Knowing your customer and evangelizing about your product or service must be suppressed. A childlike fascination with the everyday situation will serve the researcher well. It is this inquisitiveness, with truly open eyes, that leads to seeing the situation in a new way, and to seeing new opportunities.

15.5 The Process of Contextual Research

The implementation of a contextual research program is not different in structure from other research methods. Figure 15.2 shows the five major stages of contextual research.

FIGURE 15.2 THE PROCESS OF CONTEXTUAL RESEARCH IS SIMILAR TO OTHER RESEARCH PROCESSES.

1. Design the Study ▶ 2. Gather Field Data ▶ 3. Code & Analyze ▶ 4. Develop Insights ▶ 5. Report Results

15.5.1 Step 1. Designing the Research

The first step in a contextual research study is to design an approach to the fieldwork that will allow the team to collect quality data on people's activities and their context. This step should be approached creatively because it determines who will be recruited for the research and in what kind of environment one will collect rich data. In order to emphasize what we're really looking for in a field situation, let's pretend that anything is possible. Quality data would consist of a video record of a person going about an activity of interest, with an audio record of what they are thinking as they do it, combined with the knowledge of why things are like they are in the current situation (e.g., why files are set up in a particular way, why there is a list of numbers pinned to the wall, etc.) In effect, the researcher is not even present but fully comprehends what is happening.

While this ideal may not be attainable, the research design phase is used to figure out creative ways to capture data. In a real situation, the researcher seeks unfettered access to someone engaged in a particular activity, uses their interpersonal skills to build rapport, and utilizes their research skills to elicit what the subject is thinking and why the environment is the way it is.

An example of an innovative approach to selecting a context is provided by Outer Circle, a manufacturer of insulated lunch bags. Outer Circle wanted to extend its product lines into carrying hot foods away from the home. With no experience in this product category, they commissioned a contextual research study. During the research design phase, the team identified several everyday activities in which carrying hot food away from the home occurs; hot lunches that are packed in the morning, gatherings in which people bring a hot dish to pass around, and sporting events that include pregame consumption of food and beverages (tailgating). To gather information on the second scenario, a member of the research team threw a party and asked guests to bring a hot dish to pass around. Video cameras were set up in several locations to watch people arrive, unpack their dishes, and set them up on the buffet table. While guests arrived and brought their dishes into the kitchen, it was easy to discuss with guests the varied and sometimes ingenious means of packing and transporting their hot food. After sitting down to a series of wonderful, if sometimes lukewarm dishes, guests were told about the research project and engaged in another round of stories and issues related to their recent experience.

Critical steps in designing the research include:

- Identifying people who engage in activities in a context relevant to your product or service

- Figuring out how to collect data in that target context with video cameras, still cameras, and so on
- Creating a topic guide (rather than specific questions) that will be used for interviews
- Designing the protocol for interaction with participants
- Conducting a pilot field visit to test the approach

15.5.2 Step 2 Fielding the Research

Once it has been designed, tested, and refined through the pilot field visit, the research study should be fielded. Participants should be recruited and scheduled for visits by the research team. Ideally, two people will be on the research team and work together in the field. One of them will guide the field protocol, and the other will be more of a technical assistant, running the cameras, and otherwise being an observer.

When arriving in the context, the research team must be calm, courteous, and reassuring to begin building rapport immediately. Time to study the context may be limited, so building trust provides deeper access to what's going on. The research team also should be completely open about why they are there and what they hope to accomplish. Often companies have become so removed from what really goes on in the context of their products and services that contextual research must be focused on the everyday. While the context may be foreign to the researchers and even the company's development team, it is "just where I work (or live) and what I do" to those who are in that context every day.

After comfortable introductions and a description of how the time will be spent together, the research lead should get things started. Depending on the nature of the research, what happens in the field can range from "shadowing," where there is little interaction, to an interview where the participant is prompted to "show and tell"

> *In any given contextual study, there will be additional, unanticipated value from being in an environment with customers.*

about a variety of things that go on in the context. No matter what the degree of interaction, Those gathering the data must focus on having the participants engage in their everyday activities, articulate what they are thinking as they go about it, and understand why things exist as they do in that context. This will lead to a collection of "rich data."

Life Fitness, a leading producer of commercial fitness equipment, used contextual research to better understand the use of their equipment so they could define their next generation platform. The field research consisted of spending time at health club facilities engaging in exercise, and observing and engaging other exercisers in conversation. Video cameras were hung to capture the overall and individual exercise behavior at a bank of equipment.

There are often unanticipated benefits of being in the context. In this case, the research team was also able to capture video and pictures of competitive equipment while they were understanding people's behaviors. This competitive data provided Life Fitness with unexpected but valuable secondary information.

Peapod, an online grocery shopping and delivery company, provides an example of one of the pitfalls to avoid when a client participates in the fieldwork. It is beneficial to have the development team members in the field, but in practice it is critical that they understand contextual research principles and "behave." The Peapod study was being fielded to understand the in-store shopping process in order to design better tools for the shoppers—people who work for Peapod and do the actual shopping for the online customers. As the research team observed the Peapod shoppers one of Peapod's managers announced, "You see here, he is doing it all wrong." He approached the subject and grabbed the clipboard and shopping list used for reference. The Peapod manager went into management mode and sacrificed seeing how things are really done—the key goal of contextual research. When he saw that things were being done differently from what he expected, he should have questioned the established process and the context, not the worker. As it turns out, the shopping method being demonstrated right in front of him was optimized for speed, allowing the shoppers to meet the stringent time frames they were under. However, the accuracy of the orders suffered. But the Peapod shoppers knew customers were more satisfied with a timely delivery than with an accurate order that came late, so they continued with their modified process. By recognizing what was going on and not trying to correct behavior, this study produced ideas for improvement, such as grouping items on the shopping list to mimic aisle organization.

With the completion of fieldwork, the process of analysis can begin. Even with only 10–20 field visits, the research team will have more than enough data to provide surprising insights and implications.

15.5.3 Step 3 Analyzing Field Data

Having been in the field, one has learned a tremendous amount about what really goes on, what problems exist, and innovative ideas that have been developed far from corporate headquarters. Companies and the team must resist the urge to respond immediately to what has been learned. They must approach the data analysis with some rigor and detachment. The analysis will ensure coverage of the context, check or validate assumptions, and help generalize anecdotal evidence into substantiated recommendations.

The first step in data analysis is to code the data. Coding is simply the process of going through the various information sources, video, notes, and pictures, and turning them into bite-sized chunks. Often a database or structured spreadsheet can be used. The general structure of a coded piece of data includes its source, the fact or observation from the context, a comments area, and one or more fields for tagging the bite, usually with keywords. Figure 15.3 is an example of several lines of coding from a project on digital photo printers.

As the data is reviewed, "interesting" chunks are created and documented in this template. What qualifies as interesting? "Interesting" includes all of the following, and more: specific examples of how the person does something; ways of describing one's goals, activities, or setup; slang or

> *It is important to push past stereotypical descriptions of what people do and render the specific details of their everyday activity.*

colloquial language used to characterize a situation; a list the person articulates as the key aspects of a situation; a guided tour that the person give you of some part of his/her environment; a pair of people characterizing each other's behavior in a shared activity. Interesting means descriptive, authentic, characteristic, clear, tangible.

While this may seem quite broad, it can be surprising how much of our daily interactions work at the level of generalizations or stereotypes. "You know, I just organize it like everybody else, putting things where they belong." A good interviewer will have facilitated more specificity. "Put what things? Where do they belong? Why do they belong there?" The answers to these questions will be specific and useful for coding and analysis. It is always great when a participant gets down to the basics and says something simple and profound at the same time. "Look, it's not that mysterious. I don't really want to know how much time is left in my workout. After a day of working at the computer, having trouble with the systems at work, the last thing I want is flashing, blinking lights and numbers giving me "information" about my workout. I need to tune into my body, not an interface!" These descriptions, often borne out of asking helpful research participants about their situation from many different angles, having them show you what they do, really figure something out about why they do what they do. And when they share it with you, listen.

The second step is to use the coded data for identifying patterns of issues, behaviors, values, problems, workarounds, and other possible categories. Essentially, this is a pattern-recognition activity aimed at identifying issues and

FIGURE 15.3 AN EXAMPLE OF CODED INTERVIEW TAPE. A GIVEN STUDY MAY HAVE 300 TO 750 INDIVIDUAL BITES.

Participant	Description/Observation	Interpretation/Implications	Primary keyword	Secondary keyword	Time in
Bill B.	Stuff for the shoot—paper cutting, paper, cords, computer, two camera cases and lights. Fills the back of the SUV. Printer and everything besides cameras and lights fit into the two gray cases. The cases were custom made for the first dye-sub printer he had. Printers are two Kodak 8500.	Customers have equipment sets and try to find easy ways of transporting them.	equipment	mobility	00002000
Bill B.	Printers covered in boxes to protect from dust.		equipment	dust	00010800
Bill B.	Unpacking and setting up printers and computers (mock set up for the interview). Case is 120 lbs but the printers are light. Cables, paper covers, paper trays, instruction manual for the software, back-up ribbon and paper, extension cord, paper cover. Set up is generally less than 15 min from the time they walk in the door.		equipment	setup	00012600
Bill B.	USB vs. FireWire for upload speed. Files are memory intensive.		connectivity	speed	00035200
Bill B.	Paper covers are a pain but needed when people are hanging around the print area. Keeps hands off of the print while it's going through its four pass process. The covers are just something else to have to throw in the box.	Mobility and setting up in diverse environments impacts durability, cleanliness, security.	accessories	dust	00053000
Bill B.	Green pins for securing the print head during transport. They are a drag to put.	Poor ergonomics -- auto-locking print head	accessories		00062400
Bill B.	Paper trays could be larger. . . "at least 100 sheets."		accessories	capacity	00064700
Bill B.	Kodak did a good thing by matching paper capacity with ribbon output. 50 and 50. "When you change You change them both and then it's done."	One-to-one relationship between ribbon and media -- very unlike toner-based systems!	maintenance	ease of use	00072500

grouping bites within them. Once grouped, the category is analyzed in a similar fashion for more specific traits. For example, in a contextual study for Motorola on the use of mobile phones for messaging, a clear pattern of message management emerged from reviewing the coded data. The message management pattern consisted of a set of activities all aimed at dealing with the scant amount of memory available on mobile handsets at the time. Only ten messages were allowed on the phone, and they were split between the inbox and outbox. The activities were: (1) reading a message when it arrived and deciding to save it or not, (2) moving saved messages from the inbox to the outbox in order to keep messages from being bounced should the inbox fill up, (3) sending messages one wanted to retain to a friend for safekeeping until one cleared more space on the handset, and (4) trying to conceal messages that were personal in nature from friends with whom the mobile handset was shared informally. By recognizing these activities as a pattern of managing messages, the overall messaging capability was better understood through the user's context rather than the industry's technical standards. One specific feature that resulted was a "charms box," where one could store special messages under security of a personal identification number (PIN).

Bites that were related to this were tagged, collected as a set, and then looked at for patterns within the set. Issues of categorization, privacy, storage, and quick access were found within this set. Also note that this set of bites represented participants from different countries, demographics, and daily contexts. Highly diverse qualitative data can be generalized through this process.

In analyzing data, one must avoid simply responding to problems seen in the field. This one-to-one mapping of observation to response is not a sustainable strategy. Normally, many problems in the field are symptoms of a larger systemic issue. It is these higher-order issues that will lead to innovation in the next step.

15.5.4 Step 4 Creating Insights and Implications

Insights and implications are developed separately from the data analysis (see Chapter 17). In this step, one is considering the issues identified in the context in relation to the constraints and capabilities of the company. One company will develop a completely different response than another from a similar data set. This is because companies have different strategies, business models, and technical capabilities.

Taking the Motorola example a step further, insight from the message management pattern revealed an opportunity to help secure messages sent between phones. Motorola created a kind of "charms closet" on the phone, to

> *Contextual research should provide the inspiration to identify fundamentally new things a company should consider doing with their products and services.*

which the most personal and valued messages could be saved and protected by a PIN number. To another manufacturer, perhaps with fingerprint recognition technology, this same situation could be addressed by securing all messages in the phone, with only the fingerprint of the owner allowing access.

Successfully managing the creation of relevant ideas bridges the chasm between having research data and figuring out what to do about it. Companies need to involve people who are inspired by the contextual research in this part of the process. The best marketers, designers, and engineers will find the insight into the context interesting and full of implications for what could be made. Too often, individual agendas take over, ideas that people had long before the context was studied surface and are thrown into the arena. It doesn't mean that people's longstanding ideas aren't valid. Rather, the study of context should open new ground for the company and not simply be an exercise to reconsider ideas that are on the shelf. At a minimum, the study of context helps people evaluate old ideas in new ways.

To avoid this pitfall, tie ideas to principles that emerge from the research. If someone is emphasizing the need for speed in a new product, ask how speed benefits the context. Was that a particular value for which participants repeatedly demonstrated a need? Just asking this simple question can help categorize new ideas based on context from other ideas. Another especially helpful technique is to create "Ways of . . ." statements that respond to the patterns of behavior found in the context. For example, in response to the pattern that people tend to keep menus, schedules, and notes near the whiteboard where they jot down a reminder, the development team created the statement, "Ways of keeping source materials close at hand." A brainstorming session was held on this and each of the other ten "ways of" statements, which generated hundreds of ideas. From these ideas, a successful product line of over 30 SKUs was developed.

Brainstorms and development meetings should be facilitated that focus on particular categories of the contextual research. The driving question becomes, "How could we address this issue?" Generated ideas should be documented and prioritized. Ideas that bubble to the top based on voting, recurring references, and feasibility should be documented in the reporting phase of the program.

While a more complete discussion of idea generation can be found in Chapter 17, ideas should be developed on at least three levels in response to issues identified in the context: function and feature ideas, product line/platform ideas, and strategic ideas. Approaching issues identified in contextual research on these three levels increases the relevance and breadth of responses and increases the likelihood that a successful response can be developed.

15.5.5 Step 5 Reporting Contextual Research

Since contextual research broadens a product team's view beyond the product itself, the results of a study are often useful to others in the organization. Therefore, reporting becomes a significant activity to leverage the value of the study beyond its original purpose.

> *When colleagues observe a normal customer using their products in unanticipated ways, their minds open, not only to question the behavior, but also to see new solutions.*

A video report is useful for giving a strong sense of the context to those unable to be in the field. A video report can be organized in sections, each dealing with a particular topic that emerged from the research and supported with both typical and extreme examples. Video of what people really do in the context is one of the most powerful communication tools at the product manager's disposal.

A written report also should be produced, but the amount of text should be kept to a minimum. The best way to understand context is to experience it. To embody the context, a report should be highly visual, including pictures of the context and the activities that go on there. A useful structure for reporting is an executive summary followed by two-page spreads that cover distinct topics. A two-page spread can be organized with a large title, a one-paragraph introduction, examples of issues illustrated with pictures or video stills from the field, and examples of implications or possible responses (refer to Figure 15.4). The goal of these individual spreads is to cover what happens in the field, to understand why that activity is interesting or valuable to know, and to suggest possible responses. The value of "working in spreads" is that the audience can open to any page in the report and understand something significant about the context.

The reporting team also should create diagrams that embody aspects of the context and its implications. Diagrams are more than data-reporting tools. They are useful artifacts for driving discussions among development team members. An useful example is the "activity diagram" (see Figure 15.5) outlining the steps and characteristics of activities that occur in the context. A "Day in

FIGURE 15.4 EXAMPLE OF A TWO-PAGE SPREAD. A TWO-PAGE SPREAD PROVIDES AN EASY WAY TO UNDERSTAND AN ASPECT OF THE USER'S CONTEXT AND IDEAS FOR HOW THE COMPANY COULD RESPOND.

Handouts & Leave Behinds

Handouts and leave behinds are generally copies of overhead transparencies or Powerpoint presentation. Presenters are looking for ways to get the audience more engaged in their presentation.

Audience Review & Markup
Audience members often use the handout as a workbook to mark or underscore important information. They also like to summarize the presentation and use it as a springboard for new ideas.

Referencing information in handouts and booklets
After a training or sales presentation, the audience often needs to refer to information from handouts. Leave behind materials should allow the audience to quickly and easily find recalled information.

Do-It-Yourself "Meeting in a Box"
We saw several examples of professionally produced, "Meetings in a Box". The box, handed out at the beginning of a sales or training session, contains all handouts and leave-behinds. The box may include videotapes, cassettes, diskettes, and a variety of document formats.

There may be an opportunity to help users create this kind of concept without professional help.

Design Research • Presentation Products • December 1997

Consider:

- Provide participants with highlighting and note taking tools as part of a report cover.
- Presentation caddy organizes and makes mobile supplies the audience may need during a presentation.
- Useful containers for protecting & distributing materials for an entire presentation. A tidy way to distribute materials
- Label area on the handout makes it easy for participants to add the handout to their files.
- Retrofitable index helps audience members make the handout useful to themselves for later reference.
- Ways of packaging different media with a traditional report. i.e. CD pocket, VHS tape attachment, etc.
- Built in means for markup and highlighting. i.e. Sticky flags on inside cover of presentation booklet.

16 Design Research Associates • Presentation Products • December 1997

FIGURE 15.5 AN ACTIVITY DIAGRAM FOR THE USE OF STRENGTH EQUIPMENT.

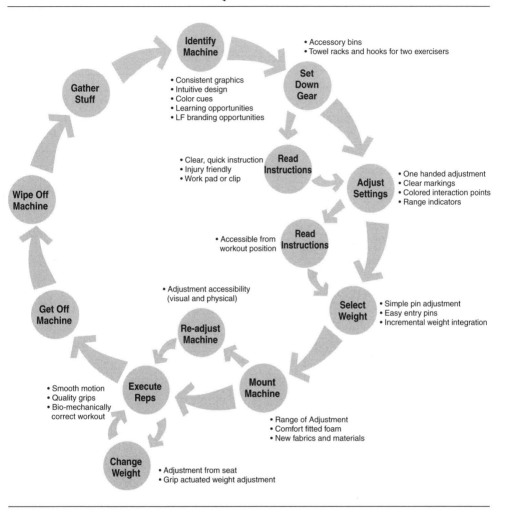

the Life" of the context is another approach that helps explain what goes on there, how it is arranged, and important characteristics of the environment. Any great report diagram has three important characteristics: it is based on evidence/data, its form makes understanding the evidence easier, and it calls out important relationships the reader should see.

15.6 The Economics of Contextual Research

What does contextual research cost and what is its return on investment? Of course, this depends on the scope and goals of a particular study. Is the study a very general one with the results expected to drive insights for multiple product lines over the course of a year or more? A study of this scope might involve 20–30 different field visits, take 12–16 weeks and cost $150,000. A smaller study, looking to generate understanding for a particular product line might involve 10–15 site visits, take eight weeks and cost less than $50,000. National and international studies increase the time slightly and the expenses significantly. Factors that affect the cost of contextual research include the number and geographic location of contexts, the extent of expected data analysis, the extent of ideation, and expenses related to travel, recruiting, and participant stipends.

Because these studies generally happen early in the overall definition and development process, specific return on investment (ROI) calculations are difficult, but certainly not impossible for a specific implementation. Specific benefits should be expected from a study, and they include:

- Ideas for unique functions or features not yet in the market and valued by customers.
- At least a handful of ideas on which intellectual property protection can be pursued in the form of patents and trademarks.
- Ideas for market positioning language, product names, and descriptions based on how people in the context think and talk about the products and services.
- Ideas and examples of new product lines that the company does not yet produce.
- Ideas for how the company could approach the product line over time. These ideas have strategic value for the company.
- A shared understanding, among a portion or all of the company, on what is really happening with the organization's products and services in the field. Many companies are so removed from everyday uses of their products that this renewed understanding helps everyone make better development decisions regardless of their functional role.

A final way of summarizing the value of contextual research is that it helps an organization generate a larger quantity of new, distinctive ideas relevant to the customer context, and that these ideas are generated earlier in the process than with other forms of research. How a company measures or values these benefits will provide a specific ROI and determine whether the investment in contextual research will provide acceptable returns and help the company grow.

15.7 Summary

Contextual research is a relatively new, but proven way to broaden a company's understanding of the role their products and services could play. It is best used when the question of what to make is the most pressing one. Contextual research requires an empathetic viewpoint and an ability to suspend an organization's focus on its own products and the expertise it believes it possess about them. It is a way to see the market with fresh eyes in order to identify opportunities beyond one's current lines of business.

The process of contextual research involves gathering rich data from everyday situations, rigorously analyzing it for significant patterns and general issues, and using these patterns to generate ideas about functions and features, product lines, and strategy. Because of their tangible nature and the fact that they are produced in the early stages of product development, the results of contextual research are relevant across the organization.

Contextual research should be included in any company's arsenal of methods they use to understand their market and develop innovative ideas on which to grow.

References

Griffin, Abbie, and Hauser, John R., "The Voice of the Customer," *Marketing Science*, 12(1): 1–27 (Winter 1993).

Robson, C., *Real World Research: A Resource for Social Scientists and Practitioner-Researchers*, Cambridge, MA: Blackwell Publishers; 2nd edition, 2002.

Spradley, J., *The Ethnographic Interview*. Boston, MA: International Thomson Publishing; 1st ed. 1997.

Squires, S. and Byrne, B., eds., *Creating Breakthrough Ideas: The Collaboration of Anthropologists and Designers in the Product Development Industry*. Westport, CT: Bergin & Garvey, 2002.

Stilgoe, John R., *Outside Lies Magic: Regaining History and Awareness in Everyday Places*. New York: Walker & Co, 1999.

Suchman, Lucy A., *Plans and Situated Actions: The Problem of Human-Machine Communication*. New York: Cambridge University Press, 1987.

Chris Conley is Assistant Professor and Director of Product Design at the Institute of Design at the Illinois Institute of Technology. He holds degrees in mechanical engineering and product design and has spent his entire career in the research and development of new products. He is a principal in Gravity Tank, a Chicago-based consulting firm providing new product definition services to manufacturers of consumer, medical, and industrial products. He leads the New Product Definition research consortium at IIT where he conducts research on understanding contexts, product conceptualization and evaluation, and the methods and tools to support these activities, especially in multidisciplinary, collaborative teams.

CHAPTER SIXTEEN

INTERACTING WITH CUSTOMERS IN THE NEW PRODUCT DEVELOPMENT PROCESS

Ian Alam

16.1 Introduction

Innovative firms interact with customers extensively to obtain necessary input for their new product development (NPD) projects. Customer input is needed to overcome the inherent risks associated with NPD, to develop a product that fulfils customer needs better than competitors do, and to manage the overall innovation process and outcome better. Yet, customer interaction is easily overlooked amid the pressure to develop new products quickly and squeeze costs from NPD programs. In addition, customer input and interaction has been among the most controversial of approaches. It has been heralded as a necessity for a successful innovation and lambasted as a useless exercise because customer inputs are often unreliable, misleading, fuzzy, and imprecise. Product managers are partly to blame for this controversy because they do not know how to interact with the customers correctly. For instance, Cooper (1999) argues that despite a significant amount of research into why new products fail, product managers have not learned their lesson and continue to make the same mistakes that lead to product failure. One such mistake is that the *customer input* is still missing in most new products. Hence, the method of customer questioning and the overall approach to customer interaction are important considerations in NPD. The objective of this chapter is to outline the strategies needed to effectively interact with customers and obtain necessary input from them for a NPD

> *Customer input and interaction is needed to develop a differentiated and unique new product.*

project. The process and techniques discussed in this chapter should be applicable to both tangible products and services.

16.2 Why Interact with Customers?

The first question that a product manager might ask is, "Why should we spend our time and resources on interacting with customers?" The answer to this question can be gleaned from the success stories of several innovation-vanguard firms such as 3M, Black and Decker, Rubbermaid, Bosch, Philips, and Sony, who rely primarily on customers for new product ideas and input (Deschamps and Nayak, 1995; McKenna, 1995). These examples and several empirical studies suggest that customer interaction in NPD can offer many benefits. Notable among them are:

- *Superior and differentiated new products:* Customer input and interaction is needed to develop a differentiated and unique new product. It is a key issue because today's customers are more sophisticated and demanding and search for superior value in a new product. For example, Gillette's innovation philosophy has been to create differentiated products that serve customers' needs uniquely. Thus, Gillette has kept tabs on its customers, closely noting their use patterns and preferences in grooming, oral care, and other day-to-day needs. Dell has also actively sought customer input for developing superior products, as evident from a recent comment of its CEO, Michael Dell: "we want to continue to be innovative and aggressive about seeking customer input and using it to develop future Dell products." Their latest innovation, a new corporate notebook, is the result of an active collaboration between Dell's customers and design engineers (Dell, 2003).
- *Reduced time-to-market:* Customer interaction may help shorten development cycle time, also known as "time-to-market" (see Chapter 12). The process of customer interaction may yield most up-to-date information about the customer preferences and tastes that are changing fast. This potentially reduces the need for design alteration and reworks in the later stages, because a firm can collect and process customer information for its NPD projects on a concurrent basis.

- *Reduced time-to-acceptance:* Customer interaction may help accelerate the market acceptance of a new product. This "time-to-acceptance" is a key success factor for many high-tech and complex new products (McKenna, 1995). One rationale for this assertion is that the interaction process may educate a customer about the specifications, attributes, and use of a new product, which in turn helps in building quick support for the innovation.
- *Long-term relationships:* Providing potential customers with the experience of participation in NPD process wins their loyalty and improves the customer-manufacturer relationship. While developing the Sunny Delight® fruit beverage, Procter & Gamble interacted with many customers. One customer, Sarah Clarke felt that P&G listened to what she had to say. So, she decided to buy the new product and also promote it to other users (Dignam, 2002).

16.3 How to Interact With the Customers?

Of interest next is the overall process of customer interaction. This entails issues such as, modes, overall style, and methods of interaction.

16.3.1 Modes of Customer Interaction

A product manager may use one or more of the following modes to interact with potential customers.

- *In-depth interviews:* Face-to-face in-depth interviews can be conducted to gather customer input on various aspects of the new products to be developed (see Chapter 14). The main objective of an interview is to translate the customers' definition of desired value into products or services. Therefore, a typical one-on-one interview probes a customer's whole situation to discover both general and detailed needs of the customers (Griffin and Hauser, 1993); that is, the focus should be on customer "problem-solving" because successful new products often emerge from a problem that was once unmet in the marketplace. Gillette is one company that has successfully used the situational interview technique. When developing its line of men's toiletries, Gillette researchers interviewed 70,000 men about what they liked in shaving creams and aftershaves. Also, many Gillette employees come to work unshaven and use shaving products in the company's on-site "Shaving Test Lab." The NPD staff then probes these employees' reactions and feedback via one-on-one interviews to draw out specific attributes, shortcomings, and advantages of each product concept. Gillette conducted thousands of such tests and interviews during the development of its Mach3® razor.

- *Focus groups and brainstorming:* To get input from a larger customer base, a firm may conduct focus groups or brainstorming sessions. The main advantage of both focus group and brainstorming is that the inherent group dynamics play a key role in generating useful information about the new products. Recently, Procter & Gamble conducted a number of focus groups to test its new Crest SpinBrush® toothbrush with an unusually large group of customers. All three modes of interaction—interview, focus group, and brainstorming—can be integrated into another mode of interaction, innovation retreat and summit, which is discussed next.

- *Innovation retreats and summits:* A firm may invite key customers to their innovation retreats and summits (see Chapter 17). Recently, a large banking firm organized a weekend retreat to identify new product opportunities. They invited executives from their client firms to attend the retreat and provide useful input on several innovation projects. Several brainstorming sessions were used to generate new product ideas. Customers also actively participated in one-on-one interviews, product demonstrations, and prototype testing during the retreat. In this regard, a manager enthusiastically remarked: "It was almost an afterthought to invite customers to our retreat. However, their participation yielded useful insight into new product opportunities, because they suggested a number of new product ideas and provided useful guidelines to the service delivery process."

- *Customers inducted into a NPD team:* Customers can join a cross-functional NPD team and provide input on various aspects of the development process. The presence of customers in a NPD team minimizes hidden knowledge, provides a better perspective for NPD decisions, and overcomes technological arrogance by developing greater empathy on the part of product development staff. Customers can also help reconcile the interfunctional conflicts by expressing their unique customer perspectives. Boeing, while developing the 777 aircraft, formed a NPD team consisting of engineers from three customer airlines and their own staffs. One such customer, British Airways, is reported to have suggested more than 100 changes to the design of the 777 aircraft and that most of those suggested changes were included in the final specifications of the aircraft (Betts, 1994).

- *Customer panels and groups:* A firm may ask selected customers to be part of a customer panel and occasionally provide input at various stages of the NPD process. Levi formed a panel of fashion-conscious young consumers in major European cities like Milan, Paris, and London, and asked them to comment on product use situations and latest trends and provide other input for its highly successful new product *Engineered Jeans* (Dignam, 2002). Similarly, P&G in the United Kingdom formed a "Community Corner" for new products, a customer club that meets through a Web site and discusses new product ideas. P&G obtained extensive customer input for its Sunny Delight® fruit beverage through this community corner.

- *Observation of customers:* A firm may obtain new product ideas and information by simply watching customers use a product. For example, Discover Card recently developed its award winning product *Discover 2GO®*, a credit card attached to a key chain that swivels in and out from a plastic key case for use and storage. The idea seems to have originated from observing customers using highly popular supermarket and drug store loyalty program cards attached to the key chains. Deschamps and Nayak (1995) provide several examples suggesting how many innovation-vanguard firms actively observe customers to obtain input for their innovation projects. While developing electric shavers, Philips routinely observes and documents how customers use the products. The power tool firm Bosch asks customers in stores for permission to visit their homes to watch them use the products.

Customers' needs and choices are often susceptible to a variety of influences, such as the number and features of alternatives and the timing of purchase. For example, customers may be less reliable in suggesting their future needs for new products in an interview or focus group situation (Simonson, 1993), whereas customer observation in a real purchase situation may better identify the needs and choices of customers. For this reason, Sony keeps realistic looking mock-ups on the shelves next to real products in their showroom in Tokyo's famous Ginza district. Sony has their NPD teams watch how customers manipulate and evaluate the mock-ups, as well as ask that the NPD team casually discuss new product features with customers.

In another case of customer observation, Johnson Controls, a manufacturer of automotive interiors, asked a group of customers to load large and bulky items into the trunk of their automobiles and critically observed and noted the use of trunk storage space. Based on their observations and other input, they developed a trunk-organizing system for the SUVs and minivans (Stevens, 1999). This technique of customer observation, sometime referred to as ethnography, can identify "unstated" or "unspoken" customer needs and detect the contradictions between what customers say and what actually they do.

A firm may obtain new product ideas and information by simply watching customers use a product.

- *Customer-manufacturer mixers:* Instead of the prolonged retreats or summits, a firm can occasionally organize informal gatherings and engage in dialogues with major customers concerning new products. Examples are occasional innovation lunches and dinners where employees and customers interact informally. An industrial firm that manufactures a variety of iron and steel products regularly invites steel fabricators, building products firms, boiler manufacturers, and similar other customers to lunch and discusses with them their needs, showing them design specifications of the products being developed and test prototypes.

- *Customer visits:* Product managers may visit their customers regularly to discuss new product opportunities. A large industrial firm that offers network and digital solutions has mandated that the managers must schedule at least one visit to a key business customer each month to discuss new product possibilities. A packaging firm, Signode Corporation, instructed its NPD team to visit all major customers to search for new product opportunities. After the completion of such visits, the team found a number of new product ideas, such as microwavable plastic products (Deschamps and Nayak, 1995). Recently, Rubbermaid sent 15 two-person teams to customers' homes to discuss and observe their home-storage practices. The group returned with 300 new product ideas in just three days (Stevens, 1999).

- *Internet-based interaction:* The Internet can also play a key role in customer interaction and allow a firm to better understand its customer needs (see Chapter 18). Recently, Polaroid used the Internet to obtain customer input for its highly innovative I-Zone® instant pocket camera, an ultraportable camera that takes miniature instant photos to be used to stick on children's backpacks, books, lockers, and so on. Polaroid created a Web site and requested that potential customers visit the Web site and assemble an ideal camera with their most preferred attributes. The outcome of this customer interaction activity was somewhat surprising for the R&D staff because the customers considered the product as "fun" and "cool" as opposed to the Polaroid's engineers who had envisaged the product to be more technologically advanced, trendy, and costly (Ozer, 2003). Likewise, BMW created a Web site called a Virtual Innovation Agency (VIA) to interact with customers. Car enthusiasts can join online discussions on the VIA Web site to share their innovation ideas with other users and BMW.

16.3.2 How to Listen to the Voice of Customers

To gain maximum benefits, product managers need to adopt an "outcome-based approach" to customer interaction. Under this approach, managers

> *Customers cannot tell a firm exactly what a product should look like because they are poor reporters of their own needs and behavior.*

would ask their customers to suggest new product benefits and outcomes they expect rather than focus on the ultimate solution or the make-up of a product (Ulwick, 2002). The main argument is that the customers cannot tell a firm exactly what a product should look like because they are poor reporters of their own needs and behavior. In contrast, Havener and Thorpe (1994) suggest that the customers can and do identify their problems but they usually can't offer solutions to their problems. Therefore, the task of a product manager is to translate the problem into a product that solves it.

Recently a multinational firm successfully applied this outcome-based strategy of customer interaction in the development of a cellular phone with camera. The following scenario characterizes the company's effort: a customer, Cathy, would like to have her digital camera with her at all times, but sometimes there are problems such as a depleted battery, or she leaves it at home by mistake.

- Cathy: *But I don't go anywhere without my cell phone; I have four kids and I am always taking pictures.*
- Outcome: A digital camera that she won't forget.
- Product: A digital camera built into a cell phone.

These comments of this customer prompted the firm to bundle her desired benefits of taking pictures and wireless communications in one product and then add another attribute of picture messaging and email capability. This was possible because the customer was asked to list the benefits she expected her cell phone to provide besides making phone calls, instead of having her comment on the ultimate design of the product. An emphasis on an outcome-based strategy of interaction results in innovative new products because such a strategy is more proficient in discovering customers' latent and unarticulated needs. An outcome-based strategy also stimulates customers to suggest ideas beyond their usual frame of mind. In contrast, the firms that adopt a solution-based interviewing approach may end up developing incremental innovations. For instance, if a firm asks its customers, what type of products they need? The customers may suggest incremental modifications to the existing products because they concentrate on existing solutions and make selections from a familiar product category; that is, the customers become presold on certain concepts and think of the existing products before answering the questions.

16.3.2 Customer Interaction as an Iterative Process

It is important that customers' needs are monitored throughout the course of the NPD, because they rarely remain completely static. Moreover, customers' voices are diverse and these diverse voices must be considered, reconciled, and balanced to develop a successful product. Another common criticism is that the customers cannot clearly articulate their require-

> *An iterative problem-solving approach to interaction is needed because it provides the opportunity to challenge, question, and clarify customer input and requirements until they make sense.*

ments and generally ask for things that are unprofitable, such as lower prices and free services. Consequently, an iterative problem-solving approach to interaction is needed because it provides the opportunity to challenge, question, and clarify customer input and requirements until they make sense. An iterative approach may also be needed to establish the relative importance of customer information, which may assist in prioritizing the customer needs.

Let's look at the technique of this iterative interaction in detail, using a liquid crystal display (LCD) computer monitor as an example. Customers' desire to free up desk space actually triggered the innovation process for the LCD monitor in a major electronics firm. The firm obtained input from the same group of customers repeatedly. During the interaction process, the customers insisted on more and more desk space, and consequently the product became slimmer. Ultimately, the slim monitor ended up with a removable base and wall-mount capability. After the space-saving feature, the firm focused on superior image quality and picture resolution features that were ranked second in importance by the customers. Finally, they considered the other less important attributes, such as horizontal/vertical viewing angle and energy efficiency. In the end, the iterative process of customer interaction created a highly innovative and successful product.

16.4 Stages of Customer Interaction

In which NPD stages should a manager interact with the customers? Overall, customer interaction may occur at all the stages of NPD, although the intensity of interaction may vary across various stages. Seemingly, customer input in the fuzzy front-end stages (see Chapter 6) of idea generation, screening, and concept development is more critical and useful than in the other later stages. For example, Philips, while developing an online children's toy in Europe, inter-acted with customers more intensely during the fuzzy front-end stages. Philips sent a team of designers and psychologists in mobile vans to various European countries to interact with both adults and children for their proposed new products. First, they hosted a series of dialogues with the selected group of people intensively to help brainstorm ideas for the new products. After gener-ating a number of product ideas, they screened them with the help of those potential customers and finally selected one new online interactive product for children. Later, the team of researchers went back to the potential customers and tested the new product concept on the same children (McKenna, 1995). In the same vein, Boeing emphasized the need for customer interaction early in the process while developing its highly successful 777 aircraft as evidenced by the comments of Boeing's manager, Alan Mulally: "Not that we did not listen to our customers in the past, but the biggest lesson we learnt was that we often listened to them late in a program. Now (for the Boeing 777), we are listening to them much earlier" (Betts, 1994).

Although managers need to interact intensely with customers earlier in the development process, they should make an effort to involve them throughout the process because customers can provide valuable input at other key stages too. Table 16.1 presents an exhaustive list of activities that a customer may be able to perform at some of the key stages of NPD process. The detail given in this table may be used as a checklist of the customer interaction activities for most innovation projects.

16.5 Selecting Customers for Interaction

What types of customers should be se-lected for interaction? There are three criteria that should be considered for customer selection. First, a firm may ob-tain input from the customers with whom they have a *close relationship* because confi-dentiality can be a major issue, especially for business-to-business products and ser-

> *A firm may obtain input from the customers with whom they have a close relationship because confidentiality can be a major issue, especially for business-to-business products and services.*

vices. A product manager can trust close customers to keep sensitive information confidential. A close customer may also display his/her commitment in con-ducting NPD activities efficiently. For instance, while developing the 777 air-craft, Boeing initially obtained input from eight different airlines from North

TABLE 16.1 CUSTOMER ACTIVITIES AT KEY STAGES OF THE DEVELOPMENT PROCESS.

Development Stages	Activities Performed by the Customers
Idea generation	Describe needs and wants; suggest desired features, benefits, attributes and preferences via brainstorming sessions; identify problems not solved by existing products; evaluate existing products by suggesting likes and dislikes; identify gaps in the market; provide a wish list (product requirements).
Idea screening and concept development	Rate the purchase intent of all the product concepts; critically react to the concepts by analyzing how they would meet customers' needs; evaluate the preliminary models, sketches, and mock-ups to crystallize the concepts; compare the concepts with competitors' offerings; suggest new product adoption criteria.
Product development	May join a NPD team to review and jointly develop the overall design and configurations; suggest improvements by identifying a product's weak/fail points; compare their wish lists with the proposed design of the product.
Product testing	Test the working prototypes by critiquing their functionality, reliability and performance; suggest final improvements and design changes; observe and participate in mock product use situation and suggest improvements; finally, rate the customers' overall acceptance of the product.
Test marketing	Provide feedback on various aspects of the marketing strategies, such as pricing, distribution, and so on, and suggest desired improvements; Give input to sharpen sales arguments and advertising themes; examine the overall salability of the new product.
Product launch	Adopt the product as a trial; provide feedback about the performance of the product along with desired improvements; provide word-of-mouth communications to other potential users; check instructions in the product manuals; refine the packaging; participate in beta tests; that is, final testing before shipment of the products.

America, Europe, and the Asia-Pacific region, but actively interacted only with its close customers such as United Airlines, British Airways, and All Nippon Airlines (Betts, 1994).

Second, customers themselves can initiate an innovation by (1) informally discussing ideas with the managers, (2) complaining about existing products, (3) discussing the new product ideas with the sales staff, and (4) providing other unsolicited suggestions. For example, a major credit card company carefully examines all the conversations its phone agents have with the customers and uses the results to develop new product ideas. A well-known firm recently introduced a highly innovative hands-free battery-operated lawnmower, which can mow a small flat lawn robotically. The firm got the idea when an elderly customer complained about how strenuous it was to mow a lawn even with a self-propelled mower and wished for a machine that would do the job automatically but would cost much less than a riding mower. In general, customers that initiate innovations tend to be knowledgeable and demanding and can articulate their needs clearly.

Third, lead users are a major source of innovative and profitable new product opportunities and thus meet a key selection criterion for interaction (von Hippel, 1986). The lead user concept is based on the assumptions that (1) the lead users have real-world experience with the needs that future profitable products must serve and with attributes they must contain, and (2) they expect to benefit substantially by obtaining a solution to their needs. Since the lead users stand to benefit substantially from the innovations, they will be highly motivated to participate in the interaction process. However, one major concern in lead user interaction can be noted. Because they are not average users, lead users may suggest ideas for highly specialized products that may have only limited appeal. To answer this concern, several case studies have proposed a systematic process for searching and involving lead users in NPD (e.g., von Hippel, Thomke, and Sonnack 1999; Urban and von Hippel, 1988). One key step of that process involves testing whether average customers in a marketplace find the product or service concept developed by lead users to be attractive.

A firm may consider multiple characteristics for selecting customers. For example, a lead user, with whom a firm has a close relationship, may initiate the innovations. Customers with multiple characteristics could be the best partners for interaction.

16.6 Problems in Customer Interaction

Despite many advantages there are problems and impediments that might occur during the customer interaction process. These impediments include:

- *Overcustomization of a new product:* Listening to customers too closely may create a risk of overcustomizing new products. To avoid this risk, the emerging trends in the marketplace as a whole need to be weighed against individual customer suggestions. A customer's positive reactions to a product concept should not be construed as an intention to use or buy that product because no money is changing hands; thus, no real commitment is necessary. Hence, one should probe customers' initial positive reactions to the product concepts through further market studies.

- *Confidentiality:* Customers, through the course of interaction, might get access to certain confidential information and proprietary skills. There is the potential that these customers might reveal the information intentionally or unintentionally to competitors. An interaction program requires mutual trust and open, collaborative relationships, as well as standards for capturing and exchanging information.

- *Identification of customers:* Locating appropriate customers for interaction is another major problem because an intimate knowledge of the market and customer contacts is necessary. A firm also needs to consider all different types of customers, end users, and even customers' customers for interaction, as illustrated in the following example. The medical products division of Philips Electronics had assumed that its only customers were doctors in hospitals. Managers later realized that services were also being provided in nontraditional environments, such as in outpatient clinics, in homes, and even on the streets for homeless people. Based on the feedback of physicians in such nonhospital environments, Philips came up with a new product, a stethoscope with improved acoustics to filter out voices, traffic, and other background noises (Tucker, 2003).

- *Lack of customer cooperation:* Customers may be disinclined to cooperate because of the conflicting objectives and intents of managers versus customers. Managers typically have the objective of developing a product that will yield maximum profit, whereas customers have the objective of developing a product that will serve their needs. Both monetary and nonmonetary incentives may be useful to get full customer cooperation. Customers may also cooperate in order to exchange feedback with other customers and remain on the cutting edge of new applications and innovations.

The above problems may be resolved by selecting customers with whom the company has a close relationship. These problems may also be resolved by entrusting the task of customer selection to the product champions because product champions are often well connected in the industry and may have forged relationships with customers already. By virtue of their position and

---

Customers. through the course of interaction, might get access to certain confidential information and proprietary skills.

connections in the industry, product champion may be able to more easily identify key customers and get appropriate assistance from them.

16.7 Summary

NPD success hinges on a firm's ability to decipher the needs of a demanding, fickle, and volatile marketplace and to respond with superior and differentiated offerings. Firms should, therefore, adopt the axiom that says "To be successful, firms should know their customers better than their customers know themselves." As a corollary to this axiom, customer interaction should become a key element in a firm's innovation activity. This chapter has proposed several customer interaction strategies in order to outline a course of action that managers can apply in their quest for successful innovations.

References

Betts, P., "The Century's Last Take-off" *The Financial Times*, March 1: 18 (March 1994).

Cooper, R. G., "The Invisible Success Factors in Product Innovation," *Journal of Product Innovation Management* 16(2): 115–133 (1999).

Dell, M. "Collaboration Equals Innovation," *Information Week*, January 27: 24–26 (January 2003).

Deschamps, J. P. and Nayak, P. R., *Product Juggernauts*, Harvard Business School Press, Boston (1995).

Dignam, C., "Prosumer Power," *Marketing*, March 14: 24–25 (2002).

Griffin, A. and Hauser J. R. "The Voice of Customer," *Marketing Science*, 12(1): 1–27 (1993).

Havener, C. and Thorpe, M., "Customers Can Tell You What They Want." *Management Review*, 83(12): 42–45 (1994).

McKenna, R., "Real-Time Marketing." *Harvard Business Review*, 87–95 (July–August 1995).

Ozer, M., "Using the Internet in New Product Development," *Research Technology Management*, 10–16 (January–February 2003).

Simonson, I., "Get Closer to Your Customers by Understanding How They Make Choices," *California Management Review*, 68–84 (Summer 1993).

Stevens, T., "Lights, Camera, Innovation," *Industry Week*, July 19: 32–38 (1999).

Tucker, R. B., "Seven Strategies for Generating Ideas," *The Futurist*, 37(2): 20–25 (2003).

Ulwick, A. W., "Turn Customer Input into Innovation," *Harvard Business Review*, 91–97 (January 2002).

Urban, G. and von Hippel, E., 'Lead User Analyses for the Development of New Industrial Products', *Management Science*, 5: 569–582 (1988).

von Hippel, E., "Lead Users: A Source of Novel Product Concepts," *Management Science*, 32: 791–805 (July 1986).

von Hippel, E, Thomke, S., and Sonnack, M., "Creating Breakthroughs at 3M." *Harvard Business Review*, 3–9 (September–October 1999).

Dr. Intekhab (Ian) Alam is Assistant Professor of Marketing at the Jones School of Business, State University of New York (SUNY) at Geneseo, New York. He received his Ph.D. from the University of Southern Queensland in Australia and a Master of Business (Marketing) degree from the Queensland University of Technology in Australia. Dr. Alam conducts research in the area of new product development. His research has been published in the *Journal of the Academy of Marketing Science, Journal of Services Marketing, Journal of Product Innovation Management, Journal of Marketing Management* and *Journal of International Marketing and Exporting*. He also has extensive consulting experience in the areas of new product development.

CHAPTER SEVENTEEN

GETTING LIGHTNING TO STRIKE: IDEATION AND CONCEPT GENERATION

Christopher W. Miller

It is about thinking outside of the box, within a box''

RICH NOTARGIACOMO, THE EASTMAN KODAK COMPANY

17.1 Introduction

Effective new product ideation is intensely focused. Ideation or "brainstorming" within NPD uses data, and the expertise and experience of key people (company and customer) to create a nexus, a pressure point in the product development cycle. It is more structured, more aggressive, and more intellectually demanding than most ideation activities. A well-populated product concept portfolio is the reward for an aggressive search for targeted new ideas. A secondary goal of ideation is to attract the resources and excitement necessary to drive that portfolio through the product development process.

"Ideation and Concept Creation" will take you through a step-by-step process for moving to a roughly screened set of new concepts. The steps are:

1. Chartering for ideation
2. Team formation, the right people to build the right ideas
3. The ideation session (ideation and initial concept building)
4. Screening, developmental thinking, and final concepts

This chapter will take the classic approach of an innovation effort sponsored by a company in a multiday format with a diverse team. The goal is to create the ideal environment for mental lightning to strike.

17.2 Chartering for Ideation: The Secret of Focus

We were able to pull the team together behind a common exciting direction. The new ideas that emerged were critical to our future success.

LINDA STEGEMAN, LUCENT TECHNOLOGIES

Ideas are infinite but our tolerance for ideation is not. Ideation is like climbing a tree; you always start at the bottom. Most of us never get past the lower branches, and that low-hanging fruit we find starts to become very familiar. There is a blurry line between low-hanging fruit and the fruit that is lying overripe on the ground. The odds are good that if you bring together the same team against the same task year after year, you will see the same idea set. Spending time on ideation "focus" is where the team will have the greatest opportunity to overcome repetition. Reconfirm your NPD team's charter and, if possible, narrow your scope to a search for ideas to a specific area that you have determined to be promising or strategically interesting (see Chapter 2). To quote Barbara Goss of Armstrong World Industries, "We had reviewed our data to the point of burnout. Then came the breakthrough. It is so obvious—the answer came from creatively framing the questions."

In the ideation charter the team should specify the market segment, unmet needs, and specific technologies that will drive ideation. Armed with these data nuggets, you can target specific high-probability branches of your idea tree. You should aim to do the following:

- Have focused project goals. Did you discover directions or opportunities in your earlier research that would suggest a more refined targeting of the charter? (Example, the NPD Charter might be targeted at *health-care software*, the ideation charter—*operating-room software*.)
- State the product development challenge as a "problem-solving task." (Example: develop an exciting set of next generation patient care software tools for the "new" operating room nurse.) Both the market segment and the technical pallet are alluded to in the few directive words of the task.
- Establish 3–5 key criteria to aid the team during the ideation process (Example: compelling need, platformable, feasibility, meaningful differentiation,

size of opportunity). These will be used during the screening process by the core team in Stage Four (see Chapter 29).

- Focus on a limited data set from previous research that will drive and focus the ideation. Limit to 10–12 compelling needs and 10–12 driving technologies.

You will create hundreds of ideas. The challenge in Stage One is to be sure that these ideas are properly targeted for the customer you seek to serve and the capability your company would like to use or develop.

17.3 Team Formation

I was surprised at how badly we needed the help of outsiders to get our ideas.

JONI SAHHAR, THE EASTMAN KODAK COMPANY

When you start your focused ideation process, you should be able to look around the room and see:

- Decision makers who own the resources needed to move the charter forward
- Implementers who can advance the ideas through to market (R&D, Marketing, Sales, Finance, Legal and Regulatory, Operations)
- Experts, guests who represent the value chain as well as key technologies
- Diversity (targeted and creative customer representation, noncompetitive product development professionals, experienced idea generators)

A frequent dissatisfaction with the ideation process is the lack of diversity in ideas. This can best be overcome by bringing in external expertise and customer idea generators. It is impossible to predict where the next ingenious idea will come from, but you increase the odds of success when you narrow your focus and broaden your team to include previously uninvolved parts of your value chain:

- There was genuine pleasure in the room as the WaterPik® team saw it's director of engineering lend his substantial expertise to help 11-year-old Noah as they designed his perfect, "Slam Dunk," showerhead. Result of the ideation–two new platform launches: the Down Pour® and the Misting Massage® shower head product lines (Figure 17.1).

TABLE 17.1 HOW MANY PEOPLE SHOULD BE AT THE INNOVATION SESSION?

Ideators: Facilitators	One-Day Yield: Idea Yield Beginning Concepts	Two-Day Yield	Three-Day Yield
8 ideators: 2 facilitators	200 ideas yield 30 beginning concepts	400 ideas yield 60 beginning concepts	600 ideas yield 90 beginning concepts
16:3	400:60	600:90	800:120
24:4	600:90	800:120	1000:140
30:5	800:120	1000:140	1200:160

(Based on unpublished records of over 200 ideation sessions over a 15-year period.)

How long should it last? Most teams pull 10–20 concepts into their portfolio. The odds favor those who can be more selective. The data shows that the 1200th idea is as likely to generate a winning concept as the first.

FIGURE 17.1 THE WATERPIK® SHOWERHEAD PORTFOLIO AFTER DEVELOPMENTAL THINKING AND CONCEPT WRITING. THE NEXT STEP FOR WATERPIK® WAS FOCUS GROUP RESEARCH.

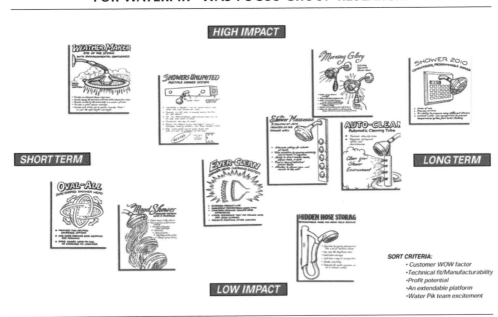

- It was Cindy Daub, a therapist and parking garage customer, who had the beginning idea for the patented precast concrete Tilt-T® from High Concrete Structures leading to the nearly 20 percent reduction in construction costs.
- The computer company NPD team went to Joshua's college dorm room to test the first mock-up of a product concept he had helped develop in their ideation session a few months before. The first product was launched in fall of 2003.

Customers are strong idea generators. Mike Johnson, of the University of Michigan, asks us to treat customers "as fellow engineers who are unencumbered by organizational and technology constraints." There is substantial evidence that "ordinary" customers are better idea generators on the scales of originality and user value than and equal on ease-of-implementation to either lead users or experts (Johnson, 2002; Kristensson, Gustafsson, & Archer, 2004).

After identifying unmet needs through ethnographic field work (see Chapter 15), Western Union wanted to retain a closeness to the customer during their

FIGURE 17.2 CUSTOMERS AND PROFESSIONALS CAN WORK SIDE BY SIDE IN AN IDEATION SESSION.

ideation and concept generation process. Five local consumers who represented the target demographic were invited into the innovation process. They were met at their homes and given short training sessions on what to expect, how to generate ideas, and how to write concepts. During the ideation session with a dozen company experts, each consumer was paired with a core team member to ensure that if concerns or questions did occur the consumers would be immediately supported in bringing their ideas forward. After concept screening, these same consumers were invited to return and describe their needs and the concepts they had helped develop to the president and his staff (Woodland, 2002).

17.4 The Ideation Session

Don't wait for lightning to strike. Get out the lightning rods!

BILL ROBSON, INNOVATION FOCUS, INC.

For every hour in ideation, you should have spent 10–100 hours in preparation. Most of the folklore on NPD is about this glamorous "moment" when the light bulb goes on. However, the best ideas bounce like ping-pong balls, they generally don't flash on like lights. Creativity can be a complex, exceedingly personal, and fragile process. Those who seek to control the power of creative thinking also can destroy it. No matter how long the list of ideas, or from how many sources you may have drawn insight, ideation will be sterile without that momentary spark of recognized genius (Prince, 1970; Osborn, 1942). In order to facilitate the ideation session, three different types of exercises are utilized: creativity, analytic, and experiential.

17.4.1 Creativity Exercises

Creativity exercises at the heart of ideation come in the form of metaphor building or irrelevant thinking followed by a forced connection to the task. For example, a Hershey's team was asked by their facilitator to go on an imaginary vacation. One subteam went on a ski vacation to the Alps and brought back a travel poster as instructed. The travel poster had snow-covered mountains with "shoosh" marks curving down the mountain side. The facilitator asked the full team to imagine what kind of candy that made them think of. One idea was "a white kiss with a chocolate stripe, a shoosh mark, curving down the side." This idea later became the Hershey's Hugs®.

Metaphor building exercises create a deviation from the straightforward listing and idea building within ideation. The initial ideas that emerge following an exercise may be impossible or far-fetched but if conceptualized can yield surprising results. Examples of exercises from among hundreds of possibilities include:

- If your technology were an animal what kind of animal would it be? What would it want to do in the market?
- Randomly open a newspaper. Look for a product idea in the middle of the page.
- List your favorite life experiences. Take the time to write about each. Invent ways to make the product like these experiences.

Vini Bansal, Head of Package Design at The Thomas J. Lipton Company was working with a team on new ways to deliver Wishbone® salad dressing to warehouse stores. His facilitator invited him to walk on an imaginary beach and find objects. A large list of objects was created. Each participant selected one object to build ideas around. Vini chose the clam shell, which eventually became the "clam-pack" case, which yielded two patents.

17.4.2 Analytic Exercises

Analytic exercises can also drive new thinking. A simple morphological analysis comparing the top customer needs from your charts (y-axis) by key technologies (x-axis) can provide an ideation road map. Build the morphology, and examine each block for logical or fantastic connections.

17.4.3 Experiential Exercises

Experiential exercises can drive creative thoughts from surprising sources. Over lunch, a group of heavy equipment manufacturers were taken on a tour of a printing plant; in another instance they examined a new fire truck for possible features. Experiential exercises generated about 20 percent of the total volume for the equipment manufacturer. British Air developed its *Business First* service based on the principles observed in a Bentley car. A packaged goods company had its ideation team start with a three-hour ethnographic exercise, going into the homes of real consumers, returning to the ideation session, and building collages about their experiences. Postsession feedback from the ideation team suggested that the resulting concepts were more "connected" to real market needs than ideation alone would have been.

After every exercise, creative, analytic, or experiential, there is an opportunity to list the ideas that have emerged. Select choices from the list and build initial product concepts.

TABLE 17.2 MORPHOLOGICAL ANALYSIS ON POTATO CHIP TRENDS:

1. Select nuggets.
2. Build the matrix.
3. Create ideas at the intersections.

| | Technology Nuggets | | |
	No-Fat and Cholesterol-Reducing Fat Substitutes	There Are 500 Varieties of Potatoes	Nitrogen Flushing Will Extend Shelf Life
Market Nugget			
Older people like salt, sour and hot	"Hot 'n' Sour low-fat chips	?	?
Ethinicisms sell • Amerimex • Yankee Chinese	?	?	?
Supermarkets want new product news, not new brands	?	?	?

FIGURE 17.3 IDEATION SESSION. IT IS IMPORTANT TO FIND A LARGE COMFORTABLE AND CONVENIENT LOCATION.

Ideation is a messy process that is best done with lots of space. A rule of thumb is to provide 80–100 square feet per participant. For a group of 24, have at least 2400 square feet set aside. Seek a 40 x 40 flexible meeting space, and divide the remainder of the space among small comfortable rooms or areas that can be used as breakout areas. Pay attention to lighting (natural if possible), ventilation (in your control), and having a large variety of foods and beverages available continuously. A local hotel or country club can usually meet these needs; however, there are several other creative options that companies have utilized. Black & Decker used an entire floor of a building that was not in use. Johnson Controls used their design lab in California. The Children's Museum of Indianapolis worked in the heart of the museum itself. Crystal Flash Energy worked in their own meeting rooms surrounded and energized by the hubbub of daily business. No matter where it is, your location should offer a rich and stimulating sensory mix, but remain free of distractions from the task at hand.

The structure of a successful innovation cycle is scripted to the minute by highly trained facilitators who are secure enough and experienced enough to take advantage of exciting developments that redirect the process. Many approaches work, but here is a process that has proven effective over three decades and hundreds of organization and product types:

17.4.4 The Ideation Schedule

Day 1 The first day is about gaining maximum breadth. It begins with aggressive broad scale idea generation building on what has been learned in the prior stages. This process may include:

- Creativity, analytic, and experiential exercises and activities involving all participants
- Expert and customer "gold fish bowls" focus groups imbedded in ideation (gold fish bowls are short breaks where the full ideation team steps back and listens to a select group discuss the underlying needs or in some cases technical capabilities.)
- Structured, high-speed facilitation of idea lists
- Targeted small groups focused on subtasks and building of beginning concepts

FIGURE 17.4 THE CLASSIC IDEATION AND CONCEPT GENERATION PROCESS.

	Day 1	Day 2	NPD core team -- Day 3
Morning	Introductions Ideation/broad	Targeted Ideation Beginning concept building	Draft Portfolio Final concept development
Afternoon	Targeted Ideation Beginning concept building	Final concept building Advisory vote, full team	Project Planning
Evening	Teambuilding	Evaluate by criteria— core team only	

This process can last from a few hours to a week. It is best when there is "hang time," a sleep cycle, within ideation and within selection and concept development this encourages creativity, integration and clarity.

Day 2 The second day is about being sure that all the bases are covered.
- Targeted break-out groups focused on specific needs or technologies
- Targeted break-out groups chasing wisps and problem solving for the unsolvable
- Initial screening through voting
- Outside guests, customer, and expert feedback
- Core team sort of beginning concepts by criteria from the charter

Day 3 The third day is a review of the screening results and concept building. A portfolio of 10–20 beginning concept clusters is selected.
- Review the results of the sort by criteria.
- Select and cluster beginning concepts for the portfolio.
- The clusters are refined into formal "concepts."
- A first cut "bubble chart" can give the team a view of the suspected portfolio value.
- Portfolio-driven action plan.

Ideation does not have to end at 5:00 P.M. on session days. Teams are likely to go off to dinner anyway, so make it a part of the ideation process. One food products team got a bus and went to five restaurants, sampling appetizers at each one. Another company took their team to a Phillies baseball game. Although it is fun to keep the ideas happening in all locations, here are some guidelines so that you don't burn out your idea generators early on in the process:

- Idea generators need rest.
- Idea generators may need time to catch up with their work.
- Push for activities that allow fluidity of social interaction.

It is extremely important to document every idea. Nothing should be lost. One Fortune 500 Company was able to review ideation data back 12 years and found a portfolio of valid concepts that at the time of creation were deemed impractical.

Use a structured facilitated innovation process. There are many strong processes (VanGundy, 1987; Matamore, 1994; Miller, 1999). Most of these are generic creative problem-solving techniques that can be easily adapted to building product concepts. Computer-assisted and Web-based techniques have been emerging for 20 years and have yet to be proven except when a team cannot be co-located for the period of the innovation session (Kahn, Miller, & Benson, 2001). The primary challenge is that programmed processes are predetermined

TABLE 17.3 IDEATION RULES OF THE ROAD.

For Ideation Management	For Creativity
Use a note pad to collect ideas and connections that could be lost.	Ideas are infinite, there is always more than one right answer.
Headline your comments so they can be captured by the facilitator, for example, What If?	Stay focused on the objective; no matter how narrow; between any two ideas there is another idea.
Be open to the ideas of others, build raw ideas into better ideas.	All ideas are connected; play with metaphors and seeming irrelevance.
Turn questions and concerns into ideas. "That would really cost" could be stated, "How do we get the cost down?"	Only those who attempt the absurd will achieve the impossible.
Time share with others, get all points of view on the table.	"Pain plus time equals humor"; don't be afraid of your past mistakes—laugh at yourself.
You can do anything but you can't do everything. Do not reject ideas, select the ones appropriate for you at this time.	Risk taking and resistance create positive balance but it takes a lot of risk takers to pull along one well-meaning voice of reason.
Be playful and physically active; the mind and the body move together.	Learning, creativity, and humor use the same mental processes of connection making.
Avoid interruptions; clear your schedule and turn off the cell phones.	Creativity takes practice and an intense desire to be good at it.

There is no such thing as a "good" idea. Ideas are pretty ugly at birth and are doomed to an early death without help. Ideas are seeds that may grow and lead you to other ideas. Never look for the big idea, only look for the next idea.

and less flexible than face-to-face facilitated processes. Videoconferencing suffers from debilitating logistics, putting the remote location at a constant disadvantage in the meeting flow. Technology, if aggressively facilitated, can make otherwise impossible groups of people possible. Experience, however, suggests that technology too often invades group intimacy and dilutes the excitement associated with ideation. Building commitment to ideas is associated with building commitment to one's fellow ideator. Commitment to action is as important as the idea itself.

17.5 Concept Screening and Developmental Thinking

I fear that I am looking at baking soda in the refrigerator in my concept set and might fail to see it.

DENNIS ESHELMAN, VICE PRESIDENT MARKETING, HERSHEY FOODS

Concept screening within the innovation session is about nurturing beginning concepts. A gardener must cull two of every three plants to adequately nurture the remainder. Some are rejects and some are defective, others don't fit your task or your team though the concept is good and valid. On a rare occasion an idea will emerge that is stronger than the task and may require a redirection of your previous thinking.

Screening should be dynamic, have distinct selection stages, and not be dependent on a single static review or pass. Here is an example of such a process:

1. *Advisory vote:* The full ideation team participates in an advisory vote at the end of all concept building. If there are 100 concepts, each individual has 10 votes. About one-third of your beginning concepts will get multiple votes and rise to the top, newer thinking generally falls second and may need special attention, and a third will get no votes and drop away.
2. *Sort:* The core team evaluates all concepts using the 3–5 unweighted rough criteria established specifically for this purpose in the ideation charter. Screening by criteria ferrets out key concepts and allows the core team important study time to carefully review all concepts. The results are tabulated and fed into the portfolio development discussion.
3. *Portfolio:* Discussion, development, and clustering ensures a set of beginning concepts that challenge the task from several angles. Be informed by, but do not allow yourself to be driven by, the tyranny of the numbers emerging from the sort. Seek the best possible solutions to the customer's problems. Match the solutions up with your organization's ability and interests. Beginning concepts may be clustered into like product sets. A portfolio should have short- and long-term opportunities with a variety of risk assessment. The core team derives the portfolio based on a discussion, balancing the objectives of the charter with the discoveries made in the ideation.

Following the creation of your draft portfolio, the beginning concepts and clusters can be drafted into final concepts. What constitutes a concept varies dramatically from one organization to the next. A concept should be enough of a statement to drive the idea into the next stage—formal development. Frequently the next step will be developmental thinking by the team focused narrowly on improving this idea. This developmental work is done with consumers, with a technical team or both. Hershey Foods took several leading concepts coming out of a baking cocoa ideation to consumers for developmental work with a group of frequent bakers. The question was not which of these concepts should move forward; rather the question was, "What else could these concepts be and how would you describe them?" One concept, a spray-on powder for

FIGURE 17.5 EARLY-STAGE CONCEPT PORTFOLIO. CONCEPTS HAVE BEEN ROUGHLY LAID OUT WITH RESPECT TO ONE ANOTHER. SOME CONCEPTS HAVE BEEN CLUSTERED WITH LIKE CONCEPTS.

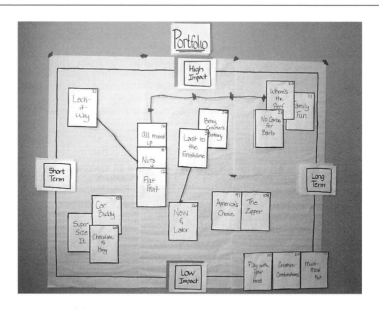

cake decoration, was changed by consumers to a "sprinkle-on," reducing the time-to-market from three years to six months. Developmental work can proceed immediately after portfolio construction.

17.6 Summary

I've been in advertising and marketing for about thirty years and if somebody had told me that two hundred beginning concepts could be generated, screened, and refined by consumers, prioritized by feasibility and business potential and distilled to about ten finished winning concepts in four days, I would have thought that there's a better chance the Jack of Spades would jump out of the deck and spit cider in my ear. (Guys & Dolls)

AL CARLSON, FORMER BRAND MANAGER THOMAS J. LIPTON COMPANY

Ideation and concept creation is an opportunity to build more than just the portfolio of concepts necessary to fill your product pipeline. Ideation is a time to build the customer-centric innovation-friendly culture necessary to drive your product ideas through to market. Throughout the NPD process, you will need to call on adherence to the voice of the customer and a willingness to invent new solutions to make your product concept a market reality. CUNA Mutual and National Liberty Corporation had been working jointly to get products to market with little success for four years. In frustration, the teams were sent into the desert for two weeks only to return with a clearer understanding of why they did not want to work together. Finally, Carol Myers, Vice President of Marketing at National Liberty and her CUNA Mutual partner, Janice Schlimgen, agreed to throw all ideas out and start from scratch. Starting with basic consumer needs and basic capabilities of the two corporations they were able to create a new untainted set of products. The first of those, "Acorn" got to market through the Veterans Life brand within three months. The team went on to launch a large variety of products. Janice and Carol agree that the joint ideation built the "team" commitment necessary to gain this shared accomplishment.

Approaching ideation with an attitude of "rigorous openness" allows you to include a variety of knowledge sources and people. The rigor will provide a focus, structured creativity and screening. The openness is not one of passive acceptance of any idea but rather an aggressive openness and excitement about where any idea might lead. Lightening strikes those who stand exposed and in the open.

References

Johnson, "Using Innovation To Create A Competitive Service Advantage," Rochester Institute of Technology Conference, 2002.

Kahn, K. B., Miller, C. W., and Benson, M. K., "Face-to-face Versus Online Concept Generation," *Visions*, 25(3): 13–14 (July 2001).

Kristensson, P., Gustafsson, A., and Archer, T., "Harnessing the Creative Potential Among Users," *Journal of Product Innovation Management*, 21: 4–14 (January 2004).

Mattimore, B., *99% Inspiration; Tips, Tales & Techniques for Liberating Your Business Creativity*, New York: Amacom, 1994.

Miller, C. W., *A Workbook for Innovation: Developing New Product Concepts*. Harrisburg, PA: The Pennsylvania Chamber of Business and Industry Educational Forum, 1999.

Osborn, A., *How to Think Up*. New York: McGraw Hill, 1942.

Prince, M., *The Practice of Creativity*. New York: Macmillan Publishing Company, 1970.

VanGundy, A. B., *Techniques of Structured Problem Solving*. New York: Van Nostrand Reinhold Company, 1987.

Woodland, C. L., "First Hand Experience or Second-Hand Information." *Quirk's Marketing Research Review*. (March 2002).

Christopher W. Miller, Ph.D., Founded Innovation Focus, Inc. (IF) in the late 1980s. Innovation Focus is an internationally recognized idea development firm, specializing in the beginning stages of new product development. For over 30 years, he has studied group dynamics and creative problem solving in product development. Prior to forming IF, he had the opportunity to work with two major corporations, Phillips Electronics and White Consolidated Industries. Today, Chris and his firm assist many of the Fortune 100 corporations to connect real market needs to their current and emerging technologies in search of new product and service ideas.

Chris has authored numerous articles and books on the topic of new product development including, Chapter 2 in the *2002 PDMA Toolbook*, "Hunting for Hunting Grounds: Forecasting the Fuzzy Front End." In 2002, Chris was named Entrepreneur of the Year by Ernst & Young. He also received the Ruth Waxman award for outstanding community service from the volunteers for Medical Engineering.

He was proud to serve as president for the Product Development and Management Association in 2004.

CHAPTER EIGHTEEN

QUANTITATIVE MARKET RESEARCH

Brian D. Ottum, Ph.D.

18.1 Introduction

The objective of the chapter is to give the practitioner an overview of some of the most useful quantitative market research tools for the initial stages of NPD. The quantitative market research tools discussed in this chapter are all a variation on the traditional survey in which customers give their numerical responses to carefully written questions. This chapter complements Chapters 14 and 15, since both qualitative and quantitative tools play a critical role in early NPD. However, qualitative and quantitative market research are quite different, each having its own strengths and weaknesses, as shown in Table 18.1.

18.2 The Quantitative Market Research Process

The four key steps in conducting any quantitative survey are (1) writing the survey questionnaire, (2) collecting the data, (3) analyzing the results, and (4) reporting. The most critical step is the first one. It takes training and experience to write a survey that is clear, unbiased, precise, and of appropriate length and difficulty. For example, a survey that asks "how much are you willing to pay for this new widget?" is undoubtedly going to get upwardly biased answers. On

TABLE 18.1 TWO DIFFERENT TYPES OF MARKET RESEARCH.

Qualitative Research	Quantitative Research
Words and images	Numbers
"Soft" data	"Hard" data
More exploratory	More confirmatory
Great for understanding unmet needs	Great for optimizing the new product's appeal
Analyzed by looking for themes and deeper meaning	Analyzed using statistics

the other hand, an experienced market researcher will use one of several 'indirect' techniques that have been shown to be much more accurate in measuring value (one of which is conjoint analysis, covered later in this chapter). A quantitative study cannot recover from a poorly written survey.

There are several ways of collecting the data. The lowest-cost, but most problematic, is the mailed survey. The biggest problem with using the mail is the very low response rate (1–5 percent is common). Do you really want to base your new prod-

> *Each data collection method has its own strengths and weaknesses.*

uct decisions on the tiny minority of unusual customers who took the time to fill out the survey? They probably aren't representative of the entire customer market. A second problem with mail is a lack of control. You really don't know who filled out that survey. For these reasons, mailed surveys are declining in usage.

In-person intercept data collection has declined in usage, but remains a good method for certain companies. Recruiting costs are low because the data collection is done where the respondents are located (they are "intercepted"). For many consumer markets, this is in the shopping mall. For business-to-business markets, this is at the conference, trade show, or meeting. If a company's customers are present in good numbers in a certain location, and have the time to respond, the in-person intercept method is a good one.

A related data collection method is also an in-person technique, but occurs in the customer's "native environment." For consumer markets, this interviewing takes place in the home. For business-to-business markets, this takes place is in the office. Going to where the respondent is makes the data collection very expensive. However, the quality of the responses is usually excellent.

Telephone interviewing has taken a beating lately. Direct marketers selling credit cards, mortgage refinancing, and windshield replacement have "poisoned the well." "Do Not Call" lists are a strong response to unwanted telemarketing. Unfortunately, the backlash has also hit the market research companies who merely gather consumer opinions (and do not sell anything). The "Do Not Call" movement has hampered the ability of companies to collect legitimate survey data. Costs have risen because a greater number of people need to be called in order to complete each survey. However, telephone interviewing remains as a quick and cost-effective tool for brief surveys (especially for business-to-business surveying when you have the phone numbers).

The fastest-growing data collection method is Web-based surveys. The speed of data collection is blindingly fast. Web-based surveys can show pictures and even video in addition to text. Unlike the in-person and mail methods, a monetary incentive often is not needed. However, programming can be expensive, especially if it is a long, one-shot survey and there are not a lot of respondents. Confidentiality is also a concern, because it is possible for competitors to get a copy of the survey. Security can be maintained by using the latest copy-protection software, by carefully controlling who is allowed to participate, and by wrapping up the data collection as fast as possible. Because Web-based surveys usually use email invitations, they are negatively affected by the rising tide of "spam" (junk email). The backlash, much like that against telemarketing, has caused the cost of Web-based surveys to increase. (See the sidebar article on "Internet-based Quantitative Market Research")

The third step in the quantitative survey process is data analysis. The mundane part of this step is inputting the data from paper surveys into an electronic database. Of course, Web and telephone surveys do this automatically as part of their process. Once the data is in the computer, statistical analysis software is used to create averages, count frequencies, and cross-tabulate the results among important groups of customers. Microsoft Excel has gotten powerful enough to do most of the key data analysis. However, sophisticated questionnaires usually require the use of specialized software like SPSS, SAS, StatPac, Statistica, NCSS, Minitab, or Wincross.

Reporting the findings is the final step in the quantitative survey process. Traditionally, this is a heavy three-ring binder report that few people read. Over the past two decades, the Microsoft PowerPoint® presentation has emerged as the preferred way to communicate the key findings of a study. Such a live presentation allows listeners to ask questions of the researcher and gain greater understanding. Some companies have started using a "workshop" instead of a data-dumping "final presentation." This workshop is typically held very soon after the end of data collection. The market researcher presents just the initial findings, and the group discusses what they mean. Questions arise, enabling the researcher to do further data analysis and get highly actionable insights. The final report is therefore much more useful to the new product development team. (Throughout this chapter, the word *product* is meant to mean either a physical product or a service sold to end users or to businesses.)

18.3 Questions Quantitative Market Research Can Answer

In the early stages of new product development, there are important questions to answer. The following table shows some of these questions, in rough chronological order, and the quantitative market research tools that help answer them. Table 18.2 shows the "quant" tools that are being used by the most innovative companies in all industries—consumer and business-to-business, product and service, and low- and high-tech industries.

Figure 18.1 illustrates how the quant tools covered in this chapter fit in with the traditional Stage-Gate® (Cooper, 1986) NPD process. The "Fuzzy Front End" first stage of NPD is Discovery (see Chapter 6). The qualitative tools covered in Chapters 14 and 15 dominate this stage. The first quant tool, segmentation, is useful at the very beginning to begin to understand the similarities and differences across the customer market. Similarly, perceptual mapping is useful for quantifying how customers think of current products (to identify opportunities). As customer needs are uncovered during the Discovery phase, they need to be quantified. The needs-ranking and Kano method tools are good for understanding these needs in detail (though both continue to be used to help scope out ideas in Stage 1).

Concept testing provides the key data needed to make the Gate 1 and Gate 2 decisions (see Chapters 21 and 22). Many simple concepts are tested for Gate

TABLE 18.2 QUESTIONS AND RESULTING TOOLS.

Early-Stage NPD Question	Quant Tool to Use
Which customers should we target?	Segmentation
What do customers think of current products[1]?	Perceptual Mapping
Which customer needs should we target for new product ideas?	Kano Method and Needs Ranking
Which of our raw ideas are the most promising to pursue?	Concept Testing
What is the optimal mix of features and price?	Conjoint Analysis

FIGURE 18.1 QUANT TOOLS WITHIN THE STAGE-GATE® PROCESS.

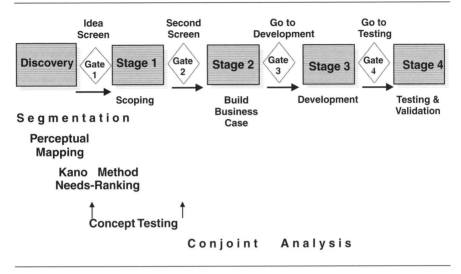

1, but Gate 2 concept testing utilizes a smaller number of detailed concept descriptions. Finally, conjoint analysis helps optimize the most promising concepts that emerge from Gate 2 concept testing.

Outside the scope of this chapter are quantitative tools that are needed for the later Development and Testing and Validation, stages of NPD. Table 18.3 shows some of the questions and some of the tools that successful companies use.

TABLE 18.3 LATER-STAGE QUESTIONS AND THEIR TOOLS.

Stage 3 and 4 NPD Question	Quant Tool to Use
What should the specifications of the new product be?	Quality function deployment
What do customers think of our prototype?	Product use testing
	Beta testing
	Extended use testing
Who will buy the new product? / Where will sales come from?	Discrete choice modeling
	Source of volume analysis
Will we sell enough to make money?	Simulated test market
	Trial sales
	Test market

By reading this chapter, the practitioner will learn the strengths and weaknesses of each quantitative (hereafter referred to as "quant") tool, as well as where to best apply it. Due to chapter length constraints, the objective is not to delve deeply into each tool. However, the practitioner should be an informed consumer of the most useful quant market research tools after reading the chapter. The treatment of each tool will contain how it works, the deliverable, and its strengths/weaknesses as well as do's and don'ts.

18.4 Segmentation: "Which Customers Should We Target?"

Segmentation is a quantitative tool for placing customers into "buckets" of similar customers so that the company can decide on which to focus during NPD (see Chapter 13). This is important because one product seldom appeals to the entire spectrum of customers. Companies find it useful to identify a target customer segment for NPD efforts. For example, the Marriott Corporation has successfully targeted its various products to distinct segments of the market:

- *Marriott Suites:* Permanent vacationers
- *Fairfield by Marriott:* Travelers on a budget
- *Residence Inn:* Extended stay customers
- *Courtyard by Marriott:* Business travelers

The first step in segmentation is to have many customers complete a survey. Kraemer (1987) suggests from 300 to over 1000. The survey can be very simple, depending on the type of segmentation desired. The list that follows gives some segmentation types, ranked from least to most useful:

- *Demographic:* Dividing customers by age, family type, income, geography, and other characteristics
- *Firmographic:* Dividing business customers by SIC code, geography, dollar sales, number of employees
- *Purchases:* Dividing customers by heavy users/light users, brands used, price paid
- *Benefits sought:* Dividing customers by what's important to them (price, performance, customer support, reliability, etc.)

Once the survey data are collected, segmentation "buckets" are created by using a statistical clustering routine. Each segment is then profiled by its defining demographics/firmographics so that the company can find them for future research or marketing efforts.

Internet-based Quantitative Market Research

Using the World Wide Web has emerged as a dominant data collection technique, due to its speed, reach and flexibility. However, it is just another data collection technique (added to telephone, mail, and in-person techniques). The quant tools presented in this chapter allow for the use of *any* data collection technique.

What is revolutionary about Web-based quantitative market research is the ability of the NPD practitioner to do the research by himself/herself. Many companies sell the capability for the practitioner to design the survey questions, create the answer scales, send out solicitations, capture the results, and even analyze the answers. The opportunity to save money by eliminating the market research "middleman" is considerable. However, a lot of low-quality surveys are the result of this "do-it-yourself" research (MacElroy, 2003). Reasons for this include:

- Surveys that are too long and tedious
- Leading or biased questions
- Poorly worded questions
- Unbalanced or illogical response scales
- The wrong respondents being chosen

When preparing a Web-based quantitative research survey, you should adhere to the principles of "netiquette." This includes (Dimetrosky et. al., 2001):

- Giving something back (for example, instant results of a question or two)
- Getting permission and opt-in (offer the choice of participating)
- Don't send spam (know whom you are sending to)
- Don't abuse respondents (send infrequent surveys, please)
- Don't sell participants' names (market research is *not* sales)
- Make it interesting (and possibly even fun)

Figure 18.2 shows a hypothetical segmentation scheme for the residential telecommunications market. Each segment is profiled by both its demographics and its attitudes toward technology. This type of segmentation is powerful for NPD because each bucket behaves quite similarly toward different new product ideas. The "Home Office," "Techno Elite," and "Technology Interested" (together representing about a quarter of households) would be the target market for an expensive cutting-edge product. On the other hand, the "Progressive Family" and "Social Families" would be the target market for new calling plans and services for households who want to keep using their current phones.

Companies that use segmentation understand the diversity of their market better, specifically identifying the most promising customers for their new product development efforts. Segmentation teaches new product developers that not all cus-

> *Market segmentation is one of the most useful theories in marketing.*

tomers think or behave the same way. Also, segmentation provides more focus for NPD efforts. One pitfall of segmentation is that it is too easy to start believing that customers are more different than they really are. The "buckets" always overlap to some degree. Also, the statistics can be misapplied to give elegant but useless results. Finally, segments can shift over time so the entire market segmentation needs to be updated periodically.

Segmentation Do's and Don'ts

DO

- Segment your customers based on the benefits they seek from products
- Target your NPD efforts to customers who have the most need for what you can uniquely offer

DON'T

- Rely on just demographics or firmographics
- Create fewer than three segments or more than eight

FIGURE 18.2 EXAMPLE SEGMENTATION OF THE TELECOMMUNICATIONS MARKET.

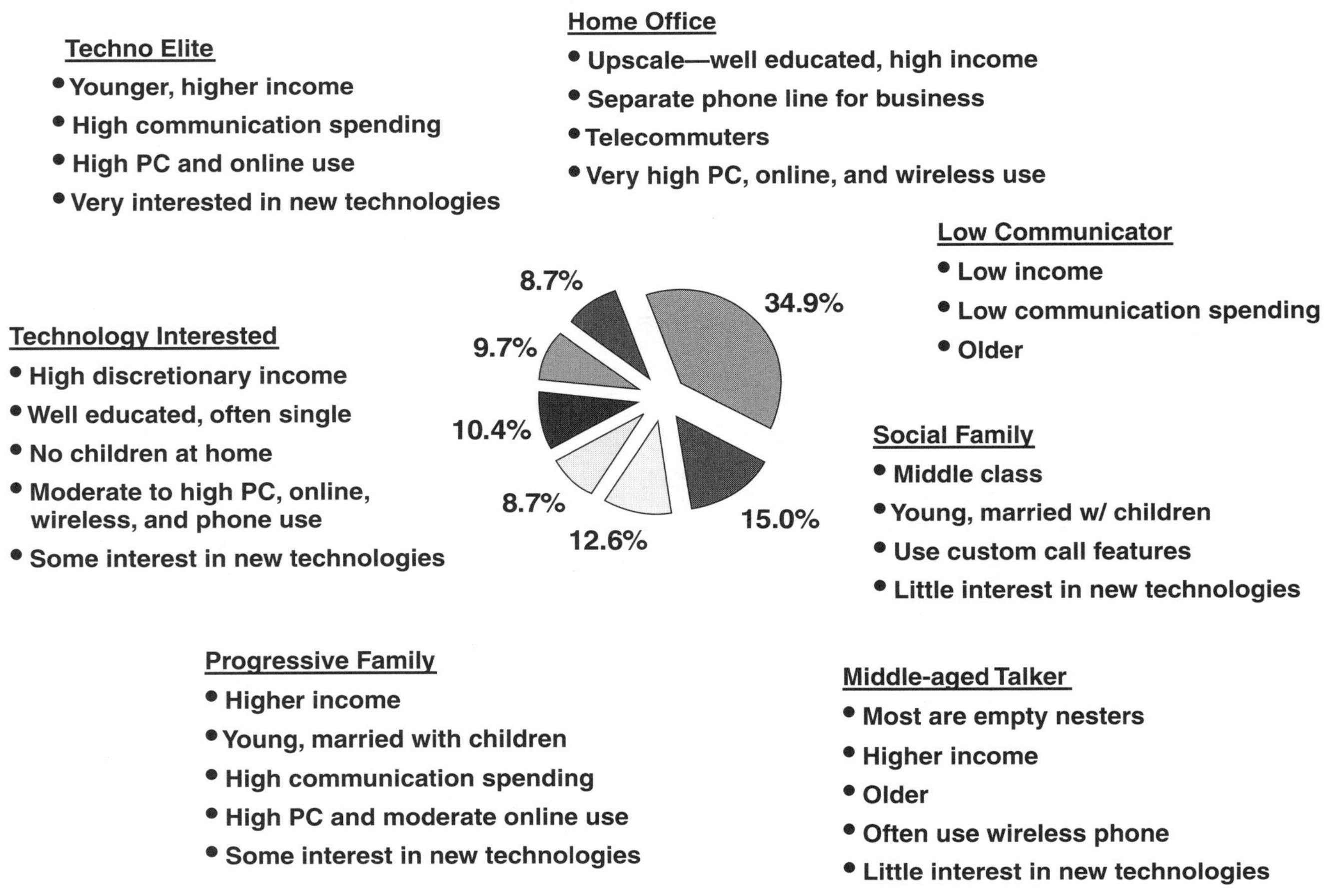

Techno Elite
- Younger, higher income
- High communication spending
- High PC and online use
- Very interested in new technologies

Technology Interested
- High discretionary income
- Well educated, often single
- No children at home
- Moderate to high PC, online, wireless, and phone use
- Some interest in new technologies

Progressive Family
- Higher income
- Young, married with children
- High communication spending
- High PC and moderate online use
- Some interest in new technologies

Home Office
- Upscale—well educated, high income
- Separate phone line for business
- Telecommuters
- Very high PC, online, and wireless use

Low Communicator
- Low income
- Low communication spending
- Older

Social Family
- Middle class
- Young, married w/ children
- Use custom call features
- Little interest in new technologies

Middle-aged Talker
- Most are empty nesters
- Higher income
- Older
- Often use wireless phone
- Little interest in new technologies

34.9%

15.0%

12.6%

8.7%

8.7%

10.4%

9.7%

18.5 Perceptual Mapping: "What Do Customers Think of Current Products?"

Perceptual mapping is a "mind map" of customer perceptions. Much like a roadmap, it shows which products are considered "close" to each other and which are far apart. Perceptual mapping works by having customers take a simple survey, which asks them to rate their impression of current products on various attributes (no more than about 20). Table 18.4 shows an example for two-seat sports cars.

The same three questions would be asked for the Porsche Boxster, Honda S2000, Lexus SC430, and Chevrolet Corvette. Statistical tools such as multi-dimensional scaling, factor (principal component) analysis, multiple discriminant analysis, or correspondence analysis are used to boil the many ratings down to a simple chart. The resulting sports car perceptual map (WRC Research Systems, 1996) might look like that shown in Figure 18.3.

The perceptual map shows that the Mazda Miata is the value leader (it's located way out on the "value" scale). The Lexus SC430 does very well for "appearance." The Porsche Boxster does well for "performance" and "appearance," but poorly for "performance" (it's located far away from "high performance"). A new product developer could use this map to see that there is a gap between the Corvette, the Lexus, and the Miata. This gap is an opportunity for a new car that has better appearance than the Miata, better performance than the Lexus, and slightly less performance and price than the Corvette.

The key deliverable from a perceptual mapping project is a visual that shows where "holes" exist in the current market so that they can be exploited with new products. It is nice to have a one-page summary of how customers think of current products. Also, the visual is better than a big table of numbers for some managers. However, perceptual mapping does have some drawbacks.

TABLE 18.4 SAMPLE PERCEPTUAL MAPPING QUESTIONS.

	Poor	Fair	Good	Very Good	Excellent
How would you rate the Mazda Miata for appearance?	1	2	3	4	5
How would you rate the Mazda Miata for performance?	1	2	3	4	5
How would you rate the Mazda Miata for value?	1	2	3	4	5

FIGURE 18.3 PERCEPTUAL MAP OF SPORTS CARS.

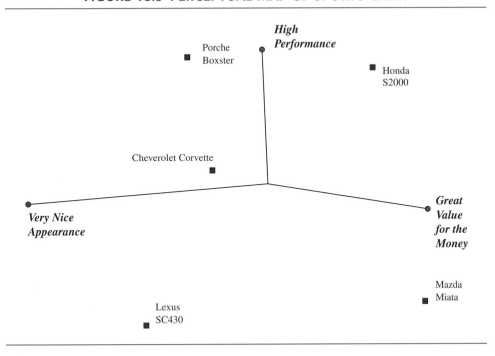

There is inherent distortion when collapsing many dimensions of a product down to the two- or three-dimensional perceptual map. Therefore, it is not 100 percent precise for all products and dimensions. Also, a complex map demands a lot of explanation.

18.6 Kano Method: "What Customer Needs Should We Target for New Product Ideas?"

One of the most daunting tasks of early NPD is to choose the customer need(s) that will be fulfilled with the new product. The Kano method is useful to classify customer needs so NPD efforts can be better focused. The Kano method asks customers to classify their needs into three categories:

- *Exciter.* A need that has the potential to delight, but that is not expected. For automobiles, an example of an exciter is being able to close electric windows even after the driver has turned off the ignition.

Perceptual Mapping Do's and Don'ts

DO

- Use a perceptual map to find out what customers think of current products, before trying to develop new ones
- Identify gaps in the market

DON'T

- Make the survey too long or tedious—build in breaks
- Use more than about eight products and 20 ratings for each

- *More is better*: Not having this need met is disliked, while getting it met is welcomed. An automotive example is fuel economy.
- *Must be*: A need that must be met in order for the new product to be acceptable. For automobiles, an example of a "must be" is safety restraints in case of collisions.

Figure 18.4 summarizes the Kano classification. The vertical axis is customer satisfaction. The horizontal axis is the degree to which the need is met (left is unmet; right is fully met). Notice that there's only upside to "exciters." But there's only downside to "must be's." So "exciters" are more exciting to new product developers than "must-be's."

As products evolve over time, needs change in their classification. For example, vehicle cup holding was a true "exciter" in the 1980s when cupholders first appeared. Then, cup holding became a "more-is-better" need, as multiple holders were added to passenger areas in the front and rear seating. Now cup holding is a "must be" need. There's little incremental benefit to adding new cupholders.

By classifying needs into these three categories, new product developers can decide which to satisfy and at what level. Developers need to be continually identifying new "exciters," refining features that address the "more is betters," and deemphasizing innovation on "must be's."

> *Kano helps identify those features that have high versus low upside potential.*

FIGURE 18.4 KANO CLASSIFICATION SYSTEM.

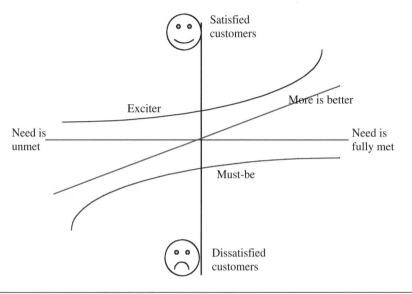

Adapted from Shiba et al., 1993.

The Kano method works by giving customers a survey to complete. They are presented with needs, and simply asked two questions about each one, for example:

"If your product had less _____, how would you feel?"
  ☐ I like it that way.
  ☐ It must be that way.
  ☐ I am neutral.
  ☐ I can live with it that way.
  ☐ I dislike it that way.

"If your product had more _____, how would you feel?"
  ☐ I like it that way.
  ☐ It must be that way.
  ☐ I am neutral.
  ☐ I can live with it that way.
  ☐ I dislike it that way.

The actual wording of the questions is customized to each individual need. But the idea is to ask about each need not being met, and then again ask about each need being fully addressed. The response scales are the same across all needs. The analysis of the survey takes two steps. First, each respondent's reaction to each *pair* of questions must be placed into one of the three buckets described above (*exciter, more is better,* and *must be*) or one of three rarely used buckets (*counterintuitive, not paying attention, don't care*). Table 18.5, from the Center for Quality of Management (1991), shows how the responses map onto the buckets.

The second analysis step is to simply tally up the number of respondents in each bucket. The bucket with the most respondents is the tag that is applied to that particular need.

By using the Kano method, new product developers will know the "exciter's" and "more is better's" they can use to target their efforts. They will also know the "must be's" that offer little upside potential. Kano is very good for understanding how customers react to changes in current products. It helps point the way to improvements that could be highly valued. It is popular with technically trained developers who enjoy data analysis and the use of intricate tools such as quality function deployment (QFD). On the other hand, Kano, on its own, cannot tell the NPD team what needs are most important to include or improve. It *classifies* needs, but does not *prioritize* them. A second weakness of Kano is a sensitivity to the wording of the questions. Customers are extremely literal. Their answers depend highly on the way the questions are asked. Kano surveys often test features when they should be testing underlying customer problems or needs.

18.7 Needs-Ranking: "What Customer Needs Should We Target for New Product Ideas?"

The Kano method helps classify customer needs, but does not tell you which needs are most important to meet. Therefore, a needs-ranking survey complements Kano. Both are ideal tools to use right after the NPD team has conducted contextual interviews/ethnography to identify many raw customer needs. Typically, contextual interviews/ethnography yields a set of 20–40 raw customer needs. However, since the interviews are totally qualitative, the team does not know which needs are most critical. And they need to know which are the top needs to be able to focus their efforts. A needs-ranking survey is simply a way of having customers rank the importance of a list of needs.

Given 20–40 customer needs, a normal rating survey is too long and tedious. No one likes to see a full page of questions with "strongly disagree" to

TABLE 18.5 KANO METHOD CLASSIFICATION MAPPING.

Need fully addressed ↓ / Need not being met →	Like it that way	Must be that way	Neutral	Live with it	Dislike it that way
Like it that way	Not paying Attention	Exciter	Exciter	Exciter	More Is Better
Must be that way	Counterintuitive	Don't care	Don't care	Don't care	Must Be
Neutral	Counterintuitive	Don't care	Don't care	Don't care	Must Be
Live with it	Counterintuitive	Don't care	Don't care	Don't care	Must Be
Dislike it that way	Counterintuitive	Counterintuitive	Counterintuitive	Counterintuitive	Not paying Attention

---

Kano Method Do's and Don'ts

DO

- Include Kano along with other tools that prioritize the importance of meeting various customer needs—use both to decide what to work on
- Word the questionnaire carefully
- Flexibly analyze the questionnaire results, taking a holistic view of each need

DON'T

- Forget that today's exciter is tomorrow's must-be
- Test features; instead, test needs
- Get bogged down in the analysis tedium of the Kano survey

"neutral" to "strongly agree" Likert scales. This results in low response rates and bad data from those fatigued respondents who actually complete the survey. A second problem with conventional rating surveys is that *all* the customer needs tend to come out as being rated important. That does not help the team prioritize its efforts.

The Web allows for a very streamlined approach that provides a much greater spread between the most and least important customer needs. First, customers read all the need statements (preferably just one simple sentence) and click on the ones that seem of personal importance to them. The next Web page shows just the needs that were clicked. Customers are then asked to allocate 100 points across the list, giving more points to needs that are more important to them. Programming allows for a calculator to show how many points have been allocated so far, and how many still remain to be allocated.

Needs ranking explicitly tells the new product development team the customer needs on which they should focus. This approach is quick and results in

---

Customers cannot directly rank a long list of their needs, but they can easily do this needs-ranking survey.

Needs-Ranking Do's and Don'ts

DO

- Use the Web if you can
- Pretest the need statements to ensure that they are clear

DON'T

- Test more than 40 needs (cut out the obvious weak needs beforehand)
- Forget to cross-tabulate the results by customer segment

---

a good spread between the most-and least-important needs. The method is very good for identifying which customers emphasize which needs.

Needs ranking is limited by the fact that customers are very literal. If a need is not expressed clearly, the importance score will suffer. Therefore, these types of surveys are highly dependent on the quality of the writing.

18.8 Concept Testing: "Which of Our Raw Ideas are the Most Promising to Pursue?"

Many companies use a haphazard and incomplete process for picking the new product ideas they will develop into new products. A better way is to test *all* the company's wild and crazy ideas in an inexpensive and quick manner. This ensures that no potential winner is discarded.

A concept is a statement about anticipated product features that will yield selected benefits relative to other products already available (Crawford and DiBenedetto, 1999). Any company, consumer or business-to-business, selling physical products or services, high-tech or low-tech, can craft its raw new product ideas into full concepts. Concepts are usually 100–150 words long and contain a simple picture or drawing. Figure 18.5 shows a good way of formatting concepts.

It is usually a good idea *not* to put a price on these early ideas, because the goal of concept testing is to get a read on customer interest in the general idea. If the idea tests well, there's plenty of time later to investigate price (and better tools—see Conjoint Analysis later in this chapter).

FIGURE 18.5 CONCEPT-WRITING TEMPLATE.

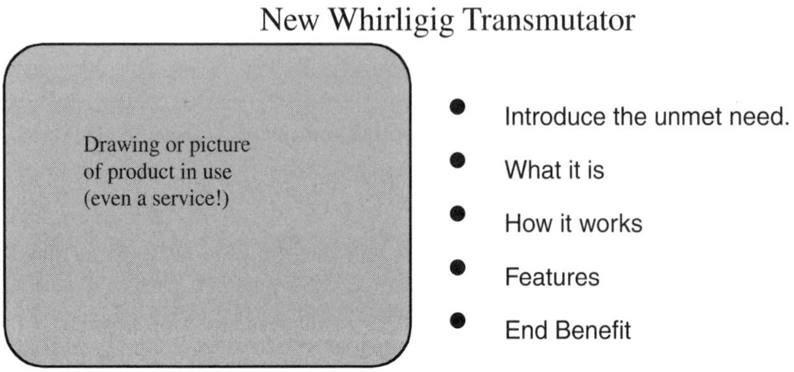

New Whirligig Transmutator

Drawing or picture
of product in use
(even a service!)

- Introduce the unmet need.
- What it is
- How it works
- Features
- End Benefit

Once 10–30 concepts are created, it is time to get them in front of customers to see their reaction. The questions to ask are on the order of "if you could buy/use such a product, how likely would you?" A five-point scale is usually used:

- Definitely not buy
- Probably not buy
- Might or might not buy
- Probably buy
- Definitely buy

Other diagnostic questions help provide understanding of the total customer reaction: uniqueness, believability, superiority vs. current products, and need for such a product.

Concept testing data can be collected in many ways: Web-based, in person, and at conferences or trade shows (excellent for business-to-business concepts).

Using concept testing, managers will know which of their new product ideas have the most promise, as well as some ways to improve them. The ones liked best are often a surprise to the companies doing the research. Concept testing improves the odds that the eventual new product will be a success.

> *Concept testing is the tool to use when ideas are in their early, rough form.*

Concept Testing Do's and Don'ts

DO

- Test as many ideas as possible (at least 50 per year)
- Test ideas prior to investigating any of them for feasibility (to keep from prematurely eliminating potential winners)

DON'T

- Be inconsistent in the concept formatting
- Test highly futuristic ideas alongside those that are just innovative

---

As in all other market research, the answer you receive depends on the question you ask. Concepts that have nicer graphics, more flowery language, or less typographical errors tend to get rated higher (regardless of the quality of their raw idea). Also, concept testing only gauges the relative appeal of the concepts tested (and therefore does not give any volume forecast).

18.9 Conjoint Analysis: "What Is the Optimal Mix of Features and Price?"

A difficult time during the development process is the setting of the final product specifications. This consists of deciding which features the new product will include and at what performance level. The conjoint analysis quant tool is excellent for this task. It also helps you to set the price.

Conjoint analysis is one of the most sophisticated quantitative market research tools available.

Conjoint analysis is a technique that uncovers how important component parts of the product are to customers by offering many different scenarios and observing what the customer does. In a way, it exemplifies the old saying "you don't know how important something is until it's gone." The first step in conjoint analysis is deciding which features to include in the study. The second step is to decide what performance level will be tested within each feature. Somewhere in the neighborhood of 12–16 total performance levels (added across all the features) is usually the limit of conventional conjoint analysis. After that, the newer and more sophisticated versions of conjoint are required.

After setting the exact features to be tested, an experimental design is chosen from either software or books. Not every possible combination is tested, usually just a carefully chosen subset (so that all the main effects can be estimated). The next step is to gather the data via the Web, in person, by mail, or by telephone. Finally, the results are analyzed with highly sophisticated statistics to identify the optimal bundle of features. The price sensitivity curve is often also defined, which can be coupled with cost data to help identify the optimal profit point.

The following illustration shows two questions (out of 16 total) from a conjoint study designed to find the optimal bicycle. In this situation, the features to be tested are brand name (well known or not), bike design style (mountain bike or hybrid), shock absorbers (both wheels, just the rear, or none at all), weight (30, 35, or 40 lbs), and price ($250, $400, $650). There are a total of 13 different performance levels (two brand names, two designs, three shocks, three weights, three prices).

Question #5 out of 16

Here is a description of a new bicycle:

- Well-known brand name
- Rugged mountain bike design with wide knobby tires
- Has shock absorbers on both the front and back
- Weighs 35 lbs
- Price is $650

If you were in the market for a new bike, how likely would you be to buy this one?

☐ Definitely   ☐ Probably   ☐ Might   ☐ Probably   ☐ Definitely
   Not Buy   Not Buy   Buy   Buy

Question #11 out of 16

Here is a description of a new bicycle:

- Well-known brand name
- "Hybrid" design with medium-width tires
- No shock absorbers
- Weighs 35 lbs
- Price is $400

If you were in the market for a new bike, how likely would you be to buy this one?

☐ Definitely   ☐ Probably   ☐ Might   ☐ Probably   ☐ Definitely
   Not Buy   Not Buy   Buy   Buy

Figure 18.6 illustrates some hypothetical results from the bicycle conjoint analysis.

These results tell us that price is most important and that the low $250 price is the favorite (no surprise!). Having a well-known brand name is the most important product-related feature. Weight and shock absorbers are a bit less important, but there are definite preferences. The customers want the lightest-weight bike, with 5 lbs extra being not very acceptable. However, customers seem to feel that one shock absorber is nearly as good as two.

Thus, the main deliverable from conjoint analysis is a highly accurate view of the trade-offs customers are willing (and not willing) to make. Conjoint analysis is an excellent tool for finding the version of the product that customers like best. It can also help show how much extra customers are willing to pay

FIGURE 18.6 WHAT'S MOST IMPORTANT IN A BICYCLE?

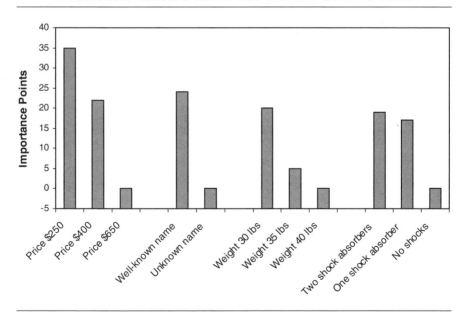

Conjoint Analysis Do's and Don'ts

DO

- Use it to optimize the product design
- Use it to help set price
- Use it to get a rough estimate of sales and cannibalization

DON'T

- Forget to create a "what if" spreadsheet to help interpret the results
- Test just one or two scenarios when you can use conjoint to predict all possible scenarios

---

for incremental features. Finally, conjoint is great for getting a rough estimate of sales at various prices.

Unfortunately, conjoint analysis is not easy to learn or use. Errors can be made during the design phase that can severely impact the final results. The analysis requires highly sophisticated statistics. Off-the-shelf software helps, but has a steep learning curve.

18.10 Summary

Quantitative market research can provide excellent guidance in answering the key NPD questions posed at the beginning of this chapter. The key task is matching the right tool to the question at hand. This chapter illustrates just a few of the many useful quantitative tools.

References

Center for Quality of Management, *Concept Engineering*. Cambridge, MA: 1991.

Cooper, Robert, *Winning At New Products: Accelerating the Process from Ideas to Launch*. Perseus Publishing: NY, 1986

Crawford, C. Merle and DiBenedetto, C. Anthony, *New Products Management*. New York: Irwin, 1999.

Dimetrosky, Scott, Khawaja, Sami, and Degens, Phil, "Best Practices for Online Survey Research." *Quirk's Marketing Research Review* pp. 36, 38–40 (January 2001).

Kraemer, Helena, *How Many Subjects?: Statistical Power Analysis in Research.* Beverly Hills: Sage Publications, 1987.

MacElroy, W., "The Democratization of Marketing Research." *Quirk's Marketing Research Review*, 22–23, 68 (February 2003).

Shiba, Shoji, Graham, Alan, and Walden, David, *A New American TQM: Four Practical Revolutions in Management.* Portland, OR: Productivity Press,1993.

WRC Research Systems, Inc., *BrandMap Software.* Downers Grove, IL: WRC Research Systems, Inc., 1996.

Brian D. Ottum is president of Ottum Research & Consulting, in Saline, Michigan. His practice is focused on new product development consulting and innovative market research tools. Ottum Research & Consulting serves clients in the packaged goods, durables, and high-technology industries. Prior to starting his own firm, Brian worked in new product development and international market research for Procter & Gamble. He holds a Ph.D. from the University of Utah, an M.B.A. from Xavier University and a B.S. from the University of Wisconsin. Brian also teaches new product development in the Executive Education program of the University of Michigan.

CHAPTER NINETEEN

EXTRACTING VALUE FROM YOUR PATENT PORTFOLIO

Laura A. Schoppe and Nancy Pekar

19.1 Introduction

Many companies have a valuable source for new product development (NPD) that often remains untapped: their portfolio of patents and other intellectual property (IP). IP is any product of human intellect: inventions, literary works (including software), trade secrets, industrial designs, and trademarks (see Chapter 20). A patent is a grant of exclusive right to an invention; the equivalent of a patent for software is copyright. This exclusive right enables the holder to prevent others from making, using, offering to sell, selling, and importing the technology. A patent is a legal property right that may be assigned, sold, or licensed to others for a fee, for payment of periodic royalties, or at not cost (i.e., donation). Therefore, a company's patent portfolio is a collection of inventions, software, and other IP that it owns and controls exclusively, unless the rights have been otherwise shared or released. More information about patents is available from the U.S. Patent and Trademark Office (USPTO) at http://patents.uspto.gov/.

Having exclusive rights to a technology can provide a significant competitive edge when developing new products. In addition to the benefits related to NPD, patents also can offer value in a related or completely new application. For example, a company that develops foam products for car seats could expand its market into recreational vehicles (e.g., boats, all-terrain vehicles), furniture (e.g., industrial furniture, theater seats, residential indoor and lawn pieces), commercial aircraft, and consumer products (e.g., toys, diapers, appliances). Another example would be using the patents for a nondestructive evaluation product for aerospace to develop new products for medicine (e.g., cranial fracture analysis, fluid-barrier penetration), heavy equipment (e.g., fracture analysis on farm, construction, factory, and other high-stress equipment), and aircraft (e.g., bolt analysis).

For companies looking to introduce new products or expand their reach into new business areas, the patent portfolio is an ideal place to start. In cases where the new product area is too far afield of the company's core business(es), the patents can be out-licensed to noncompetitors, generating royalty revenue. However, in either situation, an investment of resources is needed to reap the rewards (e.g., the R&D for NPD, the costs of pursuing and negotiating an out-license). To ensure that these resources are not wasted, a company should conduct an in-depth assessment of the patent's commercial potential. Essentially, the in-depth assessment asks: Will the product made with the patented technology ultimately be profitable? If the answer is yes, then it is worth pursuing internal NPD or out-licensing to noncompetitors. If the answer is no, then these resources—as well as the fees associated with maintaining a patent as the years go by—might be better allocated elsewhere.

However, the costs associated with conducting an in-depth assessment can be significant. The effort—purchasing market reports, consulting with experts, gathering other information, and analyzing the findings—is no small investment. Since not every patent will have sufficient commercial potential to justify NPD or out-licensing, it is not cost-effective to conduct an in-depth assessment for every patent, regardless of the size of the portfolio. Rather, a patent portfolio screening can help make a preliminary value judgment about each patent's commercial potential, identifying those patents that should receive an in-depth assessment.

> *Patent portfolio screening can help one make a preliminary value judgment about each patent's commercial potential, identifying those patents that should receive an in-depth assessment.*

19.2 Patent Portfolio Screening: What Is It? Why Do It?

Screening involves quickly examining each patent in the portfolio according to established evaluation criteria to identify—albeit on a preliminary basis—its commercial potential. This preliminary information is used to decide which patents should be selected for in-depth assessment. As indicated earlier, the assessment is used to determine more accurately a technology's commercial value and to decide whether to invest in NPD, market it for out-licensing, or do neither.

The goal of patent portfolio screening is to expend minimal time and cost in making a reasonably accurate preliminary value judgment. Spending too much time uses more resources than necessary to make a good decision about pursuing in-depth assessment. Spending too little time yields information insufficient to reduce the risks of making a bad decision. Those risks include wasting resources assessing a patent that does not have sufficient commercial potential as well as the opportunity cost associated with disregarding a patent with good, but not readily obvious, potential.

Patent portfolio screening has been most frequently used as a first step to generating revenue via out-licensing. Rather than venture into an NPD that is outside its core business(es), the company can generate fees and royalties by licensing its patents to noncompetitors. Texas Instruments, Zenith, and Dow Chemical each have licensed their unused patents to generate more than $100 million in royalty revenues (Jain, 1999). Patents that play only a minor role in a product line or are used only internally might represent big advances in another market. The minor investment in screening the patent portfolio can shine a light on major, previously unforeseen revenue opportunities.

Patent portfolio screening also is a key first step in launching a technology-driven NPD effort. In identifying a patent's preliminary commercial potential, screening confirms that the three factors essential for successful NPD—a functioning technology, patent/copyright protection for the IP, and a market that wants to use the technology—are present. In some cases, the screening process might identify lucrative new markets that the company had never considered. For example, 3M developed a new market in sticky pads for its nonpermanent adhesive innovation, which originally was developed as a way to improve acrylate adhesives (*3M Innovation Chronicles*, 1998). Information gathered during the screening process, along with the data from the in-depth assessment, will guide the NPD effort. With screening, you begin to understand the market need for the new product and, if the need is high, how it might fit into that market.

Patent portfolio screening also is an aid to understanding the company's IP resources, particularly in very large companies. Screening the portfolio might reveal patents developed in one division that solve technical challenges in another department or division. For example, a large company that needs a non-corroding flexible material for an automobile bumper might find the solution in an aluminum-alloy coating developed by the home appliance division.

Screening gives you a better handle on the entire patent portfolio, allowing the company to reap a greater return on its R&D investment.

Speaking of understanding your IP resources, the ideal time to screen your company's IP is *before* it is patented. Patenting inventions that do not provide a distinct competitive advantage or have market interest wastes resources. Just because something can be patented does not mean that it should be. By screening inventions for their commercial potential before making the patenting decision, a company can save an average of 10 percent of the total cost of the patent portfolio. For instance, Dow Chemical saved $40 million over a 10-year period by reducing patent maintenance fees (Bukowitz and Williams, 1999).

Whether applied to the entire patent portfolio (i.e., a backlog of dozens or hundreds of patents) or on an ongoing basis as new invention disclosures are received, screening quickly identifies those technologies with commercial potential inside or outside of the company's primary market(s). Expending minimal resources to screen for commercial value ensures that future resources for R&D, NPD, IP protection, and commercialization are focused on those technologies with meaningful potential. For technologies with lower potential, the screening process provides valuable feedback to inventors as to the importance of considering market need when developing their technologies.

The remainder of this chapter describes a patent portfolio screening methodology—"Getting to the Best First"—that involves conducting enough research to make an informed decision without expending resources unnecessarily. This methodology has been successfully implemented at a Fortune 200 company, one of the Big Three automotive companies, and a major research university.

19.3 The "Getting to the Best First" Methodology

This approach to patent portfolio screening involves five steps: (1) establish evaluation criteria, (2) organize the portfolio, (3) select reviewer(s), (4) evaluate the patents, and (5) rate the patents. Experience has shown that this five-step process is a fast, effective way to make an informed decision about pursuing in-depth assessment for each patent (or invention disclosure) in the portfolio.

19.3.1 Step 1: Establish Evaluation Criteria

Develop a set of evaluation criteria to use in determining the potential value of each patent consistently and according to sound economic (or other) principles (see Chapter 29). The criteria should relate directly to the company's goals. For example, if the main goal is to generate royalty revenue, then the evaluation criteria will weigh heavily the technology's potential applications/markets. If the goal is to reduce the tax burden and/or increase goodwill, then inventions with value for not-for-profit organizations should be identified for possible donation. Table 19.1 presents other samples of company goals and the related criteria.

The company determines which goals are of greatest importance and sets the threshold limits for each criterion appropriately. These criteria will help reviewers evaluate the technologies in a consistent, objective manner. By focusing on the company's goals, the criteria prevent other factors from swaying the reviewers' judgment. The screening process should not evaluate patents according to political factors such as the inventor's identity or the company division from which the technology came.

19.3.2 Step 2: Organize the Portfolio

Before the reviewers can begin screening the patents, which may number in the hundreds or thousands, the portfolio must be organized. A well-organized portfolio facilitates internal strategic planning for NPD as well as active IP management (e.g., out-licensing). Organizing the portfolio is a useful tool for looking beyond the "microscale" view of a company's products to identify its technology strengths and weaknesses. Understanding the strengths allows for a better prioritization of resources, while identifying potential weaknesses is a first step toward correcting them. As a result, the company can make informed

TABLE 19.1 SAMPLE EVALUATION CRITERIA TIED TO COMPANY GOALS.

Company Goal	Indicator	Criteria
Generate revenue	A minimum threshold in revenue	Market size
Rapid successes	A limit on how much more investment is needed before the product is ready for the market	Technology readiness
Stay within existing markets/businesses	Outside of their core market area (e.g., nonautomotive applications for an automotive technology)	Market sectors
Improve reputation in the community	Good public relations story (e.g., medical or environmental benefit regardless of revenue potential)	Goodwill
Encourage researcher innovation	Number of ways technology may be used (regardless of the revenue potential)	Credibility

choices regarding R&D, out-licensing, in-licensing, acquisitions, joint ventures, and other strategic decisions.

This step involves creating a consolidated, functional, and categorized patent portfolio:

- A portfolio that is *consolidated* integrates basic patent information, organization-specific information, and tracking information into a centralized database.
- A portfolio that is *functional* uses customized database fields for efficient sorting, searching, screening, and tracking of patents.
- A portfolio that is *categorized* brings related technologies together and allows the company to see how its core capabilities affect its patent portfolio.

Import the portfolio into a database with specific details in customized fields. This database can be linked to your patent-docketing system, or it can be set up as a separate database in a spreadsheet. Beginning with the existing citation information, set up the database fields suggested in Table 19.2 as well as any additional fields that are appropriate for your company. In addition to this electronic database, each patent should have a file folder containing the issued patent or patent application as well as whatever other background in-

TABLE 19.2 TYPICAL FIELDS FOR THE CONSOLIDATED, FUNCTIONAL, CATEGORIZED PATENT PORTFOLIO DATABASE.

- USPTO data
    - Patent number
    - Inventor name
    - Assignee
    - Issue date
    - File date
    - Abstract
    - Claims (at least one)
    - USPTO class
    - Forward references
    - Referenced patents
- Company data
    - Internal categorizations
    - Licensing status
    - Maintenance fee payment schedule
    - Associated intellectual assets, including contact information
- Technical category (broad during organizing step; reviewer assigns more specific class/cluster)

formation is available (e.g., published or unpublished papers, presentations). Although this information might not be used during the screening, it is essential if the patent is selected for in-depth assessment.

A key part of the patent database is the technical category. You can use the USPTO or World Intellectual Property Organization (WIPO) classification codes as a starting point or develop custom categories. However, at this point, the technical categories used are very broad—electronics, mechanical systems, semiconductors, avionics, advanced materials, medical devices, software—and help in assigning the patents to the proper reviewer (Step 3). More specific groupings (i.e., classes and clusters), which will consolidate patents for increased value and efficiency during the in-depth assessment, are assigned during the review process (Step 4).

The broad categories are assigned "manually" but quickly by an individual with the appropriate technical background. This person might be found within the company or be an external consultant. Although automated systems for organizing the portfolio might sound ap-

> *Only a technically savvy expert can discern what commercial applications might benefit from a particular technology.*

pealing, they have limitations. Such software packages categorize by keywords found in patent titles and abstracts. However, natural language processors are not able to pick up on subtle differences. For example, a software program would probably miscategorize a patent entitled "Method and System for Creating an Approach to a Position on the Ground from a Location above the Ground" as something related to global positioning systems (GPS) rather than as its true technical category: avionics and control systems used for landing aircraft. Only a technically savvy expert can discern what commercial applications might benefit from a particular technology. A "first pass" could be done with software, but this automated categorization must be reviewed and corrected by an expert.

The goal of this step is to organize and categorize the patents as quickly as possible. It is not necessary—and, in fact, is a waste of resources—for the expert to spend the time needed to become sufficiently familiar with the patents to use anything but a broad category. The reviewer will gain that familiarity during the screening; therefore, the reviewer is in the best position to assign the more specific technology classes and clusters. (See Step 4 for more on technology classes and clusters.)

19.3.3 Step 3: Select the Reviewer(s)

The reviewer for each broach technical category (or portion of a category) should have sufficient technical expertise to understand the capabilities of each patent. In addition, the reviewer must have the creative focus to find new—sometimes immediately obvious, sometimes far-flung—uses for a technology. However, the reviewer also should have the business experience necessary to understand the market need for the technology to solve an identifiable problem. Rather than simply enjoy technology for its own sake, the reviewer looks for the practical applications for it.

The reviewer's ability to understand the essence of the patented technology—that is, what it *enables* rather than simply what it does—is key to finding markets outside the traditional product line. Usually, it is best to call upon experts from outside the company who can provide insight into new fields. For example, having the CEO evaluate a residential plumbing company's patents likely will result in the

> *The reviewer's ability to understand the essence of the patented technology—that is, what it enables rather than simply what it does—is key to finding markets outside the traditional product line.*

technology's potential being limited to the fixtures market. In cases such as this, the CEO cannot look beyond the original use of the patent and see the technology for what it really is. An outside consultant who has expertise in, for example, advanced materials and their markets is better able to identify that the low-cost ceramics used for a sink may have applications in the jewelry, housewares, power distribution, appliances, and electronics markets. As another example, a chief technology officer in the defense industry might recognize that a foam developed for the space shuttle could be used as insulation in an aircraft fuselage but may not identify the potential advanced materials applications in recreational equipment (tennis racquets, canoes) or roofing tiles.

Similarly, it is faster and more cost-effective to have a single reviewer examine the category rather than a panel of experts. Although a brainstorming panel might identify many new products and markets for a patent, a single reviewer with the appropriate background is likely to have these same ideas. Furthermore, the costs in terms of fees and time spent assembling and coordinating a panel of experts are greater than for lining up a single qualified reviewer. Remember that the goal is to make the decision about pursuing in-depth assessment efficiently and cost-effectively. A brainstorming panel can add more value later if the patent is selected for in-depth assessment.

19.3.4 Step 4: Evaluate the Patents

Although it is easy to spend many hours or even days evaluating each patent, the reviewer should spend no more than two hours evaluating each patent. The two-hour time frame is enough for the reviewer to read the patent abstract and claims, conduct some online research, and analyze the results to effectively rate the patent's commercial potential according to the established criteria. Spending an hour or less allows time for reviewing only the title and the first claim or so of the patent, eliminating the value provided by additional research. Spending three or four hours, while providing much additional information to the reviewer, rarely results in a different evaluation than the rating made after two hours. When the portfolio includes hundreds or thousands of patents, an extra hour per patent quickly adds up to a significant level of resources. Again, the goal of portfolio screening is to rate patents' commercial potential, while expending the minimum amount of time and resources. Additional research can be conducted later if the patent is selected for in-depth assessment.

Because he or she has the required technical expertise, business experience, and creative focus (see Step 3), the reviewer consults the patent abstract and claims to identify potential new applications for the technology. The reviewer then conducts online research to identify competitors and competing technologies as well as to gain a preliminary understanding of the new market(s). Sources for this information include patent databases, corporate information services, association information, and brief Web searches using such sites as OneSource (www.onesource.com), CorpTech (www.corptech.com), Science Citation Index (www.isinet.com/isi/products/citation/sci/), and others. Keywords for searches should focus on the capabilities of the technology, not the product to which it is currently applied.

The following is an example of the level of detail obtained in screening a patent of a timing device to be used while exercising. An hour-long search is sufficient to retrieve several key pieces of information. For instance, to be competitive with other related devices, the product will need to be sold for between $20 and $50 each. The other devices offer more features but are more complex; therefore, this patent might fill a niche market. The search also would show that although the product made with the patent might be offered to individual customers online, mostly it would be used as a promotional item (e.g., a gift for subscribing to *Sports Illustrated* or buying home exercise equipment). More detailed information—specific differences between the features of existing products and the patent, who the leading distributors of promotional items are, whether to license the patent to the manufacturers of such promotional items

---

The goal of portfolio screening is to rate patents' commercial potential, while expending the minimum amount of time and resources.

or to the distributor that sells them to *Sports Illustrated*, Bowflex, NordicTrack, and the like—will be obtained if the patent is selected for in-depth assessment.

The last portion of the two-hour limit is spent analyzing the research findings. The researcher considers various analysis factors, which are related to, but different from, the evaluation criteria established in Step 1. Those evaluation criteria are used to make a business decision: How do we prioritize our resources? Which patents do we want to pursue further for NPD, out-licensing, or another option? What benefits will doing so provide to the company? The analysis factors used here examine each critical factor separately to objectively determine the patent's commercial potential and identify any issues that might exist. Such critical factors might include the following:

- IP strength
- Size, structure, and significance of the market
- Level to which the technology is currently developed
- State-of-the-art relative to competing technologies
- Ease of implementation the technology might have in a commercial manufacturing or other process
- Relevant timing for commercialization

In analyzing the information gathered about the patent, the reviewer will assign a quantitative ranking—on a scale of 1 to 10, for example—for each factor. The analysis factors themselves as well as the ranking scale will directly relate to the company's goals/evaluation criteria. For example, if a company's goal is for a new product to make $100 million per year by its second year, then timing and market are the major analysis factors of interest. A score of 10 in timing would apply for two years to market, and a score of 5 might apply for a five-year time frame. Likewise, a score of 10 would be given for a $200 million potential market size, while a score of 9 might apply for a $100 million market. Table 19.3 presents examples of analytical factors and how they might be broken down into a ranking scale.

These analysis factors are important to consider individually because a single factor could be a show-stopper. For example, a technology might be useful in a market that is a good size, be easy to implement, and have a ready customer base, but there could be significant IP issues (e.g., the pat-

> *These analysis factors are important to consider individually because a single factor could be a show-stopper.*

ent is about to expire, foreign patent protection does not exist, a provision patent deadline is approaching, a patent application was never filed) that will

TABLE 19.3 SAMPLE RANKINGS FOR COMMERCIAL POTENTIAL.

Note: This is merely an example. Companies should modify the factors and scales to reflect their specific goals, strategy, and evaluation criteria.

IP Strength*

10	No public disclosures, no similar patents, and no likely patentability or enforcement issues; globally patentable.
9	No public disclosure, some similar patents, perhaps minor patentability or enforcement issues; globally patentable.
8	Public disclosure, loss of foreign coverage, but still domestic patentability; U.S. patentable.
6–7	U.S. stat bar concerns (<3 months remaining), no other patentability issues; U.S. patentable.
3–5	Closely related patents or other patentability or enforcement issues, or critical stat bar issues; possibly U.S. patentable.
1–2	Major stat bar issues, clear public disclosure over one year ago, protection highly unlikely or major patentability or enforcement issues.

This factor is particularly important when the screening is examining invention disclosures before patenting.

Market Potential

10	The market is large and unsegmented or multiple significant markets exist and the technology is targeted to fit an identified need.
8–9	The market is large but in large segments; technology is less "end stage."
6–7	The market is medium-sized and might be fragmented; the technology is a component early in the manufacturing process rather than a final product in itself.
5	The market is reasonably sized, more fragmented; the technology is a smaller part of a final salable product.
3–4	The market is small and/or very fragmented; the technology is narrowly applicable to a few markets, with low margins of profitability.
1–2	No identifiable market.

Level of Development

10	Ready to go to market without further development (not necessarily ready to sell to end users of finished product).
8–9	Working advanced generation prototype but needs some more development to convince users of its useful potential.
6–7	Working prototype.
4–5	Inefficient but functional prototype.
3	Reduced to practice to demonstrate concept, but no working prototype.
1–2	Concept with no reduction to practice.

TABLE 19.3 (*Continued*)

Ease of Implementation

10	No new equipment needed, minimal switching costs.
8–9	New equipment/training is necessary, but the cost is worth the benefit.
6–7	New equipment necessary, and state of the art may be perceived to be "good enough" so that there will be resistance to change.
4–5	Transformation of standard operating procedures necessary to implement the new technology and company perceives it may not be worth the switching costs. Further development might help alleviate the concern.
2–3	Very high barrier to changeover or replacement; current technology is too well entrenched, there are suitable substitutes, or the industry is notorious for sluggish acceptance.
1	New factories, new training, large capital costs in general required to incorporate the technology, requires prohibitive amount of effort to change or the current technology is superior and is perceived to be so for years to come.

Timing

9–10	Very timely, demonstrated market need, market is ready for the technology.
7–8	Less timely, some market need identified.
5–6	Market is present and may accept the technology, but there is no strong pull or the market has viable substitutes available.
3–4	Technology is a little behind (past prime timing) or ahead of the cutting-edge curve (ahead of prime timing).
1–2	Technology is obsolete or too far ahead of the market being able to utilize its benefits; far too risky for the market to consider.

prevent the company from developing a commercially viable product. In this case, the technology likely would receive a low rating (see Step 5).

The reviewer supplements the analysis with two items that will aid the decision-makers as they consider the entire portfolio: (1) a very brief (two- to three-sentence) description of the technology and (2) assignment of technology classes and (if appropriate) clusters. Regarding the latter, the technology class refines the broad technical categories assigned in Step 2. For example, patents in the broad "medical devices" category would be more specifically classified as "drug delivery" or "diagnostics." Similarly, some technologies categorized as "advanced materials" may be more specifically classified as "adhesives" or "films." Within each class, the reviewer also groups patents with a similar technology type and application into clusters. Clusters combine technologies that work together to provide a unique asset that can be further evaluated and developed as a single unit. Clusters often will contain a common inventor(s), but they should not be restricted by corporate division or inventor names artificially. The focus for clustering should remain on the similarity in capability that the patents provide. The majority of the clusters will contain only one patent. The class and cluster assignments are added to the patent database fields.

19.3.5 Step 5: Rate the Patents

At this point, the reviewer is ready to rate the patent's commercial potential. The rating is essentially the intersection between the patent's quantitative rankings for the analysis factors (Step 4) and the qualitative indicators provided by the evaluation criteria (Step 1). A four-level rating system is used:

- *High:* Review suggests that a product based on the patent would be of interest in the commercial marketplace. In-depth assessment is recommended.
- *Medium-high:* Review suggests that the commercial potential of a product based on the patent is favorable. In-depth assessment is recommended if resources are available.
- *Medium-low:* The commercial potential of a product based on the patent does not appear to be particularly favorable, but readily available information cannot confirm this judgment. Conduct in-depth assessment only if resources are available after acting upon the high and medium-high patents.
- *Low:* Commercial interest in a product based on the patent appears to be limited. Do not conduct in-depth assessment.
- *Monitor:* Although the patent's commercial potential appears favorable, its stage of development and/or the readiness of the market suggests that NPD or out-licensing should be postponed. Monitor the technology's R&D and/or the market to which it would be applied before conducting an in-depth assessment.

19.4 Making the Disposition Decision

Once the screening is complete, the company's decision-makers consider the patent portfolio as a whole, determining the appropriate disposition for each individual patent or patent cluster. Because the screening provided quantitative rankings of critical analysis factors, the decision-makers can see how the evaluator arrived at the high-medium-low rating. Taking into consideration the rankings on the analysis factors and the rating related to the evaluation criteria, the decision-makers assign one of five disposition strategies:

- *Pursue NPD:* Patents with a high or medium-high rating offer a good opportunity for the company to develop a new product. Conduct in-depth assessment of other factors for NPD.
- *Pursue out-licensing:* If the product or market area with a high or medium-high commercial potential rating is an area where the company's expertise is limited or is far outside its mission, commercializing the patent via out-licensing might be preferable to NPD. Conduct an in-depth assessment to confirm viability of commercialization and begin to gather data to inform marketing campaign and licensees to target.
- *Gather more information:* For some patents with a medium-high rating and most with a medium-low rating, the information gathered in the screening process is not quite sufficient to make an effective disposition decision. If the resources are available after pursuing more favorable options, conduct an in-depth assessment to obtain a better understanding of the potential market and determine if NPD or out-licensing should be pursued.
- *Pursue other options:* Other options exist for patents besides NPD or out-licensing. In some cases, a not-for-profit organization such as a state university or a 501(c)3 research company might be able to use the technology. Donating patents to such an organization provides a tax write-off to the original owner. Of course, the Internal Revenue Service's rules about IP donation must be monitored closely to be sure the propriety and value of this option are understood. Conduct additional research to determine the appropriateness of any option.
- *Abandon patent:* If a patent has no or limited commercial potential, the company might consider releasing the patent rights to save money by not continuing to pay the maintenance fees. Conduct internal research to confirm that the patent holds insufficient internal value.

Note that if the screening process is performed at the ideal time—that is, before filing for patent protection—part of the disposition decision would address the "to patent or not to patent" question.

Within each of the three "pursue" and the "gather more information" options, the individual patents/clusters are prioritized so that resources can be directed to the best first.

19.5 Looking Ahead: In-Depth Assessment

Although the patent portfolio screening process has greatly aided and informed the decision to pursue NPD or out-licensing, launching forth with such efforts based solely on this information would be premature. Screening identifies those patents with sufficient commercial potential that directing future resources toward their analysis is cost-effective. It is now essential you assess those patents to verify the match to the market and to develop a focused strategy.

Assessment involves conducting detailed research with a variety of information sources: the inventor, the literature, patent databases, and industry experts. Whereas the patent review as part of the screening process may result in a one-page document that takes two hours to research and develop, an assessment may be more than ten pages, including interviews with industry experts (a critical in-depth market research step not performed in screening), and may take 20–25 hours to perform. Gathering this information will allow the company to determine more accurately whether moving forward with NPD or out-licensing is appropriate and, if so, to develop a strategy for most effectively and efficiently marketing the product or out-licensing opportunity.

19.6 Summary

The "Getting to the Best First" screening methodology is a fast, easy, and cost-effective way to begin understand the value of your patent portfolio. By identifying the patents that appear to have the greatest commercial potential, the screening serves as the first step in extracting that value.

The screening process provides you with an organized patent database that makes it easier to identify the company's IP resources (and needs) for future NPD and out-licensing efforts. Every patent is rated according to its commercial potential, allowing future resources to be directed toward those patents that appear to have the highest potential.

Furthermore, screening can guide future R&D decisions (see Chapter 20). If the screening showed that a market need exists or is emerging for a class of patents in the portfolio, further analysis might show that additional R&D in that area would be a sound investment. Conversely,

> *Screening can begin to guide how the company can capitalize on its strengths and eliminate or compensate for the weaknesses*

patents that received a medium-low or low screening rating due to a low market need might indicate an area where the company should consider reducing or eliminating its R&D in that area. Similarly, if the screening of an internally developed control system showed that a similar or even better system could have been purchased from a company specializing in such systems, then the company might make better make-vs.-buy decisions in the future. By illuminating a company's IP strengths and weaknesses, screening can begin to guide how the company can capitalize on its strengths (i.e., conduct more NPD and R&D) and eliminate (i.e., less R&D) or compensate for (i.e., mergers and acquisitions) the weaknesses.

In cases where the screening process has been applied to a backlog of patents, procedures can be easily implemented to make screening an ongoing process before pursuing patent protection. The steps described in this chapter can be applied to invention disclosures as they are submitted to the company's patenting or IP management office. Once the disposition decision has been made, the new technologies are added to the prioritized list of patents/disclosures according to their rating. This prioritized list should be reevaluated quarterly or semiannually to ensure that it reflects the strategic priorities of the company.

Before starting any R&D or NPD effort, check the company's patent/disclosure database to see if the solution has already been identified within the company. Consider whether some portion of the product can be addressed with technology developed by an outside company that can be accessed via in-licensing, acquisition, or joint development to reduce R&D costs.

Finally, ongoing screening ensures that you are maintaining an ongoing understanding of the marketplace. This understanding greatly enhances the creativity of the NPD team, encouraging the type of "outside-the-box" thinking that leads to revolutionary rather than evolutionary solutions to market problems with new products—be they developed internally at the company or externally by out-licensing your high-potential patents.

References

"Art Fry and the Invention of Post-it® Notes," *3M Innovation Chronicles*, (April 1998) (http://www.3m.com/about3M/pioneers/fry.jhtml).

Bukowitz, W. and Williams, R., *The Knowledge Management Fieldbook*. London: Financial Times/Prentice Hall, 1999.

Jain, A. K., "Intellectual Property: Smart Management." *Silicon India*, March, 1999.

Laura A. Schoppe is president and owner of Fuentek, LLC, based in the Research Triangle Park area of North Carolina. In her 11 years of IP management experience, Ms. Schoppe has established an impressive track record of success in moving technologies into new markets. She has managed commercial IP and technology management activities for American Standard Companies, Lockheed Martin, NASA, Rohm and Haas, Textron, Xerox, and other clients. She has experience in all aspects of IP management, particularly leading license negotiation activities to transition innovations to new products. She recently led a project to organize, screen, assess, and market a major university's portfolio of over 700 patents. She also has developed and delivered technology commercialization training programs and successfully managed several marketing materials development projects. In addition, she has 12 years of experience leading research for several defense contractors. Ms. Schoppe holds an M.B.A. from the University of North Carolina–Chapel Hill, an M.S. in mechanical and aerospace engineering from Princeton University, and a B.S. in mechanical engineering and engineering/public policy from Carnegie Mellon University.

Nancy Pekar is a writer and editor for Fuentek, LLC. She has developed technology marketing materials for various media, including brochures, Web sites, videos, and multimedia CD-ROMs. She has written outreach and "in-reach" guidebooks as well as award-winning annual reports. In addition, Ms. Pekar has edited scientific and economics reports for the Global Alliance for TB Drug Development, including a report published as a supplement to the journal *Tuberculosis*. She has prepared proceedings reports for more than ten workshops exploring the technical issues associated with hypoglycemia, diabetic retinopathy, noninvasive blood glucose monitoring, and breast cancer imaging. She also has written articles for *Government Finance Review*. Ms. Pekar is a member of the Carolina Chapter of the Society for Technical Communication and holds a B.A. in creative writing from Carnegie Mellon University.

CHAPTER TWENTY

TECHNOLOGY MANAGEMENT

Greg Evans and Patrice Gausselin

20.1 Introduction

Today's Marketing demands for *faster, better, cheaper* require better up-front strategic planning with cohesive alignment and integration between technology and strategic business planning processes. The ultimate goal of technology management is to prioritize and focus research and development efforts on technology opportunities today that will have a positive impact on corporate revenue in the future. Two key supporting processes are *technology planning* and *technology mining*. Through appropriate design and implementation, these processes can:

1. Identify resident technology and align it with current and future business needs
2. Identify gaps between resident technology and business needs
3. Identify resident technology that is no longer viable for meeting current and future business needs
4. Identify the best approach to obtain new technology, whether through internal development or external acquisition
5. Identify opportunities to expand technology usage beyond the core business

This chapter on technology management will provide practical insight into the philosophy, processes, and tools to consider when managing technology assets.

This chapter will stress the importance of ongoing, cross-functional communication, highlighting the advantages of a defined technology management process.

20.2 Technology Planning

Technology planning is a process that results in an actionable plan to leverage new and existing technologies consistent with business strategies and customer needs. It should be a systematic, cross-functional, and iterative process. The published plan will be a summary document highlighting strategic business goals, competitive industry status, internal technology position, technology opportunities, and prioritized strategies and tactical action plans. An example is provided as Table 20.1; however, the appropriate content and view must be identified for each company. It is not a one-time activity created in a vacuum by a few key staff within the technical community. Rather, it should be a collaborative effort with input from a wide variety of cross-functional areas and support from executive management. Participation from Marketing counterparts is critical to the overall alignment of R&D efforts with the marketing business vision. It is a comprehensive and ongoing innovation process, which explores opportunities inside and outside the core business. Technology planning and market business planning occur simultaneously as inputs and outputs of one another and precede the product planning process. To impact the bottom line, both processes must be aligned with the *corporate strategic goals*. These strategic goals challenge everyone to identify leading-edge, innovative, and competitive products for the future. Thus, a technology-planning process provides a means to identify technology opportunities, then focus, select and prioritize technology development efforts in alignment with strategic business and marketing goals. In summary, the purpose of technology planning is multifaceted:

- Align technology pursuits with business goals
- Proactively manage technology development
- Create new products with a competitive edge
- Enhance resource allocation
- Protect and leverage technology assets
- Provide a consistent source of ideation

Technology development is not *product development*. Rather it is a process of acquiring knowledge, which can later be utilized in the design of new products to meet market needs (Bone and Saxon, 2000). Understanding this philosophy

TABLE 20.1 TECHNOLOGY PLAN EXAMPLE.

TECHNOLOGY PLAN CORE BUSINESS LINE = Oral Care

Strategic Goals	• Maintain market share for a minimum of five years. • Expand product offering into global markets years 3–5.
Overall Competitive Position	• Competitive product launches on the rise. • Product category has been expanding in Europe and Asia, where dental care has been limited. • Competitive advertising very aggressive claims. • Strict regulations that are market specific.
Internal Technology Position	• Patented abrasive technology. • Proven product performance. • Unique dispensing technology. • One size fits all product; family usage.
Technology Opportunities	• Seek external partner for adjunct technology; whitening, delivery form and so forth. • Explore perceived benefits of current product through international consumer use testing. • Leverage dispensing technologies from another internal business area. • Update current product to be multifunctional. • Evaluate product synergism with other core products.

Technology Strategy 1—Actions	• Increase focus on global competitive intelligence.
	  1. Form CI Team; establish CI budget.
	  2. Obtain European competitive product samples.
	  3. Conduct CI search through third party.
	  4. Present findings to corporate sponsor in three months.

Technology Strategy 2—Actions	• Increase innovation resources in this core brand area.
	  1. Assign dedicated resources for six months to identify new technology direction.
	  2. Provide monthly updates to corporate sponsor.

A technology-planning process provides a means to identify technology opportunities, then focus, select, and prioritize technology development efforts in alignment with strategic business and marketing goals.

provides a perspective on the linkage between technology development and product development activities as reflected in Figure 20.1.

To ensure that all participants are on the same page, it is essential to define *technology* within a given organization for use within technology-planning processes. Consider this a working definition. To achieve the goals of technology planning, the definition should provide a connection related to a financial output of the organization. Bone and Saxon defined technology as, "scientific know-how, embodied in people, plant, patents, laboratories and equipment" (Bone and Saxon, 2000). An expanded definition that is more useful to a firm seeking long-term management of technology for profitability may define technology as, scientific know-how used to deliver value-added products for customers and businesses. Technology is what makes products functional and competitive. It may or may not be proprietary. Understanding the definition of *technology* will provide the framework for a technology-planning process. Incorporating a connection between technology and value-added products ensures that technology development will be focused on opportunities linked to strategic business plans.

A technology-planning process comprises three key areas of inputs: technology insight, competitive insight, and marketing insight. Two graphics are provided that show an overview of the complete process, Figure 20.2 depicts the inputs and outputs, and Figure 20.3 represents the flow of the processes steps in an iterative pattern.

Step 1 is the formation of a cross-functional team led by R&D. When forming the team, consider those functional areas critical to the identification and development of technology. This team should be composed of R&D staff who have both a technical background and a strategic vision, their Marketing counterparts, and perhaps consultants and industry experts. The team should

FIGURE 20.1 TECHNOLOGY DEVELOPMENT VS. PRODUCT DEVELOPMENT.

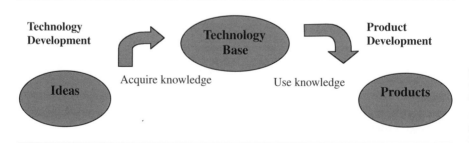

FIGURE 20.2 TECHNOLOGY-PLANNING PROCESS: INPUTS.

include people with the combined experiences and knowledge to get the job done. Team membership will vary based upon the specific field of interest. For instance, in the pharmaceutical industries, regulatory participation will be key to the team's output. Whereas for another industry, such as industrial chemicals, the Manufacturing and Technical Service areas may be appropriate to include on the team.

Step 2 requires the team to identify and categorize internal capabilities and competencies. Technology categories may be ingredient types, components, techniques, test methods, and so on that provide finished product functionality and consumer perceived value. In some cases, these technology categories will be "building blocks" or platforms upon which many products can be created. Some will be considered core competencies (Prahalad and Hamel, 1990) of your organization. It is these technology competencies that will grow or be leveraged across business segments, while others may be identified as "underutilized or quiescent." The quiescent technology may have value that will be realized through a technology mining analysis.

In Step 3, the team will align the defined technology categories with functional marketing product categories. For instance, in the personal care industry, oral care would be the functional product category, and some technology categories may be package dispensing, abrasives, surfactants, and performance testing.

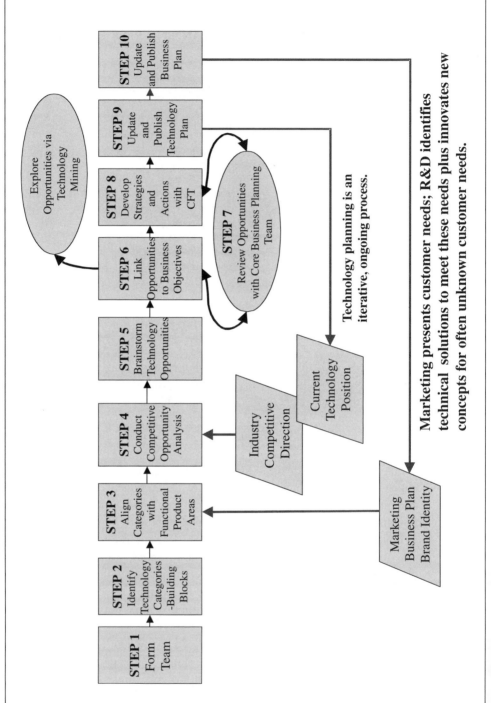

FIGURE 20.3 TECHNOLOGY-PLANNING PROCESS: 10 STEPS.

In Step 4, an in-depth review of the competitive marketplace should be completed and the internal technology position evaluated against the competitive landscape. A SWOT analysis is a common technique for evaluating overall competitiveness. The outcome is typically listed in a 2 x 2 table consisting of: "S"trengths, "W"eaknesses, "O"pportunities, and "T"hreats. An example is provided in Figure 20.4 for a consumer product. This activity provides a means to discover gaps within your technology base where new technology research will be needed to achieve future goals.

In Step 5, the cross-functional team will brainstorm new opportunities based upon their knowledge of the industry, insight from various consultant and supplier networks, competitive insight, and so forth. It is suggested that a neutral facilitator lead this brainstorming session so that all ideas are captured with none being discounted before consideration. Once all the ideas are gathered, they should be screened to group common opportunities together. Opportunities can be organized as short-, medium-, and long-term based upon technical and commercial viability.

In Step 6, the team reviews the opportunities and confirms an alignment with marketing business objectives. The team should meet to review the comprehensive list of technology opportunities against strategic business plans with sufficient dialogue that both technical and marketing aspects are thoroughly

FIGURE 20.4 TECHNOLOGY ANALYSIS: VITAMIN.

STRENGTHS	WEAKNESSES
1. Exclusive ingredients	1. Current manufacturing
2. Clinically proven performance	competency limited to tablets
3. Unique package dispensing	2. Competitors offer multiple
4. Natural, organically grown	product forms
ingredients	3. Lack of health sponsor
5. Multivitamin composition-	4. Single tablet form
potency	5. Natural product taste
OPPORTUNITIES	**THREATS**
1. License secondary technology	1. Increasing number of private label
such as gelcaps, chewables	store brands beyond name
2. Buy-out alternative product	brands
forms; retain flagship for in-	2. Extensive offerings including
house manufacturing	women's, men's, teen's,
3. Research natural flavors	children's products
	3. Consumers quickly develop brand
	loyalty

understood by the cross-functional team members. It may be necessary to create a "philosophical product prototype" to understand the merit of a given technology to a future product.

Another tool the team may opt to use is roadmaps. These provide a visual representation of how, where, and when technologies connect to products. It is often said that a picture is worth a thousand words. Roadmapping provides this picture. This technique, or tool, may be used to visualize the linkage between technologies/building blocks and business goals, it can be viewed as a stepping-stone approach for defining short-, medium-, and long-term strategies and actions for a given building block. Roadmaps also are effective guides for connecting technologies, building blocks, and competencies to customer needs (Albright and Kappel, 2003). Roadmaps are created in two dimensions with *time* as the most common x-axis variable. Multiple y-axis variables are measured against time. These may include such elements as technology options, competitive information, launch market, and resource requirements to name a few. There is significant published work in the area of roadmapping. A suggested reference on roadmapping is the Corporate Executive Board, who published an industry overview of this topic (Research and Technology Executive Council, 2002). The Research and Technology Executive Council (RTEC) identified the fact that firms utilize roadmaps to process a variety of information types including technology strategies. A Phillips Electronics example is presented in Figure 20.5. "At Phillips Electronics, roadmapping may be applied to systems,

FIGURE 20.5 TECHNOLOGY ROADMAP.

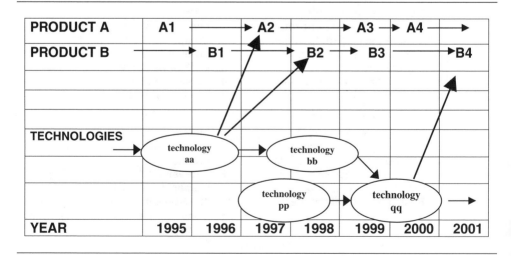

to a product range, to individual projects, to components, or to a production process" (Groenveld, 1997). The example in Figure 20.5 links technology and product over seven-year time frame. The arrows indicate the usage of a technology in a product. The evolution of technology from one generation to the next is evident. *Technology aa* is advanced to *technology bb* and further into *technology qq*. Technologies not advancing to the product stage such as *technology bb* or *technology pp* become apparent. Return on investment for these technologies may be gained through *technology mining*. In this process, opportunities to expand beyond the core business or to out-license would be explored.

In Step 7, the team will review, screen, and filter the opportunities with a core business planning team of senior level executives. When presenting the opportunities to this audience, it would be advantageous to highlight future resource requirements because these needs may have an impact on overall priorities and the selection of which opportunities to explore further. The take-away from this discussion should be a prioritized list of short-, medium- and long-term technology opportunities. Once these priority technology opportunities are established, a manageable number of *technology strategies* can be defined and tactical action plans created for each during Step 8. It is advisable not to eliminate any technology opportunities. Rather, retain these for future usage or evaluate their merit through a technology-mining process for external value.

> *It is advisable not to eliminate any technology opportunities; rather, retain these for future usage or evaluate their merit through a technology mining process for external value.*

In the final steps, an annual technology plan is published, followed by the distribution of an annual business plan to business leadership. A regular review and update should be scheduled for technology plans within your company by an internal advisory team or similar peer review group. This group should have the knowledge and vested interest in the particular business area. Doing so no less than annually is suggested to maintain alignment with the annual strategic business-planning processes. For industries with very short or very long product life cycles, the duration may be adjusted. A technology plan may take the form of a one-page summary, again, similar to Table 20.1. The intent is to highlight the strategic goals of the organization, its competitive position, the technology opportunities, and the technology strategies for a given time frame. A format should be created that is user-friendly

> *Connections between other processes and systems will ensure that Technology Plans are a valuable tool.*

and can be easily updated. Connections between other processes and systems will ensure that technology plans are a valuable tool.

20.3 Technology-Mining Process

As an outcome of effective technology planning, technology development will be aligned to support the core business. High-performance companies ensure that their business strategy is connected to a PITS (product and innovation strategy) (Cooper, 2000). By improving the strategic align-

> *Highly effective companies have learned to extract value by linking their technology-planning process with a technology-mining process.*

ment between business and technology, more-effective product developments may result, but other opportunities beyond the scope of the core business may not. Technology planning places emphasis on *creating* value by expanding or leveraging the existing technology portfolio. On the other hand, a technology-mining process places emphasis on extracting value from the existing portfolio of technologies. Highly effective companies have learned to *extract* value by linking their technology-planning process with a technology-mining process (see Figure 20.6).

During Step 2 of the technology-planning process, both building block and quiescent technologies may be identified. These technologies will merit additional evaluation through a rigorous mining process that is not limited to current business models or needs. Mining these technologies to increase shareholder value without ever expanding the technology portfolio provides the company with a significant return on investment. This can be accomplished by using the building blocks to "build" products that were overlooked by the technology-planning process, or by identifying quiescent technologies that can be offered to competitors through private labeling or outright sale of the technology. Private labeling offers the additional advantages of increasing manufacturing plant utilization as well as helping to assure that the competition is using "older" technology. Figure 20.7 depicts a proposed "macro" process map for technology mining.

There are four key components that any mining process should include and additional steps can be added to suit specific corporate culture and business needs. In essence, an effective technology-mining process must answer the questions of What?; How?; How Much?; and Who?

FIGURE 20.6 LINKED PROCESSES.

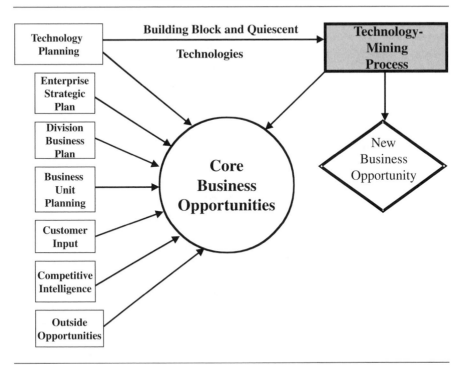

20.3.1 Opportunity Identification

Opportunity identification can be performed with any number of published methodologies that must answer the question of how a technology can be utilized in ways that are not employed by the core business. Assess each technology and determine how it could be applied to other products while conveying similar competitive or technological advantage and thus, create a product opportunity. For exam-

While many technologies will not have the same broad application as the integrated circuit, the concept of transferring technological advantage from one product application to another is the same.

ple, a building block technology such as the integrated circuit was developed by Jack Kilby (Kilby, 1964) and Robert Noyce (Noyce, 1961) to replace bulky transistors, resistors, and capacitors in computer applications. The advantage

FIGURE 20.7 TECHNOLOGY-MINING PROCESS.

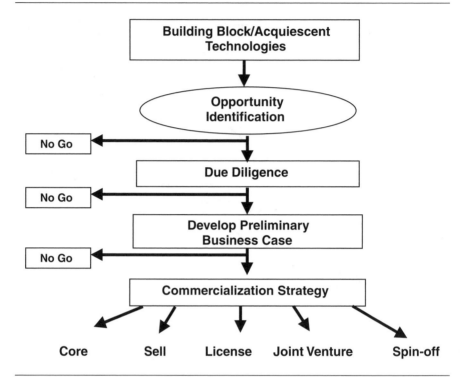

of miniaturizing electronic componentry has since been applied to countless other products ranging from wristwatches to spaceships. While many technologies will not have the same broad application as the integrated circuit, the concept of transferring a technological advantage from one product application to another is the same.

As the first step of the process, this is the only one that is mandatory, and the results of each step should be reviewed cross-functionally to decide whether to continue to invest resources in subsequent steps. Each process step acts as a filter, with only the highest potential opportunities reaching the subsequent steps that will require increased resource expenditure.

20.3.2 Due Diligence

Due diligence requires that a "litmus test" be performed by the R&D organization to validate the technical feasibility of each opportunity. This step will further refine opportunities and may identify additional ones to evaluate. The key to this step is to do preliminary evaluations in order to facilitate the development of a business case, not the development of a new product! The use of prototyping is a common means to evaluate applications. This can be done through minimum resource expenditure with the intent to create a physical facsimile of the product that can be evaluated for functionality, manufacturability, and cost. In order to perform technical due diligence, some level of market and product intelligence may also be required to ensure that the advantages offered to other products are, in fact, necessary ones. Access to this type of information through the Internet and other widely publicized media make this a far less daunting task than it might first appear. Knowing that it works and that someone will want it are key outputs for this step.

20.3.3 Preliminary Business Case

A preliminary business case is developed based on the results of due diligence. Many companies have established new business development organizations that have this sole responsibility. Unfortunately, many of these organizations are more focused upon merger and acquisition activities than the "Rembrandts in the attic" (Rivette and Kline, 1999). A preliminary business case must identify estimated market potential and resource requirements. While no formal functional group is necessary, the right skill sets must be collected from various parts of the company. Business case teams typically include representatives from R&D, Marketing, Market Research, Sales, Finance, and Legal. The challenges in getting dedicated resources for this purpose and obtaining resources that are able to separate themselves from the everyday business and paradigms it creates has resulted in many companies using external resources to develop business cases.

20.3.4 Commercialization Strategy

A commercialization strategy is developed once the preliminary business case has cleared internal hurdles and has been sanctioned by management. It proposes who and how the opportunity will be commercialized. Much has been published on developing a strategy toward licensing intellectual assets (Parr and Sullivan, 1996; World Research Group, 2002; Manfroy, 2000; O'Shaughnessy and Germaraad, 2000), but it often overlooks the core business. Avoiding the trappings of the core business mentality so as to "Think out of the Box" is imperative during the early stages of opportunity identification (Vance and Deacon, 1995). However, the challenges presented to any organization attempting to pursue licensing, joint ventures, spin-offs, and so on can be monumental, and the core business must be considered a "preferred customer."

20.4 The Organizational Structure

A discussion on technology management would be incomplete unless it included some commentary concerning organizational structure (see Chapter 8). Internal processes such as technology planning or technology mining will only be productive if the organization supports and nurtures it through structural components with committed resources. A recent study con-

> *Internal processes such as technology planning or technology mining will only be productive if the organization supports and nurtures it through structural components with committed resources.*

ducted by the Research and Technology Council of the Corporate Executive Board evaluated 20 companies representing a broad range of industries (RTEC, 2003). This study confirms that there is a growing trend for companies to restructure their R&D organizations to better capture and leverage their technology assets. Key findings include the emergence of "Technology Councils" to better use technology across business units, and the establishment of a central R&D office to coordinate a corporate-wide technology-planning process. Over half of the companies that were studied had R&D organization entities such as Technology and Business Strategy, Technology Licensing, New Business Opportunities, Technology Planning and Business Development. In fact, this evolution of the R&D organization has led, in many cases, to the appointment of a chief technology officer (CTO), who has a much broader responsibility, and expectation, than the traditional "head of R&D" (Smith, 2003). Alcoa's Paul O'Neill states that a CTO should "identify, access (and) investigate high-risk, high-return technologies possessing potential application within existing businesses or for creating new businesses" (O'Neill and Bridenbaugh, 1992). The advent of the CTO elevates technology to the "boardroom" so it can become a critical element in business strategy planning, thus making effective technology management an absolute requirement for any R&D organization that seeks to contribute to the future growth of its company.

20.5 Summary

The ultimate goal of technology management is to prioritize and focus effort on technology opportunities today that will have a positive impact on corporate revenue in the future. To accomplish this, corporations should invest in and develop tools, processes, and structure that will support the identification of technology opportunities to fuel product innovation and product-to-market excellence.

References

Albright, Richard E. and Kappel, Thomas A., "Roadmapping in the Corporation." *Research Technology Management*, 31–40 (March–April 2003).

Bone, Steve and Saxon, Tim., "Technology Strategy," *Research Technology Management*, 50–40 (July–August 2000).

Cooper, R. G., "Product Innovation and Technology Strategy." *Research Technology Management*, 38–40 (January–February 2000).

Corporate Executive Board, "Profiles of R&D Functions, Research & Technology Executive Council," July 2003.

Groenveld, P., "Roadmapping Integrates Business and Technology," *Research Technology Management*, 48–55 (1997).

Kilby, Jack S., "Miniaturized Electronic Circuits," U.S. Patent No. 3,138,743, June 23, 1964.

Manfroy, Willy, "Need Strategy for Licensing Success," *les Nouvelles* (March 2000).

Noyce, Robert N., "Semiconductor Device-and-Lead Structure," U.S. Patent No. 2,981.877, April 25, 1961.

O'Neill. P. H. and Bridenbaugh, P. R., "Credibility Between CEO and CTO—A CEO's Perspective; Credibility Between CEO and CTO—A CTO Perspective," *Research Technology Management*, 25–34 (November–December 1992).

O'Shaughnessy, James P. and Germaraad, Paul, "Tools of the Trade for Analyzing IP Opportunities," *les Nouvelles* (March 2000).

Parr, Russell L. and Sullivan, Patrick H. (Editors), *Technology Licensing "Corporate Strategies for Maximizing Value,"* Wiley Intellectual Property Series, New York: Wiley, 1996.

Prahalad C. K and Hamel, Gary., "The Core Competence of the Corporation." *Harvard Business Review* (May–June 1990).

Research and Technology Executive Council, Corporate Executive Board, "Strategies in Technology Forecasting and Roadmapping," August 2002.

Rivette, Kevin G. and Kline, David, *Rembrants in the Attic: Unlocking the Hidden Value of Patents.* Cambridged, MA: Harvard Business School Press, 1999.

Smith, Roger D., "The Chief Technology Officer: Strategic Responsibilities and Relationships," *Research Technology Management*, 28–36 (July–August 2003).

Vance, Mike and Deacon, Diane, *Thinking out of the Box.* Career Press, 1995.

World Research Group, Extracting Value from Your Intellectual Asset Portfolio Conference, Chicago, November 21–22, 2002.

Gregory S. Evans directs the technical aspects of the global product development activities for the Access Business Group, a company of Alticor. This responsibility includes overseeing a technical staff of over 220 that develop new and improved products in support of the Access Business Group's beauty and home, water and air treatment, and nutrition and wellness businesses in over 80 countries and territories. Prior to Alticor, Evans was a research supervisor for Alberto Culver Company in the Chicago area. Additionally, Evans is a member of several industry and professional organizations, including the Industrial Research Institute, the Society of Cosmetic Chemists, the Licensing Executives Society, the American Chemical Society, and the Product Development Management Association.

Patrice M Gausselin has 17 years of diverse product development experience with the Access Business Group, including formulation chemist and leadership positions within the Personal Care, Skin Care, and Cosmetics and Durables product areas. Her current responsibilities include new product development processes and tools, including technology-planning, resource management, and performance metrics for the R&D/QA division. She has presented at industry events including In-Cosmetics, the American Academy of Dermatology, and IQPC on both integrating technology and business processes and knowledge management strategies in R&D. She recently published on R&D metrics through the Corporate Executive Board, Research & Technology Executive Council. She is a member of the Society of Cosmetic Chemists.

PART FOUR

DOING THE DEVELOPMENT

Most people miss opportunity when they see it, because it comes wearing coveralls and looks like work.

THOMAS EDISON, INVENTOR AND ENTREPRENEUR, 1900

Gate decisions are high-stakes bets in which managers put their money on the NPD projects with the greatest potential payoff. Chapter 21 describes how to improve gate decisions and deal with common problems associated with gate deliverables and standards.

Winning approval in reviews of a product's development does not have to be difficult, nor does it need to be a "drop-everything-and-panic" proposition. However, it does need work. Chapter 22 delineates planning steps that go a long way toward easing the burden of putting together a winning presentation.

Decisions during development are often predicated on one or several forecasts. Chapter 23 discussess the forecasting objective and offers several types of new product forecasting approaches for establishing a sound baseline forecast.

Industrial design plays a key role during development as well. In its broadest sense, "industrial design" refers to the process of building something that works in a tangible sense, while also embodying intangible principles that work emotionally. Design strategies discussed in Chapter 24 show there are several areas critical for successful designs, as well as a few common problem areas.

Many seasoned new product development practitioners would note that industrial designers are just following what Chapter 1 lays out as key parts of developing winning new products. However, industrial design works best when, as detailed in Chapter 25, there is a good understanding of the background and motivation of industrial designers

"Human factors," "ergonomics," "usability," "user-centered design," and "interaction design" are terms with essentially the same meaning. But as Chapter 26 points out, the designer should follow good human factors design principles.

Rapid prototyping is a computer-aided technology used to create physical models from computer-aided design programs. For those practitioners considering using rapid prototyping for the first time, Chapter 27 shows how to define and assess specific needs and align them with what is best for the users' firm.

Risk analysis tools for hazard analysis and for failure modes and effects analysis (FEMA) are described in Chapter 28. The authors prescribe the use of an independent, external reviewer to provide better risk assessment of a new product's development.

CHAPTER TWENTY-ONE

GATE DECISIONS: THE KEY TO MANAGING RISK DURING NEW PRODUCT DEVELOPMENT

Jeffrey B. Schmidt

In too many firms, projects seem to acquire a life of their own. They proceed like an express train, careening down the track, slowing down at the stations (review points), but never intending to stop until they reach their ultimate destination, market launch.

ROBERT G. COOPER *(1993, P.166)*

21.1 Introduction

Most types of new product development (NPD) processes have some type of project review points (Griffin, 1997). For example, the traditional Stage-Gate® process shown in Figure 21.1 portrays the flow of NPD activities or stages (represented by rectangles) and project review points or gates (represented by diamonds). Following each stage is a gate (also called a review or decision point) where managers determine whether to proceed with developing the project (i.e., "go" decision) or to terminate the project (i.e., "kill" decision) prior to commercialization based on the projected marketing, technical, and financial performance. These managers or "gatekeepers" often constitute a cross-functional team that includes members from such areas such as Marketing, Finance, Research & Development, and Manufacturing.

While good gate decisions are the key to managing risk, gate decisions are among the least understood aspects of the NPD process, and thus, they are

FIGURE 21.1 A STAGE-GATE NEW PRODUCT DEVELOPMENT PROCESS.

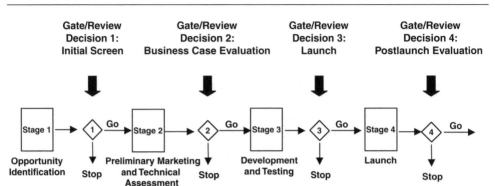

Adapted from Cooper (1990).

often poorly undertaken. In fact, gate decisions were rated as the least proficiently conducted component of the NPD process (Cooper and Kleinschmidt, 1996). Given the increasing importance of new products for many firms and the high costs to develop and launch new products, there is a need to understand how gates should be structured and how gate decisions should be made. The purpose of this chapter is to provide such understanding by introducing the topic of NPD review points, or gates, along with directions for improving an organization's NPD project continuation/termination decisions.

21.2 Gates Types and Their Components

Gates are basically part of a winnowing down process. Figure 21.2 shows the NPD funnel which depicts many new product opportunities available to an organization. As these opportunities enter the NPD process and progress through it, the weaker ones (in an absolute or relative sense) are culled by the gatekeepers such that (hopefully) far fewer products are commercialized than

---

Gate decisions are the weakest aspect of the NPD process.

FIGURE 21.2 NEW PRODUCT DEVELOPMENT FUNNEL.

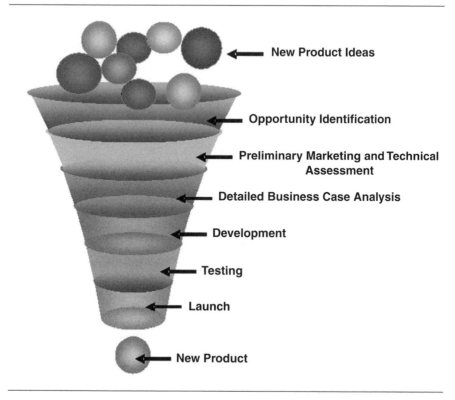

New Product Ideas

Opportunity Identification

Preliminary Marketing and Technical Assessment

Detailed Business Case Analysis

Development

Testing

Launch

New Product

were considered or even entered into the NPD process. In a recently completed study, it was found that the percentage of NPD projects drops significantly over the successive stages of development, and NPD projects for radical innovations drop off marginally faster than incremental ones. See Figure 21.3.

Two types of gates are possible. The first type of gate is called a rigid gate where all necessary criteria must be passed in order to continue the project. Indeed, it is possible in the case of a rigid gate that the failure to reach even a

The gate decisions are high-stakes bets where managers put their money on the NPD projects with the greatest potential payoff.

FIGURE 21.3 PROJECT SURVIVAL RATES OVER THE NPD PROCESS.

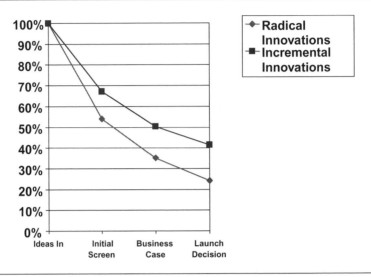

Source: Schmidt, Griffin, and Montoya-Weiss, 2003.

single threshold could derail a NPD project. The second type of gate is called a flexible or permeable gate, which allows a limited number of tasks, frequently those with long lead times, to move forward to the next stage without having to pass all criteria. Cooper (2000) and Rosenau (1996) provide good discussions of rigid and flexible gates.

Both types of gates have three components: *deliverables* (information on project progress, impediments such as technical delays, market conditions and viability, likelihood of success, etc.), *criteria (or hurdles)*, and *decisions* (that is, either a go, stop,

> *Gates consist of deliverables (information), criteria (hurdles), and Stop/Go decisions.*

or hold decision made by the gatekeepers) (Cooper 2001). The deliverables result from the NPD activities performed by functional experts. In early NPD process stages, information is likely "sketchy," not very quantitative, nor credible because the results are based perhaps on a concept and many untested assumptions. Over the course of the NPD process, the information should become more solid, since working prototypes and a variety of test results are available.

> *Gates criteria should be set by gatekeepers—not NPD team members.*

The criteria are the standards against which the deliverables are compared. To illustrate, suppose criteria of 15 percent market share in the product category and positive profits after year one are set for a new consumer packaged good. Before proceeding to the commercialization stage, the test market results could be compared to these criteria, which normally are set by gatekeepers rather than NPD team members. These criteria change in relative importance over the stages of the NPD process with marketing and technical criteria being important in the early stages and financial criteria increasing in importance at later stages (Hart et al., 2003).

The second component of gates is the criteria against which performance (projected or actual) is compared. Two types of criteria exist—"must meet" and "should meet." The former type, associated with rigid gates, is a hurdle that must be cleared to continue the project. In contrast, flexible gates are used to maintain risk without unduly delaying NPD projects. "Should meet" criteria are associated with flexible gates where the NPD project may continue for a limited time until remaining criteria are met or deliverables are completed (called permissive gates). Table 21.1 shows the six most commonly used gate criteria for three key points in the NPD process based on a survey of PDMA members.

Gatekeepers often are a team of high-level managers that controls critical monetary and personnel resources required to move the project forward (or

TABLE 21.1 TOP 6 GATE CRITERIA USED BY STAGE.

Gate 1	Gate 2	Gate 3
Market Potential (M) 86%	Technical Feasibility (T) 85%	Product Performance (T) 86%
Strategic Fit (M) 85%	Sales Objectives (F) 81%	Sales Objectives (F) 79%
Technical Feasibility (T) 84%	Product Performance (T) 79%	Quality Objectives (T) 78%
Sales Objectives (F) 81%	Product Advantage (M) 77%	Profit Potential (F) 75%
Product Advantage (M) 79%	Strategic Fit (M) 76%	Customer Acceptance (M) 73%
Profit Potential (F) 71%	ROI (F) 73%	Product Advantage (M) 72%

Notes: Gates correspond with Figure 21.1.

Numbers represent percentage of firms in sample reporting to use each criteria.

M = marketing criterion, T = technical criterion, F = financial criterion.

Source: Schmidt, Griffin, and Montoya-Weiss, 2003.

not) through their gate decisions. The separation between those performing the NPD activities and those making gate decisions is critical to maintaining control (discussed below). Resources are incrementally allocated to various projects that deserve to be continued. These gatekeepers (sometimes called the Product Approval Committee or PAC) evaluate NPD projects relative to the "must meet" and "should meet" criteria. Furthermore, comparisons often are made across the portfolio of projects currently underway such that each NPD project is prioritized. This means that sometimes promising projects are terminated, since the other projects are in process with higher potential or a better strategic fit for the organization. See Cooper et al. (1998) for an excellent treatment of portfolio management techniques (also see Chapter 3).

The PAC meets periodically to review the progress of NPD teams and projects. These meetings might be scheduled monthly, quarterly, or as needed depending on the size of the organization, the extent of NPD activity in the organization, and the distance the gatekeepers must travel to attend. Often, gate meetings run for an entire day (or multiple days!) with the PAC reviewing and prioritizing numerous projects.

Because marketing, technical, and financial information that has been generated during the preceding stage is essential to making good gate decisions, the NPD team typically is required to distribute key information and reports related to the must meet and should meet criteria to the PAC in advance of the gate meeting. This gives the PAC time to read the material and ask questions prior to the formal gate presentation. (For more information see Deck, 2002).

At the gate meeting, the NPD team leader (or selected team members) typically makes a formal presentation on the status of the NPD project. Again, depending on the organization, the time allotted for these presentations might be as long as two or three hours or as short as fifteen minutes. What has been accomplished since the last review? What are potential marketing, technical, and financial roadblocks? How are they to be overcome? What is the team's recommendation for moving ahead? What types and amounts of resources are required to complete the next stage?

This leads to the third component of gates, which is the continuation/termination decision. The ultimate responsibility of the PAC is to make a go or stop decision, often on the same day as the presentation. If the project is judged to meet the established criteria, it is prioritized. If the priority is high enough, the NPD project is permitted to move ahead to the next stage, and the necessary resources are committed. Conversely, if the project is terminated, the team members might be assigned to other projects or will have additional time to work on other projects to which they also are assigned. It should be noted that the PAC has a third option besides go or stop, namely hold. A hold decision is a temporary stop until additional information can be collected or certain problems can be remedied.

21.3 Why Are Good Gate Decisions Vital?

Making effective and efficient NPD project continuation/termination decisions is of critical important for several reasons. First, developing new products is expensive! Gillette is reported to have spent $1 billion developing its Mach 3® razor, and Boeing has spent over $10 billion on its Sonic Cruiser (which will likely never be commercialized). And Iridium, Motorola's former satellite telephone service, involved launching 66 satellites into space at a cost of $5 billion. Successful new products must recoup all of their related development, testing, and marketing costs, but they also must pay for the failures (many of which cost tens or hundreds of millions of dollars) and those NPD projects killed prior to commercialization. In extreme situations, firms might not survive if they develop the wrong products (e.g., aircraft manufacturers and pharmaceutical companies), since the cost of development is so great or because it takes years to recover and develop a successful product or technology.

Second, the cost and time to complete each subsequent stage of the NPD process frequently increases dramatically (Cooper and Kleinschmidt, 1986; Urban and Hauser, 1993). So that scarce resources are not wasted, it's best to stop NPD projects quickly if they are not going to be successful. However, PACs struggle to balance Type I errors (allowing a project to continue and it subsequently fails in the market) and Type II errors (terminating a project that would have been successful in the future had it been commercialized) (Crawford and Benedetto 2000:156).

Third, firms nearly always have many more ideas and product concepts (which are inexpensive) than available funding. The gate decisions are like high-stakes bets where managers put their money on the NPD projects they believe have the greatest chance for a payoff. Ideally, the information provided by the NPD team, and processing of that information by the PAC, along with intangibles, such as gut instinct and managerial experience, allow the gatekeepers to put the organization's resources on the projects with a greater chance of being successful.

Fourth, slow decisions lengthen product development time, and fifth, weak (i.e., noncommittal) decisions hurt new product efforts. If NPD teams must wait for approval and resources due to rescheduled or canceled meetings, or because of delayed continuation/termination decisions, the market window may close as could the opportunity to earn patents or being first to market evaporate.

While weak decisions that allow a NPD project to continue might appear to harm NPD team morale less than canceling the project, the opposite is true. What can be more demoralizing than working on a project that has little chance of success and is only weakly supported by the management? Gate decisions need to be made quickly and decisively.

Fifth, as projects move forward, it becomes increasingly difficult for managers to terminate them. "What's surprising is how many companies simply can't bring themselves to say no" (Deck, 2002:173). For various reasons, they build momen-

> *Managers often have difficulty pulling the plug on NPD projects.*

tum, and the sunk costs spent on previous stages influence future investment decisions (even though accounting and financial classes train managers to ignore costs that were incurred previously, since they are irretrievable). Gatekeepers can ignore or bias negative information and allow risky projects to continue. (See Boulding et al., 1997; Finkelstein and Sanford, 2000; Schmidt and Calantone, 2002; Simon and Houghton, 2003).

A recent example illustrates this last point. Prior to commercialization, a NPD team received negative feedback from field tests for a new product that the CEO had initiated and strongly supported. This portable field filtration product was nearly impossible to use in colder weather, since the media became very rigid. In spite of strong, negative information strongly suggesting that this product would fail, the PAC, which included the CEO, opted to launch the product nationwide. As predicted in the field tests, the product failed to gain acceptance in the market. The product was subsequently withdrawn from the market, costing the company many millions of dollars more than if it had been canceled prior to launch.

21.4 Improving Gate Decisions

Recently, a study was undertaken on PDMA practitioners which asked them about gates and gate decisions in their respective organizations (Schmidt et al., 2003). Based on responses from more than 400 new product professionals, the following suggestions (and corresponding rationale) are offered for managing risk during NPD projects. This section of the chapter draws on the results of this study, as well as other related research.

- The PAC or gatekeeper team should consist of a different set of individuals than those actually conducting the NPD activities. Individuals that spend months or years working on a NPD project tend to get emotionally attached to it, making it difficult to view progress objectively. Additionally, individuals that have access to substantial resources are needed, typically higher-level managers, most of whom are not involved in the day-to-day NPD activities.
- Have clearly defined criteria (marketing, technical, and financial) that must be met, as well as those that should be met, at each stage. Agree on these, make them explicit (i.e., put them in writing) and available to others inside the organization but outside of the NPD team. Agreeing on them in advance and making them known to others help reduce runaway NPD projects (Boulding et al., 1997).
- Have project continuation/termination decisions made by a cross-functional team rather than one person (such as the CEO). Teams generally make better decisions than individuals acting alone, since they have more information available and can use information better (Schmidt et al., 2001). Individuals from different areas of the organization have different knowledge and experience and hence different perspectives and tools.
- Separate the initial continuation/termination decision from subsequent ones by using different teams or rotating team membership. Those that begin a project by making the initial "go" decision are less likely to stop NPD projects that are performing poorly compared to those that are not responsible for starting the project (Schmidt and Calantone, 2002). Human nature drives people to protect themselves psychologically; it's difficult to admit failure to ourselves or others (such as coworkers). Therefore, continued investing in a NPD project might turn the situation around and prove to ourselves and others the "correctness" of earlier decisions and our competency.
- Development projects for more innovative new products require a higher level of monitoring (i.e., more stringent criteria; consider adding review points). Managers have a tendency to become enamored with new products that are innovative and believe innovative new products are more likely to succeed than incrementally new products (Schmidt and Calantone, 2002; Simon and Houghton, 2003). Recent research shows that, on average, significantly more gates are used when developing innovative new products compared incrementally new products (4.8 versus 3.6 gates, respectively). Table 21.2 provides additional evidence that firms tend to more highly monitor innovative NPD projects compared to incremental ones. At three major points studied, the former have more gatekeepers compared to incremental NPD projects.
- Monitoring should increase as projects move closer to commercialization due to rapidly rising costs over the NPD process. Additionally, more solid

TABLE 21.2 AVERAGE NUMBER OF GATEKEEPERS BY STAGE.

	Gate 1	Gate 2	Gate 3
Innovative NPD projects	6.2	6.9	7.3
Incremental NPD projects	5.1	5.8	6.1

Notes: Gates correspond with Figure 21.1.

Source: Schmidt, Griffin, and Montoya-Weiss, 2003.

marketing, technical, and financial information is available as the project progresses. Indeed, the results in Table 21.2 reveal a significant increase in the number of individuals on the PAC from Gate 1 to Gate 3.

- Be wary of extremely optimistic and upwardly creeping forecasts. In discussions with managers, forecasts that are very high or increase dramatically over the course of NPD projects appear to be common. In one organization, the initial sales forecasts was 3400 annual unit sales for a consumer electronics product. The forecast was subsequently revised to 7000, 10,000, 15,000, 20,000, and finally 32,000 annual units! The actual sales volume was about 4500 units, quite close to the original estimate. Certainly, as more concrete information becomes available over the stages of an NPD project, forecasts should be revised. However, forecasts that appear too ambitious or those that continue to increase significantly should be viewed with deserved skepticism. Ask hard questions before relying too much on them.

- Hold gate meetings in virtual space, rather than physical space, using asynchronous (i.e., one-way) communication methods. Most organizations hold gate meetings "face-to-face" (that is, with PAC members in the same physical location). However, research suggests that managers make better NPD continuation/termination decisions if they are not physically located in the same room at the same time (Schmidt et al., 2001). Using threaded Internet discussions, as one method of asynchronous communication, information is shared more and considered more fully since the time pressure and organizational politics are reduced. This leads to more effective decisions. While it might seem that gate decisions would be made more slowly when PAC members are not physically located in the same place at the same time, this delay is not necessarily long. Recall that the NPD teams normally provided deliverables to the PAC members prior to gate meetings. However, it must be noted that virtual gate meetings might not be feasible for organizations that develop many new products each period; in such cases, it might be easier to meet and speed up decisions by using synchronous communication.

21.5 Summary

Success in developing new products is vital for the health and survival of many organizations, and good gate decisions are vital for successful NPD programs. While most NPD processes include project review points, a high proportion of firms struggle with making effective and efficient project continuation/termination decisions. Many firms are too liberal and allow too many weak projects to continue for too long, resulting in wasted resources, missed opportunities, demoralized employees, and possible damage to brand and organizational equity when products fail in the market. If organizations develop and successfully implement gate procedures, they can manage risk during new product development. Developing an effective and efficient NPD process, including gate criteria, is not an easy task and should be based on the organization's strengths and goals along with repeated exploration, experimentation, and adjustment.

References

Boulding, William, Morgan, Ruskin, and Staelin, Richard., "Pulling the Plug to Stop the New Product Drain." *Journal of Marketing Research*, 34: 164–176 (February 1997).

Cooper, Robert G., "Stage-Gate Systems: A New Tool for Managing New Products." *Business Horizons*, 33: 44–54 (May–June 1990).

Cooper, Robert G., *Winning at New Products: Accelerating the Process from Idea to Launch*. 2nd ed. Cambridge, MA: Addison-Wesley, 1993.

Cooper, Robert G., *Product Leadership: Creating and Launching Superior New Products*. Cambridge, MA: Perseus Publishing, 2000.

Cooper, Robert G., Edgett, Scott J., and Kleinschmidt, Elko J., *Portfolio Management for New Products*. Reading, MA: Addison-Wesley, 1998.

Cooper, Robert G., *Winning at New Products: Accelerating the Process from Idea to Launch*. 3rd ed. Cambridge, MA: Perseus Publishing, 2001.

Cooper, Robert G. and Kleinschmidt, Elko J., "An Investigation into the New Product Process: Steps, Deficiencies, and Impact." *J Product Innovation Management*, 3: 71–85 (March 1986).

Cooper, Robert G. and Kleinschmidt, Elko J., "Winning Businesses in Product Development: Critical Success Factors." *Research-Technology Management*, 39: 18–29 (July 1996).

Crawford, C. Merle and Benedetto, C. Anthony Di. *New Products Management*. 6th ed. Boston, MA: Irwin McGraw-Hill, 2000.

Deck, Mark J., "Decision Making: The Overlooked Competency in Product Development," in *The PDMA Toolbook for New Product Development* Paul Belliveau, Abbie Griffin, and Stephen Somermeyer (eds.). New York: John Wiley & Sons, 2002, 165–186.

Finkelstein, Sydney and Sanford, Shade H., "Learning From Corporate Mistakes: The Rise and Fall of Iridium." *Organizational Dynamics*, 29: 138–148 (Fall 2000).

Griffin, Abbie. "PDMA Research on New Product Development Practices: Updating Trends and Benchmarking Best Practices." *J Product Innovation Management*, 14: 429–458 (November 1997).

Hart, Susan, Hultink, Erik Jan, Tzokas, Nikolaos, and Commandeur, Harry R., "Industrial companies' evaluation criteria in new product development gates." *J Product Innovation Management*, 20: 22–36 (January 2003).

Rosenau, Milton D., Jr., "Choosing a Development Process That's Right for Your Company.," in Milton D. Rosenau, Jr., Abbie Griffin, George Castellion, and Ned Anscheutz (eds.), *The PDMA Handbook of New Product Development*. 1st ed. New York: John Wiley & Sons, 1996, 77–92.

Schmidt, Jeffrey B. and Calantone, Roger J., "Escalation of Commitment During New Product Development." *Journal of the Academy of Marketing Science*, 30: 103–118 (Spring 2002).

Schmidt, Jeffrey B., Griffin, Abbie, and Montoya-Weiss, Mitzi M., "Establishing Norms and 'Best Practices' In New Product Project Review And Implications For New Product Performance." Working Paper, University of Illinois at Urbana-Champaign, 2003.

Schmidt, Jeffrey B., Montoya-Weiss, Mitzi M., and Massey, Anne P., "NPD Decision Making Effectiveness: A Comparison of Individuals, Face-to-Face Groups, and Dispersed Groups." *Decision Sciences*, 32: 575–600 (Fall 2001).

Simon, Mark and Houghton, Susan M., "The Relationship Between Overconfidence and the Introduction of Risky Products: Evidence from a Field Study." *Academy of Management Journal*, 46: 139–149 (April 2003).

Urban, Glen L. and Hauser, John R., *Design and Marketing of New Products*, 2nd ed. Englewood Cliffs, NJ: Prentice Hall, 1993.

Jeffrey B. Schmidt is Assistant Professor of Business Administration at the University of Illinois at Urbana-Champaign. He received his Ph.D. at Michigan State University, and his primary research interests are new product development, product strategy, and managerial decision making during product development. He has received multiple awards for his research in the area of new product development. Jeff has been a PDMA member for more than a decade and serves on the editorial board of the *Journal of Product Innovation Management*, and served as a director on the PDMA board and as Vice President of Academic Affairs for PDMA.

CHAPTER TWENTY-TWO

WINNING PRODUCT REVIEW APPROVAL

Bob Lonadier

22.1 Introduction

This chapter discusses the key factors involved in winning product review approval. The purpose of the chapter is to assist project leaders in ensuring that their projects have the best chance of winning approval and being taken from concept to prototype and into production. Whether the company uses a formal Stage-Gate® product development and release methodology, a less-formal product review committee, or an ad-hoc senior management review committee, all project leaders are required to prepare, present, and ultimately win approval for their projects. This chapter outlines the essential steps in a product review approval process, including a checklist of steps necessary to successfully complete a product review process, critical success factors, and pitfalls to avoid. The reader should come away with not only a detailed understanding of the "hard" criteria needed to conduct a successful product review process (see Chapter 21), but also an understanding of the "soft" skills (see Chapter 10) needed to guide a new product development process from concept into production.

22.2 Overview: The Product Review Approval Process

Every project leader faces a product review approval process. In some organizations, the process is quite formal with specific approvals that must be met at various stages of the product life cycle. In others, the process is informal, with no specific milestones that must be met. In all cases, however, the project leader is called upon to justify why the organization is expending resources to design, develop, and introduce to the market his or her product. Sometimes the review process is more of a formality to ensure that all the necessary organizations within the company are "on the same page" with regard to the product development and release process. At other times and in different organizations, successful product reviews can make the difference between a product making it from concept to prototype to production and project cancelation. Project leaders, with their multiple responsibilities and time constraints, often underrate the significance of a product review approval process and therefore tend to underinvest in preparation for the review. This is unfortunate not only because it sometimes results in projects being canceled that would have otherwise been viable in the marketplace, but also because the time and effort invested in successfully defending a product review pays dividends over the entire life of the project. Done correctly, material created in preparation for a product review approval process can be reused throughout the product life cycle and becomes just as valued a communication piece as the product requirements document.

22.3 The Seven Steps to Winning Product Review Approval

Winning product review approval is straightforward if you understand and implement the following seven steps:

- Identification of critical success factors, key influencers, and stakeholders
- Background preparation and research
- Building a winning product review team
- Preparing the product review presentation
- Internal selling
- Giving the product review presentation
- Follow-up and feedback

This chapter will guide you through each step in the process. This approach is essentially the same regardless of the stage in the product life cycle, from concept development to release to ongoing maintenance and end of life.

22.3.1 Critical Success Factors, Key Influencers, and Stakeholders

This section addresses how to identify the key elements necessary to win product review approval. First, we will review the leader's role in gaining product approvals.

22.3.1.1 The Leader's Role. Project leaders are asked to wear many hats in the performance of their duties. They need to be adept at understanding design and development issues, taskmasters who pay minute attention to details about resource allocations and project schedules. They also need to be skilled at marketing and positioning their product, work well with manufacturing to meet demand and wrestle production problems to the ground, and be astute businesspersons who can make key business decisions that affect the company's revenue and profitability. Effective project leaders also are good salespeople for their products, both internal and external, to the organization. All of these talents are fully utilized in winning product approval.

The project leader is the chief salesperson responsible for selling the company on the continued funding of their product. Like regular account managers, they do not do it all by themselves but pull together an effective team of development, finance, marketing, manufacturing, customer support, sales, and even legal staff

> *The first step in winning product review approval is to put together a plan for Identifying Stakeholders, Key Influencers, and Critical Success Factors.*

to make the sale. The project leader is like the orchestra conductor who strives to get the very best music out of the different instrument sections, keep everyone on the same page, and deliver a harmonious and consistent solution that is greater than the sum of its parts. Practice, too is a very important part of the final performance as few project leaders can walk in to a project review session ill prepared and expect to emerge unscathed.

22.3.1.2 Identifying Stakeholders and Key Influencers. Most organizations strive to have the key stakeholders on the product approval review team. Even the best organizations cannot have the foresight to identify all possible stakeholders and require them to be part of the review team. Senior management's time is very precious, and they cannot always be present when important project approval decisions are made. Each project is different, and it may not be possible to predict with any certainty each organization that will be affected by a product introduction. Where the product is in its life cycle also affects which group(s) within the organization are affected. Therefore, it is incumbent upon the project leader to identify the key stakeholders *as early as possible in the product* *review approval process.* Table 22.1 summarizes how to look for stakeholders and influencers.

How can you identify stakeholders beyond those on the product review team? If you are the project leader for an existing product line and the product under review is an extension of that product, then you can look at the interactions that you currently have with different organizations. A simple metric can be to identify those groups of people that you are already in contact with and develop your stakeholder list from there.

For new products and/or products targeted at new markets, the task is somewhat more challenging. For new products, it is important to understand what groups are likely to be affected by the introduction of the product and how. Does the product require the same or different sales capability as existing products? Does it require the same or different customer support model as existing products? Does it require new manufacturing processes? Suppliers? New markets almost always require a different selling strategy if not an entirely different distribution channel. Marketing programs will have to be substantially modified or created anew. Usually these groups are already part of the development and release process, but it is amazing the oversights that occur sometimes when putting together a product proposal.

22.3.1.3 Key Influencers and Their Status. Key influencers differ from stakeholders in that the project review process may not directly affect them. Do not, however, make the mistake of ignoring these important people in the organi-

TABLE 22.1 USING THE PROJECT/MARKET MATRIX TO IDENTIFY STAKEHOLDERS.

	Existing Product	New Product
Existing Market (same customers)	Look at the types of daily interactions you have to identify and understand the key stakeholders.	How are the various organizations affected by the differences in the new product introduction?
New Market (different customers)	What sales, marketing, and postsales support changes does this new market require? How are prospective customers reached and demand fulfilled?	Who are the champions behind this new thrust? What new organizations are being created to deal with the new market and product introductions?

zation, for influencing them may have the greatest impact on whether or not your project is approved. Early in my career I ignored the production manager's input when putting together my proposal for a software product line; since software production is not usually on the critical path of a successful release, I thought it was an area that I could safely ignore. However, unbeknownst to me the production manager was recently tapped by the CEO to improve efficiency within the organization. Suddenly, this person had the power to almost unilaterally kill projects that did not fall within the new efficiency guidelines. Ignoring his input meant putting my project review into certain peril.

Key influencers are sometimes difficult to spot on an organizational chart, but by observing behavior and talking to people you can almost always identify them. Is there one "go to" person within the organization that everyone consults for advice? Their opinion about your project proposal may matter more than that of the people on the review committee. Who does senior management consult when they have difficult business decisions to make? Whose opinion do you respect within the organization? Usually others respect that person's opinion as well.

22.3.1.4 *Influencing the Influencers.*
As with any selling process, there is the requirement to satisfy both the tangible and intangible aspects of the customer's needs. Understanding the intangibles in the sales process is what often separates the merely good salespeople from the top performers. Since you are now in the role of salesperson for your product, you need to take the time to understand what's in it for the key influencers. Often, the needs of the influencers are in close alignment with the goals of the organization and your product line as a whole. As a key player, the influencer wants to be involved in important decisions and feel as if he or she has some control or input over the final outcome of the product direction. We will discuss in greater detail the project review approval process, but the more that you can involve the influencers early and more deeply in the process, the greater your chance for success.

Critical success factors are those factors that will most readily spell the difference between success and failure for the project approval. Often, success lies in identifying those key influencers and stakeholders and winning them over, but critical success factors can also mean hitting major project milestones or meeting cost and/or performance targets that are essential to moving the product forward. In new markets, early alpha and beta customer trials or even conditional purchase orders can be required to substantiate customer demand. The important idea is to identify those critical success factors well in advance of putting together the project approval presentation.

22.3.2 The Review Approval Process in Detail

In the ideal case, the work for winning project approval has already been done before the presentation is ever made. If the project plans are well constructed, the market and product requirements documents properly prepared, the engineering functional specifications completed in sufficient detail, the project plan complete, the marketing and sales training plans done, then the product review process is merely a compilation of pieces of these documents. The reality, though, is usually quite different; incomplete product specifications combined with time-to-market pressures and tactical demands on the project leader's time leaves little or none available when it comes time to present information for product approval. Usually there is a last-minute crush to pull together the necessary documents and little or no time to prepare, practice, and presell the presentation.

This handbook is written with both the ideal case and reality in mind. Winning project approval begins with putting together a mini-business-plan for the project under review. The mini-business-plan components are as follows:

- Executive Summary
- Market Opportunity Identification
- Purchase Justification and Key Selling Proposition
- Key Features and Benefits
- Development Cost and Time
- Sales Forecast, Profit and Loss Statement
- Go-to-Market Strategy
- Key Dependencies and Assumptions
- Regulatory requirements (if required)
- Risks
- Appendices and Backup Material

Your company may have a particular format that business plans must follow—these are generic guidelines. Not every business plan component will be required for each phase of the product life cycle. The preceding list represents the complete set of issues that need to be addressed for a new product introduction, for example. For products further along in the life cycle, typically a subset of these will be included, almost certainly a financial impact statement and a risks and impact section is included in every presentation. The next sections go into each in more detail.

22.3.2.1 Executive Summary. The executive summary is a short synopsis of what the project plan is all about. The name executive summary was coined because it often is the only section of the proposal presentation that senior management reviews! Therefore, it needs to be concise and action-oriented, and not more than a page or a slide in length. This will increase your chances that a busy executive will read (and agree) with your proposal. Of course, if additional detail is needed, it is contained in the rest of the presentation. Sometimes, it is helpful to write this section last after you have completed all the other sections to get an idea what the key points of the proposal will be.

22.3.2.2 Market Opportunity Identification. There are many risks in developing a new product, but they fall mostly into two categories: development and market risk (see Chapter 28). Development risk is simply: Can we build it? Can we design it, implement it, manufacture it on time and at a cost the customer is willing to pay? Market risk is much harder to measure. Assuming that the product is developed according to specification, is there enough demand to justify the development cost and return a profit to the company? Companies have moved beyond the "Field of Dreams" approach to product development (If you build it, they will come) to one that relies on market opportunity identification. This section quantifies the overall potential market for the product and qualifies key market characteristics so those potential customers can be readily identified and sold to.

22.3.2.3 Purchase Justification and Key Selling Proposition. The key selling proposition is that unique set of benefits that will make the specific sale for the product. Even with a broad market defined for your product, you still need to identify the key selling propositions for the product. This will be useful later on in the go-to-market strategy section as well.

22.3.2.4 Key Features and Benefits. This should come directly out of your product requirements document—what are the key features, functions, and benefits that the target audience cares about in the product.

22.3.2.5 Development Cost and Time. This should be readily available from the engineering/development plan. For the purposes of the presentation, you typically only need to document key delivery milestones, manpower estimates, and associated cost. Keep the detailed project schedule available as a backup, if needed.

22.3.2.6 Sales Forecast, Profit and Loss Statement. The sales forecast is a key part of the presentation, since at the end of the day everything comes down to dollars and cents (see Chapter 23). Finance, Sales, and Engineering all provide critical input to this section. If possible, try to include nominal, pessimistic, and optimistic forecasts to help management understand the risks involved.

22.3.2.7 Go-to-Market Strategy. How is your product going to be brought to market (see Chapter 30)? Should you use the existing sales channels or do you need to build new ones? Does this product need to be marketed and if so, how? Here is where you outline the critical areas of the go-to-market plan, particularly anything new/or requiring a specific budget. This will also be useful later in the launch-planning phase of the project.

22.3.2.8 Key Dependencies and Assumptions. It is very important to identify the critical dependencies and any assumptions that you have made in preparing this project proposal. Often, since you are so close to the "action," it is difficult to identify them yourself; this is where the project approval team and your peers can be helpful in identifying them for you. Don't try to hide these in the presentation; make sure that everyone knows about them and deals with them accordingly.

22.3.2.9 Regulatory Requirements (If Required). Some regulated industries (such as health care, pharmaceuticals, and government applications) have strict regulatory requirements that need to be included as part of the overall project plan. Others, such as electronics, may not be as strict but still require approvals for export, and so on. Make sure that these are documented and included in the project timetables and costs.

22.3.2.10 Risks. This is a very important section of the presentation. It is imperative that you clearly identify all of the project risks and (especially) how you plan to mitigate them (see Chapter 28). Do not avoid or try to downplay this section; if you do, you may lose credibility with your audience, making the job that much harder.

22.3.2.11 Appendices and Backup Material. This is a good place to put all the material that you created but had to leave out due to time constraints. Don't be afraid to refer to it during and after the presentation.

22.3.3 Pulling Together the Product Review Team

Successful project leaders are skilled at pulling together ad-hoc teams across disciplines to solve a particular problem; this is a perfect time to put those team-building skills to good use (see Chapter 9). Here are some sample organizations to consider drawing resources from:

- Finance
- Sales Administration
- Marketing
- Engineering
- Manufacturing
- Customer Support
- Project Management
- Development/R&D

Often, the cross-functional team is already composed of members of these groups. Getting finance involved early in the process is critical. Usually there is a financial analyst on staff, particularly in larger companies, who can be invaluable in pulling together the numbers that tell your story. Management loves nothing more than data. If you can present relevant data on your project, they will be more comfortable with your presentation. Just make sure that it is relevant and not too detailed; otherwise, you can get bogged down in explaining the nuances of the data and its sources and forget to focus on your key points.

22.3.4 Preparing the Project Approval Presentation

Most organizations will have a template to follow for pulling together product review approval presentations. Often, this will decide what information is important to present for approval. Usually it follows closely the mini-business-plan description discussed earlier. Be specific in asking the audience what you are expecting of them during the presentation and what action you want them to take as a result. There is usually a fixed amount of time in which to give the presentation; plan for enough time at the end of the presentation for at least 15 minutes of Q&A and discussion. A good rule of thumb is two minutes per slide, although this can easily turn into three or more if the slides are dense or controversial, which is all the more reason to presell the presentation. Allow enough lead time in order for the work to be completed well in advance of the presentation date.

22.3.5 Internally Selling the Project

If you have sales experience, the next phase may come naturally to you. For most project leaders, however, this is the most challenging, but also the most important phase. Rather than focus on this essential step, project leaders usually overinvest in their plans, only to wonder why approval was so difficult to obtain, or in the worst case, see their otherwise sound product plans get rejected. Internal selling is not that different from external selling and can give you an appreciation of what your salespeople go through every day!

The most important aspect of winning product review approval is preselling the presentation (see Chapter 10). Since most project leaders are managing multiple tasks and deadlines, there is a tendency, conscious or not, to put off preparing the review presentation until the last minute. This is a big mistake, because it does not leave you time to presell the presentation. If you are fortunate enough to have a dedicated or assigned project review team, then you can use much of that effort to also sell the various constituencies on the merits of your product. It is only human nature that people want to (1) help and (2) feel a part of a winning team. The more involved you can get other key stakeholders in the development of the presentation, the easier time you will have winning approval. Make sure that you leave enough time to dry run the presentation in private with key decision-makers; they may not have had a chance to review it yet. This may be difficult, since senior management's time is precious and there is a tendency not to want to "double-up" on their time, once for the private review and then again for the public. Just as often, though, once the senior manager has seen the presentation in private he or she will not even bother to show up, granting approval in abstention. This can be a great convincer to others present in the room. "Sarah could not make it to today's meeting, but has already seen then proposal and has signed off on it," is a great way to build consensus. Depending on the possible objections, it can also be useful to have an advocate in the room speaking on your behalf. Thus, it is important to know which way the votes are likely to swing in advance. I remember early in my career putting together a product review approval presentation for an OEM software product that we would buy and resell as part of our total solution. It was not until I got before the presentation review committee that I learned that the finance hurdle rate for gross margin was 50 percent. My product was at 40 percent—knowing that going in would have saved me considerable embarrassment and/or allowed me to put together arguments for overcoming that objection.

Preselling is also a great way to uncover hidden agendas and potential issues before you get into the formal meeting. This way you can come prepared to address this issue up front for the broader group. For example, if during the presell you discover that many people are concerned about technical feasibility, you can use the session to demonstrate a working prototype, allocate resources to create one, or postpone the meeting until such a prototype can be built. After all, no point in wasting management's time (and yours) on a presentation that is certain not to be approved.

22.3.6 Giving the Presentation

If you've done your homework, giving the presentation should be the easiest part of the process. There still are a few important items left to cover, so don't lose focus this close to your destination!

22.3.6.1 Preparation Before the Presentation. You've pulled together the perfect project review team, developed the killer presentation, and presold the presentation to key stakeholders and influencers. Now, there are just a few important steps to follow in advance of the big event. Most companies require you submit the proposal in advance, and it is circulated before the presentation. Don't assume that everyone has read it, instead assume that no one has read it; that is why preselling is so important. If you've made any changes to the presentation between the presell and the final delivery make sure you communicate to those you spoke with personally. It's also a great way to reinforce key selling points and help overcome any remaining objections. "I incorporated your feedback on possibly using too optimistic a demand profile and reran the numbers using a nominal, worst-, and best-case demand scenario. The project is still NPV positive after three years with a 12 month breakeven in the worst-case scenario, so I feel pretty good about the planning assumptions." This is also a good time to confirm that your supporters are going to be present at the meeting and supporting you.

22.3.6.2 Practicing the Presentation. An important step that people often skip and then later regret is the dry-run presentation. The purpose of the dry run is threefold: to ensure that all of the supporting material is ready, that you can run through the pace and flow of the presentation and make sure you are comfortable with it, and to get valuable feedback from trusted third parties to strengthen the presentation. This dry-run should not be broadcast to the world, but instead it should be focused on a close circle of friends who will tell you what they really think and help bullet-proof the presentation. This is an excellent time to invite your manager to see all the hard work you've been doing and to help prepare him/her for battle on your behalf in the main ring.

22.3.6.3 Delivering the Presentation. If you've done all the necessary preparation, presold the presentation to key stakeholders and influencers, prepared and delivered the dry run, and incorporated feedback, then the actual presentation should be a piece of cake. A few tips to keep in mind. First, make sure that you pace yourself during the presentation to leave plenty of time left for Q&A at the end. I like to leave time in between key points in the slides to ask if there are any questions during the talk and then to make sure that I am leaving 10–15 minutes for Q&A regardless of how many questions were asked during the pitch. If you can assign someone to write down questions (and answers), that will free you to spend time focused on the discussion. Second, do not (I repeat, do not) become defensive at any time during the presentation. Your job is to educate, inform, and persuade; if the audience detects even the slightest defensiveness, they will suspect that your proposal has bigger problems that are not being uncovered here. Do not let objections go unanswered (this is what the dry run is good for), but at the same time don't go into a defensive mode. Sometimes you win, sometimes you lose, but you never should let them see you sweat.

It is also a good idea to check in with the audience and make sure that you are pacing yourself correctly. If everyone has reviewed, is familiar with, and is comfortable with the early content in the presentation, then you can fast-forward to the next section. And don't be surprised if you are asked to jump around in the presentation flow. During the dry run, you should be able to get a sense of how and where the interruptions will be but always expect the unexpected; it is a positive sign if people are engaged and asking questions.

22.3.7 Follow-up and Feedback

Usually you will either receive approval or conditional approval during the presentation. Often the approval is tied to a major event, the funding of a business plan or the staffing of a development team, for instance. Assuming that the outcome of the presentation is favorable, the next steps are to move ahead in the product development process with an eye toward the subsequent stage. If the approval is conditional, then you may need to come back before the review committee to demonstrate that the conditions have been met. Occasionally, this is done in a separate meeting, but typically it is "carried over" into the next formal review session. The product review committee will usually distribute the results of the meeting but remember to personally keep the stakeholders in the loop. Regardless of the outcome, follow-up with the key stakeholders and influencers and thank them for their participation and support. They will be the ones that can help you with a favor down the road, not the least of which is the next milestone in the review process.

22.4 Summary

Winning product review approval does not have to be difficult, nor does it need to be a "drop everything and panic" proposition. If you are doing a good job as a day-to-day project leader, then putting together an effective presentation that wins approval need not be difficult or time-consuming. Plus, you can reuse many elements of the presentation in your go-to-market campaign, sales training and collateral, competitive analysis, and follow-on approval presentations. Remember that bad project leaders don't plan to fail, they just fail to plan. A little planning a preparation can go a long way toward easing the burden of developing a winning product review approval presentation.

Robert Lonadier has over 15 years of experience in product management and advising high-technology companies on business strategy and new product development. Robert has worked with and for companies such as Intel, AT&T, IBM, Alcatel, Lockheed, Citrix, as well as numerous start-ups. Robert has an undergraduate engineering degree from MIT and an M.B.A. from its Sloan School of Management.

CHAPTER TWENTY-THREE

APPROACHES TO NEW PRODUCT FORECASTING

Kenneth B. Kahn

23.1 Introduction

Forecasts are an elemental part of the new product development process because most, if not all, go/no-go decisions during the process require some kind of forecast on which to base these decisions. New product forecasting, therefore, cannot be avoided nor ignored. Still, many companies consider new product forecasting to be a baneful effort that is characteristically inaccurate due to the uncertainties related to market acceptance, technical feasibility, and company capability to bring the new product to fruition. Successful new product forecasting is possible, though. Those companies that have been more successful with their new product forecasting effort manifest such success by way of select, meaningful techniques and a cross-functional, systematic process (see Chapter 1). In the present chapter, the topic of new product forecasting is addressed, along with how a company may achieve a better, more meaningful new product forecast.

The organization of the chapter is as follows: The chapter begins with a discussion of establishing a definition around what is to be forecast. Various techniques available and considerations surrounding the decision to use a particular technique versus another are then discussed. This is followed by general considerations for the new product forecasting, including guidelines on new product forecast accuracy and what constitutes a successful new product forecasting process.

23.2 Establish the Forecasting Objective

The first step towards successful new product forecasting is to establish the forecasting objective. This will clarify the purpose and intent of the forecast so that a meaningful forecast can be made—meaningful

> *The first step towards successful new product forecasting is to establish the forecasting objective.*

in the sense that the forecast is presented in a usable and understandable form. Otherwise, an innumerable set of forecasts can be developed, leading to confusion over which forecast should be employed. The forecasting objective helps to clarify the type of forecast to be made, the forecasting level at which the forecast will be applied, the forecasting time horizon, the forecasting interval, and the form in which the forecast should be.

Several types of new product forecasts are possible and can be broken down in terms of *potential* versus *forecast*, and *market* versus *sales*. *Potential* represents a maximum attainable estimate, whereas *forecast* represents a likely attainable estimate. *Market* represents all companies within a given industry marketplace, whereas *sales* pertains to only the respective focal company. The following new product forecast definitions are provided:

- *Market potential*: The maximum estimate of total market volume reasonably attainable under a given set of conditions.
- *Sales potential*: The maximum estimate of company sales reasonably attainable within a given market under a given set of conditions.
- *Market forecast*: A reasonable estimate of market volume attainable by firms in that market under a given set of conditions.
- *Sales forecast*: A reasonable estimate of company sales attainable within a given market under a given set of conditions.

During the new product forecasting effort, one or all of the above may be of interest. The key is to clarify through the objective what is needed at particular points during the NPD process.

Once what is to be forecast is established, this forecast needs to be further defined in terms of level, time horizon, interval, and form. *Forecasting level* refers the focal point in the corporate hierarchy where the forecast applies. Common levels include the stock keeping unit (SKU) level, stock keeping unit per location (SKUL) level, product line level, strategic business unit (SBU) level, company level, and/or industry level. *Forecasting time horizon* refers to the time frame for how far out one should forecast. New product forecasts could correspond to a single point in the future or a series of forecasts extending out for a length of time (the latter is more common). Examples include a 1–2 year time horizon, which is typical for most fashion products; 2–5 years for most consumer product goods; and 10 plus years for pharmaceutical products. One reason for the longer time horizon for pharmaceuticals is the length of time surrounding drug patents. *Forecasting time interval* refers to the granularity of the forecast with respect to the time bucket as well as how often the forecast might be updated. For example, a series of forecasts can be provided on a weekly, monthly, quarterly, or annual basis. *Forecasting form* refers to the unit of measure for the forecast. Typically, new product forecasts early on are provided in a monetary form (e.g., US $) and later in the process provided in terms of unit volume for production purposes. Some new product forecasts also can take the form of narrative scenarios that describe a future event.

23.3 Forecasts During the New Product Development Process

Decisions differ across the different stages of the new product development process, and similarly, forecasts too will differ across product development process stages. Early on in the process the forecasting focus will be market potential. Such forecasts are normally in dollars and used to answer the question of whether an opportunity is good for a company to pursue. Marketing and Finance departments would play key roles in establishing forecasts at this early stage.

During the concept generation and pretechnical evaluation stages, forecasts investigate sales potential in answering the question of whether an idea is good for the company to pursue. Again, forecasts at this point would normally be in the form of dollars and under the auspices of Marketing and Finance departments.

Entering the technical development and launch phases, unit sales forecasts would become critical in order to plan for the launch and ensure adequate supply through the channel. At this point, the Operations and Supply Chain department would play a key role in developing these sales forecasts to drive operational decisions. Specific testing, such as product testing during technical development and market testing during the commercialization, would help the company to qualify key assumptions and better estimate unit demand and sales revenues from such unit demand.

23.4 Forecasting Techniques

One will find that there are numerous forecasting techniques available. Among the multiple ways in which to categorize these techniques, one way is to organize new product forecasting techniques into the three categories of judgmental techniques, quantitative techniques, and customer/market research techniques. Figure 23.1 presents the more popular techniques associated with each of these three categories.

Judgmental techniques represent techniques that attempt to turn experience, judgment, and intuition into formal forecasts. Six popular techniques within this category include jury of executive opinion, sales force composite, scenario analysis, the Delphi method, decision trees, and assumptions-based modeling:

- *Jury of executive opinion*: A top-down forecasting technique where the forecast is arrived at through the ad-hoc combination of opinions and predictions made by informed executives and experts.
- *Sales force composite*: A bottoms-up forecasting technique where individuals (typically salespeople) provide their forecasts. These forecasts are then aggregated to calculate a higher-level forecast.
- *Scenario analysis*: An analysis involving the development of scenarios to predict the future. Two types of scenario analysis include the exploratory and normative approaches. Exploratory scenario analysis starts in the present and moves out to the future based on current trends. Normative scenario analysis leaps out to the future and works back to determine what should be done to achieve what is expected to occur.
- *Delphi method*: A technique based on subjective expert opinion gathered through several structured anonymous rounds of data collection. Each successive round provides consolidated feedback to the respondents, and the forecast is further refined. The objective of the Delphi method is to capture the advantages of multiple experts in a committee, while minimizing the effects of social pressure to agree with the majority, ego pressure to stick with your original forecast despite new information, the influence of a repetitive argument, and the influence of a dominant individual.
- *Decision trees*: A probabilistic approach to forecasting where various contingencies and their associated probability of occurring are determined—typically in a subjective fashion. Conditional probabilities are then calculated, and the most probable events are identified. The example in Figure 23.2 shows two scenarios under consideration, option A and option

FIGURE 23.1 A SAMPLE OF NEW PRODUCT FORECASTING TECHNIQUES.

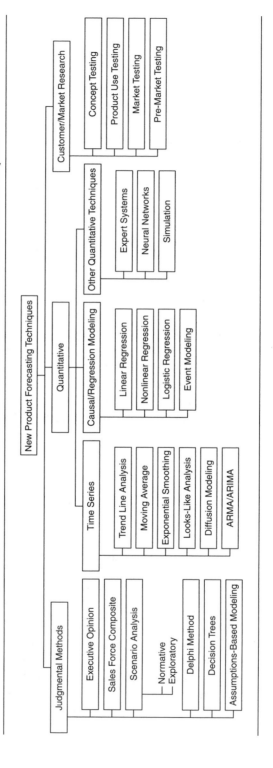

FIGURE 23.2 FORECASTING USING A DECISION TREE APPROACH.

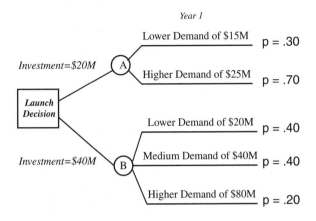

Expected Return after Year 1

E[A] = (.30*$15M) + (.70*$25M) – $20M = $22M – $20M = **$2M**

E[B] = (.40*$20M) + (.40*$40M) + (.20*$80M) – $40M = $40M – $40M = **$0**

B. A has two demand scenarios with their associated probabilities of occurrence, B has three demand scenarios with their associated probabilities. Using a decision tree approach, option A looks more attractive because the forecast for expected revenue is $2 million, versus no revenue in the case of option B.

- *Assumption-based modeling:* A technique that attempts to model the behavior of the relevant market environment by breaking the market down into market drivers. Then, by assuming values for these drivers, forecasts are generated. These models are also referred to as chain models or market breakdown models. Figure 23.3 illustrates the ATAR model, which stands for the drivers of awareness, trial, availability, and repeat purchase, and is commonly used to forecast consumer packaged goods (see Kahn, 2000; Crawford and di-Benedetto, 2003). As illustrated, the ATAR model begins with an overall market size and uses these drivers to break down the market size proportionally.

FIGURE 23.3 AN EXAMPLE OF AN ASSUMPTIONS-BASED FORECASTING: THE ATAR MODEL.

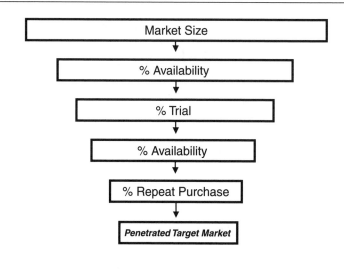

Formula

Unit Sales = (Market Size) * (% Awareness) * (% Trial) * (% Availability)
         * (% Repeat Purchase) * (# Bought Per Period)

$ Profit = (Revenue − Unit Cost) * Unit Sales

Quantitative techniques are broken into the three subcategories of time series, "causal"/regression modeling, and other quantitative techniques. Time series techniques analyze sales data to detect historical "sales" patterns and construct a representative graph or formula to project sales into the future. Time series techniques used in association with new product forecasting include:

- *Trend line analysis*: A line is fit to a set of data. This is done either graphically or mathematically.
- *Moving average*: A technique that averages only a specified number of previous sales periods.
- *Exponential smoothing techniques*: A set of techniques that develop forecasts by addressing the forecast components of level, trend, seasonality, and cycle. Weights or smoothing coefficients for each of these components are deter-

mined statistically and are applied to "smooth" previous period information (see Makridakis et. al., 1997; Mentzer and Bienstock, 1998).

- *Looks-like analysis (analogous forecasting)*: A technique that attempts to map sales of other products onto the product being forecast. Looks-like analysis is a popular technique applied to line extensions by using sales of previous product line introductions to profile sales of the new product. Figure 23.4 shows a product line's sales curves for two prior product launches, proportioned by month across the first ten months of sales. An average sales curve would be extrapolated from these data and used to forecast sales for the next line extension.

- *Diffusion models*: Models that estimate the growth rate of product sales by considering various factors influencing the consumer adoption process. Considerations taken into account include the rate at which mass media (the coefficient of innovation) and word of mouth (the coefficient of imitation) affect lead users, early adopter, early majority, late majority, and laggard customer segments. Different types of diffusion models exist, including the Bass Model, Gompertz Curve, and Logistic Curve. Diffusion models are also referred to as technology S-curves (see Morrison, 1996; Mahajan, Muller, and Wind, 2000).

- *Autoregressive moving average (ARMA)/autoregressive integrated moving average (ARIMA) models*: A set of advanced statistical approaches to forecasting, which incorporate key elements of both time series and regression model building. Three basic activities (or stages) are considered: (1) identifying the model, (2)

FIGURE 23.4 LOOKS-LIKE ANALYSIS.

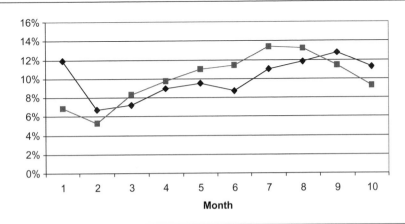

determining the model's parameters, and (3) testing/applying the model. Critical in using any of these techniques is understanding the concepts of autocorrelation and differencing. ARMA/ARIMA models are also referred to as Box-Jenkins Techniques (see Makridakis et. al. 1997).

"Causal"/regression modeling techniques use exogenous or independent variables and through statistical methods, develop formula correlating these with a dependent variable. The term "causal" is used very loosely because these models are predicated on correlational relationships and not true cause-and-effect relationships. Four popular techniques within this subcategory include:

- *Linear regression*: A statistical methodology that assesses the relation between one or more managerial variables and a dependent variable (sales), strictly assuming that these relationships are linear in nature. For example, price may be an important driver of new product sales. The relationship between price and the quantity sold would be determined from prior data of other products within the product line and then used to predict sales for the forthcoming product.
- *Nonlinear regression*: A statistical methodology that assesses the relation between one or more managerial variables and a dependent variable (sales), but these relationships are *not* necessarily assumed to be linear in nature.
- *Logistic regression*: A statistical methodology that assesses the relation between one or more managerial variables and a binary outcome, such as purchasing versus not purchasing. A logistic regression model calculates the probability of an event occurring or not occurring.
- *Event modeling*: Often a regression-based methodology that assess the relation between one or more events, whether company-initiated or unaffiliated with the company, and a dependent variable (sales). For example, a promotion used with prior product launches would be analyzed and the bump in sales caused by this promotion statistically determined. The expected bump in sales would be correspondingly mapped to the sales of the new product.

The other category contains those techniques that employ unique methodologies or represent a hybrid of time series and regression techniques. A sample of these forecasting techniques include:

- *Expert systems*: Typically computer-based heuristics or rules for forecasting. These rules are determined by interviewing forecasting experts and then constructing "if-then" statements. Forecasts are generated by going through various applicable "if-then" statements until all statements have been considered.

- *Neural networks*: Advanced statistical models that attempt to decipher patterns in a particular sales time series. These models can be time-consuming to build and difficult to explain. In most cases, these models are proprietary.
- *Simulation:* An approach to incorporating market forces into a decision model. "What-if" scenarios are then considered. Normally, simulation is computer-based. A typical simulation model is Monte Carlo simulation, which employs randomly generated events to drive the model and assess outcomes.

Customer/market research techniques include those approaches that collect data on the customer/market and then systematically analyze these data to draw inferences on which to make forecasts. Four general classes of customer/market research techniques include:

- *Concept testing*: A process by which customers (current and/or potential customers) evaluate a new product concept and give their opinions on whether the concept is something that they might have interest in and would likely buy. The purpose of concept testing is to proof the new product concept.
- *Product use testing*: A process by which customers (current and/or potential customers) evaluate a product's functional characteristics and performance. The purpose of product use testing is to proof the product's function.
- *Market testing*: A process by which targeted customers evaluate the marketing plan for a new product in a market setting. The purpose of market testing is to proof the proposed marketing plan and the "final" new product.
- *Premarket testing*: A procedure that uses syndicated data and primary consumer research to estimate the sales potential of new product initiatives. Assessor and BASES are two proprietary new product forecasting models associated with premarket testing. BASES is commonly employed in the consumer products goods industry.

23.5 New Product Forecasting Strategy

While there are a number of forecasting techniques available, it is important to realize that not all of them are appropriate for every forecasting situation. Qualitative techniques are quite adaptable, but very time-consuming; they would, therefore, not be appropriate in situations where a

> *While there are a number of forecasting techniques available, it is important to realize that not all of them are appropriate for every forecasting situation.*

severe time constraint exists. Quantitative techniques require data, and rely on the critical assumption that current data will correspond to future states; if meeting these requirements is not feasible, quantitative techniques would not be meaningful. Customer/market research tools are time-consuming and expensive to use. Budget constraints could seriously hamper what degree of customer/market research may be applied. A toolbox approach is therefore recommended for applying new product forecasting techniques.

To assist in decisions related to new product forecasting, a variation of the product-market matrix is tailored to reveal four new product forecasting situations (refer to Figure 23.5). Mapping market uncertainty and product technology uncertainty on the two dimensions of current and new reveals four cells, each of which is represented by one of the following new product forecasting strategies: sales analysis, life-cycle analysis, customer and market analysis, and scenario analysis.

Sales analysis is associated with the situation of current market and current product technology, where the uncertainties of market and product technology are lowest. Cost reductions and product improvements would populate this cell. The nature of these products would mean that sales data would be available because the product has previously existed. Analysis would focus on looking for deviations and deflections in sales patterns based on previous cost reductions and improvements in the product. Quantitative techniques such as times series and regression could be quite useful and manifest objective forecasts.

Product life-cycle analysis is associated with the situation of the current market and new technology. Line extensions are associated with this cell and represent higher product technology uncertainty. Because of understanding of the current marketplace, analyses would attempt to overlay patterns of previously launched products in the product line onto the new line extensions. These

FIGURE 23.5 NEW PRODUCT FORECASTING STRATEGY.

patterns would characterize a launch curve or life-cycle curve by way of looks-like analysis or analogous forecasting.

Customer/market analysis would be necessary in the case of current technology and a new market due to higher market uncertainty. The purpose of this forecasting strategy would be to understand the new market and, thus, reduce such uncertainty and manifest greater understanding about the new market. Various customer/market research studies might be engaged along with the use of assumption-based models in an attempt to specify market drivers, which would be validated by the customer/market research performed. Products in this cell would include new use and new market products (market extensions).

A scenario analysis strategy would correspond to the situation of a new market and new product technology, representing high market and product technology uncertainties akin to new-to-the-company (new category entries) and new-to-the-world products. Scenario analysis would be employed to paint a picture of the future and future directions to be taken. Note that a scenario analysis strategy should not be confused with just the use of scenario analysis; rather the intent of forecasting in this situation is to develop various scenarios on which to base the NPD decision. Given a lack of data, potential difficulty in identifying the specific target market, and questions regarding technology acceptance, subjective assessment techniques would play a major role here.

It should be recognized that forecasting techniques have applicability in each of the cells, depending on the specific situation. Customer/market research could be of great benefit in understanding the market for cost reductions, product improvements, and line extensions. Subjective assessment techniques can be readily applied to all types of new products. The issue is to recognize the resources necessary and outcome desired, for example, subjective assessment techniques may not provide enough detail to forecast next year's sales of a product improvement. Hence, the intent of the proposed framework is to offer a strategy to facilitate the new product forecasting effort by suggesting the application of those techniques that appear to be most appropriate. In no way should techniques be viewed as exclusive to only those cells indicated.

23.6 New Product Forecasting Benchmarks

Even with a plethora of techniques and a keen strategy, new product forecasting is characteristically associated with low accuracy (high forecast error). As shown in Table 23.1, the overall average accuracy

New product forecasting is characteristically associated with low accuracy.

TABLE 23.1 PERCENT FORECAST ACCURACY AND FORECAST HORIZON FOR NEW PRODUCT FORECASTS

Type of New Product	Average % Accuracy Achieved (Standard Deviation, Sample Size)	Forecast Horizon in Months (Standard Deviation, Sample Size)
Cost improvements	71.62 (sd = 22.46, n = 29)	21.15 (sd = 21.15, n = 40)
Product improvements	64.88 (sd = 23.63, n = 45)	19.96 (sd = 18.20, n = 102)
Line extensions	62.76 (sd = 22.25, n = 45)	20.84 (sd = 18.58, n = 97)
Market extensions	54.33 (sd = 24.02, n = 42)	23.58 (sd = 21.26, n = 93)
New category entries (new-to-the-company)	46.83 (sd = 24.31, n = 30)	34.56 (sd = 35.21, n = 45)
New-to-the-world	40.36 (sd = 24.72, n = 39)	36.08 (sd = 35.96, n = 93)

n = sample size   sd = standard deviation

across the six types of new products was 58 percent, with cost improvements generally being 72 percent accurate; product improvement forecasts 65 percent accurate; line extension forecasts 63 percent accurate; market extension forecasts 54 percent accurate; new category entry (new-to-the-company) forecasts 47 percent accurate; and new-to-the-world products 40 percent accurate. Note that these mean values of new product forecasting accuracy were collected by asking respondents to indicate the average forecast accuracy achieved one year postlaunch (see Kahn, 2003). The nature of these accuracy percentages reaffirms the fact that new markets are more troublesome to forecast (i.e., market extensions, new category entries, and new-to-the-world products) than those where a current market is being served (i.e., cost improvements, product improvements, line extensions).

The overall average forecast time horizon for these forecasts is approximately 26 months. As shown in Table 23.1, the average time horizons for cost improvements, product improvements, line extensions, and market extensions were below this average (21 months, 20 months, 21 months, and 24 months, respectively), while the average time horizons for new category entries and new-to-the-world products were above this average (35 months and 36 months, respectively). These results suggest that forecasts for new category entries and new-to-the-world products are characteristically longer term in nature, and correspondingly, more strategic in nature than forecasts for the other types of new products.

In terms of process characteristics, benchmarking research suggests that in almost two-thirds of companies the Marketing department has responsibility for the new product forecasting effort. Even if not responsible, the Marketing department is heavily involved in the new product forecasting effort, with the departments of Sales, Sales Forecasting, and Market Research also having an appreciable level of involvement in the new product forecasting effort. In terms of technique usage, companies typically use more than one new product forecasting technique—on average, 2–4 forecasting techniques. The purpose of using multiple techniques is to ascertain a good baseline for the new product forecast by way of reconciling the forecasts derived by each respective forecasting technique. Research, though, suggests that the greater the number of techniques used does not simply lead to higher new product forecast accuracy or greater satisfaction with the new product forecasting process, so simply increasing the number of forecasting techniques employed does not manifest successful forecasting; up to four forecasting techniques appears to be sufficient.

23.7 The New Product Forecasting Process

While applying an appropriate forecasting technique will benefit the new product forecasting effort, there are further considerations. Various uncertainties inherent in the new product should be accounted for, including potential cannibalization effects and market penetration to be achieved, along with finding pertinent data and having the time to perform the necessary analyses to address these and other uncertainties. The way in which successful companies have done this is through a process perspective, specifically creating a structured, systematic new product forecasting process. Such a process builds on experiences from prior new product forecasts, cross-functional communication (especially with Marketing), and customer feedback; together within a process these enable organizational learning and understanding on which to make a credible and realistic forecast.

Assumptions management is an important part of the new product forecasting process. The process would clearly specify assumptions and make them transparent so that there is company understanding of what underlies these assumptions. After launch, successful forecasting companies would then implement tracking systems that closely monitor and control these assumptions to determine if forecasts will come to fruition or whether a deviation is occurring. Transparency of assumptions is particularly valuable for clarifying whether the forecast is based on sound rationales or optimism.

Successful forecasting companies also realize that new product forecasts should not be point forecasts, but rather, conceived as ranges. These ranges typically become more narrowed as the product approaches and enters the launch phase. For example, pessimistic, likely, and optimistic cases could be connected with the monitor and control of assumptions to determine which scenario is playing out.

Finally, best-in-class companies are constructing databases to collect, track, and reflect on new product rollouts, especially consumer packaged goods industries. Such a database is crucial to the validation of new product forecasting assumptions, as well as documenting new product forecasting accuracy. Tying this internal database with syndicated data, market share and competitor data may be retained to enable more robust analyses. The database also enables other sophisticated analyses related to brand preference, price elasticities, and geographic rollout scenarios. The issue is having the discipline to establish and keep up with the maintenance of the database with data feeds on new product launches.

23.8 Summary

New product forecasting is certainly not easy, and there is no silver bullet when it comes to new product forecasting. However, companies who employ appropriate techniques coupled with a well-structured new product forecasting process show a greater propensity for new product forecast success. Techniques play the key role

> *Companies who employ appropriate techniques coupled with a well-structured new product forecasting process show a greater propensity for new product forecast success.*

of establishing a sound initial baseline forecast. The new product forecasting process, then, refines and augments this baseline forecast. Together, these two elements help to manifest the best possible new product forecast on which to drive new product decisions.

References

Crawford, Merle and diBenedetto, Anthony, *New Products Management*, Boston: McGraw-Hill/ Irwin, 2003.

Kahn, Kenneth B., *Product Planning Essential*, Thousand Oaks, CA: Sage Publications, 2000.

Kahn, Kenneth B., "An Exploratory Investigation of New Product Forecasting Practices," *Journal of Product Innovation Management*, 19: 133–143 (March 2002).

Lilien, Gary, Rangaswamy, Arvind, and Van den Bulte, Christophe, *Diffusion Models: Managerial Applications and Software*, Institute for the Study of Business Markets Report #7-1999.

Mahajan, Vijay and Muller, Eitan, Wind, Yoram, *New-Product Diffusion Models*, International Series in Quantitative Marketing, Volume 11, Boston: Kluwer Academic Publishers, 2000.

Makridakis, Spyros G., Wheelwright, Steven C., and Hyndman, Rob J., *Forecasting: Methods and Applications*, New York: John Wiley & Sons, 1997.

Mentzer, John T. and Bienstock, Carol C., *Sales Forecasting Management*, Thousand Oaks, CA: Sage Publications, 1998.

Morrison, Jeffrey, "How to Use Diffusion Models in New Product Forecasting," Journal of Business Forecasting, 6–9 (Summer 1996).

Kenneth B. Kahn, Ph.D. is Associate Professor of Marketing in the Department of Marketing, Logistics, and Transportation at the University of Tennessee, Knoxville, and is a cofounding director of UT's Sales Forecasting Management Forum, which emphasizes education and research in the areas of sales forecasting and market analysis. His teaching and research interests concern product development, product management, sales forecasting, and interdepartmental integration. Dr. Kahn has published in a variety of journals, including the *Journal of Product Innovation Management*, and is author of the book *Product Planning Essentials*. His industrial experience includes serving as an industrial engineer and project engineer for the Weyerhaeuser Company and as a manufacturing engineer for Respironics, Inc.

CHAPTER TWENTY-FOUR

ENHANCING NEW PRODUCT DEVELOPMENT SUCCESS THROUGH INDUSTRIAL DESIGN STRATEGY

Robert W. Veryzer

24.1 Introduction

"Design" or "industrial design" is (or can be) an element in a company's overall business strategy. In its broadest sense, design refers to how something is tangibly constructed to function operationally while embodying intangible elements to function emotionally. Thus, design encompasses technical aspects along with form, user interaction, ergonomics, semiologic (meanings and signs), and other aesthetic aspects. The distinctions between "engineering design" and "industrial design" reflect the different orientations and training underlying the approaches to these two different aspects of products. Although such distinctions are applicable in terms of education, skills, and company organizations, in practice there is often a strong connection between the two. The consequence of what occurs with respect to "design" has a significant impact on the entire new product development effort and the ultimate success (or failure) of a product or brand in the marketplace.

User-oriented design, much like marketing, may be thought of as a consumer-centric tool that can help a firm achieve its goals (see Chapters 14, 15, 16). Most discussions of strategy are cast in terms that do not reflect the specific dynamics of the design challenge underlying new product development. Because of this, they are often of only limited value in terms of their ability to help guide decision-making with respect to the resolution of design-related issues. This is particularly true for industrial design considerations, since often these involve issues that are not easily quantified, but have a significant bearing on qualitative acceptance by consumers. This chapter examines the impact of design on business strategy and its relationship to effectively achieving the overall product goals for firms engaged in developing products for consumers and businesses.

24.2 Goals and Design Strategy Prerequisites

There are a variety of goals that an entity may have; however, for the most part these goals may be thought of as extending out on a continuum that ranges from maximization of financial return (for example, return on investment, profit) to building brand equity (for example, brand value

> *Design delivers value by embodying products across functional and emotional dimensions in ways that match or anticipate consumer's goals.*

and consumer trust) and extending toward more universal or altruistic goals (for example, to solve people's or company's problems, enhance quality of life, or improve the lives and existence of others—people, animals, the environment). Such a continuum, which moves out from company-centric to encompass objectives with an ever broader impact, represents "value," and it is usually necessary that financial return for the operating entity (for the company or organization to continue) be coupled with one or more of the broader goals (for example, enhance quality of life, solve problems) in order for a product to be viable in terms of offering value that others will embrace. These *mission goals* form the basis of the enterprise and can be distinguished from the strategies or *strategic goals* that design may be used to help execute and accomplish.

Along with mission goals, there are a number of prerequisites for design strategy formulation with respect to new product development. These generally fall into six categories: opportunity, directional consistency or fit, financial return, technical feasibility, competitive opening, and risk (see Table 24.1).

These prerequisites involve considerations and conditions that need to be understood before an effective design strategy may be determined. "Risk" can also be considered as a separate prerequisite even though it is comprised of the accumulated risks (or probabilities with respect to positive or negative outcomes) of the other categories of prerequisites and the uncertainties inherent in the interaction between these various component categories (for example, projected market need and recognition of the opportunity by competitors/lead time).

TABLE 24.1 DESIGN STRATEGY PREREQUISITES.

- **Opportunity:** Existence of market need (existing vs. projected), market attractiveness, existence and identification of a target market, market phase (e.g., product life-cycle stage), timing, infrastructure (e.g., distribution channels, business model), regulatory, social, political, and environmental trends and regulation.
- **Directional Consistency or Fit:** Encompasses compatibility with and appropriateness for mission goals, brand architecture, and brand positioning as well as any policies or existing strategic goal directives.
- **Financial Return:** Encompasses expected commercial value, costs, profit margin, estimated revenue, time-to-payback, business model, and so on.
- **Technical Feasibility:** Technical hurdles, core competencies, available technologies, patents, potential alliances, and so on.
- **Competitive Opening:** Differential advantage, entry costs/barriers, revenue barriers, cost structure, vulnerability to predatory pricing, patent and proprietary knowledge protection, recognition of the opportunity by competitors/lead time, potential for competitive response, the nature of the industry (e.g., structure, dominance, sophistication, basis for competition—price, aesthetics, features, safety).
- **Risk:** Risk is the probability as a function of all of the factors named above.

24.3 Fundamental Design Strategies

A number of useful ways for considering "design strategy" have been presented by people such as Porter (1996), Borja de Mozota (1998), as well as many others. Although there are numerous approaches for characterizing strategy, there are essentially five fundamental "strategies" that

> *Strategy should be considered in terms of how design positions a product and how specific design executions can be used to achieve particular strategies.*

may be undertaken in the execution of design in order to move a concern toward its primary mission goal(s). The five fundamental strategies are:

- *Cost advantage:* Designing products so as to result in a cost advantage. The emphasis is on designing the product in order to minimize component and production costs. Design impact on costs (both product/components and production processes) allows a basic strategy of cost domination to be employed.
- *Design eminence:* Design that establishes an identifiable and unique product image. The emphasis is on differentiating the product using primarily ergonomics, innovative concepts, and aesthetics that embody both consumers' needs and brand values. Value is added through design elements that en-

hance product usability as well as perception (e.g., visual, tactile, auditory senses), and evoke emotive reactions to reinforce the product's brand message (for example, high performance, power, sophistication) as well as resonate with target consumer values. A design-eminence strategy can involve establishing design styles, trends, or fashions, as well as changing brand perceptions.

- *Feature leadership:* Design based on innovation and introducing leading-edge products emphasizing new features. This strategy involves pursuing new solutions and often pushing the frontier in terms of applying or developing technology. Agile, forward-thinking along with willingness to move past, and even cannibalize, sales of previous products is required.

- *Specific appropriateness (or concentration):* This strategy relies on design that delivers the optimal product for a narrow product space (e.g., product category or requirements of a particular type of user). The focus of design efforts to execute a concentration strategy is on gaining an integral understanding of the needs of specific customer segments relevant to the narrow product space and then developing significant points of difference that can be used to distinguish a product from other products available to customers in the segment. The key here is the difference arising from the improvements in the product's (or service's) fit and performance—that is, the design objective is to produce a more "appropriate" product.

- *Desirable alternative:* Design of products consistent with an established product category or category leader. Such an approach, which is often referred to as that of a "market challenger" or "market follower" is the reality for many product offerings. Competing in a particular category and offering choice alternatives that increase the selection of available products, while not pushing strongly in terms of any one of the other possible strategies, can be a viable and even profitable approach to satisfying mission goals. This strategy is more likely to succeed when there is sufficient room in the market (for example, in an expanding or growth market). When a market becomes more competitive, such as when the market is no longer expanding or is not stable due to new competitive entrants, a firm employing this strategy alone is likely to have to adopt or overlap another strategy in order to compete. Although not necessarily leading in terms of features, form, user interaction, semiotic (meanings and signs), or style aspects, this strategy relies on executing them better or in a sufficiently different way from other leading companies to a degree that attracts customers.

In effect, each of the strategies involves or may result in a "position" for a product—for example, low cost, performance leader, most beautiful, preferred alternative, leading-edge, and so on. In addition, each may result in outstanding (perhaps even "award-winning") design, and each can require utilizing the full range of design skills and tools for implementation. The five strategies represent the basic approaches that, when considered with respect to the various product design situations discussed in the next section, provide a framework for formulating specific product design strategies.

24.4 General Product Design Situations

In formulating design strategy, it is imperative that the product design situation be considered. Product design situations, which have been discussed by various researchers (e.g., Gilles and Gilles, 1989; Veryzer, 1998), may be grouped into four general categories that reflect different considerations and challenges. These are:

- *Renovative design:* This involves the updating or overhaul of an existing product with little change with respect to the technology employed or the functionality delivered.
- *Adaptive design:* This involves adjusting an existing product to new circumstances or a changed situation (e.g., improvements in technological capabilities, reorienting the design direction of an existing product). In the more extreme cases, adaptive design can entail a drastic shift in the design direction of a product.
- *Evolutionary design:* Involves the design of new products, where the progression from previous products that exist is relatively continuous in terms of product capabilities delivered, the technology employed, and design direction (e.g., form and appearance).
- *Discontinuous design:* This involves a dramatic break in the progression from the course of previous products. Discontinuous design situations may be further subdivided into three cases: (1) primarily technological discontinuity (such products may be perceived as being essentially the same as previously existing products even though they utilize revolutionary new technology—solid state televisions were an example of this when they were initially introduced), (2) primarily commercial discontinuity (products perceived as being highly innovative even though they utilize little new technology but uniquely package it for an unmet consumer need—the SONY Walkman® is an example of this), and (3) both commercial and technical discontinuities (the Segway Human Transporter is an example this type of discontinuous design).

It is important to note that all four of these design situations relate to new products, each involving differing levels of utilization of an existing product base or components.

24.5 Design Strategy Formulation

The fundamental design strategies discussed previously along with the four general types of product design situations yield a Design Strategy Matrix that reveals the basic strategy options available with respect to design (see Table 24.2). The Design Strategy Matrix indicates which strategies are appropriate for a particular design situation. For example, with the development of digital cameras, which were (are) discontinuous in several ways, essentially five strategies are available to firms with respect to how they orient their design as they create products for this category. Design can be carried out that results in presenting a product to customers that offers: low cost, design eminence (in terms of image, ergonomics, and so on), advanced new features, a particularly appropriate fit to customers' needs, or a desirable alternative to other comparable product offerings. The way that a strategy is executed differs depending on the specific design situation involved. For example, as indicated in Table 24.2, a feature leadership strategy for a discontinuous design (product) involves a distinctly different challenge from that of a renovative design situation.

There are various ways of operationalizing each of the different strategies. For example, OXO International achieves design eminence through ergonomic design that establishes an identity in addition to providing comfortable, "easy-to-use" products. The iMAC employed a design eminence strategy using color, transparent materials, and shape to gain attention and market share—and throw the competition slightly off-balance, at least for a time. Likewise, Euro-Pro's Shark vacuum products employ specific cues such as the silver color and smooth, oblong shape to establish an identity in a crowded product category. Approaches such as "modularity" or modular design can be used to carry out different design strategies. For example, using common platforms may lead to economies of scale and design efficiencies that can produce a significant cost advantage. Modularity could also be used to provide feature benefits that might come with interchangeable parts that allow consumers to customize or create products, which can result in design eminence or even feature leadership. Thus, design strategies may be enacted in various ways through different applications of the basic elements of design in order to address the challenges involved in any of the design situations or contexts surrounding the new product being developed.

TABLE 24.2 DESIGN STRATEGY-SITUATION MATRIX.

	Fundamental Strategies				
	Cost Advantage	Design Eminence	Feature Leadership	Specific Appropriateness (Concentration)	Desirable Alternative
Design Situations: Existing Product Base					
• Renovative Design	Maintain or increase cost advantage	Maintain or update existing image	Sustain current product version as next generation is designed	Sustain current product offering, keep product viable	Respond to competitors' changes and maintain product viability
• Adaptive Design	Increase cost advantage, design for component and manufacturing cost savings	Adjust or revamp design in order to revitalize or reposition brand or product	Convey product advantages and functionality to build brand image	Upgrade in order to ensure that gap does not open up that allows competition into the product space	Adjust and improve product to make it more competitive
New Product Formulation					
• Evolutionary Design	Formulate cost structure that allows competitive advantage	Evolve product identity within current brand image	Reinforce or enhance brand identity and convey new functionalities	Advance the product category	Introduce and define points of competitive differentiation
• Discontinuous Design	Develop new cost structure that changes the competitive situation substantially	Define new form/category direction with image as key component	Define and convey new product form/category (also creates brand leadership role)	Define and convey new product form/category (can lend itself to a consumer-centric brand image)	Introduce significant point of difference for new product form

> *Effective design strategy requires alignment of the strategy to be pursued with a particular product design situation.*

The strategies represent "orientations" toward design, and each may be executed in a manner that gives a firm's product(s) a differential advantage in the marketplace in addition to shaping brand image. Certainly, it is desirable for a product to be designed so as to be superior with respect to all of the dimensions inherent in each of the strategies, but it is often difficult, if not impossible, to deliver all these dimensions simultaneously—trade-offs are usually required (for example, cost advantage vs. feature leadership). Even so, overlapping two or more strategies is possible and can help to place a product offering in a unique position not currently served by competitive offerings. These strategies may also be applied more broadly at the firm level as a design orientation across all products. Braun does this with respect to design eminence's being a cornerstone of its overall strategy. Subaru is an example of a company that applies a specific appropriateness or concentration strategy in its focus on relatively narrow segments of users with products well tailored to the needs of the customers in the segment. Firms like Samsung Electronics and Logitech have been successfully combining both a desirable alternative and design eminence strategy with increased emphasis on elevating the image and utility of their products. Over time, as more and more of their products exhibit even greater design eminence, the perception of these firms and their "brand" will be more significantly affected—examples of product design strategy helping firms achieve their mission goals and build brand equity.

Whether a firm employs different strategies for different products, applies a single strategy across all of its products, or a combination of strategies, the result—if the execution is effective—is to position their product(s) in terms of how they are perceived by customers and how they are considered relative to competitive product offerings. Overall, the strategy employed, its appropriateness for the specific design situation to which it is applied, and the design execution to carry it out, must be correctly aligned if the design strategy is to be effective in helping a firm achieve its mission goal(s).

24.6 Key Success Considerations and Potential Pitfalls

In pursuing any of the design strategies discussed, there are several factors critical for success as well as a few common problems areas. These are general considerations that hold across the implementation of all of the strategies and all of the design situations. In order to help ensure successful application of a design strategy the following should be considered:

- Alignment of mission goal and the strategy selected.
- Assessment of strategy prerequisites and their implications or impact on shaping and limiting strategy options (for example, financial return requirements, technical feasibility, brand positioning).
- An in-depth understanding of the true nature of the product opportunity—especially in terms of what customers' actual needs are—as well as the competitive situation.
- An appreciation of how design may be used to mitigate specific risk factors (for example, designing a product so as to minimize storage and shipping costs or repair costs).
- Leveraging platform use for other products (such as was done with the Dodge Neon automobile platform used as the basis for the Chrysler PT Cruiser) and platform flexibility.
- A compelling design vision—for example, the 1963 Sting Ray Corvette evolved out of the secret "Q"-Corvette design project undertaken to create a new design theme for the Chevrolet sports car. The design was the result of inspiration and dedication to a vision of what the car could be, and some 40 years later the car retains some of the influence of that earlier design vision and still benefits from the design eminence that it helped establish.

There are also pitfalls that need to be avoided if the strategy selected is to be successful, some of these are:

- Applying a strategy without regard to the differing requirements for the different design situations.
- Mistiming or missing the window of opportunity for a particular strategy or the particular type of execution employed to effect a strategy. For example, the appeal of "retro" product designs may be fading for the time being even as some automakers are poised to introduce retro models.
- Execution breakdowns. The Pontiac Aztek design did not scale up well to the size of automobile it was eventually introduced as, and the execution of the design did not effectively convey sufficiently desirable value in terms of its appearance. Problems in the way a strategy is carried out in terms of the physical elements of a product should not be overlooked or left unaddressed.
- Lack or loss of focus. Unclear or ambiguous understanding of the situational-strategic context surrounding the design effort can severely undermine the result of the process.

24.7 Summary

Design, and particularly industrial or "product" design, can be a significant element in the strategic mix for any company wishing to achieve its goals. The task of formulating design strategy involves its own orientation and set of concerns. In addition to taking a company's mission goal(s), target consumer values, brand positioning, and relevant circumstances into

> *Design strategy involves its own set of considerations—a clear understanding of the situation-strategic design context can vault a firm ahead in the market, whereas a misalignment can be costly in terms of suboptimal or negative design outcomes.*

consideration, devising design strategy requires an appreciation of the specific challenges associated with the type of design being undertaken (renovative, adaptive, evolutionary, or discontinuous). An appreciation of the specific design strategies and considerations related to the various contextual situations can help firms further clarify their strategic thinking in order to more successfully differentiate and position their products through design. By aligning design context and strategy, firms can more effectively enhance industrial design's contribution to the product development process, the products it produces, the brand equity it builds, and the business it creates.

References

Borja de Mozota, Brigitte, "Structuring Strategic Design Management: Michael Porter's Value Chain," *Design Management Journal*, 9(2), 26–31 (Spring 1998).

Gilles, Willem and Paquet, Gilles, "On Delta Knowledge," in *Edging Toward the Year 2000: Management Research and Education in Canada*, Canadian Federation of Deans of Management and Administrative Studies, 1989.

Porter, Michael E., "What is Strategy?," *Harvard Business Review*, 61–78 (November–December 1996).

Veryzer, Robert W., "Discontinuous Innovation and the New Product Development Process," *Journal of Product Innovation Management*, 15: 304–321 (1998).

Robert W. Veryzer, Ph.D. is Associate Professor of Marketing/New Product Development in Rensselaer Polytechnic Institute's Lally School of Management & Technology, Troy, New York. His research focuses on product design, new product development, radical innovation, and various aspects of consumer behavior. His articles appear in leading professional journals such as the *Journal of Consumer Research* and *The Journal of Product Innovation Management* (he is a recipient of *The Journal of Product Innovation Management* Thomas P. Hustad Best Paper Award), and is coauthor of the book *Radical Innovation: How Mature Firms Outsmart Upstarts* (Harvard Business School Press). His work experience includes product planning and product management positions with *Fortune 500* firms as well as design and new product development consulting.

CHAPTER TWENTY-FIVE

BUILDING A BRIDGE TO THE END USER: HOW INDUSTRIAL DESIGNERS CONTRIBUTE TO PRODUCT DEVELOPMENT

Joseph Juratovac

25.1 Introduction

Industrial design is a discipline, distinct from engineering, that combines creative and intuitive elements of the visual arts with practical knowledge of markets, human behavior, materials, and manufacturing to create product designs of high value. It is important to note that the specific training for industrial designers produces a mind-set that is quite distinct from that of the engineering disciplines. Understanding the unique contributions of industrial designers will build a case for their substantive involvement in the product development team.

Industrial designers are employed by corporations and consulting firms, many of which also offer product development and engineering services. Some companies use both in-house industrial design groups and industrial design consultants; reasons for this vary, but include providing a fresh view of the product and problem-solving to the project team and/or resolving issues with overcapacity due to limited internal resources.

Industrial design is employed in various ways and at various points in the product development process. Involving industrial designers throughout the development process is the ideal way to maximize the value that industrial design can bring to the finished product. This chapter will describe a number of key points where industrial designers can make major contributions to the process.

25.2 Background and Motivation of Industrial Designers

Industrial designers can be used best when you have a good understanding about what makes these individuals tick. The education and affinities of industrial designers are at least partly responsible for their distinct view of the world, and in particu-

> *The ability to create unique and simple solutions to complex problems is greatly emphasized in design education.*

lar, their user-centric role in the world of product development.

Training for industrial designers includes a combination of visual arts (two- and three-dimensional expression, drawing, painting, and sculpture) and liberal arts (history, psychology, sociology, and literature). Their education also includes applied sciences such as physics, materials and processes, and human factors. An industrial design curriculum, found in many universities, as well as in more arts-based colleges, focuses on a range of problem-solving projects that teach the student analytical methods, a holistic approach, researching the user's experience, "out-of-box thinking," methods of communicating ideas, and presentation techniques to express a design concept. Practical skills, such as drawing, building models in a variety of media (cardboard to wood to foam), and using computer-aided design tools are a major portion of the designer's education, all focused on effective means of developing and communicating a design.

The designer's eye seeks balance, proportion, visual interest, harmony of line and form, texture, and color. In addition to these visual elements, industrial designers' training includes developing sensitivity to tactile aspects of a product or object, how it feels to use a product or a feature, its touch, sound, and other experiential characteristics. The ability to create unique and simple solutions to complex problems is also greatly emphasized in a designer's education.

Through this training, a "user-centric" mind-set develops. The function of the final product is crucial to its use, but it is viewed from the perspective of how a person perceives and uses the object: the design of a hammer is developed from how a person would hold, swing, and store the tool, rather than only by analyzing how hard or fast it drives a nail. Industrial designers consider both the "outside-in" viewpoint—designing a product from the user's point of view—as well as the "inside-out" approach that engineers might take, which is to study the function of the product, tool, or device. The designer is trained to integrate both form and function into the concept as a holistic solution.

A common definition of design is "creative problem-solving." Industrial designers are trained to analyze a problem and approach it from many angles—

thinking in a broad, "big picture," "systems" manner and making certain that they are solving the right problem. For example, while a problem statement might be to "design a better chair," an industrial designer might broaden the problem statement to, "design a means of supporting a person in a sitting position," which might allow a more innovative range of potential solutions. Inquisitive by nature, designers ask a lot of questions, such as "why?" and "what if?" to explore the boundaries of the problem and better understand (and challenge) constraints. For those focusing on a straightforward solution, this may seem annoying, but this is not the intent. The designer wants to try to arrive at the best, most novel solution and seeks to investigate all the possibilities.

How does this individual affect the product development process? Let's walk through the product development continuum.

25.3 Up-Front Involvement: Before Product Definition

A growing area of interest is the motivation of companies to seek ways to innovate, expand beyond their traditional market spaces, use their technologies in new ways, and by other means transform their businesses to secure new profits. These activities often lie outside the traditional sequence of product development activities, and industrial designers can play a key part in them. In phased product development processes, this is often referred to as "Phase Zero" and is a nebulous state because all an organization has at this time is a general desire to produce something new and different.

The "what if?" mind-set of industrial designers is well suited for exploring alternative directions, investigating new applications, and seeking out unmet user needs that require novel solutions. User research (observation) is used as a stimulus for new insights into other potential solutions. Industrial designers are skilled at extrapolation, examining trends and combining them with markets and technologies to create new concepts. Designers are able to "suspend reality" when needed to set aside what is currently feasible to explore what is possible in the future. Outputs of these investigations can be captured and communicated in many ways (described later in more detail in the "Rapid Visualization" section).

Outputs of this front-end involvement can be the description of a new product or service concept that becomes the basis for a business plan or product definition for a product development effort.

25.4 Collect and Analyze User Needs: Walk a Mile in Their Shoes

The collection and analysis of user needs is at the core of industrial design activities in new product development. A thoughtful process of researching user needs ensures that the product development team is solving the right problem for the right users.

> *Researching user needs ensures that the development team is solving the right problem for the right users.*

Industrial designers are highly motivated to identify and consider unmet needs before launching into the design of something new. Research methodologies can be formal or informal, depending on the needs of the project. Industrial designers might lead the user research or work with specialists to design and conduct the research. The objective of this inquiry is to be able to "walk a mile in the shoes" of the end user and to understand "all" the users.

Understanding how people use a product is a major concern, but it is also important to understand why, when, and where a product is used, particularly the environment in which a product is used. Developing a piece of medical equipment requires the designer to understand how the doctor or nurse would interact with the product, as well as to understand how this product fits into an overall procedure, where it might be positioned relative to the patient and other equipment, how it might need to be transported, and so forth. Beyond the immediate users, who purchases or specifies the equipment? Who services the equipment? Understanding the variation in users, varying sizes, motivations, levels of knowledge, and sophistication is the goal of user research—not to specify a "typical user," but to identify "most likely" users and learn as much from them as possible.

A common form of user research involves qualitative market research, for example focus groups, in which small groups of targeted users are gathered for a guided discussion (see Chapters 14, 15, and 16). Focus groups are an effective means of learning about people's reactions to existing products and services, in that a reasonable population of people's insights can be collected in a fairly short amount of time and in various geographic locations. Industrial designers will often work with market research firms to design the research and questionnaires, usually with a different perspective. It should be noted that focus groups should not be used for innovative direction, because people tend to respond in terms of today's context and initially have difficulty accepting something new and disruptive to the norm. Also, in terms of research into future territory, or to gauge emotional perceptions, methods using individual responses are preferable, to avoid issues with group dynamic influences.

User research has a slightly different focus from traditional market research to understand fundamental aspects of product use, including how a function is performed currently, how environmental factors influence the product or process, how the user responds emotionally to the product, and what key benefits would best address the needs of the user. User research would include questions such as: How do you do this currently? If you could, how might you do this differently? Why do you do this certain behavior? Why do you want this certain thing added to this device? Probing questions cause users to explain their interactive behavior with a product or why they want more from this product. And using this research properly may lead to far more satisfied customers down the line.

Ethnographic research, based on cultural anthropology, focuses on observing what people do, in their "natural habitats," and applying that knowledge to improve existing products, to add useful attributes and features to products, or even to uncover unmet needs that require totally new products. This form of research is favored because it places a higher value on what people do than what they say they do. Industrial designers convert those observations into unspoken "needs," which become the basis for new product (or feature or service) concepts.

The collecting of user needs is followed by various methods of documenting, analyzing, and presenting needs in a form that can be readily understood and used by the development team. Scenarios are an effective way to summarize user needs in a story-based approach that lets the team visualize "real" users, "walk a mile in their shoes," and understand the attributes that are likely important to them (see Figure 25.1).

Industrial designers provide the "voice of the customer" throughout the product development process and provide stewardship of the user needs (see Chapter 14).

25.5 Understanding Brand Essence, Promise and Positioning

Because industrial designers are instrumental in transforming brand characteristics into visual expressions, they make it a point to understand brand attributes, brand promise to the consumer, and strategic brand positioning direction. Likewise, designers are interested in the target consumers' perception of the company's verbal brand values as well as the consumers' own personal-identity-related desires. The designer's role is to then incorporate the brand identity values and the consumer perceptions and desires as fundamental criteria in the concept generation and development process.

FIGURE 25.1 SCENARIOS ARE VALUABLE FOR ILLUSTRATING HOW USER CHARACTERISTICS DRIVE DESIRED PRODUCT ATTRIBUTES.

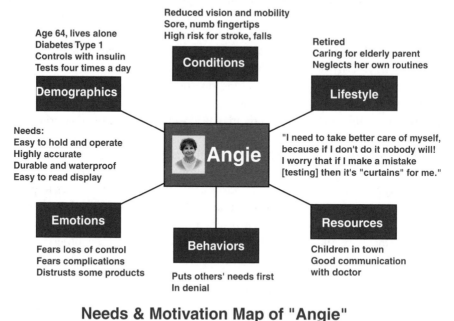

Age 64, lives alone
Diabetes Type 1
Controls with insulin
Tests four times a day

Demographics

Reduced vision and mobility
Sore, numb fingertips
High risk for stroke, falls

Conditions

Retired
Caring for elderly parent
Neglects her own routines

Lifestyle

Needs:
Easy to hold and operate
Highly accurate
Durable and waterproof
Easy to read display

Angie

"I need to take better care of myself, because if I don't do it nobody will! I worry that if I make a mistake [testing] then it's "curtains" for me."

Emotions

Fears loss of control
Fears complications
Distrusts some products

Behaviors

Puts others' needs first
In denial

Resources

Children in town
Good communication
with doctor

Needs & Motivation Map of "Angie"

25.6 Concept Generation and Development

Industrial designers' most identifiable activity, as well as admittedly the most fun, is brainstorming, or the conceptualization of product concepts (see Chapter 17). Concept generation commonly follows product definition and user needs gathering, but can occur at nearly any point in the product development process.

In general, concept generation is the free-form exploration of new ideas, using various methodologies to rapidly generate a wide range of ideas in a short

> *With training and support, small groups can generate impressive numbers of ideas in a short amount of time.*

amount of time. This is often performed in a group setting, with all participants tossing in ideas and building on others' ideas. Brainstorming sessions have a few, inviolable rules, including "no idea is a bad idea." To allow new ideas to surface, participants have to let go of the instinctive process of prejudgment, to the extent that their ideas won't be judged until they have been developed, dissected, and discussed, and later evaluated. Industrial designers use brainstorming sessions to develop multiple configurations of a design, conceptualize different aesthetic approaches, dream up new product solutions, and work out small details.

Outputs of brainstorming might be words, diagrams, sketches, and even crude models. The focus is on methods that quickly convey an idea and let the creator move on to think of more ideas. "Covering the walls" is the goal and the result of a fertile brainstorming session, as a large wall is an effective means of viewing all ideas, building upon them, and grouping similar ideas (see Figure 25.2). Properly prepared and managed, a small group can generate an impressive number of ideas in a short amount of time. For the output to be meaningful, there should be some general boundaries and criteria established in context of the basic problem at hand.

FIGURE 25.2 COVERING THE WALLS (OR TABLE) WITH THE OUTPUT OF A BRAINSTORMING ACTIVITY.

Concept development activities follow a pattern of divergence followed by convergence. Diverging is the mental process of expanding on the problem statement to allow the widest variety of ideas; converging is the process of taking disparate elements, or seeds of ideas, combining them into more complete ideas, and reviewing those against project objectives. Knowing when to diverge, how much, and how long is a critical, learned skill of design teams. There is a tension between the need to explore all possible avenues in solving a problem and the need to settle on a known, or favored direction, and proceed to the design process. Product development schedules create the need to innovate within a tight timeframe, with the realization that people cannot tinker with an idea indefinitely and need to get new products to market in a timely fashion. The philosophical differences of industrial designers and engineers can be in conflict, for example, when an engineer or project manager wants to pick an idea and move forward with it, while the industrial designer wants to carefully evaluate all the potential solutions and not hastily pick the "wrong" idea to move forward. Using this tension wisely can benefit the quality of the end product.

25.7 Rapid Visualization

Industrial design concepts are communicated in a number of forms. Sketches are a common method of two-dimensional communication for which designers are well known; perspective drawings in pencil, marker, or other media are a common way to rapidly develop sketches. Industrial designers are trained in a number of methods to quickly express ideas and seek the fastest way to help others visualize an idea or a design. Sketches are effective tools that help industrial designers see the design and allow them to explore many alternatives, such as viewing an object from many angles (see Figure 25.3).

With an idea more fully developed, project needs may dictate a more refined image of the product. A variety of media and approaches can be used to create renderings, which are more controlled, colorful, and dramatic, and most often intended for presentations. In the earlier days of the profession, renderings were produced using watercolors, gouache (a water-based paint), pastels, and charcoal. Renderings have evolved with the use of magic markers. Markers add speed, punch, and vibrancy, and while they may limit the designer's palette somewhat to the colors on hand and don't have the infinite modulation of color that paints provide, markers are a very effective way to communicate ideas.

As in most other areas of product development, computerized tools have transformed industrial design by giving designers additional means for communicating design ideas faster and more effectively. Sophisticated illustration

FIGURE 25.3 EXPLORING CONCEPTS THROUGH QUICK PENCIL SKETCHES.

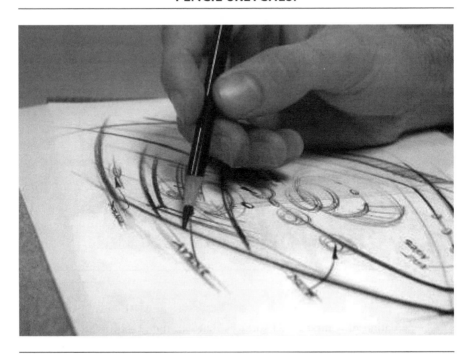

programs and image-modification programs allow more controlled, easily edited images; text can be included to produce notes, and subtle details such as color gradients and textures are easily added. Common packages at the time of this writing include Adobe Photoshop® for image editing and Adobe Illustrator® and Macromedia FreeHand for vector-based illustrations.

Three-dimensional design tools are another aspect of industrial design that have transformed the design process and provided new opportunities (see Figure 25.4). Programs originally intended for 2-D drafting have evolved into 3-D modeling tools. Surface modeling programs have introduced terms like NURBS (non-rational uniform B-splines) to the industrial design field, permitting the

Computerized tools give designers additional means for communicating design ideas.

FIGURE 25.4 PHOTOREALISTIC RENDERING PRODUCED FROM ALIAS STUDIO SOFTWARE.

creation of complex 3-D surfaces that can then be translated to solid modeling programs used in mechanical design (see Chapter 27). A model, created in a 3-D surfacing package, is a powerful entity because it enables several downstream uses that are helpful to enhancing the design and development process. A model built in Alias®, the most common package, allows a surface model to be used to create photorealistic, ray-traced renderings; provides the surface geometry to machine or build actual models; and can be modified to produce an animation, show the product in use, or allow it to be viewed from a variety of angles.

Industrial design is also a model-intensive discipline. The designer's ability to think in 3-D is augmented by his/her ability to build objects in three dimensions. Just as an industrial designer needs to create sometimes dozens of sketches to develop a design and explore variations, he/she also needs to see, feel, and hold the form to get a true sense of scale and proportion. Rough models are often constructed in parallel with concept sketches to help visualize the product and accelerate the design process. "Model early, model often" is a commonly used phrase that emphasizes the value of modeling in the design process, and models serve many purposes in product development. Models can be used to communicate internally with a project team or on a one-on-one basis with a design colleague, as a presentation tool to clients or outside investors, and as a means of presenting an idea to potential users. Models can range from a 15-minute rough foam, hand-carved volumetric model, to a detailed, accurate, painted appearance model mimicking the look, feel, and textures of a manufactured product that can take weeks to construct.

25.8 Industrial Design Through the Development Process

As the development process progresses from initial concepts to detailed design, industrial designers continue to support the

> *Model early, model often.*

creation of the product in many ways. Through the development of concepts using sketches, models, and/or CAD, the preferred concept begins to emerge. Refinement of the concept(s) evolves through reviews with engineering and marketing team members. Concepts may also be validated through individual user interviews and focus groups as well as user testing of functional models (see Figure 25.5). Industrial designers provide inputs to product requirements that represent the voice of the customers.

In the detail design phase of product development, industrial design works iteratively with mechanical designers and engineers to establish not only the "skin" of the product but also the size and layout of components. Years ago,

FIGURE 25.5 APPEARANCE MODEL CNC MACHINED FROM 3-D DATABASE.

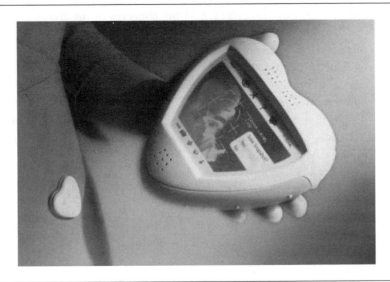

the industrial design direction would be established for a new product and then passed on to engineering. This "over-the-wall" process would often result in the design changing radically from the original intent. In other cases, the layout would be established and the industrial designer contracted to put a skin over it—the "make-it-pretty" method. This resulted in industrial designers only being able to make surface alterations to the product, with limited impact on the product's manufacturability, usability, and market success.

In the current, team-based, interdisciplinary process, a design can be passed back and forth several times as the layout and design of the product evolves. Through this iterative exchange, industrial designers focus on dictating the location of key features or components to optimize the design and appeal for the end user. Attention to ergonomics is a critical skill the industrial designer brings to the design, such as understanding the product's interaction with hand anthropometrics or the location and angle of a display screen to optimize readability and minimize fatigue.

The design process is the integration (and sometimes conflict) of what is practical (functional and manufacturable) and what is desirable (appealing and innovative). The final design can evolve quite markedly from the original concept through this exchange, as both parties strive to respect the others' point of view and develop a "win-win" strategy. In this situation, it may be desirable to share models of the revised design with key users to make sure that the benefits originally addressed are still provided by the new design. Industrial designers, or perhaps marketing team members, may collect user feedback at multiple points in the development process and communicate the response to the development team. If feedback is conclusively negative, the design may require further changes to reflect the concerns of the consumers.

Another challenge in the detail design phase is revealed in the name of the phase itself. The majority of the development team's work at this point is spent working through dozens of details, internal and external to the product. Maintaining the holistic, or "big picture" view of the product is important to maintain the original intent of the design, the essential elements of the concept that people found appealing. Components may grow or need to be repositioned. Materials may change based on functional or cost requirements. Industrial designers are trained to be able to focus in on details, yet zoom back and view the overall design as it evolves, and they are often the ones who speak up when the design deviates from the intended path. The industrial designer may suggest revisions to the design to recapture that original intent. With the macroissues resolved, the industrial designer then turns his/her attention back to resolving small, subtle details in the quest for quality.

Attention to ergonomics is a critical focus for industrial designers.

25.9 Industrial Design and Product Usability

The increasing level of technology has enabled dramatic improvements in product performance and features. Unfortunately, these benefits come at a cost of exponentially higher levels of complexity. The running joke about people not being able to understand how to change the flashing "12:00" on their VCR display is a popular example of products having wonderful features that ordinary users cannot access without significant amounts of training or sifting through a thick instruction manual. The challenge in product development is how to offer ever-increasing new and improved features and functionality, yet make the products intuitive and easy-to-learn and operate. Beyond the annoyance and confusion that results from a confusing product-use experience, there can be safety implications, for example with medical products, where user error can result in serious health complications or worse.

A high premium has been placed on ease of use, and industrial designers play a role in the development of simpler products. Industrial designers partner with human factors specialists to review and refine the ease of use of the product (see Chapter 26). Human factors engineers skilled in cognitive psychology are a key resource, providing the technical rigor to focus on usability. At the earliest stages of concept development, essential questions are asked, such as what functions must be performed, how should certain functions be accessed, which functions are more important, which operations are performed most often, and so forth. Concepts are developed, in the form of storyboards and flow charts, to organize the sequence of operations and develop a diagram of choices. Animations and simulations can be created as a way to model a prototype interface, to allow an interface concept to be developed and evaluated (see Figure 25.6).

Usability tests with prototype interfaces are an effective way to test one interface approach against another, providing user feedback early in the

Usability tests are an effective method to test one interface approach against another and provide feedback early in the development process.

FIGURE 25.6 SIMULATED USER INTERFACE ON A TOUCH-SCREEN DISPLAY.

development process and reducing the risk potential. Simulations can mimic all or a portion of an interface, and research protocols can be designed to evaluate the interactions.

For example, a user interface development team debated the merits of two data entry options used to program a medical device. They decided to simulate and test both. Simulations were created to allow a test subject to program the device after a small amount of training. The protocol was developed to time their responses and record errors. Two groups of users were recruited to try each interface simulation, both controlled by a touch-screen CRT display. The results indicated the interface approach with more buttons—numeric buttons like those on a telephone—was faster to program with fewer errors. Usability testing provided the assurance that the correct option was chosen, saving costly redesigns later on.

25.10 Design Refinements for Manufacturing and Product Launch

As the design progresses through the detail design stage and transitions to manufacturing, industrial design continues to play a role. This role is somewhat diminished in intensity, but continues to ensure that the design intent is maintained. Industrial designers should participate in contact with vendors, molders, fabricators, and the assembly line personnel to communicate the design quality expected beyond what is expressed in the drawings or database. Again, the industrial designer's motivations are to maintain a focus on the details so that they are resolved correctly while maintaining a holistic view of the product and its anticipated appeal to the end user. Creativity is still required at this late stage, as attention is shifted to fine-tuning the final look and functional aspects of the product.

Industrial designers are also an effective link to marketing because they often support the market launch activities (see Chapter 30). The designer's influence can extend to related items such as packaging, manuals, and other promotional and marketing materials, with an intimate knowledge of the users and the market. Keeping industrial designers involved with graphic designers in the development of these materials helps to carry the user-centric intent and brand theme throughout the entire product introduction.

Even after product introduction, industrial designers should stay involved. If product development is considered a continuum, the design team can learn a great deal that can be applied to the memory bank of accumulated knowledge. Understanding the market's reaction, watching the product in use, and gathering user feedback are valuable activities that provide information that can be applied to product line extensions, future product planning, or planning minor revisions to the introduced product.

25.11 Summary

Industrial design is most effective as a contributor to product success when it is an integral part of the development process, not a support function. Some final points:

- *Industrial design provides a link to the users:* In the course of product development, many concerns take precedence: schedule, budget, technical issues, manufacturing, distribution, and budget. It is very easy to forget for whom the product is designed! Industrial designers are the user advocates, the individuals who blow the whistle when changes occur that affect ease of use, conflict with the original key benefits, or significantly alter the established design's intent.
- *Industrial designers are communicators:* The various means of visual expression generated by industrial designers speak much louder than words to communicate product concepts, illustrate different design approaches, provide

visualization of brand strategy, build consensus, attract customers, and create brand trust.

- *Explore multiple conceptual directions early in the process:* The exploration process, developing many different solutions to a problem, energizes industrial designers. They embrace the "hunt" for the ideal design solution because the best path to a solution may not be the easiest or most obvious. Encourage the team to generate multiple approaches early in the development process, where true innovation occurs and mistakes are not as costly.
- *Design refinement is key—to a point:* Product refinement is critical to a successful product, but one can't tinker forever. Resolving details, fine-tuning aspects of the design for user delight is very important, but so is sticking to a reasonable schedule. There will be a constant struggle for how good is "good enough," or preferably, "great enough."
- *Industrial designers strive for simple elegance:* Simple, easy-to-use, and attractive products should be the goal of product development. Despite the fact that simplicity is uncomplicated, arriving at products that are intuitive, easy to use, and beautiful is complicated work. Industrial designers understand this dichotomy, and their design process includes a major emphasis on user interaction that boils the concept down to its essentials, while at the same time creating an emotional experience.

Industrial design is a discipline that recognizes the difference between making a product that simply meets requirements and creating products that exceed expectations, delight the customer, and build brand equity.

References

Coates, Del, *Watches Tell More than Time: Product Design, Information, and the Quest for Elegance,* New York: McGraw-Hill Trade, 2002.

Industrial Designers Society of America & Business Week, *Innovation: Award-Winning Industrial Design,* New York: St. Martin's Press, 1997.

Industrial Designers Society of America, *Design Secrets: 50 Real-Life Product Design Projects,* Gloucester, MA: Rockport Publishers, 2001.

Norman, Donald A., *The Design of Everyday Things,* New York: Basic Books, 2001.

Norman, Donald A., *Why We Love (or Hate) Everyday Things,* New York: Basic Books, 2003.

Web Sites

Design Council, UK
http://www.design-council.org.uk/

Design-oriented links
http://www.designaddict.com/design_addict/index.cfm

Design-oriented site
http://www.core77.com/

Industrial Design Society of America
http://www.idsa.org/

Joseph Juratovac is a program manager specializing in user research and industrial design for Product Development Solutions group at Battelle Memorial Institute. Mr. Juratovac holds 13 patents and has developed the user research and industrial design capabilities within Battelle. He manages design programs for clients in the medical, consumer, and energy markets. Mr. Juratovac received his industrial design degree from the University of Cincinnati and has juried professional design competitions.

CHAPTER TWENTY-SIX

HUMAN FACTORS ENGINEERING CONSIDERATIONS IN NEW PRODUCT DEVELOPMENT

Mary Hoffman Pancake

26.1 Introduction

A successful product manager strives to increase profits by reducing problems throughout the product development life cycle. Products that minimize error and injury are safer and more usable—and better positioned to increase sales and improve customer satisfaction. These major benefits can happen consistently when the product manager uses human factors as an integrated design team member from the start.

Many devices found responsible for accidents reflect more than mechanical and/or electrical failure—they reflect little or no time paid to human factors design. In fact, the Food and Drug Administration (FDA) and the Department of Defense (DoD) deemed this discipline an area of vital importance to the development process and require an established human factors engineering program as part of the product development process.

Because many project managers may be unfamiliar with human factors, this chapter will introduce the value of human factors in the product development process and the elements of an effective human factors engineering program. It is recommended that this chapter be supplemented with more detailed information. (Suggestions are listed at the end of this chapter.)

26.2 What Is Human Factors?

Human factors (HF) is the knowledge of human characteristics relevant to product design. The application of this knowledge is referred to as human factors engineering (HFE). HFE is the integration of human physical and cognitive characteristics into the design, development, test, and evaluation of products. The goal of human factors is optimizing product performance and safety under operational conditions.

Ergonomics is a term synonymous with human factors. It originated in England around the same time that the term human factors originated in the United States. These are used interchangeably with other terms, such as usability, user-centered design, human system integration, and interaction design. All these terms have essentially the same meaning, focusing on the human elements in product design.

Human Factors Engineering is more than just a collection of information or design principles. HFE specialists use a variety of tools and techniques for analyzing the information and generating user requirements and specifications. It involves a process for translating user needs into requirements and specifications for the human-system interface. HFE uses an iterative evaluation process for ensuring that user needs are met.

26.3 What Value Does Human Factors Engineering Add? What's in it for Me?

HFE will save your company money. As you look at elements in the product life cycle, HFE not only reduces product development costs, use of HFE has been

> *Human factors engineering equals good economics.*

shown to reduce costs associated with customer service elements of the product life cycle.

Usability and safety leads to user acceptance and a preferred product. Effective use also leads to efficiency and increased productivity, job satisfaction, and improved quality of life. This leads to a competitive advantage, enhanced reputation, and loyal customers. Implementing a human factors engineering program early in the product development cycle, rather than during validation, reduces overall product development costs and time to market. It is much easier and faster to *make revisions early* in the design cycle rather than *after* the product is manufactured.

Human factors engineering addresses the safe, effective, and economical use of products. The objective of HFE is to minimize, with the goal of eliminating, use errors that not only impact product performance, but may also lead to injuries or death. By striving to achieve this goal, future company resources for reporting, follow-up, interacting with customers, recalls, and liability expenses are reduced.

All these benefits equate to reduced expenditures and increased sales.

26.4 What Is the Impetus Behind Human Factors? Who Thinks This Is Important?

Many organizations require, or at least highly recommend, the implementation of an HFE program during product development. These organizations have discovered the benefits of human performance requirements when integrated early in the design process.

Good HFE practices are of such concern to the FDA that they have incorporated a requirement in 21CFR 820.30. The FDA has been an advocate of HFE since 1975, with early concern stemming from use errors in anesthesia delivery. Per the Code of Federal Regulations (CFR), manufacturers are required to establish and maintain procedures "to ensure that the design requirements are appropriate and address the intended use of the device, including the needs of the user and patient" (820.30c) and "for verifying and validating the device design to ensure that the devices conform to the user needs and intended uses with the production units tested under actual or simulated use conditions" (820.30g). This requires a process to be in place that ensures adequate consideration of human factors in the design and development of medical devices.

The United States Army has an extensive MANPRINT (MANpower and PeRsonnel INTegration) program. MANPRINT is the Army's human systems integration program that fulfills the requirements of DoD Directive 5000.2. This is a comprehensive program that integrates manpower, personnel capabilities, training, system safety, health hazards, human factors engineering, and soldier survivability into the system life cycle. The objectives of the program are to improve soldiers' performance, improve total system performance, and reduce the cost of ownership. MANPRINT addresses the entire life cycle of the product, from concept inception through maintenance and disposal. Although this was originally implemented for military systems, it is an all-inclusive approach to product development, since it focuses on the optimization of total system performance to include the human and machine.

There are a number of guidance documents, standards, and regulations relevant to human factors engineering. The International Organization for Standardization (ISO), Association for the Advancement of Medical Instrumentation (AAMI), and Department of Defense (DoD) publish relevant standards. Some of these are listed at the end of the chapter.

26.5 Usability (How Useful Is it?)

The ultimate objective of human factors engineering in product design is to develop a usable product. From "ISO 13407–Human Centered Design Processes for Interactive Systems," the definition of usability is the "extent to which a product can be used by specified users to achieve specified goals with effectiveness, efficiency, and satisfaction in a specified context of use." Per ISO 13407, the goals of usability are:

- *Effectiveness:* The accuracy and completeness with which users achieve specified goals
- *Efficiency:* The resources expended in relation to the accuracy and completeness with which users achieve goals
- *Satisfaction:* The comfort and acceptability of use
- *Learnability:* The ability to use the system help or manuals to perform the task
- *Intuitiveness:* The ability to perform the tasks with limited explanation
- *Helpfulness/supportiveness:* The ability to overcome problems that arise
- *Controllability:* The perceived feeling of being in control/tracking performance
- *Avoiding excessive mental load:* The perceived mental effort or physical indicators (i.e., auditory, visual, or verbal)
- *Avoiding excessive physical load:* Physical measures such as heart rate, respiration, and weight
- *Safety:* The ability to operate the system safely

26.5.1 How Does a Product Achieve Usability?

Product usability is optimized when the user is the central focus of the product development process. That is not to say all other performance and budgetary requirements are minimized, but rather the user and the context of use must be considered early in the product development cycle as requirements are being defined. By identifying user-centered requirements, appropriate allocation of function between user and product can be established and factored in to the product architecture.

User input is the key to optimizing user acceptance and is an iterative process. Waiting until the product is ready for validation is too late—it will be very costly in both time and money to implement the input from users at that late stage of the development cycle. Then reality sets in; cost and schedule win, and user needs are not incorporated. Your device just lost qualities that may make or break its sales. The moral of this story is: Get user input early and often. Common sense, intuition, or appointing the design team as "users" is too limited and not based on scientific knowledge of human abilities and limitations. The design team needs to understand the intended user population to ensure product safety, effectiveness, and satisfaction.

Who are the users to consider when designing a product? Anyone who interacts with the product or system. These may be operators, maintainers, or even persons on whom the product is being used (for example, the patient). Cultural,

> *The user should be the central focus of the product development process.*

sociological, educational, and physical characteristics of the potential users need to be considered in the design. All these characteristics play a role in how users interact with the device.

In what context will the product be used? Context of use addresses:

- User population
- Tasks to be performed
- Social, organizational, and physical environment
- When (date and time) the product will be used.

This information is obtained by *talking to users*. It is amazing how much you can learn by talking to users who have a totally different perspective than the product de-

> *Get user input early and often.*

velopers. In order to design a usable product, the product development team needs to understand how, when, where, and why the product will be used by the intended population. It is important to know whether the product will be used in the home, office, school, hospital, or battlefield. Further, the characteristics of that environment, such as lighting, noise, vibration, and so on, need to be specified so that the device can be used effectively, efficiently, and to the users' satisfaction. It is important to consider all possible contexts in which the product may be used in its life span. This will enhance marketability and possibly extend the life of the product.

User input can be obtained in many ways. Interviews and observations of the users' actual environments are extremely useful in understanding the context of use. Focus groups are invaluable to provide feedback on concept models or early prototypes. Users from the intended population are critical for formal usability testing in the lab or field with mature prototypes or production units.

26.6 Human Factors Engineers as a Part of the Project Team: What Do They Do?

The human factors engineering specialist needs to be an integral part of the product team. In the concept phase, the HFE professional works with the project team to perform studies and analyses to identify user needs. In the design phase, the HFE

> *HFE translates users' needs, standards, and guidelines into project-specific requirements and specifications.*

team member defines user requirements and specifications by applying scientific standards and guidelines that optimize the function of the product for human use. It is their responsibility to translate the users' needs, standards, and guidelines into project-specific specifications and requirements for the rest of the team (Chapanis, 1996). The HFE professional works closely with the safety engineer throughout the program to evaluate use errors for the likelihood of misuse, injury, or death. It is critical that the HF engineer be involved in the risk analysis, since much of the HFE information is helpful in assessing user-related hazards. As part of verification and validation, HFE tests the design against the user-related specifications and requirements using prototypes and the final production units.

There are a number of tools and techniques applicable to the identification and testing of user requirements. In addition to cost and schedule, the availability of equipment and users factor into the decision of what methods to employ.

26.7 When Is Human Factors Considered in the Product Life Cycle?

Human factors should be considered at every stage of the product life cycle. That does not mean that at every phase of the program a comprehensive HFE effort is required. As with the entire program approach, HFE elements are tailored to the

> *HFE elements are tailored to the project based on requirements, schedule, and budget.*

specific project, based on requirements, schedule, and budget. Table 26.1 lists

TABLE 26.1 TYPICAL HFE ACTIVITIES IN THE PRODUCT DEVELOPMENT CYCLE.

Discovery Process and Product Strategy	Product Requirements	Design and Development	Verification and Validation	Manufacturing	Quality Assurance and Regulatory	Product Launch and Support
Elicit information from product user community: Research user needs, capabilities, and context of use. Use focus groups, interviews, and questionnaires Use HFE audit / benchmark competition Use quality function deployment (QFD)	**Apply knowledge of human abilities to define product performance:** Assess and prioritize user needs. Define ergonomic requirements. Reference HF guidance and standards. Perform preliminary task analysis	**HFE design input and user input / evaluations:** Perform functional allocation. Perform task analysis and workload assessment. Apply ergonomic principles and data to maximize product performance. Obtain iterative user input via simulations and rapid prototypes.	**Verify specifications:** Expert HFE review User assessments **Validate requirements:** Field studies to evaluate product in real-life scenarios	**Workplace layout and workstation design:** Apply HFE guidance and standards to optimize manufacturing efficiency. Perform task analysis and workload assessment.	**Identify use errors:** Evaluate products for potential safety and health risks or damage that could result from misuse or abuse of the product.	**Product usage processes:** Provide labeling and packaging guidelines Provide input to user and maintenance manuals Provide input to training documentation Design customer feedback surveys and questionnaires

typical HFE activities conducted during the stages of the product development cycle. Table 26.2 lists typical HFE document deliverables expected during product development.

26.8 Tailoring Human Factors Engineering to Your Company's Needs

No two product development projects are exactly alike and thus no two human factors programs are the same. The more complex the user interface and greater the impact of errors results in a more substantial human factors engineering effort, both

> *At a minimum, sufficient HFE is needed to ensure product safety and effectiveness in a traceable manner.*

in terms of development cost and time (see Figure 26.1). At a minimum, sufficient HFE effort is needed to ensure product safety and effectiveness in a traceable manner.

It is therefore essential that a human factors engineering program include the following elements:

- HFE member of the project team responsible for user-related issues
- Participants from the intended user population
- User-related requirements, task analysis, and functional allocation, most importantly those related to safe use
- Studies, analyses, and tests that assess user performance and identify hazards
- Verification and validation test data for user-related requirements

It is a business decision whether to hire experienced HFE staff or rely on outside consultants. Whatever the approach, HFE expertise must be integrated into the project team to achieve product usability, safety, and cost-effective design.

26.9 Summary

Ironically, the influence of human factors engineering in product design should be transparent to the end user. When a product is well designed, users don't complain about it and probably don't even compliment it—it's expected. However, when a product is confusing to use or is uncomfortable, you will *always* hear about it—either in customer complaints or lack of sales!

TABLE 26.2 TYPICAL HFE DELIVERABLES DURING THE PRODUCT DEVELOPMENT CYCLE.

Discovery Process and Product Strategy	Product Requirements	Design and Development	Verification and Validation	Manufacturing	Quality Assurance and Regulatory (Safety) Issues	Product Launch and Support
HFE Plan User needs (profiles and context of use) HFE benchmark of existing products	HFE design guidelines User requirements document Task analysis	Theories of operation User interface specifications (hardware and software elements) User evaluation plan(s) and report(s)	Usability test plan Usability report HFE design changes based on field studies	Work instructions Workstation layout	Use error analyses	Labeling and packaging specifications Manuals and training curriculum Customer feedback surveys

FIGURE 26.1 USER REQUIREMENTS DRIVING HFE TIME AND COST.

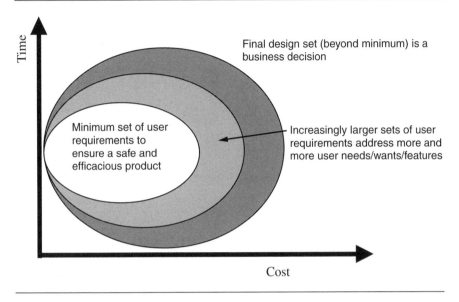

Product usability is dependent not only on a dedicated HFE team member and a good HFE program plan, but the goal of product usability and thus product success, must be valued by the entire team—including the customer and management. User needs must drive the team for a new product's success.

References

ANSI/AAMI HE48, *Human Factors Engineering and Preferred Practices for the Design of Medical Instrumentation.* Arlington, VA: AAMI, 1993.

ANSI/AAMI HE74, *Human Factors Design Process for Medical Devices.* Arlington, VA: AAMI, 2001.

Army Regulation 602-1, *Human Factors Engineering Program.* Department of the Army, 1991.

Army Regulation 602-2, *Manpower and Personnel Integration (MANPRINT) in the System Acquisition Process.* Department of the Army, 2001.

Booher, H. (Ed.), MANPRINT: *An approach to system integration.* New York: Van Nostrand Reinhold, 1990.

Chapanis, A., *Human Factors in Systems Engineering.* New York: John Wiley & Sons, Inc., 1996.

DoD Directive 5000.2, *Operation of the Defense Acquisition System,* Department of Defense, 2003.

ISO 13407, *Human-Centered Design Processes for Interactive Systems.* International Organization for Standardization, 1999.

MIL-HDBK-46855A, *DoD Handbook—Human Engineering Program Process and Procedures*, Department of Defense,1999.

MIL-STD-1472F, *Design Criteria Standard Human Engineering*. Department of Defense, 1999.

Sawyer, D., *Do It By Design—An Introduction to Human Factors in Medical Devices*. U.S. Department of Health and Human Services, Food and Drug Administration, Center for Devices and Radiological Health, 1996.

Web sites

FDA's Human Factors Program:
http://www.fda.gov/cdrh/humanfactors/

Human Factors and Ergonomics Society:
http://www.hfes.org/

Human Systems Information Analysis Center:
http://iac.dtic.mil/hsiac/

U.S. Army's MANPRINT Program:
http://www.manprint.army.mil/manprint/

Mary Hoffman Pancake is a project manager at Battelle Memorial Institute, a nonprofit research and development company headquartered in Columbus, Ohio. Since 1989, she has been involved with product usability and safety for military and medical industry clients. Hoffman Pancake has a B.S. in biophysics from the University of Scranton and a M.S. and Ph.D in biomedical engineering from the Ohio State University.

CHAPTER TWENTY-SEVEN

DESIGN BECOMES REALITY— RAPID PROTOTYPING

Raymond Sander

27.1 Introduction

This chapter serves as a primer for those interested in adding or considering the use of rapid prototyping processes in their business. Rapid prototyping refers to methods and technologies that improve an organization's capabilities to produce models or components for product development efforts.

Though "product development" can include a wide range of products, from banking services to fast food, use of the word "prototyping" in this chapter refers to tangible product development. The text refers to physical products, such as medical devices, consumer products, electronics, appliances, and so on.

Historical perspectives on these processes will guide readers through a needs assessment for usage and help them determine when to use a service bureau or purchase rapid prototyping equipment.

This chapter does not include a comprehensive study of rapid prototyping technologies, but rather offers a "big picture" understanding of these technologies, so readers can evaluate the appropriateness of each method for their business needs. High- and low-end machines are covered and not necessarily in a "good, better, best" format. Rather, the rapid prototyping processes are described in an order that may make better sense for meeting one's immediate needs versus spending ten times the cost for a process that may be overkill.

27.2 What Is Rapid Prototyping?

By definition, rapid prototyping (RP) is a computer-aided technology used to fabricate physical models from CAD (computer-aided design) programs. Quite simply, rapid prototyping creates a 3-D model of whatever the design program dictates.

But rapid prototyping is more than just a technological process. Rapid prototyping allows one to include the tactile process—to actually hold the result—soon after computer generation. The tactile process evokes emotion, ideas, issues, and new thoughts that may not have come to the surface as readily as with a two-dimensional model, if at all.

> *Holding a 3-D model evokes emotions, ideas, and issues that may not occur when viewing a 2-D model.*

Rapid prototyping allows the "what if" thought processes, as well as general problem solving, to occur earlier in the product development process and at a lower cost. What manager wouldn't want to benefit from this technology?

27.3 Rapid Prototyping—How Is It Used?

Rapid prototyping is literally "technology complementing technology." For example: What good would a word-processing program be on the fastest computer if you couldn't print out the text? How would the document be shared with others if everyone had to gather around a computer screen to view it? Complementing technologies make the "good" "better" and the "better" "best." So it is with rapid prototyping.

> *Rapid Prototyping is literally technology complementing technology.*

The advantages of computer-aided design (CAD) over manual mechanical drawing are so great that no one would want to do without the technology. Without computer-aided design, making changes to the drawing was a painful and slow process, making it difficult to find vendors to cut parts or make molds without a CAD database.

Rapid prototyping in the CAD world is like having a three-dimensional printer. In a matter of hours, a virtual model can now be "printed" into a 3-D physical model. Designers no longer need to wait until the mechanical design is complete to send parts out—only to find out that a necessary detail was forgotten, or that subcomponents don't fit just right. Today, product development schedules demand a more rapid time-to-market, and products need to be designed and tested much sooner. Improvements to the design need to happen early in the design process. CAD programs allow the designers more flexibility to pursue the "what ifs." Rapid prototyping techniques allow development team members to see and touch many alternatives in the same day.

Mistakes are vital to the innovative design process. Rapid prototyping processes allow one to learn from "mistakes" and improve the design early in the process, when it is least expensive. The cost of sim-

> *Mistakes are vital to the innovative design process.*

ple concept models created in early Phase 1 versus the cost at the detail design phase is significant. Rapid prototype users can concurrently "print" out parts to validate their size, shape, fit, ergonomics, and so on. With modeled parts in hand early in the design process, team members have excellent visual aids for client meetings—allowing improved communication about components clients can actually see and touch. This can also reduce time-to-market milestones. While the design is evolving, issues and problems can be recognized and addressed, keeping the CAD database cleaner and eliminating the need to change interfacing parts. Prototypes can be used with focus groups and to update clients, as well as to work out the fit with interfaced components. Best of all, rapid prototyping can eliminate "concession" decisions downstream, which frequently lead to a less than ideal product.

Clients and design teams from different locations are often brought together using teleconferencing and/or videoconferencing. After completing a teleconference, the use of rapid prototyping allows one to email or FTP early prototype concepts to a service bureau located close to the client's location where parts can be printed out—typically saving a shipping day. Rapid prototyping requires a new way of thinking about the use of everyday terms. Designers may say, "We can fax parts now." And this is possible with rapid prototyping—but at the receiving end of the transmission, the "fax" takes 3-D form. All of this allows the speeding up and sharing of information that is more accurate during the product development process. Rapid prototyping becomes an excellent tool to pinpoint a client's needs or preferences. The sooner a client has a model in his/her hands and can discuss it, the more information a designer has to work with, which allows more quality to be built into a product.

All rapid prototyping technologies need a three-dimensional CAD database. This database does not need to be complete with every detail, but drawings need to be at the point at which one could view the part successfully and provide initial feedback. For example: some design teams start with a volumetric or simple "shelled" form.

The other thing these technologies share is that they are all additive processes. Traditional machining is subtractive: starting with a block of material and removing mass until the desired shape is produced. Rapid prototyping starts out with raw material (powder, resin, paper, wax, metal, or plastic) and builds the part layer by layer until it is complete. These layers are most commonly around 0.003″ but can be as small as 0.0005″. The layer thickness is a trade-off between detail and time to build.

27.4 How Does Rapid Prototyping Work?

Regardless of the specific machine/process, the basic steps used for rapid prototyping are the same:

1. **A surface or solid model CAD file must be generated.**
   - Generally, solid model programs such as *Pro Engineer*® and *Solid Works*® create a better STL file than a surface modeler. The term "water tight" refers to how close surfaces are joined in a surface CAD program. This can be a source of problems when working with rapid prototyping. If you are working with a surface modeler CAD program, you should increase the system default tolerance to 6–8 decimal places and establish good drawing practices. Some CAD designers take surface shortcuts that may seem like time-saving decisions at the moment, but create problems after the file gets more complicated and moves into rapid prototyping.
   - When working with an assembly of parts, rapid prototyping gives the user the option to create them as one part or as individual parts. Some RP machines can make parts with various colors to highlight and differentiate features.
2. **This file must be saved as an STL file.** This is a conversion option in the CAD program and usually requires nothing more than following the "Save As" command.
   - The STL file was first created for the stereolithography rapid prototyping process but has been adopted as the standard for present day RP files.
   - The output STL file is a series of triangles or facets. The size of these facets can be controlled by settings during the conversion process. The settings would be found in export options and described as resolution or deviation.
   - There are STL viewers (such as SolidView®) that view and validate STL files. If the viewer identifies an incorrect setting, it can save a day in time

and the cost of the part. If a user doesn't like a part's resolution, it can be resaved at a tighter tolerance setting and viewed/verified again. It is a true WYSIWYG (what you see is what you is what you get) approach. The viewer will display exactly what the rapid prototyping machine will use to build a specific part. If an STL file is prepared for in-house or RP service bureau use, it should definitely be viewed before it leaves its originator.

3A. **If you are using an RP service bureau, the STL file is now ready to transmit.**

  OR

3B. **If you are using a company machine, continue the process.**

4. **The STL file is opened into the software program supplied with the RP machine.**

   - The files are automatically processed, oriented, and sliced into layers. Note that each machine has a build envelope and can run as many parts as can be orientated in this envelope. They can be the same or different parts.
   - The machine is then set to run. Once initiated, the machine cannot be stopped to add additional parts. To help monitor costs, a display provides information such as total run time, completion time, and volume.
   - Removal, cleaning, and postprocessing of the parts. The amount of post-processing a part requires depends on the process and, as we will learn later, is an important consideration for the selecting a process.
   - Depending on the rapid prototyping process, some postproduction may be required. This may be additional curing, cleaning off supports, sanding/bead blasting, dissolving wax, or permeating the part with a resin to stiffen it.

5. **Incorporate a plan to model early and often—not just to validate design.** The use of early models can resolve more than engineering and design concerns. Models can help resolve internal component packaging, volume, and ergonomic issues. By sharing early models with those in marketing and manufacturing, product developers can get specialized feedback on a design much earlier in the process.

Sharing early models with others allows one to gather specialized feedback much earlier in the development process.

27.5 Overview of Commercial Rapid Prototyping Systems (High End)

The high-end rapid prototyping machines produce prototypes as close to the real part as possible without computer numerical control (CNC) machining them from the desired material for the project. The machines are best suited for service bureaus or large companies who can keep them running on a daily basis. This article does not contain a complete listing of every current rapid prototyping machine—only the major systems (by their unique process nature) are listed here.

27.5.1 Stereolithography (SLA)

Today one of the most common, highly recognized, and widely used RP processes is stereolithography. Introduced in the mid-1980s, it catapulted the rapid prototyping revolution forward. Stereolithography's strengths are in the accuracy of the part produced and its excellent surface finish. The SLA machine builds parts by passing a low-power laser beam, controlled by the computer, into a vat of a photo reactive resin. When the laser beam hit this resin, it solidifies. As each layer is printed, the build platform is lowered, a sweeper bar levels a new layer of uncured resin over the first, and the process is repeated until the part is complete. SLA's require "bridgework" constructed to keep unattached pieces from floating away. The pieces will become attached as further levels are printed. This bridgework is very thin and is removed during the postprocessing cleanup. As with most rapid prototyping processes, the SLA machine can build multiple parts arranged throughout the build envelope. Build envelopes range from 10″ × 10″ × 10″ to the current largest machine of 20″ × 20″ × 24″. Early materials were brittle, but now parts can be built from a variety of formulations for rigid, durable, and even in some cases clear optical, quality. SLA machines provide some of the more expensive rapid prototyping processes and most often are found at service bureaus and large corporations.

The SLA process should be considered for models that require high definition, need close tolerance, and use as patterns for RTV molding. This process is also a good choice for working models when built with a resin that matches the developing product's performance needs.

Reconsider using stereolithography in early design studies. The cost of SLA parts is higher, which prohibits making many for concurrent design study models. It is also not as fast as the conceptual modeler machines. Rapid prototyping vendors also may delay the start of one customer's build to combine it with another customer's order to maximize their build volume.

27.5.2 Selective Laser Sintering (SLS)

The selective laser sintering (SLS) process is very similar to SLA. Both use a computer-controlled laser, but the SLS process uses a powder instead of a liquid. Selective laser sintering parts are very strong and have good aesthetic quality with a slight textured surface similar to that of a sugar cube. The build size is 15″ × 13″ × 18″. The laser sinters (heats and fuses) the powder, producing a solid layer cross-section of the part. The process is repeated by the spreading a new layer of powder, and these new layers are sintered to the previous layer. These powders can be plastic, metal, or a rubberlike substance. Because selective laser sintering can make metal parts, it is truly unique. It can make fast mold inserts for prototype injection molding and low-run injection tooling. SLS makes strong parts for durable fit and function prototypes. No bridgework is required with this process because the unsintered powder supports the part while it is constructed. SLS machines are also expensive and are typically found in larger corporations and service bureaus.

The SLS process is used for models requiring the strength of or near thermoplastic specifications, for working models, and when rapid tooling is required.

Evaluate using the SLS process in early design from a cost and speed standpoint. When these models require finish painting, the powdery surface finish needs an extended effort to achieve a finished model appearance.

27.5.3 Fused Deposition Modeling (FDM)

The fused deposition process is, in essence, a computer numerical control (CNC) hot-melt glue gun, a very simple process with little that can go wrong. FDM users like the strength of the acrylonitrile-butadiene-styrene (ABS) polymer material, making it a good choice for functional models. The gain in strength comes at the expense of surface finish. Functioning on the same principle of building in layers, the fused deposition modeling deposits semi-melted material across the layer cross-section—building the part. Once the layer is complete, the part is lowered and the process is repeated layer by layer until the model is complete. Common materials extruded with the FDM process are ABS (including medical grade), polycarbonate, investment casting wax, and an elastomer. FDM build envelopes range from 8″ × 8″ × 12″ to the largest current machine of 23.6″ × 19.7″ × 23.6″. Fused deposition modeling machines can start at less than $100,000 and are found in service bureaus and many midsized companies. Also, FDM machines can be used in any office environment without special venting.

Use the FDM process for designs requiring strength and working models. FDM is a good choice for an in-house machine, due to its affordable purchase cost. FDM modelers are affordable for most company budgets. If finish painting is needed, FDM models show build steps, and the bottom (first layer built) surface is textured and rough.

27.5.4 Overview of Concept Modeler Systems (Lower End)

Concept modeler systems can be generally described as 3-D printers. These are the least expensive of the rapid prototyping processes. They are by and large office-friendly and can be found next to plotters, as well as in the Model Shop. Concept modelers generally produce very inexpensive parts for early up-front form evaluation, as well as fit. The materials used are not as strong as those used with high-end rapid prototyping systems. Concept modelers are usually faster at running builds. Due to their low cost, these systems are not usually found at service bureaus, but are installed in small to large companies.

27.5.5 Z-Corporation (Z-Corp)

The Z-Corp machine is a powder-based machine that works well with solid shapes, as well as ribbed walls greater than 0.030″. Build envelopes range from 8″ × 10″ × 8″ to that of the current largest machine, which is 20″ × 24″ × 16″. A major advantage of the Z-Corp process is its speed. It outperforms all other rapid prototyping methods, producing models in one-tenth of the time as an SLA machine. Its limitations involve surface quality. Because it uses a powder, the surface is very grainy. This machine is best used for concept model generation, form, and fit. Newer machines can print in color (without any secondary operations), which is excellent for assemblies. Z-Corp parts are normally cured with wax or thin cyanoacrylate glue and with some extra postprocessing can be permeated with urethane resin to simulate flexible rubber parts.

Use the Z-Corp process for conceptual models when speed is crucial, and a finish model surface is not required. Due to its relatively low cost, the Z-Corp process is a good choice when many models are required. Z-Corp models can be permeated with urethane rubber to replicate flexible parts without any molds, as well as being printed in multiple colors. Z-Corp modelers are affordable for most company budgets.

The Z-Corp process may not be the best choice for very close tolerance parts, parts requiring high strength, and models requiring a finished paint surface.

27.5.6 Solidscape (formally Sanders Prototype)

Known for its high accuracy and detail this thermal inkjet printer has the edge when making lost wax masters for medical and jewelry-like parts. The trade-off is speed for this 32–63 microinches (RMS) surface finish. Layers are as thin as they come building parts 0.0005″ at a time. Parts produced from the Solid-scape are not very strong requiring investment casting to complete the part. The build envelope 12″ × 6″ × 8.5″.

27.5.7 3-D Systems Inkjet

3-D Systems produces several inkjet-style printers—their first was the Actua®. The Actua built parts from hard wax with impressive detail, though the parts were brittle. 3-D Systems replaced the Actua with the ThermoJet® printer. With a maximum model size of 10″ × 7.5″ × 8″, the Thermojet builds with a thermopolymer that is much stronger than the previous Actua models. Surface quality details from the ThermoJet are very good. Two choices of material allow users options for making investment castings, as well as rapid models. 3-D Systems' newest release is a network-controlled system called InVision SI2®. This jet printer offers an in-between process designed to provide a bridge from the high-end SLA to the quicker concept modeler.

The ThermoJet® modelers are affordable for most company budgets. ThermoJet printers are a good choice for concept models, extremely fine detail, or for making patterns for RTV molding. If thin wall parts require strength and a speedy build time is required, you may want to use another process.

27.5.8 Objet

Objet is a jet-type concept modeler, but uses a photopolymer similar to the SLA. The Objet produces smooth, detailed prototypes at fast-build rates. After the Objet deposits the material to a single layer, a UV bulb along the jetting bridge emits UV light, curing each layer. The newer Objet printers can build in thin layers down to 0.0006″, producing extremely fine detail.

Objet modelers are affordable for most company budgets and produce SLA-like models. They can be used for RTV patterns, but output models are not as clean and crisp as those from stereolithography. Conceptual models require finer details and thin walls. Overall, the Objet modeler is still new and has yet to establish a track record.

27.6 Which System Is Right for My Business?

For those considering rapid prototyping for the first time or who have been using one or more of these processes described in this chapter, it is necessary to define and assess specific needs and budget. If you have been using outside service bureaus for rapid prototyping models, record and track all those expenses and trends for types of RP models used. This helps when analyzing actual expenses and return on investment, and will point you in the direction of the process that best suits your current needs.

When evaluating the alternatives, *think about your use of rapid prototyping.* Look back at each use of rapid prototyping and evaluate how that model worked out. Were there issues with the quality of the model? Were your needs based around design and form study or engineering a working model? Would you have benefited by making more models to explore the decision-making process? Did the cost of the model put a burden on the project? What went wrong (and right) when obtaining your previous models? What space can you provide if you buy a RP system? Can you afford this purchase? Consider the real "cost" of a mistake made in the design process: redesign time, labor, and scheduling.

> *Consider the "real cost" of a mistake made in the design process: time for redesign, labor, and rescheduling.*

Avoid any decisions that are influenced by those who resist change in your organization. Listen to their concerns, of course, but realize that some people fear change or will choose a simple change over what might be best. Many companies that have moved into owning a rapid prototyping machine find they average 6–10 times the amount of models built in-house after purchasing the machine than prior to going outside. Because the quickly learn the value prototyping more often.

Can you get by without it? A question with which many have struggled. You will need to assess your business and your competition. Are your timelines too long, and would you like to compress them? To save time, today's teams need to update the product development process and use the power of current rapid prototyping processes. One of the biggest opportunities to reduce time is in what some call the "Fuzzy Front End." Implementing an aggressive concept model stage early, when there is freedom in your design, directs the downstream efforts of your team based on good information and will likely do so with fewer changes. Do you find that past designs resulted from concessions versus time? Adhering to the motto, "Model Early, Model Often" will greatly accelerate product development and lead to high-quality, fault-free designs.

If the questions above lead you to the high-end processes, and budget is a problem, you can partner with a service bureau in your area to meet those needs. Notice the word "partner." It is in your best interest for the service bureau to be a part of your team—clearly understanding how you work and your specific needs. Most service bureaus will insist on having one person handle your account, resulting in a valuable relationship, because this person will handle problem files for you and represent you to their company. We own both concept modelers and SLAs at Battelle, yet still use outside vendors.

As you familiarize yourself with rapid prototyping, you'll want to build a list of resources to stay current with this ever-changing technology. I suggest that you start with the University of Utah's Rapid Prototyping home page at http://www.cc.utah.edu/~asn8200/rapid.html#COMM. This site has a large list of commercial service providers. You can also contact RP machine manufacturers and have representatives visit your business. They will help you locate a local vendor, and you can start a relationship for future business.

Please refer to the "References" section for additional RP resources.

27.7 Costs and Staffing

Most of the high-end rapid prototyping machines will start around $180,000 and can cost as much as $750,000 for the largest machines. Concept modelers start around $30,000 and run up to $80,000. The cost of producing parts ranges from $0.70 per cubic inch and can go up to $3.50 per cubic inch. Most companies already have surface or solid model CAD systems, which is a requirement for rapid prototyping. Files sent to a rapid prototyping machine must be originated in 3-D. Maintenance on the laser systems requires that the laser be replaced at the 5000–7000 hour intervals along with power supply and diodes. The cost for this can be in the $26,000 range and should be budgeted in operation costs. Most concept modeler machines have small consumable replacement costs for items such as printer heads.

All rapid prototyping machines require a small amount of time to train staff, usually when the machine is delivered. Though the new machine can be up and running in a very short time, an operator's skills still need to be developed. Part orientation and STL file verification will take time to master in order to produce the highest-quality parts. Although it is possible to have all 3-D CAD people trained to run the rapid prototyping machine, it may be best to have two or three people handle these responsibilities exclusively. Not only does this allow them a sense of pride and ownership, but they will also learn from each other. These key people should join one of the rapid prototyping e-forums on the Web (one that is specific to the machine in your business). There is a wealth of knowledge to be gleaned from these forums, and they allow one to stay abreast of shows and seminars.

27.8 Summary

Promises, promises! One of the first rapid prototyping workshops I attended in the late 1980s offered a great presentation entitled "The Good, the Bad, and the Ugly." It was a very honest and up-front presentation of one company's account of what worked and what didn't. Material, machines, education, and processes have come a long way since the 1980s.

Though some of what others have learned about using various rapid prototyping processes can be applied to other situations, in the end, one must carefully evaluate what works best for each company. Your first selection may not be what works best for your company, products, or culture. This should not be viewed as a failure, but should motivate you to continually evaluate your RP processes against other emerging or established processes in locating the process that is closest to ideal.

Even with rapid prototyping, one can end up with "ugly" from time to time. By adhering to good standard work practices, developing a dedicated rapid prototyping staff, and continually refining methods to identify client needs, rapid prototyping will become vital to the success of product development.

References

Smith, Preston G. and Reinertsen, Donald G., *Developing Products in Half the Time, New Rules, New Tools,* New York: Van Rostrand Reinhold, 1998.

Web Sites

New Product Dynmaics, Rapid Prototyping List Servers:
http://www.newproductdynamics.com/organizations.htm#Listservers

New Product Dynmaics, Using Conceptual Modelers for Business Advantage:
Preston G. Smith
http://www.newproductdynamics.com/TCT4-01/TCT4-01.pdf

University of Utah, Rapid Prototyping:
http://www.cc.utah.edu/~asn8200/rapid.html

University of Utah, Rapid Tooling:
http://www.cc.utah.edu/~asn8200/rt.html

Take advantage of technologies and strategies that enhance the product development process and improve time-to-profit.

Wholers Associates, Inc
http://www.wohlersassociates.com/index.html

Fast Models, Big Value:
Cover story *Design News* (09-08-03 issue)
http://www.manufacturing.net/dn/index.asp?layout=article&articleid=CA318815

The interface of Medical Imaging, Finite Element Analysis (FEA), Computer-Aided Design (CAD) and Rapid Prototyping:
http://www.sussex.ac.uk/Units/biomodel/research/index.html

BioMedical Modeling:
http://www.biomodel.com/

3-D Systems
http://www.3dsystems.com/

Objet:
http://www.objet.co.il/home.asp

Stratasys
http://www.stratasys.com/NA/index.html

Z-Corp:
http://www.zcorp.com/

Ray Sander is the lead model maker for Battelle Product Development Solutions group. With over 25 years experience in pattern, model making, silicone tooling, and manufacturing, he has world-class mechanical skills and diverse options to parts design and manufacturing. His extensive background experience includes rapid development of functional prototypes for all levels of product development, visual/appearance models for market research, customer focus groups, human factors design and user-interface development, and low-volume prototype/production runs of urethane and epoxy cast parts. Sander has been selected as one of *Medical Device and Diagnostic Industry* (MDDI) magazine's 100 notable people in the medical device industry for 2004.

CHAPTER TWENTY-EIGHT

RISK TOOLS FOR TECHNICAL DEVELOPMENT: HAZARD ANALYSIS AND FMEA

Steven R. Nelson and Fritz Eubanks

28.1 Introduction

A well planned and executed risk analysis activity should be part of any significant product development project. Sometimes it's required, as in the development of medical devices. Regardless of requirement, you owe it to your customer, your company, and yourself to produce a safe product on time, within budget, and that meets the needs of its users. Effective use of risk analysis helps you meet these goals.

Risk analysis serves as the project manager's binoculars to see into the future. By spending time and money early to examine what might go wrong and how it might happen, you can make effective plans to avoid those problems and/or minimize their impact, while staying on schedule and budget. For example, Battelle's Product Development Solutions has developed an effective risk assessment methodology as part of their standard model for new product development to ensure that each product under development has appropriate attention paid to safety and performance issues (see Figure 28.1).

The problems you don't identify early will cause the most trouble.

FIGURE 28.1 BATTELLE PRODUCT DEVELOPMENT METHODOLOGY (INCLUDING RISK ASSESSMENT).

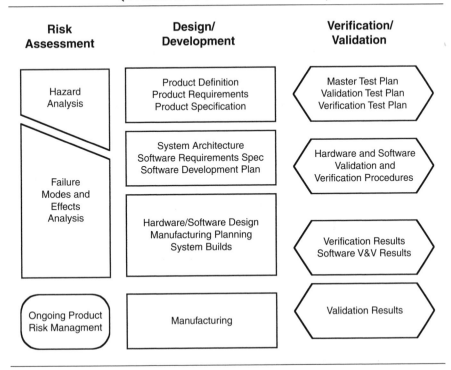

28.2 Risk Analysis Tools—Hazard Analysis and Failure Mode and Effects Analysis

When using binoculars, you keep both eyes open to get an accurate view. It also can be said that you look at everything twice. The same is true in an effective risk analysis program. First, an early view of the product's development "landscape" is taken to identify general problem areas to be handled while keeping development on track—this is the role of the hazard analysis (HA). As shown in Figure 1, the HA is performed prior to any significant development effort. Wasted development effort and cost can be driven to a minimum using this approach. Later in the development process, the Hazard Analysis is replaced by the failure modes and effects analysis (FMEA) in which a more detailed view of each part of the design is taken to make sure that it is serving its purpose and working appropriately with the other parts of the design.

28.2.1 Hazard Analysis (HA)

A hazard analysis is a technique that allows the product development team to identify, prioritize, and develop mitigation strategies for potential risks very early in the product development cycle. The team starts by looking at how the product might negatively affect the user or environment (potential hazards or risks) and then produces scenarios about how the actions of the product could produce those hazards (causes). This is often referred to as a "top-down" look because it starts with a wide focus and then narrows down to specifics. The hazard analysis should be performed as soon as a clear understanding exists about basic product functionality. The results of the HA are used to help complete the product specification and test plan. All of these documents should be started at the same time. Figure 28.2 shows a typical hazard analysis format.

The ID column is used to assign a unique number to each line to make it easy to identify a line when communicating with others.

The risk assessment team's first task it to examine the product or system to decide what hazards it might produce. Often, product development teams have trouble separating hazards from causes. For example, is electric shock a hazard or a cause? To illustrate the answer, we'll use Ben Franklin's maxim "for want of a nail the shoe was lost, for want of a shoe the horse was lost, for want of a horse the rider was lost."

Hazards are the risks the project team wants to control. They should be defined as globally as possible. In this case, the lost rider (death) is the hazard. The lost shoe and lost horse are intermediate hazards that the team should not spend time and

> *The hazard is the result or effect that directly affects the user of the product.*

resources on because they are subsets of the more global, or final, hazard. Potential hazards examined must include deficiencies in safety (injuries) and could include deficiencies in performance (insufficient throughput) or customer dissatisfaction (product produces too much noise).

FIGURE 28.2 HAZARD ANALYSIS WORKSHEET.

ID	Potential Hazard	Cause(s)	S	O	RI	Mitigation

In staying strictly with Franklin's original maxim, one would identify the lost nail as the root cause. But Franklin was really warning against neglect in this lesson. Team members must develop the ability to ask questions that cover a number of possibilities. *Why was the nail lost? Did the blacksmith not shoe the horse properly? Did the rider fail to perform normal checks of the shoes to make sure they were not damaged or had loose nails? Was the design, construction, or material of the nail inadequate to the task? Was the horse ridden over terrain unsuitable to the types of shoes used?* The team needs to answer all these questions to identify the root cause.

So, is electric shock a hazard or a cause? An electric shock involves the delivery of electrical energy to a person from the product. It's a hazard, but likely an intermediate one. The causes that the

> *The cause is the initiator or root that leads directly to the hazard.*

product development team should consider might include the failure of insulation or guarding of a live electrical line or component. These causes provide the team with something that they can address in terms of making changes to the design to prevent the hazard. The final hazard should be described in terms of what this electrical energy does to the person. Thus, the hazard is likely some level of injury to the user.

Severity (S) is a numerical rating describing the degree of damage caused by the hazard. The severity scale should be tailored to the product under development and the hazards it might pose, which will be different for each company. For example, a diagnostic medical device not only carries with it the potential for harm to the operator but also the potential to provide a false reading and potentially harm the patient by misleading the physician. A useful technique used to handle this kind of analysis is to create a list of severity categories (for example, personal injury, incorrect analysis, product performance, etc.) and criteria for the levels in each (see Figure 28.3). Not all categories need to be completely filled in with criteria, and the criteria at each severity level should represent about the same level of "damage" (note that moderate injury is rated as an incorrect positive indication and a system failure—all about the same level of "badness" in this example). In Franklin's maxim, rather than leave the hazard as "rider was lost" we used "death" as the hazard, thus leaving no doubt that the proper severity level is 5.

The number of severity (or other evaluation ratings like occurrence or detectability) levels used is up to the project team. A sufficient number of levels must be used to maintain adequate discrimination between the severity levels (with five distinct levels of injury possible, a minimum of five levels of severity must be used). Many standard texts use 10 levels, while the authors have found that fewer levels are often sufficient. The benefit from using fewer levels is that

FIGURE 28.3 SEVERITY LEVELS FOR VARIOUS HAZARD CATEGORIES AND CRITERIA.

Severity Levels	Hazard Categories and Criteria		
	Injury	Analysis	Performance
5	Death		
4	Serious	Incorrect negative	
3	Moderate	Incorrect positive	System failure
2	Minor	Inconclusive result	Decreased throughput
1	Annoyance	Clearly wrong	Adjustment required

the project team takes less time in scoring each line, thus increasing the cost-benefit ratio of the risk assessment effort.

Occurrence (O) is a numerical rating describing the chance that the cause will occur and that it will lead to the hazard. In our example, the question is: How likely is the loss of a nail and that this loss will lead to the death of the rider? While the severity scale spans the extremes from ultimately serious to annoyance, the occurrence scale should be limited to low probabilities. How many people will buy a toaster if they receive a minor shock even 1 percent of the time they use it? Even the highest occurrence level will not happen very often. The HA team needs to develop an occurrence scale appropriate for the product. The rating scale shown in Figure 28.4 is an example of a scale that might be appropriate for a medical device.

FIGURE 28.4 OCCURRENCE SCALE.

Occurrence	Description	Alternate Description
5	Occasional	As likely as getting a traffic ticket
4	Unlikely	As likely as being in a serious traffic accident
3	Remote	As likely as being killed in a serious traffic accident
2	Improbable	As likely as being struck by lightning
1	Almost Unbelievable	As likely as being hit by a meteor

Some practitioners advocate the use numerical odds as the criteria for choosing the rating in this column (for example $1:10,000$). To maintain the credibility of the hazard analysis, if the team elects to use this approach, they should be able to show a history with similar products, simulations, analysis, or testing to justify their selection of a rating. Often in new product development efforts, the information available to the team at the time the hazard analysis is initiated is often insufficient to produce a valid analysis to justify the rating.

The *risk index* (*RI*) is simply the product of the severity and occurrence ratings. The basic theory is that higher the risk index, the more attention should be paid to the potential hazard. The team pays attention to the potential hazard by defining a *mitigation* strategy to reduce the severity of the hazard or reduce the chances of it occurring. Ultimately, the person who has product responsibility must make the final decisions about what levels of risk are acceptable because he/she will answer for problems with the product's safety and performance. In making this decision, examine both the overall risk index and the severity column. The higher the risk index, the higher the degree of risk, and the more attention the item should be given. However, the hazards that have very high severity consequences (such as death) should have a mitigation strategy devised for them regardless of their overall risk index. General rules of thumb are poor substitutes for an intelligent decision made for each product by the person or company responsible for that product's safety and performance.

Because many critical risk areas will be multidisciplinary in nature, the hazard analysis team should include representation from each technical area involved in the product's development. The team leader is responsible for scheduling and running meetings, team composition, and making sure that the team has the information they need to make appropriate decisions. One obvious piece of information needed is an accurate description of the product under evaluation. Since the hazard analysis is performed early in the development cycle, different team members may have different concepts in mind. The team leader needs to present the team with a single conceptual design so that all the members are evaluating the same product.

The hazard analysis team brainstorms possible hazards that could be produced by the product. Hazards should be listed and combined until you reach the top-level hazard. Try to drive your selection of hazards to closely match one of those severity levels. Next, the team lists a set of causes that might lead to these hazards. This list should be reviewed to eliminate the intermediate level causes; the goal is to identify root causes in order to devise an effective set of mitigation strategies, keeping in mind that there may be different root causes for different hazards and several potential root causes for a specific hazard.

There are several kinds of hazard or risk for which one must plan. These may be described as "known-knowns" (risks that are self evident), "known-unknowns" (risks that may be hidden or variable, but have been seen before in similar projects or products), and "unknown-unknowns."

The last category is the most difficult to evaluate and may cause the most problems. For example, the user or developer of a chainsaw will easily identify the risk associated with the moving chain; however, the user or developer of a microwave oven might have no idea that it poses a risk to someone with a pacemaker. The team should try their best to look beyond the obvious risks—it is up to the team to protect the user.

Scoring the hazards and causes occurs next. If the team has been able to define the hazard as one of the severity levels, then scoring in the severity column is finished. Otherwise, the team needs to pick the level that most closely matches the hazard. The most contention usually arises in selecting the occurrence rating. Whenever possible, the project team should acquire hard data to properly evaluate the occurrence scores. However, very early in the development of a new product, hard data may not be available. Then experience and judgment must be used, and team consensus must be reached. Allow each person to express his or her view before coming to a conclusion. It can be tempting for the leader to push the team to a quick decision without full discussion. This behavior negates the major benefit of using a team of intelligent, skilled professionals to evaluate the product. It is important to understand that consistency of scoring is more important than the absolute score given for a particular hazard/cause because the RI for various hazards/causes will be compared to decide which are the worst and should be addressed.

28.2.2 Design Failure Mode and Effects Analysis (DFMEA)

A design FMEA is a technique that allows the product development team to systematically examine each important aspect of the product to identify, prioritize, and set mitigation strategies for potential design weaknesses. One of its key features is that the team systematically examines every part used in the design, so if done properly the team is reasonably assured that there are no gaps left in the analysis.

The design FMEA is usually done later in the development cycle than the hazard analysis, but don't wait for the design to be completed before the DFMEA is done—it will be too late to realize the main advantages offered by this technique. Use the results of the FMEA to help complete the product specifications and test plans, and influence the design. Figure 28.5 is an example of a design FMEA worksheet (normally on one line, but shown on two lines for clarity).

FIGURE 28.5 FMEA WORKSHEET.

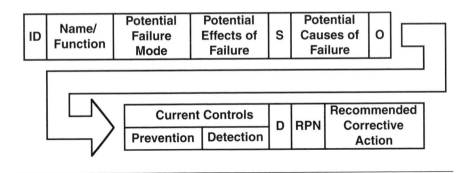

To complete the DFMEA, the team examines each part of the product using the bill of materials. For each part, the team completes the column entries in turn (for example, all of the important functions of the part are listed *before* the team starts listing the potential failure modes). Examining the product starting with each part and working towards the global product function is often referred to as a "bottoms-up" approach, which complements the "top-down" look provided by the HA.

The columns of ID, Severity, Causes, and Occurrence are the same as for the hazard analysis. The column for the Recommended Corrective Action is the same as the HA Mitigation column. The Potential Effects column is the same as the HA Hazard column.

The name of the part and its important functions are listed in the second column. Each part may have several functions in addition to the obvious ones— examine the parts in contact with the one under evaluation to define interface functions. For example, a bolted joint may be obviously used to hold a cover plate onto a device, but if a gasket is on the cover plate to prevent leakage, the bolted joint also functions to provide the force necessary to compress the gasket and maintain the seal. It is up to the team to choose which functions performed by the part are important. Just as in the hazard analysis, issues of safety must always be addressed, but issues of performance and customer satisfaction can also be evaluated and may be critical to the success of the product in the marketplace.

The *Current Controls* columns list the methods currently in place to prevent the failure mode from happening or to detect it if it does. These controls could cite specific sections of the requirements or specifications document. Also, references to test procedures or results, experience with the same part used in the same environment and manner, or results of computer simulations or other

FIGURE 28.6 EXAMPLE OF A DETECTABILITY RATING SCALE.

Detectability Level	Description
5	Only detectable by user in field
4	Detectable during final inspection
3	Detectable during assembly
2	Detectable during part production
1	Detectable during design

analysis can also provide evidence of controls. The column is divided into prevention and detection to allow the team to derive a numeric score for occurrence (related to the prevention controls) and detectability (related to the detection controls) more easily.

The column labeled D is the *Detectability* column. Essentially, this column is a numerical rating of the team's opinion of how likely your company is to detect a problem with the product before it reaches the end user. The earlier in the development process—the more likely that you can detect the problem—the lower the detectability rating. Figure 28.6 is an example Detectability rating scale.

The RPN column stands for *Risk Priority Number* and is the equivalent of the risk index in the hazard analysis. It is simply the product of the severity times the occurrence times the detectability. When determining whether a particular issue should be addressed with a recommended corrective action, the same rules apply in the FMEA as in the HA. While all three factors (severity, occurrence, detectability) contribute equally to the RPN, when designing a corrective action you should try to concentrate on reducing the severity or occurrence scores first. It's always better to eliminate or significantly reduce the potential for harm than try to catch a problem in assembly or final testing.

28.3 A Few Final Thoughts

The techniques described here are tools, and as with any other tool, it is the responsibility of the user to execute it properly for professional results. When performing a risk assessment, keep the following in mind:

Your attitude: Completing the forms for a HA or FMEA can be somewhat tedious (several companies offer software that may help relieve some of the tedium). The team needs to approach the development of a hazard analysis or failure modes and effects analysis with a positive attitude so they can exercise the creativity needed to produce a high-quality result. As the leader of the product development team, you should make sure that the team understands the importance of the HA or FMEA and how it will help them during the development of the product. You might encourage the team to view the work as if they were solving the crime in a mystery novel. This technique helps keep the team interested and focused, while encouraging them to use their knowledge of the product's operation creatively to produce a high-quality risk assessment.

Stay balanced: Some models still describe an FMEA as a means to identify all failure modes and all causes for a product. More realistic definitions, such as the one used by the Automotive Industry Action Group (AIAG, 2001: 9), understand that the FMEA is an analytical technique used "to ensure that, to the extent possible, potential failure modes and their associated causes/mechanisms have been considered and addressed." In deciding how much effort to spend on risk assessment, you should consider the following:

- How risky is this product?
  (A chain saw is likely more risky than a cordless screwdriver.)
- How complex is the product?
  (A car is more complex than a bicycle.)
- How different is it from other products we have successfully had in the field for years? (A small variation of a standard product may not require extensive risk assessment. But be wary of even standard products if used in a new environment or by a different set of end users.)
- How important is it to the company that this product succeed?
  (Try to keep an executive mindset—as the product development leader, your view must be that product success is life or death.)

As the product development manager, you need to make sure that the effort spent in accomplishing the risk assessment pays back a useful dividend to your overall product development program. A project that incorporates a good risk assessment activity should proceed more quickly and at a lower cost than one without it. A reasonable decision might be to direct between 2 percent and 10 percent of the overall product development effort on risk assessment.

Use an independent reviewer: This article was edited before it was published in this book. This independent, external review undoubtedly improved the article (even if the authors didn't particularly enjoy the process). The same holds true for the HA or FMEA. The project team members are the experts on the design and must provide the bulk of the technical risk assessment input, but they sometimes become too focused on details or enamored with the design approach selected. A reviewer who is *not* part of the development team should be included on the risk assessment team—the more independent, the better. Ideally, this reviewer should have no stake at all in whether the product actually goes to market. The reviewer should be willing to question anything and not accept easy or vague answers. Providing answers to those questions will force the product development team members to confront problems that may have been overlooked. Confrontation results in a better risk assessment.

28.4 Summary

This article only scratches the surface of risk assessment activities that might be appropriate for your product development efforts. Instructional seminars and books are widely available to instruct you and your team in how to accomplish a hazard analysis or failure mode and effects analysis (some will have a different approach than described here). To start you on the path, a few key references are listed following this section.

References

AIAG, *Potential Failure Mode and Effects Analysis (FMEA) Reference Manual.* 3rd Ed., 2001.

ANSI/AAMI/ISO 14971:2000, "Medical devices—Application of risk management to medical devices," Arlington, VA: Association for the Advancement of Medical Instrumentation (AAMI), 2000.

IEC 812, "Analysis techniques for system reliability—Procedure for failure mode and effects analysis (FMEA)," Geneva, Switzerland: Bureau Central de la Commission Electrotechnique Internationale (CEI), Geneva, Switzerland, 1985.

Stamatis, D. H., *Failure Mode and Effect Analysis: FMEA from Theory to Execution.* ASQ, Milwaukee, WI: Quality Press, 1995.

Tan Hiap Keong, Risk Analysis Home Page, http://home1.pacific.net.sg/~thk/, downloaded on 7/8/2003.

Steven R. Nelson has 25 years of experience leading commercial and government projects ranging in size from $5000 to $5 million. For 16 years, he has worked to transition the very formal and expensive government risk analysis and management tools into the commercial product development environment.

He founded Decision Support to assist and train commercial clients in the use of these techniques. Mr. Nelson has a degree in mechanical engineering from the Ohio State University.

Fritz Eubanks is a mechanical engineer at Battelle Memorial Institute involved in system-level design and analysis of both medical and commercial products, with emphasis on hardware and software risk assessment activities, such as safety hazard analyses and failure mode and effects analyses. His postgraduate studies in engineering life-cycle design concentrated on methods and tools used to evaluate engineering designs for ownership quality and cost issues, such as assembly, serviceability, and recyclability. He also has extensive knowledge of aerospace equipment repair and maintenance developed during his eight years with the U.S. Air Force Logistics Command.

PART FIVE

FINISHING THE JOB

Look to the end, no matter what it is you are considering.

SOLON, QUOTED IN HERODOTUS, *HISTORIES* 500 BC

Many firms struggle to measure the results of improvements of their new product development practices. Chapter 29 shows a systematic approach to choosing metrics that help identify waste and drive continued improvements.

From the customer's viewpoint, the launch of a new product must appear smooth and its value proposition compelling. However, inside the firm launch is a hectic time of many activities that must be managed and synchronized. Chapter 30 gives six steps for the firm to follow for a well-planned and well-executed launch.

Supply chain and distribution are important to a product's success during and after it's launch. Many firms overlook how important this is. Chapter 31 discusses how to integrate supply chain issues into product launch strategy to provide a "lean launch." Such launches react quickly to emerging customer needs and market demands.

Chapter 32 describes how to design a program to assess a new product's performance in the marketplace as soon as possible after launch. This program can tell the firm how well the product is doing. More importantly it can tell where the product needs improvement if the sales forecast is not good.

Product life-cycle management is a multifaceted discipline, one, which many companies underemphasize and underfund. Chapter 33 shows how to assign knowledgeable individuals to the postlaunch phase to ensure peak returns from new product introductions and management of the product life cycle.

The last phase in the life cycle of a product line is its discontinuance. In Chapter 34 the reader is guided through a proven process for discontinuing an active product line with minimal negative impact to customers and the firm.

CHAPTER TWENTY-NINE

USING AN EFFECTIVE METRICS PROGRAM TO SUPPORT BUSINESS OBJECTIVES

Amy Chan

29.1 Importance of an Effective, Efficient Product Development Metrics Program

Over the past decade, companies have made significant progress in improving their product development practices. Yet many companies are still struggling to measure the results of their R&D spending and question whether they really know what their product development capabilities are, which areas to measure, and how to get the most from those metrics. In addition, most companies have improved their product development processes, and competition from "fast followers" has increased. The focus on Six Sigma improvement is also driving many companies to bring better management to research and development. These factors intensify the need for an effective and efficient metrics program.

A metrics program enables fact-based analysis to identify gaps in new product development capabilities, define how much improvement is needed, and prioritize improvement activities. Metrics help identify waste and drive improvements. Monitoring performance levels allows management to set clear improvement goals and understand the organization's performance relative to other divisions and to the competition. A metrics program delivers a range of valuable benefits by helping companies to:

Metrics help identify waste and drive improvements.

- *Assess overall development performance:* Gauge product development capabilities and identify performance gaps.
- *Prioritize improvement investments:* Improvement activities can be prioritized and assessed based on strategic alignment, investment requirements, and associated returns.
- *Monitor industry best practices:* Companies with external benchmarking can compare their performance with best-in-class companies to gain or retain a competitive advantage.
- *Improve operational reliability:* A set of predictive measures can help companies anticipate development performance problems and take corrective action.
- *Enable behavioral change:* Clearly defined metrics help a company stay focused on a common set of measurable performance goals by helping each department understand how its performance ties into the entire organization's business performance, and by creating the basis for aligning incentives to desired performance.

29.2 Key Challenges to Implementing a Successful Metrics Program

Despite the benefits of a metrics program, many companies are not using metrics to their full advantage. PRTM's benchmarking subsidiary, The Performance Measurement Group, LLC (PMG), recently surveyed 40 companies of various sizes in a wide range of industries. (The Performance Measurement Group, 2002). Findings showed that although over 70 percent of companies use metrics to review project results, only 55 percent use metrics for planning and goal setting. Furthermore, only 41 percent use metrics for external benchmarking, and just 38 percent use metrics to link their strategy to individual goals. These numbers tell us that although many companies are tracking metrics, few are leveraging their full potential. There are four primary reasons for this:

- Metrics used are not the right ones.
- Tracking mechanisms are inadequate.
- Bottom-line implications of performance are not considered.
- Management process is missing.

29.2.1 Metrics Used Are Not the Right Ones

What are performance metrics? They are indicators that monitor the impact of your efforts on the business in which you work. They are measures of performance, motivators of behavior, the focal point for directing improvement efforts, and the medium for communicating with other organizations. Performance metrics focus on fact-based rather than intuitive decision making and provide irrefutable evidence of problems and areas for improvement. Effective metrics are easily understood, communicable, quantifiable, and recordable, and allow automated data collection when possible. They reinforce adherence to agreed-upon business practices. In addition, effective metrics directly support overall business objectives, measure the results of a team's (or individual's) effort, and provide balance across conflicting objectives (i.e., excel in core competencies and maintain reasonable performance in other areas).

It is critical to establish a balanced set of metrics to ensure that the decision-making team has appropriate information to make the right decisions. The metrics should be balanced across multiple dimensions, including:

- *Historic performance and leading or predictive indicators:* Historical metrics such as actual time-to-market are useful for measuring performance and analyzing trends, but predictive measures, such as project complexity and project risk, can help companies anticipate product development performance problems and take corrective action.
- *Project, portfolio, and technology metrics:* All three metrics must be considered together. Companies that focus mainly on project-level metrics, for example, typically make suboptimal product decisions, since portfolio and technology-level metrics are absent.
- *Dimensions of productivity, time, cost, and quality:* A team that is measured only against schedule will meet the dates, but potentially put at risk product quality, cost, features, and other important factors.

A subset of metrics should be selected and designed as "benchmarkable" so that performance can be compared across products, divisions, and companies. Companies often designate some metrics for internal use only. These internal metrics are not used for external benchmarking purposes.

Many companies struggle with selecting the right number of metrics and often err on the side of tracking too many. Tracking too many metrics is more dangerous than tracking too few. Reports containing too many metrics hinder understanding of "the big picture." Teams become overly focused on the metrics themselves, rather than the real goal of delivering value to the marketplace.

It is a good practice to start with a few metrics and add more as you mature in your ability to derive the implications of a broader metrics set.

Developing a single scorecard or dashboard of key metrics avoids these problems by using the metrics that drive best-in-class performance, focusing attention on a few key metrics (e.g., productivity, time, cost, quality), and layering levels of detail for various levels of management.

29.2.2 Tracking Mechanisms Are Inadequate

It is important to understand that companies can only compare metrics that their current processes support. For example, a company cannot measure budget variance (plan vs. actual project cost) if it does not have project-accounting processes. Budget variance is a good metric to measure, but if data are not collected at the project level in a consistent fashion across projects, then budget variance cannot be created. Appropriate processes must be in place to collect and support metrics in a meaningful and practical way.

In the last several years, significant advances have been made in product development information systems in such areas as resource management, performance management, and product life-cycle management. Although these systems overcome many of the problems associated with implementing a successful metrics program, many companies are slow to adopt them. A recent study conducted by PMG showed that only 24 percent of respondents are using enterprise-wide systems to track metrics.

> *A recent study shows that only 24 percent of companies are using enterprise-wide systems to track metrics.*

Other challenges? Many companies struggle to manually collect accurate and reflective information. Or they invest significant time collecting one component of a metric, when appropriate proxies could be just as effective. For example, if customer satisfaction for a company cannot be measured at a software company, then measuring the number of critical software bugs could be as effective when the prevalence of critical bugs is directly related to customer satisfaction.

It is best practice to leverage data that are a natural by-product of processes, referring to the cost variance metric example provided earlier. Companies should avoid measuring theoretically interesting metrics that have no practical basis. Moreover, trying to measure metrics where data cannot be readily collected will not work. If current processes do not provide the critical data that need to be measured, these processes will require adjustments. Processes allow appropriate metrics performance measurement.

29.2.3 Bottom-Line Implications of Performance Are Not Considered

Successful improvement programs are grounded in facts—not "guesstimates"—to avoid unproductive and demoralizing "program-of-the-day approaches," and they provide a clear linkage to results. Un-fortunately, most managers rely on intui-

> *Unfortunately, most managers rely on intuition and experience rather than facts to determine how to create or sustain value.*

tion and experience rather than facts to determine how to create or sustain value. Decisions are typically based on a view of assets, liabilities, and revenue—often without linking to process-based capabilities and competencies. This re-liance on the most basic metrics promotes only linear, incremental improvement and inhibits the ability to perceive the need for changes and make them in time to respond to threats and opportunities. Metrics are a powerful means of man-aging and improving basic business practices.

For an effective metrics program, the benefits of achieving targeted metrics performance must be directly or indirectly linked to the income statement or balance sheet. The metrics must be tied to overall business objectives. It is also important to use and focus on metrics that can measure performance and iden-tify gaps between performance and objectives, although there is no set rule on how to accomplish this. The following two examples demonstrate how two companies with different business objectives might take totally different ap-proaches to metrics.

In the first example, the company's business strategy is to produce leading-edge products, and its product development strategy is to be the first to launch products to the market. This company might want to focus on tracking metrics such as *research and development spending, percentage of R&D spending on more innovative products* (e.g., radical innovations, new product lines, and major upgrades of current products), and *percentage of revenue derived from products with significant differ-entiation* relative to the competition, because it may spend relatively more on R&D to consistently develop pioneering products. The company would also want to drive shorter *time-to-market* and *product life cycles* because it wants to launch products with new features ahead of competitors, and continually re-place product lines. In the second example, the company's business strategy is to be the low-cost producer, and its product development strategy is to intro-duce competitive products following other companies' product introductions. This company might want to focus more on a high *component reuse rate* and low *capital expenditure*, while spending less time on the product concept, design, and development phases of product development. Since the two companies have different business objectives, it makes sense for them to focus on different sets of metrics.

Often companies reward A, while hoping for B. Metrics programs can significantly modify an organization's behavior, but the modified behavior often fails to deliver the intended outcome due to poor linkage with business strategy. Performance targets should be based on market "facts," such as best-in-class performance, current performance, and strategy.

When setting priorities, companies should take a decathlon approach. To win a decathlon, an athlete chooses one or two events to excel in and tries to achieve an acceptable level of performance in the remaining events. The same is true for companies: Choose the metrics in which you can achieve best-in-class performance, and then aim for a moderate advantage on the remaining metrics.

PMG's survey shows that companies are making progress in using metrics programs as part of ongoing product development management. Yet, although 68 percent of respondents have incorporated metrics programs, only 47 percent are measuring the financial impact of improvement programs. Without measuring the outcome of improvement efforts, these companies have no way of knowing which initiatives have the greatest impact.

29.2.4 Management Process Is Missing

Companies often neglect to put in place a process for gleaning the appropriate metrics data from their product development process. An effective project-level process specifies major milestones and the time each project phase should take, considering project complexity and scope. The management process enables companies to benchmark a project's product development performance against others with similar characteristics, resolve deficiencies identified by metrics, and measure progress towards goals.

Companies with portfolio- and project-level processes provide a framework and common language, which are critical to effective metrics measurement. Metrics data are a natural by-product of those processes.

29.3 How to Implement a Metrics Program

A successful metrics program requires a comprehensive approach that defines the decision structure, organization, process metrics tracking, and templates that can be used to measure, analyze, improve, and control the product development process.

Companies can start by defining the program objectives, picking the right metrics, and then developing a complete solution. The ten-step, three-phase approach shown in Table 29.1 builds on the best practices observed in com-

TABLE 29.1 TEN-STEP PERFORMANCE MEASUREMENT APPROACH.

Phase	Step	Objectives/Issues Addressed
Phase 1: Define detailed definitions	1. Define metrics program. 2. Define strategy and high-level objectives. 3. Define balanced performance meterics. 4. Determine present process capability.	• Define metrics program charter and work plan. • Define metrics program objectives that articulate how the company will benefit from metrics. • Link the company's strategy and high-level objectives to performance metrics. • Measure the right metrics. • Assess the current metrics and leverage then where possible.
Phase 2: Implementation	5. Define decision-making structure. 6. Establish data collection and reporting process. 7. Define metrics tracking systems.	• Define who will review the current performance to identify improvement opportunities. • Ensure timely, fact-based, and operateional decision. • Define the tasks and responsibilities for data collection, analysis, and reporting to ensure efficient metrics tracking. • Ensure adequate tracking.
Phase 3: Rollout	8. Pilot metric process. 9. Conduct ongoing performance reviews. 10. Implement contrinuous improvement.	• Identify the first set of improvement targets and test the new performance measurement process. • Identify improvement opportunities and take corrective actions. • Review and improve the metrics and the measurement process as necessary to meet changing business needs. • Track the bottom-line impact of the improvement program.

panies with successful metrics programs, and resolves the four problems discussed earlier. Each phase consists of different objectives.

Phase 1—Define Detailed Definitions: Identify the metrics needed to evaluate current performance and set targets that will drive the organization. As shown in Figure 29.1, companies with the best performance measurement outcomes choose metrics that balance the key dimensions of quality, productivity, time, and cost—and externally benchmark these metrics. They not only track historic performance but also identify key predictive measures.

Phase 2—Implementation: Identify data-collection mechanisms and metrics management responsibilities to support ongoing metrics calculation and tracking. Implementation should provide answers to the following questions: Who will collect the data? Who will send the reports? What systems will be used? Who will review the data?

Phase 3—Rollout: Identify key opportunities for improvement, and implement new business processes aimed at helping the selected areas meet the target performance levels.

FIGURE 29.1 SAMPLE PRODUCT DEVELOPMENT PERFORMANCE METRICS.

Process Performance	
Business Results	**Product/Project Attributes**
Productivity	**Cost**
Pipeline throughput per $MM of R&D Spending (# of projects released, normalized for project size, i.e., platform, major, minor)	*Project cost vs. target *Development costs vs. plan (e.g., labor, common direct expense, etc.)
	Time *Time-to-market vs. plan (schedule slippage)
% of revenue from new products ("New" products are those that have not reached peak production. Timelines vary by industry.)	
	*Cycle time by project type and phase
Goal attainment (the % of projects in the portfolio that meet or exceed goals regarding price, quality, revenue, etc.)	
	Quality
Resource utilization (the % of labor allocated to revenue-generating projects)	*First pass yield *Warranty cost and return rates

> *Companies with the best performance measurement outcomes choose metrics that balance the key dimensions of quality, productivity, time, and cost.*

29.3.1 Reaping the Value of Metrics

Experience working with various businesses indicates that companies that benefit from successful metrics programs:

- *Align metrics with the organization's success criteria:* Individuals ranging from CEOs to product managers and engineers must understand how their performance can affect the organization's overall performance.
- *Define a manageable set of metrics that balances the key dimensions of quality, productivity, time, and cost:* Each metric should have a positive impact on the organization's performance. Too many metrics can distract management from the all-important bigger picture. Often, companies can add more metrics to collect data as the organization progresses.
- *Create simple, explicit, understandable metrics definitions:* These definitions allow those involved in the metrics program to communicate in the same language.
- *Define the program objectives up-front:* For example, is the objective of the program to identify a gap, or to set a performance goal? Companies must identify what they are trying to accomplish with their metrics program. Also, they must align their metrics with their business objectives.
  Example:
  - Objective: Reduce time-to-market (TTM) by 20 percent
    Metric used: TTM: Weeks from concept through general availability
  - Objective: Understand schedule predictability across various projects
    Metric used: Schedule Slip Rate: [(Actual TTM minus Planned TTM) divided by Planned TTM], project team's perception of business impact of schedule slip rate
- *Define accountability and targets for each metric and tie performance to individual goals, reviews, and compensation:* Accountability helps set the basis for action.
- *Identify ongoing improvement opportunities using metrics programs and monitor the bottom-line impact to maintain momentum:* Reestablish performance targets when necessary.
- *Increase the visibility into operational metrics and develop a complete solution that defines the decision-making structure, organization, process, tracking mechanisms, and reporting templates.*

- *Benchmark regularly:* Do this internally to set standards and measure success, externally to identify predictive measures (e.g., trends) and gain a competitive advantage.
- *Review metrics results on a regular basis by setting up a mechanism for formal senior management reviews:* The improvement goals should be focused, concrete, and tangible.

29.4 Summary

Implementing a successful metrics program can be challenging—especially at the beginning—but companies must remember that those challenges often can be overcome through appropriate planning and target setting. Fact-based management is not easy, and there is no "one-size-fits-all" scorecard. Your metrics program must be tailored to your processes, practices, policies, and objectives. While setting a target performance level may not be clear-cut, companies can start with "best-in-class" and tailor that to an aggressive but achievable goal based on current performance levels. Merely implementing a metrics program does not guarantee success, though. Following a systematic approach enables companies to reap the full value of their metrics program.

Reference

The Performance Measurement Group, *PMG's Scorecard Users Guide*, 2002.

Amy Chan is a senior analyst at The Performance Measurement Group, LLC, a PRTM company. She has several years' experience working with companies to collect product development metrics and interpret their benchmarking results to identify and quantify potential improvement opportunities.

Amy has worked with many companies to analyze and correlate product development and innovation topics across several industries. She recently coauthored reports on collaborative development practices and how companies are using product development metrics to measure their R&D output. Amy is a member of the 2003 PDMA Comparative Performance Assessment Study research project team.

Amy holds a BS degree in business administration from Boston University.

The author wishes to thank Michelle Roloff—PMG general manager, PRTM's Mark Deck—director, Mark Strom—director, and Katey Goehringer—manager, for their support with this chapter.

CHAPTER THIRTY

MANAGING NEW PRODUCT AND SERVICE LAUNCH

Sue Nagle

Strategy gets you on the playing field, but execution pays the bills.

GORDON EUBANKS

30.1 Introduction

Because launch is the time when an organization begins to recover its investment in a product or service, and success is often determined in its first weeks in the marketplace, managing launch is a critical part of product development. However, organizations are just beginning to understand and institutionalize best practices in managing new product and service launches.

From the customer's viewpoint, the launch of a new product or service must appear smooth and its value proposition compelling. However, internal to a company, launch is a hectic time with many activities, which must be managed and synchronized. Fixing launch process problems has been compared to repairing a merry-go-round without shutting it down (Nagle, 2001). Fortunately, there are methods to ensure that launch is both well managed and well executed.

By following six steps, companies can increase new product and service revenue and improve return on investment on new product and service development costs. They are:

1. Establish goals.
2. Create an effective launch process.

3. Define appropriate launch team structure and roles.
4. Choose suitable launch managers.
5. Select the right sponsorship team.
6. Implement continuous improvement.

30.2 Establishing Goals

The up-front definition of measurable goals allows all those associated with the launch to know how they will be held accountable as well as when they will be successful. In many cases, the cross-functional

> *For an innovation like this to take place, companies need first to establish the right metrics.*

program goals already exist in the original business case for the service or product. These typically include a suite of metrics, such as overall return on investment, time-to-breakeven, an appropriate measure for quality, and a revenue and profit profile. In addition, measurable supporting interim goals should be added, and proactively affected by the launch team. Examples include a target for time-to-volume for end customers (*not* channel partners), a target time for reduction-to-zero defects, customer service calls as a percentage of units in the field, and marketing program response rates. For international offerings, targets may include time-to-volume overseas and overseas-to-domestic sales ratio, because research has shown that overall product success is dependent on positive performance in these areas (Oakley, 1997). No set formula exists for determining these goals—they will largely be shaped by the offering, market, and industry structure.

Both experience and training emphasize the importance of establishing measurable goals, but in practice goal setting is frequently skipped, presumably in an effort to avoid the lengthy discussions necessary to establish targets. The following example describes how setting the right launch goals helped Kraft to achieve measurable results.

Kraft recently announced a speed-to-shelf incentive plan which changes the approach for compensation paid to retailers for shelving new product at launch. Instead of paying the industry-standard 100% upon acceptance of product, retailers will receive 50% upon acceptance and 50% after the new product is on the shelf. Projected gains include increasing Kraft's return on invested capital by a factor of two to three by decreasing delay from marketing campaign to product availability, and reducing the three to four month ship-to-shelf time by at least one third (Thompson, 2002).

For an innovation like this to take place, companies need first to establish the right metrics (see Chapter 29). Had Kraft chosen first-customer-ship date or sales-in to retail customers, the benefits described would probably have never been discovered. Instead, by focusing on understanding and improving a metric such as time-to-volume for end customers, an enormous benefit will be reaped.

In short, choosing how launch will be measured is challenging yet worth the effort.

30.3 Creating an Effective Launch Process

Designing an effective process is one of the most challenging, creative, and rewarding aspects of launch-related projects. In part, this is because the best process must be tailored to the company: its culture, customers, its industry, and the types of solutions that it provides. The need to consider proven best practices across industries heightens the challenge. Finally, the process must be defined and implemented at a level of detail and structure that is useful for both launch teams and executives.

Launch spans the time from development of the launch plan to the review of success in the market, as shown in Figure 30.1. When the launch begins, most strategic decisions have been made: target customers, product definition and differentiation, and much of the channel, operations and customer service approach have been defined. The business case has been documented and agreed upon. However, the business case has yet to be achieved, and typically

FIGURE 30.1 LAUNCH OVERVIEW.

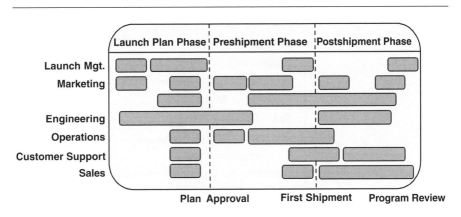

a significant proportion of total spending takes place during the launch. Given these facts, a successful launch depends on revisiting assumptions and making the right choices in the few key remaining decisions, finding and resolving outstanding issues, and flawless execution. An effective launch process systematizes each of these.

30.3.1 Launch Plan Phase

In the first phase, launch begins with a cross-functional team kick-off to overview goals for a program, bring forward any outstanding issues, and create the launch plan. The precise timing for this kick-off varies depending on the specific service or product being launched, and may be triggered by reaching the appropriate milestone in development. A sample launch plan format is shown in Figure 30.2. This plan summarizes the launch team's assessment and recommended path forward, with Launch Management, Marketing, Engineering,

FIGURE 30.2 SAMPLE LAUNCH PLAN FORMAT.

Sample Launch Plan Contents
Executive Summary........................ 1
Value Proposition........................... 2
Goals and Measures....................... 2
Project Plan and Resources.............. 3
Customer Trials.............................. 4
Pricing Strategy............................. 4
Competitive Assessment.................. 4
Rollout Strategy............................. 5
Communication Plan....................... 5
Channel Strategy and NPI Plan.......... 6
Operations Ramp........................... 6
Sales Training Plan......................... 7
Customer Service Plan.................... 7
Obsolescence Plan......................... 8
Outstanding Issues and Risks........... 8

Sales, Distribution, and Customer Service components. Because the launch plan represents the commitments and plans for the entire launch, the members of the management sponsorship team review the document formally.

In composing the launch plan, the launch team works to uncover and resolve outstanding issues, as well as to systematically revisit and refine initial assumptions. The team may spend several sessions reviewing the project plan and brainstorm-

> *Choosing a rollout strategy is one of the most important decisions made during launch.*

ing outstanding risks and prospective responses. Earlier decisions about rollout strategy, pricing strategy, product positioning and channel strategy are revisited and refined in the context of the current market. Finally, details behind outstanding plans are fleshed out and agreed upon: the communication plan is developed and reviewed, training plans are finalized, and sessions are scheduled. If not already agreed upon, any specific incentives for the sales force are put in place (Cooper, 2001).

Choosing a rollout strategy is one of the most important decisions made during launch. Choices include whether to go to market via a "hard launch" (launch across many markets simultaneously) or a "soft launch" (a series of discrete launches

> *Thorough testing reduces risk of failure in every aspect of the launch.*

across individual markets). In its final form, the launch plan includes specific market sequence and timing. Factors such as market readiness, location of target customers, and service or product availability play into this decision. If the product will be introduced across international markets, the choice of initial targets for international introduction should take into account recent research on effects of higher takeoff rates in countries such as Denmark and Sweden (Yu, 2003).

Obtaining the right customer feedback in its many forms throughout the product development process (i.e., from the "Fuzzy Front End" prior to concept development all the way through to commercialization) is critical to market success (see Chapters 14, 15, and 16). Thus, market, beta, and creative testing with target customers needs to be a part of the launch. Testing critical aspects of the customer experience and business processes warrants vigorous planning and diligent execution. For example, beta tests are used not only for product or service feedback, but also to test customer support, sales training in the sign-up process, order-deliver-return cycle, and so forth. Risk of failure must be reduced in every aspect of the launch.

30.3.2 Preshipment Phase

After the launch plan is approved, the launch transitions to Preshipment phase and its focus on flawless execution. In a blur of activity, customer feedback on products and programs continues to flow into the company, engineering works to resolve last-minute discoveries, prelaunch introductions occur, marketing campaigns are readied, the sales force is trained and begins introductions, service or manufacturing pilot efforts and ramp-up begin, customer service representatives are trained . . . the launch team works tirelessly to uncover problems and resolve them prior to launch. At times, conflicts arise between quality and launch date demands, particularly for event-based launches. At this time, both dedicated individuals and creative teamwork are critical to choosing the best path forward. Finally, the service is activated or the first product ships and sales begin to ramp!

30.3.3 Postshipment Phase

The Postshipment phase typically lasts from 3–9 months, depending on the offering and the industry (see Chapter 31). In the Postshipment phase, the sales force relentlessly sells the offering, marketing campaigns continue, and customer service representatives begin their efforts in earnest. Engineering and Operations continue to resolve uncovered problems. Launch teams continue to meet to review progress on goals defined up-front, share ideas, and resolve any uncovered issues. As appropriate, the team feeds suggestions back to new product development personnel. As the team concludes its work, team members review (1) program results to date versus goals, and (2) learning with the sponsorship team.

30.3.4 Approach to Creating an Effective Process

Designing and implementing an effective launch process requires a significant effort. Figure 30.3, outlines one successful approach.

Assessing current practices consists of administering interviews and benchmarking questionnaires with key launch personnel, executives, and customers to evaluate current launch performance. Next, a team of key personnel "decomposes" the launch into each of its many activities, recording it all on paper, and assembles them into key steps. (Facilitated working sessions help to ensure that this creative work moves forward productively.) Third, a team works to fully define each step, its owner, and any helpful tools using best practices as

FIGURE 30.3 CREATING AN EFFECTIVE LAUNCH PROCESS.

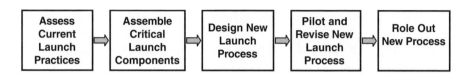

input. Fourth, the process is tried out on a launch and revised with input. At last, the organization rolls out the new launch process.

30.4 Defining the Launch Team

Clearly defining the roles and goals of launch team members, implementing a structure for launch teams, and choosing launch team membership are all critical to the success of the new product or service.

Traditional roles for effective launch teams include both managing the launch from plan through postlaunch review, and

> *Successful launch teams work together to proactively uncover problems or risks, and find solutions both inside and outside individual team members' functional roles.*

raising and resolving critical issues prior to the product or service reaching the market. Successful launch teams work together to proactively uncover problems or risks, and find solutions both inside and outside individual team members' functional roles. Team members meet periodically to communicate and assess progress but do most of their work outside of the meeting. They communicate program progress, issues, goals, and action items within their functions. When necessary, they escalate roadblocks and propose alternative solutions to management sponsors. Team accountability does not disappear when the product reaches the market but continues through the sales, service, and support ramp-up until the team has reviewed results of the launch.

Goals for the launch team are set and measured either by each individual team or by standard metrics within a company, as discussed in the "Establishing Goals" section. If launch team members do not report to the person leading the launch effort, the launch manager provides input to individual performance reviews. Typical input areas include performance on the team (overall effectiveness, functional representation, communication, problem-solving skills, conflict resolution, and collaboration) and team execution-to-goals.

The team's success in resolving issues is heavily dependent on strong functional representation, so a cross-functional team structure is the most effective (see Chapter 9). However, designated launch team structure for a company will vary depending on the organization, the product development process, the launch budget, and the complexity of the product or service.

As a guideline, launch teams contain: (1) the minimum number of people necessary to effectively represent functions with significant time commitment or impact on launch success, and (2) the people who are required to make progress/resolve issues at every launch meeting. For line extensions, a pared-down team structure is frequently the best option if certain functions are not involved in the effort. Consider the following example:

> Athletic Footwear sells and markets sports shoes and boots across multiple retailers, while outsourcing manufacture and design of its shoes to a single company. Athletic Footwear typically spends $3–5 million in marketing per launch. Typical teams might consist of a launch manager plus one representative each from Marketing (representing Finance), Sales Training (representing all of Sales), Logistics, Quality Assurance, Customer Service, and perhaps an appropriate representative of Manufacturing/Design from the supplier. Athletic Footwear decides to spend $20 million launching a new line of footwear targeted to urban professionals commuting to work. This launch requires heavy marketing efforts to expose consumers to a new product in an underserved market. Athletic Footwear is heading into uncharted territory, where it doesn't know the customer, channels, or competition as well as it does the existing market. CEO Joe Smarty realizes that he needs to modify the standard team structure to ensure success. He adds a member of sales management to provide input on new channel and customer needs, and a representative of Athletic Footwear's longstanding public relations firm to support Marketing in this critical effort.

Once a launch team structure is defined, the right team members are chosen and committed to each specific launch. Along with defining a best-practice process and gaining support from executives, the talent on the team will determine its success. Skills to keep in mind while recruiting team members internally or externally include an ability to collaborate across functions, leadership, project management ability, and leverage/respect within the function.

30.5 Choosing Launch Managers

The launch manager is arguably the single most important person for a product's success. An effective launch manager builds a strong, shared vision within the launch team. He/she helps to create a cohesive and committed team, which identifies and aggressively overcomes functional and organizational hurdles to meet the established goals. That individual also serves as the point person responsible for running team meetings and dealing with personnel issues, and ensures communication within the team, within the organization, and with management sponsorship. In short, the launch manager is a people motivator and project manager who understands how to get things done from both a technical and a political standpoint.

> *An effective launch manager builds a shared vision, helping create a team which aggressively overcomes hurdles.*

A great launch manager can come from any function, as long as that individual has the stature to operate effectively within the organization. The most important skills include leadership, problem-solving, conflict resolution, and project management abilities. Leadership skill enables the launch manager to motivate the launch team. Problem-solving and conflict resolution skills are critical to a leader ensuring that the team works together effectively. Project management skills are critical because launch is a time when numerous activities and related action items must be properly identified, tracked, resolved, and communicated.

30.6 Selecting the Sponsorship Team

The management sponsorship team fills a vital need for launch success. These executives review the plans and progress of the team, remove roadblocks, and help prioritize the effort within the scope of other initiatives. This governing body ensures that the launch team is both accountable for and empowered to effectively execute the launch. Behind the scenes, sponsorship team members frequently mentor launch team members.

> *The sponsorship team ensures that the launch team is both accountable for and empowered to effectively execute the launch.*

Choosing the sponsorship team is highly organizationally dependent, but there are several guidelines to bear in mind:

- *Members are the final decision-makers and have authority over resources:* In medium and large organizations, this team is frequently two levels above launch team members.
- *Less is more:* This team should consist of the minimum number of people necessary to make decisions for functions affected. In other words, avoid functional duplication. This will also help in scheduling meetings.
- *Encourage consistency of sponsorship team membership across launch programs:* This allows the team to learn to work together effectively in making decisions across the business portfolio.

Effective sponsorship teams typically include one executive each from Engineering, Finance, Marketing, Operations, and Sales, and a general manager. Depending on the organization, it may make sense to add seats for one to two other functions.

30.7 Ensuring Continuous Improvement

Ensuring continuous improvement across your company's launch portfolio is the final step to successful launch. The mechanisms to do so are relatively simple, but implementing them requires discipline and a true commitment to organizational

> *Implementing continuous improvement requires discipline and a true commitment to organizational learning.*

learning. In the long run, a company's product and service launch performance will greatly benefit from this focus.

After the company fully defines and documents the process, the sponsorship team designates an owner. This owner periodically reviews and updates the process with feedback on best practices from teams and management, as well as lessons learned from individual program reviews and external benchmarking data. In general, the sponsorship team reviews and approves both process metrics and changes to the process. This ensures organizational buy-in.

30.8 Summary

A well-planned and well-executed launch is critical to success in the marketplace and achieving program goals. As in many sound management approaches, there are no hard and fast rules, only guidelines. Having said this, based on our experience, companies can increase new product and service revenue and improve return on investment on total new product costs through following six steps. By (1) establishing goals, (2) creating an effective launch process, (3) defining the launch team structure and roles, (4) choosing suitable launch managers, (5) selecting the right sponsorship team, and (6) implementing a good continuous improvement program, companies can improve their business results.

References

Cooper, Robert, *Winning at New Products*, Boston, MA: Perseus Publishing, 2001.

Nagle, Sue, "Market Launch Planning: Repairing the Merry-Go-Round," *PRTM's Insight* (Spring 2001).

Oakley, Paul, "High-tech NPD Success Through Faster Overseas Launch," *Journal of Product & Brand Management*, 6(4): 260–274 (1997).

Thompson, Stephanie, "Kraft Speeds New Product Launch Times," *Advertising Age*, 73: 1–2, (November 18, 2002).

Yu, Larry, "Rates of Takeoff in Europe," *Sloan Management Review*, 44(4): 10 (Summer 2003).

Sue Nagle is a director with Perrin-Nagle Associates in Boulder, Colorado. Sue's consulting background includes increasing sales productivity, improving product development return on investment and effectively launching new products and services. She has a diverse portfolio of publications and invited talks, has fulfilled professional engagements spanning five continents, and currently serves as an Executive in Residence with C. U. Boulder's Leeds School of Business. Prior to consulting, Sue held positions in product management for Hewlett-Packard and design engineering for Pitney Bowes. Her education includes an M.B.A. from the Sloan School of Management and an M.S. and B.S. in Mechanical Engineering from MIT. She lives in Boulder with her husband and daughter.

CHAPTER THIRTY-ONE

MANAGING THE SUPPLY CHAIN IMPLICATIONS OF LAUNCH

Roger J. Calantone, C. Anthony Di Benedetto, and Theodore P. Stank

31.1 Introduction

The launch stage for new consumer product launches is risky and typically the most expensive stage in the new product development process. Accordingly, launch represents a major factor in determining the success of new consumer products (see Chapter 30).

A particular launch consideration is the clean hand-off between the development team to the team that will manage the product postlaunch. This hand-off heavily underlies a company's propensity for achieving new product success. By hand-off, we mean that tactical decisions

> *Supply chain capabilities support successful launches and minimize losses from unsuccessful ones.*

made at launch must align with the strategy that justified the product's development. For example, distribution logistics must be in place, a reliable demand forecast for the new product must be made to guide manufacturing ramp-up, and promotional activities aimed at both the consumer and the trade must be appropriately timed. While many of these launch aspects have been well studied and understood by product development professionals, the importance of supply chain and distribution logistics to product launch success have been largely overlooked.

There is much to be gained by a more thorough consideration of supply chain capabilities to support successful launches and minimize losses from unsuccessful ones. As we will discuss later in this chapter, integrating supply chain capability issues explicitly into product launch strategy is central to "lean launch" methods. Lean launch methods involve the use of a flexible supply chain system to react quickly to emerging customer needs and market demands. Companies have been adopting lean launch methods for some time now, and given the success seen so far, lean launch will be an increasingly important part of consumer launch strategies in the near future.

Overall, our objectives in this chapter are as follows:

- To describe the potential pitfalls at the launch stage
- To outline the development of launch strategy to manage these pitfalls
- To present the advantages of lean launch and flexible supply chain processes in launch strategy development
- To illustrate the successful application of lean launch methods
- To draw managerial insights and conclusions regarding the benefits of lean launch

31.2 Pitfalls at the Launch Stage

Traditionally, product launch is managed using anticipatory methods, that is, manufacturing, marketing, and supply chain/distribution decisions are made in advance of the launch based on early forecasts of demand.

Three negative, yet avoidable, outcomes of traditional anticipatory launch are possible. In instances where a product is both technically and financially successful across a broad range of market segments, unplanned out-of-stock problems are likely to materialize. Even when a product has widespread success, product popularity and adoption rates are likely to vary between market segments. Replenishment inventory needed for markets experiencing rapid penetration may not be available due to preintroduction inventory commitment to other segments. When products are highly successful, manufacturing and logistics capacity may not be able to keep up with demand because of scheduling lead-time and material procurement inflexibility. If inventory is available in the aggregate, product may still be out-of-stock on retail shelves in specific markets, while it is overstocked in other markets. For at least the time it takes to reposition inventory to where it is needed and to ramp-up manufacturing support, launch success may be in jeopardy. For products that are neither technical nor financial successes, preallocation of inventory results in overstock. In this case, inventory is positioned forward in the channel resulting in excess reclamation expense.

Launch of the Advantix camera provides an illustration of the problems associated with the coordination of consumer promotions and trade support with manufacturing and distribution ramp-up. A consortium of camera makers, including Kodak and Fuji, developed the Advantix system, and its upcoming launch in early 1996 was kept secret, causing some retailers to be skeptical of the new product. Additionally, early reviews of the system were modestly positive at best. Consortium members, including Fuji, kept sales projections and production plans relatively modest. When retailers did get to see the camera in February 1996, however, they were very impressed, and demand for cameras and accessories was much higher than anticipated. Manufacturers went into back order and the anticipated April shipping date was missed. Since products were unavailable, retailers were reluctant to do the planned in-store promotions, and consortium members pulled back on consumer advertising until the production could be sufficiently ramped up. Unfortunately, none of the consortium members increased production quantities enough, resulting in poor consumer availability as late as August 1996, though by late summer the ramp-up problems had been remedied. In short, the camera makers missed the whole peak summer season of 1996 (Crawford and Di Benedetto 2003:429).

Realize that new product introductions are seldom clear-cut successes or failures. Products may initially only appeal to a narrow segment of the target market, such as a specific geographic region or usage group, as contrasted to the broader market to which they are presented. Financial success depends on sufficient penetration to cover manufacturing, inventory, and promotional start-up costs.

Therefore, products that experience limited technical success, but have a potential for achieving broader appeal over time, may fail at launch due to the inability to focus resources (including logistical support), generate sufficient segmental revenue, and cover market rollout costs.

A launch of a new cracker product provides an example of the pitfalls of anticipatory launch strategies. Two variants of a new thin cracker were introduced prior to the year-end holiday season. One variant was flavored similarly to the established cracker brand, while the other was onion-flavored. The manufacturing process for the products involved production of the regular-flavored cracker with an additional flavoring process for the onion-flavored variant. Significant inventory of each variant was sold to retailers and forward deployed for the expected holiday sales. The market enthusiastically received the regular-flavored cracker. The onion-flavored version, however, was not well received and sales lagged behind those of the regular variant by a considerable margin.

Unfortunately, the supply chain was unable to fully replenish the regular-flavored version resulting in out-of-stock situations, while high levels of onion-flavored stock remained on retail shelves until after the holiday season. The combination of reclamation costs for unused onion-flavored inventory and out-of-stock costs for the regular-flavored cracker resulted in limited financial success of the overall launch.

31.3 Launch Strategy

At a macro level, the launch strategy is simply the decision to launch or not launch the product. More specifically, launch strategy decisions will be concerned with both product and market issues: the level of innovativeness of the new product, the targeted market, the competitive positioning, and so forth (Di Benedetto, 1999). On the engineering side, launch strategy is supported by market tests that confirm the adequacy of the product prototypes as evidenced in internal alpha testing or beta testing with select customers. On the marketing side, launch strategy requires knowledge of the ability of the product to satisfy the customer's value proposition, in requisite quantities, at a price with sufficient margin over cost to provide an adequate financial return to justify the production and marketing investments the commercialization stage requires. This stage of the new product development process requires actual financial returns rather than just the promise of returns. The launch strategy needs another component in order to calibrate the cost basis of the decision, namely, the scale of the launch with regard to the size of the potential addressable market is required. As shown in Figure 31.1, the challenge is to get close to the "right size" of the market, to properly scale both the size of the marketing investment and the size of the production and distribution facility.

Often, demand and profit assessment, and the decision to develop and launch the product, are supported by teardown analysis. For example, in a traditional teardown analysis of a new sport-utility vehicle (SUV) aimed at consumers, a car maker will buy several competitive models, move them to a central location, and "tear them down" to individual components. Each part is cost estimated, leading to a very good projection of material costs per unit. The type of labor involved is also assessed (i.e., whether human labor or robotics were used), and a labor cost per unit estimated. But in a complete teardown analysis, the car maker would project the total size of the SUV market, and then assess the total unit costs at various levels of production (keeping in mind that average total cost would decrease as production increased). The car maker can then make an intelligent decision as to whether the SUV should be

FIGURE 31.1 CONSEQUENCES OF MATCH BETWEEN LAUNCH SIZE AND MARKET SIZE.

		Actual Market Size	
		LOW	HIGH
Launch Size	LOW	Commercial Failure	Opportunity Cost
	HIGH	Cost Overrun, Commercial Failure	Commercial Success

launched. For example, if the firm believes that it can get 10 percent of the SUV market with this new product, how many units does that translate to? What would be the average total cost incurred? And, given the going selling price, could the company make a large enough profit to generate target net present values, or to pay back the development costs in the desired period?

The forecasting and management challenge is to properly size the launch for the market demand (see Chapter 23). When this is impossible, that is, when we cannot know the market reality in advance of the launch sizing decision, we must try to increase the flexibility of the production response tactics for marketing and distribution resource allocation. This will permit the firm to rapidly respond to early sales success without overcommitting to inventory during the introductory rollout phase. Closely monitoring sales trends, through the use of point-of-sale (POS) information, can assist the firm in responding in a timely manner to sales fluctuations. These efforts can be further facilitated by regional rollouts that build a response to demand slowly, and slowly ramp up productive and distributive capacity, again while avoiding overcommitment. The opportunity cost scenario and the overcommitment scenario are both addressed by a variety of supply chain strategies, discussed later. For now, suffice it to say that flexibility and staged market commitment are necessary to a right-sized launch strategy. The next section describes how lean launch methods can help firms achieve the required level of supply chain flexibility as described here.

31.4 The Flexible Supply Chain and Lean Launch

Advanced supply chain capabilities offer an alternative way to support a successful new product launch as well as contain loss when products fail to meet expectations. The lean launch method involves development of a flexible supply chain system capable of rapidly responding to early sales success to limit commitment of inventory

> *The lean launch method involves a flexible supply chain capable of rapidly responding to early sales success and limiting the commitment of inventory during introductory rollout.*

during introductory rollout. Flexible supply chain logistics systems are characterized by coordinated source, make, and deliver operations that drastically cut raw material to consumer cycle times and enable the firm to respond to actual market needs rather than anticipate demand with inventory.

Postponement is the basic principle driving the development of lean launch strategies. Leading-edge firms increasingly use postponement as the logic for flexible operations that enable quick reaction to

> *Postponement is a key principle driving lean launch.*

customer needs and actual market demand. Postponement delays finalization of product form and identity to the latest possible point in the marketing flow and postpones commitment of inventory to a specific location to the latest possible point in time. Cutting lead times can reduce uncertainty and increase operational flexibility so that products can be produced to order or at least manufactured at a time closer to the point when demand materializes. The volatility of demand for new products can be managed by reducing lead times, which shorten the forecasting horizon and lower the risk of error. (Bowersox, Stank, and Daugherty, 1999)

Postponement of time and form can be employed. In time postponement the key differential is the timing of inventory deployment to the next location in the distribution process. In contrast to anticipatory shipment to distribution warehouses based on forecast, the goal of time postponement is to ship exact product quantities from a central location to satisfy specific customer requirements. The practice of shipping exact quantities to specific destinations greatly reduces the risk of improper inventory deployment and eliminates duplicate inventory safety stocks throughout the channel. Time postponement provides inventory-positioning flexibility by alleviating the need for forward deployment of inventory to cover total forecasted sales. Positioning flexibility allows firms to strategically position only limited inventory in the market and selectively replenish stock based on closely monitored sales information. Benefits from time postponement may be realized regardless of whether one or multiple new product variants are launched. (Bowersox, Stank, and Daugherty, 1999)

Form postponement provides product variation flexibility by alleviating the need to lock in feature design prior to gaining some understanding of a product's market appeal. Assembly, packaging, and labeling postponement are options in which firms initially manufacture products to an intermediate or neutral form with the intent to delay customization until specific customer orders are received. Benefits from form postponement become significant when introducing multiple product variants. Postponement of product differentiation reduces the need to stock inventory of all product variations. For example, computers are often assembled, packaged, and labeled to conform to specific configurations during customer order processing. Demand variations from forecasted volumes for each product variant following launch can be accommodated without the out-of-stock or overstock risk associated with traditional anticipatory launch strategies.

Form postponement may also involve forward deployment of materials or components to support final customized manufacturing to specific customer requirements. The shipment of house paint to retailers as a neutral base with subsequent mixing to customer-specified colors provides the classic example of postponing form until end-consumer purchase. International shipments that necessitate language-specific labels and support materials, such as instruction manuals, also frequently utilize form postponement. Such products are shipped in bulk quantities to a regional distribution center where labeling and packaging are completed as customer orders are processed.

The application of lean launch strategies is being driven by key competence in five areas of supply chain management (Bowersox, Closs, and Stank 1999). These include collaborative relationships, information systems, measurement systems, internal operations, and external operations—all representing critical elements of a firm's supply chain strategies, structures, and processes. Competence in collaborative relationships requires a willingness on the part of supply chain partners to create structures, frameworks, and metrics that encourage cross-organizational behavior. This consists of sharing strategic planning and operational information as well as creating financial linkages that make firms dependent upon mutual performance. Suppliers, manufacturers, third-party providers, and customers are encouraged to identify and partner with firms that share a common vision and are pursuing parallel objectives pertaining to partnership interdependence and the principles of collaboration. Efforts must focus on providing the best end-customer value, regardless of where along the supply chain the necessary competencies exist. This collaborative relationship perspective is key to developing effective supply chain structures that align the functional operations of multiple firms into an integrated system.

Supply chains capable of supporting lean launch also depend upon the availability of sophisticated and economical information technology that allows businesses to quantify sales, define requirements, and trigger production and inventory replenishment twenty-four hours a day, seven days a week. Such systems provide the input needed for short-, mid-, and long-term plans, which translate strategic goals and objectives into action and work to guide each operating area. Effective information systems provide thorough, accurate, and timely information from customers, material and service suppliers, and internal functional areas regarding current and expected conditions. Managers with access to data throughout the supply chain and the hardware and software needed to process it are better positioned to gain rapid insight into demand patterns and trends. Accessibility allows integrated operational decisions to be made in complex global supply chains. Rather than relying upon forecasted sales, inventory replenishments are driven by precise sales information regarding specific stock items in the market. The success of such technology and planning integration rests upon a firm's ability to manage information on supply chain resource allocation through seamless transactions across the total order-to-delivery cycle. It requires adaptation of technological systems to exchange information across functional boundaries in a timely, responsive, and usable format and to extend such internal communications capabilities to external supply chain partners.

Measurement system integration is also required to manage coordinated supply chain lean launches (see Chapter 29). These systems must track performance across the borders of internal functional areas and external supply chain partners; measuring both the operations of the overall supply chain and the financial performance of individual firms. Measurement systems must also reflect the operational performance of the overall supply chain and the financial performance of individual firms. Integrated performance measurement provides the basis for calibrating the many parts of the supply chain. Good metrics and strong measurement systems serve to provide timely feedback, so management can take corrective action and drive integrated operations.

Greater coordination of internal source, produce, and deliver operations also enables lean launch applications. Integration of internal operations provides a firm with the ability to seamlessly link activities across internal functional areas in order to achieve synergies that lead to better performance in meeting customer requirements. Internal integration is achieved by linking operations into a seamless, synchronized operational flow, encouraging front-line managers and employees to use their own discretion,

> *Greater coordination of internal source, production, and delivery operations enables lean launch applications.*

within policy guidelines, to make timely decisions. Empowered employees have the authority and information necessary to do a job, and they are trusted to perform work without intense over-the-shoulder supervision, enabling them to focus resources on providing unique and customer-valued product/service offerings that competitors cannot effectively match. Coordination of procurement and production techniques such as concurrent engineering and design, supplier partnerships, agile manufacturing and improved transportation performance has the potential to create flexible processes that enable firms to accommodate actual market needs rather than rely on anticipatory forecasts.

The need to reduce redundancies and achieve greater economies of scale in launch operations is not limited to internal activities alone. External integration synchronizes the core competencies of selected supply chain participants to jointly achieve improved service capabilities at lower total supply chain cost. The goal is to outsource specialized activities that previously were developed and performed internally. After outsourcing activities are identified and appropriate suppliers are chosen, systems and operational interfaces between firms must be synchronized to reduce duplication, redundancy, and dwell time (the ratio of days inventory sits idle in the supply chain relative to the days it is productively being used). Synchronization requires extensive information sharing between firms to standardize processes and procedures. Additionally, synchronization ensures that all activities are conducted by the supply chain entity that best creates the service and cost configuration to meet customer requirements. Innovative firms have utilized the principles of response-based logistics to customize product and service offerings without increasing manufacturing capacity or stock levels. The following examples illustrate how these principles have been applied in two diverse industries (from Bowersox, Stank, and Daugherty, 1999).

31.5 Computer Industry Illustration

Dell Computer's approach to manufacturing and distribution has become the PC industry source model. Dell assembles computer systems as end consumers order them, thus reducing or eliminating anticipatory inventory commitment. As a direct marketer, Dell uses no resellers. In contrast, most PC vendors build, test, package, and ship systems to resellers. The reseller holds products in inventory in anticipation of customer purchase. Historically, that stocking period averages 6–8 weeks. At the time of sale, the system is opened and modified to meet the purchaser's specification.

Dell takes a very different approach to marketing its product, which necessitates using a lean launch method. Dell's strategy has been to focus almost exclusively on corporate customers. In contrast, most of their competitors have committed substantial resources to reaching consumers through conventional retail distribution. Dell developed flexible manufacturing techniques that allow the company to build computers to order. To support this assemble-to-order strategy, they run a lean manufacturing operation. By working closely with suppliers, component and material inventories are minimized. The close relationships and support of suppliers have allowed Dell to operate with nearly no work-in-process inventory. In fact, Dell averages less than one day's inventory and component parts stock supply. They "pull" parts from suppliers just as they are needed for production. Replenishment requirements are instantaneously forwarded to suppliers based on actual orders.

Assembling systems to order means that there is no finished inventory in the channel to manage. Transitioning from a finished-goods inventory model to assemble-to-order with channel-assisted computer system configuration has become the industry model. Other competitors in the PC industry are moving to emulate Dell's direct sales model. For example, prior to its merger with Hewlett-Packard, Compaq had moved toward a build-to-order manufacturing strategy to reduce the time it takes the company to deliver product to corporate clients. By postponing build to stock and moving final assembly forward in the channel, Compaq hoped to avoid problems associated with forecasting demand and holding extensive inventories. Since the merger, HP has worked extensively with resellers to set up a channel assembly program. The intent is to leave assembly in the hands of resellers so that HP has no finished goods inventory. Gateway has developed a program that allows components to be merged while in transit. Transportation carriers complete the merging prior to final delivery. All of these examples are forms of lean launch formats for new products based on supply chain management principles.

31.6 A Lean Launch Illustration: Benetton

Apparel manufacturer Benetton has enhanced its competitiveness in a highly competitive market through lean launch application. Benetton's agents in various countries utilize electronic data interchange (EDI) to transmit orders to Italy on a daily basis. Based on this market information, Benetton is able to precisely track sales and react to demand by manufacturing only those garment styles, colors, and sizes being sold. Computer-aided design (CAD) and computer-aided manufacturing (CAM) make their manufacturing operation fast and flexible. From the time a garment is designed to when it is actually manufactured can take as little as a few hours. State-of-the-art software allows designs to be created in-house and be quickly fed to computer-controlled garment cutters and knitting machines.

Benetton utilizes form postponement to apply dyes. Traditionally, manufacturing of clothing starts with dyeing of the yarn, followed by knitting into garments. Because of the short cycle associated with seasonal clothing sales, it is difficult to restock retailers with the right color and size assortment. The traditional anticipatory process potentially yields excess inventories of unpopular colors, while at the same time increasing the risk of out-of-stocks on popular colors, historically resulting in lost sales opportunities or overstocks that require extensive markdown. Benetton, however, manufactures garments from bleached yarn and delays dyeing until market information on color preference is available through their EDI linkages with market-based agents.

Benetton's sophisticated manufacturing system is supplemented with a highly responsive logistics system. Their distribution center is highly mechanized. To the largest extent possible, all work processes are standardized. For example, garments are packed in one of two standard sized boxes; bar-coding and preaddressed customer labels are utilized to speed processing. To facilitate logistics, Benetton entered into a joint venture with a service company to manage international forwarding and customs clearance. EDI technology is used to transmit documentation before actual shipments arrive at entry ports thus facilitating speedy clearance through customs and routing on to retail outlets. The system provides a significant reduction in physical distribution costs and reduces lead times to United States markets by greater than 50 percent (Pepper, 1991).

31.7 Summary

The pressure is increasingly on firms to meet customer needs and marketplace demands quicker and more completely than the competition. Many firms see the development and launch of successful new products as their lifeblood, and their ability to identify and meet emerging customer needs and demands quickly as a key component of their competitive strategy. Until relatively recently, however, new product launch has been "business as usual" in many firms: marketing, manufacturing, and distribution channel decisions pertaining to launch had been made in anticipatory fashion based on early forecasts.

By including distribution and logistics more fully on the launch team, firms can become more adept at increasing supply chain flexibility and improve effectiveness and efficiency of the new product launch. Those firms employing lean launch methods have been able to accelerate time-to-market and cut lead times drastically, thereby enabling the firm to match emerging customer needs more rapidly. By postponing major decisions as long as possible, even large firms can seem to turn on a dime, match product features and production to customer demand much more effectively than before, and reduce costs through cheaper distribution and reduced manufacturing change orders gained by postponement. The Dell and Benetton examples illustrate how some of the best lean launch firms do it, and provide a starting point for analysis of one's own company in search of ways to "get lean" during the launch phase.

In sum, launch is a key stage in the new product development process and deserves a much more strategic view.

References

Bowersox, Donald J., Closs, David J., and Stank, Theodore P., *21st Century Logistics: Making Supply Chain Integration A Reality*, Oak Brook, IL: The Council of Logistics Management, 1999.

Bowersox, D. B., Stank, Theodore, and Daugherty, Patricia, "Lean Launch: Managing Product Introduction Risk Through Response-Based Logistics," *Journal of Product Innovation Management*, 16: 557–568 (1999).

Crawford, C. Merle and Di Benedetto, C. Anthony. *New Products Management*, 7th ed. Burr Ridge, IL: Irwin/McGraw-Hill, 2003.

Di Benedetto, C. Anthony. "Identifying the key success factors in new product launch." *Journal of Product Innovation Management*, 16: 530–544 (1999).

Pepper, C. B. "Fast Forward." *Business Monthly*, 25–30 (February 1991).

Roger Calantone holds the Eli Broad University Chair in Business at Michigan State University. He is Distinguished University Faculty and is director of the Broad Information Technology Management Program (ITMP). He teaches Research Methodology, Technology-Product Development, and Decision Support Systems to business and engineering students and runs practicum programs for product commercialization. He is the author of over 200 academic articles and proceedings. He is a PDMA-Certified New Product Development Professional and is a long-time member of the Product Development & Management Association, IEEE, and Beta Gamma Sigma. He has consulted for numerous firms and has received numerous research grants and awards.

C. Anthony Di Benedetto is Professor of Marketing, Fox School of Business and Management, Temple University. He earned a B.Sc. in Chemistry, an M.B.A., and a Ph.D. in Marketing and Management Science from McGill

University. His research interests include improving the new products process, new product launch, and international marketing strategy. He has served as Vice President of Publications for the Product Development & Management Association (PDMA), editor of the PDMA newsletter *Visions*, and as abstracts editor for the *Journal of Product Innovation Management*. He is currently editor of the *Journal of Product Innovation Management*.

Theodore Stank is the John H. Dove Distinguished Professor of Logistics at the University of Tennessee. Dr. Stank's research interests focus on the strategic implications associated with integrated logistics and supply chain management concepts, specifically related to integration, information exchange, and operational responsiveness. He is a coauthor of *21st Century Logistics: Making Supply Chain Integration a Reality* and has published over 55 articles in academic and professional journals. He previously worked for Abbott Laboratories, served as an officer in the U.S. Navy, and provided consulting and executive education services for numerous manufacturing and logistics firms.

CHAPTER THIRTY-TWO

MARKET TESTING AND POSTLAUNCH EVALUATION FOR CONSUMER GOODS

David W. Olson

32.1 Introduction

After the long months (or in some cases years) of development, having survived the perils of prelaunch consumer testing (see Chapter 18) and the seemingly endless treacheries of internal politics (see Chapter 10), the product may finally be launched into the marketplace. In an ideal world, previous research will already have ensured that a genuine consumer need exists for the product (or service), and consumer testing will have proven that the new product delivers successfully on that need. In reality, though, even with the most thorough prelaunch research program, the marketer inevitably faces many more unknowns than knowns when he/she launches a new product. (See Table 32.1 and Chapter 30) In this chapter, we describe the process of designing a program to assess the new product's performance in the marketplace as soon as possible after launch, to tell the team and company management: (1) how well the product is doing; and, more important, (2) where its performance needs improvement if the sales prognosis is not good.

32.2 Goals for Postlaunch Evaluation

In designing a program for evaluating the new product's performance following launch, there are several key overall goals to keep in mind.

TABLE 32.1 TYPICAL "KNOWNS" PRELAUNCH VERSUS POSTLAUNCH.

Key Factor	Prior to Launch	After Launch
Concept Interest	√	
Product Acceptance	√	
Purchase Cycle/Use-Up Rate		√
Name, Packaging	√	
In-Store Visibility		√
Positioning/Advertising	√	
Cannibalization		√
Pricing	√	
Trade Acceptance		√
Competitive Response		√

32.2.1 The Right Performance Metrics

For everyone, the new product's *sales* will doubtless be the single most important measure of the brand's performance (although there are significant pitfalls; see Section 32.5.1). However, in addition to sales, the marketer will want to consider

> *The marketer must define the crucial measures of performance specific to this particular case, to guide postlaunch evaluation.*

other measures of performance that are early leading indicators of likely sales performance (examples are discussed in Section 32.5.2). What these other metrics might be depends very heavily on the specific product category involved. For example, in some cases, quick initial trade acceptance may be an absolutely crucial step toward success; in such cases, the marketer should set specific goals for the number or percent of accounts accepting the new product and use this to gauge the new product's early performance. In other cases, sales may be direct from manufacturer (e.g., catalog or online sales), in which case, of course, trade acceptance is irrelevant.

32.2.2 Valid and Predictive Measures

Obviously, the marketer must try to ensure that the measures being obtained are reliable, valid, and predictive measures of performance. *Reliability* refers to the measurement device itself and whether its measures are stable or are subject to high degrees of random measurement error or fluctuation. If a measure is unreliable, it will show poor test-retest stability (i.e., if a new and independent reading is taken, it may show very different results from the first measurement). *Validity* and *predicitivity* refer to whether the metrics themselves measure accurately what they purport to measure—in this case, new product success—and whether they can help predict future performance. Many new products are inappropriately evaluated using measures that are low in reliability and/or validity, which can give results that are either overly rosy and inflated, or unfairly and prematurely negative and damaging. Even sales audits (measures of store sales), typically considered the "hardest" measure of performance, can often be inaccurate if not collected in the proper way; the marketer must be continually vigilant on this score.

32.2.3 Speed of Reading Performance

There is clearly a strong desire for a *quick* read of the product's performance soon after it is launched, whether in the test market or nationally. However, the earlier the attempt to read the product's performance, the more difficult it is to get an accurate and valid assessment of longer-term performance. Early buyers are not necessarily reflective of the important larger mainstream mass of consumers, and it takes time for products to be incorporated into buyers' purchase repertoires. For this reason, consumer response models (see Section 32.3) become essential tools for the new product marketer, because they provide a means to gather early consumer response data to project longer-term (i.e., first-year) sales.

32.2.4 Actionable Diagnostics

The postlaunch evaluation program should be designed to provide a *clear* indication of where the product is performing well—aspects of the marketing program to leave alone—*as well as clear signals of the problem areas that need improvement.*

> *Validity, speed of reading, and actionable diagnostics are key criteria for postlaunch measurement.*

Fortunately, methods exist to provide such clear learning (e.g., diary, scanner, or internet panels; telephone or Internet surveys; customer response cards; etc.); unfortunately, such methods cost money, sometimes considerable sums. Nevertheless, seen in the context of the entire marketing budget, such research is actually a small fraction of the project costs and should be considered an essential part of the overall cost of launching a new product.

32.3 Consumer Response Models

The key to obtaining a quick, yet predictive measure of a new product's performance after launch is understanding the consumer adoption process, *or consumer response model*, at work in the marketer's category. As a very valuable exercise, the marketer should diagram or lay out the sequence of events that will occur when the product is launched and that will contribute to the product's sales performance.

32.3.1 Packaged Goods

The typical model for packaged goods is the awareness—trial—repeat model (see Figure 32.1). It assumes that the adoption process for such products follows these steps. First, consumers are made aware of the new product (usually via advertising). Next, some proportion of those aware of the brand decide to try it (i.e., buy it the first time). Then, some of those triers will decide to buy the

FIGURE 32.1 TYPICAL AWARENESS-TRIAL-REPEAT MODEL FOR PACKAGED GOOD.

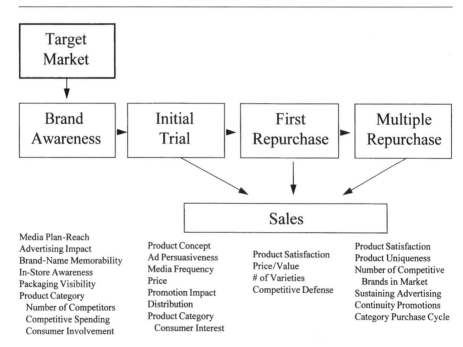

Media Plan-Reach
Advertising Impact
Brand-Name Memorability
In-Store Awareness
Packaging Visibility
Product Category
 Number of Competitors
 Competitive Spending
 Consumer Involvement

Product Concept
Ad Persuasiveness
Media Frequency
Price
Promotion Impact
Distribution
Product Category
 Consumer Interest

Product Satisfaction
Price/Value
# of Varieties
Competitive Defense

Product Satisfaction
Product Uniqueness
Number of Competitive
 Brands in Market
Sustaining Advertising
Continuity Promotions
Category Purchase Cycle

product again, and eventually adopt it into their buying repertory. The marketer can use this model to set specific performance goals on awareness, trial, and repeat purchase prior to launch. He/she can then measure these variables (e.g., in a telephone or online tracking study; see Section 32.5.1) and can begin to pinpoint the product's strong and weak areas. For instance, if awareness is below expectations or goals (see Section 32.5.1), the marketer can examine those aspects of the program designed to generate awareness: the advertising, the packaging visibility, public relations, and so on. If trial-given awareness is below expectations, the marketer should reexamine the selling proposition, pricing, and promotion effectiveness. And if repeat purchasing is below expectations, it may signal a serious problem in postuse satisfaction, but may also reflect problems with out-of-stock conditions in the stores or a weak price-value equation. (Of these factors, repeat purchase is usually most critical to long-term success for new packaged goods products.)

32.3.2 Consumer Services

A different kind of response model might apply to services; Figure 32.2 shows one possible formulation of an adoption model of new menu items offered in fast-food restaurants such as McDonald's, Burger King, or Wendy's. In some

FIGURE 32.2 MODEL OF NEW SERVICE AT RETAIL OUTLET.

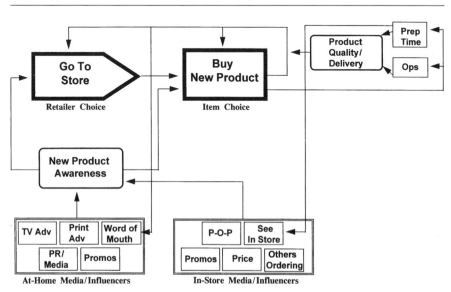

ways the model resembles the packaged goods model, in that at-home media such as TV and print advertising are assumed to generate consumer awareness of the new item. However, the impact of that awareness is potentially both on the choice of restaurant to visit (i.e., "I want to try that new sandwich, so I'll go to McDonald's") and on the decision of which item to buy once the consumer is in the store (i.e., "Hmmm, instead of my usual Big Mac®, I think I'll try this new sandwich that I heard about on TV last week"). The whole in-store environment is assumed to be more important as well in this case, as consumers scan the menu boards to make their decisions and see others buying or not buying the new item. And finally, in this case, the consistency of quality of product delivery becomes a particularly crucial variable for ultimate consumer acceptance. If the new item's sales are initially sluggish, it may lead to a deterioration of the quality of delivery of that service to those who do try it (i.e., because the service staff do not get a sufficient amount of experience in preparing the new product to learn to "do it well," and because the sandwiches may sit for a long time in the holding bins, leading to a reduction in delivered quality). This feedback loop, thus, becomes a very important aspect of evaluating a new menu item early on; ongoing quality control monitoring is essential in this case to flag this potential problem.

Other services (e.g., financial services) will have yet another configuration for how the adoption process works; the specific model must be tailored to the individual situation.

32.3.3 Durables

Another model applies, obviously, to durables where repeat purchase or replacement sales are not important to early sales performance. In these cases, the role of the salesman, the impact of direct marketing,

> *Different response models need to be developed for different types of launches.*

the effect of special interest group word of mouth, and the influence of publicity (e.g., reviews in specialized trade magazines) all play an important role in the new product's eventual sales performance. Models of durable adoption developed by Professor Frank Bass and his colleagues serve as a good starting point in constructing a launch model for durables (Bass, 1969). As with services, a detailed model specific to the type of durable needs to be developed, to provide a yardstick against which the new product should be measured after it is introduced.

32.3.4 Consumer Response Models: Summary

Even if it seems difficult or impossible to define *specific* measures of acceptance which are likely precursors of sales, it is still a very worthwhile exercise to try to lay out that adoption model. It provides guidance on where the marketer might look in trying to understand shortfalls in sales performance after launch, even if the process is more based on judgment and guesswork than on hard data. Setting performance criteria on these measures should be done, to the extent possible, based on past corporate or competitive performance, for example:

- What was the average trade acceptance of the past five launches we have made?
- How many special-interest magazines reviewed our product, and how many were positive reviews?
- What levels of consumer awareness, trial, and repurchase have been associated with successful, versus unsuccessful, launches in the past?

If it has not already been done, a historical analysis of past launches, both corporate and competitive, should be undertaken to provide these sorts of benchmarks. This provides a very valuable framework, then, for assessing the new product's performance.

> *Use past history to set reasonable target objectives on key measures.*

32.4 Test Marketing vs. National Launches

The marketer must decide whether to introduce the product in a limited area, rather than immediately launching it nationally. The benefits of test marketing are ones of lower cost; reducing risk exposure (e.g., of possibly sullying the company's name or image among consumers or trade customers, etc.); obtaining a "success story" to use to obtain favorable trade acceptance in expansion areas; gaining early operational and logistical experience in manufacturing, distributing, and commercializing the new product or service; and permitting assessment of specific marketing elements to modify prior to full national launch. The drawbacks of test marketing are ones of opportunity cost, competitive exposure, and possible unreliability of reading performance (e.g., if competitors try to make the test unreadable by heavy defensive promotions, etc.). In addition, test marketing may simply not be possible for some products (e.g., automobiles). Industrial and business-to-business products typically call for a very different approach, using pilot or prototype testing, followed by beta testing (Stern, 1991).

At one time, test marketing was standard operating procedure for major manufacturers (in those situations where it was feasible). In recent years, indications are that the popularity of test marketing has been declining (*Profit-Building Strategies*, 1993). One factor is the high costs of test marketing these days due to factors such as the imposition of slotting fees by retailers, the high fixed costs of advertising (e.g., commercial production), and the costs of limited production runs. There also are increased pressures from corporate management to skip test marketing and launch products nationally to meet stockholder expectations or annual volume goals and to prevent competitive preemption (Power, 1992). And the Internet combined with online home shopping has opened up some interesting alternatives to traditional test marketing (Miller, 2002). Nevertheless, for many new products, test marketing remains an important and valuable step in the product's evaluation.

32.4.1 Selecting Test Markets

It can be said that there are two ways to go about selecting sites for the test market: the scientific, "right" way; and the way it tends to be done in practice. In the scientific way, cities would be chosen to be

> *Test markets chosen for expediency overstate the product's true sales potential.*

representative of the United States as a whole (as a rule of thumb, normally those cities should represent from 0.5–1.5 percent of the U.S. population). The key matching criteria usually are, in order of importance: category sales development (CDI), brand or corporate sales development (BDI), and demographics such as age, socioeconomic status, ethnicity, and other demographics. Additional matching criteria might include regional diversity (e.g., selecting a mix of east coast, west coast, and midwestern markets), trade channel issues (e.g., matching as closely as possible the degree of concentration of key supermarket chains), media issues (e.g., equalizing the coverage of local TV and print media), and others. If this "scientific" approach were employed, the new product's sales performance in the test market might be expected to approximate its performance if launched nationally, subject to some likely chronic overstatement (see Section 32.4.2).

Unfortunately, in the real world, test market cities are more often selected for reasons of expediency. Very often, a company's "best" markets are chosen, because they are more likely to achieve good distribution in those markets. In these cases, it can be expected that the new product's performance will be considerably stronger than it is likely to be nationally. (Of course, if the purpose of the test market is more to gain early operational and logistical experience or to develop a "success story" to use with the trade in expansion markets than to obtain a true gauge of the product's national sales potential, it makes sense to conduct those tests in the company's best markets.) All of these issues need to be kept in mind when test market results are being evaluated (Weinblatt, 1995).

32.4.2 Adjustments of Test Market Results

It has been demonstrated that test market sales performance is almost always higher than subsequent national sales performance. *As a rule of thumb, test market sales should be reduced by 15 percent even if the markets are chosen to be representative of the country as a whole.* This inflation is due to the unusual attention that test markets tend to receive by the company (e.g., trade support and other means to merchandise the product). If the markets are not reflective of the country as a whole, but are unusually strong areas for the manufacturer, sales must obviously be further discounted. (The unadjusted, inflated sales figures can—and should!—be used for the purpose of trying to convince retailers in expansion markets to stock the new item.) Sophisticated statistical modeling of test market sales results can be done to yield a better projection of the product's likely sales performance if launched nationally.

32.4.3 Types of Test Markets

There are basically two choices in test marketing for a manufacturer whose products are sold through distribution channels not controlled by the manufacturer (e.g., as is the case for most packaged goods). In

> *Marketers can use traditional or controlled store testing in test marketing.*

traditional test marketing, the new product is sold in to trade accounts using the company's regular sales force, and advertised and promoted as if it were a national launch. In *controlled store testing*, outside companies are hired by the manufacturer to handle the product's distribution and merchandising, with no reliance on the company's sales force. The latter approach ensures good distribution for the product and that it is well displayed and always in stock. These companies may also coordinate local or marketwide merchandising programs. In addition, it is possible to set up special tests of alternative advertising, pricing, promotions, and so on, which are administered by the controlled-store-testing companies. In short, controlled store testing provides a "best-case" scenario for the new product (which may not, and indeed probably *will not*, be matched by the company's own sales force).

32.4.3.1 Electronic or Scanner Test Markets. In some cases, test market areas have been established (by Nielsen and IRI) that permit highly sophisticated testing of new products and their marketing programs in supermarkets (Maturi, 1990). These areas use scanner panels (records of individual household buying patterns obtained via scanning of Universal Product Code symbols on packages), and one (IRI's BehaviorScan service) further links into local cable systems to permit testing of alternative television campaigns. These provide the ultimate in in-depth assessment of the new product in a limited geographical area, as a precursor to a national expansion.

32.4.3.2 Online Testing. The newest alternatives to traditional test marketing use the Internet as both a means of delivering advertising exposures for new products, and a direct link to purchasing generated by that advertising using home-shopping services. While these methods offer great advantages in cost and time compared to test marketing, the artificiality of both the advertising exposure and the shopping experience for most products (e.g., packaged goods) means that they must be treated with caution until their predicitivity can be fully assessed. Particularly for products often bought over the Internet (e.g., software), these methods may have great promise.

32.4.4 Other Limited Geography Sales Tests

Mention should be made of other types of tests that can be conducted, particularly for manufacturers whose sales and distribution process do not involve retail partners. If the product is a catalog item or is marketed via direct response and fulfilled directly by the manufacturer, new items can be tested in limited runs of catalogs to gauge consumer acceptance. On an informal level, products can be tested in individual sites, among a limited set of key prospects. More formally, clusters of individual stores can be used together with local advertising to conduct real-world tests at much less cost than traditional test marketing (Needel, 1991).

32.4.5 Test Marketing: Summary

Test marketing should be strongly considered prior to launching a new brand nationally. Although expensive, it is still far less expensive than a national launch. With the right evaluation program in place, extremely valuable learning can be obtained on how to improve a new product's performance before it is launched nationally; instead, if a brand is launched nationally with a defective marketing program, it is very difficult to rectify the problems on the fly in the heat of pressure from top management, from the field force, and from trade customers to "fix it—and FAST!!"

At the same time, ways to accelerate learning from test marketing and guide modifications to the marketing program constantly need to be sought. Too often, corporate management—correctly—sees test markets as inconclusive and likely to delay the whole process. The key is finding ways to measure test market performance quickly and accurately. In the next section, we discuss some of these assessment methods.

32.5 Assessment Methodologies

In this section, we outline some of the ways to measure postlaunch performance, whether the product is being test marketed or has been launched nationally.

32.5.1 Sales

Obviously, the first measure everyone will be interested in is the product's initial sales level. Increasingly, such information is available quickly, even within a matter of a week or so, via improvements in information technology. However, while actual sales is an important metric, it can frequently be misleading. Factory shipments may be a poor indicator of actual consumer takeaway, due to pipeline inventory. Initial consumer sales will reflect primarily early consumer trial of the new product (if it is a packaged good); these can be artificially hyped by short-term consumer or trade promotions and thus make things appear rosier than they really are.

For most packaged goods, the sales velocity inevitably peaks in the first couple of months and then falls off (see Figure 32.3) as trial flattens. Many companies read sales the first month or so and then extrapolate them erroneously, assuming that they can but only grow in subsequent months. Understanding the month-by-month sales growth and decline curves is essential to projecting sales accurately.

For nonpackaged goods or services, reading early sales as a means to gauge future success can be equally or even more treacherous. The initial sales will probably come from "early adopters" or innovators, whose reaction to the product may not be reflective of later adopters or laggards.

FIGURE 32.3 SALES AS FUNCTION OF TIME FOR NEW BRAND LAUNCHES.

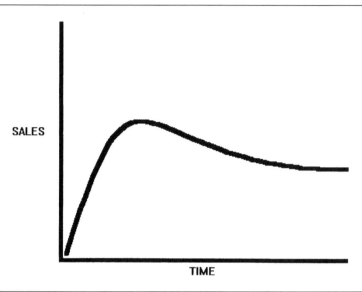

The company should examine the past period-by-period sales growth history for similar launches as a way to gauge the new launch's likely future sales performance based on results to date. It is likely that it will require at least six months to produce an accurate estimate of the new product's first-year sales performance if sales alone are the barometer. This ability to read and forecast performance improves if other information is obtained during the first few months following launch, as discussed in the next section.

32.5.2 Sales Surrogates or "Leading Indicators"

Consumer research can be conducted to ascertain the magnitude of consumer response to the launch in the initial months following launch. This information can be used as input into sales forecasting models, which can provide very accurate estimates in most cases of eventual long-term (or at least first-year) sales. It also provides key diagnostic learning about the product's areas of strength and weakness.

32.5.2.1 Consumer Tracking. These surveys, typically conducted via telephone (or, increasingly, online) in the test market or nationally, obtain measures of consumer awareness, advertising awareness, trial, reasons for buying or not buying, repurchase (if applicable), repeat intentions, product likes and dislikes, and so on. Based on these early reads, the measures can be extrapolated and used as inputs into forecasting models to project sales. Equally or even more importantly, these data can be used to identify performance strengths and weaknesses. Table 32.2 outlines some typical measures, and how to interpret results.

Figure 32.4 provides information assembled over a period of years by the author during his career with the Leo Burnett Company, relating brand awareness measures to advertising spending (gross rating points [GRPs]). It can be used as a means to gauge whether the new product is attaining satisfactory brand awareness. If it is not, other measures in the tracking questionnaire can be examined to identify the most likely causes of the low brand awareness (e.g., by examining advertising awareness, product visibility in the store, etc.). A similar collection of data shows typical trial levels at given levels of awareness (see Figure 32.5). Again, a shortfall in trial should lead the investigator to examine tracking study measures of price satisfaction, reasons for not trying, ability to locate the product in the store, and so on.

In this way, tracking data can show where the problems really are and give the marketer a focus for efforts to strengthen the program. Although not inexpensive (such tracking studies may cost from $10,000 to $100,000 and more), they can provide invaluable learning. Strong consideration should be given to building the cost of such studies into the launch program for the new product.

32.5.2.2 Panels. As discussed earlier, in some cases it is possible to obtain individual household purchase data, from scanner-based panels (Nielsen or IRI), paper-and-pencil diaries, or, most recently, online panels. These can be very expensive, but generally provide better data than telephone tracking studies (which rely on self-reported purchase behavior). On the other hand, these panels do not provide the attitudinal data (e.g., reasons for buying or not buying) that the tracking studies provide. If panels are used, some additional research is needed to flesh out the problems and point the way to corrective actions.

32.5.3 Other Performance Measures

In addition to tracking studies or panels, which can provide data that can be used to project sales performance, other measures are very useful in gaining insight into why a new product is performing as it is. These include: customer inserts with mail-back questionnaires, monitoring of 1-800 customer complaints or comments, and interviews, formally or informally, with field force reps and trade customers. Also, very typically, qualitative research (usually focus groups) is conducted among buyers and nonbuyers to try to identify barriers to success.

TABLE 32.2 NEW PRODUCT TRACKING STUDY QUESTIONNAIRE.

Question Wording	Guidelines for Interpreter
Screener: "In the past X months, you have bought (category) ?" "Are you aged 21–55?" (or other demographic controls) **Category Usage, Awareness, etc.:** "In the past X months, how many times have you bought (category)?" "What brands of (category) have you ever heard of?" "Have you even heard of (brand)?" (ask for 4–6 brands) "Have you ever bought (brand)?" (ask for same 4–6 brands) "In the past X months, which brands of (category) have you bought?" "About how many (packages, times, etc.) have you bought (brand) in the past X months?" "On which of the following occasions do you use (category)?"; "Which members of your household use (category)?" etc. **Ad Awareness:** "Do you recall seeing any advertising for (brand)?" (Ask for brands respondent is aware of.) "Please describe to me the advertising for (brand)." (Record verbatim) "Do you recall seeing any (coupons, other promotions) for (brand)? "Where did you see the advertising for (brand)?" **Ever Bought:** IF YES: "Why did you first try (brand)?" (Record verbatim.) "When did you first buy (brand)?" "How many times have you bought (brand)?" "When did you last buy (brand)?" "How likely are you buy (brand) again?" (Definitely to Definitely Will Not Buy—5 point scale) "What do you like about (brand)? What dod you dislike?" "Did you use (coupons, other promotions) to buy (brand)?" "How would you rate (brand) on (attributes)?" IF NO: "Did you look for the product in the store? Did you find it?" "Why didn't you try (product)?" "How likely are you to try (brand) in the future?" (5-point scale)	**Demographics** • Base analysis on category buyers • Analyze by demographic groups • Analyze by heavy vs. light buyers • Unaided awareness . . . usually very low for new brands • Plot vs. GRPs or past launches (Exhibit 6) • Plot vs. Awareness or past launches (Exhibit 7) • Past month penetration • Calculate share of market for new brand • Analyze trial, repeat of new brand by usage segments • Norm: Ad Awareness = 67% of Brand Awareness • Norm: Proven Awareness = 50% of Claimed • Norm: Coupon Awareness = 20% of Brand Awareness • Norm: 70–80% on TV for TV launches • Look for specific reasons, even if fairly small in % • Analyze repurchase by time of first purchase • Norm: 50% repeat among earlier triers • Look for continued buying among early triers • Take 100% of "Definitely's and 50% of "Probably's— • Norm = 50% • Look for specific likes and dislikes, even if small % • Norm: 30% Fair to Poor Value • Norm: 25% of Trial from Promotions • Analyze specific attributes • Norm: "Found" = 2/3 of "Looked For" • Look for specific reasons, even if small % • Norm: 10–15% Definitely Will Try

FIGURE 32.4 TV GROUPS VS. AIDED BRAND AWARENESS.

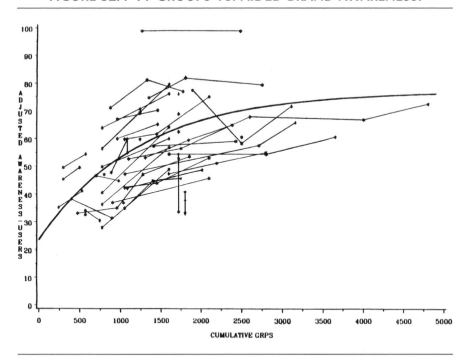

Such research, while useful to generate theories about possible problems, should not be relied on to identify the magnitude of problems; more quantitative data (e.g., from tracking) are called for. Table 32.3 is a summary of some of these measurement methods, how they are conducted, how they are used, and their primary drawbacks.

32.6 Case History

In some cases, smart, insightful postlaunch research has been used to pinpoint potentially fatal problems with the launch, to provide guidance on how to overcome those problems, and to turn would-be failures into successes. In one case, a number of years ago the Kellogg Company launched a new cereal brand, called Cracklin' Bran, into two test markets. In both, it achieved a dismal share of market—only about one-half of its minimum acceptable share—and might easily have been abandoned.

FIGURE 32.5 BRAND AWARENESS VS. TRIAL.

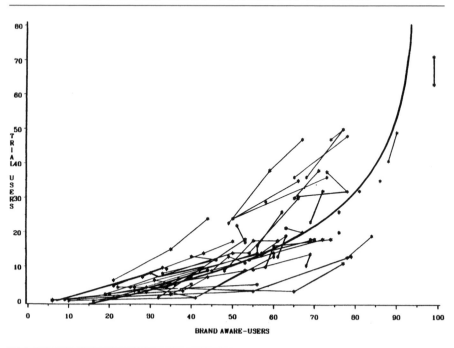

BRAND AWARE-USERS

However, in-market tracking showed the sales problem to be due almost entirely to a very low awareness performance among consumers; in all other respects, the product seemed viable (in particular, those few who became aware of it and tried it showed very high levels of liking, translating into high repeat purchases). Further postlaunch detective work suggested two areas for improving brand awareness: (1) improving the advertising, which was not clearly communicating the product's concept of being a delicious bran cereal (this, despite prelaunch copy research, which indicated the advertising to be very strong); and (2) modifying the media plan, which was too heavily concentrated in certain time periods on television and not providing the broad-based exposure necessary for strong awareness. New advertising was developed, and radio was added to the media mix to broaden the advertising's reach. Another test market was opened six months later, and, to the client and agency's delight, the new product achieved much higher awareness, which translated into stronger trial and sales—and the product achieved its sales goals in this market. It was launched

TABLE 32.3 METHODS TO READ MARKETPLACE PERFORMANCE.

Measure	Source	Use	Drawbacks
Straight factory sales	Accounting department	Short-term financial results	Misleading early on
Trial and repeat purchase	Tracking studies/ dairy or scanner panels	Forecasting and projection, user characteristics	Expensive, forecasting error/limitations
Awareness, attitudes, reasons for buying or not buying	Tracking studies, ad hoc surveys, mail-back consumer insert cards, 1-800 calls	Diagnosis of problems, focus on areas of improvement	Expensive to collect, errors in interpretation
Strengths and weaknesses of specific marketing elements	Focus groups, one-on-one interviews with consumers or customers	Hypothesis generation, definition of problems, evaluation of potential solutions	Errors in interpretation, nonprojectability of findings

nationally about nine months later, and continues to be a strong brand about 25 years later. (It was renamed Cracklin' Oat Bran in the early 1980s, to take advantage of the "hot" health trend in oat bran at that time. The process keeping brands current throughout their life cycle is a very different, but an equally important topic than that of how to launch a successful brand in the first place.) The sales generated by this product in the quarter century since its national launch total well over $1 billion, a rather nice return on a total post-launch research investigation, which perhaps cost the equivalent of $60,000 in today's dollars.

32.7 Summary

Obviously, not every launch merits or can afford a sizeable postlaunch budget. However, even more modest research programs can provide the sort of essential information on performance which marketers can use to pinpoint and fix problems quickly. Or, they can show the product's poor sales are inherent in the launch and not easily remedied, in which case the product can be abandoned without wasting good money. The new product marketer should plan, before the product is launched, how he/she is going to obtain the crucial learning, early on, to help guide decisions about how to address problems out in the market. Such money can be among the very best-spent in the entire launch budget.

References

Bass, Frank M., "A new product growth model for consumer durables," *Management Science*, 15(1): 215 (1969).

Maturi, Richard J., "How to improve the odds for new product debuts," *Investor's Daily*, 8 (April 24, 1990).

Miller, Jim and Lundy, Sheila, "Test marketing plugs into the Internet," *Consumer Insight*, 20–23 (Spring 2002)

Needel, Stephen, "Leveraging store-level scanner data for test marketing," presentation at the Third Annual ARF Behavioral/Scanner Data Workshop, Advertising Research Foundation, New York, June 5–6, 1991.

Power, Christopher, "Will It sell in Podunk? Hard to Say," *Business Week*, 46 (August 10, 1992).

Stern, Aimee L., "Testing goes industrial." *Sales & Marketing Management*, 30 (March 1991).

"Test marketing a new product: when it's a good idea and how to do it. *Profit-Building Strategies for Business Owners*, 14 (March 1993).

Weinblatt, Ira, "Beware of macho testing," *New Product News*, 12 (January 8, 1995).

David Olson is principal of his own consulting firm, David Olson Consulting, which specializes in market research, market planning, and sales forecasting for new products. In his 28-year career with the Leo Burnett Company, he helped such clients as Procter & Gamble, Kellogg's, Pillsbury, Maytag, RCA, and McDonald's with their new product launches, using a proprietary expert system forecasting method and planning process, which he developed. He is a graduate of Harvard University, and has been a frequent speaker at conferences and seminars. He is a former board member of PDMA and has served as webmaster for pdma.org since the inauguration of its Web site in 1996.

CHAPTER THIRTY-THREE

OVERVIEW AND CONTEXT FOR LIFE-CYCLE MANAGEMENT

Bill Ausura, Bob Gill, and Steven Haines

33.1 Introduction

Because funding for new product innovations comes primarily—if not exclusively—from profits derived from products currently in the marketplace, it is critical that companies do their best to optimize postlaunch life-cycle management (for simplicity, designated as "LCM" throughout the remainder of this chapter). Not focusing on good postlaunch product management creates high degrees of risk for new product innovation and development programs in any company over the long-term. Moreover, lack of attention to product and customer profitability can adversely affect overall corporate performance. Despite these obvious imperatives, many companies have no one assigned to manage the product after the product has been launched into the marketplace. Their business paradigm can best be described as a "throw it over the wall" situation, where there is not hard-and-fast accountability for product profit and loss management. It is highly recommended that companies officially assign someone or some team of people to each individual product that has been launched, in order to ensure that the actual results for the product during its postlaunch life cycle live up to the expectations and goals assigned the product during the original project/product business case development and decision-making.

33.2 Life-Cycle Management: Work Areas and Work Structures

LCM may be the most challenging dimension of product management, namely because it includes such a multitude of different and varied activities. But these can be grouped into three broad work areas: (1) ongoing P&L management of an

> *Life-cycle management is by far the most complex and difficult assignment in the product management business function.*

existing product ("postlaunch product management"), (2) introducing enhancements and derivatives, and (3) providing input into the planning for the next new product to which existing customers are likely to be migrated. Ongoing P&L management tends to be almost a full-time job on most products. But most LCM managers are also asked to be the project manager or oversee the project team that introduces derivatives or enhancements for their assigned products. And many of the enhancement and derivative projects take almost as much time and effort as the original new product development and introduction project. Finally, since the LCM manager is the one person who lives with the product and its markets, customers, and day-to-day issues, he/she is in the best position to provide guidance for planning a migration or replacement product. Adopting best practices for managing product enhancements and derivatives can result in the life-cycle curves of long-lived products often looking like Figure 33.1 instead of a single S-curve.

Many industries assign LCM responsibilities to a single manager after the cross-functional new product development (NPD) project team has completed its product planning, development, and launch activities. The reasons are varied: little insight into how much work the LCM job entails, higher priorities set for NPD versus LCM, lack of resources, and so on. But companies that maintain cross-functional teams to manage products after their launch and throughout their life cycles tend to have a more balanced and successful product management discipline, as well as better ability to manage their broader portfolios of new and existing products and services. Some companies utilize the original NPD cross-functional team to migrate over into the LCM phase (although this is not the "norm"). This practice provides an excellent work transition, since that NPD team will already have intimate knowledge and experience with the product and its market drivers and positioning. Those teams will have the greatest ability to immediately make quick decisions and trade-offs, especially during the critical growth phase of LCM, where "crossing the chasm" from early adopters to mass markets is imperative. The one potential drawback to utilizing the same cross-functional team to do new product

FIGURE 33.1 S-CURVES OF MULTIPLE ENHANCEMENTS AND DERIVATIVES.

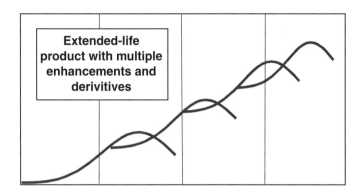

Extended-life product with multiple enhancements and derivitives

Source: Kotler 1997, p. 364.

introduction and postlaunch life-cycle management is that there are personality differences that make people who do one or the other of NPD versus LCM most effective in just one of these areas (Onkvisit and Shaw, 1989). Ignoring this can cause inefficiencies in teams if they are assigned to do things which their personalities don't fit.

33.3 Postlaunch Product Management

As products evolve through NPD processes and ultimately get launched, the support plans provided by the various functional organizations are synchronized. As with the transmission of an automobile, the synchronization of the gears (the functional plans) becomes critical as the product increases its velocity in the market. The role of the product manager becomes that of an operational business manager, general manager, or "mini-CEO," interfacing with all the business functions that have an impact on product results.

We recommend that a cross-functional team structure be used to manage products during the postlaunch life cycle, similar to the NPD project teams that are often used to plan and introduce products (Katzenbach and Smith, 1994; also see Chapter 9). Cross-functional life-cycle management teams simply get at issues and problems more quickly than people working in functional silos, and this tends to enable better long-term fixes for life-cycle problems and challenges. If a cross-functional team work model is used in the postlaunch time period, the product manager's responsibility extends to oversight of that team (like a board of directors), managing or overseeing four key areas or dimensions of LCM. These areas include:

1. Marketing the product
2. Servicing and supporting the product
3. Keeping score (of product performance and financials)
4. Operations oversight

To help put these dimensions into perspective, a pictorial model is provided in Figure 33.2. This shows the major activities and related subactivities within each of these four key areas. The importance of the interdependence of these activities cannot be emphasized enough. The dynamics of the marketplace, coupled with the often asynchronous activities of the other business functions

FIGURE 33.2 LCM DIMENSIONS.

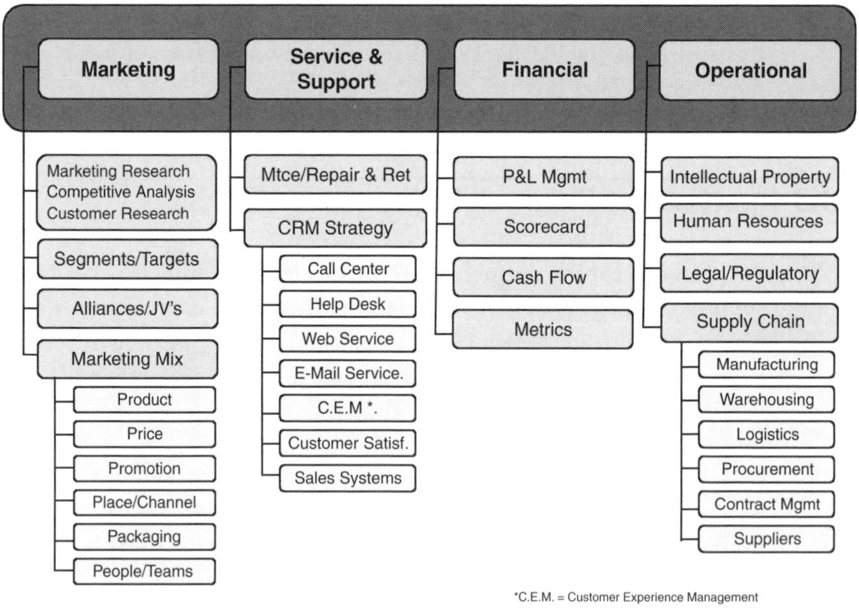

Marketing	Service & Support	Financial	Operational
Marketing Research / Competitive Analysis / Customer Research	Mtce/Repair & Ret	P&L Mgmt	Intellectual Property
Segments/Targets	CRM Strategy	Scorecard	Human Resources
Alliances/JV's	Call Center	Cash Flow	Legal/Regulatory
Marketing Mix	Help Desk	Metrics	Supply Chain
Product	Web Service		Manufacturing
Price	E-Mail Service.		Warehousing
Promotion	C.E.M *.		Logistics
Place/Channel	Customer Satisf.		Procurement
Packaging	Sales Systems		Contract Mgmt
People/Teams			Suppliers

*C.E.M. = Customer Experience Management

Source: © 2004 Sequent Learning Networks.

of the organization, can lead to inefficiencies due to poorly established or agreed-upon goals or improperly established communication channels. This is why a strong cross-functional team structure and high-quality execution are so important. The team serves as the main mechanism for communicating information about the performance of the business (the product) and in making replanning decisions. In order to manage effectively, the team members must inherit or bring with them some key items from the NPD phases of work when they enter the life-cycle phase. A *Product Master Plan* © is therefore recommended, which includes the business case and all functional department support plans. This plan book is essentially the repository of all material relating to the NPD project and the product it produces. The departmental *support plans* are the various documents team members create to outline what they plan to do to support the product through the development and introduction phases as well as into the postlaunch life-cycle period.

33.3.1 Dimension 1: Marketing the Product

During the product planning and development phases, a marketing plan should have been prepared. The purpose of the marketing plan is to define the market, competitors, target market segments, and positioning, with the goal of creating a roadmap for optimizing the performance of the product in the market. Further, the marketing plan contains the major dimensions of the marketing mix, such as prod-

> *In postlaunch product management, marketing is one of the most important dimensions; without intense attention to product marketing, it is highly unlikely that the product will meet its business commitments over the life cycle.*

uct, price, promotion, place (McCarthy, 1996), which are adjustable business "levers" used by product teams as they monitor and respond to market conditions. Because the marketplace is dynamic and unforgiving, a dynamic marketing plan with adjustments as needed becomes that much more important.

One of the most important issues in this dimension area has to do with the overall determination of exactly where the product is situated in its life, or its point along the life-cycle curve. One way companies set this up during the product-planning process is to establish a series of conditions that are likely to materialize, and thus act as a trigger to an adjustment to the marketing mix. An example of this would be "If sales grow at a rate of more than 10 percent per month, then the product will be classified as being in the growth phase." Without these conditional statements in the product plans, it becomes a difficult exercise to determine the specific phase a product is in, and the team is exposed to higher levels of risk because it may respond with actions that could be inappropriate for a given life-cycle phase.

Another one of the key areas for the marketing function has to do with the nurturing and promotion of a durable brand. A brand is generally a collection of attributes of either a product or a company held together by messages, images, logos, experiences, and other identifiers that create a perception of the company and can be is etched into the minds of the customers or the marketplace. Consumer brands are some of the most familiar. We all know Coca-Cola® even though we might not be consumers of their products. The same is true for IBM, Mercedes Benz, Kleenex®, Pampers®, or any other company or product we see in our daily lives, in our trips to the grocery store, the department store, or to the Internet. Marketing plans and programs should be aligned with the established brand strategies for the enterprise (Hiebing and Cooper, 1997).

33.3.2 Dimension 2: Servicing and Supporting Products

One of the most important dimensions of managing products is maintaining a clear focus on customer satisfaction, loyalty, and retention. Much of the available research and literature have asserted that it takes more money and is much more difficult to acquire a customer than to keep a customer (Kotler, 1997), provided that the customer is strategically valuable and/or profitable.

> *Managing the customer experience is a key issue for product life-cycle management; knowing how to ensure that customer "touch points" create positive images of your product and company is essential.*

The term "customer relationship management" (CRM) has been applied for several years to define the domain of customer interactions, namely through the Marketing, Sales, and Customer Service functions. Despite the hype surrounding the automation of the service and support functions, the overarching strategy of the organization is to make sure that the perceptions that were intended (via value proposition communication, product positioning, and marketing messages) actually match the perceptions of the target audience. If there are gaps between the perceptions you originally intended customers to have and their actual perceptions, then customer satisfaction will be affected. The more their satisfaction is negatively affected, the greater the likelihood that customers won't remain loyal, become repeat customers, nor will they recommend your products and services to others.

Service and support are delivered through several customer touchpoints. It is at these points where metrics can be established and perceptions measured. Further, it is usually at these points where the product or service is actually delivered. These touchpoints can include call centers, Web sites, retail stores, customer service desks, sales person visits, service technician visits, help desks, and billing departments.

In an ideal world, customers should have hassle-free service, be able to easily communicate with the company in a timely manner, have no hold times on the phone, or be able to interact with the company over the Internet and intuitively secure whatever product or service they wish. Unfortunately, in the modern economy, cost cutting and economic pressures often result in minimal staffing and poorly designed programs for supporting customers, thereby negatively affecting the overall customer experience. The best market research and the best technologies, yielding the perfectly designed product or service, all mean little if customers cannot contact your company in a manner in which they choose and experience an interaction that is satisfying.

For companies considering the automation of CRM functions, it is imperative that the processes be fully understood. All interrelationships, work flows, and dependencies should be established and diagrammed so that each area can be visualized and understood. One way of establishing the interrelationships is to break them into business operating scenarios or key business flows. The workflows should include whatever inputs, activities, and outputs are required as work moves through the "system." It cannot be emphasized enough that people should actually be carrying out the work for each of these scenarios in order to better understand both the efficiencies and inefficiencies. Once the areas for improvement are identified, the enterprise can be ready to entertain the automation of those functions.

A key concern for successful CRM initiatives is accessibility to timely data. Most companies have data in disparate databases due to the evolution of data storage needs, reorganizations, mergers, and other events. In order for CRM initiatives to be successful, it is important to understand where the needed data repositories rest, what systems are dependent on the data, and how often the data are refreshed.

Another critical concern is defining the kind of information that is required, as in the case of customer sales information. The sales organization needs such data to understand buying patterns and opportunity targets. The same sales data are needed by the customer service function in order to establish call queue prioritizations and customer treatment. And sales data are needed by marketing teams as they seek to establish promotional budgets for different market targets. Sales automation systems are useful for collecting such data due to the hierarchy of contacts, leads, prospects, and opportunities and the ability to perform roll-ups and drill-downs to enable views by executives and managers within the sales function. Other systems will be needed to allow customer service teams to have up-to-date customer names and contact information to achieve a more personalized approach in their interactions with customers. Marketing teams also need up-to-date customer data in order to understand the buying habits, purchasing decisions, and other information to enable reevaluation of segment characteristics.

Overall, CRM initiatives require a comprehensive, complete data storage component where all business data are stored and updated, so that the dependent functions can have timely access to accurate, up-to-date information on which to make business decisions. The customer service and support functions should be closely melded within the body of the cross-functional team. When it comes to balancing investments, it is wise to make sure that funds are spread uniformly along the value chain so that customers don't end up with the short end of the stick. This will enable the company to have the best chance of optimizing the value of its embedded customer base.

33.3.3 Dimension 3: Keeping Score (of Product Performance and Financials)

Financial performance reporting and analysis represent the underlying foundation for any business. As owner of a product "minibusiness," the product manager relies on input from the Finance and Marketing representatives on the cross-functional team to provide relevant, timely information based upon standard corporate formats and agreed-upon metrics for measuring product performance. Some of those metrics may relate to revenue, number of units sold, market share, gross margin, expense line items, product return rate, and profit. Customer profitability and customer lifetime value are key focal points (especially to Service and Support teams).

When a new product or derivative product is created, a business case should be completed. The business case addresses the strategic, market, technical, and economic feasibility for the product. Often, the business case and legacy documentation are "lost" in later years as people change jobs. It is recommended that business cases be kept in a repository (e.g., the product master plan). These cases should serve as a basis for retrospective (6–12 months postlaunch) and ongoing monthly reviews by the life-cycle managers and their teams as they attempt to ensure the product lives up to its originally projected financial returns.

One of the recommended methods for conducting the monthly reviews is to use a *product scorecard*. A product scorecard is a vehicle used to make com-

A "product scorecard" is an invaluable instrument in monthly reviews.

parisons among the original business case for the product (and associated forecast data), the in-year business plan, monthly results, and year-to-date results. Using this approach affords the product manager and the cross-functional team visibility into each of the line items so that they can assess how each of those items is affecting the business. It allows the team to identify and track trends, abnormal business situations, and out-of-boundary conditions. By seeing appropriate levels of granularity, the team is able to focus on areas of concern so that changes can be made to the marketing mix or other elements of the product. A typical product scorecard for a hardware product might be formatted as shown in Table 33.1.

Periodic retrospective reviews and annual reviews should be held less frequently than monthly scorecard sessions, but with more in-depth scrutiny. The retrospective review should be done 6–18 months after the product launch (Cooper, 1993). It serves to assess the accuracy and completeness of the original business case, as well as to provide a learning experience for future cases. In addition, perhaps one or two times per year the core team should review the original business case assumptions as well as assumptions being used to develop ongoing period (1-year, 1-3 year, etc.) business plans that surface new trends or competitive activity. This review also helps product teams learn how to improve other business cases, which will be done for future projects.

A particularly critical area of financial management during LCM, especially on hardware products, is cost reduction programs. Even on services and software products, expense and operating cost reductions can be pursued to continue to improve or maintain margins over the postlaunch life cycle. When the original market-based product pricing is done, full life-cycle target costs should be identified, and these should be identified with the primary objective of ensuring that the product will yield the desired product profit margins over time. In order to achieve the returns projected in the product business case, it will usually be necessary to implement a *series* of cost reduction programs throughout the postlaunch life cycle, rather than a single cost reduction effort. In most cases, the life-cycle product managers and their teams are held accountable for ensuring that these programs are created and implemented. Successful implementation of these cost reduction programs is again usually more effective and efficient if all the members of a cross-functional team are collectively pursuing them instead of a single business function such as product management or finance attempting to push the other organizations.

TABLE 33.1 TYPICAL PRODUCT SCORECARD.

Original Business Case	In-Year Business Plan	YTD Plan	YTD Actual	YTD Variance	Line Item	Month Plan	Month Actual	Month Variance
					Units			
					Price/Unit			
					TOTAL REVENUE			
					Cost of Goods Sold			
					• Material			
					• Labor			
					• Overhead			
					TOTAL COGS			
					GROSS MARGIN			
					GM %			
					DIRECT EXPENSES			
					• Marketing			
					• Sales			
					• Cust Svce			
					• Product Dev			
					• Dep'n/Amortization			
					TOTAL DIR EXPS			
					Indir/Allocated Exps			
					TOTAL EXPENSES			
					NET OPER PROFIT			

33.3.4. Dimension 4: Overseeing Operations

Operational oversight concerns the actual running of the business. It includes business functions such as human resource management, legal and regulatory, intellectual property management, and supply chain management. One of the most important areas of operational oversight is understanding and interpreting the plans and activities occurring across the supply chain. Supply chain management is the oversight of materials, information, and finances as they move in a process from raw materials all the way to the eventual consumer (see Chapter 31). It involves coordinating and integrating these flows within and among companies. The goal of an effective supply chain management system is to minimize inventory and other costs, maximize product availability, and optimize efficiency in product movement from beginning to end of the chain. Supply chain decisions are usually made over a variety of time horizons— short-, medium-, and long-term. Short-term activities and decisions constitute the day-to-day operations of the business. Medium- and long-term supply chain decisions are usually more strategic in nature, such as setting up a new factory. During the product life cycle, product managers should have a fairly strong understanding of the manner in which the supply chain operates, including manufacturing and production processes, methods, and capacities; plant locations; warehousing capabilities; inventory methods and inventory level guidelines; logistics and transportation methods (inbound and outbound); and quality control metrics and measurements.

33.4 Introducing Enhancements and Derivatives

Leading-edge companies create product enhancements and line extensions on specific product platforms in order to maintain a competitive position and extend the product life cycle (Burgelman, Maidique, and Wheelright, 2001). Key decisions include agreeing on product requirements, timing, and value proposition of the proposed product improvement. Some best practices include:

- Continually monitoring customer needs throughout the product life cycle and determining if new customer needs or gaps can be addressed through current product line extensions as opposed to a full new product development initiative
- Using customer service call centers, the Sales organization, and a CRM system as a prime drivers and information sources for product improvements
- Using a "fast-track" product development process to reduce time-to-market in situations where the level of risk is low

Roles and responsibilities for product improvement initiatives during LCM are ideally shared across several functions. For example, Marketing would initiate any additional, needed market/customer research, gather and summarize customer and product performance information, and prepare a mini-business-plan. Engineering would provide design alternatives, cost estimates, and development resources to complete the improvement. The product manager would ensure that all inputs are secured and coordinate the overall product improvement project.

In short, a company's product improvement effort should be an integral part of life-cycle management. Two areas to watch out for are one, waiting too long before initiating product improvements, and two, getting little or no added value from improvement initiatives. In the first area, early warning systems can be used to detect volume erosion and/or detect potential competitive initiatives. In the second area, ongoing customer contact through sales and customer support should be maintained and relied on to identify and prioritize product requirements.

To achieve successful product improvements as part of a programmatic LCM program, the following steps are prescribed.

First, review and update the market segment portfolio and market and technology trend analysis developed during the product-planning phase to verify your company's competitive position in the market. Gather and summarize customer and product feedback collected from current product returns, sales, and customer service. From this information, identify key customer needs or gaps. Prioritize key unmet needs and map to any required new product features/attributes. Review the product line plan to identify current initiatives that might already be in process to address unmet needs.

Next, develop a working prototype or preliminary design plan for the product improvement. Estimate the scope, time, cost, and level of risk. Create a mini-business-plan of record with recommendations to address unmet customer needs. Determine whether "fast-track" or full phase reviews are appropriate. Fast-track projects such as product enhancements are lower risk. If a fast-track approach is recommended, get buy-in from gate reviewers that the project can continue under a fast-track review process.

Once a path forward is agreed to, create a mini-business-plan of record that describes the project scope, schedule, and resource requirements, and submit to a "fast-track" or full-phase review team as appropriate. Gatekeepers agree to accept, reject, or ask for additional information to support the project. The findings and recommendations are documented and sent to the project team. If the business case is accepted, funding should follow. Once funding commitments are secured, the project can be undertaken and the enhancement or derivative product can eventually be introduced to augment the original product.

33.5 Providing Input into the Planning for the Next New Product to Which Existing Customers Are Likely to be Migrated

One of the major responsibilities of life-cycle product managers and their teams is inputting information to other individuals or teams who may be working on new, replacement, or migration products. The life-cycle product manager should be in the best position to understand target markets and customers using his/her product. Therefore, this manager has the most knowledge about market and customer needs for planning or design phase products that are targeted at replacing products currently in life-cycle management phases. In most cases standard market and product requirement assessments can be significantly shortened by utilizing the information and expertise available from the current life-cycle product manager.

33.6 The Last LCM Step: Executing Product Discontinuation and Final Exit

Almost all products naturally will evolve to a decline phase of their life cycle unless some overt, proactive event or action precipitates an early withdrawal from the market. Similar to the business or market "triggers" that usually define when a product moves from one phase to another on

> *The product exit is simply an implementation of a plan that should have been documented much earlier in the product life cycle.*

the life-cycle curve (e.g., from growth into maturity), many companies and teams define key "trigger events," which serve to signal that a product is in the decline stage and worthy of being considered for a near-term exit from the marketplace. If these trigger events begin to occur, the product team meets to decide if a product exit is called for, and begins doing the necessary planning for final product withdrawal. Some companies actually make the creation of a draft exit plan a requirement for approving a product development project, before the final business case for development funding has been completed (the go/no go decision). While this may seem early, the rationale is to ensure that everyone is aligned on the long-term product plan from the very beginning, including an estimate of how long the product should exist for active selling, and how the product will eventually be taken out of service (see Chapter 34).

Key steps for a typical product exit include many of the following:

- Identification of existing major customers, including any significant remaining contract liabilities
- Preparation of an announcement package, internal and/or external as required, designed to allow a graceful customer migration to replacement products or services
- Identification of all close-down activities and systems, and execution of the required close-down processes and procedures on those systems
- Discontinuation of all active marketing and sales activities
- Disposition of all inventories, product liabilities, and intellectual property as appropriate depending on the type of product and business conditions

33.7 Roadblocks to Achieving Best-in-Class LCM

There are numerous reasons why companies sometimes don't focus as much attention as they should on postlaunch life-cycle management, and thus, don't become effective in optimizing product financial returns once the product launch has occurred. One of the most obvious is in the people area. Compared to the more highly visible, glamorous area of new product development (NPD), LCM seems mundane to many people, often regarded as a maintenance function, and offering little chance of recognition or career advancement. Also, in many companies this impression is reinforced by upper-level managers through the manner in which they mete out monetary and nonmonetary incentives and rewards to people in NPD versus LCM job assignments. Even if these external influences are ignored, the basic dynamics of the LCM job, with its day-to-day problems, constant interruptions, and financial results pressures often tends to provide a less than acceptable balance of positive versus negative personal job satisfaction and feedback for many people. To make matters worse, the opportunities for learning NPD best practices far outweigh those for LCM, because industry conferences, training, and most available written material tend to be focused primarily on NPD topical areas. Comparatively speaking, there are far fewer resources available in the area of product life-cycle management because the issues which must be addressed in this area often tend to be variable based on the type of industry and products being managed. And because this disparity of source material and resources has existed for years, the number of experienced workers and coaches in LCM continues to trail those with NPD skills and experience. To close the learning gap, companies must first recognize the need for and importance of this business function, better understand its multiple dimensions, and seek to upgrade their skills and experience in this key area.

33.8 Summary

Product life-cycle management is a multifaceted discipline, one that many companies tend to underemphasize and underfund. New product planning and product development are usually highly favored as assignments over product life-cycle management responsibilities, although the latter is key to providing a steady stream of revenue to fund new product initiatives. It is critical that businesses assign knowledgeable, experienced resources to the postlaunch phase of product management in order to achieve optimal returns from both new product introductions and product life-cycle management activities. It is equally critical that companies define the roles, accountabilities, and procedures for doing top-notch life-cycle management in their particular business or industry. This will ensure that the people assigned to manage their LCM products have the necessary tools, knowledge, skills, and experience to do their jobs.

References

Burgelman, R. A., Maidique, M. A., Wheelwright, S. C., *Strategic Management of Technology and Innovation*, 3rd ed. New York, NY: McGraw-Hill/Irwin, 886–891, 2001.

Cooper, R. G, *Winning at New Products*, 2nd ed. Reading, MA: Addison-Wesley Publishing, 117–118, 1993.

Hiebing, R. G., Jr. and Cooper, S., *How to Write a Successful Marketing Plan*. Lincolnwood, IL: NTC Business Books, Intro page xxx, 1997.

Katzenbach, J. and Smith, D., *The Wisdom of Teams*. New York, NY: HarperBusiness, 11–26, 1994.

Kotler, P., *Marketing Management: Analysis, Planning, Implementation, and Control*. Upper Saddle River, NJ: Prentice Hall, 1997.

McCarthy, E. J., *Basic Marketing: A Managerial Approach*. 12th ed. Homewood, IL: Irwin, 1996.

Onkvisit, S. and Shaw, J., *Product Life Cycles and Product Management*. Westport, CT: Greenwood Press, 131–132, 1989.

Whiteley, R. C., *The Customer Driven Company*. Reading, MA: Addison-Wesley Publishing, 50–61 1991.

Bill Ausura is president of Product & Portfolio Professionals, a New Jersey-based consulting firm specializing in product and portfolio management. A PDMA New Product Development Professional, he is currently president of

PDMA's NY/NJ local chapter. His last corporate position was Director of Product Management and Product Marketing Practices at Lucent Technologies. Bill spent 35 years in various Marketing, Sales, and Operations positions, most of it in hardware product development and management of computer and telecommunications equipment at Lucent Technologies, AT&T, and other companies. He currently advises, develops courses, and teaches for Sequent Learning Networks (www.sequentlearning.com), a company specializing in professional education of product and portfolio managers and their teams.

Bob Gill is managing partner at InterMatrixPDP Inc., a Boston-based management consulting company providing new product development and product life-cycle management (PLM) solutions. Bob sits on the PDMA Executive Committee as Immediate Past President and is a regular contributor to national and international forums, speaking on a wide range of NPD and PLM issues. He coauthored the chapter on product strategy in the *PDMA Handbook*, published in 1996. Bob has a B.S. in engineering from Northeastern University and an M.B.A. from Suffolk University. He lives in Newton with his wife Virginia and sons Jason, David, and Stephen

Steven Haines is the founder and president of Sequent Learning Networks, a company focused on product management and marketing training. He has more than 20 years of product management and marketing experience across a broad range of industries. Steven's last corporate position was Sr. Director of Product Management at Oracle, and prior to that, he spent 12 years in product management at AT&T, improving the profitability and market stature of several advanced technology products. At AT&T, he participated in the benchmarking of product management and development practices. Steven was an adjunct professor of Marketing and Management at Rutgers University for 12 years. He is director of chapter finance for PDMA, and VP-Finance & Marketing in the New York PDMA chapter. Steven holds a B.S. in management from SUNY Binghamton, and an M.B.A. in corporate finance from Pace University.

CHAPTER THIRTY-FOUR

PRODUCT OBSOLESCENCE AND DISCONTINUATION

Elizabeth Jackson

34.1 Introduction

The last phase in the life cycle of a product line is its discontinuance. Little has been written in product management articles and textbooks about this important phase of product life. This chapter will guide you through a proven process to obsolete an active product line with minimal negative impact on customers and the company.

At first glance, it seems that the discontinuance or obsolescence of a product line is simply a matter of ceasing to produce it any more. On the face of the results, that is what really happens. However, there are many ramifications to both the internal and external organizations affected by the product obsolescence. This critical stage of product life-cycle planning is frequently overlooked, leaving customers stranded and unable to plan for future purchases. A lack of communication about discontinued products can and will turn customers away in future buying decisions (Ausura,2003). Internal systems will also be clogged with unused and unnecessary raw materials, component parts, and documentation.

The three objectives for this chapter are to help the reader:

- Evaluate which products are likely candidates for obsolescence
- Understand the scope of the potential impact of product obsolescence to customers and to the company

- Implement an obsolescence event by providing a step-by-step process to successfully obsolete an active product line.

34.2 Ownership of the Obsolescence Process

As overall managers of a product family, product managers own the analysis and decision of whether to discontinue a product line. Armed with knowledge about the product, the market, and the annual con-

> *The product manager is in a unique position to manage a product obsolescence event.*

tribution to revenue, the product manager is in a unique position to bring the facts concerning a product line to the organization, to propose the obsolescence of a product family, and to manage the obsolescence event. The product manager will evaluate a number of factors to determine which products are candidates for obsolescence.

34.3 Evaluating Products for Obsolescence

To evaluate products for obsolescence, various questions should be asked that include: Does the Product sell? Is the product out-of-date? What about competition?

34.3.1 Does the Product Sell?

The most fundamental reason to discontinue a product is lack of sales. If no one is buying a product, it usually follows that a company should stop producing it and no longer offer it for sale. This lack of in-

> *The most fundamental reason to discontinue a product is lack of sales.*

terest may be due to a number of factors, but only a few reasons to continue production of a low-performing product are valid and warrant consuming the resources required to maintain production capability and inventory, and to support sales. Don't be lured into the trap of inaction by pandering to sentiment and emotion that because "we've always made them" production can't ever stop. According to the profile of its products, each company should establish guidelines for acceptable levels of annual sales dollars and units sold. These parameters will help determine which products are candidates for obsolescence.

These obsolescence guidelines must be tempered with industry, product, and customer knowledge. If a fixed value of sales dollars alone were to be the criteria for obsolescence, the purveyors of low-priced items would frequently plan the discontinuance of products whose revenue is, in fact, substantial overall for that industry. Likewise, the unit sale count among industry groups cannot logically be measured against one another. Comparing the unit sales of nuts and bolts with automobiles will not yield any usable data.

One of the best places to obtain these sales data is from a company database that tracks both dollar and units sold. If a product to be discontinued has a direct replacement, it is advantageous to have the sales history of the older models recognized as the historical data for the newer products, providing continuity for product future portfolio decisions.

34.3.2 Is the Product Profitable?

A thorough look into the profitability of a product line will also help the product manager decide whether to keep a line active. Margin calculations derived from the annual sales dollars and the cost of goods sold will contribute valuable insight as to whether the line is a candidate for discontinuance. A simple margin calculation, commonly called SMAGS (sales margin as a percentage of gross sales), can be calculated by subtracting the product cost from the sell price (actual dollars the company received from the sale), divided by the sell price (× 100 to yield the margin percentage). As with sales dollars and units sold, the acceptable margin level will vary by industry.

$$\left(\frac{\text{Sell price} - \text{cost}}{\text{Sell price}} \right) \times 100$$

SMAGS Calculation

Some products with low margins are destined to be permanent members of the product line. The product may give the | *Evaluate product profitability.* |

company a competitive advantage; perhaps the company owns the market for that model. No one else sells one quite like it. Maintaining those lower-margin models in the line rounds out the product portfolio so that customers can satisfy their requirements with one brand label.

If a decision is made to maintain a low-margin product, the best course of action is to repair the cost structure of the product. Bring a cross-functional team together to find a way to lower the cost of the goods through detailed analyses of the production, component part, and distribution costs. Develop and implement a tactical plan to bring the margin into the acceptable range for the company. A value analysis exercise will help identify customer-focused opportunities to reduce product cost (Severson, 2002).

34.3.3 Is the Product out of Date?

Reviewing the current technology applicable to a product group will also assist the product manager in deciding whether to initiate an obsolescence program (Lehmann and Winer, 2002). Computer manufacturers and computer accessory companies do not support all revisions of software and hardware products. A good case in point is the $5^1/_4$-inch floppy disk technology. Since the introduction and acceptance of $3^1/_2$ inch disks and CD-ROMs, the larger media have disappeared from the market. The hardware to support the use of the $5^1/_4$-inch disks as well as the manufacturing equipment to produce them was discontinued.

A different solution for a product's intended use may also drive obsolescence. A new invention can take the place of any product line. Remember the lessons learned in the home video market. The first home video format was the Betamax tape. Betamax was soon replaced by VHS tapes, and now DVDs are taking over the market. Betamax players have been discontinued; VHS is less common and will be rendered obsolete by DVDs some time in the future.

34.3.4 Planned Obsolescence

Another reason to plan for the obsolescence of a product is the internal development of its successor. It is especially important in high-tech companies to understand where a product lies in its life cycle. If the cycle is in decline, and the product is one of the company's primary

> *The development of a product's successor is often a reason to plan for obsolescence.*

platforms, the development of its successor is critical to ensure the continued success of the organization (McGrath, 2001). When a corporation decides to invest in the next generation of a product line, the project justification and development should include a plan for the disposition of the current version. Development of the new revision may be provoked by any of the variables discussed here, but if the existing product is not discontinued, there will be competing lines from the same company.

Good management of planned product obsolescence can be observed in the chemical industry. When product lines are to be replaced by a new series of similar chemicals with enhanced performance or lower cost (and correspondingly higher margins), a product obsolescence program is planned. The product manager and a cross-functional team gather to manage the obsolescence program. One manufacturer produces several years' worth of inventory before the old product is rendered obsolete and production is shut down. This extensive product overlap gives the manufacturer a long time to manage the internal and external transition to the new chemical series.

34.3.5 What about the Competition?

A thorough analysis of similar product lines offered by competitors will aid in the decision of whether to discontinue a product. If the analysis reveals that no competitor is selling a similar product and other company criteria for obsolescence are met, it may be prudent to suspend production and sales. There may be, however, a scenario in which no competitor offers a similar product and a company enjoys 100 percent market share because the product is superior or the market is too small to support competitive models. Intimate market knowledge will help make such determinations. If competitors sell a similar product, even though company criteria may indicate possible obsolescence, careful consideration must be given when deciding the fate of product. It is frequently desirable to maintain the perception of offering a full range of products, providing the buying public with one-stop shopping.

Maintaining competitive brands sold by the same company may be a corporate philosophy. Food manufacturers often foster brand loyalty at a high level. Their cereal market consists of numerous products under the one banner and the variety of cereals under that name keeps the consumer loyal at the parent brand level.

Gathering competitive information is an important aspect of a product manager's responsibility. In a business-to-business environment, good sources of industrial intelligence include the examination of the actual product or product catalogs, trade shows, suppliers, plant tours, reverse engineering, browsing Internet sites, and interviews with outside salespeople. The importance of sales contacts should not be minimized. Salespeople are the link to end customers; they're the people who really know what is going on in the marketplace (Lehmann and Winer, 1997). Consumer product research can be accomplished by comparison shopping. Go to where the products are sold and assess products for sale. In either case, at the start of the survey, develop a list of attributes to be compared and questions to be answered. This will ensure that each product will be evaluated by the same criteria. The survey should encompass information about specific features (colors, size range, material, accessories), price, availability, procurement method, manufacturing location, quality, and workmanship.

34.3.6 Some Final Considerations

As products are identified for possible obsolescence, there are other issues that must be considered before a final decision is made. Maybe it's just good business to continue to provide these products. If the primary consumer is a customer of much influence and importance in your customer base and wants you to continue to offer a product for sale, carefully evaluate the threat of losing the additional business from that customer.

Another consideration is continued sales after obsolescence. Decide in advance whether to sell the product as a custom order for a specified period. A never-ending cycle of postobsolescence production will emerge if a clear policy is not communicated. If a product needs postobsolescence component availability, develop a plan now. The magnitude of this extended sales plan can alter the obsolescence path.

34.4 Product Support After Obsolescence

Some creative solutions to after-obsolescence product support are available. When a manufacturer of small appliances chose to not support parts and other service for its older models of their standard home meat slicer, customers needing replacement parts for models more than 20 years old were directed to return the worn model at their own expense with a description of the repair problem. The company, in return, sent a new slicer to the customer. It was more cost-effective to send a new machine than to support 20 years of component part revisions.

Automobile manufacturers sell replacement and repair parts for seven years after the model year, enabling consumers to maintain their cars and trucks with factory-built components. After that period, many after-market manufacturers produce components for automotive maintenance. An entire industry has grown around this need to supply after-market parts for automobiles. The sales volume and complexity of motor vehicles makes this an attractive industry, but not every product can be supported so extensively.

There are many creative solutions to after-obsolescence product support.

34.5 Impact on Internal Systems and External Customers

After the decision to obsolete a product is made, the real work begins. The success of an obsolescence plan depends largely on careful timing. The amount of advance

> *Careful timing is critical to a successful obsolescence plan.*

notice provided is purely an individual industry and company decision. It is common knowledge that as the automobile industry rolls out a new model year of cars and trucks, there is no new production of the previous model year. The vehicles available are limited to the stock on hand. In other industries, it may be prudent to provide advance notice of obsolescence, especially component parts used in larger, complex systems. Using the automotive example again, system integrators providing automotive manufacturing lines will use controls and components as specified by the end-user. Up to one year may lapse between specification and the start of production. Ample notice of any planned obsolescence is critical to maintaining a specification position for these manufacturing systems.

There are many internal manufacturing, procurement, and communications systems and documents that support active products. These processes and documents must be identified. Provisions and schedules for changing and deleting them should be developed. The detailed obsolescence process that follows addresses these individual components of production, procurement, distribution support, and advertising. The scope of the internal obsolescence effort will become evident as the company navigates through a product obsolescence event.

34.6 The Obsolescence Process and Responsibilities

Figure 34.1 shows the timeline used for the obsolescence of an active product line at a durable goods manufacturing company. The product line was to be made obsolete because a new generation of a similar

> *Consider both external and internal interests when developing the obsolescence timeline.*

product with features more closely matching the competition had been introduced four years prior. Most customers had converted to the new models. The product manager decided to consolidate sales into the new product line, reduce the SKU count, and eliminate some unique components and tooling. The termination of production of this line also aided the manufacturing process by removing the need for a separate line to produce these products.

FIGURE 34.1 PRODUCT OBSOLESCENCE TIMELINE.

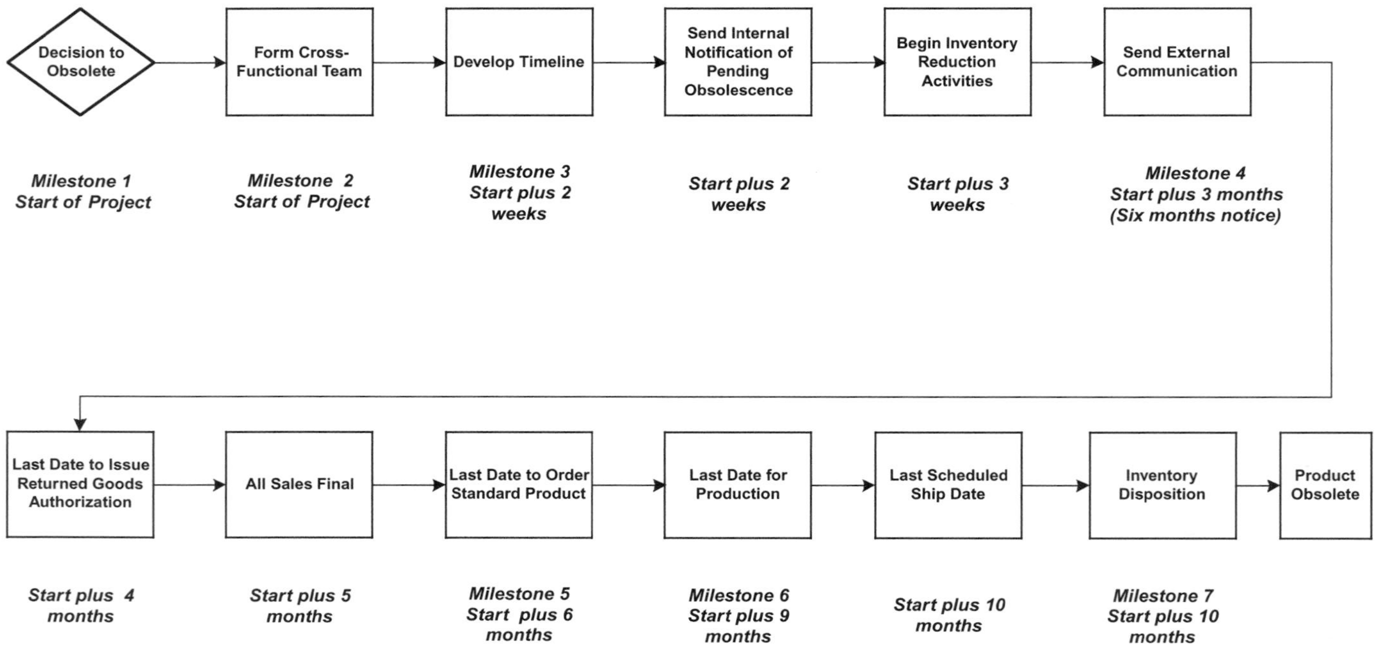

The *first* milestone in the timeline is the product manager's decision to obsolete a product line. The *second* is the formation of a cross-functional team to help manage the process. This team should include the product manager and representatives from Finance, Master and Manufacturing Planning, Logistics, Purchasing, Information Technology, Sales Support, and Communications. The product manager is charged with introducing the program including the rationale for obsolescence, the provisional timetable, the product return policy, and the policy regarding future custom orders.

The *third* milestone is the development of the working timeline. The team is charged with gathering the information necessary to finalize the timetable. Early communication of this timeline is critical. Give your customers and internal systems as much advance notice as possible. Many variables will have an impact the on the timetable:

- Future commitments to customers
- Seasonal variations in customer buying patterns
- Amount of raw material and component parts on hand
- Raw material and component parts committed from suppliers
- Value of finished goods inventory on hand
- Scheduled publication date of printed materials
- Other team commitments that may affect their availability to implement the process

When the team has gathered the pertinent data that may influence the project timeline, the product manager executes milestone number *four*, release of the notification of pending obsolescence. This important communication is distributed internally and externally and includes:

- Product description
- Key dates of the program
- Complete list of the models affected
- Detailed return policy
- Cross-referenced list to suggested replacement models
- Policy regarding future custom orders
- Name and address of a company contact

At milestone *five* no more orders are accepted for standard product. Milestone *six* is the scheduled end of production. The final milestone, number *seven*, is the disposition of any remaining inventory.

Numerous activities must be scheduled to coordinate the end of production with the obsolescence date communicated to customers. Table 34.1 lists the

TABLE 34.1 PRODUCT OBSOLESCENCE ACTIVITIES.

Activity	Background Activities
Broadcast internal notice of future obsolescence	• Provide a product cross-reference list so that internal sales can begin to transition customers to the recommended substitute product.
Minimize stock levels	• Lower warehouse safety stock levels. • Lower purchased component order quantities. • Schedule minimal production quantities. • Review orders with future release dates to schedule production. • Begin to balance finished goods with associated component parts to reduce potential inventory liability. • Consolidate warehouse storage locations. • Plan the master forecast to reflect the obsolescence date.
Send notice of future obsolescence to customers	• Form a team to manage the obsolescence activities.
Begin enforcing of last date to issue Returned Goods Authorization (RGA)	• Change MRP system to deny further authorizations of returns.
Communicate to customers that all future sales are final and no returns are permitted	• Add text to sales orders notifying customers that all sales will be final after the scheduled date. • Add obsolescence notification text to purchase orders. • Only add inventory to satisfy firm orders. • Deny order cancelations or negotiate cancelation fees. • Communicate how to dispose of inventory at vendor and other sales locations.
Block entry of sales orders after last date to order	• Remove models from visibility on electronic data interface (EDI) systems. • Remove references from Web site, and catalog and price list databases. • Notify second-party sellers to remove models from catalogs, advertising, and in-store displays. • Notify distributors and vendors to remove models from ordering databases.
Cease production of standard models	• Remove safety stock requirements. • Begin to shut down the production line.
Dispose of remaining inventory	• Eliminate finished goods, unique raw materials and component parts, and consigned inventories. • Notify internal departments of disposition.
Begin follow-up internal activities	• Remove documentation from transactional databases. • Dispose of tools, dies, fixtures, and unique manufacturing equipment. • Archive product data. • Notify suppliers to return documentation and tools. • Review for discontinuance any fees connected with product such as patents, certifications. or other contracts.

sequence of activities that the manufacturing company used to successfully obsolete the active product line.

34.7 Summary

Product obsolescence, the final stage of the product life cycle, is key to maintaining a profitable product offering. The product manager analyzes the status of sales, margins, and the competitive position of products before deciding to obsolete a line. The activities required to facilitate a product discontinuance will vary by organization according to the processes in place for planning and scheduling production, procurement, communication, and advertising. Careful attention to all these facets of the organizational structure will ensure continued customer satisfaction and minimal internal disruption. Early and continued involvement of the cross-functional obsolescence team brings together the necessary expertise to gather complete process and system information and to address the changes required for obsolescence. Completing the follow-up activities to rid active files and databases of obsolete product information will minimize data clutter.

By developing an integrated, comprehensive life-cycle plan that includes a structured obsolescence procedure for the company's product portfolio, product managers can ensure the continued health of the company's total product offering. Managing product obsolescence in addition to the introduction and life-span activities of the products is critical to the preservation of company profitability and market position.

References

Ausura, Bill, "Recapturing 'true' life-cycle portfolio management; The path to more successful product development," *Visions*, 27: 8–11 (April 2003).

Lehmann, Donald R. and Winer, Russell S., *Analysis for Marketing Planning*, 5th ed., New York: McGraw-Hill 244–247, 2002.

Lehmann, Donald R. and Winer, Russell S., *Product Management*, New York: Times Mirror Higher Education Group, 99–137, 1997.

McGrath, Michael E., *Product Strategy for High Technology Companies*, 2nd ed., New York: McGraw-Hill 78–83, 2001.

Severson, Roger J., Cost Improvement Using Value Analysis Seminar, 2002.

Elizabeth Jackson is a product manager at Hoffman Enclosures, Inc., an Anoka, Minnesota-based manufacturer of electrical and electronic enclosures.

She is a 20+-year manufacturing professional and has held other positions that include manufacturing engineer, technical training specialist, and design engineer. Ms. Jackson has more than ten years of experience in new product development, including the justification, design, launch, and support of numerous successful product lines. She holds a B.S. from Cardinal Stritch University and has been a member of PDMA since 2001.

PART SIX

PDMA RESEARCH ON NPD

No great thing is created suddenly, any more than a bunch of grapes or a fig. If you tell me that you desire a fig, I answer that there must be time. Let it first blossom, then bear fruit, then ripen.

EPICTETUS, ROMAN PHILOSOPHER, 106 AD

Sixteen years ago the PDMA planted two new product development research programs. These programs blossomed into what today are the Outstanding Corporate Innovator (OCI) award and the Comparative Performance Assessment Study (CPAS).

Since 1988, the OCI committee has selected over 29 firms as OCI award winners. Summarized in Chapter 35 are the lessons learned from these firms, which must meet the following four OCI standards:

1. A continued record of success in launching new products over a five-year period.
2. Significant company growth delivered by its successful new products.
3. A sound new product development process in place.
4. Unique and innovative features of their approach to product development that make it suitable for that firm.

The Comparative Performance Assessment Study began its existence as a best practices study first completed in 1990 and then repeated in 1995. The results of the two studies provided the basis for over a 100 briefings at conferences worldwide. The best practice research was moved to the PDMA Foundation in 2003 and repositioned as a comparative performance study. Chapter 36 reports on the analysis of first results from the 2003 CPAS.

CHAPTER THIRTY-FIVE

LESSONS LEARNED FROM OUTSTANDING CORPORATE INNOVATORS

Outstanding Corporate Innovator Award Committee:
Douglas Boike, Thomas Hustad, Stan Jankowski, Sally Evans
Kay, John Moran, Albert Page, Norman Parker

35.1 Introduction

Lessons learned from leading practitioner companies are often a very effec-tive technique for companies facing challenges in launching or improving their new product development performance. The PDMA's Outstanding Cor-porate Innovator award companies can provide a valuable set of such learning experiences for companies. The objective of this chapter will be to survey the learning from sixteen years of Outstanding Corporate Innovator award winners of the PDMA. This award has been in place since 1988 and annually recognizes select companies on the basis of their innovation success in new product de-velopment. Each year's award winners have shared their lessons learned in presentations at the PDMA Annual International Conference. This chapter will summarize the key lessons learned and provide real-life case studies of these leading companies.

35.2 Introduction to the OCI Award

The PDMA initiated its Outstanding Corporate Innovator (OCI) Award in 1988. Over sixteen years, twenty-nine companies have been selected as award winners. They are shown in Table 35.1. Together, they represent a group of

TABLE 35.1 PAST OCI AWARD WINNERS.

Year	Award Winner
1988	Merck & Co.
1989	Hewlett-Packard
1990	Advanced Cardiovascular Systems Division of Eli Lilly (now Guidant)
	Harris Corporation, Broadcast Division
	New PIG Corporation
1991	Safety-Kleen Corporation
1992	Keithley Instruments
	Marriott Corporation—Lodging Group
1993	Apple Computer
	Nabisco
	NordicTrack
1994	Bausch & Lomb Eyewear Division
	Chrysler Corporation
	Welch Allyn
1995	Fluke Corporation
	Pepsi-Cola Company
	Senco Products, Inc.
1996	Kodak
1997	Herman Miller
	3Com (US Robotics)
1998	Cincinnati Machine Tool
1999	Maytag Corporation
2000	EXFO Electro-Optical Engineering Inc.
	Rockwell Collins
2001	Hunter Douglas Window Fashions Division
2002	Teknion
	BMW Group
2003	Harley Davidson
	Dow Chemical

outstandingly successful organizations, chosen because they have met the four criteria for an OCI award winner:

- A sustained record of success in launching new products over a five-year period
- Significant company growth delivered by its successful new products
- A sound new product development process
- Unique and innovative features to their approach to product development that make it particularly suitable for the organization

Each year the OCI winners are presented their awards at a special session at PDMA's annual International Conference. Part of the award ceremony includes a keynote presentation by the winning companies, which highlights their practices, processes, lessons learned, and the impact their product development efforts have had on their businesses.

35.3 Similarities and Differences in Practices of Award Winners

35.3.1 Summary of Common Practices/Beliefs among Award Winners

In a retrospective look at these past OCI award winners, it first appears that each of the companies is distinctly different from each other. Yet after some reflection, there are a number of important characteristics and similarities across the set. All of the winners had in place processes, systems, and resources that reflected the following notable best practices:

- A well-defined product development process unique to their market and technology environment (see Chapters 4 and 5)
- A strong commitment to cross-functional teams as the fundamental organizational construct for executing new product development (see Chapters 9 and 10)
- Strong voice of the customer input (see Chapters 13, 14, 15, 16, 17, and 18)
- A robust process at the front-end to drive innovation in their product portfolio (see Chapters 3, 19, and 20)
- A strong linkage of new product development to the company's corporate strategy, therefore, ensuring top management commitment (see Chapter 2)

While a clear set of common practices can be defined across the population of past award winners, it also appears the implementation detail of these common practices varied across the group, driven by their market, technology, and organizational environments. In many cases, the chosen solutions are quite distinctive and provided the greatest learning for the new product development community.

35.3.2 Well-Defined Product Development Processes

In reflecting upon past winners, in every case the winning company has been able to present a well-defined product development process reflecting the following attributes:

- Clear charter and strategy alignment for new product development
- Multiple phase gates
- Clear definition of milestones and phase activities
- Expected timelines for different class and/or complexity programs
- Ongoing monitoring of process performance with a goal towards continually improving cycle time performance (see Chapter 12)

At the same time however, there are at least three different levels of rigor and attention to fast cycle time and innovation across the population of award winners. Figure 35.1 depicts a framework for describing these differences.

In this framework, one model of process discipline appears to be most appropriate for very mature industries and development organizations. A very good example of this is Rockwell Collins, a 2000 award winner. It operates in the defense and aerospace electronics business, an industry that that moves at a measured pace, however, one that welcomes technological innovation. Rockwell Collins is a long recognized leader in this industry and has developed a series of leading products by implementing a very structured technology and product development process. Their process for complex system development

FIGURE 35.1 CHARACTERISTICS OF NEW PRODUCT DEVELOPMENT PROCESSES OF AWARD WINNERS.

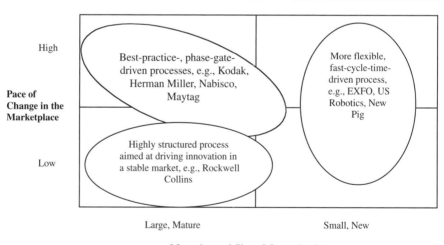

activities is shown in Figure 35.2 along with goals they have set for performance improvement. Key attributes of the process include:

- A very well-defined requirements definition process at the front end of their overall process
- A very structured phase-based development process that is supported by very robust technology-based tools and online project management systems
- An ongoing focus on continuous new product development process improvement
- Measured cycle time goals and objectives for project tracking and resource planning

All in all, they represent a very good model for a company facing a similar set of market, technology, and organizational constraints.

FIGURE 35.2 SYSTEM DEVELOPMENT PROCESS FOR ROCKWELL COLLINS.

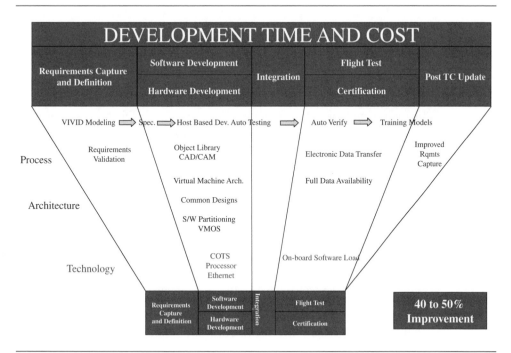

Source: Copyright Rockwell Collins.

Another class of companies operates in the classic middle ground of mature organizations playing in a rapidly changing market. These companies face the challenge of maintaining process discipline while driving innovation and rapid cycle time. Given the sizes of many of these organizations, a standard approach is to install a robust stage-gate process with a strong orientation towards cycle time reduction and reliable product delivery. Several recent award winners typify this class of company—Eastman Kodak, Herman Miller, Nabisco, Maytag. As an example, Figure 35.3 shows the key elements of the new product commercialization (NPC) process for Herman Miller, a leading office furniture designer and manufacturer. This very fine example highlights all of the key required elements and their phasing for a successful product development and launch effort. While considerable detail is required, there is a strong attention to moving through phase-gate milestones reliably and quickly, while retaining the level of innovation in the product.

Finally, the last class of company tends to be those smaller, younger companies operating in very rapidly changing markets. Several of the award winners (companies such as Teknion, EXFO, and US Robotics) have played in this space. In nearly every case, they have been characterized by:

- Flexible, very fast cycle time–driven processes
- Strong culture and commitment to success
- More attention to achieving results quickly, so as to drive multiple product iterations in the market place

In these companies, the actual process map that is followed is important; however, what is more important is to understand the culture and drive towards excellence manifest by all in the organization. Figure 35.4 shows the New Products Assault Process for EXFO, a fast and nimble fiber-optics test equipment manufacturer. While traditional in general structure, the process is exercised with a high degree of focus on ever-decreasing cycle time and continual monitoring of the overall portfolio. The culture of the organization is captured in the "assault" value statement in the process title.

In summary, sound processes are central to success; however, the level of discipline in design and application often must vary depending upon the organization size and degree of market and technology change.

35.3.3 Commitment to Cross-Functional Teams

In a similar fashion, all of the award-winning companies have shown a great deal of dependence upon teams as the primary organizational construct for

FIGURE 35.3 HERMAN MILLER NEW PRODUCT COMMERCIALIZATION PROCESS.

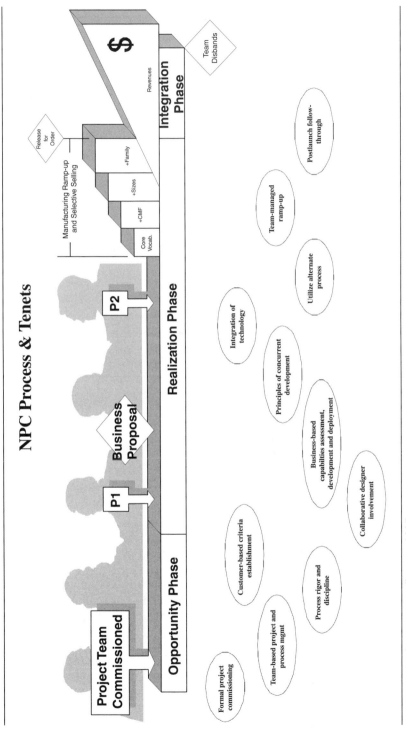

NPC Process & Tenets

Source: Copyright Herman Miller Inc., 1997.

FIGURE 35.4 EXFO NEW PRODUCTS "ASSAULT" PROCESS.

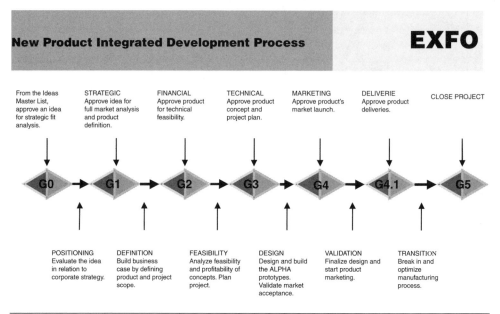

Source: Copyright EXFO Electro-Optical Engineering, Inc.

completing new product development. Various team structures were utilized by the winners; however, they customarily included:

- Cross-functional roles and responsibilities
- Shared goals and objectives
- Co-location to the extent possible
- Team building and training

Again, however, we see a difference in the structure, discipline, and flexibility of the team structures across different market and organizational environments.

Figure 35.5 displays some of the differences we see. As with process design and discipline, larger, more established companies seeking innovation as well as reliable product design and delivery will form cross-functional teams using functionally aligned resources. In these cases, the assignment to the team is often on a sustaining basis; however, the team members will often retain some organizational alignment to their functional homes. This preserves some level of resource management ability as well as retains core competencies and dis-

FIGURE 35.5 CHARACTERISTICS OF TEAM STRUCTURES OF AWARD WINNERS.

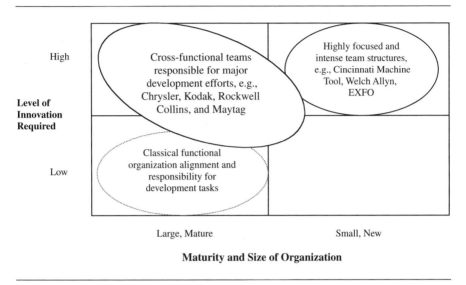

For organizations that are heavily involved in rapid cycle time, highly innovative product development work, the cross-functional team becomes a more intense experience. In several of our award winners, such teams take on lives of their own, setting new norms for behavior and process performance. For

ciplines. Generally, a dedicated program manager is put in place to lead and guide the cross-functional teams. In some cases, team members may sit on multiple teams depending upon the size of the organization and the scope of the projects. Often, co-location is used as a means to bring team members together for extended periods of time for improved communication and coordination. Upon the completion of a project, resources often will move back under the direct control of their functional owners, awaiting the next assignment to a project. Figure 35.6 depicts the team structure used by Teknion, another award-winning office furniture equipment manufacturer to implement their new product development process. As can be seen, a core team is formed for each major development project, supported by representatives from each of the major functions in the organization. These representatives work as members of functionally oriented satellite teams in support of the core team. They are further supported by a product planning management team (the "3 Amigos") and an Implementation Team.

For organizations that are heavily involved in rapid cycle time, highly innovative product development work, the cross-functional team becomes a more intense experience. In several of our award winners, such teams take on lives of their own, setting new norms for behavior and process performance. For

FIGURE 35.6 TEKNION TEAM STRUCTURE.

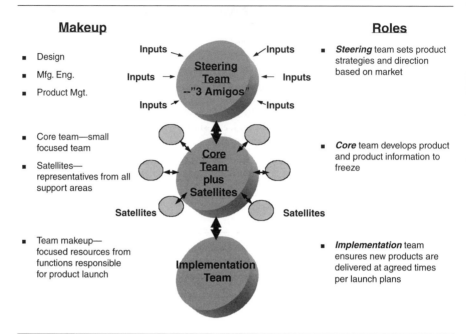

Source: Copyright Teknion.

example, Cincinnati Machine Tool coined the term "Killer" teams to describe the mission and intensity of the teams they had formed to undertake their "Wolfpack" product development process. Such a team structure is shown in Figure 35.7. The "rules of engagement" for such teams indicates the level of autonomy and accountability that they enjoy:

• Total responsibility for the success of the project
• Responsibility to make their own decisions on investments and resources
• Totally self-contained—have access to all resources that they need
• Always co-located, strong team orientation and culture
• Focus on extremely fast cycle time and decision-making process
• "Take no prisoners" mentality

It is also important to recognize that such team structures can be disruptive to the balance of a more traditional organization and, therefore, should only be used in those circumstances requiring a high degree of commitment and innovation.

FIGURE 35.7 CINCINNATI MACHINE TOOL "KILLER" TEAM STRUCTURE.

Integral Part of Operation

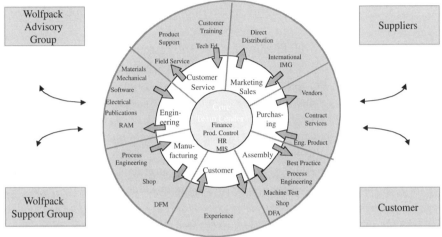

Source: Reprinted with permission of Milacron, Inc.

One further example of a best practice has been provided by Dow Chemical, the 2003 winner. Dow uses teams extensively to drive innovation in a traditionally conservative industry. One technique they use is to consciously profile and select all team members on the basis of their skill, risk, and innovation makeup. For extremely innovative projects, they form teams composed of those with a high degree of risk-taking. For more traditional projects, they form teams with a high degree of process discipline and execution orientation. As a result of such team selection efforts, they have transformed a traditionally conservative business into a highly innovative growth business.

In summary, a blend of cross-functional teaming approaches exists in the range of best practices. The approach to be taken should be carefully selected based on the market, technology, and organizational environment factors facing the development organization.

35.3.4 Strong Voice of the Customer Input

Voice of the customer was also an important element of the award-winning companies. Understanding customers and markets and their needs and requirements has long been recognized as critical to the success of a new product development effort. The linkage between sound market analysis and understanding and new product success is well demonstrated. Award-winning companies have made "customer focus" a high priority in their product development processes. These companies demonstrate this philosophy by giving the customer high priority in development. They accomplish this by:

- Continually refining insights into the customer needs, behaviors, preferences, expectations, and economics—particularly separating needs and wants, so as to move beyond readily identifiable extensions to existing product forms
- Focusing value propositions on meeting those needs and achieving a superior customer experience
- Effectively capturing, analyzing, and disseminating an understanding of the customer throughout the organization
- Focusing resources, and aligning measurement and reward systems on activities that maximize long-term customer value

In a broad range of examples, the following best-practice customer research techniques were employed:

- Customer surveys and research on desired product attributes and features
- Ethnographic studies of customer needs and behaviors
- Customer testing of new products prior to introduction
- Extensive customer satisfaction monitoring and tracking

Using a characterization framework for market research and analysis described in Chapter 16 of this book, Figure 35.8 summarizes several of the more innovative techniques employed by the award winners. As can be seen, many of these best practices demonstrate a very high priority for understanding the voice of the customer. Maytag, the 1999 award winner, provides one of the best examples of a holistic program, employing techniques such as:

- Carefully monitored ethnographic studies of home owners in actual day-to-day living conditions dealing with common laundry and related cleaning tasks
- Structured in-market tests of early product concepts
- Lead user research to explore responses of early adopters to new product concepts
- Focus and orientation of product evolution to drive consumers to "want-in" new products before their old products "wear out"

FIGURE 35.8 SAMPLING OF BEST PRACTICES IN MARKET RESEARCH AND ANALYSIS.

Stage 1: Synthesize and discover	Stage 2: Validate and sharpen	Stage 3: Prioritize and develop
Broad needs surveys ■ Preferences and attributes ■ Buying behavior Ethnographic studies ■ Lab-based ■ In-site monitoring Trend analyses Problem analysis techniques Scenario analysis	Focus groups ■ Specific value propositions ■ Product concepts ■ Feature trade-offs	Surveys ■ Attribute experiments (e.g., conjoint design) ■ Feature trade-offs Specific testing ■ In-market concept tests ■ Prototypes ■ Lead User research
OCI Best Practices ■ Harley User's Group (Harley Davidson) ■ Extensive appliance usage studies (Maytag) ■ Business traveler needs studies (Marriott) ■ Driver ergonomic studies (BMW)	**OCI Best Practices** ■ Extensive market taste testing and focus groups (Nabisco and Pepsi-Cola) ■ Extensive consumer research (Eastman Kodak) ■ Physician's panels and in-house office mockup (Welch Allyn)	**OCI Best Practices** ■ Rapid prototyping and in-market testing (Dow Chemical and Bausch & Lomb) ■ Lead user research and testing of new office environments (Teknion & Herman Miller)

As a result of Maytag's drive to "want-in", they reported that 80 percent of their new high-end product sales were to households where the previous models were still functioning.

In every case, an award-winning company regarded the voice of the customer as a key factor in driving their success.

35.3.5 A Robust Front-End Innovation Process

Each of the award-winning companies displayed significant innovation for their respective industries. In many cases, this level of performance was directly attributable to a very strong and robust front-end innovation process. Such processes often operate at the front end of a company's product development process seeking to identify and qualify new product concepts that can be supported with strong customer need and achievable technology and manufacturing.

Figure 35.9 depicts the key steps in Maytag's innovation processes. As representative of best practices, such a process has the following attributes:

- Strong linkage to voice of the customer (see the earlier discussion)
- Openness to technology and product concepts from outside the organization
- Focus on developing and maintaining a portfolio of new product concepts—to continually fill the pipeline and drive new business success
- An organizational commitment to innovation—from the salesperson to the manufacturing worker
- Training and organizational aids to support the innovation process

As a further example of a truly "out-of-the-box" front-end process, NordicTrack, an award winner in 1993, operates a totally externally oriented process. All of their new product concepts are gleaned from an inventor's net-

FIGURE 35.9 MAYTAG'S INNOVATION PROCESS.

Maytag Product Innovation Process Overview

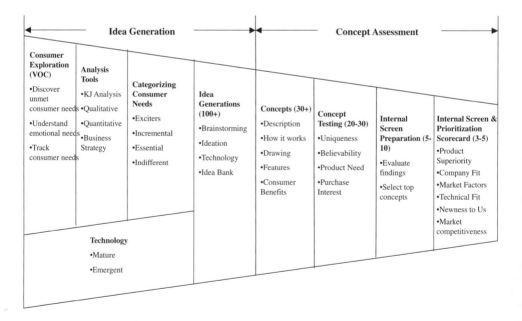

Source: Copyright © 1999–2004 Maytag Corporation.

work that submits ideas to their new product review process for evaluation and subsequent prototyping for the most promising concepts. The inventors, in turn, were promised yes or no answers to their submissions in very short period of time—creating an environment of rapid cycle time and continual drive for innovation. This process has generated a successful series of products for their marketplace (e.g., physical exercise equipment) that have been characterized as truly innovative.

In summary, the front-end innovation displayed by a development organization is most crucial to the success of the entire business and represents a very strong statement of corporate priority.

35.3.6 Strong Linkage to Business Strategy

Finally, consistent with this level of commitment to innovation and new product development, every one of the award-winning companies displayed a very strong linkage of new product development to business strategy. New product development was always viewed as crucial to the company's growth and success (see Chapter 29).

As such, top management involvement and commitment was a central component of award-winning companies. In many cases, the senior executives of the respective businesses represented their companies at the awards ceremony and made their company presentations. Table 35.2 summarizes many of the pronouncements of company CEO's and top-level executives in regard to the role that new product development plays in their success. As the quotes demonstrate, successful companies have found new product development to be essential to their success. Moreover, the linkage of product development to business strategy becomes a fundamental management principle.

35.4 Summary of Business Impact

As we look at the best practices of award-winning companies, we also need to look at the impact their efforts have had on business success. In all cases, we have been fortunate to have profitable and market-leading companies selected as award winners. On a more quantitative basis, however, we have observed that award winners have enjoyed significant growth in sales as a result of their new product development focus. Table 35.3 summarizes the reported sales impact of many of the award-winning companies. The data clearly shows impacts of 20 to 50 percent or more over five-year periods.

TABLE 35.2 TOP MANAGEMENT COMMITMENTS TO INNOVATION AND NEW PRODUCT DEVELOPMENT.

- "Intelligent innovation, operating excellence and supportive culture are the key drivers of business growth"—Maytag CEO
- "No other company approaches new product development the way NordicTrack does"—VP of Product Planning & Development, NordicTrack
- "The BMW Group introduces at least one technological breakthrough per year to strengthen its position as a technology leader"—VP Technology Development, BMW
- "We have established a very strong culture that welcomes exploration, quick identification of failure and unorthodox approaches to discovery"—VP Dow Chemical
- "Our strategy is focused on delivering innovative new products to the market ahead of competitors. Up-front 'strategic fit' and 'portfolio management' reviews of potential new projects insure that all NPD efforts are focused on differentiated market driven opportunities and strict adherence to a Stage Gate process ensures rapid delivery of innovation to the market"—VP R&D EXFO
- "Our company culture is based on the belief that innovative, proprietary products will continue to be key to our success. The voice of the customer is ingrained into our culture and defines our NPD activities"—VP New Products, Hunter Douglas
- "From Day One at Teknion, NPD has been the cornerstone. We will not rest"—President/CEO Teknion

TABLE 35.3 THE SALES IMPACT OF NEW PRODUCTS OVER A FIVE-YEAR PERIOD.

OCI Award Winner	Actual	Predicted**
Safety Kleen	45%	36%
Hewlett-Packard	60%*	68%
Keithley Instruments	70%	67%
Marriott	30%	39%
NordicTrack	95%	52%
Bausch & Lomb	40%	54%
Herman Miller	44%	54%
Maytag	65%	55%
Dow Chemical	20%	TBD

* Sales increase over a two-year period.
** As predicted by the regression model described in Reference 1.

Moving beyond these reported figures, an analysis conducted by Page (2003) has further substantiated that these sales growth estimates are appropriate. In his research, Page has validated the following five hypotheses using 26 separate reports of sales impact:

- The impact of new product programs has been increasing over time
- High technology companies will have a greater impact from new product programs than other companies
- And lower technology and service type companies will have a lower impact from new product programs than do other companies
- Companies that perform better have higher impact new product programs than do other companies
- And companies that do not perform well have lower impact new product programs than do other companies

In fact, the results of Page's regression analysis (see Table 35.3) shows that the OCI award-winning companies did better than the averages computed by the model. This substantiates the ongoing success enjoyed by many of our award-winning companies.

35.5 Summary

In summary, applying lessons learned from leading practitioner companies is often a very effective method for companies facing challenges in launching or improving their new product development performance. The PDMA's Outstanding Corporate Innovator award companies provide a valuable set of such learning experiences for other companies.

Our analysis has found that all of the winners had in place processes, systems, and resources that reflected the following notable best practices:

- A well-defined product development process unique to their market and technology environment
- A strong commitment to cross-functional teams as the fundamental organizational construct for executing new product development
- Strong voice of the customer input
- A robust process at the front end to drive innovation in their product portfolio
- A strong linkage of new product development to the company's corporate strategy, therefore, ensuring top management commitment

While a clear set of common practices were defined across the population of past award winners, it also appears the implementation detail of these common practices varied across the group, driven by their market, technology, and organizational environments. In many cases, the chosen solutions are quite distinctive and provided the greatest learning for the new product development community. The unique solutions, we believe, in fact show that a key best practice is to mold a company's new product development process to the unique market, competitive, and technology situation facing the business.

Given such distinctive practices, it is also clear that exemplary performance has been enjoyed by these companies, most notably in sales growth due to new products.

In conclusion, the Outstanding Corporate Innovator award companies provide a wonderful learning experience for new product development professionals.

Reference

Page, Albert L. and Jun Yu., "Benchmarking the Sales Impact of New Products," in *The Business of Product Development: People, Process and Technology Across the Life Cycle* edited by Gloria Barczak. PDMA Research Forum Proceedings 121–126 (October, 2003).

Sally Evans Kay has spent over 25 years in corporate new product development and innovation within various industries. Her experience includes strategy and process development as well as new opportunity/new technology identification, analysis, and development. Sally has been active in the PDMA as an officer and director and member of the Outstanding Corporate Innovator and Certification committees. Prior to focusing on new product development, her career included assignments in R&D, finance, and marketing.

Tom Hustad is Professor of Marketing at Indiana University's Kelley School of Business. He served as the 1981 president of the PDMA and is founder of the *Journal of Product Innovation Management*. PDMA's international headquarters was based at Indiana University under his leadership from 1984–1996. He was appointed a Crawford Fellow of Innovation in 1993. His students have created a number of products familiar to consumers.

Douglas G. Boike is President of Triad Consulting, Inc., a management consulting firm focused on process improvement in manufacturing and new product development. He formerly was a director with Mercer Management

Consulting, responsible for its supply chain practice. He has also held operations and technology management positions with Xerox Corporation and B/E Aerospace. Dr. Boike has held a number of positions within the PDMA, most recently serving as secretary/treasurer of the PDMA Foundation. Dr. Boike earned a Ph.D. in engineering science from Dartmouth College, an M.Eng. in engineering management from Rochester Institute of Technology and a B.AA in physics from Kalamazoo College.

Norman Parker has served on PDMA's Outstanding Corporate Innovator selection committee for two years. He is the Director of Marketing for Johns Manville's Roofing System Division in Denver, Colorado. Prior to Johns Manville, he worked for Hunter Douglas and Milliken & Company, where he held leadership roles in product development, product management, and operations.

Albert L. Page is a Professor of Marketing at the University of Illinois Chicago, where he co-teaches a unique client-centered Interdisciplinary Product Development course. He has been researching and teaching in the area of product development since 1975 and has been a member of the PDMA since 1976, serving as its president in 1994 and 1995.

Stan Jankowski, former Global Director of Strategic and Economic Planning for a Fortune 50 firm, is currently president of N.O.V.A. Consulting Co. LLC, Traverse City, Michigan. Mr. Jankowski provides new product strategy support and conducts new product opportunity identification and analyses studies and competitive research for major corporations. He also develops and provides customized new product identification and evaluation skills development programs and coaching for NPD professionals. A past director of the Product Development & Management Association, Mr. Jankowski currently serves as the chairperson of the PDMA Outstanding Corporate Innovator Award (OCI) Selection Committee.

John Moran is VP Marketing for tradeattache.com an Internet-based international directory of manufacturers, distributors, importers, and exporters. Mr. Moran is an engineering graduate of the U.S. Merchant Marine Academy and holds an M.B.A. degree in marketing. He is a past chairman of the Product Development & Management Association (PDMA) organization's prestigious Outstanding Corporate Innovator (OCI) Award.

CHAPTER THIRTY-SIX

FIRST RESULTS FROM THE 2003 COMPARATIVE PERFORMANCE ASSESSMENT STUDY (CPAS)

Marjorie Adams-Bigelow

36.1 Introduction

New products and services are critical to a business's long-term success. In support of this critical element within a business, a major aspect of the PDMA's charter is to help firms and product development professionals increase their understanding and management of new product development. Under this charter, the PDMA sponsored studies of product development best practices in 1990 and 1995. This research has resulted in many presentations and articles covering the state of product development practices, including a chapter by Thomas Hustad (1996) in the *PDMA Handbook of New Product Development* (Volume 1), entitled "Reviewing Current Practices in Innovation Management and a Summary of Selected Best Practices."

Given the changes in new product development practices that have taken place in firms since 1995, and the opportunity to examine these changes over time, the PDMA Foundation, during 2003, conducted the Comparative Performance Assessment Study (CPAS). The 2003 survey updated and broadened the scope of the previous research. This chapter presents first findings and is based on 201 responses, primarily from PDMA members, received at the time of writing this chapter in December 2003. (By the second quarter of 2004, more than 400 responses are expected from both PDMA and non-PDMA respondents.). This sample includes:

- 52 percent products companies, 15 percent primarily services companies, and 33 percent companies with a mixture of products and services
- 52 percent business-to-business (B2B), 30 percent primarily consumer companies, and 18 percent with a mix of B2B and consumer
- 32 percent primarily high tech, 41 percent primarily low-tech companies, and 27 percent a mixture of high tech and low tech.

36.2 Introduction to the Survey

A 16-page survey and glossary of terms were sent to U.S. PDMA practitioner members in May 2003, and to those who expressed interest on the PDMA Web site. The survey was conducted at the business unit level, and focused on four major topics within new product development:

- The process by which products are development internally
- The Fuzzy Front End and portfolio management
- Organizing for product development
- Tools/methodologies supporting product development

Products refer to both manufactured goods and services.

In addition, the survey included questions related to new product outcomes and business unit characteristics that enable comparisons among companies of different sizes, technology base, customer focus, and different levels of success.

Finally, for many of the questions, distinctions were made between radical innovations, more innovative projects, and incremental innovations.

Radical innovations include:

- New-to-the-world products (also called *breakthrough products*)

More innovative projects include:

- New product lines, which are new to your organization
- Additions to existing product lines
- Major revisions and next generation advances of products currently produced by your organization

Incremental innovations include:

- Incremental Improvements to products currently produced by your organization

- Repositionings of products currently produced by your organization
- Cost reductions of products currently produced by your organization

36.3 New Product Development Practices

This review summarizes new product development practices across all business units and highlights the practices used by the most successful business units.

Who are the most successful business units? We used the outcome measures from the survey to characterize those business units that were "the best." These most successful business units were defined in terms of their success within their industry, success with their new product development programs relative to their expectations, and performance in terms of market success (sales and profitability). These measures capture performance relative to their competitors, their own expectations, and in their customers' eyes (see Chapter 29). To be characterized as one of the most successful business units, they were:

- The most successful or in the top third in their industry for NPD success, *and*
- Above the mean for their new product program success, *and*
- Above the mean for market financial success from new products

Forty-three respondents (23.0 percent) met these criteria. A total of 144 respondents were categorized as "the rest" of the business units. Fourteen business units were not categorized because they left too many of the applicable questions blank.

36.3.1 Outcomes

How successful are our respondents? Overall success with new products has been fairly consistent since 1995 for PDMA Members (Hustad, 1996). Of those new products that are launched, success rates have improved very little, from 55.9 to 56.8 percent. Sales from new products introduced in the last five years as a percentage of total sales have increased from 27.9 to 30.1 percent, an 8 percent increase. It is interesting to note that in the 1995 survey as reported in Hustad (1996), respondents projected that in the next five years the percentage of new product sales would rise to 37.3 percent of total sales. They did not meet that rather lofty goal, but at least the trend was in the right direction. Table 36.1 shows the numbers from each PDMA survey.

The "Best" are significantly better than the rest. Almost three-quarters of their launched new products are successful, versus about half for the rest of the

TABLE 36.1 NEW PRODUCT SUCCESS RATES.

Criterion	Percentage—1995 for PDMA Members	Percentage—2003 for PDMA Members/Web Interest
Percentage of new product introduced into the market during the past five years that were successful	55.9%	56.8%
New product sales as a percentage of total sales	27.9%	30.1%

companies, and over half of their sales come from new products, versus less than a quarter for the rest of the companies. Their success rates are enviable. And perhaps their greatest achievement is their ability to progress from ideation to commercialization. We will discuss this ability in more detail in the next section, in which we will discuss the new product development process.

What kinds of projects are included in the NPD portfolio? As in 1995, the largest percentage of projects are product improvements. The percentage of new-to-the world products declined from 10 percent to 8 percent, and overall, the more innovative new products declined relative to the more incremental new products, perhaps a reflection of our current economic situation. Figure 36.1 shows the breakout by product type of the projects in our respondents' new product portfolio. Overall, the portfolios across the years are more similar than different.

36.3.2 The Process by Which Products Are Developed Internally

Eighty percent of respondents have a formal process for conducting new product development, up from nearly 75 percent of PDMA responding companies in the 1995 study (Hustad, 1996). While this once was a differentiator between the best performers and other companies, companies now view having a process as a necessary aspect of product development. Considerations now are how to make the process flexible enough to be responsive to a variety of situations, and how to keep the process from becoming stale (see Chapter 4). As shown in Figure 36.2, for those who have a formal process:

- 65 percent of the time they use a facilitating "process owner" to help the cross-functional teams move through stages and management reviews (see Chapter 5).

FIGURE 36.1 PROJECTS IN THE NPD PORTFOLIO.

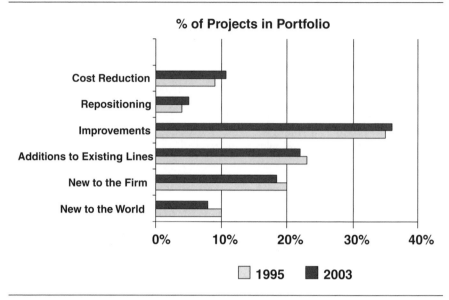

1995 ■ 2003

- 50 percent of the time they have conditional decisions for which the conditions are specifically stated in addition to go/no go decisions.
- 45 percent of the time they are prepared to skip stages or combine gates based on carefully selected criteria. This occurs more often for incremental projects (58 percent of the time).
- 40 percent of the time they have overlapping gates based on carefully selected criteria. This also occurs more often for incremental projects (46 percent of the time).

The "best" performers are more likely to use overlapping gates for new product development projects, but are no more likely than other business units to have process owners, use conditional decisions, or skip stages/combine gates.

A key trend in new product development is the use of collaborative development partners. Our respondents use collaborative development partners 51 percent of the time for radical innovations, 42 percent of the time for more innovative projects, and only 25 percent of the time for incremental innovations. For their collaborative projects, they use formal partnership agreements 54 percent of the time for radical innovations, 42 percent of the time for more innovative projects, and 34 percent of the time for incremental innovations.

FIGURE 36.2 PERCENTAGE OF THE TIME FORMAL PROCESS INCLUDES PROCESS OWNER, CONDITIONAL DECISIONS, SKIPPED OR COMBINED GATES, AND OVERLAPPING GATES.

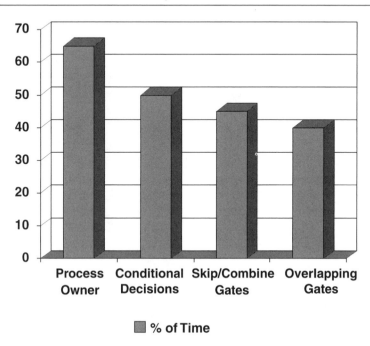

How often do our respondents redesign their process? There are no trends in this regard and no difference between the "best" and the rest of the companies. As shown in Figure 36.3, the largest number of respondents (29 percent) said they redesigned on an ongoing basis, followed by every two years (18 percent), every five years (17 percent), business units who have not redesigned their process (14 percent), and every year (12 percent).

A key aspect of the new product development process is moving new products through the stages of the process. A rich set of ideas is important, but they must be managed well so that there are sufficient resources to manage each project as it progresses. The earlier an idea is killed, the less costly that project is (if it will be killed eventually). It is important to make good decisions as early as possible.

We often hear that 1 in 10 new products are successful. These quoted numbers are talking about the number of ideas that become successful new

FIGURE 36.3 REDESIGN PROCESS.

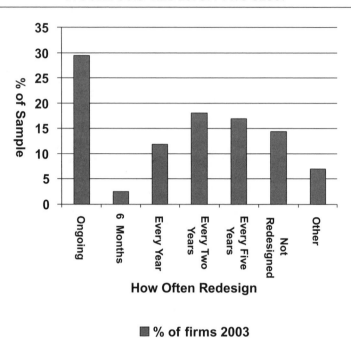

% of firms 2003

products. From the numbers in the "Outcome" section of this chapter, close to but less than 50 percent of those new products that are launched are failures. That is the result to focus on. Killing projects early on in the development process is not a negative, but is necessary in order to have sufficient resources for those projects that continue in the pipeline.

How many projects make it from ideation to become a successful new product? These data from PDMA members indicate that 7.8 ideas are needed for each success. That is up from 6.6 in 1995. The big difference in 2003 is that more projects are getting killed during idea screening. Only 64 percent of ideas proceed to business analysis versus 75 percent in 1995. For all of the other stages, as shown in Table 36.2 and Figure 36.4, 2003 and 1995 percentages are very close.

Overall, 7.8 ideas are needed for one new product success. For the "Best" performers, only 4 ideas are needed versus 10.3 ideas for the rest of the companies. As shown in Table 36.3, they have a lower percentage for idea screening, but a much higher percentage for all of the other stages.

TABLE 36.2 MORTALITY CURVES: 1995 VERSUS 2003.

Stage of the Development Process	Percentage of Projects Advancing to the Next Stage	
	1995	2003
Idea Screen	75%	64%
Business Analysis	67%	68%
Development	73%	72%
Test & Validation	83%	85%
Commercialization	85%	84%
Success in Market	56%	57%

A good process starts with a strong up-front process. The overall data and the data for the "Best" performers both indicate improvement in the Fuzzy Front End processes. We find further support for that conclusion in the next section of this chapter, where we specifically examine the front-end processes.

FIGURE 36.4 MORTALITY CURVE FOR NEW PRODUCT DEVELOPMENT PROJECT: IDEA GENERATION THROUGH SUCCESS.

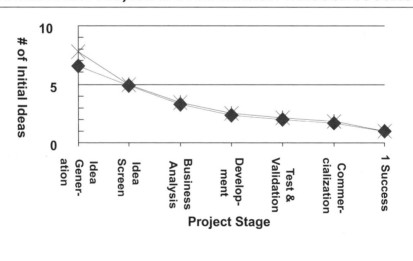

TABLE 36.3 MORTALITY CURVES: THE BEST VERSUS THE REST.

Stage of the Development Process	Percentage of Projects Advancing to the Next Stage	
	The Best	The Rest
Idea Screen	62%	66%
Business Analysis	79%	64%
Development	83%	69%
Test & Validation	94%	81%
Commercialization	92%	80%
Success in Market	73%	52%

36.3.3 The Fuzzy Front End and Portfolio Management

A key aspect of the Fuzzy Front End (see Chapter 6) is whether business units have a specific strategy that directs and integrates the entire new product program. It all needs to start with a new product strategy that is integrated with the overall business strategy (see Chapter 2). In 2003, 77 percent of respondents have a specific strategy, up from 63 percent in 1995. Within those business units characterized as the "Best" performers, 83 percent have a specific strategy versus 73 percent of the rest. These numbers are very encouraging.

Less encouraging are the responses related to the existence of a well-defined, structured process for portfolio management (see Chapter 3). Portfolio management is necessary to make sure that the projects in the pipeline match the strategy that has been developed. Only 53.5 percent of respondents have a well-defined structured process for portfolio management. Less than half of the participants (47 percent) have both a strategy and a portfolio management structured process. And the "Best" performers do not differ from the rest in this regard—only 50 percent of them have both a strategy and a well-defined portfolio management process.

Those who have a process use a variety of portfolio management techniques. Discounted cash flow is used the most, for 72 percent of the projects; options pricing, valuing the projects as options with distinct phases (or stages), is used the least, for 31 percent of the projects. The usage of eight portfolio management techniques is shown in Table 36.4. One encouraging finding is that participants who do not feel that they have a well-defined process, do utilize portfolio management tools. They have the beginnings of a portfolio management system.

Looking more specifically at the strategies of the business units (see Chapter 2), respondents categorized their innovation strategy as one of the following Miles & Snow strategy types (1978):

TABLE 36.4 USE OF PORTFOLIO MANAGEMENT TECHNIQUES.

Portfolio Management Technique	% of Projects
Discounted Cash Flow	72%
Rank Ordering Projects	65%
Payback Period / Breakeven Time	61%
Strategic Buckets	52%
Checklists	51%
Scoring Models	49%
Bubble Diagrams or Portfolio Maps	42%
Options Pricing or Expected Commercial Value	31%

- We value being first with new products, markets and technologies, even though not all efforts prove profitable. We respond rapidly to early signals concerning areas of opportunity (30 percent of respondents are "First to Market").
- We are seldom first to market with new products. However, by carefully monitoring the actions of major competitors, we are frequently a fast follower, bringing a more cost-efficient or perhaps more innovative product into the market very rapidly (40 percent of respondents are "Fast Followers").
- We attempt to locate and maintain a secure niche in a relatively stable product or service area. We try to protect our niche by offering higher quality, superior service, lower prices, etc. We ignore industry changes that have no direct influence on current areas of operations (21 percent of respondents have a "Niche Strategy").
- We are usually not as aggressive in maintaining established products and markets as our competitors. Rather, we respond in those areas when forced to by environmental pressures (8 percent of respondents are just "Reactive").

Figure 36.5 compares the data from 2003 and 1995. We see significantly more Fast Followers, perhaps reflective of the economy (as we have found with some other results). By definition the reactive business units lack a strategy and do not pursue new products. The other three strategies can be successful new product strategies, although having a niche strategy will limit the business unit's ability to grow over time. There are no reactive strategies among our "Best" performers (zero percent versus 11 percent for the rest of the companies), and a higher percentage of business units who are first to market (42 percent of the best versus 24 percent for the rest of the companies). The percentage of Fast Followers and those with a niche strategy are similar for the two groups.

In this part of the survey, we asked about processes used for both idea generation and screening (see Chapter 17). Within idea generation, we asked

FIGURE 36.5 STRATEGY TYPES.

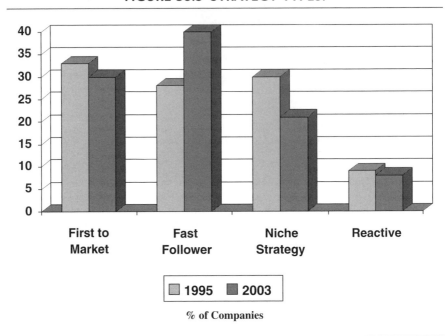

% of **Companies**

about the level of formally planned idea generation activities and whether these activities were designed to fill identified gaps or to generate new ideas in general, as well as what percent come without specific prompting from a wide variety of sources. Overall, more ideas are actively generated than come without specific prompting, more ideas are generated using formal processes than informal processes, and more ideas are generated to fill identified gaps than because the business unit needs more ideas in general. Specifically:

- 33 percent of the ideas are actively generated by formally planned activities to fill identified gaps in the existing product portfolio. (The percentage for the "Best" performers is higher for radical innovations and more innovative projects than for the rest of the business units, but equivalent for incremental innovations.)
- 13 percent of the ideas are actively generated by formally planned activities because in general more ideas are needed.
- 18 percent of the ideas are generated by informal activities to fill identified gaps in the existing product portfolio.

- 11 percent of the ideas are generated by informal activities because in general more ideas are needed. (The percentage for the "Best" performers is less for all types of projects than for the rest of the Business units.)
- 22 percent of the ideas come without specific prompting from a wide variety of sources.
- 3 percent of the ideas come from other methods.

Moving on to idea screening, we asked about the formality of the process, and the formality of the budget (budget allocated directly, indirectly, or not allocated). We find that almost two-thirds of respondents use a formal process and that more of them allocate budgets directly than indirectly or not at all. Specifically:

- 35 percent use a formal process with a budget allocated directly for this activity.
- 14 percent use a formal process with a budget allocated indirectly.
- 13 percent use a formal process with no allocated budget.
- 7 percent use an informal process with a budget allocated directly for this activity.
- 12 percent use an informal process with a budget allocated indirectly
- 18 percent use an informal process with no allocated budget.
- 1 percent chose other.

An interesting finding with these data is that the "Best" performers tend to use more formal processes with an allocated budget for more innovative projects and incremental innovations, but use more informal processes with an indirect process for radical innovations than the rest of the respondents.

These findings support our findings in the "Process" section regarding the increased level of kills in the idea screening phase of product development. More projects are being killed earlier. This should be reflected in overall cost savings to a firm's new product development program, but will not be reflected in the financials of individual new products.

A key aspect of the new product development process is how a business unit organizes for product development. We will discuss organizational structures and practices in the next section.

36.3.4 Organizing for Product Development

How do our business units organize for product development (see Chapter 8)? A single dominant function is the most utilized structure. For radical innovations that function is equally likely to be R&D or Marketing; for more innovative projects and for incremental innovations Marketing tends to dominate. While the role of R&D declines as the level of innovativeness declines, the role of Engineering increases.

The specific structures included in the survey and their relative usage are detailed below. Because business units may use a combination of structures during a project, these percentages add to more than 100 percent. Specifically:

- 55 percent of the time, a single dominant function drives development of new products and solicits other functions as needed.
- 40 percent of the time there is a sequential workflow through each function.
- 35 percent of the time a "New Product Committee" of functional resource owners is assembled.
- 32 percent of the time a separate New Product department with permanent multifunctional staff is used.
- 25 percent of the time project management is treated as a separate function ("Project office") and a "New Product Committee" of functional resource owners is assembled.
- 19 percent of the time a distinct division or venture with its own Profit and Loss Statement is used.

The "Best" performers do not differ significantly from the rest of the respondents for any of these categories.

Looking specifically at project leadership, a part-time project leader is the most utilized leadership practice, followed by a professional project/program manager whose only job is project management. The specific leadership practices and their relative usage are detailed below. Because business units may use a combination of leadership practices during a project, these percentages add to more than 100 percent. Specifically:

- 43 percent of the time a part-time project leader who had other duties is used.
- 31 percent of the time a professional project/program manager whose only job is project management is used.
- 26 percent of the time the team is self-directed.
- 25 percent of the time a project champion who could reside anywhere in the organization moves the project along.
- 21 percent of the time a full-time project leader borrowed from a full-time position for a single project is used.
- 20 percent of the time a process owner serves as the leader. (This is the only category in which the "Best" performers differ significantly from the rest of

the respondents. The "Best" are less likely to use a process owner as leader— 12 percent of the time versus 23 percent for the rest.)

The differences between radical innovations, more innovative projects, and increment innovations were not very large. The largest difference was in the use of a full-time project leader (Not surprisingly, full-time project leaders were used 26 percent of the time for radical innovations, 23 percent of the time for more innovative projects, and only 15 percent of the time for incremental innovations).

Key to the success of a new product development project is the use of effective cross-functional teams and effective leaders (see Chapters 9 and 10). We asked about seven specific practices for product development teams and seven for the product development leaders. The questions about teams relate to how teams work together, both across teams and over time, and how the teams work within the broader organization. The questions about leaders relate to how leaders in different roles support innovation. Overall, usage is fairly high, employed more than 50 percent of the time for most practices. In every category, the "Best" performers used the practice more than the rest of the respondents, and for all but four of the categories the results were statistically significant. Tables 36.5 and 36.6 describe each of the practices, their usage, and the difference between the "Best" performers and the rest. These lists provide 16 practices that are more prevalent within the "Best" performers and add specificity to the well-known advice to use cross-functional teams with strong management support.

How are teams rewarded? Similar to the 1995 survey, the rewards continue to focus on nonfinancial rewards. The most common forms of rewards are completion dinners, newsletter recognition, and plaques/pins. Given the prevalence of new ventures since 1995, and increasing need to protect valuable new product development resources, more use of financial rewards might have been expected, but did not materialize.

The next section of this chapter focuses on the tools and techniques that support new product development.

36.3.5 Tools/Methodologies Supporting Product Development

We continue to see more tools and methodologies supporting product development. In this section, we will discuss three categories of tools/methodologies:

- Market Research
- Engineering, R&D, and Design
- Technology

TABLE 36.5 PRODUCT DEVELOPMENT TEAM PRACTICES.

Practice	Percent of Time Practice Is Employed: Total	Percent of Time Practice Is Employed: Best	Percent of Time Practice Is Employed: Rest	Statistically Significant (at the .05 level or better)?
Cross-functional team training	32%	38%	30%	No
Team members fit their expertise to the project.	61%	66%	58%	No
Team members understand the concerns of other functions.	55%	63%	52%	Yes
Cross-team exchange of lessons learned occurs.	42%	50%	39%	Yes
Clear goals and objectives are established for teams.	64%	70%	61%	No (significant at the .1 level)
Team goals and objectives are related to SBU strategy.	64%	75%	61%	Yes
Quick start-up team formation occurs.	46%	50%	44%	No

For market research tools (see Chapters 13–16 and 18), the most utilized tool in this survey is beta tests. Voice of the customer, which was the most utilized tool in 1995, is third this year, behind beta tests and site visits. Alpha testing, early tests with others in the firm, was the fourth ranking tool this year (it was not previously included). Web-based versions of the market research tools represented the least utilized tool; however, we expect their usage will show an increase in the next survey. The "Best" performers use many of these tools significantly more and do not use any to a lesser extent. Table 36.7 includes the rankings for market research tools/methodologies for this survey and 1995, and indicates which tools are used to a greater extent by the "Best" performers.

Engineering, R&D, and Design tools are not utilized at all by some companies. For others, they are critical to their success. "Best" performers utilize each of these tools significantly more (at the .05 or better level). Failure Mode and Effect Analysis is the most utilized tool followed closely by Simultaneous/

TABLE 36.6 PRODUCT DEVELOPMENT LEADERSHIP PRACTICES.

Practice	Percent of Time Practice Is Employed: Total	Percent of Time Practice Is Employed: Best	Percent of Time Practice Is Employed: Rest	Statistically Significant (at the .05 level or better)?
Project management leadership training	37%	46%	33%	Yes
Technology managers support innovation by ensuring their people participate actively and effectively on teams.	60%	74%	54%	Yes
Manufacturing managers support innovation by ensuring their people participate actively and effectively on teams.	49%	55%	45%	No
Marketing managers support innovation by ensuring their people participate actively and effectively on teams.	62%	72%	57%	Yes
Senior business unit managers support innovation by ensuring that structure, processes, and other organizational mechanisms support the innovation team.	54%	66%	49%	Yes
Senior managers support innovation by making sure that available resources flow smoothly to innovation projects.	52%	64%	48%	Yes
Senior managers make long-term investments in technology, manufacturing, etc., to support ongoing innovation.	52%	69%	46%	Yes—largest difference between best and rest

Concurrent Engineering, and Design for Manufacturing, Assembly, Testing, DFX. Six Sigma analysis is the least utilized Engineering, R&D, and Design tool. Table 36.8 includes the rankings for these tools.

Technology tools range from those commonly used, project management systems, CAD/CAE, and document management systems (the three most utilized technology tools), to those used infrequently, including virtual reality/

TABLE 36.7 MARKET RESEARCH TOOLS/METHODOLOGIES.

Tool/Technique	Rank 2003	Rank 1995	Used Significantly More by "Best" Performers (.1 level of significance or better)
Beta testing (tests of working models by users)	1	4	Yes
Customer site visits (observe and interview at their workplace)	2	2	No
Voice of the customer (1-on-1 in-depth interviews for needs)	3	1	No
Alpha testing (early tests with users)	4	Not included	Yes
Focus groups (interview as a group for needs)	5	5	No
Concept tests (customer evaluation of concept statements)	6	3	No
Lead users (analysis and/or inclusion)	7	Not included	No
Gamma testing (testing with the ideal product)	8	Not included	Yes
Ethnography (observe customers and their environment for needs)	9	Not included	Yes
Test markets	10	6	No
Concept engineering (formal method for concept development)	11	Not included	Yes
Trade-off analysis (conjoint, discrete choice modeling)	12	7	No
Pretest markets (including STM, information acceleration)	13	8	No
Creativity sessions (professionally moderated)	14	Not included	No
Web-based versions of above tools	15	Not included	Yes

virtual design/CAVE technology, Web-based sourcing management software, and remote collaborative design systems (the three least utilized technology tools). As with the market research tools/methodologies, the "Best" performers use many of these tools significantly more and do not use any to a lesser extent. Table 36.9 includes the ranking for these tools and indicates which tools are used to a greater extent by the "Best" performers.

TABLE 36.8 ENGINEERING, R&D, AND DESIGN TOOLS/METHODOLOGIES.

Tool/Technique	Rank 2003	Rank 1995
Failure mode & effect analysis (FMEA)	1	4
Simultaneous/concurrent engineering	2	2
Design for manufacturing, assembly, testing, DFX	3	1
Value analysis/value engineering (VA/VE)	4	3
Quality function deployment (QFD)	5	5
Six Sigma analysis	6	Not included

TABLE 36.9 TECHNOLOGY TOOLS.

Tool/Technique	Rank 2003	Rank 1995	Used Significantly More by "Best" Performers (.1 level of significance or better)
Project management systems	1	Not included	No
Computer-aided design/ engineering (CAD/CAE)	2	1,3 (separate last time)	Yes
Document management systems	3	Not included	Yes
Rapid prototyping systems	4	2	Yes
Performance modeling and simulation systems	5	4	Yes
Product data management systems	6	Not included	Yes
Resource management systems	7	Not included	Yes
Configuration management systems	8	Not included	Yes
Knowledge management systems	9	Not included	Yes
Customer needs/ requirements analysis software	10	Not included	No
Product portfolio management software	11	Not included	No
Remote collaborative design systems	12	Not included	Yes
Web-based sourcing management software	13	Not included	No
Virtual reality/virtual design/ CAVE technology	14	5	No

36.4 Summary

This PDMA best practices research dates to 1990 and draws on research conducted even earlier by Booz, Allen & Hamilton. This survey benefits from being able to benchmark against the previous results, but it also has been expanded to include current topics such as collaboration, portfolio management, team, and leadership issues between teams and over time, and a broader inclusion of tools and methodologies that support product development. This is a descriptive survey, and we need to be careful not to draw inappropriate conclusions. That said, what conclusions can we draw from these data?

1. First, and not to be discounted, the PDMA membership cares deeply about new product development. The time taken to complete this survey (30–60 minutes per respondent) and the response rate achieved among the membership is admirable.
2. Firms have come a long way, but can still learn from current processes, successes, and failure, and from each other.
   - 80 percent of respondents have a formal product development process. Given that these respondents are primarily PDMA members, those numbers are probably higher than those of the general population, but indicative of a general trend. Those firms that have achieved this very necessary first step can now focus on making this process more flexible—knowing when they can skip gates, have overlapping gates, use conditional decisions, and making sure they do not let their process get stale.
   - 77 percent of these respondents have a specific strategy for their new product activities, a very large increase from 1995's 63 percent. This strategy needs to have a link to specific development projects. One such link is a process for managing the portfolio of projects, and the results in this area are disappointing, as less than half of the respondents have both a strategy and a portfolio management system.
   - The Fuzzy Front End is less fuzzy. There is significant use of formal processes for idea generation and selection, while leaving some room for unstructured creativity. This result is supported in the data regarding percentage of ideas that progress to the next stage—more ideas are being eliminated during idea screening.
   - Cross-functional teams are a key element to effective new product development. This survey goes beyond that finding and suggests practices that are important across teams, over time, and to ensure effective project leadership. Tables 36.5 and 36.6 provide a nice summary of those practices.

- Product development is at least as important, if not more important, in hard times as it is in good times. However, we do see, with these data, some shift in investment dollars from more- to less-innovative new products and from more-expensive to less-expensive tools and methodologies that support product development. Are those trends a function of the economic situation? If so, firms need to learn from those who continue to invest in new products.
- The "Best" performers in our survey have admirable results and continue to invest in tools, techniques, methodologies, and training. There is more research that can be conducted about how they do this, but it does appear anecdotally that they do not try to do everything well, but focus on selected aspects of their process. They are not in less-competitive industries with favorable environmental circumstances; they act differently.

The CPAS project is still in process. As we continue to collect and analyze survey data, we look forward to sharing our findings with you, and receiving your feedback. To find out more about participating in the survey or to obtain further information or results, refer to www.pdma.org.

References

Hustad, Thomas P., "Reviewing Current Practices in Innovation Management and a Summary of Selected Best Practices," in *The PDMA Handbook of New Product Development* edited by Milton Rosenau. New York: John Wiley & Sons, Inc., 489–511, (1996).

Miles, Raymond E. and Snow, Charles C., *Organization Strategy, Structure, and Process*, New York: McGraw-Hill Book Company, 1978.

Additional Publications from Previous PDMA Research on Best Practices:

Griffin, Abbie, "Product Development Cycle Time for Business-to-Business Products," *Industrial Marketing Management*, 31:2, 291–304 (March 2002).

Griffin, Abbie, "PDMA Research on New Product Development Practices: Updating Trends and Benchmarking Best Practices," *Journal of Product Innovation Management*, 14:6, 429–458 (November 1997).

Markham, Stephen and Griffin, Abbie, "The Breakfast of Champions: Associations Between Champions and Product Development Environments, Practices and Performance," *Journal of Product Innovation Management*, 15:5, 436–455 (September 1998).

Page, Albert L., "Assessing new product development practices and performance: Establishing crucial norms," *The Journal of Product Innovation Management*, 10:4; 273–291 (July 1993).

PDMA members may obtain copies of these articles by accessing *JPIM* Online through the PDMA Web site. Go to www.pdma.org, log into the "Members Only" section, and click on "JPIM Online." PDMA members have access to all *JPIM* content electronically.

Acknowledgments

This chapter relies on data gathered for the 2003 CPAS as well as data gathered for the 1995 survey. Abbie Griffin served as principal investigator for the 1995 survey. In addition, she, along with Doug Boike, Michelle Roloff, Davis Webb, and Brian Ottum, served on the Advisory Committee for the 2003 study. Amy Chan served as project manager for the development of the online survey for the 2003 study. Thanks to Abbie, Doug, Michelle, Davis, Brian, and Amy for all of their hard work during 2003 and for making the development process for this new product so much fun. Thanks also to Abbie for her thoughtful and prompt comments on the draft of this chapter.

The PDMA Foundation, a not-for-profit 501(c) (3) organization, provided financial support for this research.

Marjorie Adams-Bigelow is the project director of the 2003 PDMA Comparative Performance Assessment Study (CPAS). Previously, she was a professor at the Darden Graduate School of Business, University of Virginia. She also worked for nine years at Booz, Allen & Hamilton, in client staff and marketing positions. Dr. Adams has held a number of positions within PDMA including service as a board member for three years, chair of the Nominating Committee, and Co-chair of the 2000 PDMA Conference held in New Orleans. Dr. Adams has a Ph.D. in marketing from the Wharton School, University of Pennsylvania, an M.B.A. from the University of Chicago, and a B.A. in mathematics and economics from the University of Virginia.

ABOUT THE PRODUCT DEVELOPMENT & MANAGEMENT ASSOCIATION (PDMA)

The PDMA is a nonprofit professional organization dedicated to serving people with an interest in new products. Professionals, executive managers, and academics in the field recognize the PDMA as the global leader in communicating knowledge and tools for the benefit of people and organizations that develop new products and services. Founded in 1976, the PDMA membership is over 2000 product development professionals and academics from all sectors of the economy in over 20 countries worldwide.

PDMA's mission is to improve the effectiveness of people engaged in developing and managing new products—both new manufactured goods and new services. This mission includes facilitating the generation of new information, helping convert this information into knowledge that is in a usable format, and making this new knowledge broadly available to those who might benefit from it. A basic tenet of the Association is that enhanced product innovation represents a desirable and necessary economic goal for firms that wish to achieve and retain a profitable competitive advantage in the long term.

The development of new products and services involves an integrated set of unique activities. The PDMA is the only organization that solely focuses on addressing this challenge by providing:

- National conferences
- Regional and local conferences and meetings

- Publications
- Awards for achievements in new product development
- Sponsored research
- Body of Knowledge
- Certification as a New Product Development Professional (NPDP)
- Certification education and training

PDMA's membership is unique in several ways. It represents the best new products professionals from the most widely admired and accomplished new products companies in the world, from the largest to the smallest, and from capital goods to high technology and software to package goods to services of all kinds. PDMA's members include the field's foremost academics and service providers. Whereas most other professional associations are vertical organizations specializing in one industry or one function, PDMA's membership is horizontal and multifunctional, as is the current state of the new product field. This unique characteristic allows PDMA to address innovation management issues in the same way as new product development teams do in practice.

PDMA fills an information void in the business world. Practitioners turn to PDMA to find the answers they cannot get anywhere else. Through PDMA's national and international meetings, local area chapter meetings, publications, awards, sponsored research programs, Body of Knowledge, and New Product Development Professional certification program, PDMA offers members the opportunity to learn about the strategies, processes, and organizational issues that are involved in product development. Members usually describe PDMA's greatest value to them as being the networking opportunities it offers. The online membership directory is the only place in the world where you can gain access to over 2000 new product professionals.

Conferences and Meetings

Annual International Conference. At the annual PDMA International Conference, traditionally held in October of each year, executives and academics from organizations that are leaders in innovation present cutting-edge ideas, research, and case studies. Certification training and examinations are available at the conference. Various workshops offer effective training for managers at all levels of experience.

Jointly sponsored conferences. In addition to the annual conference, PDMA jointly sponsors several meetings throughout the year, each focusing on an important new product issue. Conferences also are held to disseminate the information contained in PDMA's *Handbook of New Product Development*, the *ToolBook for New Product Development*, and Comparative Performance Assessment Study research results (see Chapter 36).

Local chapter meetings. With more than a dozen regional chapters throughout the country, PDMA sponsors over 35 local meetings annually, offering an excellent opportunity for local involvement and exchange of ideas.

Publications

Journal of Product Innovation Management. The award-winning *Journal of Product Innovation Management*, published six times a year, brings its readers the theory and practice that will enable them to operate at the cutting edge of effective management practice. The *Journal* takes a multifunctional, multidisciplinary, international approach to the issues of innovation, and draws on the work of authors from all over the world. Contents include articles by practitioners and academics, abstracts of relevant articles published elsewhere, and reviews of newly published books on new product development. The complete contents of the journal are available electronically to all PDMA members. From the PDMA member area of PDMA's Web site (www.pdma.org), click on "JPIM Online." The electronic archive is full-text searchable.

Visions. PDMA's quarterly news magazine, *Visions*, offers views from practitioners on new product development and updates members on chapter news, regional meetings, and upcoming events. The electronic archive of *Visions* is available at www.pdma.org.

PDMA Glossary. The PDMA glossary (available at www.pdma.org; also see the glossary following this appendix) is the most comprehensive definitional listing of terms, phrases, and acronyms associated with all aspects of new product development.

Awards

Crawford Fellows. The PDMA confers honorary recognition to select individuals who have made unique contributions to advancing the field of new product development. This honor is named after the founder of the PDMA, Professor Emeritus C. Merle Crawford.

Outstanding Corporate Innovator Award. The only program of its kind, the Outstanding Corporate Innovator Award (see Chapter 35) recognizes leading companies that have consistently sustained growth through innovation over a period of at least five years. Recipients receive their awards and present their successful innovation programs at PDMA's Annual International Conference. Recent recipients have included Bausch &Lomb, Chrysler, Welsh Allyn, Nabisco, Nabisco, Hewlett-Packard, Mariott Corporation, Merck, Apple Computer, Eli Lilly, and Harley Davidson.

Thomas P. Hustad JPIM Best Paper Award. Each year the board of directors of the PDMA and the Editorial Board of the *Journal of Product Innovation Management* awards the article they feel most advances the state of the art of new product development the Thomas P. Hustad *JPIM* Best Paper Award. The award winner is announced at the PDMA Annual International Conference.

Dissertation Proposal. The PDMA supports academic research through an annual dissertation competition. Current doctoral students compete for a $ 2500 grant to support their dissertation research. The winners report their results at PDMA's Annual International Conference. Through this competition, PDMA attracts beginning scholars into the field of product development.

Sponsored Research

PDMA initiated research on best practices in new product development in 1990. This research was repeated and updated in 1995, resulting in three academic publications of the results and nearly 100 presentations to practitioner audiences globally. In 2003, PDMA initiated its Comparative Performance Assessment Study (CPAS). The purpose of this ongoing study of new product development is to allow industry-by-industry comparisons to be made.

Body of Knowledge (BOK)

The purpose of the PDMA Body of Knowledge is to organize, distill, and provide ready access to the continuously evolving core knowledge needed and

used by product development and management professionals and their organizations. The BOK includes generally agreed to definitions and summaries of
important concepts, tools, methodologies, and processes, organized to provide
a foundation upon which to capture and build knowledge, as the field evolves.
It provides access to related reference information around key topic areas and
linkages to the latest writings and presentations on the topic of new product
development.

Certification as a New Product Development Professional (NPDP) and Certification Training

PDMA has the only certification program for the NPD professional. PDMA
certifies individuals as being New Product Development Professionals (NPDP).
NPDP certification confirms mastery of NPD principles and best practices, enabling better job performance and career/promotion opportunities. It recognizes growth, professional development, and competence in NPD. One first
qualifies to become NPDP certified through acquiring bachelor's degree and
obtaining at least two years of work experience. An individual becomes certified
by passing a 200-question multiple choice test that shows competent knowledge
in six areas of new product development:

- New product strategy
- Portfolio management
- New products process
- Tools and metrics
- Market research
- Teams, people, and organizational issues

The PDMA offers classes and workshops that prepare individuals for the
certification test. Some of these are offered in conjunction with chapter meetings
and events, and one is offered every year at the PDMA Annual International
Conference.

Membership and Further Information

To obtain membership or other information about the PDMA, visit the Association's Web site at www.pdma.org or call the Association at (800) 232-5241.

THE PDMA GLOSSARY FOR NEW PRODUCT DEVELOPMENT

Accidental Discovery: New designs, ideas, and developments resulting from unexpected insight, which can be obtained either internal or external to the organization.

Adoption Curve: The phases through which consumers or a market proceed in deciding to adopt a new product or technology. At the individual level, each consumer must move from a cognitive state (becoming aware of and knowledgeable about a product), to an emotional state (liking and then preferring the product) and into a conative or behavioral state (deciding and then purchasing the product). At the market level, the new product is first purchased by the innovators in the marketplace, which are generally thought to constitute about 2.5 percent of the market. Early adopters (13.5 percent of the market) are the next to purchase, followed by the early majority (34 percent), late majority (34 percent) and finally, the laggards (16 percent).

Affinity Charting: A "bottom-up" technique for discovering connections between pieces of data. An individual or group starts with one piece of data (say, a customer need). They then look through the rest of the data they have (say, statements of other customer needs) to find other data (needs) similar to the first, and place it in the same group. As they come across pieces of data that differ from those in the first group, they create a new category. The end result is a set of groups in which the data contained within a category is similar, and the groups all differ in some way. See also Qualitative Cluster Analysis.

Alliance: Formal arrangement with a separate company for purposes of development, and involving exchange of information, hardware, intellectual property, or enabling technology. Alliances involve shared risk and reward (e.g., codevelopment projects).

Alpha Test: Preproduction product testing to find and eliminate the most obvious design defects or deficiencies, usually in a laboratory setting or in some part of the developing firm's regular operations, although in some cases it may be done in controlled settings with lead customers. See also Beta Test and Gamma Test.

Alpha Testing: A crucial "first look" at the initial design, usually done in-house. The results of the Alpha Test either confirm that the product performs according to its specifications or uncovers areas in which the product is deficient. The testing environment should try to simulate the conditions under which the product will actually be used as closely as possible. The Alpha Test should not be performed by the same people who are doing the development work. Since this is the first "flight" for the new product, basic questions of fit and function should be evaluated. Any suggested modifications or revisions to the specifications should be solicited from all parties involved in the evaluation and considered for inclusion. As the testing is done in-house, special care must be taken to remain as objective as possible.

Analytical Hierarchy Process (AHP): A decision-making tool for complex, multicriteria problems in which both qualitative and quantitative aspects of a problem need to be incorporated. AHP clusters decision elements according to their common characteristics into a hierarchical structure similar to a family tree or affinity chart. The AHP process was designed by T. L. Saaty.

Analyzer: A firm that follows an imitative innovation strategy in which the goal is to get to market with an equivalent or slightly better product very quickly once someone else opens up the market, rather than to be first to market with new products or technologies. Sometimes called an imitator or a "fast follower."

Anticipatory Failure Determination (AFD): A failure analysis method. In this process, developers start from a particular failure of interest as the intended consequence and try to devise ways to ensure that the failure always happens reliably. Then the developers use that information to develop ways to better identify steps to avoid the failure.

Applications Development: The iterative process through which software is designed and written to meet the needs and requirements of the user base or the process of enhancing or developing new products.

Architecture: See Product Architecture.

Asynchronous Groupware: Software used to help people work as groups, but not requiring those people to work at the same time.

Attribute Testing: A quantitative market research technique in which respondents are asked to rate a detailed list of product or category attributes on one or more types of scales such as relative importance, current performance, and current satisfaction with a particular product or service. The purpose of this technique is to ascertain customer preferences for some attributes over others to help guide the design and development process. Great care and rigor should be taken in the development of the list of attributes, and it must be neither too long for the respondent to answer comfortably nor so short that it lumps too many ideas together at too high a level.

Audit: When applied to new product development, an audit is an appraisal of the effectiveness of the processes by which the new product was developed and brought to market. See Chapter 14 of *The PDMA ToolBook I*.

Augmented Product: The core product, plus all other sources of product benefits, such as service, warranty, and image.

Autonomous Team: A completely self-sufficient project team with very little, if any, link to the funding organization. Frequently used as an organizational model to bring a radical innovation to the marketplace. Sometimes called a "tiger" team.

Awareness: A measure of the percent of target customers who are aware that the new product exists. Awareness is variously defined, including such definitions as recall of brand, recognition of brand, and recall of key features or positioning.

Back-Up: A project that moves forward with the lead project to provide an alternative asset should the lead project fail in development. It is intended for the same marketplace and moves either in synchrony or with a moderate time lag. A back-up has essentially the same mechanism of action performance as the lead project. Normally a company would not advance both the lead and the back-up project through to the marketplace, since they would compete directly with each other.

Balanced Scorecard: A comprehensive performance measurement technique that balances four performance dimensions: (1) customer perceptions of how we are performing, (2) internal perceptions of how we are doing at what we must excel at, (3) innovation and learning performance, and (4) financial performance.

Benchmarking: A process of collecting process performance data, generally in a confidential, blinded fashion, from a number of organizations to allow them to assess their performance individually and as a whole.

Benefit: A product attribute expressed in terms of what the user gets from the product rather than its physical characteristics or features. Benefits are often paired with specific features, but they need not be.

Best Practice: Methods, tools, or techniques that are associated with improved performance. In new product development, no one tool or technique ensures success; however, a number of them are associated with higher probabilities of achieving it. Best practices likely are at least somewhat context specific. Sometimes called "effective practice."

Best Practice Study: A process of studying successful organizations and selecting the best of their actions or processes for emulation. In new product development it means finding the best process practices, adapting them, and adopting them for internal use. Refer to Chapter 35.

Beta Test: An external test of preproduction products. The purpose is to test the product for all functions in a breadth of field situations, and find those system faults that are more likely to show in actual use than in the firm's more controlled in-house tests. See also Field Testing.

Beta Testing: A more extensive test than the Alpha, performed by real users and customers. The purpose of Beta testing is to determine how the product performs in an actual user environment. It is critical that real customers perform this evaluation, not the firm developing the product or a contracted testing company. As with the Alpha Test, results of the Beta Test should be carefully evaluated with an eye toward any needed modifications or corrections.

Bowling Alley: An early growth stage strategy which emphasizes focusing on specific niche markets, building a strong position in those markets by delivering clearly differentiated "whole products," and using that niche market strength as a leverage point for conquering conceptually neighboring niche markets. Success in the bowling alley is predicated on building product leadership via customer intimacy.

Brainstorming: A group method of creative problem-solving frequently used in product concept generation. There are many modifications in format, each variation with its own name. The basis of all of these methods uses a group of people to creatively generate a list of ideas related to a particular topic. As many ideas as possible are listed before any critical evaluation is performed.

Brand: A name, term, design, symbol, or any other feature that identifies one seller's good or service as distinct from those of other sellers. The legal term for brand is *trademark*. A brand may identify one item, a family of items, or all items of that seller.

Brand Development Index (BDI): A measure of the relative strength of a brand's sales in a geographic area. Computationally, BDI is the percent of total national brand sales that occur in an area divided by the percent of U.S. households that reside in that area.

Breadboard: A proof-of-concept modeling technique that represents how a product will work, but not how a product will look.

Break-Even Point: The point in the commercial life of a product when cumulative development costs are recovered through accrued profits from sales.

Business Analysis: An analysis of the business situation surrounding a proposed project, which usually includes financial forecasts in terms of discounted cash flows, net present values, or internal rates of returns.

Business Case: The results of the market, technical, and financial analyses, or up-front homework. Ideally defined just prior to the "go to development" decision (gate), the case defines the product and project, including the project justification and the action or business plan.

Business-to-Business: Transactions with nonconsumer purchasers such as manufacturers, resellers (distributors, wholesalers, jobbers, and retailers, for example) institutional, professional, and governmental organizations. Frequently referred to as "industrial" businesses in the past.

Buyer: The purchaser of a product, whether or not he or she will be the ultimate user. Especially in business-to-business markets, a purchasing agent may contract for the actual purchase of a good or service, yet never benefit from the function(s) purchased.

Buyer Concentration: The degree to which purchasing power is held by a relatively small percentage of the total number of buyers in the market.

Cannibalization: That portion of the demand for a new product that comes from the erosion of the demand for (sales of) a current product the firm markets.

Capacity Planning: A forward-looking activity that monitors the skill sets and effective resource capacity of the organization. For product development, the objective is to manage the flow of projects through development, such that none of the functions (skill sets) creates a bottleneck to timely completion. Necessary in optimizing the project portfolio.

Centers of Excellence: A geographic or organizational group with an acknowledged technical, business, or competitive competency.

Certification: A process for formally acknowledging that someone has mastered a body of knowledge on a subject. In new product development, the

PDMA has created and manages a certification process to become a New Product Development Professional (NPDP).

Champion: A person who takes a passionate interest in seeing that a particular process or product is fully developed and marketed. This informal role varies from situations calling for little more than stimulating awareness of the opportunity, to extreme cases in which the champion tries to force a project past the strongly entrenched internal resistance of company policy or that of objecting parties.

Charter: A project team document defining the context, specific details, and plans of a project. It includes the initial business case, problem and goal statements, constraints and assumptions, and preliminary plan and scope. Periodic reviews with the sponsor ensure alignment with business strategies. See also Product Innovation Charter.

Checklist: A list of items used to remind an analyst to think of all relevant aspects. It finds frequent use as a tool of creativity in concept generation, as a factor consideration list in concept screening, and in ensuring that all appropriate tasks have been completed in any stage of the product development process.

Chunks: The building blocks of product architecture. They are made up of inseparable physical elements. Other terms for chunks may be modules or major subassemblies.

Clockspeed: The evolution rate of different industries. High-clockspeed industries, such as electronics, see multiple generations of products within short time periods, perhaps even within 12 months. In low-clockspeed industries, such as the chemical industry, a generation of products may last as long as 5 or even 10 years. It is believed that high-clockspeed industries can be used to understand the dynamics of change that will in the long run affect all industries, much like fruit flies are used to understand the dynamics of genetic change in a speeded-up genetic environment, due to their short life spans.

Cognitive Modeling: A method for producing a computational model for how individuals solve problems and perform tasks, based on psychological principles. The modeling process outlines the steps that a person goes through in solving a particular problem or completing a task, which allows one to predict the time that it will take or the types of errors an individual may make. Cognitive models are frequently used to determine ways to improve a user interface, to minimize interaction errors, or to reduce time required by anticipating user behavior.

Cognitive Walkthrough: Once a model of the steps or tasks a person must go through to complete a task is constructed, an expert can roleplay the part of a user to cognitively "walk through" the user's expected experience. Results from this walk-through can help make human-product interfaces more intuitive and increase product usability.

Collaborative Product Development: When two firms work together to develop and commercialize a specialized product. The smaller firm may contribute technical or creative expertise, while the larger firm may be more likely to contribute capital, marketing, and distribution capabilities. When two firms of more equal size collaborate, they may each bring some specialized technology capability to the table in developing some highly complex product or system requiring expertise in both technologies. Collaborative product development has several variations. In customer collaboration, a supplier reaches out and partners with a key or lead customer. In supplier collaboration, a company partners with the provider(s) of technologies, components, or services to create an integrated solution. In collaborative contract manufacturing, a company contracts with a manufacturing partner to produce the intended product. Collaborative development (also known as codevelopment) differs from simple outsourcing in its levels of depth of partnership in that the collaborative firms are linked in the process of delivering the final solution to the intended customer.

Colocation: Physically locating project personnel in one area, enabling more rapid and frequent decision-making and communication among them.

Commercialization: The process of taking a new product from development to market. It generally includes production launch and ramp-up, marketing materials and program development, supply chain development, sales channel development, training development, training, and service and support development.

Competitive Intelligence: Methods and activities for transforming disaggregated public competitor information into relevant and strategic knowledge about competitors' position, size, efforts, and trends. The term refers to the broad practice of collecting, analyzing, and communicating the best available information on competitive trends occurring outside one's own company.

Computer-Aided Design (CAD): A technology that allows designers and engineers to use computers for their design work. Early programs enabled 2-dimensional (two dimensions) design. Current programs allow designers to work in 3-D (3 dimensions), and in either wire or solid models.

Computer-Aided Engineering (CAE): Using computers in designing, analyzing, and manufacturing a product or process. Sometimes refers more narrowly to using computers just at the engineering analysis stage.

Computer-Enhanced Creativity: Using specially designed computer software that aids in the process of recording, recalling, and reconstructing ideas to speed up the new product development process.

Concept: A clearly written and possibly visual description of the new product idea that includes its primary features and consumer benefits, combined with a broad understanding of the technology needed.

Concept Generation: The processes by which new concepts, or product ideas, are generated. Sometimes also called idea generation or ideation.

Concept Optimization: A research approach that evaluates how specific product benefits or features contribute to a concept's overall appeal to consumers. Results are used to select from the options investigated to construct the most appealing concept from the consumer's perspective.

Concept Statement: A verbal or pictorial statement of a concept that is prepared for presentation to consumers to get their reaction prior to development.

Concept Study Activity: The set of product development tasks in which a concept is given enough examination to determine if there are substantial unknowns about the market, technology, or production process.

Concept Screening: the evaluation of potential new product concepts during the discovery phase of a product development project. Potential concepts are evaluated for their fit with business strategy, technical feasibility, manufacturability, and potential for financial success.

Concept Testing: The process by which a concept statement is presented to consumers for their reactions. These reactions can either be used to permit the developer to estimate the sales value of the concept or to make changes to the concept to enhance its potential sales value.

Concurrency: Carrying out separate activities of the product development process at the same time rather than sequentially.

Concurrent Engineering (CE): When product design and manufacturing process development occur concurrently in an integrated fashion, using a cross-functional team, rather than sequentially by separate functions. CE is intended to cause the development team to consider all elements of the product life cycle from conception through disposal, including quality, cost, and maintenance, from the project's outset. Also called simultaneous engineering.

Conjoint Analysis: Conjoint analysis is a market research technique in which respondents are systematically presented with a rotating set of product descriptions, each of which contains a rotating set of attributes and levels of those attributes. By asking respondents to choose their preferred product and / or to indicate their degree of preference from within each set of options, conjoint analysis can determine the relative contribution to overall preference of each variable and each level. The two key advantages of conjoint analysis over other methods of determining importance are: (1) the variables and levels can be either continuous (e.g. weight) or discreet (e.g. color), and (2) it is just about the only valid market research method for evaluating the role of price (i.e. how much someone would pay for a given feature).

Consumer: The most generic and all-encompassing term for a firm's targets. The term is used in either the business-to-business or household context and may refer to the firm's current customers, competitors' customers, or current nonpurchasers with similar needs or demographic characteristics. The term does not differentiate between whether a person who is a buyer and one who is a user target. Only a fraction of consumers will become customers.

Consumer Market: The purchasing of goods and services by individuals and for household use (rather than for use in business settings). Consumer purchases are generally made by individual decision-makers, either for themselves or others in the family.

Consumer Need: A problem the consumer would like to have solved. What a consumer would like a product to do for them.

Consumer Panels: Specially recruited groups of consumers whose longitudinal category purchases are recorded via the scanner systems at stores.

Contextual Inquiry: A structured qualitative market research method that uses a combination of techniques from anthropology and journalism. Contextual inquiry is a customer needs discovery process that observes and interviews users of products in their actual environment.

Contingency Plan: A plan to cope with events whose occurrence, timing, and severity cannot be predicted.

Continuous Improvement: The review, analysis, and rework directed at incrementally improving practices and processes. Also called Kaizen.

Continuous Innovation: A product alteration that allows improved performance and benefits without changing either consumption patterns or behavior. The product's general appearance and basic performance do not functionally change. Examples include fluoride toothpaste and higher computer speeds.

Continuous Learning Activity: The set of activities involving an objective examination of how a product development project is progressing or how it was carried out to permit process changes to simplify its remaining steps or improve the product being developed or its schedule. See also Learning Organization.

Contract Developer: An external provider of product development services.

Controlled Store Testing: A method of test marketing where specialized companies are employed to handle product distribution and auditing rather than using the company's normal sales force.

Convergent Thinking: A technique generally performed late in the initial phase of idea generation to help funnel the high volume of ideas created through divergent thinking into a small group or single idea on which more effort and analysis will be focused.

Cooperation (Team Cooperation): The extent to which team members actively work together in reaching team level objectives.

Coordination Matrix: A summary chart that identifies the key stages of a development project, the goals and key activities within each stage, and who (what function) is responsible for each.

Core Benefit Proposition (CBP): The central benefit or purpose for which a consumer buys a product. The CBP may come either from the physical good or service, or it may come from augmented dimensions of the product. See also Value Proposition.

Core Competence: That capability at which a company does better than other firms, which provides them with a distinctive competitive advantage and contributes to acquiring and retaining customers. Can include technical, organizational, supply chain, operational, financial, marketing, partnership, or other capabilities. The purest definition adds "and is also the lowest cost provider."

Corporate Culture: The "feel" of an organization. Culture arises from the belief system through which an organization operates. Corporate cultures are variously described as being authoritative, bureaucratic, and entrepreneurial. The firm's culture frequently affects the organizational appropriateness for getting things done.

Cost of Goods Sold (COGS or CGS): The direct costs (labor and materials) associated with producing a product and delivering it to the marketplace.

Creativity: "An arbitrary harmony, an expected astonishment, a habitual revelation, a familiar surprise, a generous selfishness, an unexpected certainty, a formable stubbornness, a vital triviality, a disciplined freedom, an intoxicating steadiness, a repeated initiation, a difficult delight, a predictable gamble, an ephemeral solidity, a unifying difference, a demanding satisfier, a miraculous expectation, and accustomed amazement" (George M. Prince, *The Practice of Creativity*, New York: Harper, 1970). Creativity is the ability to produce work that is both novel and appropriate.

Criteria: Statements of standards used by decision-makers at decision gates. The dimensions of performance necessary to achieve or surpass for product development projects to continue in development. In the aggregate, these criteria reflect a business unit's new product strategy.

Critical Assumption: An explicit or implicit assumption in the new product business case that, if wrong, could undermine the viability of the opportunity.

Critical Path: The set of interrelated activities that must be completed for the project to be finished successfully. These activities can be mapped into a chart showing how long each task takes and which tasks cannot be started before other tasks are completed. The critical path is the set of linkages through the chart that is the longest and determines how long a project will take.

Critical Path Scheduling: A project management technique, frequently incorporated into various software programs, which puts all important steps of a given new product project into a sequential network based on task interdependencies.

Critical Success Factors: Those critical few factors that are necessary for, but don't guarantee, commercial success.

Cross-Functional Team: A team consisting of representatives from the various functions involved in product development, usually including members from all key functions required to deliver a successful product, typically including Marketing, Engineering, Manufacturing/Operations, Finance, Purchasing, Customer Support, and Quality. The team is empowered by the departments to represent each function's perspective in the development process.

Crossing the Chasm: Making the transition to a mainstream market from an early market dominated by a few visionary customers (sometimes also called innovators or lead adopters). This concept typically applies to the adoption of new, market-creating, technology-based products and services.

Customer: One who purchases or uses a firm's products or services.

Customer-Based Success: The extent to which a new product is accepted by customers and the trade.

Customer Needs: Problems to be solved. These needs, either expressed or yet to be articulated, provide new product development opportunities for the firm.

Customer Perceived Value (CPV): The result of the customer's evaluation of all the benefits and all the costs of an offering as compared to that customer's perceived alternative. It is the basis on which customers decide to buy things.

Customer Site Visits: A qualitative market research technique for uncovering customer needs. The method involves going to a customer's work site, watching as a person performs functions associated with the customer needs your firm wants to solve, and then debriefing that person about what they did, why they did those things, the problems encountered as they were trying to perform the function, and what worked well.

Customer Value Added Ratio: The ratio of WWPF (worth what paid for) for your products to WWPF for your competitors' products. A ratio above 1 indicates superior value compared to your competitors.

Cycle Time: The length of time for any operation, from start to completion. In the new product development sense, it is the length of time to develop a new product from an early initial idea for a new product to initial market sales. Precise definitions of the start and endpoint vary from one company to another, and may vary from one project to another within the company.

Dashboard: A typically colored graphical presentation of a project's status or a portfolio's status by project resembling a vehicle's dashboard. Typically, red is used to flag urgent problems, yellow to flag impending problems, and green to signal on projects on track.

Database: An electronic gathering of information organized in some way to make it easy to search, discover, analyze, and manipulate.

Decision Screens: Sets of criteria that are applied as checklists or screens at new product decision points. The criteria may vary by stage in the process.

Decision Tree: A diagram used for making decisions in business or computer programming. The "branches" of the tree diagram represent choices with associated risks, costs, results, and outcome probabilities. By calculating outcomes (profits) for each of the branches, the best decision for the firm can be determined.

Decline Stage: The fourth and last stage of the product life cycle. Entry into this stage is generally initiated by technology advancements, consumer or user preference changes, global competition, or environmental or regulatory changes.

Defenders: Firms that stake out a product turf and protect it by whatever means are possible, not necessarily through developing new products.

Deliverable: The output (such as test reports, regulatory approvals, working prototypes, or marketing research reports) that shows a project has achieved a result. Deliverables may be specified for the commercial launch of the product or at the end of a development stage.

Delphi Processes: A technique that uses iterative rounds of consensus development across a group of experts to arrive at a forecast of the most probable outcome for some future state.

Demographic: The statistical description of a human population. Characteristics included in the description may include gender, age, education level, and marital status, as well as various behavioral and psychological characteristics.

Derivative Product: A new product based on changes to an existing product that modifies, refines, or improves some product features without affecting the basic product architecture or platform.

Design for the Environment (DFE): The systematic consideration of environmental safety and health issues over the product's projected life cycle in the design and development process.

Design for Excellence (DFX): The systematic consideration of *all* relevant life cycle factors, such as manufacturability, reliability, maintainability, affordability, testability, and so on, in the design and development process.

Design for Maintainability (DFMt): The systematic consideration of maintainability issues over the product's projected life cycle in the design and development process.

Design for Manufacturability (DFM): The systematic consideration of manufacturing issues in the design and development process, facilitating the fabrication of the product's components and their assembly into the overall product.

Design of Experiments (DOE): A statistical method for evaluating multiple product and process design parameters simultaneously rather than one parameter at a time.

Design to Cost: A development methodology that treats costs as an independent design parameter, rather than an outcome. Cost objectives are established based on customer affordability and competitive constraints.

Design Validation: Product tests to ensure that the product or service conforms to defined user needs and requirements. These may be performed on working prototypes or by using computer simulations of the finished product.

Development: The functional part of the organization responsible for converting product requirements into a working product. Also, a phase in the overall concept-to-market cycle in which the new product or service is developed for the first time.

Development Change Order (DCO): A document used to implement changes during product development. It spells out the desired change, the reason for the change and the consequences to time-to-market, development cost, and cost of producing the final product. It is attached to the project's charter as an addendum.

Development Teams: teams formed to take one or more new products from concept through development, testing, and launch.

Digital Mock-Up: An electronic model of the product created with a solids modeling program. Mock-ups can be used to check for interface interferences and component incompatibilities. Using a digital mock-up can be less expensive than building physical prototypes.

Discontinuous Innovation: Previously unknown products that establish new consumption patterns and behavior changes. Examples include microwave ovens and the cellular phones.

Discounted Cash-Flow (DCF) Analysis: One method for providing an estimate of the current value of future incomes and expenses projected for a project. Future cash flows for a number of years are estimated for the project, and then discounted back to the present using forecasted interest rates.

Discrete Choice Experiment: A quantitative market research tool used to model and predict customer buying decisions.

Dispersed Teams: Product development teams that have members working at different locations, across time zones, and perhaps even in different countries.

Distribution: The method and partners used to get the product (or service) from where it is produced to where the end-user can buy it.

Divergent Thinking: Technique performed early in the initial phase of idea generation that expands thinking processes to generate, record, and recall a high volume of new or interesting ideas.

Dynamically Continuous Innovation: A new product that changes behavior, but not necessarily consumption patterns. Examples include Palm Pilots, electric toothbrushes, and electric hair curlers.

Early Adopters: For new products, these are customers who, relying on their own intuition and vision, buy into new product concepts very early in the life cycle. For new processes, these are organizational entities that were willing to try out new processes rather than just maintaining the old ones.

Economic Value Added (EVA): The value added to or subtracted from shareholder value during the life of a project.

Empathic Design: A five-step method for uncovering customer needs and sparking ideas for new concepts. The method involves going to a customers' work sites, watching as they perform functions associated with the customer needs that your firm wants to meet, and then debriefing the customer about what they did, why they did those things, the problems they encountered as they were trying to perform the function, and what worked well. By spending time with customers, the team develops empathy for the problems that customers encounter trying to perform their daily tasks. See also Customer Site Visits.

Engineering Design: A function in the product creation process where a good or service is configured and specific form is decided.

Engineering Model: The combination of hardware and software intended to demonstrate the simulated functioning of the intended product as currently designed.

Enhanced New Product: A form of derivative product. Enhanced products include additional features not previously found on the base platform, which provide increased value to consumers.

Entrance Requirement: The document(s) and reviews required before any phase of a stages and gates development process can be started.

Entrepreneur: A person who initiates, organizes, operates, assumes the risk, and reaps the potential reward for a new business venture.

Ethnography: A descriptive, qualitative market research methodology for studying the customer in relation to his or her environment. Researchers spend time in the field observing customers and their environment to acquire a deep understanding of the lifestyles or cultures as a basis for better understanding their needs and problems.

Event: This marks the point in time when a task is completed.

Event Map: A chart showing important events in the future that is used to map out potential responses to probable or certain future events.

Excursion: An idea generation technique used to force discontinuities into the idea set. Excursions consist of three generic steps: (1) step away from the task, (2) generate disconnected or irrelevant material, and (3) force a connection back to the task.

Exit Requirement: The document(s) and reviews required to complete a stage of a stages and gates development process.

Exit Strategy: A preplanned process for deleting a product or product line from the firm's portfolio. At a minimum it includes plans for clearing inventory out of the supply chain pipeline at a minimum of losses, continuing to provide for after-sales parts supply and maintenance support, and converting customers of the deleted product line to a different one.

Explicit Customer Requirement: What the customer asks for in a product.

Factory Cost: The cost of producing the product in the production location including materials, labor and overhead.

Failure Mode Effects Analysis (FMEA): A technique used at the development stage to determine the different ways in which a product may fail, and evaluating the consequences of each type of failure.

Failure Rate: The percentage of a firm's new products that make it to full market commercialization, but which fail to achieve the objectives set for them.

Feasibility Determination: The set of product development tasks in which major unknowns (technical or market) are examined to produce knowledge about how to resolve or overcome them or to clarify the nature of any limitations. Sometimes called exploratory investigation.

Feature: The solution to a consumer need or problem. Features provide benefits to consumers. The handle (feature) allows a laptop computer to be carried easily (benefit). Usually any one of several different features will be chosen to meet a customer need. For example, a carrying case with shoulder straps is another feature that allows a laptop computer to be carried easily.

Feature Creep: The tendency for designers or engineers to add more capability, functions, and features to a product as development proceeds than were originally intended. These additions frequently cause schedule slip, development cost increases, and product cost increases.

Feature Roadmap: the evolution over time of the performance attributes associated with a product. Defines the specific features associated with each iteration / generation of a product over its lifetime, grouped into releases (sets of features that are commercialized). See also Product Life-Cycle Management.

Field Testing: Product use testing with users from the target market in the actual context in which the product will be used.

Financial Success: The extent to which a new product meets its profit, margin, and return on investment goals.

Firefighting: An unplanned diversion of scarce resources, and the reassignment of some of them to fix problems discovered late in a product's development cycle.

Firm-Level Success: The aggregate impact of the firm's proficiency at developing and commercializing new products. Several different specific measures may be used to estimate performance.

First-to-Market: The first product to create a new product category or a substantial subdivision of a category.

Flexible Gate: A permissive or permeable gate in a Stage-Gate® process that is less rigid than the traditional "go-stop-recycle" gate. Flexible gates are useful in shortening time-to-market. A permissive gate is one where the next stage is authorized although some work in the almost-completed stage has not yet been finished. A permeable gate is one where some work in a subsequent stage is authorized before a substantial amount of work in the prior stage is completed.

Focus Groups: A qualitative market research technique where 8–12 market participants are gathered in one room for a discussion under the leadership of a trained moderator. Discussion focuses on a consumer problem, product, or potential solution to a problem. The results of these discussions are not projectable to the general market.

Forecast: A prediction, over some defined time, of the success or failure of implementing a business plan's decisions derived from an existing strategy.

Function: (1) An abstracted description of work that a product must perform to meet customer needs. A function is something the product or service must do. (2) Term describing an internal group within which resides a basic business capability such as engineering.

Functional Elements: The individual operations that a product performs. These elements are often used to describe a product schematically.

Functional Pipeline Management: Optimizing the flow of projects through all functional areas in the context of the company's priorities.

Functional Reviews: A technical evaluation of the product and the development process from a functional perspective (such as mechanical engineering or manufacturing), in which a group of experts and peers review the product design in detail to identify weaknesses, incorporate lessons learned from past products, and make decisions about the direction of the design going forward. The technical community may perform a single review that evaluates the design from all perspectives, or individual functional departments may conduct independent reviews.

Functional Schematic: A schematic drawing that is made up of all of the functional elements in a product. It shows the product's functions as well as how material, energy, and signal flow through the product.

Functional Testing: Testing either an element of or the complete product to determine whether it will function as planned and as actually used when sold.

Fuzzy Front End: The messy "getting started" period of product development, when the product concept is still very fuzzy. Preceding the more formal product development process, it generally consists of three tasks: strategic planning, concept generation, and especially, pretechnical evaluation. These activities are often chaotic, unpredictable, and unstructured. In comparison, the subsequent new product development process is typically structured, predictable, and formal, with prescribed sets of activities, questions to be answered, and decisions to be made.

Fuzzy Gates: Fuzzy gates are conditional or situational, rather than full "go" decisions. Their purpose is to try to balance timely decisions and risk management. Conditional go decisions are "go," subject to a task being successfully completed by a future, but specified, date. Situational gates have some criteria that must be met for all projects, and others that are only required for some projects. For example, a new-to-the world product may have distribution feasibility criteria that a line extension will not have. See also Flexible Gates.

Gamma Test: A product use test in which the developers measure the extent to which the item meets the needs of the target customers, solves the problems(s) targeted during development, and leaves the customer satisfied.

Gamma / In-Market Testing: Not to be confused with Test Marketing (which is an overall determination of marketability and financial viability), the In-Market Test is an evaluation of the product itself and its marketing plan through placement of the product in a field setting. Another way of thinking about this is to view it as an in-market test using a real distribution channel in a constrained geographic area or two, for a specific period of time, with advertising, promotion, and all associated elements of the marketing plan working. In addition to an evaluation of the features and benefits of the product, the components of the marketing plan are tested in a real-world environment to make sure they deliver the desired results. The key element being evaluated is the synergy of the product and the marketing plan, not the individual components. The Market Test should deliver a more accurate forecast of dollar and unit sales volume, as opposed to the approximate range estimates produced earlier in the Discovery phase. It should also produce diagnostic information on any facet of the proposed launch that may need adjustment, be it product, communications, packaging, positioning, or any other element of the launch plan.

Gantt Chart: A horizontal bar chart used in project scheduling and management that shows the start date, end date, and duration of tasks within the project.

Gap Analysis: The difference between projected outcomes and desired outcomes. In product development, the gap is frequently measured as the difference between expected and desired revenues or profits from currently planned new products if the corporation is to meet its objectives.

Gate: The point at which a management decision is made to allow the product development project to proceed to the next stage, to recycle back into the current stage to better complete some of the tasks, or to terminate. The number of gates varies by company.

Gatekeepers: The group of managers who serve as advisors, decision-makers and investors in a Stage-Gate® process. Using established business criteria, this multifunctional group reviews new product opportunities and project progress, and allocates resources accordingly at each gate. This group is also commonly called a Product Approval Committee or Portfolio Management Team.

Graceful Degradation: When a product, system, or design slides into defective operation a little at a time, while providing ample opportunity to take corrective preventative action or protect against the worst consequences of failure before it happens. The opposite is catastrophic failure.

Gross Rating Points (GRPs): A measure of the overall media exposure of consumer households (reach times frequency).

Groupware: Software designed to facilitate group efforts such as communication, workflow coordination, and collaborative problem-solving. The term generally refers to technologies relying on modern computer networks (external or internal).

Growth Stage: The second stage of the product life cycle. This stage is marked by a rapid surge in sales and market acceptance for the good or service. Products that reach the growth stage have successfully "crossed the chasm."

Heavyweight Team: An empowered project team with adequate resourcing to complete the project. Personnel report to the team leader and are co-located as practical.

Hunting Ground: A discontinuity in technology or the market that opens up a new product development opportunity.

Hunting for Hunting Grounds: A structured methodology for completing the Fuzzy Front End of new product development.

Hurdle Rate: The minimum return on investment or internal rate of return percentage a new product must meet or exceed as it goes through development.

Idea: The most embryonic form of a new product or service. It often consists of a high-level view of the envisioned solution needed to solve the problem identified by a person, team, or firm.

Idea Exchange: A divergent thinking technique that provides a structure for building on different ideas in a quiet, nonjudgmental setting that encourages reflection.

Idea Generation (Ideation): All of those activities and processes that lead to creating broad sets of solutions to consumer problems. These techniques may be used in the early stages of product development to generate initial product concepts, in the intermediate stages for overcoming implementation issues, in the later stages for planning launch, and in the post-mortem stage to better understand success and failure in the marketplace.

Idea Merit Index: An internal metric used to impartially rank new product ideas.

Implementation Team: A team that converts the concepts and good intentions of the "should-be" process into practical reality.

Implicit Product Requirement: What the customer expects in a product, but does not ask for, and may not even be able to articulate.

Importance Surveys: A particular type of attribute testing in which respondents are asked to evaluate how important each of the product attributes are in their choice of products or services.

Incremental Improvement: A small change made to an existing product that serves to keep the product fresh in the eyes of customers.

Incremental Innovation: An innovation that improves the conveyance of a currently delivered benefit, but produces neither a behavior change nor a change in consumption.

Individual Depth Interviews (IDIs): A qualitative market research technique in which a skilled moderator conducts an open-ended, in-depth, guided conversation with an individual respondent (as opposed to in a [focus] group format). Such an interview can be used to better understand the respondent's thought processes, motivations, current behaviors, preferences, opinions, and desires.

Industrial Design (ID): The professional service of creating and developing concepts and specifications that optimize the function, value, and appearance of products and systems for the mutual benefit of both user and manufacturer (Industrial Design Society of America).

Information: Knowledge and insight, often gained by examining data.

Information Acceleration: A concept-testing method employing virtual reality. In it, a virtual buying environment is created that simulates the information available (product, societal, political, and technological) in a real purchase situation at some time several years or more into the future.

Informed Intuition: Using the gathered experiences and knowledge of the team in a structured manner.

Initial Screening: The first decision to spend resources (time or money) on a project. The project is born at this point. Sometimes called "idea screening."

In-Licensed: The acquisition from external sources of novel product concepts or technologies for inclusion in the aggregate NPD portfolio.

Innovation: A new idea, method, or device. The act of creating a new product or process. The act includes invention as well as the work required to bring an idea or concept into final form.

Innovation-Based Culture: A corporate culture where senior management teams and employees work habitually to reinforce best practices that *systematically* and *continuously* churn out valued new products to customers.

Innovation Engine: The creative activities and people that actually think of new ideas. It represents the synthesis phase when someone first recognizes that customer and market opportunities can be translated into new product ideas.

Innovation Steering Committee: The senior management team or a subset of it responsible for gaining alignment on the strategic and financial goals for new product development, as well as setting expectations for Portfolio and Development Teams.

Innovation Strategy: The firm's positioning for developing new technologies and products. One categorization divides firms into prospectors (those who lead in technology, product and market development, and commercialization, even though an individual product may not lead to profits), analyzers (fast followers, or imitators, who let the prospectors lead, but have a product development process organized to imitate and commercialize quickly any new product a prospector has put on the market), defenders (those who stake out a product turf and protect it by whatever means are possible, not necessarily through developing new products), and reactors (those who have no coherent innovation strategy).

Innovative Problem Solving: Methods that combine rigorous problem definition, pattern-breaking generation of ideas, and action planning that results in new, unique, and unexpected solutions.

Integrated Architecture: A product architecture in which most or all of the functional elements map into a single or very small number of chunks. It is difficult to subdivide an integrally designed product into partially functioning components.

Integrated Product Development (IPD): A philosophy that systematically employs an integrated team effort from multiple functional disciplines to develop effectively and efficiently new products that satisfy customer needs.

Intellectual Property (IP): Information, including proprietary knowledge, technical competencies, and design information. This provides commercially exploitable competitive benefit to an organization.

Internal Rate of Return (IRR): The discount rate at which the present value of the future cash flows of an investment equals the cost of the investment. The discount rate with a net present value of 0.

Intrapreneur: The large-firm equivalent of an entrepreneur. Someone who develops new enterprises within the confines of a large corporation.

Introduction Stage: The first stage of a product's commercial launch and the product life cycle. This stage is generally seen as the point of market entry, user trial, and product adoption.

ISO-9000: A set of five auditable standards of the International Organization for Standardization that establishes the role of a quality system in a company and which is used to assess whether the company can be certified as compliant to the standards. ISO-9001 deals specifically with new products.

Issue: A certainty that will affect the outcome of a project, either negatively or positively. Issues require investigation as to their potential impacts, and decisions about how to deal with them. Open issues are those for which the appropriate actions have not been resolved, while closed issues are ones that the team has dealt with successfully.

Journal of Product Innovation Management: The premier academic journal in the field of innovation, new product development, and management of technology. The *Journal,* which is owned by the PDMA, is dedicated to the advancement of management practice in all of the functions involved in the total process of product innovation. Its purpose is to bring to managers and students of product innovation the theoretical structures and the practical techniques that will enable them to operate at the cutting edge of effective management practice.

Kaizen: A Japanese term describing a process or philosophy of continuous, incremental improvement.

Launch: The process by which a new product is introduced into the market for initial sale.

Lead Users: Users for whom finding a solution to one of their consumer needs is so important that they have modified a current product or invented a new product to meet the need themselves because they have not found a supplier who can solve it for them. When these consumers' needs are portents of needs that the center of the market will have in the future, their solutions are new product opportunities.

Learning Organization: An organization that continuously tests and updates the experience of those in the organization, and transforms that experience into improved work processes and knowledge that is accessible to the whole organization and relevant to its core purpose. See Continuous Learning Activity.

Life-Cycle Cost: The total cost of acquiring, owning, and operating a product over its useful life. Associated costs may include: purchase price, training expenses, maintenance expenses, warrantee costs, support, disposal, and profit loss due to repair downtime.

Lightweight Team: A new product team charged with successfully developing a product concept and delivering to the marketplace. Resources are, for the most part, not dedicated and the team depends on the technical functions for resources necessary to get the work accomplished.

Line Extension: A form of derivative product that adds or modifies features without significantly changing the product functionality.

Long-Term Success: The new product's performance in the long-run or during some large fraction of the product's life cycle.

"M" Curve: An illustration of the volume of ideas generated over a given amount of time. The illustration often looks like two arches from the letter M.

Maintenance Activity: That set of product development tasks aimed at solving initial market and user problems with the new product or service.

Manufacturability: The extent to which a new product can be easily and effectively manufactured at minimum cost and with maximum reliability.

Manufacturing Assembly Procedure: Procedural documents normally prepared by manufacturing personnel that describe how a component, sub-assembly, or system will be put together to create a final product.

Manufacturing Design: The process of determining the manufacturing process that will be used to make a new product.

Manufacturing Test Specification and Procedure: Documents prepared by development and manufacturing personnel that describe the performance specifications of a component, subassembly, or system that will be met during the manufacturing process and that describe the procedure by which the specifications will be assessed.

Market Conditions: The characteristics of the market into which a new product will be placed, including the number of competing products, level of competitiveness, and growth rate.

Market Development: Taking current products to new consumers or users. This effort may involve making some product modifications.

Market-Driven: Allowing the marketplace to direct a firm's product innovation efforts.

Market Research: Information about the firm's customers, competitors, or markets. Information may come from secondary sources (already published and publicly available) or primary sources (from customers themselves). Market research may be qualitative or quantitative (see the entries for these two types of market research).

Market Segmentation: Market segmentation is defined as a framework by which to subdivide a larger heterogeneous market into smaller, more homogeneous parts. These segments can be defined in many different ways: *demographic* (men versus women, young versus old, or richer versus poorer), *behavioral* (those who buy on the phone versus the Internet versus retail, or those who pay with cash versus credit cards), or *attitudinal* (those who believe that store brands are just as good as national brands versus those who don't). There are many analytical techniques used to identify segments such as cluster analysis, factor analysis, or discriminate analysis. The most common method is simply to hypothesize a potential segmentation definition and then test whether any differences that are observed are statistically significant.

Market Share: A company's sales in a product area as a percent of the total market sales in that area.

Market Testing: The product development stage when the new product and its marketing plan are tested together. A market test simulates the eventual marketing mix and takes many different forms, only one of which bears the name *test market*.

Maturity Stage: The third stage of the product life cycle. This is the stage where sales begin to level off due to market saturation. It is a time when heavy competition, alternative product options, and (possibly) changing buyer or user preferences start to make it difficult to achieve profitability.

Metrics: A set of measurements to track product development and allow a firm to measure the impact of process improvements over time. These measures generally vary by firm but may include measures characterizing both aspects of the process, such as time-to-market and duration of particular process stages, as well as outcomes from product development such as the number of products commercialized per year and percentage of sales due to new products.

Modular Architecture: A product architecture in which each functional element maps into its own physical chunk. Different chunks perform different functions, the interactions between the chunks are minimal, and they are generally well-defined.

Monitoring Frequency: The frequency with which performance indicators are measured.

Morphological Analysis: A matrix tool that breaks a product down by needs met and technology components, allowing for targeted analysis and idea creation.

Multifunctional Team: A group of individuals brought together from different functional areas of the business to work on a problem or process that requires the knowledge, training, and capabilities across these areas to successfully complete the work. See also Cross-Functional Team.

Needs Statement: Summary of consumer needs and wants, described in customer terms, to be addressed by a new product.

Net Present Value (NPV): Method to evaluate comparable investments in very dissimilar projects by discounting the current and projected future cash inflows and outflows back to the present value, using the firm's discount rate or cost of capital.

Network Diagram: A graphical diagram with boxes connected by lines that shows the sequence of development activities and task interrelationships. Often used in conjunction with a Gantt Chart.

New Concept Development Model: A theoretical construct that provides for a common terminology and vocabulary for the Fuzzy Front End. The model consists of three parts: the uncontrollable influencing factors, the controllable engine that drives the activities in the Fuzzy Front End, and five activity elements: Opportunity Identification, Opportunity Analysis, Idea Generation and Enrichment, Idea Selection, and Concept Definition.

New Product: A term subject to opinions and practices, but most generally defined as a product (either a good or service) new to the firm marketing it. Excludes products that are only changed in promotion.

New Product Development (NPD): The overall process of strategy, organization, concept generation, product and marketing plan creation and evaluation, and commercialization of a new product. Also frequently referred to just as "product development."

New Product Development Process (NPD Process): A disciplined and defined set of tasks and steps that describe the normal means by which a company repetitively converts embryonic ideas into salable products or services.

New Product Development Professional (NPDP): A New Product Development Professional is certified by the PDMA as having mastered the body of knowledge in new product development, as proven by performance on the certification test. To qualify for the NPDP certification examination, a candidate must hold a bachelor's or higher university degree (or an equivalent degree) from an accredited institution and have spent a minimum of two years working in the new product development field.

New Product Idea: A preliminary plan or purpose of action for formulating new products or services.

New Product Introduction (NPI): The launch or commercialization of a new product into the marketplace. Takes place at the end of a successful product development project.

New-to-the-World Product: A good or service that has never before been available to either consumers or producers. The automobile was new-to-the-world when it was introduced, as were microwave ovens and pet rocks.

Nominal Group Process: A brainstorming process in which members of a group first write their ideas out individually, and then participate in a group discussion about each idea.

Nondestructive Test: A test of the product that retains the product's physical and operational integrity.

Nonproduct Advantage: Elements of the marketing mix, other than the product itself, that create competitive advantages. These elements can include marketing communications, distribution, company reputation, technical support, and associated services.

Operational Strategy: Operational Strategy is an activity that determines the best way to develop a new product while minimizing costs, ensuring adherence to schedule, and delivering a quality product. For product development, the objective is to maximize the return on investment and deliver a high quality product in the optimal market window of opportunity.

Operations: A term that includes manufacturing but is much broader, usually including procurement, physical distribution, and, for services, management of the offices or other areas where the services are provided.

Operator's Manual: The written instructions to the users of a product or process. These may be intended for the ultimate customer or for the use by the manufacturing operation.

Opportunity: A business or technology gap that a company or individual realizes, by design or accident, that exists between the current situation and an envisioned future in order to capture competitive advantage, respond to a threat, solve a problem, or ameliorate a difficulty.

Outsourcing: The process of procuring a good or service from someone else, rather than the firm producing it themselves.

Outstanding Corporate Innovator Award: An annual PDMA award given to firms acknowledged through a formal vetting process as being outstanding innovators. The basic requirements for receiving this award, which is given yearly by the PDMA, are: (1) sustained success in launching new products five years, (2) significant company growth from new product success, (3) a defined new product development process, that can be described to others, and (4) distinctive innovative characteristics and intangibles.

Pareto Chart: A bar graph with the bars sorted in descending order that is used to identify the largest opportunity for improvement. Pareto charts distinguish the "vital few" from the "useful many."

Participatory Design: A democratic approach to design that does not simply make potential users the subjects of user testing, but empowers them to be a part of the design and decision-making process.

Payback: The time, usually in years, from some point in the development process until the commercialized product or service has recovered its costs of development and marketing. While some firms take the point of full-scale market introduction of a new product as the starting point, others begin the clock at the start of development expense.

Payout: The amount of profits and their timing expected from commercializing a new product.

Perceptual Mapping: A quantitative market research tool used to understand how customers think of current and future products. Perceptual maps are visual representations of the positions that sets of products hold in consumers' minds.

Performance Indicators: Criteria on which the performance of a new product in the market is evaluated.

Performance Measurement System: The system that enables the firm to monitor the relevant performance indicators of new products in the appropriate time frame.

Performance / Satisfaction Surveys: A particular type of market research tool in which respondents are asked to evaluate how well a particular product or service is performing and / or how satisfied they are with that product or service on a specific list of attributes. It is often useful to ask respondents to evaluate more than one product or service on these attributes in order to be able to compare them and to better understand what they like and dislike about one versus the other. This information can become a key input to the development process for next generation product modifications.

PERT (Program Evaluation and Review Technique): An event-oriented network analysis technique used to estimate project duration when there is a high degree of uncertainty in estimates of duration times for individual activities.

Phase Review Process: A staged product development process in which first, one function completes a set of tasks, then passes the information they generated sequentially to another function, which in turn, completes the next set of tasks and then passes everything along to the next function. Multifunctional teamwork is largely absent in these types of product development processes, which may also be called baton-passing processes. Most firms have moved from these processes to Stage-Gate® processes using multifunctional teams.

Physical Elements: The components that make up a product. These can be both components (or individual parts) and minor subassemblies of components.

Pilot Gate Meeting: A trial, informal gate meeting usually held at the launch of a Stage-Gate® process to test the design of the process and familiarize participants with the Stage-Gate® process.

Pipeline Alignment: The balancing of project demand with resource supply.

Pipeline Inventory: Production of a new product that has not yet been sold to end consumers, but that exists within the distribution chain.

Pipeline Loading: The volume and time phasing of new products in various stages of development within an organization.

Pipeline Management: A process that integrates product strategy, project management, and functional management to continually optimize the cross-project management of all development-related activities.

Pipeline Management Enabling Tools: The decision-assistance and data-handling tools that aid managing the pipeline. The decision-assistance tools allow the pipeline team to systematically perform trade-offs without losing sight of priorities. The data-handling tools deal with the vast amount of information needed to analyze project priorities, understand resource and skillset loads, and perform pipeline analysis.

Pipeline Management Process: This consists of three elements: pipeline management teams, a structured methodology, and enabling tools.

Pipeline Management Teams: The teams of people at the strategic, project, and functional levels responsible for resolving pipeline issues.

Pipeline (Product Pipeline): The scheduled stream of products in development for release to the market.

Platform Product: The design and components that are shared by a set of products in a product family. From this platform, numerous derivative products can be designed. See also Product Platforms.

Platform Roadmap: A graphical representation of the current and planned evolution of products developed by the organization, showing the relationship between the architecture and features of different generations of products.

Porter's Five Forces: Analysis framework developed by Michael Porter in which a company is evaluated based on its capabilities versus competitors, suppliers, customers, barriers to entry, and the threat of substitutes. See Michael Porter, *Competitive Strategy*, New York: The Free Press, 1998.

Portfolio: Commonly referred to as a set of projects or products that a company is investing in and making strategic trade-offs against. See also Project Portfolio and Product Portfolio.

Portfolio Criteria: The set of criteria against which the business judges both proposed and currently active product development projects to create a balanced and diverse mix of ongoing efforts.

Portfolio Management: A business process by which a business unit decides on the mix of active projects, staffing, and dollar budget allocated to each project currently being undertaken. See also Pipeline Management.

Portfolio Map: A chart or graph which graphically displays the relative scalar strength and weakness of a portfolio of products or competitors in two orthogonal dimensions of customer value or other parameters. Typical portfolio maps include price versus performance, newness to company versus newness to market, and risk versus return.

Portfolio Rollout Scenarios: Hypothetical illustrations of the number and magnitude of new products that would need to be launched over a certain time frame to reach the desired financial goals; accounts for success / failure rates and considers company and competitive benchmarks.

Portfolio Team: A short-term, cross-functional, high-powered team focused on shaping the concepts and business cases for a portfolio of new product concepts within a market, category, brand, or business to be launched over a 2–5 year time period, depending on the pace of the industry.

Preproduction Unit: A product that looks like and acts like the intended final product, but is made either by hand or in pilot facilities rather than by the final production process.

Process Champion: The person responsible for the daily promotion of and encouragement to use a formal business process throughout the organization. This person is also responsible for the ongoing training, innovation input, and continuous improvement of the process.

Process Managers: The operational managers responsible for ensuring the orderly and timely flow of ideas and projects through the process.

Process Map: A workflow diagram that uses an x-axis for process time and a y-axis that shows participants and tasks.

Process Mapping: The act of identifying and defining all of the steps, participants, inputs, outputs, and decisions associated with completing any particular process.

Process Maturity Level: The amount of movement of a reengineered process from the "as-is" map, which describes how the process operated initially, to the "should-be" map of the desired future state of the operation.

Process Owner: The executive manager responsible for the strategic results of the NPD process. This includes process throughput, quality of output, and participation within the organization.

Process Reengineering: A discipline to measure and modify organizational effectiveness by documenting, analyzing, and comparing an existing process to "best-in-class" practice, and then implementing significant process improvements or installing a whole new process.

Product: Term used to describe all goods, services, and knowledge sold. Products are bundles of attributes (features, functions, benefits, and uses) and can be either tangible, as in the case of physical goods; intangible, as in the case of those associated with service benefits; or can be a combination of the two.

Product and Process Performance Success: The extent to which a new product meets its technical performance and product development process performance criteria.

Product Approval Committee (PAC): The group of managers who serve as advisors, decision-makers, and investors in a Stage-Gate® process: a company's NPD executive committee. Using established business criteria, this multifunctional group reviews new product opportunities and project progress, and allocates resources accordingly at each gate.

Product Architecture: The way in which the functional elements are assigned to the physical chunks of a product and the way in which those physical chunks interact to perform the overall function of the product.

Project Decision Making and Reviews: A series of go/no-go decisions about the viability of a project and the ability to provide a product that meets the marketing and financial objectives of the company. This includes a systematic review of the viability of a project as it moves through the various phase stage gates in the development process. These periodic checks validate that the project is still close enough to the original plan to deliver against the business case.

Product Definition: Defines the product, including the target market, product concept, benefits to be delivered, positioning strategy, price point, and even product requirements and design specifications.

Product Development: The overall process of strategy, organization, concept generation, product and marketing plan creation and evaluation, and commercialization of a new product.

Product Development & Management Association (PDMA): A not-for-profit professional organization whose purpose is to seek out, develop, organize, and disseminate leading-edge information on the theory and practice of product development and product development processes. The PDMA uses local, national, and international meetings and conferences, educational workshops, a quarterly newsletter (*Visions*), a bimonthly scholarly journal (*Journal of Product Innovation Management*), research proposal and dissertation proposal competitions, *The PDMA Handbook of New Product Development*, and *The PDMA ToolBook I for New Product Development* to achieve its purposes. The association also manages the certification process for New Product Development Professionals (www.pdma.org).

Product Development Check List: A predetermined list of activities and disciplines responsible for completing those activities that is used as a guideline to ensure all the tasks of product development are considered prior to commercialization.

Product Development Engine: The systematic set of corporate competencies, principles, processes, practices, tools, methods, and skills that combine to define the "how" of an organization's ability to drive high value products to the market in a competitive timely manner.

Product Development Portfolio: The collection of new product concepts and projects that are within the firm's ability to develop, are most attractive to the firm's customers, and deliver short- and long-term corporate objectives by spreading risk and diversifying investments.

Product Development Process: A disciplined and defined set of tasks, steps, and phases that describe the normal means by which a company repetitively converts embryonic ideas into salable products or services.

Product Development Strategy: The strategy that guides the product innovation program.

Product Development Team: A multifunctional group of individuals chartered to plan and execute a new product development project.

Product Discontinuation: A product or service that is withdrawn or removed from the market because it no longer provides an economic, strategic, or competitive advantage in the firm's portfolio of offerings.

Product Discontinuation Timeline: The process and timeframe in which a product is carefully withdrawn from the marketplace. The product may be discontinued immediately after the decision is made, or it may take a year or more to implement the discontinuation timeline, depending on the nature and conditions of the market and product.

Product Failure: A product development project that does not meet the objective of its charter or marketplace.

Product Family: The set of products that have been derived from a common product platform. Members of a product family normally have many common parts and assemblies.

Product Innovation Charter: A critical strategic document, the Product Innovation Charter (PIC) is the heart of any organized effort to commercialize a new product. It contains the reasons the project has been started, the goals, objectives, guidelines, and boundaries of the project. It is the "who, what, where, when, and why" of the product development project. In the Discovery phase, the charter may contain assumptions about market preferences, customer needs, and sales and profit potential. As the project enters the Development phase, these assumptions are challenged through prototype development and in-market testing. While business needs and market conditions can and will change as the project progresses, one must resist the strong tendency for projects to wander off as the development work takes place. The PIC must be constantly referenced during the Development phase to make sure it is still valid, that the project is still within the defined arena, and that the opportunity envisioned in the Discovery phase still exists.

Product Interfaces: Internal and external interfaces affecting the product development effort, including the nature of the interface, action required, and timing.

Product Life Cycle: The four stages that a new product is thought to go through from birth to death: introduction, growth, maturity, and decline. Controversy surrounds whether products go through this cycle in any predictable way.

Product Life-Cycle Management: Changing the features and benefits of the product, elements of the marketing mix, and manufacturing operations over time to maximize the profits obtainable from the product over its lifecycle.

Product Line: A group of products marketed by an organization to one general market. The products have some characteristics, customers, and uses in common and may also share technologies, distribution channels, prices, services, and other elements of the marketing mix.

Product Management: Ensuring over time that a product or service profitably meets the needs of customers by continually monitoring and modifying the elements of the marketing mix, including: the product and its features, the communications strategy, distribution channels, and price.

Product Manager: The person assigned responsibility for overseeing all of the various activities that concern a particular product. Sometimes called a brand manager in consumer packaged goods firms.

Product Plan: A detailed summary of all the key elements involved in a new product development effort such as product description, schedule, resources, financial estimations, and interface management plan.

Product Platforms: Underlying structures or basic architectures that are common across a group of products or that will be the basis of a series of products commercialized over a number of years.

Product Portfolio: The set of products and product lines the firm has placed in the market.

Product Positioning: How a product will be marketed to customers. The product positioning refers to the set of features and value that is valued by (and therefore defined by) the target customer audience, relative to competing products.

Product Rejuvenation: The process by which a mature or declining product is altered, updated, repackaged, or redesigned to lengthen the product life cycle and in turn extend sales demand.

Product Requirements Document: The contract between, at a minimum, marketing and development, describing completely and unambiguously the necessary attributes (functional performance requirements) of the product to be developed, as well as information about how achievement of the attributes will be verified (i.e. through testing).

Product Superiority: Differentiation of a firm's products from those of competitors, achieved by providing consumers with greater benefits and value. This is one of the critical success factors in commercializing new products.

Program Manager: The organizational leader charged with responsibility of executing a portfolio of NPD projects.

Project Leader: The person responsible for managing an individual new product development project through to completion. He or she is responsible for ensuring that milestones and deliverables are achieved and that resources are utilized effectively. See also Team Leader.

Project Management: The set of people, tools, techniques, and processes used to define the project's goal, plan all the work necessary to reach that goal, lead the project and support teams, monitor progress, and ensure that the project is completed in a satisfactory way.

Project Pipeline Management: Fine-tuning resource deployment smoothly for projects during ramp-up, ramp-down, and mid-course adjustments.

Project Plan: A formal, approved document used to guide both project execution and control. This document details planning assumptions and decisions, facilitates communication among stakeholders, and indicates approved scope, cost, and schedule deadlines.

Project Portfolio: The set of projects in development at any point in time. These will vary in the extent of newness or innovativeness.

Project Resource Estimation: This activity provides one of the major contributions to the project cost calculation. Turning functional requirements into a realistic cost estimate is a key factor in the success of a product delivering against the business plan.

Project Sponsor: The authorization and funding source of the project. The person who defines the project goals and to whom the final results are presented—typically a senior manager.

Project Strategy: The goals and objectives for an individual product development project. It includes how that project fits into the firm's product portfolio, what the target market is, and what problems the product will solve for those customers.

Project Team: A multifunctional group of individuals chartered to plan and execute a new product development project.

Prospectors: Firms that lead in technology, product, and market development and commercialization, even though an individual product may not lead to profits. Their general goal is to be first to market with any particular innovation.

Protocol: A statement of the attributes (mainly benefits; features only when required) that a new product is expected to have. A protocol is prepared prior to assigning the project to the technical development team. The benefits statement is agreed to by all parties involved in the project.

Prototype: A physical model of the new product concept. Depending upon the purpose, prototypes may be nonworking, functionally working, or both functionally and aesthetically complete.

Psychographics: Characteristics of consumers that, rather than being purely demographic, measure their attitudes, interests, opinions, and lifestyles.

Pull-Through: The revenue created when a new product or service positively affects the sales of other existing products or services (the obverse of cannibalization).

Qualitative Cluster Analysis: An individual- or group-based process using informed intuition for clustering and connecting data points.

Qualitative Marketing Research: Research conducted with a very small number of respondents, either in groups or individually, to gain an impression of their beliefs, motivations, perceptions, and opinions. Frequently used to gather initial consumer needs and obtain initial reactions to ideas and concepts. Results are not representative of the market in general or projectable. Qualitative marketing research is used to show why people buy a particular product, whereas quantitative marketing research reveals how many people buy it.

Quality: The collection of attributes, which when present in a product, means that a product has conformed to or exceeded customer expectations.

Quality Assurance / Compliance: Function responsible for monitoring and evaluating development policies and practices, to ensure they meet company and applicable regulatory standards.

Quality-by-Design: The process used to design quality into the product, service, or process from the inception of product development.

Quality Control Specification and Procedure: Documents that describe the procedures and the specifications by which a finished subassembly or system will be measured and must meet before judged ready for shipment.

Quality Function Deployment (QFD): A structured method employing matrix analysis for linking what the market requires to how it will be accomplished in the development effort. This method is most frequently used during the stage of development when a multifunctional team agrees on how customer needs relate to product specifications and the features that deliver those needs. By explicitly linking these aspects of product design, QFD minimizes the possibility of omitting important design characteristics or interactions across design characteristics. QFD is also an important mechanism in promoting multifunctional teamwork.

Quantitative Market Research: Consumer research, often surveys, conducted with a large enough sample of consumers to produce statistically reliable results that can be used to project outcomes to the general consumer population. Used to determine importance levels of different customer needs, performance ratings of and satisfaction with current products, probability of trial, repurchase rate, and product preferences. These techniques are used to reduce the uncertainty associated with many other aspects of product development.

Radical Innovation: A new product, generally containing new technologies, that significantly changes behaviors and consumption patterns in the marketplace.

Rapid Prototyping: Any of a variety of processes that avoid tooling time in producing prototypes or prototype parts and therefore allow (generally nonfunctioning) prototypes to be produced within hours or days rather than weeks. These prototypes are frequently used to test quickly the product's technical feasibility or consumer interest.

Reactors: Firms that have no coherent innovation strategy. They only develop new products when absolutely forced to by the competitive situation.

Realization Gap: The time between first perception of a need and the launch of a product that fills that need.

Render: Process that industrial designers use to visualize their ideas by putting their thoughts on paper with any number of combinations of color markers, pencils, and highlighters, or by using computer visualization software.

Reposition: To change the position of the product in the minds of customers, either on failure of the original positioning or to react to changes in the marketplace. Most frequently accomplished through changing the marketing mix rather than redeveloping the product.

Resource Matrix: An array that shows the percentage of each nonmanagerial person's time that is to be devoted to each of the current projects in the firm's portfolio.

Resource Plan: Detailed summary of all forms of resources required to complete a product development project, including personnel, equipment, time, and finances.

Responsibility Matrix: This matrix indicates the specific involvement of each functional department or individual in each task or activity in each stage.

Return on Investment (ROI): A standard measure of project profitability, this is the discounted profits over the life of the project expressed as a percentage of initial investment.

Rigid Gate: A review point in a Stage-Gate® process at which all the prior stage's work and deliverables must be complete before work in the next stage can commence.

Risk: An event or condition that may or may not occur, but if it does occur will impact the ability to achieve a project's objectives. In new product development, risks may take the form of market, technical, or organizational issues.

Risk Acceptance: An uncertain event or condition for which the project team has decided not to change the project plan. A team may be forced to accept an identified risk when they are unable to identify any other suitable response to the risk.

Risk Avoidance: Changing the project plan to eliminate a risk or to protect the project objectives from any potential impact due to the risk.

Risk Management: The process of identifying, measuring, and mitigating the business risk in a product development project.

Risk Mitigation: Actions taken to reduce the probability and/or impact of a risk to below some threshold of acceptability.

Risk Tolerance: The level of risk that a project stakeholder is willing to accept. Tolerance levels are context-specific. That is, stakeholders may be willing to accept different levels of risk for different types of risk, such as risks of project delay, price realization, and technical potential.

Risk Transference: Actions taken to shift the impact of a risk and the ownership of the risk response actions to a third party.

Roadmapping: A graphical multistep process to forecast future market and / or technology changes, and then plan the products to address these changes.

Robust Design: The design of products to be less sensitive to variations, including manufacturing variation and misuse, increasing the probability that they will perform as intended.

"Rugby" Process: A product development process in which stages are partially or heavily overlapped rather than sequential with crisp demarcations between one stage and its successor.

S-Curve (Technology S-Curve): Technology performance improvements tend to progress over time in the form of an "S" curve. When first invented, technology performance improves slowly and incrementally. Then, as experience with a new technology accrues, the rate of performance increase grows and technology performance increases by leaps and bounds. Finally, some of the performance limits of a new technology start to be reached and performance growth slows. At some point, the limits of the technology may be reached and further improvements are not made. Frequently, the technology then becomes vulnerable to a substitute technology that is capable of making additional performance improvements. The substitute technology is usually on the lower, slower portion of its own "S" curve and quickly overtakes the original technology when performance accelerates during the middle (vertical) portion of the "S."

Scanner Test Markets: Special test markets that provide retail point-of-sale scanner data from panels of consumers to help assess the product's performance. First widely applied in the supermarket industry.

Scenario Analysis: A tool for envisioning alternate futures so that a strategy can be formulated to respond to future opportunities and challenges.

Screening: The process of evaluating and selecting new ideas or concepts to put into the project portfolio. Most firms now use a formal screening process with evaluation criteria that span customer, strategy, market, profitability, and feasibility dimensions.

Segmentation: The process of dividing a large and heterogeneous market into more homogeneous subgroups. Each subgroup, or segment, holds similar views about the product, and values, purchases, and uses the product in similar ways.

Senior Management: That level of executive or operational management above the product development team that has approval authority or controls resources important to the development effort.

Sensitivity Analysis: A calculation of the impact that an uncertainty might have on the new product business case. It is conducted by setting upper and lower ranges on the assumptions involved and calculating the expected outcomes.

Services: Products, such as an airline flight or insurance policy, which are intangible or at least substantially so. If totally intangible, they are exchanged directly from producer to user, cannot be transported or stored, and are instantly perishable. Service delivery usually involves customer participation in some important way. Services cannot be sold in the sense of ownership transfer, and they have no title of ownership.

Short-Term Success: The new product's performance shortly after launch, well within the first year of commercial sales.

Should-Be Map: A version of a process map depicting how a process will work in the future. A revised "as-is" process map. The result of the team's reengineering work.

Simulated Test Market: A form of quantitative market research and pretest marketing in which consumers are exposed to new products and to their claims in a staged advertising and purchase situation. Output of the test is an early forecast of expected sales or market share, based on mathematical forecasting models, management assumptions, and input of specific measurements from the simulation.

Six Sigma: A level of process performance that produces only 3.4 defects for every one million operations.

Slip Rate: Measures the accuracy of the planned project schedule according to the formula: Slip Rate = ([actual schedule/planned schedule] −1) * 100%.

Specification: A detailed description of the features and performance characteristics of a product. For example, a laptop computer's specification may read as a 90 megahertz Pentium, with 16 megabytes of RAM and 720 megabytes of hard disk space, 3.5 hours of battery life, weight of 4.5 pounds, and an active matrix 256 color screen.

Speed-to-Market: The length of time it takes to develop a new product from an early initial idea for a new product to initial market sales. Precise definitions of the start and endpoint vary from one company to another, and may vary from one project to another within a company.

Sponsor: An informal role in a product development project, usually performed by a higher-ranking person in the firm who is not directly involved in the project, but who is ready to extend a helping hand if needed, or provide a barrier to interference by others.

Stage: One group of concurrently accomplished tasks with specified outcomes and deliverables, as part of the overall product development process.

Staged Product Development Activity: The set of product development tasks commencing when it is believed there are no major unknowns and that result in initial production of salable product, carried out in stages.

Stage-Gate® Process: A widely employed product development process that divides the effort into distinct time-sequenced stages separated by management decision gates. Multifunctional teams must successfully complete a prescribed set of related cross-functional tasks in each stage prior to obtaining management approval to proceed to the next stage of product development. The framework of the Stage-Gate® process includes work-flow and decision-flow paths and defines the supporting systems and practices necessary to ensure the process's ongoing smooth operation.

Standard Cost: See Factory Cost.

Stop-Light Voting: A convergent thinking technique in which participants vote their idea preferences using colored adhesive dots. Also called preference voting.

Strategic Balance: Balancing the portfolio of development projects along one or more of many dimensions such as focus versus diversification, short- versus long-term, high versus low risk, extending platforms versus development of new platforms.

Strategic New Product Development (SNPD): The process that ties new product strategy to new product portfolio planning.

Strategic Partnering: An alliance or partnership between two firms (frequently one large corporation and one smaller, entrepreneurial firm) to create a specialized new product. Typically, the large firm supplies capital, and the necessary product development, marketing, manufacturing, and distribution capabilities, while the small firm supplies specialized technical or creative expertise.

Strategic Pipeline Management: Strategic balancing, which entails setting priorities among the numerous opportunities and adjusting the organization's skill sets to deliver products.

Strategic Plan: Establishes the vision, mission, values, objectives, goals, and strategies of the organization's future state.

Strategy: The organization's vision, mission, and values. One subset of the firm's overall strategy is its innovation strategy.

Subassembly: A collection of components that can be put together as a single assembly to be inserted into a larger assembly or final product. Often the subassembly is tested for its ability to meet some set of explicit specifications before inclusion in the larger product.

Success: A product that meet's its goals and performance expectations. Product development success has four dimensions. At the project level, there are three dimensions: financial, customer-based, and product technical performance. The fourth dimension is new product contribution to overall firm success.

Support Service: Any organizational function whose primary purpose is not product development but whose input is necessary to the successful completion of product development projects.

SWOT Analysis: "Strengths, Weaknesses, Opportunities, and Threats" Analysis. A SWOT analysis evaluates a company in terms of its advantages and disadvantages versus competitors, customer requirements, and market/economic environmental conditions.

System Hierarchy Diagram: The diagram used to represent product architectures. This diagram illustrates how the product is broken into its chunks.

Systems and Practices: Established methods, procedures, and activities that either drive or hinder product development. These may relate to the firm's day-to-day business or may be specific to product development.

Systems and Practices Team: Senior managers representing all functions who work together to identify and change those systems and practices hindering product development and who establish new tools, systems, and practices for improving product development.

Target Cost: A cost objective established for a new product based on consideration of customer affordability. Target cost is treated as an independent variable that must be satisfied along with other customer requirements.

Target Market: The group of consumers or potential customers selected for marketing. This market segment is most likely to buy the products within a given category. These are sometimes called "prime prospects."

Task: The smallest describable unit of accomplishment in completing a deliverable.

Team: That group of persons who participate in the product development project. Frequently each team member represents a function, department, or specialty. Together they represent the full set of capabilities needed to complete the project.

Team Leader: The person leading the new product team. Responsible for ensuring that milestones and deliverables are achieved, but may not have any authority over project participants.

Team Spotter's Guide: A questionnaire used by a team leader (or team members) to diagnose the quality of the team's functioning.

Technology-Driven: A new product or new product strategy based on the strength of a technical capability. Sometimes called "solutions in search of problems."

Technology Roadmap: A graphic representation of technology evolution or technology plans mapped against time. It is used to guide new technology development for or technology selection in developing new products.

Technology Stage Gate (TSG): A process for managing the technology development efforts when there is high uncertainty and risk. The process brings a structured methodology for managing new technology development without thwarting the creativity needed in this early stage of product development. It is specifically intended to manage high-risk technology development projects when there is uncertainty and risk that the technology discovery may never occur and therefore the ultimate desired product characteristics might never be achieved.

Technology Transfer: The process of converting scientific findings from research laboratories into useful products by the commercial sector. May also be referred to as the process of transferring technology between alliance partners.

Test Markets: The launching of a new product into one or more limited geographic regions in a very controlled manner, and measuring consumer response to the product and its launch. When multiple geographies are used in the test, different advertising or pricing policies may be tested and the results compared.

Think Links: Stimuli used in divergent thinking to help participants make new connections using seemingly unrelated concepts from a list of people, places, or things.

Think-Tank: Environments, frequently isolated from normal organizational activities, created by management to generate new ideas or approaches to solving organizational problems.

Thought Organizers: Tools that help categorize information associated with ideas such that the ideas can be placed into groups to be more easily compared or evaluated.

Three R's: The fundamental steps of Record, Recall, and Reconstruct that most creative minds go through when generating new product ideas.

Threshold Criteria: The minimum acceptable performance targets for any proposed product development project.

Thumbnail: The most minimal form of sketching, usually using pencils, to represent a product idea.

Time-to-Market: The length of time it takes to develop a new product from an early initial idea for a new product to initial market sales. Precise definitions of the start and end point vary from one company to another, and may vary from one project to another within the company.

Tone: The feeling, emotion, or attitude most associated with using a product. The appropriate tone is important to include in consumer new product concepts and advertising.

Tornado: A mid- to late-growth stage strategy that follows the "bowling alley" and which describes an often frenzied period of rapid growth and acceptance for a product category. Activities of the tornado phase include commoditization of a product to become an industry standard, competitive pricing to maximize share and low cost volume distribution channels. Success in the tornado is related to maintaining previously established product leadership and complementing it with operational excellence in a variety of strategic areas.

Total Quality Management (TQM): A business improvement philosophy that comprehensively and continuously involves all of an organization's functions in improvement activities.

Tracking Studies: Surveys of consumers (usually conducted by telephone) following the product's launch to measure consumer awareness, attitudes, trial, adoption, and repurchase rates.

TRIZ: The acronym for the Theory of Inventive Problem Solving, which is a Russian, systematic method of solving problems and creating multiple-alternative solutions. It is based on an analysis and codification of technology solutions from millions of patents. The method enhances creativity by getting individuals to think beyond their own experience and to reach across disciplines to solve problems using solutions from other areas of science.

Uncertainty Range: The spread between the high (best case) and low (worst case) values in a business assumption.

User: Any person who uses a product or service to solve a problem or obtain a benefit, whether or not he or she purchases it. Users may consume a product, as in the case of people using shampoo to clean their hair or eating potato chips to assuage their hunger between meals. Users may not directly consume a product, but may interact with it over a longer period of time, like a family owning a car, with multiple family members using it for many purposes over a number of years. Products also are employed in the production of other products or services, where the users may be the manufacturing personnel who operate the equipment.

Utilities: The weights derived from conjoint analysis that measure how much a product feature contributes to purchase interest or preference.

Value: Any principle to which a person or company adheres with some degree of emotion. It is one of the elements that enter into formulating a strategy.

Value-Added: The act or process by which tangible product features or intangible service attributes are bundled, combined, or packaged with other features and attributes to create a competitive advantage, reposition a product, or increase sales.

Value Analysis: A technique for analyzing systems and designs. Its purpose is to help develop a design that satisfies users by providing the needed user requirements in sufficient quality at an optimum (minimum) cost.

Value Chain: As a product moves from raw material to finished good delivered to the customer, value is added at each step in the manufacturing and delivery process. The value chain indicates the relative amount of value added at each of these steps.

Value Proposition: A short, clear, and simple statement of how and on what dimensions a product concept will deliver value to prospective customers. The essence of "value" is embedded in the tradeoff between the benefits a customer receives from a new product and the price a customer pays for it.

Vertical Integration: A firm's operation across multiple levels of the value chain. In the early 1900s, Ford Motor Company was extremely vertically integrated, because it owned forests and operated logging, wood finishing, and glass-making businesses. They made all of the components that went into its automobiles, as well as most of the raw materials used in those components.

Virtual Customer: A set of Web-based market research methods for gathering voice-of-the-customer data in all phases of product development.

Virtual Product Development: Paperless product development. All design and analyses are computer-based.

Virtual Reality: Technology that enables a designer or user to "enter" and navigate a computer-generated 3-D environment. Users can change their viewpoint and interact with the objects in the scene in a way that simulates real-world experiences.

Virtual Team: Dispersed teams that communicate and work primarily electronically may be called virtual teams.

Vision: An act of imagining, guided by both foresight and informed discernment, that reveals the possibilities as well as the practical limits in new product development. It depicts the most desirable, future state of a product or organization.

Visionary Companies: Leading innovators in their industries, they rank first or second in market share, profitability, growth, and shareholder performance. A substantial portion (e.g., 30 percent or more) of their sales are from products introduced in the last three years. Many firms want to benchmark these firms.

Visions: The new product development practitioner-oriented magazine of the PDMA.

Voice of the Customer (VOC): A process for eliciting needs from consumers that uses structured in-depth interviews to lead interviewees through a series of situations in which they have experienced and found solutions to the set of problems being investigated. Needs are obtained through indirect questioning by coming to understand how the consumers found ways to meet their needs, and more important, why they chose the particular solutions they found.

Whole Product: A product definition concept that emphasizes delivering all aspects of a product that are required for it to deliver its full value. This would include training materials, support systems, cables, how-to recipes, additional hardware / software, standards and procedures, implementation, applications consulting—any constitutive elements necessary to assure the customer will have a successful experience and achieve at least minimum required value from the product. Often elements of the whole product are provided via alliances with others. This term is most often used in the context of planning high-technology products.

Workflow Design Team: Functional contributors who work together to create and execute the work-flow component of a Stage-Gate® system. They decide how the firm's Stage-Gate® process will be structured, what tasks it will include, what decision points will be included, and who is involved at all points.

Workplan: Detailed plan for executing the project, identifying each phase of the project, the major steps associated with them, and the specific tasks to be performed along the way. Best practice workplans identify the specific functional resources assigned to each task, the planned task duration, and the dependencies between tasks. See also Gantt Chart.

Worth What Paid For (WWPF): The quantitative evaluation by a person in your customer segment of the question: "Considering the products and services that your vendor offers, are they worth what you paid for them?"

Acknowledgment: Some of the definitions for terms in this glossary have been adapted from the glossary in *New Products Management*, by C. Merle Crawford and C. Anthony Di Benedetto. Terms, phrases, and definitions generously have been contributed to this list by the PDMA Board of Directors, the design teams for the PDMA Body of Knowledge, the editors and authors of *The PDMA ToolBooks I and II for New Product Development* (John Wiley & Sons, 2002, 2004), the editors and authors of *The PDMA Handbook of New Product Development* (John Wiley & Sons, 1996, 2004) and several other individuals knowledgeable in the science, skills, and art of new product development. We thank all of these volunteer contributors for their continuing support.

AUTHOR INDEX

Page numbers in italics indicate citations in reference sections.

SUBJECT INDEX

Accelerate to Market (ATOM), 65
Acceptance, 65
Accountability, 16
Activity diagrams, 243, 245
Advance specifications, 166
Advisory vote, 275
Agility, 176
Alcoa, 65
Alignment, 39–40, 62, 64, 87, 115, 323, 325, 326
All-out speed, 176
Ambassadors, 154
Ambiguity, 148
Analogous forecasting, 369
Analysis:
    choice, 198
    conjoint, 198, 297–300
    of contextual research, 238–241
    data, 281
    DFME, 436–438
    financial, 9
    hazard, 431–436
    by industrial designers, 392–394
    market, 191–209
    morphological, 269, 270
    qualitative, 196–198
    quantitative, 198–200
    risk, 430–440
    scenario, 365
    SWOT, 37
    trend line, 368
Analytic exercises, 269
Analyzer BU, 35

Anger, 225
Angioplasty business, 122–123
Appleton Papers, 65, 68
Arenas, 18
ARMA/ARIMA models, *see* Autregressive moving average/autoregressive integrated moving average models
Assertiveness, 155
Assessment, 39, 55–56, 67, 489–495
Assumption-based modeling, 367–368
ATAR model, *see* Awareness, trial, availability, and repeat purchase model
ATOM (Accelerate to Market), 65
Attitude, 438–439
Attributes, 5, 164, 166–168
Attribute experiments, 198–199
Audi, 164
Authority, 180
Autregressive moving average/autoregressive integrated moving average (ARMA/ARIMA) models, 369, 370
Awareness, trial, availability, and repeat purchase (ATAR) model, 367–368

Balance, 9–10, 22, 40, 51, 115, 439

Banking industry, 204–209
Bargaining, 155
Barriers, team, 133–136
Baseline schedules, 181
BASES model, 371
Bell Labs, 197
Benchmarks/benchmarking, 67, 68, 98, 133, 134, 373–375
Benefits, 5, 355
Benefit accrual, 67
Benefits-sought segmentation, 284
Benetton, 475–476
Best practices, 67, 68
Black & Decker, 86, 87, 271
"Blind men and the elephant," 30–31
Blueprinting, service, 100–102
BMW, 96, 254
Body of Knowledge (BOK), 570–571
Boeing, 252, 257, 343
BOK, *see* Body of Knowledge
Bosch, 253
Bounding box, 179
Box-Jenkins Techniques, *see* Autregressive moving average/autoregressive integrated moving average models
Brainstorming, 141, 242, 252, 325, 394–395
Brands, 393
Braun, 385

Also available from the PDMA...

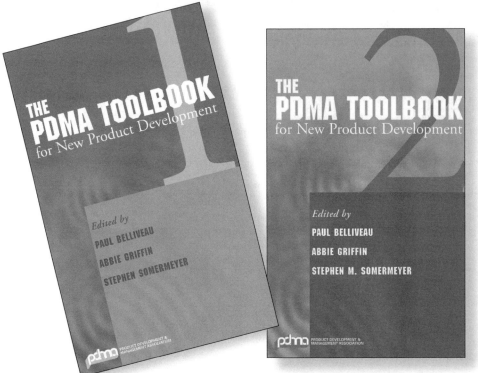